RAF Bomber Command Profiles

10 Squadron

RAF Bomber Command Profiles

10 Squadron

Chris Ward
with
Ian Macmillan

This edition first published 2019 by Mention the War Ltd., 12 Newcastle Street, Merthyr Tydfil, CF47 0BH

Copyright 2019 © Chris Ward.

The right of Chris Ward to be identified as Author of this work is asserted by him in accordance with the Copyright, Designs and Patents Act 1988.

The original Operational Record Book of 10 Squadron and the Bomber Command Night Raid Reports are Crown Copyright and stored in microfiche and digital format by the National Archives. Material is reproduced under Open Licence v.3.0.

All rights reserved. No part of this publication may be reproduced, stored in a retrieval system, transmitted in any form or by any means, electronic, mechanical or photocopied, recorded or otherwise, without the written permission of the copyright owners.

This squadron profile has been researched, compiled and written by its author, who has made every effort to ensure the accuracy of the information contained in it. The author will not be liable for any damages caused, or alleged to be caused, by any information contained in this book. E. & O.E.

Cover design: Topics - The Creative Partnership www.topicsdesign.co.uk

A CIP catalogue reference for this book is available from the British Library.

ISBN 9781911255499

Also by Chris Ward:

Dambusters- The Definitive History of 617 Squadron at War 1943-1945
by Chris Ward, Andy Lee and Andreas Wachtel, published 2003 by Red Kite.

Dambuster Crash Sites
by Chris Ward and Andreas Wachtel, published 2007 by Pen and Sword Aviation.

Dambusters. Forging of a Legend
by Chris Ward, Andy Lee and Andreas Wachtel, published 2009 by Pen and Sword Aviation.

Images of War: 617 Dambuster Squadron at War
by Chris Ward and Andy Lee, published 2009 by Pen and Sword Aviation.

1 Group Bomber Command. An Operational History
by Chris Ward with Greg Harrison and Grzegorz Korcz, published 2014 by Pen and Sword Aviation.

3 Group Bomber Command. An Operational History
by Chris Ward and Steve Smith, published 2008 by Pen and Sword Aviation.

4 Group Bomber Command. An Operational History
by Chris Ward, published 2012 by Pen and Sword Aviation.

5 Group Bomber Command. An Operational History
by Chris Ward, published 2007 by Pen and Sword Aviation.

6 Group Bomber Command. An Operational History
by Chris Ward, published 2009 by Pen and Sword Aviation.

Other RAF Bomber Command Profiles published by Mention the War Ltd.
75(NZ) Squadron
83 Squadron
101 Squadron
103 Squadron
106 Squadron
115 Squadron
138 Squadron
300 Squadron
617 Squadron

Contents

Introduction 11
Narrative History 13
September 1939 14
October 1939 16
November 1939 19
December 1939 22
January 1940 24
February 1940 25
March 1940 26
April 1940 30
May 1940 37
June 1940 48
July 1940 58
August 1940 62
September 1940 69
October 1940 77
November 1940 81
December 1940 85
January 1941 89
February 1941 93
March 1941 96
April 1941 101
May 1941 105
June 1941 110
July 1941 116
August 1941 122
September 1941 127
October 1941 133
November 1941 137
December 1941 140
January 1942 143
February 1942 146
March 1942 151

April 1942 153
May 1942 158
June 1942 165
July 1942 172
August 1942 175
September 1942 180
October 1942 186
November 1942 190
January 1943 196
February 1943 200
March 1943 204
April 1943 210
May 1943 216
June 1943 223
July 1943 228
August 1943 236
September 1943 245
October 1943 253
November 1943 257
December 1943 262
January 1944 266
February 1944 270
March 1944 275
April 1944 283
May 1944 287
June 1944 293
July 1944 305
August 1944 314
September 1944 320
October 1944 326
November 1944 332
December 1944 337
January 1945 344
February 1945 349

March 1945 355

April 1945 362

Author's Notes (NB: entries are denoted in the main narrative by an asterisk) 368

Miscellany of 10 Sqn Photographs 370

Stations, Commanding Officers and Aircraft 381

Operational Record 382

Aircraft Histories 383

Key to Abbreviations 395

This book is dedicated to the memory of Ken Secker, wireless operator in the crew of F/O D. S. Brown RCAF. They joined 10 Squadron at RAF Melbourne on the 21st of July 1944, and undertook the last of their 32-sortie tour of operations on New Year's Day 1945. Post-war, Ken served as a police officer and was the last-surviving member of his crew when he passed away on his 96th birthday on the 17th of February 2018.

Rest in peace.

Sgt K Secker RAF Wireless operator
F/O D S Brown RCAF Pilot
F/O R Webster RCAF Navigator
F/O K Purney RCAF Bomb-aimer
Sgt D Hansom RAF Flight engineer
Sgt N Williams RAF Mid-upper gunner
Sgt T Fenwick RAF Rear gunner

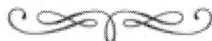

Introduction

RAF Bomber Command Squadron Profiles first appeared in the late nineties, and proved to be very popular with enthusiasts of RAF Bomber Command during the Second World War. They became a useful research tool, particularly for those whose family members had served and were no longer around. The original purpose was to provide a point of reference for all of the gallant men and women who had fought the war, either in the air, or on the ground in a support capacity, and for whom no written history of their unit or station existed. I wanted to provide them with something they could hold up, point to and say, "this was my unit, this is what I did in the war". Many veterans were reticent to talk about their time on bombers, partly because of modesty, but perhaps mostly because the majority of those with whom they came into contact had no notion of what it was to be a "Bomber Boy", to face the prospect of death every time they took to the air, whether during training or on operations. Only those who shared the experience really understood what it was to go to war in bombers, which is why reunions were so important. As they approached the end of their lives, many veterans began to speak openly for the first time about their life in wartime Bomber Command, and most were hurt by the callous treatment they received at the hands of successive governments with regard to the lack of recognition of their contribution to victory. It is sad that this recognition in the form of a national memorial and the granting of a campaign medal came too late for the majority. Now this inspirational, noble generation, the like of which will probably never grace this earth again, has all but departed from us, and the world will be a poorer place as a result.

RAF Bomber Command Squadron Profiles are back. The basic format remains, but, where needed, additional information has been provided. Squadron Profiles do not claim to be comprehensive histories, but rather detailed overviews of the activities of the squadron. There is insufficient space to mention as many names as one would like, but all aircraft losses are accompanied by the name of the pilot. Fundamentally, the narrative section is an account of Bomber Command's war from the perspective of the bomber group under which the individual squadron served, and the deeds of the squadron are interwoven into this story. Information has been drawn from official records, such as group, squadron and station ORBs, and from the many, like myself, amateur enthusiasts, who dedicate much of their time to researching individual units, and become unrivalled authorities on them. I am grateful for their generous contributions, and their names will appear in the appropriate Profiles. The statistics quoted in this series are taken from The Bomber Command War Diaries, that indispensable tome written by Martin Middlebrook and Chris Everitt, and I am indebted to Martin for his kind permission to use them.

Finally, let me apologise in advance for the inevitable errors, for no matter how hard I and other authors try to write "nothing but the truth", there is no such thing as a definitive account of history, and there will always be room for disagreement and debate. Official records are notoriously unreliable tools, and yet we have little choice but to put our faith in them. It is not my intention to misrepresent any person or Bomber Command unit, and I ask my readers to understand the enormity of the task I have undertaken. It is relatively easy to become an authority on single units or even a bomber group, but I chose to write about them all, idiot that I am, which means 128 squadrons serving operationally in Bomber Command at some time between the 3rd of September 1939 and the 8th of May 1945. I am dealing with eight bomber groups, in which some 120,000 airmen served, and I am juggling around 28,000 aircraft serial numbers, code letters and details of provenance and fate. I ask not for your sympathy, it was, after all, my choice, but rather your understanding if you should find something with which you disagree. My thanks to you, my readers, for making the original series of RAF Bomber Command Squadron Profiles so popular, and I hope you receive this new incarnation equally enthusiastically.

Special thanks are owed to Dick King, custodian of the 10 Squadron Association photograph archive, from where the majority of the photos came, and to the archive section of the Yorkshire Air Museum at Elvington for the others. Also, to Association member and former 10 Squadron serving officer, Ian Macmillan, for reviewing the contents of the book and adding his insights and further information. My appreciation, as always, to my gang members, Andreas Wachtel, Steve Smith, Greg Korcz and Clare Bennett for their unstinting support, without which my Profiles would be the poorer. Finally, my appreciation to my publisher, Simon Hepworth of Mention the War Publications, for his belief in my work, untiring efforts to promote it, and for the stress I put him through to bring my books to publication.

Chris Ward. Skegness, Lincolnshire. June 2019.

Narrative History

Originally formed on the 1st of January 1915, 10 Squadron operated various training aircraft until posted to France in July of that year. It fulfilled an artillery observation and tactical reconnaissance role, with some light bombing activity until the end of hostilities, and returned to the UK in February 1919, for eventual disbandment in December. Reformation took place on the 3rd of January 1928, and the squadron continued in existence from that point on. In March 1937, and while based at Dishforth in Yorkshire, the squadron became the first to take delivery of the twin-engine Armstrong Whitworth Whitley, the type with which it would enter the impending conflict under the banner of 4 Group.

When war came on the 3rd of September 1939, the squadrons of 4 Group alone had the necessary training and experience in night flying to venture deep into hostile territory, the rest of the Command having been prepared for daylight operations in line with the Douhet Theory. In his 1921-published book, Command of the Air, the Italian air theorist, General Giulio Douhet, proposed that future wars would be won by air forces, operating independently of ground forces, sending armadas of self-defending bombers in daylight to reach the enemy heartland in sufficient numbers to bomb it into submission. Among advocates of the theory was Arthur Harris, the future commander-in-chief of RAF Bomber Command, Billy Mitchell in America and Walter Wever in Germany. Fortunately, for the outcome of the war, Wever was killed in a flying accident in 1935, and the Luftwaffe developed a tactical rather than strategic bomber force, which was perfect for a short war as in Blitzkrieg, but inadequate for a prolonged conflict.

10 Sqn Whitley K1789. Forced landing in a field during cross-country training flight while based at Dishforth, 1st December 1937. Repaired and not struck off charge until 6th November 1943.

September 1939

At the outbreak of war 4 Group's five operational units were 10, 51, 58, 77 and 102 Squadrons, with 78 Squadron held back as a group pool training unit to feed fresh crews into the front-line. Known as "Shiney Ten", 10 Squadron was commanded by W/C Staton, a First World War pilot, who had been born in Staffordshire in August 1898, and had been in post since June 1938. The requirements of what the American press would refer to as the "Phoney War" dictated that only paper weapons could be dropped on German soil, for fear of reprisals and damage to civilian property. Consequently, leaflet operations, known as "nickels", would characterize 4 Group's early contribution to the war, and, despite the ineffectiveness of such operations in persuading the Germans to capitulate, they would provide much useful experience and training in night flying and navigation over a blacked-out enemy homeland. The squadron was called into action for the first time on the 7th, when eight Whitleys were made ready for a leafleting operation over north-western Germany, although it was actually between 00.35 and 01.10 on the 8th that they departed Dishforth, with W/C Staton and S/L Whitworth the senior pilots on duty. The other pilots on this momentous occasion were F/O Bickford, P/O Nelson, and Sgts Chandler, Craig, Johnson and Verstage, and all reached their respective target areas, which included Cuxhaven, Wilhelmshaven, Kiel and Lübeck. Searchlights and ineffective anti-aircraft fire were reported at many locations, and the blackout in the Cuxhaven area and across the Schleswig-Holstein peninsular was described as not effective. All returned safely, F/O Bickford the last to land, at 09.00, after calling in at Manby to refuel.

Four crews were briefed for a nickel operation over southern Germany, which was to be launched from Reims on the night of the 9/10th, and took off from Dishforth between 07.55 and 08.25 with F/L Allsop the senior pilot on duty. F/Sgt Harcourt-Powell and P/O Nelson landed first at Tangmere, from where the former took off again almost immediately, but P/O Nelson's K9027 was declared to be unserviceable because of problems with the auxiliary tanks, and F/O Parkin and P/O Willis ferried K9031 down as a replacement, before taking the disgraced K9027 back to Dishforth. The 4 Group ORB recorded Stuttgart and Nuremberg as the destinations for the 10 Squadron effort, two aircraft for each, but poor weather kept the Whitleys on the ground at Reims and delayed the operation until the evening of the 10th. They flew out over the Franco/German frontier at between 16,000 and 20,000 feet in good visibility, with a thin layer of cloud well below them at 7,000 feet, and experienced ineffective searchlight activity and a little anti-aircraft fire. Three of the crews reached their briefed targets, two at Nuremberg and one at Stuttgart, while the fourth failed to make it all the way to the latter and delivered their nickels on reaching Frankfurt. 78 Squadron joined 10 Squadron at Dishforth on the 15th, after a spell at Ternhill, and resumed its training duties.

There was little activity thereafter for 10 Squadron until the 24th, when F/O Phillips and Sgt Verstage were briefed for nickelling duties over Hamburg and Bremen, but also to create an A.R.P. (air-raid personnel) disturbance in Berlin and carry out a reconnaissance of blacked-out aerodromes. They took off at 22.10 and 22.35 respectively, before setting course for north-western Germany, where they experienced challenging weather conditions, which included electrical storms. On return, both crews received incorrect D/F (direction-finding) bearings from Linton-on-Ouse and Leconfield, which were at ninety degrees to what was correct, and this led to F/O Phillips flying a course parallel to the English coast, sometimes as far east as Dutch waters. Fortunately, his fuel state allowed him to orbit over the North Sea until daylight arrived to provide him with a visual reference, and he eventually touched down at Dishforth at 07.25, after more than nine hours aloft.

10 Sqn Whitley

10 Squadron was the first to operate the Whitley when it entered RAF service in 1937. It was a significant improvement over its open-cockpit predecessor, the Heyford.

Length: 69.26 ft
2 x Rolls-Royce Merlin X V-12 piston engines
Max Range: 1,501 miles
Service Ceiling: 26,001 ft
Rate-of-Climb: 938 fpm

Crew: 5
Width: 83.99 ft
Max Speed:; 200 kts
Weight (Empty): 19,350 lb
Weight (MTOW): 33,501 lb

Four crews were briefed for a further reconnaissance operation over Hamburg and Bremen on the night of the 30th, and took off between 20.12 and 20.21 with S/L Whitworth the senior pilot on duty. After completing their sorties in very challenging weather conditions, Sgt Chandler and crew returned to Dishforth without difficulty, while the three others experienced the same inaccurate D/F bearings mentioned above and were sent roaming all over the west coast of Scotland before two of them eventually reached home. K9027, containing the crew of F/Sgt Cattell, whose navigator was S/L Pollock-Gore, ran out of fuel near Bolton, and was force-landed on farmland. In the moonlight a farm house was seen to be in the Whitley's path, and the pilot managed to swing it sufficiently to avoid contact. The crew was able to walk away from the badly damaged aircraft, which, it seems, was eventually returned to flying duties. During the course of the month the squadron carried out four operations and dispatched eighteen sorties without loss.

Whitley K9019 1/2 October 1939

October 1939

Bomber Command HQ sent orders to 4 Group HQ on the 1st to drop nickels over area 2 in Germany, which comprised Berlin, Potsdam and Spandau. The task was handed to 10 Squadron, which would, thereby, have the honour of being the first to overfly Germany's Capital city, and W/C Staton, Sgt Craig, Sgt Johnson and F/L Allsop departed Dishforth at five-minute intervals from 22.00, before setting course for northern Germany. They encountered broken cloud over the North Sea, which, built to ten-tenths with tops at 18,000 feet over enemy territory. Icing accretion became a constant danger and the extreme cold froze the manually-operated turrets and actuating gear, turning the operation into an ordeal for the crews. Three completed their sorties as briefed from around 20,000 feet and returned home between 07.00 and 07.10 to make their reports and thaw out. F/L Allsop and crew were last heard from by W/T at 05.05, when a fix put K9018 some 180 miles off the Northumberland coast at St Abb's Head. The message suggested that they had been defeated by the weather, and had jettisoned their leaflets over Denmark, thus violating that country's neutrality. Coastal Command conducted a search in the area of the last fix, but found nothing, and the first of many 10 Squadron failures to return over the ensuing five years and seven months was officially posted missing at noon.

Nine crews were briefed on the 15th for a nickelling operation that night over northern Germany, five for Berlin, and two each for Hamburg and Magdeburg. Sgt Chandler's sortie was scrubbed after he became medically unfit to fly, leaving three other crews to take off between 17.20 and 17.40 for either Hamburg in the north-west or Magdeburg in the east. F/L Bickford's sortie lasted twenty minutes and was curtailed by an oil leak from the front turret that covered the windscreen. Sgt Verstage and crew returned after half an hour with a fuel problem, and took off again at 18.45, by which time the Berlin-bound quintet had set off between 18.00 and 18.40 with S/L Whitworth the senior pilot on duty. Of the seven crews continuing on, only that of Sgt Johnson was able to complete their sortie at Berlin as briefed, the others all limping home between 21.05 (S/L Whitworth) and 03.35 (F/O Phillips) to report either technical issues or an inability to obtain a fix to establish their position over enemy territory.

NACH HITLERS STURZ

Die Lebensfrage für das deutsche Volk ist heute:

SOLL DER KRIEG VERLÄNGERT ODER ABGEKÜRZT WERDEN?

Hitler will verhindern, dass der Deutsche dies selbst entscheidet. Er kann ihn aber nicht hindern, Fragen zu stellen.

Hier sind sieben wichtige Fragen — und die Antworten.

Kann Hitlerdeutschland auf einen Kompromissfrieden rechnen?

Nein. In dem Vertrag von London haben England und Russland mit der Billigung der Vereinigten Staaten noch einmal erklärt, dass sie niemals mit dem Hitlerregime oder irgend einer anderen deutschen Regierung verhandeln werden, die sich nicht unzweideutig von allen Angriffsabsichten lossagt.

Bedeutet Hitlers Niederlage Deutschlands Zerstörung?

Nein. Immer wieder, zuerst im September 1939, zuletzt am 21. Mai 1942, hat die britische Regierung erklärt, dass sie zwei Ziele hat:
1. die Hitlertyrannei zu vernichten,
2. allen Völkern Europas, auch dem deutschen, nach dem Krieg den Aufbau eines Staates zu ermöglichen, der jedem Einzelnen unparteiische Gerechtigkeit, Rede- und Koalitionsfreiheit sichert und ihn vor Arbeitslosigkeit und wirtschaftlicher Ausbeutung bewahrt.

Hitlers Niederlage bedeutet also nicht die Zerstörung Deutschlands, sondern die Rettung Deutschlands vor der Zerstörung.

Wird England das deutsche Volk dem Bolschewismus ausliefern?

Die britische und die russische Regierung haben sich im Artikel V des Londoner Vertrags verpflichtet, sich nicht in die inneren Angelegenheiten anderer Staaten einzumengen, nachdem Hitlers Kriegsmaschine zerstört und eine Wiederholung von Angriffen unmöglich gemacht ist. Die Vereinigten Staaten nehmen dieselbe Haltung ein. Damit ist die „bolschewistische Gefahr" als das entlarvt, was sie schon immer war: ein Propaganda-Schreckgespenst.

Bedeutet Hitlers Niederlage Arbeitslosigkeit und Inflation für Deutschland?

In der Welt von heute hängt der Wohlstand eines jeden Volkes vom Wohlstand aller anderen ab. Es kann keinen dauernden Frieden und keinen Wohlstand geben, solange ein Volk versucht, sich zum Herrenvolk zu machen. In der Roosevelt-Churchill-Erklärung haben sich England und die Vereinigten Staaten in ihrem eigenen Interesse verpflichtet, nach dem Kriege keine wirtschaftliche Benachteiligung der Unterlegenen zuzu-

'After Hitler's Fall' leaflets dropped over enemy territory were known as 'Nickels'. Whitleys of 10 Sqn were the first RAF aircraft to visit Berlin in October 1939 on such a mission.

The destinations for six of the squadron's Whitleys on the night of the 18/19th were Bremen, Hamburg and Hannover, for which they took off between 22.40 and 23.50 with S/L Whitworth the senior pilot on duty. F/L Bickford's sortie to Hannover developed into an epic battle against the freezing conditions and electrical storms in the ice-bearing cloud, the tops of which reached a towering 20,000 feet. Despite remaining airborne for more than ten hours, the sortie was ultimately unsuccessful, largely as a result of the continuing unreliability of the direction-

1939 publicity shot of an Armstrong-Whitworth Whitley

finding signals from England. Four other crews returned between 05.50 and 07.40, but only that of F/Sgt Harcourt-Powell was able to report successfully completing their sortie.

As events were to prove, P/O Nelson and crew had also managed to deliver their leaflets according to brief, but the engines had cut out at 18,000 feet on the way home, and only restarted at 1,500 feet. Not trusting that they would take the aircraft home, it was decided to divert away from enemy territory, and a forced-landing was ultimately carried out near Amiens in north-eastern France. The crew was unhurt and the Whitley only slightly damaged, and they returned to Dishforth together on the 24th, the day on which briefings were held for the next nickelling operation to be undertaken that night. Hamburg, Berlin and Magdeburg provided the destination for four aircraft, which departed Dishforth between 17.30 and 17.45 with S/L Whitworth the senior pilot on duty. F/Sgt Harcourt and crew returned early at 21.00 with W/T failure, and the nickels were transferred to K9033, which took off at 22.00 in the hands of F/L Bickford and crew. They were also forced to abandon their sortie and returned ninety minutes later after the conditions caused the port engine air-intake to freeze. Meanwhile, the remaining three crews pressed on and completed their sorties before returning safely between 01.20 and 01.40.

F/L Bickford and crew were in action again on the night of the 31st, taking off at 23.00 to reconnoitre Jade Bay, the Elbe and Weser Estuaries and Hamburg. The Hamburg element of the sortie was completed before low cloud intervened and obscured the coastal region. Sgt Craig and crew departed Dishforth at 23.55, by which time the cloud had increased to make their brief impossible to fulfil. Both crews experienced great difficulty in establishing their position over

England in the conditions of low cloud, and Sgt Craig eventually landed at Driffield. During the course of the month the squadron operated on five nights, and dispatched twenty-four sorties for the loss of one Whitley and crew. The winter of 1939/40 would prove to be harsh in the extreme, and Whitley crews were to suffer unbelievable discomfort from the extreme cold inside their unheated aircraft. It speaks great volumes for the courage and determination of the crews, who pressed on deep into enemy territory, and often spent ten hours or more in the air.

November 1939

The new month began with a royal visit on the 1st, His Majesty King George VI arriving in time for lunch accompanied by the Chief-of-the-Air-Staff (CAS), Air-Chief-Marshal (ACM) Sir Cyril Newall, the Commander-in-Chief (C-in-C) Bomber Command, ACM Sir Edgar Ludlow-Hewitt, and the Air-Officer-Commanding (A-O-C) 4 Group, Air Commodore (A/C) Coningham. After lunch the party was introduced to W/C Staton, who led the king to the B Flight crew room, where he was presented to a number of crews, and discussed recent operations. Thereafter, he was led to a hangar, where the remainder of the squadron personnel were assembled, before spending a considerable time exploring a Whitley. He appeared to be most interested by the cockpit, and commented on "the enormous number of gadgets".

Propaganda Map. The first raid on Berlin in WWII was a 'Nickel' (leaflet) raid from RAF Dishforth on 1/2 October 1939. One of 10 Squadron's four Whitley aircraft on the raid failed to return. The artist Rex Whistler was inspired by this event to adapt his published drawing to create this version specific to 10 Squadron.

HM George VI visited the Squadron twice within a month in November and December 1939. His first visit was to RAF Dishforth and the second was to the forward base at Villeneuve, France - codenamed 'Sister'.

Operationally, this was to be a very low-key month, but the boredom was relieved for some by a bombing and fighter affiliation exercise on the 6th conducted over the Irish sea in conjunction with 41 Squadron. Following the recent difficulties with the Leconfield D/F equipment, Sgt Johnson and crew carried out trials on the 9th, flying to a point one hundred miles north of Leconfield and returning, and then a hundred miles to the east and returning, periodically requesting a bearing from Leconfield to check against bearings from Linton-on-Ouse. The exercise was useful in demonstrating that a number of bearings were still inaccurate. Air-firing training at Acklington occupied some crews on the 14th and 15th, before the first operation was posted on the 20th. The plan was for one aircraft each to drop leaflets over Stuttgart and Frankfurt in southern Germany and Hamburg and Bremen in the north-west, and carry out a reconnaissance of the areas. F/L Bickford, P/O Nelson and F/Sgt Cattell and their crews took off at 10.30 to head for Mildenhall, where they would refuel before the two last-mentioned departed in the afternoon to carry out their brief in the south. The attachment was led by W/C Staton, who had flown as a passenger in F/L Bickford's Whitley, which was to be held as the reserve aircraft. In the event, adverse weather conditions would cause the cancellation of the two sorties until the following evening. Meanwhile, F/O Paterson and Sgt Johnson and their crews departed Dishforth at 14.30 to fulfil their briefs over Hamburg and Bremen, where they encountered ten-tenths low cloud, which prevented the reconnaissance aspect of the sorties from taking place. P/O Nelson and F/Sgt Cattell carried out their tasks on the evening of the 21st in conditions of three-tenths cloud and a half moon, before returning safely to make their reports.

A Whitley Cockpit

Orders were received at 4 Group HQ on the 23rd to prepare for an attack on the pocket battleship Deutschland, sister ship to the Admiral Scheer and the soon-to-be-famous Admiral Graf Spee. The task was handed to seven Whitleys from 10 Squadron, eight from 51 Squadron, four from 77 Squadron and five from 102 Squadron, and was to be carried out as soon as conditions allowed and a reconnaissance of the north-western German naval ports had taken place. Six of the Dishforth element took off between 07.25 and 07.46, one section led by W/C Staton and the other by F/L Bickford, and made their way north to Kinloss to refuel and await further instructions from Coastal Command. Sgt Johnson remained at Dishforth to lead the 51 Squadron element, which was late, and he took off without them, only to be forced to return with technical issues. P/O Willis had an unspecified flying accident on the 26th, and, after sitting out the period on the ground, the 10 Squadron element returned to Dishforth on the 28th, to be replaced at Kinloss by 99 Squadron. During the course of the month the squadron launched just four sorties without loss.

W/C William Ernest Staton, CB, DSO & Bar, MC, DFC & Bar
Commanding Officer from 10th June 1938 to 10th July 1940.

December 1939

B Flight was on stand-by on the 3rd when orders were received to send four aircraft and one reserve to a forward base at Villeneuve-les-Vertus, situated some twelve miles south of Reims in France, which was code-named "Sister". This move was in preparation for a nickelling operation over Prague and Frankfurt. S/L Whitworth was the senior pilot involved, but W/C Staton travelled south with Sgt Johnson as detachment commander, leaving F/L Bickford in temporary command of the squadron. They carried with them supplies for four days, but bad weather prevented the operation from taking place. Three crews were ordered to return to

Dishforth on the 5th, while the two remaining ones remained at "Sister" until Saturday the 8th, in order to be present for a visit by King George VI and the Duke of Gloucester, before returning home on the following day. In the meantime, F/L Bickford and Sgt Craig took off from Dishforth shortly after 15.00 on the 6th to deliver nickels over Bremen and Hamburg. F/L Bickford's K9035 suffered an issue with the airscrew variable pitch control, probably because of the freezing conditions, which reached minus 32 degrees at 22,150 feet. This left the rear gunner with frost-bitten hands, but, despite the privations, they completed the sortie according to brief. Sgt Craig and crew were subjected to heavy anti-aircraft fire over Sylt, and also had to endure the intense cold, but arrived home safely to report fulfilling their brief. W/C Staton was among those remaining at "Sister", and, when His Majesty moved towards five crews assembled in a square in front of a Whitley parked closest to the inspection, he was received by the 10 Squadron commanding officer. His Majesty recognised the members of the squadron, whom he had met so recently at Dishforth, asked many questions and showed great interest in forthcoming operations.

The YMCA tea-lady is given a 'helping hand' passing a cuppa to a Whitley's crew.

From dawn on the 10th crews were put on stand-by for patrols over the North Sea, but were stood down on the 11th. F/Sgt Cattell and crew took off at 22.40 on the 13th to patrol the island of Sylt, but turned back on reaching Borkum, where freezing conditions were encountered at between 1,000 and 1,500 feet. They climbed to 4,000 feet to escape the icing, and then experienced great difficulty in locating Dishforth on arriving back home, but landed safely at 02.50. F/L Phillips and crew took off eight minutes after F/Sgt Cattell, also bound for Sylt, where accurate anti-aircraft fire straddled the Whitley without causing damage. They encountered the same challenging conditions of low-lying mist while searching for Dishforth, but landed safely at 05.45.

Six Whitleys were made ready on the 17th for patrol duties over Borkum and Sylt, and took off between 13.15 and 16.30 with S/L Whitworth and crew first away. W/C Staton was the senior pilot on duty, departing at 15.05, and he would report dropping two flares over Borkum, the second eliciting a response in the form of a special kind of searchlight consisting of three separate beams, which failed to latch onto the aircraft but illuminated the cockpit. A convoy of around forty ships was seen to be steaming northwards off Flamborough Head by S/L Whitworth and crew, while F/Sgt Harcourt-Powell and crew spotted two Heinkel 111s heading towards England, one of which turned onto the Whitley's tail, but failed to open fire. The weather conditions and visibility remained good throughout the operation, which was concluded with the safe return of Sgt Craig and crew at 23.20. A similar operation to the same area was mounted on the 19th involving four Whitleys, with S/L Whitworth the senior pilot on duty. Take-offs took place between 14.30 and 17.00, and all reached the Borkum/Sylt region to encounter a little searchlight activity and anti-aircraft fire, mostly from the vicinity of Wilhelmshaven. No damage was done, and all aircraft returned to find challenging conditions for landing, which would cause the cancellation of two further patrols.

The 23rd brought sea patrols for two 10 Squadron crews, F/L Bickford and F/Sgt Harcourt-Powell departing Dishforth at 11.45 and 12.05 respectively, before setting course for the target area on an east-north-easterly heading to a final position some fifty miles north of Sylt. They were both safely back on the ground by 18.34 after uneventful sorties during which they sighted only one neutral merchantman between them. 10 Squadron's final operation of the year took place on New Year's Eve and involved the crews of F/L Phillips, F/O Nelson, Sgt Craig and Sgt Parsons, whose brief was to carry out a security patrol over Sylt, Heligoland and Norderney. They took off in the early afternoon, and returned safely in the evening, whereupon F/L Phillips reported dropping a flare and a single bomb on what appeared to be a flare-path in the vicinity of Cuxhaven. During the course of the month the squadron dispatched twenty sorties on six patrols without loss.

January 1940

There would be very little operational activity to occupy the crews of Bomber Command until the end of February, by which time the harsh winter conditions had begun to relent and loosen their grip. Four crews were put on stand-by at Dishforth for a North Sea sector sweep, but the threat of fog saw them stand down. It was the 4th before the first operational activity of the year could be mounted by 10 Squadron, Sgt Verstage and F/O Paterson taking off at 15.10 to cross the North Sea as a tactical pair before splitting up to deliver leaflets over Hamburg and Bremen respectively. They were thirty miles out from the English coast when a leaking oxygen bottle forced F/O Paterson to turn back, and he landed at 16.35 to effect repairs, before taking off again within the hour. Meanwhile, Sgt Verstage and crew had noted lights in Holland, before observing two weak searchlights on Heligoland, and poor blackout to the north of the River Elbe. They delivered their nickels as briefed and returned home, spotting a triple-beamed searchlight flashing on and off and the lights of a convoy or fishing fleet. F/O Paterson and crew also observed many land and marine lights as they flew close to the Dutch coast, and reported severe anti-aircraft fire over Bremen, along with two blue searchlights in the vicinity of Wesermünde. On return, low brake pressure persuaded F/O Paterson to deliberately undershoot the landing, but he overdid it, and K9020 struck a tree before coming heavily to earth, breaking the starboard undercarriage, and, as a result, causing damage to the starboard main-plane, tail-plane and propeller. F/Sgt Cattell and crew carried out a patrol in the Sylt-Norderney-Borkum area on the 5th, taking off at 14.03 and landing eight-and-a-half hours later after an uneventful sortie.

10 Squadron in 1940 at Dishforth – Whitley V with Merlin engines

A number of patrols were briefed out over the ensuing two weeks, but adverse weather conditions caused their cancellation, and it was the 19th before a sortie could be launched. F/Sgt Harcourt-Powell and crew took off at 15.07 for a security patrol in the Borkum-Wangerooge-Sylt region, but ran into a thick band of snow-bearing cloud that came down to sea-level and persuaded them to turn back. This was the final operational activity of a month which had produced just three sorties without loss.

February 1940

Dishforth spent most of the new month in a state of unserviceability through ice and snow on the runway or boggy conditions when occasional thaws occurred. A number of operations were briefed but cancelled, and even training flights were severely curtailed. At 22.45 on the 26th, S/L Whitworth and crew took off to deliver leaflets to Berlin, and landed at "Sister" a little over eight hours later after a successful, but uneventful sortie. This proved to be the only operational activity of the month.

March 1940

Ground and Technical Staff.

W/C Staton was sent on twelve days' leave on the 1st, and the squadron was placed temporarily in the hands of S/L Beaman. Also on this day, Sgt Johnson and F/L Bickford were briefed for reconnaissance and nickelling sorties over Berlin, and took off at 17.30 and 18.30 respectively. Both returned at 03.15, F/L Bickford doing so safely, while K9026 crashed in a field a quarter of a mile short of the runway after both engines cut out through petrol starvation. The Whitley hit a tree before making contact with the ground and skidded across the field to stop against the far hedge and just short of another tree. The aircraft sustained considerable damage, but the crew walked away unhurt. At debriefing both crews reported extensive searchlight activity over enemy territory and generally poor blackout discipline.

During the morning of the 3rd, S/L Beaman took the station Magister for a trip to Catterick, but force-landed in a small field after the engine cut. He was unhurt, and the Magister would soon be returned to active duty. The squadron was about to re-equip with Mk V Whitleys, and the initial five were flown over from the Armstrong Whitworth works at Baginton, Coventry by 2 Ferry Pool pilots during the afternoon and evening. Sgt Hillary was the senior pilot of K9022 during a training exercise, although it was second pilot, Sgt Keast, who was in control when the Whitley overshot the flare-path at Dishforth and came to grief at 21.10. Neither sustained injury, but the Whitley was extensively damaged and was declared to be beyond economical repair. The Mk V Whitleys had been delivered "incomplete", and instructions were received on the 4th that the squadron was not to keep them, as it was considered that it would take too long to make good the deficiencies. A working party arrived on the station during the morning to carry out modifications to the TR9F equipment in the Mk IVs, and this allowed the squadron to be screened and the crews to be allowed forty-eight hours leave on a two-hour recall.

Elaborate 'Nose Art' was to come later. 10 Squadron's first bombing raid of WWII was on the German seaplane base at Hörnum, Sylt on 20 March 1940, accompanying 51 Sqn.

At last, on the 16th, preparations were put in hand at Dishforth for the month's next operational activity to be carried out that night. S/L Whitworth, F/L Phillips and Sgt Verstage, the last-mentioned as a reserve, flew down to "Sister" as a staging post for a nickelling and reconnaissance trip to Prague, while six other Whitleys were made ready for reconnaissance sorties over the Ruhr. The Prague-bound duo took off at 19.00, while Dishforth dispatched its six Whitleys between 19.00 and 20.15 with F/L Bickford the senior pilot on duty and last away. The route to Czechoslovakia was via Mannheim, Nuremberg and Pilsen, and it was noted that the blackout was much more effective than of late. The weather conditions were not ideal, with cloud presenting some difficulties, and the fixes from Le Bourget were found to be out by between sixty and a hundred miles. This led to S/L Whitworth almost certainly dispensing his leaflets south of Prague, but F/L Phillips enjoyed better luck, and his presence over Prague caused the local radio station to be taken temporarily off the air. A number of the Ruhr-bound crews were routed in over Borkum and the Ems Estuary to Oldersum, before heading south to Salzbergen and then towards Duisburg over the Rhine between Wesel and Orsoy. It seems that others reached the Ruhr via a southern route over Luxembourg, and the area reconnoitred covered Gelsenkirchen in the north-east to Bonn in the south-west. Adverse weather conditions prevented all from landing anywhere in England, and all eight of the Dishforth crews landed at "Sister" between 01.00 and 03.31. The weather conditions at Dishforth were so marginal that W/C Staton ordered the nine crews to remain at "Sisters" until the 18th, when they took off at fifteen-minute intervals from 11.55 to return home, landing beneath a 600-foot cloud base between 15.55 and 18.40. K9031 took off in the hands of F/Sgt Cattell and crew, but was forced to return because of a problem with a propeller. They landed safely at Amiens-Glisy aerodrome to find that one blade had lost six inches from the tip.

The first opportunity to drop bombs on a German land target came in retaliation for a Luftwaffe attack on elements of the Royal Navy at Scapa Flow on the 16th, during which a stray bomb had inadvertently killed a civilian on the Orkney island of Hoy. The British response was to attack the German seaplane base at Hörnum on the southerly tip of the island of Sylt, where no civilian property was at risk. A force of thirty Whitleys was made ready on the 19th, of which fifteen would be launched from Dishforth, eight representing 10 Squadron and seven 51 Squadron, while Driffield would provide the remaining fifteen from 77 and 102 Squadrons. The 4 Group attack was allowed a four-hour window, and would be followed up later by twenty Hampdens of 5 Group in a two-hour slot. Seven of the 10 Squadron Whitleys were loaded with two 500 and two 250 pounders each, while the eighth, containing S/L Whitworth and crew, would carry two small bomb containers (SBCs) of 4lb incendiaries and four 250 pounders. W/C Staton was the senior pilot on duty and was the first into the air to be followed by Sgt Verstage, F/L Phillips, Sgt Parsons, S/L Whitworth, F/O Nelson, F/L Bickford and Sgt Craig between 19.20 and 20.03. W/C Staton was fired on from a flak ship on the approaches to the target when at 2,500 feet, and then arrived in the target area twenty minutes ahead of schedule. He decided to orbit and watch the Driffield aircraft carry out their attacks, before dropping his bombs in the face of light flak that reached 8,000 feet, and observing them to fall short of the crane on the jetty. Further intense light flak was seen to come from a position a thousand yards north-west of the target. There was also a concentration of batteries in the centre of the island at Westerland, and, at one point, the searchlights were arranged in a line facing westwards, behind which a light flak unit was firing. On return W/C Staton reported lighting up the target with flares and blinding the searchlights. S/L Whitworth delivered all of his bombs and one container of incendiaries, but an error by the bomb-aimer caused the other container to hang up. They spent forty-five minutes trying to persuade the SBC to drop, but without success, and no one was certain that any bombs had fallen away until they arrived home to check. The remaining crews made similar reports concerning the defences, and all claimed to have bombed in the target area, some observing hits on sheds and the slipway. Once all of the post-raid reports had been collated, they seemed to suggest that the operation had been an outstanding success, and news of it was duly splashed across the front pages of the national press. It was not possible to carry out a reconnaissance until the 6th of April, by which time no evidence of damage could be detected, and this would be the first of countless examples of overly enthusiastic claims of success by bomber crews. However, the propaganda value to the folks at home was massive.

There was just a single reconnaissance/nickelling operation to occupy the squadron before the month ended, and this involved six crews, who took off between 18.50 and 20.27 on the 22nd to reconnoitre the River Rhine and the Ruhr Valley with S/L Whitworth and F/Ls Bickers and Phillips the senior pilots on duty. They flew out through heavy ice-bearing cloud, which prevented Sgt Parsons from climbing beyond 7,000 feet, and he was fifty miles out from the coast on a course for Borkum when he decided to turn back to land fifty-five minutes after taking off. The conditions were also responsible for the loss of S/L Whitworth's D/F aerial, which forced him to turn back on reaching Borkum, and he landed safely after a round trip of some five-and-a-half hours. Sgt Hillary had to climb to 18,000 feet to escape the cloud, and was then shadowed by enemy fighters throughout his time over Germany, one closing to two hundred yards, at which point he ducked into cloud to escape its attentions. On emerging into clear air, the fighter was still there, but did not attack and broke away as anti-aircraft fire took over. The conditions had improved markedly for the four Whitleys by the time the industrial Ruhr hove into sight and visibility became excellent. The area to be covered stretched from Borkum in the north to Gelsenkirchen in the east and Saarbrücken in the south, taking in all of the Ruhr manufacturing centres and Cologne, and occupying between seven and ten hours of flight time. F/L Phillips and Sgt Craig landed at Amiens-Glisy, the latter after violating the neutrality first of Holland and then of Luxembourg through engine trouble which threatened to force them down in Germany, and the former also crossed northern Holland because of a navigation error. The other two Whitleys lobbed in at Abingdon, and all returned to base later in the day to report observing the glow from so many blast furnaces and coking ovens, that their precise locations could not be pinpointed, and also described being subject to heavy flak and searchlight activity over Düsseldorf and the Siegfried Line. It was also agreed that the weather conditions over England and the North Sea were the severest yet encountered.

S/L Hanafin reported to the squadron on posting on the 26th, and he would assume the role of flight commander. During the course of the month the squadron operated on four occasions, dispatching twenty-four sorties without loss, and registered the destruction of just one Whitley as a result of the training crash.

Bombing up at Villeneuve - Vertus Airfield in France, (Codename Sister) 25 miles south of Reims during the period Oct 1939-Mar 1940 when 10 Squadron used it as a forward operating base. After D-Day it was used by the USAAF C-47's but little remains today.

10 Sqn Whitley

April 1940

At the start of the new month operations and training exercises were posted and then cancelled because of the weather. The station commander, G/C Hopcraft, became ineffective due to illness on the 4th, and W/C Staton took temporary command of Dishforth, while 10 Squadron was put into the hands of S/L Whitworth. It was the 6th before the first operation was mounted, and this involved P/O Prior and the newly-arrived Sgt MacCoubrey and their crews conducting a reconnaissance of the Dortmund-Ems/Mittelland Canals region north of the Ruhr as far as Datteln and Recklinghausen at the north-eastern end of Germany's industrial heartland. The latter took off at 19.40, and entered enemy airspace via Borkum as normal, but, despite fine and clear weather conditions, they found it too dark to pick out ground detail from between 4,000 and 10,000 feet, and they returned home after eight-and-a-half hours aloft, discovering on landing that a connecting rod in the port engine had broken a few minutes earlier and was protruding through the crank-case. K9032 had taken off at 20.50, and was running short of fuel as F/O Prior brought it in over the north Lincolnshire coast with the intention of force-landing after nearly nine hours in the air. The Whitley struck a tree two miles south of Grimsby at 05.44, and was wrecked in the ensuing crash, although, happily, without injury to the crew, who were able to walk away.

4 Group HQ moved from RAF station Linton-on-Ouse on the 7th, and took up residence at the imposing red-brick former manor house, Heslington Hall in York. On the 9th the German invasion of Norway and Denmark brought an end to the shadow boxing which had characterized events since September, and it was the signal for the strategic bombing war to begin hesitantly, but in earnest. It took German forces just six hours to subdue Danish resistance after sending in

First Line Servicing

forces by ground, sea and air, while the Norwegians would resist for two months, supported by British and French forces. The Royal Navy tried to do its best after the horse had bolted, and, prevented by the distance from directly supporting the British and French response at Narvik in the north, Bomber Command would target airfields in the south which were being used by the enemy to bring in troops and supplies, and also attack shipping on the main routes from Germany. This would bring about the first mining sorties by RAF Bomber Command, initially by Hampdens of 5 Group, and this was a campaign which would endure for almost the entire period of the war and be highly effective. The codename for mining was "gardening", mines were referred to as "vegetables", and, the regions into which Europe's coastal areas from the Pyrenees in the south-west to the Polish border in the north-east were divided, were given horticultural and marine-biological names.

Orders were received on the 11th for Dishforth and Driffield to prepare twenty-two Whitleys for operations that night against shipping, according to the 4 Group ORB, at Trondheim, however, this was beyond the range of Whitleys, and the actual target area was in the Kattegat, between Kiel Bay in the south and Oslo in the north. Sgt Johnson's K9034 became unserviceable with engine trouble and had to be scrubbed, leaving five 10 Squadron participants to take off between 18.55 and 20.13 with F/L Bickford the senior pilot on duty, and S/L Hanafin flying as his navigator. All reached the target area, where skies were clear, but extreme darkness produced challenging conditions for identification of ground detail and likely targets. F/L Bickford dropped all of his bombs on lights which were thought to be a ship near the entrance to Oslo Fjord, but no results were observed. No bombs were dropped by the rest of the 10 Squadron

Whitley rear turret

element, but P/O Cattell jettisoned his "safe" over the North Sea after a failing engine threatened to bring the Whitley down. In the event, all returned safely between 03.30 and 05.08 to report on blackout conditions and enemy defences. An operational order was issued on the 14th for six Whitleys from 51 Squadron and three from 10 Squadron to attack road and rail junctions in Germany close to the Belgian and Dutch frontiers to delay the enemy advance through the Low Countries. The operation was cancelled, but, had it taken place, would have been the first direct attack on mainland Germany and a politically sensitive action.

The squadron made ready six Whitleys on the 15th to attack Stavanger aerodrome that night in concert with six others from 102 Squadron at Driffield. They took off between 19.25 and 19.55 with F/Os Nelson and Paterson the senior pilots on duty, but Sgts Craig and Hillary returned early with communications failures, while F/O Paterson abandoned his sortie because of an engine issue, and ultimately landed at Waddington after overshooting Dishforth. F/O Nelson and crew battled through towering cloud on the way north, but had still not found clear skies by the time they reached 20,000 feet, and also opted to turn back. P/O Parsons and crew reached the target area but were unable to identify the aerodrome in the adverse weather conditions and the absence of accurate D/F fixes, and jettisoned their bombs in the North Sea on the way home. Only Sgt Johnson and crew managed to complete their sortie as briefed, finding clear skies and excellent visibility above 12,000 feet on the way out, and dropping their bombs on the north-east runway after arriving to find fires already raging in or near a hangar. The attack took place in the face of considerable light flak but just a single searchlight, and they returned safely after a round-trip of more than seven-and-a-half hours.

W/C Staton put himself on the Order of Battle for the night of the 16/17th as the lone 10 Squadron representative among two from 51 Squadron briefed to attack the aerodromes of Fornebu and Kjeller, situated respectively to the south-west and north-east of Oslo. He took off

Armstrong Whitworth Whitley Mk V with the Nash and Thompson Type FN4 rear turret.

at 19.10, and flew into low cloud, snow storms and severe icing as he approached Norway, which prevented him from identifying the targets. He claimed that would have required a clear, moonlit night and an altitude of at least 5,000 feet to pick out his targets, and blamed the many small islands for creating the difficulties in establishing position. He was able to observe great shipping activity at Drammen, further to the south-west, counting eight ships berthed at the wharves, one anchored in the Fjord and another in the process of turning about. The ice accretion was so bad, that some remained on the Whitley after landing, and the crew described large chunks being flung off the propellers and crashing against the fuselage. The operation was repeated two nights later by F/L Bickford, P/O Parsons and Sgt Craig and their crews, who departed Dishforth between 20.15 and 20.30. On reaching Oslo Fjord, they found fog down to 300 feet, which completely obscured the ground in the target area. F/L Bickford brought his bombs back to a landing at Leuchars in Scotland, where he found Sgt Craig already thawing out, having jettisoned his load on the way back. P/O Parsons observed a dummy flare burning near Leuchars, which was visible from forty miles away, but pressed on to land at Dishforth at 06.10.

Briefings took place at Dishforth on the 20th, at which five crews from 51 Squadron and six from 10 Squadron learned that they were to return to Oslo Fjord that night for another attempt at the aerodromes at Fornebu and Kjeller, with Sola airfield at Stavanger as an alternative. They were told also that 58 Squadron at Linton-on-Ouse would be supporting the operation with three

Whitleys in formation

Whitleys. S/L Whitworth was to be the senior pilot among the 10 Squadron element, and the recently-commissioned P/O Cattell, who was to act as a reserve, found himself on the Order of Battle after Sgt Verstage reported sick late on. F/O Phillips was drafted in as the new reserve pilot, with members of both his and Sgt Vertage's crew, but their involvement was cancelled because of insufficient time to brief them. Sgt MacCoubrey's aircraft became unserviceable, and he and his crew were transferred to the Whitley prepared for Sgt Verstage. The five Whitleys departed Dishforth either side of 20.30, but P/O Warren and crew arrived back fifty

Ground crew at work

minutes later with a fuel feed problem, which, having been rectified, allowed them to take off again at 21.50. Sgt MacCoubrey's generator had been troublesome from the start of the sortie, and eventually forced him to turn back when an hour out, leaving just four crews to press on to the target. F/O Nelson made landfall at Fredrikstad, situated on the eastern bank of Oslo Fjord, but found low cloud obscuring it and the aerodromes, so headed westwards to Sola airfield, where he dropped six 250 pounders onto the south-western stretch of the runway. As he flew out to sea, he encountered a balloon barrage, which had been run-up from ships to a height of 12,000 feet when the attacking force was seen to approach. He flew back towards Scotland in clear skies until fifty miles from the coast, and landed at Leuchars after a round-trip of nine hours. P/O Cattell and crew also attacked Sola airfield, delivering their bombs onto the intersection of the runways, before landing at Leuchars at 05.40. P/O Warren and S/L Whitworth saw shipping in Oslo Fjord, but did not carry out an attack and brought their bombs back, touching down at Leuchars at 05.55 and 06.56 respectively.

Sgt Johnson and crew were briefed with others on the 22nd for an operation that night against Fornebu and Kjeller aerodromes, and would ultimately find themselves the sole 10 Squadron participants in the night's activity. They took off at 20.35, and flew north at 4,000 feet in excellent visibility under clear skies and a full moon. Kjeller aerodrome could not be identified, but moderately intense light flak greeted them in the vicinity of Fornebu, and a few bursts of heavy flak were also felt. An annoying blue searchlight was extinguished by the gunners, before an uneventful return flight was conducted at 2,500 feet, ending at Kinloss for refuelling.

Preparations were put in hand on the 23rd for operations that night against Fornebu and Kjeller aerodromes, shipping in Oslo Fjord and Aalborg aerodrome in northern Denmark, for which 10 Squadron briefed four and two crews respectively. The Oslo element took off between 19.31 and 19.50 with S/L Hanafin and F/L Bickford the senior pilots on duty, the former flying the first sortie in a Whitley Mk V, and they were followed into the air at 21.47 and 21.58

A Whitley Mk V (This aircraft belonged to 10 OTU at RAF Abingdon)

respectively by F/O Nelson and Sgt MacCoubrey. F/O Nelson's sortie lasted only a matter of minutes after his air speed indicator (a.s.i) failed, leaving the others to fly out in clear conditions with very little cloud. S/L Hanafin and Sgt Craig found the Oslo target area with ease, the latter delivering his bombs onto Fornebu aerodrome in the glare of searchlights, but failing to observe their bursts because of the need to take violent evasive action to dodge the flak. S/L Hanafin spotted two vessels in the Fjord and attacked one of them, which was believed to be a 250-tonner, and observed hits close to the funnel. He then followed up with a strafing pass, after which the ship was seen to run aground. He found that Kjeller aerodrome appeared to be out of service, and an observation of Fornebu was rendered impossible by the same intense searchlight activity experienced by Sgt Craig. Low cloud and rain produced

challenging conditions for S/L Hanafin's eventual landing at Leuchars, while Sgt Craig put down at Kinloss. F/L Bickford attacked the alternative target, the aerodrome at Kristiansand, and observed his bombs to hit the north-eastern end of the runway and the corner of a hangar. F/L Phillips also attacked this target and registered hits on the runway and hangar before returning to Kinloss. Sgt MacCoubrey found a number of searchlights operating at Aalborg aerodrome, but the sound of his approach prompted many more to spring into life accompanied by a spirited flak response. He dropped all of his bombs onto the ring of searchlights positioned around the aerodrome, and managed to escape without damage, but failed to pick up the divert signal to land at Kinloss because of the bad weather at Dishforth. As a result, he landed at base with extreme difficulty in conditions of low cloud and ground mist. P/O Warren attacked Aalborg aerodrome from 15,000 feet, confirming the cone of searchlights around it and the excellent visibility, and landed at Leuchars at 05.10 in rain and low cloud with a base at 500 feet.

Dishforth was ordered to provide a dozen Whitleys for operations against Fornebu aerodrome on the 30th, 10 and 51 Squadrons responding with six each. The 10 Squadron element took off between 19.12 and 19.47 with S/Ls Hanafin and Whitworth the senior pilots on duty, and were more than an hour into the outward flight when a recall signal was sent out at 21.00 to S/L Hanafin, F/L Phillips and Sgt MacCoubrey, after the NCO i/c armoury reported that they had taken off with the safety pins still attached to the long-delay-fused bombs. The armourer responsible was put immediately under open arrest, and the three aircraft duly landed between 22.45 and 01.45, Sgt MacCoubrey having reached the Norwegian coast at the time of the recall. S/L Whitworth and Sgts Johnson and Craig all reached the target in excellent conditions to be greeted by intense searchlight and flak activity, and delivered their bombs onto the aerodrome and hangar, which was observed to be in flames. The weather deteriorated during the return trip, and the trio landed at Dishforth under a cloud base of 500 feet. During the course of the month the squadron operated on nine occasions, dispatching thirty-five sorties for the loss of a single Whitley in a landing crash.

May 1940

The Norwegian campaign continued on the night of the 1/2nd, for which 10 Squadron made ready six Whitleys to attack the aerodrome at Stavanger, while six aircraft from the Driffield squadrons attended to Fornebu from a forward base at Kinloss. The Dishforth element took off between 22.05 and 22.50 with W/C Staton the senior pilot on duty, and all reached the target area to find good conditions for bombing. F/L Bickford was the first to arrive and made a gliding attack, which caught the defences completely by surprise, and, it was only after the incendiaries had set fire to buildings and aircraft, that a searchlight and anti-aircraft response was forthcoming. P/O Warren described a considerable amount of moderately accurate ground-fire as he bombed from 6,000 feet. He had flown over a convoy some 150 miles short of the Norwegian coast, but had decided not to attack. Through an electrical fault, only one bomb fell from S/L Hanafin's bomb bay, and that fell onto a runway. F/O Nelson delivered his entire load onto the aerodrome and watched it set off small fires, while W/C Staton put one stick in front of a hangar and the other along the side of a wood where aircraft were parked. F/O Phillips favoured a glide approach, and also aimed at the perimeter of the aerodrome to hit aircraft at their dispersals, before returning safely with the others to land at either Driffield or base between 04.40 and 05.35.

Five new Whitley Mk V aircraft, P4955, 56, 58 59 and 60, were delivered by Ferry Pool pilots on the afternoon of the 4th, shortly before four crews attended briefing for the night's activity. Sgt MacCoubrey took off at 19.27 bound for a security patrol in the Borkum-Wangerooge region of the east Frisians, and he was followed into the air at 19.36 by Sgt Hillary and crew, who were to carry out a similar task further north over the island of Sylt, taking in the seaplane bases at Hörnum, Rantum and List. They were to be shadowed later by Sgt Johnson and Sgt

10 Squadron at Leeming, summer 1940. The Station Commander, G/C W E 'Bull' Staton is 5th from right front. Another nickname for him was 'King-Kong'

Craig respectively, who would take off at 21.19 and 21.50. They flew out in clear and fine weather with just a little cloud over the enemy coastal area, but Sgt Craig was forced to turn back when around a hundred miles short of his objective, after his starboard engine overheated. Sgt MacCoubrey and crew encountered intense searchlight and flak activity over Borkum, along with ground haze, which prevented identification of ground detail. They descended to 600 feet and dropped flares, but were still unable to penetrate the haze, and continued on with their patrol at 7,000 feet without further incident. Sgt Johnson and crew arrived later after flying out at 4,500 feet, and encountered the same conditions, before returning safely from an uneventful sortie. Meanwhile, Sgt Hillary and crew had crossed the North Sea at 10,000 feet, before descending to 5,000 feet to make landfall on the Danish island of Rømø to the north of Sylt. Haze reduced visibility, and a further reduction in height to 2,000 feet provided no improvement, although the aircraft remained at this altitude for the remainder of the patrol.

At noon on the 5th the squadron was told to stand down for seven days while a full conversion took place onto the Mk V Whitley. By the time the Squadron was declared operational again, the ill-fated Norwegian campaign had ended, and a new, intense phase of the war had begun. The storm broke on the 10th, when German ground forces advanced across the Low Countries at first light, supported by tactical air power, and overran the weak Dutch and Belgian defences. The Battle and Blenheim squadrons of the Advanced Air Striking Force had been held back on their French airfields, allowing the Germans to set up strong defences around the canals and bridges over the Maas at Maastricht in Holland and the Meuse at Sedan in France. By the time they were thrown into the fray, they were hopelessly outmatched by the Luftwaffe, and, beginning on the 11th, Battles, in particular, were shot out of the sky in huge numbers by intense ground fire and marauding ME109s and 110s. Within days the Battle squadrons would be effectively knocked out of the campaign, and the 2 Group Blenheims would also experience a torrid time. Bomber Command responded on the night of the 10/11th by sending Whitleys to bomb bridges across the Rhine at Rees and Wesel and attack columns of transport heading westwards at Goch and Geldern. On the following night the first attack on a German town was carried out by Hampdens and Whitleys against road and rail communications targets in Mönchengladbach.

10 Squadron was not involved in these first forays into mainland Germany, but was ordered to prepare six Whitleys on the 12th for operations that night against road junctions in the area between the Rhine and the Dutch frontier. They took off between 20.35 and 21.31 with W/C Staton and S/Ls Hanafin and Whitworth all on the Order of Battle. Their destinations were at Gladbeck and Cleves (Kleve), situated north-west of the Ruhr, which S/L Whitworth failed to locate despite largely clear skies and after spending two hours searching as far east as Düsseldorf, where the blackout was described as excellent. The rear gunner spotted two twin-engine enemy fighters, picked out fleetingly by searchlights, and fired at them without observing results. This aircraft landed at Manston because of concerns about fuel after seven hours aloft with a seemingly faulty petrol gauge. W/C Staton located the secondary target at Cleves and bombed it from 5,000 feet, also noting an enemy aircraft at 00.20 between Emmerich and Cleves, which did not attack. He described searchlights arranged in two-kilometre-squares with a searchlight at each intersection. If he flew in any direction for more than two minutes the searchlight immediately ahead would illuminate his track before the others opened up into a curtain of light. He confirmed heavy but inaccurate flak in the border region, and that Rotterdam was burning. F/O Phillips carried out his attack at Gladbeck from 7,000 feet, also describing the blackout as complete, while S/L Hanafin delivered part of his bomb load, two 500 and six 250

Flak damage to a Whitley's wingtip

10 Sqn Whitley

10 Sqn Whitley take off, 1940

pounders, also at Gladbeck. F/L Bickford let his load go from 9,000 feet, and Sgt Johnson reached the target area only for an alarming drop in oil pressure in one engine to persuade him to turn immediately for home, where he was the last to land, at 06.00.

Orders were received at Dishforth on the 15th to make all available aircraft ready for operations that night. 10 Squadron responded with thirteen Whitleys, but, because of the continuing sickness of P/O Cattell and the refusal of Group to allow W/C Staton to fly, only twelve crews could be assembled, and the spare Whitley was loaned to 51 Squadron. The first element of six, which included the 51 Squadron crew of F/L Budden, took off between 19.57 and 20.09 with F/O Paterson the senior pilot, and the Ruhr as their destination, where the objectives were oil plants at Wanne-Eickel/Herne and Gelsenkirchen, marshalling yards at Schwerte, south-east of Dortmund, and the electrical power station at Reisholz, to the south-east of Düsseldorf. Alternative targets were blast furnaces and any marshalling yards that presented themselves in the general target area. The second element departed Dishforth between 20.07 and 20.18 with S/Ls Hanafin and Whitworth the senior pilots on duty. They had been briefed to attack enemy communications in the Dinant and Turnhout regions of southern and northern Belgium respectively, specifically to cause as many blockages and delays as possible by bombing road bridges across the canals and rivers.

There were clear skies over the Ruhr with the usual ground haze, but P/O Parsons and Sgt Hillary located Gelsenkirchen and bombed from 6,000 and 7,000 feet respectively, the former observing two bomb-bursts on the perimeter of the target, which was probably the Nordstern oil plant, while the latter saw no results. Sgt Craig and crew found a long, moving line of military transports south of Düsseldorf, which they bombed from 5,000 feet, while P/O Warren and crew spent two hours stooging around in search of their primary or alternative target in the same area, before coming upon the German-occupied aerodrome at Gilze-Rijen in southern Holland on the way home and bombing it from 9,000 feet, observing five bursts. On return they reported making landfall between The Hague and Rotterdam, both of which were burning furiously. F/O Paterson also experienced great difficulty in identifying their briefed target, and bombed the glow of one of a number of blast-furnaces at the eastern end of the Ruhr from 5,000 feet. Although no results were observed, the light from the furnaces highlighted tall chimneys nearby. Sgt Verstage and crew located Gelsenkirchen fairly easily, and made two unsatisfactory runs across their target at 6,000 feet, before beginning a third and accurate one. It was at this point that searchlights, which had been dormant, suddenly sprang into life in a blaze of light, and the target was lost in the glare. After fifteen minutes a burning military objective was sighted and attacked, but no results were observed.

Meanwhile, over Belgium, the weather conditions were as those over the Ruhr, and P/O Nelson and crew bombed their primary target at Dinant from 3,000 feet, observing no results but feeling the shock wave from their bomb-bursts. Sgt MacCoubrey and crew were over their target at Dinant between 23.45 and 00.30, bombing from 7,000 feet without observing results. Sgt Johnson and crew were at 5,000 feet over northern Belgium attacking their secondary target, a road leading to a bridge over a river, or, more likely, the Antwerp-Turnhout Canal. The hazy conditions had hindered their attempts to locate the target, but, at least, there was an absence of the searchlights they had encountered over Antwerp. S/L Whitworth and crew failed to identify their briefed targets in southern Belgium, possibly because of the glare from a circle of a dozen searchlights at Dinant, but came upon a main cross-road south of the town, which they attacked with two salvoes from 4,000 feet at 00.05. The bombs were seen to fall short and into an adjacent wood, which was observed to catch fire. S/L Hanafin located his primary target, a bridge over the River Meuse at Dinant, and bombed it from 6,500 feet between 23.50 and 00.21, choosing to jettison the bombs lives to ensure their departure, after experiencing bomb-release problems in P4957 in the past. F/L Bickford and crew bombed the railway at Dinant from 5,000 feet before returning to spend two hours establishing their position, firstly near Waddington and eventually at Dishforth, ultimately landing safely at 03.50.

The entire operating strength of the squadron, fourteen crews, was called to briefing on the 17th to learn that Bremen was to be their destination that night, where an oil plant was the primary target. Alternative targets in the event of bad weather would be any aerodromes on the Frisian Islands. They took off between 20.04 and 21.03 with W/C Staton the senior pilot on duty and first away, but S/L Hanafin crashed after the undercarriage-retract lever was accidentally knocked as the Whitley bounced along the grass track in the early stages of its take-off run. It sank onto one wing and turned completely round before coming to a halt, severely damaged, but without injury to the occupants. The others pressed on in excellent weather conditions, W/C Staton locating the oil plant with ease by means of the River Weser and the shape of the adjacent docks. He was over the target from 00.04 to 00.35, and made six attempts in the face of intense searchlight activity before delivering his attack. He and Sgt Johnson were operating in concert, and it was while Sgt Johnson was acting as a decoy to attract the searchlights, that W/C Staton made a steep diving turn before gliding down from 8,000 to 5,500 feet on a west to east heading, and then turning on a south to north track to drop two 500 and six 250 pounders plus incendiaries from 1,500 feet. They were seen to straddle the aiming-point and a number of direct hits were claimed, but the Whitley sustained some non-critical flak damage to the starboard wing and fuselage as it completed the bomb-run. Sgt Johnson also made a glide approach from 7,000 down to 3,000 feet, and his bombs were seen to explode among buildings to the west of the target. His aircraft also sustained flak damage, which included a burst tyre, and this led to a forced-landing at base, again, without crew casualties, and, in this instance, without serious damage to the Whitley. Sgt Hillary and crew spent fifteen minutes over the primary target, and bombed it from 5,000 feet at 00.50, while F/O Paterson and crew dropped their load in two sticks from 4,000 feet between 00.45 and 01.30 after making numerous runs. They were unable to observe the results, as taking evasive action became a greater priority in the face of intense searchlight and flak activity. Sgt Verstage and crew carried out a glide approach to deliver their bombs from 5,000 feet, observing some to fall among fires in the docks a mile south-east of the oil plant, and the others onto a nearby railway. F/O Nelson and crew glided from 10,000 to 3,800 feet before releasing their bombs, the fall of which could not be identified in the glare of searchlights. Sgt MacCoubrey and crew delivered their load in a salvo from 4,600 feet, but also saw no results in the haste to escape the flak and searchlights. Sgt Craig and crew were over the target for ten minutes from 00.05, and dropped their incendiaries first from 6,000 feet, before letting the 250 and 500 pounders go into the fires caused by them. S/L Whitworth was undertaking his final sortie with the squadron, and dropped his bombs from 6,000 after shedding two thousand feet in a glide. P/O Parsons dropped his load from 2,000 feet and F/L Bickford from 4,200 feet after a long glide, while F/L Phillips's attack lasted for forty minutes from 00.10

and was carried out at 5,000 feet. P/O Warren failed to locate the primary target because of navigational problems, and bombed the aerodrome on Borkum from 5,000 feet at 02.14. All aircraft returned safely, many bearing the scars of battle, but a feeling of satisfaction at the night's work probably pervaded the crew room.

On the 18th, a gloriously hot day with a gentle breeze, S/L Whitworth and F/Ls Bickford and Phillips were awarded the DFC. On the same day, S/L Whitworth and Sgts Craig and Verstage were posted to Linton-on-Ouse to join 78 Squadron, which was about to be released from its Group Pool training role and enter the fray as a front-line bomber unit. For S/L Whitworth this would be a temporary posting, which would see him return to 10 Squadron in mid-June. In the meantime, he was succeeded as B Flight commander by F/L Bickford, who was promoted to acting squadron leader rank. The postings set off a number of crew changes, starting with S/L Bickford taking over the crew of Sgt Verstage, while the newly-appointed captain, F/O Henry, would replace S/L Bickford with F/O Wakefield as temporary second pilot. S/L Whitworth's former crew was to be captained now by the newly-appointed F/O Smith, with the yet-to-arrive F/O Hyde as second pilot, and the also yet-to-arrive F/O ffrench-Mullen acting as second pilot to F/O Parkin with the former crew of Sgt Craig.

Whitley P4964 clipped a hedge and crashed on landing in the hands of P/O Warren on the 19th, but no serious damage was done, and no injuries were reported. The two above-named pilots arrived on posting from 78 Squadron on the 20th, and were allotted to A and B Flights respectively. The squadron was ordered to make ready six Whitleys for that night's operations against bridges or enemy vehicle and troop concentrations around the River Oise in the Ribemont, Hannapes and Catillon area of north-eastern France. They were part of a Bomber Command effort involving ninety-two aircraft, and took off either side of 21.00 with S/L Hanafin the senior pilot on duty, but a navigational error led F/O Nelson and crew astray and into an area protected by barrage balloons. Rather than continue and risk damage or cause disruption to Fighter Command activities, they decided to land, and did so at Anstey in Leicestershire at 22.20. The others pushed on in favourable weather conditions, and S/L Hanafin located the bridge at Hannapes at 00.20, before spending thirty minutes manoeuvring into a favourable position for an attack. The bombs were released from 4,500 feet in two sticks, the first of which was seen to fall close to the bridge. Sgt MacCoubrey and crew also found this target and attacked from the same altitude without observing results. F/O Paterson and P/O Parsons identified the bridge at Ribemont, the former bombing it from 2,000 feet at 00.15, while the latter arrived more than an hour later and carried out an attack from 4,000 feet. Sgt Hillary and crew came upon a bridge at Mont-d'Origny and bombed it from 6,000 feet at 01.20, before return to claim direct hits.

Ten crews were called to briefing on the 21st, when the target for four of them was revealed to be a railway junction/marshalling yards at Rheydt, situated south of Mönchengladbach on the south-western corner of the Ruhr, while the other six were to attack the marshalling yards at Jülich, a small town to the north-east of Aachen. The intention was to impede movement of enemy reinforcements and supplies, and, in pursuance of that, alternative targets were any marshalling yards or railway junctions in the general target areas. They were part of a Bomber Command commitment of 124 aircraft, and took off between 20.37 and 20.55 with S/L Bickford the senior pilot in the first element, and S/L Hanafin in the second, before heading south across

Lincolnshire to exit the Suffolk coast at Orfordness. F/L Phillips and P/O Warren arrived at the target within a minute of each other at 23.50 to be greeted by fine weather conditions with ground haze, along with moderately intense light flak and numerous searchlights in the general area. S/L Bickford and F/O Nelson soon also arrived, and the quartet delivered their payloads from between 3,000 and 7,000 feet over a period lasting until F/L Phillips finally turned away at 00.45. F/O Nelson claimed direct hits on the railway yards, while F/L Phillips observed some bomb-bursts, and P/O Warren and crew reported a large fire developing as they made their attack, which they believed to be a decoy site to attract the raid away from the intended target.

Meanwhile, some twenty miles to the south, the attack at Jülich was in progress from between 00.01 and 00.35 and was delivered from heights ranging from 4,500 to 7,000 feet. There were mixed opinions concerning the amount of flak and searchlights in the target area and around towns on the route, but F/O Smith's P4960 was struck by shrapnel from a bursting heavy flak shell while being held in a cone. The rear turret was put out of action, and its occupant sustained a wound to his arm, but, on examination in hospital, this would prove not to be serious. It was, however, the first operational casualty to be recorded by the squadron since the start of hostilities. P/O Cattell's P4955 was approached from astern by four single-engine fighters, which came within four hundred yards and made seven attacks, without, the crew believed, scoring any hits. It was only after returning safely that three bullet holes were discovered in the fuselage. S/L Hanafin and crew reported being attacked by a Henschel 126, which closed in to four hundred yards at 23.30 when north of Breda at 7,000 feet on the way out, but a brief exchange of fire resulted in no damage and the enemy broke off the attack and disappeared.

Targets on either side of the Franco-Belgian frontier were posted for attention on the 22nd, for which 10 Squadron detailed eleven crews. Sgt Johnson and crew would drop out late on because of sickness, and their place be taken by a 51 Squadron crew. They took off between 20.30 and 20.48 with W/C Staton the senior pilot on duty, and headed for Orfordness on their way to the Ardennes region, where a railway junction at Hirson and a road out of Givet were the primary targets. Alternative targets were any transport and troop movements east of a line from Mons through Marbeuge, La Capelle, Le Cateau and the Foret de Mormal. They arrived in the target area between 23.30 and 00.30 to be greeted by clear skies with a little ground mist, and most spent a considerable time making sure to deliver the most effective attacks possible, which they did mostly from between 4,000 and 7,000 feet. F/O Nelson and crew attacked the road leading east out of Givet from 1,800 feet, but were unable to observe the results. Not all were able to identify the primary targets, but all but on found alternatives amongst those specified at briefing. Only F/O Parkin and crew retained their bombs after failing to locate a suitable objective through the layers of ground mist, and, on return, reported intense anti-aircraft fire between Charleroi and Maubeuge.

The futile attempts to impede the enemy advance towards Paris continued on the 24th, when fifty-nine Whitleys, Hampdens and Wellingtons were sent to attack communications targets between Germany and the battle front in France. 10 Squadron made ready a dozen Whitleys, which departed Dishforth between 21.46 and 22.04 with S/Ls Bickford and Hanafin the senior pilots on duty. They had been briefed to attack road junctions at locations on both sides of the Franco-Belgian frontier between Mons and Avesnes, or a railway junction at Hal in northern Belgium. S/L Hanafin spent forty minutes trying to establish his position over the last-mentioned target in conditions of five-tenths cloud at 10,000 feet, but was persuaded by an engine defect to retain his bombs and return home. F/Os Smith and Nelson and S/L Bickford were able to identify this target and attacked it from 6,000 to 7,000 feet between 00.30 and 00.58, but only F/O Smith was able to confirm his bombs straddling the junction. The others bombed road junctions at Avesnes, Aulnoye, Mons, Bavai and Binche from between 2,000 and 10,000 feet, and Sgt MacCoubrey and crew were the last to turn for home at 02.12 after watching the second of their two sticks fall within a hundred yards of the railway at Avesnes.

Orders were received on the 25th for the squadron to make ready eleven Whitleys for operations that night over the Ruhr, at Monheim and Reisholz to the south of Düsseldorf, and at Emmerich, situated on the East Bank of the Rhine to the north. They took off between 20.37 and 20.49 with S/L Hanafin the senior pilot on duty, but F/O Smith had to turn back shortly after crossing the Norfolk coast after the second pilot became violently sick. Sgt Johnson, P/O Cattell and F/L Phillips headed for the Emmerich area, where they found around twenty searchlights encircling the town, which contained oil-storage facilities. Sgt Johnson and F/L Phillips attacked an aerodrome to the east of the town from 8,000 and 6,000 feet respectively, while P/O Cattell bombed a fire some twenty-five miles to the south of the town and a railway junction at Zevenaar across the Dutch border to the north-west. S/L Hanafin dropped his bombs over Leverkusen from 14,000 feet, probably aiming for the I.G Farben chemicals works where synthetic oil was being produced, and he claimed hits. P/O Parsons and Sgt Hillary had been briefed for an oil refinery at Monheim, which they bombed from 9,000 and 12,000 feet respectively, having spent fifty minutes over the target between midnight and 01.00. F/O Paterson attacked Bickendorf aerodrome near Cologne from 10,000 feet just after midnight, while Sgt MacCoubrey had emptied his bomb bay over an unidentified marshalling yard near Duisburg from 14,000 feet a few minutes earlier. F/O Henry and P/O Warren aimed their loads at the oil refinery at Reiszolz from 12,000 and 14,000 feet respectively, before all returned home safely to make their reports.

On the evening of the 26th the evacuation of British and French military personnel from the beaches of Dunkerque began. Earlier in the day, W/C Staton had received confirmation of the award of a Bar to his DSO. The Command ordered an assault on communications and oil targets on the 27th, and eleven crews from 10 Squadron learned at briefing that they would be heading for the Ruhr to attack marshalling yards at Duisburg, Dortmund and Neuss. They took off between 20.18 and 20.29 with S/Ls Bickford and Hanafin the senior pilots on duty, but F/O Nelson and crew had reached only as far as Bircham Newton in Norfolk when running into an electrical storm and suffering a lightning strike, which fused the W/T aerial and temporarily incapacitated the pilot. The second pilot took over, and landed the Whitley safely at Bircham Newton, where an inspection took place. The others pressed on via Great Yarmouth to enemy territory, and roamed far and wide over it between 22.55 and 01.00 without any discernible pattern. P/O Cattell and crew bombed the marshalling yards at Neuss from 8,000 feet, while S/L Bickford went for Lohausen aerodrome to the north of Düsseldorf, bombing it from 10,000 feet. F/O Parkin and crew found a coking plant ten miles north-west of Dortmund, and attacked it from 9,000 feet, and F/L Phillips and P/O Parsons identified the marshalling yards at Dortmund as the recipient for their loads from 8,000 and 10,000 feet respectively. While outbound at 12,000 feet over Utrecht at 23.10, S/L Hanafin and crew were approached by two single-engine enemy fighters, which followed the Whitley, one on each side, for ten minutes. In order to resolve the matter, S/L Hanafin throttled back to stalling speed, and the starboard enemy aircraft at once attacked. The rear gunner, Aircraftman Oldridge, returned fire, and watched the assailant fall away in flames, the first enemy aircraft to be brought down by a Bomber Command crew. S/L Hanafin and crew continued with their sortie, and chose a railway junction at Dorsten to bomb from 10,000 feet. Sgts MacCoubrey and Hillary attacked the marshalling yards at Duisburg from 10,000 and 12,000 feet respectively, and this left just P/O Warren and crew unaccounted for. They had failed to locate a suitable target through the industrial haze and searchlight glare, and had set course for Flushing on the island of Walcheren, where they intended to bomb the aerodrome. Between 02.00 and 02.10 they found themselves over a flare-path, which they took to be Flushing, and dropped their bombs from 8,000 feet, only to decide, after further calculations, that it was more likely Schiphol, situated south of Amsterdam. However, a fix acquired over Anglesey told a different story, and reports of an attack by an unidentified aircraft on the 3 Group training station at Bassingbourn in Cambridgeshire confirmed a very embarrassing "friendly fire" incident.

As a result of the above "black" posted by P/O Warren, he lost his status as crew captain, and was appointed second pilot to Sgt Johnson, while F/L Harrington was elevated to captain. All serviceable aircraft were flown over to Topcliffe for dispersal on the evening of the 31st, and operations would be launched from there until further notice. During the course of the month the squadron operated on eleven nights and dispatched 104 sorties without loss.

Whitley N1349 was a 10 OTU aircraft based at Abingdon. Many 10 Sqn crews trained there prior to joining the operational squadron at Dishforth.

June 1940

The new month began with gloriously hot weather and the award of the DFC to F/O Nelson and P/O Cattell on the 1st. There was some difficulty in arranging transport for air and ground crews between Dishforth and Topcliffe, some four miles to the north-east, but S/L Bickford and crew were the first to leave Dishforth by road after learning at briefing that their target was the Ruhr oil plant at Homberg, situated to the north-west of Duisburg. Seven other crews were shipped over thirty minutes later in a bus and Bedford lorries, and they were able to watch S/L Bickford and crew take off at 21.30 to act as "target finder" and illuminator for the following aircraft. S/L Hanafin was the senior pilot on duty among the main element, which departed Topcliffe between 22.02 and 22.23 to fly out over Orfordness and into the most unfavourable weather conditions over western Germany. S/L Bickford found a band of rain-bearing cloud between 2,000 and 7,000 feet which completely obscured the ground. Despite being over the target area at 3,000 feet between 00.19 and 00.56, and knowing by DR (dead-reckoning) that the oil plant was somewhere beneath him, he realized that there was no point in releasing the illuminator flares as a signal to the others, and abandoned his sortie, bringing his bombs home. S/L Hanafin, Sgts Johnson and Hillary, P/O Parsons and F/O Parkin all also retained their bombs after searching in vain for a gap in the cloud. P/O Cattell found a piece of sky where the cloud base was at 4,500 feet, from where he spotted what appeared to be a marshalling yard upon which to drop his bomb load in a single stick. Heavy ground fire persuaded him to ignore the outcome and head for home, and he arrived back at Topcliffe at 04.35, uncertain as to the precise location of his attack. Another gap in the cloud allowed F/L Phillips to catch sight of a road some four miles north-east of Homberg, which he bombed from 5,000 feet without observing the results.

The same target was posted on the 2nd with S/L Bickford again briefed to perform a target identification and illumination role for five other 10 Squadron aircraft and six from 51 Squadron. He took off at 21.30 at the end of another fine summer's day, and was followed into the air between 21.41 and 22.06 by the five other 10 Squadron participants to exit the English coast as usual via Orfordness. The weather conditions over the western Ruhr were in complete contrast to those of twenty-four hours earlier, and S/L Bickford began to release flares over the target at 00.40, continuing to do so for twenty minutes from heights ranging between 4,000 and 6,000 feet. Inevitably, S/L Bickford's presence attracted a hostile reception, and his Whitley was hit several times by shrapnel from exploding flak shells, as a result of which, the rear gunner sustained serious wounds. F/O Nelson and crew arrived ahead of S/L Bickford and carried out their attack on the oil plant between 00.30 and 01.00 from 8,500 feet. They were prevented by searchlight glare from determining the precise fall of their bombs, but it was thought that they hit a railway junction close to the target. Sgt MacCoubrey and crew followed up between 01.10 and 01.30, delivering their bombs from 12,000 feet, but, again, without observing the results. F/O Smith arrived somewhat late over Krefeld, and observed an alternative target to the south, east of Düsseldorf, which he claimed had been illuminated by S/L Bickford, although this does not seem likely. It was a railway line, which, in the event, became lost from sight, but the River Rhine was clearly visible, and he dropped his load onto a railway bridge from 9,000 feet. Sgt Johnson, who had the contrite P/O Warren beside him in the cockpit, found the illuminating flares to be of no assistance in identifying the primary target, and he attacked a railway junction one mile to the east from 9,000 feet, observing the bombs to burst between the junction and a railway bridge over the Rhine. P/O Cattell and crew began their bombing run on the primary target, but lost it in the searchlight glare. They made six further runs, but failed to locate it, and ended up delivering all of their bombs in a single stick across the marshalling yards at Krefeld from 9,000 feet. Meanwhile, S/L Bickford was keen to obtain medical attention for his rear gunner, whose pain had been dulled by a morphine injection, and he landed at Bircham Newton as the first available station with medical facilities.

Leeming, a new bomber station situated on the A1 some eight miles south-east of Richmond, was about to be handed to 4 Group, and an "opening-up" party proceeded there on the 3rd in preparation for the arrival of 10 Squadron as its first resident unit early in July. Meanwhile, the largest effort by the Command in a single night to date saw a mixed force of 142 aircraft made ready to attack multiple targets in Germany. 10 Squadron dispatched eight Whitleys from Topcliffe between 21.15 and 21.35 with S/L Hanafin the senior pilot on duty. Their target for the third night running was the Homberg oil plant, which they reached via the usual outward route, and found excellent weather conditions with an intense searchlight and flak response. They carried out their attacks from between 7,000 and 12,000 feet, F/L Harrington, F/O Parkin and P/O Parsons finding the target already well alight as they made their approaches. The squadron participants were over the target sometime between 00.06 and 01.20, and F/O Nelson's rear gunner reported the fires still visible from sixty miles into the return trip. On his way home F/L Phillips had to contend with a failing port engine, which eventually stopped, leaving the Whitley sinking towards the waves of the North Sea. They were directed by D/F to Wattisham in Suffolk, where a beacon, floodlight and flares were in place long before the aircraft was heard approaching. Those on the ground could see the Whitley plainly, but the crew was unable to establish its position, despite flying over the airfield and being informed of that by flying control. P4963 ultimately crashed while trying to land at Battisford some three miles to the north-east of Wattisham, injuring all but the wireless operator, who would provide all of the initial report of the incident. The rear gunner, P/O Fields, was removed from the aircraft and died almost immediately, while F/L Phillips and the two other crew members were taken to Ipswich hospital.

10 Squadron's participation in operations on the night of the 4/5th was cancelled, but W/C Staton, S/L Bickford and F/O Smith took part in the first of a number of 4 Group air-defence exercises, in which the 4 Group A-O-C, Air Commodore Coningham, flew as observer with W/C Staton. On the 5th the group ordered ten Whitleys from Dishforth and eleven from Driffield to be made ready for operations against enemy communications in the area of the Somme, the former to target the town of Doullens. The five 10 Squadron participants took off between 20.20 and 21.24 with S/L Hanafin the senior pilot on duty, and headed south to exit the English coast over Shoreham. Weather conditions over northern France were good with clear skies and some ground haze, but crews had no difficulty in identifying the target area. F/L Harrington and crew were the first to arrive, and spent thirty-five minutes over the target either side of midnight, carrying out their attack from 6,000 feet in the light of flares delivered by another aircraft. The bombs were seen to burst in the north-east corner of the town, and these were backed up by those falling from Sgt Johnson's aircraft, delivered in two sticks from 5,500 feet between 23.48 and 00.45. P/O Parsons and F/O Nelson arrived in the target area almost an hour later, and dropped their bombs onto the town from 6,000 feet between 00.35 and 01.30. S/L Hanafin found two alternative targets close to Doullens, it is believed at Beauval to the south, on which two 250 pounders were dropped, and Orville to the south-east, which received four 500 and four

Ops room possibly Dishforth

250 pounders, two of which hit a railway junction, while the remainder fell between two roads leading out of the town.

Nine crews attended briefing on the 6th to learn that three marshalling yards at Wedau, south of Duisburg, Euskirchen, south-west of Cologne and Rheydt were to be the targets for that night. They took off from both Dishforth and Topcliffe between 21.04 and 21.20 with S/L Hanafin the senior pilot on duty. F/L Harrington and crew had been airborne for forty minutes when the captain became ill had had to hand over the controls to his second pilot, P/O Jeremiah. F/L Harrington would be interviewed by the station medical officer before being sent to Catterick military hospital. The others pressed on to exit the English coast over Orfordness, with, it seems, Sgt Hillary, Sgt MacCoubrey and F/O Smith assigned to Euskirchen, although the squadron ORB cites Aachen as being attacked by the two last-mentioned crews. There were two major marshalling yards in Aachen, situated some twenty-five miles to the west of Euskirchen, and the route to the target would have passed close to them. The bombing was carried out from 8,000 and 10,000 feet respectively between 00.28 and 01.05, F/O Smith observing bomb bursts on the eastern end of a tunnel a couple of miles south-west of the city. F/O Parkin had his bombs hang up over the Wedau yards, which was only discovered on the way home over Belgium. They found an already-burning oil tank at Ghent, and released the bombs from 10,000 feet, observing them to set off further fires. By the time that S/L Hanafin and crew identified the Wedau yards, no flares were left to illuminate it, and it was decided, therefore, to seek an alternative target, and a smaller railway yard soon presented itself close by to the west. This was bombed from 9,000 feet, but no results were observed, probably because of the volume of glare from the forest of searchlights in operation. P/O Cattell and crew had no difficulty in locating the Wedau yards, and delivered their load in a single stick from 9,000 feet across the northern end, observing a large explosion as a result. F/O Henry and Sgt Johnson attacked the yards at Rheydt from 11,000 and 9,000 feet respectively, without observing results, and all aircraft had returned safely home by 04.00.

Operations against marshalling yards continued on the night of the 8/9th for which 10 Squadron made ready eight Whitleys, along with one other, which P/O Cattell and crew would take to join a 51 Squadron element briefed to attack a concentration of tanks and stores in the Forest of Gobain. The main element, bound for the marshalling yards at Essen-Frintrop, Wedau and Rheydt took off between 21.15 and 22.00, although S/L Bickford's intended departure from Topcliffe ended with P4962 swinging violently until the undercarriage collapsed. The crew walked away with only a minor injury sustained by the second pilot, and, despite the Whitley being severely damaged, it would, eventually, be returned to flying condition. The others got away safely, and headed out via the usual route, but S/L Hanafin and crew landed at Hemswell with an oil leak in the front turret. Repairs were carried out, and they took off again only for the problem to recur and leave a film of oil across the windscreen, at which point, the sortie was abandoned. Meanwhile, P/O Cattell and crew had departed last at 22.38, and were adopting the same route on the way to their target in France.

The crews of the main element found their respective target areas under generally clear skies with mist partially obscuring ground detail. F/O Paterson, P/O Parsons and F/O Nelson had been assigned to the yards at Rheydt, but the first-mentioned failed to locate it despite searching for an hour, and he dropped his bombs shortly after 01.00 from 10,000 feet onto what was believed to be an aerodrome to the south-east. P/O Parsons did manage to locate the primary target, and attacked it from 10,000 feet, believing his bombs to hit the northern end. F/O Nelson dropped four 250 pounders on these yards, also from 10,000 feet, and the rest of his load onto the aerodrome at Eindhoven in southern Holland, where hits were observed as enemy aircraft were in the process of taking off. Sgt Hillary and F/O Smith located the Wedau yards, and carried out their attacks from 8,000 and 10,000 feet respectively, believing the bombs to have fallen into the target, although searchlight glare rendered a positive assessment difficult. F/Os Henry and Parkin were also experiencing intense searchlight activity over Essen, but identified the yards in a north-western suburb, and attacked them from 11,000 and 9,500 feet respectively, the former observing bursts on the northern end, and the latter on a junction a mile and a half to the north-east. Many miles to the west, P/O Cattell and crew found the forest at Gobain to be already well alight, and bombed it from 5,000 feet, the first stick all high-explosives and the second all incendiaries

W/C Staton and F/O Nelson were ordered to stand down from the operation on the 9th, the former on the orders of the station commander and the latter because of his impending investiture. Nine crews presented themselves for briefing, which had to be carried out twice after the target changed at the last minute to the hindrance of enemy troop and transport movements in France. S/L Hanafin, F/O Paterson, P/O Parsons and Sgt Hillary and their crews were assigned to targets in the Libramont area of southern Belgium, while F/Os Smith, Parkin, Henry and P/O Cattell and their crews were to ply their trade at Neufchateau, some five miles to the south. Finally, Sgt Johnson and crew were to attack a suitable objective at Sedan, situated five miles inside France, and the take-off by all aircraft from Topcliffe was accomplished safely between 21.24 and 21.40. Weather conditions in the target area were generally good, but strong defensive positions ensured that the crews would run the gauntlet of searchlights and intense ground fire. S/L Hanafin arrived on the stroke of midnight, and dropped the first five bombs from 500 feet, before attacking again with the remaining five from 5,000 feet. F/O Paterson and P/O Parsons delivered their bombs from 2,000 and 4,500 feet respectively, while Sgt Hillary attacked an alternative target, a cross-roads some six miles south of Neufchateau, from 4,000 feet without observing results. F/O Smith was unable to locate Neufchateau in the ground mist, but followed the river to the town of Givet, which he bombed from 7,000 feet and observed bursts in the built-up area. A similar difficulty led to F/O Parkin bombing Namur from 1,500 feet after searching for some time for a suitable alternative, but F/O Henry and P/O Cattell located their primary target, and bombed it from 9,000 and 3,500 feet respectively. Meanwhile, Sgt Johnson had found a road bridge across the River Meuse at Pont Maugis, south of Sedan, and attacked it from 5,000 feet without observing results.

The squadron was not to be involved in operations on the 10th, the day on which Italy declared war on Britain, but instructions were received to fit eight Whitleys with auxiliary petrol tanks by 10.30 on the 11th. F/O ffrench-Mullen was elevated to captain status to take over the crew of F/L Harrington, who was still in Catterick hospital. Eight crews were transported to Topcliffe, where they took off between 14.03 and 15.00 for the Channel Island of Guernsey with W/C Staton and S/L Hanafin taking the lead. They would be joined there by elements of 51 and 58 Squadron, while 77 and 102 Squadrons would use Jersey airport as their forward base for that night's operation to Italy. The brief for the thirty-six Whitley crews was to attack industrial targets, particularly the Fiat works, in Turin. This left five crews available for other operations against enemy troop movements in northern France, and they departed Topcliffe between 20.41 and 20.47 bound for Shoreham and then the Amiens region. F/O Parkin got only as far as Hucknall in Nottinghamshire, where engine trouble forced him to land to try, in vain, to effect repairs. F/O Paterson had probably reached the French coast before a similar problem forced him to turn back and land at Tangmere. The others pressed on to encounter cloudy conditions and ground mist, and F/O ffrench-Mullen and F/Sgt Witt carried out an attack from 10,000 and 4,000 feet respectively, the latter observing his bombs to fall between a road and rail junction just outside the town on the north-western approaches. P4954 failed to return with the crew of Sgt Keast, and was found to have been hit by flak before crashing near Abbeville without survivors.

Meanwhile, the rest of the squadron had taken off from Guernsey between 20.10 and 21.05 and set course for the Alps, flying through thunderstorms and severe icing conditions on the way. This prevented S/L Hanafin from climbing above 12,000 feet, and it was at this time that the trailing aerial was struck by lightning. The wireless operator sustained a small burn to the hand, but the rear gunner, who had been leaning on his guns, suffered shock that left him sufficiently incapacitated to persuade the captain to abandon the sortie. P/O Parsons and F/Os Smith and Henry also struggled for the necessary height to clear the Alps, and they, too, turned back towards Guernsey. P/O Cattell managed to haul his Whitley to 17,000 feet, where he found himself in thick cloud and unable to reach any higher. Deciding that it would be unwise to continue and risk crashing into a snow-covered peak, he also set course for Guernsey. W/C Staton did reach Turin to find thick banks of cloud between 5,000 and 8,000 feet, and spent sixty-five minutes in the target area dropping flares to make sure of his position. It was in the light of his very last flare that he dropped his bombs from 4,000 feet, observing them to burst at the southern end of the target and produce green fires accompanied by large columns of smoke. Sgt MacCoubrey and crew reached 18,000 feet, and found the port of Genoa under drifting cloud with tops at 15,000 feet. The bombs were dropped onto the docks, and were seen to burst on the eastern end. Sgt Johnson and crew also located Genoa, where they attacked the Ansaldo works, one of Italy's foremost producers of war materials, from 15,000 feet, setting off explosions, which continued after they had turned for home. These three 10 Squadron crews were among just ten to report bombing in the target area, where no significant damage resulted.

S/L Whitworth returned to the fold from 78 Squadron on the 12th, and immediately resumed command of B Flight. He was the senior pilot on duty among five crews from 10 Squadron briefed for operations over northern France on the 13th. P/Os Parsons and Cattell and F/Sgt Witt took off at 21.10 to attack road and river crossings at Chateau-Thierry on the road between Reims and Paris, and were followed into the air fifteen minutes later by S/L Whitworth and Sgt Johnson. The first element bombed the target from 4,000 feet, but cloud and searchlight glare made it difficult to assess the results. Sgt Johnson failed to locate the primary target because of the cloud and haze, and eventually back-tracked to bomb a location at Ville-en-Tardenois, south-west of Reims, where a large explosion was observed. S/L Whitworth experienced similar difficulties in locating the primary target, and, after stooging around for a considerable time at 2,000 feet, abandoned the sortie and turned for home.

German forces marched unopposed into Paris on the 14th to begin a four-year-long occupation of the French Capital. Meanwhile, crews were being briefed at Dishforth for two operations that night, the first to disrupt river traffic and destroy barges and tugboats on the Rhine between Bingen and Mannheim in south-west central Germany, and the second to support ground forces in a futile effort to save France from imminent collapse. The former involved the use of "W" bombs, which are believed to be mines for use against canal and river traffic, which had to be dropped within narrow parameters of height and speed to prevent them from breaking up on impact. The latter involved a return to the Chateau-Thierry area to attack road and railway crossings, while an alternative objective was a river crossing over the Seine at Les Anderlys south-east of Rouen. S/L Hanafin was the senior pilot on duty as the Germany-bound element of five took off at 20.40, but it was soon discovered that the W/T equipment was not operating, and he was forced to abandon his sortie. The others pressed on in cloudy skies, which cleared as the target area drew near, and F/O Parkin and crew spent eighty minutes over the Rhine, without being able to hold the river in view for long enough to complete a bombing run. They decided to return with the load intact, leaving the others to try their luck. F/O Paterson and crew searched for almost thirty minutes before finding a stretch of the Rhine north of Worms, where they dropped their bombs from 700 feet, observing them to fall into the water. They also reported that the fuselage container, presumably a small bomb case (SBC) of incendiaries, fell out at the same time, and also ended up in the river. F/O Smith and crew delivered their hardware into the river from 500 feet south of Oppenheim, while Sgt MacCoubrey flew around for forty minutes at 7,000 feet seeking a suitable target to attack from a lower level. Unfortunately, the intense anti-aircraft fire prevented them from descending, and they became the third of this element to be forced to return home empty-handed. Of the France-bound contingent, P/O Parsons, P/O Cattell and Sgt Johnson were recalled after an hour in order to save them for an operation on the following night, leaving F/Sgt Witt to drop his bombs in a single stick on Chateau-Thierry from 6,000 feet, and S/L Whitworth to do likewise at the alternative of Les Anderlys.

The night of the 17/18th became the first of five consecutive nights involving Whitley activity over Germany, for which 10 Squadron made ready ten aircraft, seven for a repeat of the special Rhine operation of the 14th against river traffic in company with 51 Squadron, and three to join others to cause maximum nuisance in the Ruhr by attacking the Nordstern and Scholven-Buer oil plants in the north of Gelsenkirchen, and the marshalling yards at Wedau in Duisburg. Those bound for the Rhine took off from Topcliffe between 20.35 and 20.47 with S/L Hanafin the senior pilot on duty, and they were followed into the air either side of 21.30 by S/L Whitworth, F/Sgt Witt and Sgt Hillary. There were no early returns to deplete the effort, and all crews reached their respective targets in good weather conditions before searching for a suitable target. F/O ffrench-Mullen and crew searched for fifty minutes before descending to 700 feet to deliver their "W" bombs in two runs in the face of intense searchlight and moderate flak activity. The defences prevented S/L Hanafin from venturing below 9,000 feet, and kept F/O Henry, P/O Cattell and F/O Smith at 2,000, 4,000 and 4,500 feet respectively, which was far too high for an effective attack with "W" bombs, and all four were persuaded to abandon their sorties and bring their bombs home. F/O Paterson arrived on the scene at about the same time, shortly before 00.30, and came down to 450 feet to deliver his bombs within ten minutes, while Sgt Johnson and crew cruised back and forth for thirty minutes before sneaking down to 800 feet to let their bombs go. Weather conditions in the Ruhr were good, apart from the usual industrial haze, and all three crews attacked at Gelsenkirchen from between 8,500 and 10,000 feet, observing their bombs to burst in the target area and set off fires.

Orders were received on 4 Group stations on the 18th to prepare thirty-eight aircraft for operations that night over the Ruhr, where marshalling yards and oil plants were to be the objectives. 10 Squadron was required to provide four Whitleys only, and they departed Topcliffe shortly before 21.30 with S/L Whitworth the senior pilot on duty. Their destination was the marshalling yards at Schwerte, situated on the south-eastern corner of the Dortmund conurbation, which all reached to find favourable weather conditions but intense searchlight and flak activity. S/L Whitworth was the first to carry out an attack, delivering his bombs in a single stick from 10,000 feet between 00.46 and 01.00 without observing their fall. F/O ffrench-Mullen and F/Sgt Witt were on the scene within minutes and also attacked from 10,000 feet, while Sgt Hillary and crew ventured down to 4,000 feet, from where they observed their first stick to hit the yards and create fires, and their second to cause a large explosion among buildings adjacent to the railway. All returned safely to relate their experiences at debriefing, F/O ffrench-Mullen and F/Sgt Witt claiming hits on the yards and a railway junction, the former reporting flak damage to the port wing.

Six crews were called to briefing on the 19th, to learn that their primary target was an aluminium works at Ludwigshafen, situated on the Left Bank of the Rhine opposite Mannheim in southern Germany. They took off between 20.45 and 21.00 with S/L Hanafin the senior pilot on duty, but lost F/O Parkin and crew to a failing starboard engine almost immediately, and they were back on the ground within fifty minutes. Sgt Johnson and crew were delayed by taking evasive action to dodge the many searchlight and flak concentrations outbound, and opted to bomb the briefed alternative target of the marshalling yards at Koblenz. They attacked from 8,000 feet in good weather conditions shortly before 01.00, and observed their bombs to fall slightly north-east of the target. S/L Hanafin and crew also cited a delay as their reason to head straight for Koblenz, and they had already bombed from 9,000 feet by the time that the Johnson crew turned up. The flight commander and his crew would return safely at 04.47 to claim hits on a bridge to the east of the target. F/O Paterson and crew were the only ones to reach the primary target, which they attacked in a single stick from 11,000 feet at 00.40, causing a large fire. F/O Henry and crew were unable to locate the factory, and sought out an alternative target, eventually aiming two sticks from 10,000 feet at a marshalling yards an estimated thirty miles to the north at around 00.45. F/O Smith and crew were at the mid-point of the sea crossing outbound when engine issues forced the decision to bomb a last resort target, for which, according to the squadron ORB, Amsterdam aerodrome was selected. This is believed to be an error, and it was, in fact, the docks at Antwerp that P4960 was circling with F/O Smith occupying the bomb-aimer's position. As the bombing run began, the rear gunner reported smoke issuing from the starboard engine, and the second pilot noticed the temperature rising rapidly, at which point, he throttled back and called for the bombs to be jettisoned. A course was set for the nearest point on the English coast, while an SOS signal was sent and requests were made for a Q.D.M from Honington. They crossed the coast ten miles north of Orfordness at 8,000 feet with F/O Smith back at the controls, and homed in on Honington, which, as luck would have it, was blacked out because of an air-raid warning. The Whitley arrived over the station at 1,200 feet, and it was during the second circuit that the airfield was recognised by the outlines of the hangars and bomb dump. The final approach was made from 800 feet, but F/O Smith realized that he had undershot by some distance, and, with the starboard engine now dead, was unable to regain height. The Whitley crashed into trees at Ampton Park, three miles from the threshold, and broke in two before being consumed by fire. F/O Smith was killed, and two members of the crew sustained face and hand burns, while two walked away physically unscathed.

His Royal Highness Group Captain the Duke of Kent arrived at Dishforth for lunch on the 20th, and was escorted around the station by W/C Staton. The primary target for that night was the marshalling yards at Hamm, situated to the north of the eastern end of the Ruhr, to which the squadron dispatched eight Whitleys between 21.33 and 21.55 with S/Ls Hanafin and Whitworth the senior pilots on duty. They encountered ten-tenths cloud over enemy territory, and, despite this becoming broken to some extent by the time they reached the target area, the crews of S/Ls Hanafin and Whitworth and F/Os ffrench-Mullen and Paterson failed to identify it, and both flight commanders brought their bombs home. F/O ffrench-Mullen and crew found a railway junction at Fröndenberg, some fourteen miles to the south, upon which they delivered three sticks from 2,500 feet between 01.00 and 01.40. F/O Paterson and crew eventually found an unidentified road junction, which they bombed in two sticks from 8,000 feet at 01.20. It was left to F/O Parkin and the three NCO pilots to locate and attack the primary target, which they did from between 8,000 and 11,000 feet between 00.50 and 01.30, before returning safely to report successfully hitting the yards.

Seven Whitleys were made ready for operations on the 21st, and they took off between 21.30 and 21.50 with S/L Whitworth the senior pilot on duty. They were bound for an oil plant at Bochum in the heart of the Ruhr as their primary target, and a similar objective further north at Salzbergen as the alternative. F/O Parkin and crew were just thirty minutes out when a starboard engine problem forced them to turn back, while P/O Cattell and crew had reached the target area when an engine issue forced them to abandon their sortie. They sought a last-resort target, and found Schiphol aerodrome on the way home, which they bombed from 8,000 feet. F/O ffrench-Mullen and crew experienced intercom failure, and ended up bombing an unidentified marshalling yard near Bocholt from 10,000 feet. The cloud and haze presented challenging conditions for the remaining crews to identify ground detail in, but F/O Henry found the marshalling yards at Wanne-Eickel, north-east of Gelsenkirchen, and bombed them from 10,000 feet. F/Sgt Witt and crew attacked a marshalling yard in the Bochum area from 8,000 feet, and this left just S/L Whitworth and Sgt Hillary to positively identify and bomb the primary target. The former delivered four 500 and two 250 pounders onto the oil plant from 10,000 feet and observed a large blue flash, before dropping the remaining four 250 pounders onto the marshalling yards at Wanne-Eickel. Sgt Hillary and crew released their load in three sticks from 12,000 feet, but seemed to miss the mark.

The signing of the armistice at Compiegne on the 22nd signalled the official defeat of France, and, for the first time since the opening of the German offensive in the west, no Bomber Command aircraft operated that night. 10 Squadron made ready eight Whitleys on the 23rd and briefed the crews for attacks on an aluminium works at Ichendorf, a western suburb of Cologne, with coking ovens, blast furnaces and marshalling yards as alternative targets. They took off between 21.32 and 21.45 with S/L Whitworth the senior pilot on duty, and made their way to Germany to find low cloud and hazy conditions, which, together with searchlight glare, made target-identification difficult. P/O Cattell and crew did manage to locate it, and were the first to arrive, at 00.30, to deliver their bomb load in two sticks from 8,000 feet. Neither stick found the mark, the first hitting a railway line and the second causing a series of vivid blue flashes. As they turned away at 00.40, S/L Whitworth and Sgt Johnson and their crews dropped their 500 and 250 pounders from 10,000 feet without observing their fall. Sgt Hillary and crew were the last to arrive at the primary target, and attacked it with three sticks from 12,000 feet between 01.00 and 01.15, observing bursts in the general area. F/O Parkin found a railway junction for his bombs, which he delivered from 10,000 feet, and it may have been the same one attacked by F/O Henry immediately north of the primary objective. F/O Paterson and crew, who were operating with the squadron for the last time before being sent on attachment to 78 Squadron, located an unidentified blast furnace near Düsseldorf to aim for from 8,000 feet, while F/Sgt Witt and crew picked out an unidentified factory in the target area to attack from 8,000 feet, which resulted in a very large explosion accompanied by an immediate outbreak of fire.

Six crews were bussed over to Topcliffe on the evening of the 25th to take part in that night's operations, which, for P/O Parsons and Sgt MacCoubrey and their crews, was against the Focke-Wulf aircraft factory at Bremen, with the marshalling yards at Oldenburg as an alternative. F/Os Parkin and Henry, P/O Cattell and Sgt Johnson and their crews had been given the aluminium works at Cologne/Ichendorf as their primary target and the I.G. Farben chemicals works at Leverkusen as the alternative. They were airborne between 21.26 and 21.44 and all reached their respective target areas to find unhelpful weather conditions which included thick ground haze. F/O Parkin came upon a railway junction at Bergheim at midnight while on his approach to Cologne, and, in view of the conditions, decided to drop two 500 and three 250 pounders upon it from 11,000 feet, observing them to fall accurately. He then continued on for a matter of five minutes to Ichendorf, which would have been identified by the nearby Quadrath Power Station, and delivered the remainder of his load there, without seeing the results through the nine-tenths cloud. F/O Henry was unable to locate the primary target, but the part of Leverkusen containing the chemicals works lay under a clear patch of sky, which enabled him to drop a first stick from 10,000 feet at 00.31 and a second stick from 9,500 feet four minutes later, the latter causing a minor explosion in the north-east corner of the factory. P/O Cattell crossed the Dutch coast in cloud at 12,000 feet, and found the Ichendorf factory to be under ten-tenths cloud, which persuaded him to turn back and bomb the aerodrome at Haamstede on the island of Schouwen in the Scheldt Estuary. The attack was carried out in a single salvo from 6,000 feet and the bombs were seen to burst on a hangar. Sgt Johnson found complete cloud cover all the way, and turned back when east of the target, before reducing height to 7,000 feet and spending thirty minutes searching for the primary or a worthwhile alternative. He was unsuccessful and brought his bombs home.

Meanwhile, P/O Parsons had located the Focke-Wulf factory at Bremen, and delivered his load in two sticks from 9,000 feet between 00.35 and 00.39 in the face of a spirited searchlight and flak defence. He did not observe the fall of the bombs, but believed them to be accurate. Thwarted by thick haze over Bremen, Sgt MacCoubrey set course for the marshalling yards at Osnabrück, which he also failed to locate, and decided to bomb the aerodrome on the Frisian island of Borkum. He dropped all of his 250 pounders from 10,000 feet at 01.20, believing them to have burst close to a hangar, and followed up with the four 500 pounders four minutes later without being able to plot their fall.

4 Group orders on the 27th required five Whitleys each from 10 and 51 Squadrons to be made ready for an attack that night on the inland docks at Duisburg-Ruhrort. The 10 Squadron element took off from Topcliffe between 21.42 and 21.52 with S/L Whitworth the senior pilot on duty. All reached the target area to find good and clear weather conditions but intense searchlight glare, which rendered target identification something of a challenge. Despite this, all attacked the primary target from between 8,000 and 13,000 feet between 23.35 and 01.25, Sgt MacCoubrey and crew delivering their load in four separate runs during twenty-five minutes spent over the target. Returning crews claimed hits on the western end of the docks in particular, and one reported bursts near warehouses on the southern edge. Just four crews were required for operations on the 28th, and they departed Topcliffe either side of 21.00 with the recently posted-in F/O Nixon the senior pilot on duty. They set course for Frankfurt, where an explosives factory in the south-western suburb of Höchst was their designated target. Extreme darkness and searchlight glare created challenging conditions for target identification, but all located the factory, and F/O Nixon chose a glide approach from 11,000 down to 8,000 feet to deliver his bombs in a single stick in the face of an intense flak response. P/O Cattell made four runs, the final one at 01.35 from 10,500 feet, while Sgt Johnson took two runs to empty his bomb bay from 11,000 feet between 00.55 and 01.00. P/O Parson's bombs also went down at 01.00 in a single stick from 9,000 feet after a straight run across the aiming-point, before he and his crew returned safely with the others.

The final operation of a hectic month for the Whitley brigade was briefed on the evening of the 30th, for which 10 Squadron detailed nine crews. Their target was the marshalling yards at Hamm, for which they took off from Topcliffe between 21.29 and 21.41 with S/L Whitworth the senior pilot on duty. He encountered eight-tenths cloud over the target, along with intense searchlight and flak activity, which prevented him from identifying it or the alternative of Rotterdam docks, and he returned his bombs to store. Sgt Johnson employed flares to improve his chances of locating the primary target beneath ten-tenths cloud, but he eventually gave up and headed for Rotterdam, which also eluded him. F/O Nixon brought his bombs home to report a cloud base at 4,000 feet over Hamm, which had prevented him from identifying it. F/Sgt Witt made two gliding runs across the aiming-point at 00.30 and 00.40, and observed the first stick to fall over the northern end of the yards. Sgt Hillary made three attacks between 00.55 and 01.08 and observed two sticks to fall in the target area after the first had burst to the north of the town. F/O Henry favoured a gliding attack from a starting point of 14,000 feet, and let his load go in a single stick, believing them to have struck home in or near the target. Sgt MacCoubrey's first run was in a glide from 12,000 to 10,000 feet, and those bombs appeared to be accurate, while the second stick produced a small fire in the northern end of the yard. P/O Parsons and F/O Prior each carried out a single attack, the former from 8,000 feet, from where he observed his bombs to burst across the centre of the yards. The latter glided down to 6,000 feet on a south to north heading a few minutes later, and watched his bombs also burst within the target area. During the course of the month the squadron operated on twenty occasions, dispatching 149 sorties for the loss of three Whitleys and one complete crew.

July 1940

It was at this point that the Battle of Britain began, and Bomber Command would play its part by continuing the offensive against communications and industrial targets in Germany, and airfields in the occupied countries. 10 Squadron was ordered to make ready three Whitleys on the 2nd for operations that night against the marshalling yards at Hamm, with concentrations of invasion barges at Rotterdam as the alternative target. They took off from Topcliffe at 21.30 with S/L Hanafin the senior pilot on duty and the newly-promoted F/L ffrench-Mullen also on the Order of Battle. Cloud and thick haze prevented S/L Hanafin and F/L ffrench-Mullen from locating the primary target, the former finding a self-illuminated target of opportunity in the Ruhr to bomb from 9,500 feet, while the latter brought his bombs home. F/Sgt Witt came upon a gap in the cloud, the base of which was at 8,000 feet with haze below, and carried out an attack from that altitude, observing his bombs to burst across the southern extremity of the yards.

Three 10 Squadron crews attended briefing on the 5th to learn that Merville aerodrome in north-eastern France was to be their target that night. They departed Topcliffe between 21.33 and 21.42 with P/O Cattell the senior pilot on duty, but not one was able to locate the target in conditions of low cloud, and all brought their bombs home. The move to the squadron's new home at Leeming was completed on the 8th, but, for the time-being, operations would continue to be launched from Dishforth. Also on this day, Sgt MacCoubrey and P/O Cattell and a number of their crew members were posted to 19 O.T.U at Kinloss and 10 O.T.U at Abingdon respectively for a rest from operations. Five crews were briefed for an attack on the Howaldtswerke shipbuilding yard at Kiel that night, which would be carried out in concert with elements of 51 and 58 Squadrons. They departed Dishforth between 20.45 and 21.05 with S/L Whitworth the senior pilot on duty, and reached the target to find six-tenths cloud with a base at 6,000 feet, below which, the visibility was good. Searchlight and flak activity was intense and accurate, and, together with the cloud, prevented all but P/O Parsons from carrying out an attack. Bombs were dropped by this crew on parts of the Kiel yard, but no assessment could be made. F/Sgt Witt and crew were unable to establish their position on the Baltic coast, and took their bombs home after running out of time. F/O Nixon and crew also returned their bombs to store after the Kiel defences made an attack impossible. S/L Whitworth was making his approach from the north over Eckernförde, when a piece of shrapnel penetrated the cockpit, and hit his parachute harness, before ricocheting off to hit him below the left eye. The bombs were dropped immediately onto the southern outskirts of Eckenförde, while the crew assessed the damage to the Whitley. They found that the rudder controls had been cut and the radio equipment and fixed aerial had been destroyed, despite which, a safe return was made. The last message from F/L ffrench-Mullen and crew was received at 01.45 and was to report the sortie being abandoned. N1496 failed to arrive back at Dishforth and was posted missing later that morning. The good news eventually filtered through that the entire crew had survived as PoWs after the Whitley had been shot down into the sea off Heligoland at 02.05 by Ofw Paul Förster of IV/NJG.2.

On the 10th W/C Staton's long period in command of the squadron came to an end on his posting as station commander at its new home of Leeming. His tenure would last until December, when he would be appointed ADC to His Majesty King George VI. After taking a starring role in the propaganda film, Target for Tonight, alongside G/C "Speedy" Powell and W/C "Pick" Pickard, acting Air Commodore Staton would be posted in July 1941 to Java as SASO HQ Far East, and, in March 1942, be captured by the Japanese, in whose hands he underwent a torrid time, being moved sixteen times from camp to camp. Happily, he would survive the war and live a long life to pass away in July 1983. S/L Whitworth was appointed to succeed him as 10 Squadron's commanding officer in a temporary capacity, pending the arrival of a permanent successor.

Six 10 Squadron crews were briefed at Dishforth on the 12th for operations that night against the Krupp-Germania Werft shipyard at Kiel. They took off between 20.45 and 20.51 with S/L Hanafin the senior pilot on duty, and set course for the Danish coast via the Frisian Islands. Sgt Hillary and crew turned back almost immediately because of an oil leak in the front turret, and, despite efforts on the ground to rectify the problem, it became too late to send the crew back into the air. S/L Hanafin abandoned his sortie because of bad weather and the mistaken belief that the crew was short of oxygen bottles. F/Sgt Witt and crew reached the target area to find five-tenths cloud at 6,000 feet and ten-tenths at around 10,000 feet, and they also had to contend with intense anti-aircraft during the bombing run. The bombs were dropped in a single stick onto the eastern side of Kiel harbour, probably in the same spot as those delivered by F/O Nixon, who confirmed the state of the cloud and the ferocity of the defences. P/O Parsons was unable to locate the primary target through the cloud, and headed for Sylt as an alternative, where the conditions defeated him also, and he brought his bombs home. It was a similar story for F/O Prior, who attempted to find Westerland aerodrome instead, but was defeated by the cloud and icing conditions and also returned his bombs to store.

The primary target for the night of the 13/14th was the oil plant at Monheim, situated to the north-east of Cologne, east of the Rhine, while a Bayer chemicals factory west of the river was given as an alternative. Just three 10 Squadron crews were briefed, and they took off shortly before 21.30 with S/L Whitworth the senior pilot on duty. The ORB is short on detail, but records that all aircraft reached the primary target and returned safely home to report delivering their bombs according to brief, but not observing the results because of the weather conditions. Four Whitleys were made ready on the 14th for an operation that night against an aircraft park on the aerodrome at Diepholz, situated between Bremen to the north-east and Osnabück to the south-west. They took off between 21.10 and 21.14 with S/L Hanafin the senior pilot on duty, and all arrived in the target area to find favourable weather conditions with five-tenths cloud. S/L Hanafin carried out a glide approach from 16,000 down to 11,000 feet, and dropped the bombs in a single stick, two of them being observed to hit the aerodrome. P/O Parsons made three bombing runs, the first two at 11,000 feet, when two and four 250 pounders respectively were released, while the third was a gliding attack down to 9,000 feet from where the four 500 pounders were dropped. F/Sgt Witt also favoured a gliding approach, and delivered his bombs during two runs from 6,000 and 5,000 feet, the result of which was a fire two miles to the south of the target and the burst of a 500 pounder among buildings accompanied by a blue flame. F/O Nixon reported a small fire resulting from his attack, but no other detail was recorded in the ORB.

F/L Raphael reported to the squadron for flying duties on the 16th during a period of reduced operational activity. With the Battle of Britain gaining momentum overhead, and the country gripped by "invasion fever", Bomber Command stations were put on invasion stand-by, which required each to have aircraft at readiness from dusk until dawn on a rota basis. The first record of invasion stand-by for 10 Squadron appeared in the ORB entry for the 19th, and this arrangement would continue through to the 25th of October, by which time the threat of invasion had diminished. Nine crews were called to briefing on the 20th, and learned that their primary target for that night was a Blohm & Voss aircraft factory at Wenzendorf, situated to the south-west of Hamburg. It seems that the operation was to be launched from Leeming for the first time, with S/Ls Hanafin and Whitworth the senior pilots on duty. The former was the first to depart at 21.12, but returned five minutes later for an undisclosed reason, before taking off again at 21.20. The others followed him into the air over the ensuing seven minutes, but a late change of aircraft left Sgt Green and crew on the ground until 21.54, and this would cause them to be late and prevent them from carrying out an attack. They were, however, hit by flak at 12,000 feet, which left the rear turret jammed. Sgt Hillary and crew also brought their bombs back after failing to locate either the primary or secondary targets. S/L Whitworth and crew arrived in the target area to find ten-tenths cloud above their flight level of 12,000 feet, but good visibility below, and carried out their attack in a glide and in the face of intense searchlight and moderate flak activity. It was only after they landed that the bombs were discovered to be still on board, and the fault was traced to a blown fuse in the electrical supply to the bomb racks. The remaining crews found patches of low cloud drifting across the target, and this combined with searchlight glare to make identification difficult. S/L Hanafin dropped his bombs in a single stick from 11,000 feet while on a due-north heading, after which a terrific fire was observed that remained visible for forty miles into the return flight. F/O Henry and Sgt Johnson made two runs, but were unable to pinpoint the fall of their bombs, while F/O Prior carried out four attacks on a variety of headings, and observed some bombs to hit the northern end of the target. F/O Nixon dropped his load in a single stick from 9,000 feet, but was prevented by the cloud from observing the results, and P/O Somerville, who had recently been elevated to captain status, made a similar report on his safe return home.

Later on the 21st W/C S.O. "Sid" Bufton arrived from 10 O.T.U to assume command of the squadron as successor to W/C Staton. Born in 1908, Bufton had joined the RAF in 1927, and had been a Welsh international hockey player between 1931 and 1937. He put himself on the Order of Battle on the 22nd to fly as second pilot to Sgt Johnson, one of eight crews briefed to attack the Focke-Wulf aircraft factory at Bremen or oil refineries at Hamburg and Hannover as alternatives. They took off between 21.19 and 21.31, and all reached the target area to encounter five to nine-tenths cloud, but, otherwise, good visibility and accurate heavy calibre flak. The primary target was attacked by F/O Henry, Sgt Hillary, Sgt Johnson, F/O Prior and F/O Nixon from between 10,000 and 14,000 feet either in a single or in multiple runs, and some bombs were observed to hit buildings and the adjacent airfield, although the cloud hampered a detailed assessment. P/O Somerville was unable to locate the primary target, and flew eastwards to Hannover, where the oil refinery, probably at Misburg in the eastern suburbs, was attacked in two runs from 9,500 and 13,000 feet through five-tenths cloud. Some bursts were observed, but pinpointing them was rendered impossible by searchlight glare. F/Sgt Witt and crew also failed to locate the primary or secondary targets, and bombed what was believed to be Diepholz aerodrome as a last-resort. Sgt Green and crew spent so much time searching for the primary target, that there was none left to find a secondary or last resort, and an oil leak in the front turret helped the decision to return with their bomb load intact.

Hamburg was posted as the destination for 10 Squadron on the 24th, where the battleship Bismarck and the merchantmen Europa and Bremen were the intended targets, while the Bismarck's sister ship, Tirpitz, believed to be at berth in Wilhelmshaven, was designated the alternative target. Eight of the originally-detailed nine Whitleys departed Leeming between 21.15 and 21.34 with S/L Whitworth the senior pilot on duty, and W/C Bufton again flying as second pilot to Sgt Johnson. Not for the last time during the war at this target, towering, ice-bearing cloud and electrical storms would play a major part in the outcome of the operation, although it was an engine issue that forced Sgt Hillary and crew to turn back when just ten minutes out from Flamborough Head. The others reached the enemy coast to find a bank of cloud between 3,000 and 18,000 feet blocking their way and extending to cover the target area. Each crew spent time over the target without ever breaking free of the cloud, and, after being tossed about by the electrical storms and battling ice-accretion, six of the crews turned back, and, with the exception of Sgt Green, brought their bombs home. The icing conditions caused Sgt Green's starboard engine to cut out, and this, combined with being a target for a flak barrage, confirmed the need to jettison the bombs. P/O Parsons and crew also abandoned their attempt to locate the primary target, but found themselves over Wilhelmshaven, where they dropped a flare by DR (dead-reckoning), upon which the defences opened up with unreasonable hostility. The front turret had iced up, which made identification difficult, but it was eventually confirmed that it was Wilhelmshaven beneath, and a single stick of bombs was dropped. There was no chance of assessing the outcome as evasive action became the priority, and this Whitley escaped damage to arrive home safely with the others.

W/C Bufton was elevated to crew captain status on the 26th and P/O Warren, who was still serving his punishment for the "blue-on-blue" incident, was assigned to his crew as second pilot, while Sgt Johnson and crew were screened from operations pending their posting for a rest at an O.T.U. The 28th brought news of an influx of pilots, observers (navigators) and air gunners, and, among them, was S/L Ferguson, who arrived on the 30th ultimately to assume command of A Flight. Decorations were announced on the 31st, F/O Henry and P/O Parsons receiving the DFC, Sgt Johnson a Bar to his DFM and Sgts Hillary and MacCoubrey a DFM each. During the course of the month the squadron dispatched forty-nine sorties on nine operations for the loss of one Whitley and crew.

August 1940

10 Squadron remained on the ground on the night of the 1/2nd while other elements of 3 and 4 Groups attended to seven targets in the Ruhr. Orders were received at Leeming on the 2nd to prepare seven Whitleys for an operation that night against the oil refinery at Salzbergen near Osnabrück, with W/C Bufton the senior pilot on duty supported by S/L Hanafin. However, at some point before take-off, G/C Staton sent for W/C Bufton and told him to stand down, leaving just six crews to depart for the target either side of 22.00. They flew out over Flamborough Head, each carrying the standard bomb load of four 500 and six 250 pounders, a proportion of them fitted with long-delay fuses of between two and eight hours. F/Sgt Witt and crew turned back after an hour because of a jammed rear turret, and S/L Hanafin was at 15,000 feet and well into the outward flight when an overheating starboard engine persuaded him to curtail his sortie, both returning their bombs to store. F/O Prior and crew spent forty minutes over the target, and delivered their bombs in three sticks from 13,000 feet, observing them to fall short of the northern, southern and eastern boundaries. F/O Henry's load went down in a single stick, which set off the defences, and he was prevented from observing their fall by low cloud, haze and through taking evasive action. P/O Parsons and Sgt Hillary had similar stories to tell, but reported that their bombs, delivered in a single stick, had set off fires.

Group ordered the squadron to make ready seven Whitleys for operations on the 5th, and they were each loaded with two containers of incendiaries on wing-racks and the usual mix of high explosives. The crews were briefed to attack the Dornier aircraft factory in the Hansastadt (free trade) city and port of Wismar, situated on Germany's Baltic coast some thirty miles east of Lübeck. They took off between 20.46 and 21.10 with W/C Bufton the senior pilot on duty and F/L Raphael and S/L Ferguson undertaking their first operation with the squadron, the latter as second pilot to the former. All reached the target area, where varying amounts of cloud and haze provided difficult conditions for some crews, while all faced an intense searchlight and flak response. W/C Bufton had all but two bombs hang up, and P/O Somerville was unable to identify the aiming-point and brought his load home. The others, according to the squadron ORB, managed to deliver their attacks in the general target area, some observing bursts and fires, but the group ORB reported that two unnamed crews bombed alternative targets, a fuel storage depot at Kiel and an aerodrome at Neumünster on the Schleswig-Holstein peninsular.

There were no operations from Leeming thereafter until the 11th, when eight crews were briefed to attack a synthetic oil refinery at Gelsenkirchen in the Ruhr. A standard bomb load in each Whitley was supplemented by fifty cans of "Razzle" pellets, a new incendiary device designed to set fire to forests and crop fields, on this occasion in the general area of Cologne. They took off between 20.41 and 21.14, F/Sgt Witt and crew last away having been drafted in at the last minute as a reserve after P/O Cairns's aircraft became unserviceable. W/C Bufton was the senior pilot on duty, with S/L Ferguson flying as second pilot to Sgt Hillary, and they flew out over Hornsea on the Yorkshire coast to make landfall again in the Amsterdam region. The target was found to be under four to nine-tenths cloud with a base at 7,000 feet, and five crews managed to deliver their loads in two sticks from around 11,000 feet, although without pin-pointing their fall. W/C Bufton had difficulty in identifying the aiming-point despite dropping flares and incendiaries, and he proceeded to the Razzle area with his bombs still on board to deliver the pellets from above cloud. Sgt Hillary was unable to locate either the primary or secondary targets, and attacked an aerodrome at Krefeld as a last resort before proceeding also to the Razzle area to deliver his from 12,000 feet. The others dropped their Razzles from above cloud, and none was able to offer an assessment of the device's effectiveness. An unanticipated disadvantage of Razzle was that pellets tended to lodge in control surface hinges, and catch fire when they dried out, as they were intended to, and a number of Whitleys suffered slight fire damage on return to their stations that morning. Although the Command would persist with Razzle for some time, employing it particularly in the Black Forest region of south-western Germany, it would soon be decided that it did not possess war-winning potential, and would be consigned to the "It was worth a try" file. Information was received that morning that ten Whitleys would be required on the 13th for operations over Italy, and that they must be ready to depart from Leeming at 13.30.

When The Times newspaper was published on the morning of the 13th it contained the news that F/L ffrench-Mullen and his crew were safe and on extended leave in a PoW camp. At the appointed time the participants in the night's operation took off from Leeming for the forward base at Abingdon, from where the attack on the primary target, the Fiat aero-engine factory at Turin, would be launched, with the Fiat airframe factory briefed as the alternative objective. W/C Bufton was the senior pilot on duty, supported by F/L Raphael, with S/L Ferguson flying on this occasion as second pilot to F/O Prior. Take-off from the Oxfordshire forward base began at 20.40, but Sgt Green and crew returned there at 00.32 after abandoning their sortie when the rear turret door blew open and was damaged. F/O Henry and crew arrived back at 03.50 to report also turning back, in their case because of engine problems which prevented them from climbing above 14,000 feet to clear the Alps. They described the cloud at 8,500 feet on the way out with clear skies over a brightly-lit Geneva, and an otherwise uneventful sortie. F/O Nixon attacked the primary target from 5,000 feet, observing all but one bomb to hit the southern end and one the northern end. They reported their incendiaries causing many fires, and as many as twenty-five were counted burning at the same time. P/O Cairns made two runs, and observed the second stick to hit the northern end of the target, while F/O Prior attacked with three sticks delivered from 7,000 feet, the same height as that favoured by F/L Raphael. P/O Somerville went in at 8,000 feet, one thousand feet above the seven-tenths cloud layer, making two runs without observing the results. W/C Bufton descended to 4,000 feet to make his two passes across the target, and he observed hits on the main factory buildings, reporting that his incendiaries started many fires, soon after which, two large explosions occurred. F/Sgt Witt dropped his bombs in three sticks from 5,000 feet, and saw hits on the southern end and on the main buildings in the centre. A message was received by W/T from P/O Parsons that he and his crew had attacked the target, but had lost an engine in an engagement with a fighter. The Whitley struggled all the way to within one mile of the Kent coast with a severely damaged starboard aileron, which broke off as the pilot was preparing to make a forced landing on the beach at Dymchurch Redoubt. The loss of control sent P4965 crashing into the sea, and, although three members of the crew survived to be rescued, P/O Parsons DFC and his co-pilot, Sgt Campion, were lost, their bodies eventually coming ashore on the French coast for burial.

As the Battle of Britain increased in intensity, the Luftwaffe had launched "Unternehmen Adlerangriff" (Operation Eagle Attack), on the 13th, principally to destroy RAF Fighter Command on the ground and in the air. On the 15th, seventeen bombers caused havoc at Driffield in a raid that destroyed three hangars, two barrack blocks, part of the officers' mess and nine

Whitleys, and killed fifteen people. Meanwhile, the squadron ORB tells us that preparations were put in hand at Leeming to send four Whitleys back to Italy that night, two to attack the Fiat aero-engine works at Turin and two the Caproni airframe factory in Milan. The 4 Group ORB describes the targets as blast furnaces in Turin, Milan and Genoa. A further nine 10 Squadron Whitleys were detailed for an operation to Munich, and both undertakings were to be launched from the forward bases of Abingdon and Honington respectively. The two elements departed Leeming in mid-afternoon, arriving at their respective forward bases to top up the fuel tanks for the long round trip. However, reports of unfavourable weather over southern Germany caused the Munich operation to be cancelled at 18.00, and the nine aircraft and crews returned immediately to Leeming.

The Turin-bound quartet of S/Ls Hanafin and Whitworth and Sgts Green and Towell took off from Abingdon between 20.20 and 20.30, and encountered eight-tenths cloud at 5,000 feet from the French coast until it developed into ten-tenths at 8,000 feet later on. All crews completed the long flight out to the target area, but S/L Whitworth was unable to locate the primary or secondary targets at Turin because of low cloud. He proceeded a further seventy-five miles to the south-east to the port of Genoa, where he attacked a blast-furnace from 6,500 feet in three runs. Sgt Towell and crew did manage to identify the Fiat works, and attacked it with a single stick from 2,500 feet. They observed explosions and fires inside the factory, which could be seen for ten minutes into the return flight. S/L Hanafin attacked the Caproni works in two passes from 3,500 feet, observing his incendiaries to break through the glass roof, and the high explosives to cause fires and explosions which continued as he turned for home. A message was received from Sgt Green and crew to confirm that they had successfully attacked the Milan target, but nothing more was heard from them, and N1497 failed to return home. It was learned later that the Whitley had crashed in Italy killing the second pilot, F/O Higson, who, American sources suggest, was at the controls, and delivering the rest of the crew into enemy hands. It was also reported that the crew was allowed to attend the military funeral of their colleague. The remaining three aircraft returned to Tangmere, Reading and Abingdon between 05.57 and 06.33 to complete round-trips of between nine and ten hours.

The squadron was ordered to make ready nine Whitleys on the 16th for another long-range operation that night, this one to Jena in eastern Germany to attack the Karl Zeiss optical works. The same crews detailed for Munich were briefed, while their Whitleys were each loaded with two 500 and five 250 pounders and one container of incendiaries. They took off between 20.33 and 20.42 with F/L Raphael the senior pilot on duty and F/O Warren restored to captain status after serving his term of punishment. The 10 Squadron crews would not be alone in the skies over Germany on this night, as Bomber Command dispatched 150 aircraft, including forty-two others from 4 Group assigned to the same and other industrial targets in eastern and southern Germany. All from Leeming reached the target area after flying across enemy territory over ten-tenths cloud, but opinions were divided concerning the visibility in the target area. F/O Henry and crew described the conditions as good, providing easy identification of the primary objective, which they attacked in four runs from between 5,000 and 6,000 feet. Bomb bursts were seen to straddle the factory and fires were observed as the Whitley turned for home. In contrast, Sgt Howard and crew were unable to locate the aiming-point despite a thorough search, which was not aided by the failure of the flares to ignite, and they delivered their nickels before returning home with their bombs. F/L Raphael reported varying amounts of cloud between eight and ten-tenths, but found the target from a height of 6,500 feet, and made two runs on reciprocal headings north-west to south-east and back. They were attacked by a night fighter from Weimar aerodrome situated some ten miles north-west of Jena, and shot it down with three bursts of fire from the rear turret in a one-sided engagement witnessed by the crew of F/O Prior, who had S/L Ferguson beside him as second pilot. A navigational error caused the Warren crew to spend too much time searching for the primary, and they bombed an aerodrome at Saalfeld, located to the south-west of Jena, as a last-resort target. P/O Cairns and crew brought most of their load home after failing to locate the primary target in the cloudy and hazy conditions, and found a brightly-lit factory at Mellingen, a few miles west of Jena, for their incendiaries.

The others attacked the primary target from between 7,000 and 11,000 feet, and, with the exception of F/O Nixon and crew, returned safely. A message was received from P4955 at 00.30 stating that the port engine was unserviceable, and another, at 00.35, confirmed that they had attacked the target. A D/F-fix based on an S.O.S call from the Whitley at 03.24 located it over the Scheldt Estuary, after which nothing more was heard. A BBC news bulletin at 23.59 on the 17th reported that the German authorities were offering a reward for information or the capture of RAF airmen who had come down in the Zevenbergen region close to the Scheldt, and it was assumed that this referred to the Nixon crew. It had actually crashed at Rijsbergen, some ten miles south of Zevenbergen, just two minutes after the S.O.S. signal, and the crew was eventually rounded up and sent into captivity.

An aluminium factory at Rhinefelden was the objective for ten Leeming Whitleys on the night of the 18/19th, which took off between 19.58 and 20.35 with W/C Bufton and S/L Whitworth the senior pilots on duty. Nestling on the German/Swiss frontier close to Basle, this represented another long-range operation for the "Whitley Boys", but weather conditions were favourable, if hazy, and W/C Bufton reported that identification of the target was rendered easy. He carried out two runs at 5,000 feet, and watched his bombs fall into the target and result in explosions and sheets of white flame. S/L Whitworth picked up the target from a point west of Basle, and also made two runs, both at 4,000 feet, and observed many explosions and fires resulting from his bombs. F/O Warren made his three runs from 1,500 feet, and claimed that all of his bombs found the mark, after which, many explosions and fires were seen. The other crews were thwarted by the ground haze and failed to find the primary target, or, in some cases, the secondary target, which was the aerodrome at Freiburg. Sgt Howard and crew identified the latter, and made two passes at 8,000 feet without being able to pinpoint the fall of his bombs, and P/O Cairns also attacked the secondary target, in his case in two runs from 6,000 feet, and he saw his bombs hit hangars. F/L Raphael and crew were the third to arrive at this location, and they attacked in two runs from 8,000 feet to leave further fires, one with brilliant, white flames, which he believed were from an ammunition dump. F/O Prior and Sgt Towell each reported bombing an aerodrome at Habsheim (untraced), while F/O Henry and P/O Somerville found no worthwhile targets, and brought their bombs home.

Continuing night attacks by the Luftwaffe on 4 Group stations prompted the decision on the 23rd to move 77 and 102 Squadrons from Driffield to new homes, and reduce Driffield to a Care & Maintenance status. Ten Whitleys were made ready at Leeming for a long-range operation that night, and crews flew them down to Abingdon as a forward base. S/Ls Hanafin and Ferguson were the senior pilots on duty as they took off between 19.59 and 20.11 with the Merille Magneto Works in Milan's Sesto San Giovanni district to the north-east of the city

Air Vice Marshal Sidney Osborne Bufton, CB, DFC (12 January 1908 – 29 March 1993) was a senior commander in the Royal Air Force. He played a major part in establishing the Pathfinder project, over the objections of Arthur Harris. He served in World War II as Officer Commanding 10 Squadron 1940-41.

centre as their primary target, and an airframe factory at Sesto Calende, on the southern tip of Lake Maggiore, as the alternative. P/O Cairns and crew were the first to return early after experiencing a fuel-feed problem from the overload tank to the starboard engine, and they were followed home at 21.55 by P/O Somerville and crew with an unserviceable rear turret, S/L Hanafin at 22.07 with exactor trouble, and, finally, at 22.55 by Sgt Towell and crew, who had picked up P/O Somerville's signal and misinterpreted it as a recall. Those reaching the Milan area were confronted by ten-tenths cloud, through which Sgt Witt saw a diffused red glow, onto which he delivered his bombs in a single salvo without observing the results. F/O Warren could not identify the aiming-point through the cloud, thunderstorms and haze, and dropped his bombs blindly from 8,000 feet at 00.08. F/O Henry made two runs across the target at 8,000 feet at 00.21 and 00.26, dropping a container of incendiaries on the first and the high explosives and nickels on the second, and was able to report a large fire as he retreated to the north-west. Sgt Howard and crew spent too long trying to scale the Alps, and decided to head for the secondary target situated some thirty miles short of Milan, but ran out of time here and jettisoned the bombs live over the general area. F/L Raphael and crew were the last to reach the primary target, which they located with great difficulty, before identifying it by its white roof and making two runs across it at 7,500 feet at 00.36 and 00.40. S/L Ferguson and crew attacked the secondary target in two runs at 01.00 and 01.06 from 8,000 feet, and observed fires and explosions, which could not be confirmed as coming from the airframe factory.

After a night off, orders were received on the 26th to return to Italy for another crack at the primary and secondary targets, for which six Whitleys were made ready and sent to a forward base at Harwell. Here, two became unserviceable, and one was replaced by a reserve aircraft, meaning that just five took off at 20.00 with F/L Raphael the senior pilot on duty. Conditions in the target area proved to be a great improvement on those experienced forty-eight hours earlier, and the white factory roof stood out clearly in the light of flares. Four crews attacked in either two or three runs from between 6,500 and 11,000 feet between 00.35 and 01.15, and P/O Cairns and crew reported explosions at the western extremity of the target and a large cloud of

Whitley T4263 ZA-E

white smoke rising to 6,000 feet resulting from the previous aircraft's bombs. There was no news of Sgt Howard and his crew in P4990, and they were duly posted missing at 09.30 on the 27th. Within hours news was received that the Italian authorities were reporting the shooting down of a Whitley at Valera near Varese, situated within a few miles of the secondary target, and that there were no survivors.

Four crews were called to briefing at Leeming on the 28th to be told that the Ruhr was to be their destination that night, P/O Cairns and F/O Warren assigned to a synthetic oil plant at Dortmund, while P/O Somerville and F/L Raphael went for a similar target at Reisholz, a south-eastern district of Düsseldorf. F/L Raphael would be carrying a special night camera to capture, for the first time in 4 Group, the results of the raid. They took off between 23.05 and 23.35, and flew out over Flamborough Head to reach the target area after flying through rain for most of the way. They were greeted by spirited searchlight and flak activity, and were hampered by cloud and intense darkness, but managed to identify their primary targets. P/O Cairns made two runs at 10,000 feet either side of 03.00, and observed large explosions near the aiming-point, while F/O Warren attacked in three passes from 11,000 feet, observing one stick to overshoot and two to fall close to the target. P/O Somerville dropped two sticks from 8,000 feet, and F/L Raphael three sticks from 9,000 and then 8,000 feet, observing large explosions and fires, before returning safely with a series of good quality photographs.

The last night of the month brought an operation against the synthetic oil refinery at Wesseling near Cologne, with the I.G. Farben chemicals and explosives factory at Leverkusen as the alternative objective. Six crews were briefed, and they took off either side of 21.00 with W/C Bufton the senior pilot on duty and F/L Tomlinson elevated to captain status after flying thus far as second pilot to Sgt Witt. They flew out over Withernsea, and reached the target area to find intense darkness and hazy conditions, which hampered their search for the primary target. P/O Somerville did manage to locate it, and carried out two passes at 8,000 and 10,000 feet between 00.05 and 00.10, observing bursts and explosions. F/L Tomlinson was over the target between 00.25 and 00.35, and delivered three sticks from 10,000 feet, which appeared to cause some fires to break out. F/O Warren arrived as F/L Tomlinson was completing his attack, and also carried out three passes, in his case at 9,000 feet between 00.35 and 00.51, and observed bomb bursts but no detail. P/O Cairns attacked the secondary target from 4,000 and 8,000 feet, before dropping the last of his bombs on an aerodrome about eight miles to the north-west. F/L Raphael bombed an aerodrome ten miles south-west of Cologne and searchlight concentrations at Rheydt and Hertogenbosch, while W/C Bufton found a factory and blast-furnace at Spich, a south-eastern suburb of Cologne, and bombed them over a forty-minute period from 9,000 feet. During the course of the month the squadron operated on eleven nights, dispatching seventy-nine sorties for the loss of four Whitleys and three complete crews.

September 1940

The squadron occupied itself with training on the 1st and 2nd, before receiving orders on the 3rd to prepare for operations that night over Italy, with briefing set for 11.00. Possibly because this was the first anniversary of the declaration of war, the target was changed during the morning to Berlin, and the briefing put back until 16.00. Six crews were detailed initially, but W/C Bufton was added to the Order of Battle, and he would have S/L McNair from 4 Group HQ as his second pilot. Their Whitleys were loaded with two 500 and six 250 pounders each, and took off between 20.30 and 20.45 before setting course for Flamborough Head for the North Sea crossing. They entered Germany via the Emden area, and made their way between Bremen and Hannover to Berlin, where a power station at Friedrichsfelde, in the city's eastern extremity, was the designated target and a nearby gas works the alternative. Berlin was found to be covered by ten-tenths cloud with a base at 3,000 feet, which prevented F/O Warren from locating the primary target, and he eventually bombed a railway line on the eastern side of the Capital. P/O Cairns and crew spent twenty minutes over Berlin either side of 00.30, but also failed to locate the primary target, and found an aerodrome through four-tenths cloud near Magdeburg, which they attacked with a single stick from 10,000 feet at 01.15. P/O Somerville and crew were confronted by a two-hundred-foot thick band of seven-tenths cloud at 7,500 feet over Berlin, through which they identified their aiming-point and delivered their bombs in a single stick from 8,000 feet at 00.40. They claimed one large fire in the vicinity of the target, but intense searchlight and flak activity persuaded them to leave the area without delay. P/O Thomas and crew failed to locate either the primary or alternative targets, and were on their way home at 8,000 feet when they came across a factory at Osterburg, between Berlin and Bremen. They dropped their load in a single stick at 02.05, claiming direct hits with their 500 pounders. S/L Whitworth carried out two attacks on the alternative target, delivering four 250 pounders from 8,000 feet at 00.21, and photographing the resulting large fire, before releasing the remainder of his load at 00.35. F/L Tomlinson and crew were thwarted by the same cloudy conditions over Berlin, but found Spandau marshalling yards two miles to the south-west of the primary target, upon which they dropped their bombs in two passes from 9,000 feet. They arrived back over Yorkshire short of fuel after 9½ hours in the air, and it became necessary to force-land P4967 at Nether Sylton near Northallerton at 06.45. The Whitley was written off, but the crew walked away to tell their story. After W/C Bufton and his crew had landed at 06.05, they reported that they also had failed to find the primary and alternative targets after searching extensively, and had tried unsuccessfully to hit a nearby searchlight concentration from 5,000 feet at 02.05. Sometime later they had attacked an aerodrome south of Bremen, without observing results, and, thus, very little had been achieved by the squadron despite the effort expended.

An oil depot at Salzhof, situated on the north-western fringe of Berlin, was posted as the primary target for the night of the 6/7th, and five Whitleys were duly loaded with two 500 and five 250 pounders each along with one container of 4lb incendiaries. They took off at 20.30 with F/L Raphael the senior pilot on duty, and set course via the usual route for Germany's capital, and arrived to find the cloud base to be at around 3,000 feet. A large break in the cloud cover allowed some crews to identify the primary target, but they had to run the gauntlet of intense searchlight and flak activity. F/O Warren and crew carried out their attack in two passes from 5,000 feet, guided by fires already burning, after which the rear gunner reported an increase in the intensity of the conflagration. P/O Somerville dropped his entire load from 8,500 feet in a single pass,

10 Squadron operational crews September 1940

while P/O Cairns made two runs across the aiming-point from 6,500 and 5,500 feet, both crews observing bursts followed by fires. F/L Raphael and crew were unable to identify the briefed aiming-point, but found a nearby searchlight and flak concentration to bomb from 7,000 feet, and they, too, observed large bursts, which prompted the searchlights to be doused and the flak to fall silent. P/O Thomas and crew sent a message at 01.25 to report "task completed", and they were fixed at the position 03.40E at 04.40, which would place them at a point roughly equidistant between the Dutch and English coasts. They were posted missing at 09.30, and, despite an extensive search, no trace of P4935 and its crew was ever found.

Marshal of the Royal Air Force Lord Trenchard arrived at Leeming at 10.45 on the 8th for an official visit. At noon, G/C Staton addressed the crews to inform them of information received from American sources in Rome concerning the fate of F/O Higson and crew, who had failed to return from Turin on the night of the 15/16th of August. The report confirmed that their aircraft had been hit by flak, and that F/O Higson had ordered his crew to bale out, knowing that he was unlikely to make it out himself. The Whitley had exploded on impact, killing the pilot, who was given a burial with full military honours by the Italians in the presence of his crew. Six crews were briefed for the night's operation at 17.00, only for the target to be changed and a second briefing called for 20.30. With invasion fever now at its peak and the Battle of Britain approaching its climax overhead, the most-pressing campaign was the destruction of concentrations of barges and other invasion craft being assembled in the ports along the Dutch, Belgian and French coasts. The destination for the 10 Squadron crews on this night was Ostend, and they departed Leeming either side of midnight with S/L Hanafin the senior pilot on duty. The weather conditions proved to be challenging, with ten-tenths ice-bearing cloud up to 13,000 feet and electrical storms, and this prevented S/L Hanafin and crew from identifying the target, despite searching for almost ninety minutes. They brought their bombs home, as did the crews of F/O Wood, F/L Raphael and F/O Prior, who were also defeated by the ten-tenths cloud that obscured the ground. P/O Cairns and his crew found the cloud base at 4,000 feet, and came below it through rain to identify the seawalls at the mouth of the river, before making a first attack from 3,500 feet at 01.50 and a second from 3,000 feet six minutes later. Three direct his were observed on ships due west of the Basin de Chasse following the first pass, while evasive action prevented an assessment of results from the second one. On return at 04.53, P5094 overshot the runway after the flaps failed to deploy, and came to rest across the Great North Road after crashing through the boundary fence. With the exception of P/O Cairns, who sustained a broken knee and had to be dragged from the burning wreckage by the wireless operator, all walked away unscathed. P/O Somerville and crew also came below the cloud base in a glide down to 2,500 feet to deliver their entire load in a single stick, guided by fires from a previous aircraft, and their bombs were seen to burst across the north of the target and set off further fires.

Seven crews were called to briefing at Leeming on the 11th, where they learned that the dockyards and shipbuilding yards at Bremen were to be their targets, for which they took off between 19.28 and 19.45 with W/C Bufton and S/L Hanafin the senior pilots on duty. They represented half of the 4 Group force assigned to this target, and arrived in its vicinity to find up to five-tenths cloud and haze, and intense searchlight and flak activity. The crews carried out their attacks between 22.10 and 23.00 at heights ranging from 8,000 to 12,000 feet, delivering their bombs in one, two or three passes on a variety of headings. They reported many explosions across a number of basins and wharves, and fires which remained visible for some eighty miles into the return journey. F/L Tomlinson reported hits on warehouses and five ships, but, during violent evasive action, it seems that the rear gunner became convinced that the Whitley was doomed, and took to his parachute.

On the 13th, S/L Whitworth was posted to Dishforth to take command of 78 Squadron at the end of an outstanding tour as B Flight commander with 10 Squadron. His time with 78 Squadron would end in mid-February 1941 with a posting to HQ 4 Group as a staff officer. Later in 1941, he would act as an advisor to the USAAC in America, before returning to the operational scene briefly as the commanding officer of 35 Squadron in January 1942. He might, perhaps, be best known, particularly through the portrayal of him in the 1955 feature film, The Dam Busters, for his time as station commander at Scampton during the formation of 617 Squadron in March 1943 and the launching of Operation Chastise, the epic attack on the Ruhr dams in mid-May. On the 10th of May, Scampton had been re-designated as a Base, rather than a station, and G/C Whitworth would remain as Base commander until being appointed as Deputy Director of Bomber Operations in late August. His successor as B Flight commander at 10 Squadron was S/L Ferguson, while S/L Tom Sawyer, a pilot with more than a thousand hours of service-flying behind him, was posted in from an instructing role at Abingdon for his first taste of operations, and was assigned to B Flight to gain experience before succeeding S/L Hanafin as A Flight commander.

On the 14th, S/L Hanafin was awarded the DFC, and was not among the ten pilots and crews called to briefing that day. S/L Ferguson, F/L Tomlinson and F/O Wood were told initially that they would be operating over Hamburg, while the remainder were assigned to "barge-busting" in the Belgian port of Antwerp, but the Hamburg element was cancelled later because of adverse weather conditions over north-western Germany, and the crews reassigned to Antwerp. They took off between 19.30 and 19.41 with S/L Sawyer flying as second pilot to Sgt Wright, a young and inexperienced captain who had only just been elevated to that status after completing the obligatory number of "second dickey" trips. S/L Ferguson and crew were twenty miles out from Spurn Head on the Humber Estuary when starboard engine failure forced them to jettison the bomb load and ditch in the North Sea at 21.00. They all managed to clamber into the dinghy, and then took the necessary measures to attract rescuers. Meanwhile, the rest of the squadron carried on to find some cloud over the Belgian coast but fine, clear weather conditions and moonlight over the target itself, and were able to identify the aiming-point by ground features. They carried out their attacks in the face of intense light flak, most delivering their bombs in a number of passes from heights ranging from 4,500 to 12,000 feet between 21.35 and 22.25, before returning safely to report hitting the docks area and observing many explosions and fires among the quays, locks and shipping. On their way home Sgt Willis and crew spotted a series of distress signals over the sea at 23.45, and circled the spot at 1,000 feet dropping flares, while seeing nothing on the surface. They descended to sea level to gain an accurate fix at 00.05, and sent an S.O.S signal which prompted a trawler to set off in search and find S/L Ferguson and crew at around 00.30. They were dropped ashore at Grimsby late on the 15th, and were picked up by a squadron transport to be taken back to Leeming during the afternoon of the 16th. At debriefing they reported that P4966 had remained afloat for five minutes before being claimed by the cold North Sea. F/O Warren was screened from operations on the 16th pending his posting to 7 Squadron after the current moon period. The Battle of Britain had reached its climax on the 15th, when running battles involving a total of 1,200 enemy aircraft took place throughout the day until dusk, and the loss of sixty aircraft finally persuaded Hitler to abandon all thoughts of invading Britain. This was not the end of the Battle of Britain, however, but the intensity waned dramatically until it ended finally and officially in October.

10 Squadron called ten crews to briefing on the 17th in preparation for that night's operation to bomb the battleship Bismarck at Hamburg, or her sister ship, Tirpitz, at Wilhelmshaven. F/O Wood was unable to take-off because of an engine issue, leaving the remaining nine to depart between 22.07 and 22.23 with W/C Bufton the senior pilot on duty, and S/L Sawyer again accompanying Sgt Wright and crew. P/O Landale and crew were soon back in the circuit with an unserviceable rear turret, leaving the others to press on to the target, skirting the German Frisian islands, which responded with a flak barrage. The approach to Bismarck's dry dock was via the River Elbe, which led from the estuary for some fifty-five miles in a south-easterly direction right into the heart of Germany's second city. From Cuxhaven and Brunsbüttel at the mouth of the estuary, the shoreline was dotted with heavy flak batteries, which gave their individual attention to the Whitleys for twenty-eight minutes as they headed for the target at 130 m.p.h. It was an uncomfortable experience for the crews on this dark night with up to ten-tenths cloud, and W/C Bufton delayed his attack for twenty minutes while he waited for a gap to reveal the ground below. From that point most of the crews were able to carry out their attacks under clearer skies, but Sgt Wright and P/O Jones must have arrived later, and were unable to locate either the primary or secondary targets because of cloud, haze and a smoke screen. Having been instructed at briefing to bomb only on positive identification of the target, they bombed aerodromes at Schillighörn and Midlum respectively as alternatives. The other crews were less diligent, and, after failing to locate the vessel, delivered their bombs in one or two passes over the general target area, some reporting bursts as much as five thousand yards from

where the Bismarck was believed to be. The attacks were carried out at heights ranging from 6,000 to 12,000 feet between 00.30 and 01.23, after which all returned home, some displaying battle damage courtesy of the Hamburg flak. P/O Steyn and crew reported identifying the Bismarck only after bombing some dock gates through a gap in the clouds, and confirmed that she was not berthed at the location suggested by the intelligence section at briefing, but was moored to a buoy in a basin situated some distance to the east, which probably was the principal reason for the others not finding her.

F/L Phillips reported to B Flight on the 18th for flying duties, and he would take over F/O Warren's crew, while S/L Hanafin was screened pending his posting to instructional duties at Abingdon on the 1st of October. Targets presented to ten crews at briefing on the 20th were all marshalling yards, at Hamm and Soest, north-east and east respectively of the Ruhr, and Ehrang in the southern Rhineland close to the Luxembourg frontier. W/C Bufton, F/O Prior and Sgts Snell and Willis were assigned to the last-mentioned and took off between 21.14 and 21.42, F/O Prior last away having been delayed by a technical malfunction. Despite taking off last, it seems that F/O Prior and crew were the first to arrive in the target area, before the weather took a hand. They made two runs across the aiming-point in conditions of one-tenth cloud and haze, and delivered six 250 pounders from 10,000 feet at 00.35 and the two 500 pounders from a thousand feet lower just a minute later. W/C Bufton and crew searched in vain for a few minutes at heights between 6,000 and 10,000 feet, before eventually attacking an aerodrome at Trier from 5,000 feet at 01.36 and a factory one mile east of Maastricht from 8,000 feet at 01.45, although the interval between the two attacks appears to be too short for the distance covered. Sgt Snell and crew located the primary target, which they attacked with six 250 pounders from 7,000 feet at 01.30, before pulling away in the mistaken belief that they had sustained flak damage. When this was found not to be the case, they dropped the two 500 pounders on what they believed was Cologne. The deteriorating weather conditions in the target area, which consisted of ten-tenths

The remains of Whitley V P5094 which crashed at Dishforth early on 9 September 1940, as a result of hydraulic failure. It came to rest across the A1 Great North Road adjacent to the Yorkshire base. Because the subsequent fire and explosion occurred some 10 minutes after the aircraft came to rest, the only crew injury was to the captain, P/O Cairns, who suffered a broken leg. He was rescued by his wireless operator Sgt Nicholson.

cloud with a base at 2,000 feet and rain storms, also thwarted the efforts of Sgt Willis and crew to locate the marshalling yards, and they bombed the docks at Antwerp in two sticks from 9,000 feet as a last resort target at 02.30 and 02.40. Sgt Wright and P/O Steyn found much more favourable conditions at Soest, the latter picking out the nearby and one-day-to-be-famous Möhne reservoir to the south. Sgt Wright arrived first and dropped his full load in a single salvo from 10,000 feet at 00.35, observing the bombs to strike the ground some mile-and-a-half south of the aiming-point, while P/O Steyn made two runs at 9,000 feet at 01.15 and 01.20, and watched his bombs hit the yards and adjacent railway track. On the way home, the Wright crew ran into a towering bank of cumulo-nimbus cloud, which threw the Whitley around and caused the pilot to vent noxious gas into the cockpit as he became increasingly unable to control his sphincter muscle and the aircraft. S/L Sawyer took over the controls, and, once safely back on the ground, ordered his less experienced colleague to spend at least ten hours in the Link Trainer in simulated bumpy conditions. Meanwhile, S/L Ferguson, F/O Wood, F/O Landale and P/O Jones had all located the yards at Hamm, despite finding patchy six-tenths cloud at 14,000 and 5,000 feet, and carried out their attacks in one, two or three runs from between 5,000 and 13,000 feet between 00.50 and 01.05. P/O Jones and crew reported hits on railway tracks, but the others were unable to assess the results of their efforts.

Briefing at Leeming on the 22nd involved eleven crews, ten for a raid on the Vereinigte Aluminiumwerke plant at Lauta, a town situated some thirty miles north of Dresden in eastern Germany, while the newly arrived F/L Phillips was to carry out a freshman sortie to Brussels. *(The term "freshman" to describe a sprog crew was widely in use in Bomber Command, and is used in this book because of its familiarity to readers. However, in 10 Squadron records the term "nursery" was employed instead).* In the event, the freshman sortie and five others were cancelled early on because of concerns about the weather, and a seventh was scrubbed just before take-off began at 19.09. This left just S/L Ferguson, F/Os Prior and Landale and P/O Steyn to represent the squadron, the first-mentioned taking off thirty minutes late after experiencing an intercom problem. Weather conditions outbound were challenging with cloud and violent thunderstorms along the route, but three crews managed to locate the general area of the primary target, all arriving at around the same time to carry out their attacks in three passes from between 9,000 and 11,000 feet at around 23.15. One large fire was claimed along with a number of smaller ones, and the adjacent railway track was also hit, but cloud prevented a more detailed assessment, and only P/O Steyn and crew would be credited with a successful attack. The weather conditions persuaded S/L Ferguson to seek an alternative target en-route to the primary, and he bombed a railway siding at Halle, a hundred miles west of Lauta, from 10,000 feet at 00.37, and also delivered ten tins of "Razzle" over woodland.

Three Whitleys were made ready for freshman sorties on the 23rd, and S/L Sawyer, F/L Phillips and P/O Bridson were briefed for an attack on the docks and invasion craft at Calais, with Boulogne as the alternative. They departed Leeming between 22.12 and 22.22, and flew out in good weather conditions to find just two-tenths cloud at around 3,000 feet over the French coast. They each selected Boulogne as their target, pinpointing the seawall, and carried out their attacks in a number of passes from between 7,000 and 10,000 feet either side of 00.30 in the face of a spirited flak defence. Many bomb bursts and fires were seen along the quayside, across basins and among dockside workshops, and the raid was deemed to be a success.

Berlin was posted as the destination for the Command's main strength of 129 aircraft on the night of the 23/24th, which 4 Group supported with twenty-nine Whitleys. Crews were optimistically briefed for eighteen precision targets within the city, and it would be only after the infamous Butt Report in eleven months-time that the futility of such requirements would be fully realized. 10 Squadron did not take part, but made ready a dozen Whitleys on the 24th, and loaded each of them with six 250, two 500 pounders and ten tins of razzle, while the crews were being briefed to attack an electrical power station at Finkenherd in Berlin's north-western suburbs, and, failing that, a similar target at Charlottenburg or the Siemens factory closer to the city centre. They took off between 18.58 and 19.19 with S/L Sawyer the senior pilot on duty, and flew out over Flamborough Head only for F/O Wood to turn back early on with a starboard engine issue. The others pressed on to reach the target area, where low cloud and rainstorms prevented all but one crew from identifying the primary target. Sgt Willis and crew made two runs across the aiming-point, the first from 9,500 feet at 23.35 and the second ten minutes later from a thousand feet lower, and observed bomb bursts near the target, after which they dropped tins of Razzle to the south of the city. F/O Prior aimed part of his load on the Siemens factory from 9,000 feet at 00.12, before cloud slid in to prevent a further attack, and he eventually deposited the rest on Hamburg docks from 7,000 feet at 01.00. P/O Steyn's P5055 developed engine problems over Berlin when at 9,000 feet, and lost two thousand feet immediately, which prompted him to empty his bomb bay over a dual-carriageway in the centre of Berlin. F/O Landale and crew bombed a bridge close to Tempelhof aerodrome in two passes at 10,000 feet either side of midnight, while P/O Jones and crew attacked a railway junction near Magdeburg and Sgt Wright and crew bombed the south-western suburbs of the Capital from 11,000 feet. S/L Sawyer followed up on Sgt Wright's attack, attracted by the resultant fires, while F/L Tomlinson found a blast-furnace in the south-eastern suburbs of Berlin, and dropped his load in a single salvo. P/O Bridson identified the Charlottenburg power station and attacked it in three passes from 12,000 feet between 23.35 and 23.43, and Sgt Snell bombed a railway junction at Treptow from 5,000 feet at 00.40. All returned safely, landing either at West Raynham or Bircham Newton, except for Sgt Snell, who put down in a ploughed field near Watton without damage to the aircraft.

The squadron stayed at home on the night of the 25/26th, while other elements of the group attacked targets in north-western Germany, on the Baltic coast and at Berlin. Orders were received at Leeming on the 27th to prepare ten Whitleys for operations that night against Channel ports and one for a freshman sortie to be used by Sgt Towell and crew. The primary target for the 10 Squadron element was Lorient with Cherbourg as an alternative, while Le Havre would be the destination for the Towell crew. The main element took off first between 19.20 and 19.46 with W/C Bufton the senior pilot on duty, and this left just Sgt Towell and crew on the ground until their departure at 22.00. Weather conditions over the French coast were good with clear skies, and attacks were carried out in multiple passes on the primary target from 4,500 to 10,000 feet between 22.00 and 23.29. Returning crews reported many fires and particularly concentrated bombing of the docks at the Pont-de-Caudan, where a number of enemy submarines were spotted. Sgt Towell and crew encountered low cloud over Le Havre, which all-but obscured the ground, but the port was identified through a gap, and a single pass was made at 11,000 feet at 00.55, during which six 250 and two 500 pounders were released and observed to straddle the docks.

On Sunday the 29th, G/C Staton, W/C Bufton and the squadron officers attended a service in the station church at Dishforth for the dedication of a memorial plaque to F/L Allsop's crew, which had been lost a year earlier. The squadron detailed twelve Whitleys and crews for operations on the night of the 30th, ten for Berlin and two for freshman sorties to Le Havre. The primary "Big City" aiming-point was the Air Ministry building, with the Finkenherd power station as the alternative target and the Spandau B.M.W works as the last resort. W/C Bufton and both flight commanders were on the Order of Battle as they began taking off at 18.00, but S/L Ferguson and F/O Prior were delayed until 18.38, the former because of late bombing-up and the latter through a recalcitrant engine. Before they departed the freshman crews of P/Os Brant and Peers set off for Le Havre at 18.25. P/O Jones and crew were back on the ground at 18.42 complaining of an unserviceable rear turret, although no defect was found during testing on the ground. P/O Peers was crossing the English coast outbound when an engine failed, and he jettisoned his load into the sea before landing at Abingdon. P/O Brant and crew pushed on to the French coast, and delivered an attack on Le Havre in three passes through seven-tenths cloud between 21.45 and 21.50 from 10,000 feet.

While this was in progress, the main element was heading for Berlin after flying out over Flamborough Head and encountering heavy cloud during the outward leg. Nine-tenths cloud over Berlin, with a base as low as 700 feet, hampered attempts to identify the primary target, and S/L Ferguson went for the Spandau factory, which he bombed in three sticks shortly after midnight. Sgt Towell and crew attacked the primary target through a gap in the cloud from 12,000 feet in a number of runs either side of midnight, and reported their bombs falling onto a railway station, probably at Potsdam. Sgt Wright also managed to locate the primary target, releasing his bombs through the cloud in a single stick in the face of an intense searchlight and flak response. F/O Prior was unable to locate the primary target in the cloudy conditions, but found the power station, which he bombed from 12,000 feet, while F/L Tomlinson and F/O Wood attacked targets of opportunity within the city. F/L Phillips bombed the marshalling yards at Schöneberg, south-west of the city centre, in two passes at 13,000 feet, but, with cloud tops at around 10,000 feet, it was difficult to observe the results. W/C Bufton was on his way home near Bremen when he spotted a factory with a blast-furnace at Verden, and dropped his bombs in a single pass from 10,000 feet at 00.15. Fires were observed, and the entire factory was ablaze as the Whitley headed towards the coast. A message was received at 23.00 from Sgt Snell to confirm a successful attack, but nothing further was heard, and it was some time later that news came through that both pilots had been killed in the crash of T4130 on German soil, and that the three survivors were in enemy hands. Meanwhile, F/O Wood and crew had overflown England and Wales, and had ditched N1483 in the Irish Sea off Waterford after twelve hours and forty minutes aloft. Fortunately, they were picked up by a trawler and eventually delivered to Holyhead later in the day. During the course of the month the squadron operated on twelve nights and dispatched ninety-six sorties for the loss of four Whitleys and one crew.

October 1940

A number of operations were posted at Leeming during the first week of the new month, but were cancelled because of doubtful weather conditions. S/L Sawyer would eventually succeed S/L Hanafin as A Flight commander after completing the requisite number of freshman sorties, but, in the meantime, it was decided by the station commander on the 7th that F/L Tomlinson would stand in temporarily. Nine crews attended briefing later that morning, five to learn that they were to attack barges, shipping and the docks at Lorient, while four others were given the Fokker aircraft factory in Amsterdam as their primary target with Schiphol aerodrome as an alternative. Those bound for the Brittany coast took off first either side of 19.30 with S/L Ferguson the senior pilot on duty, and headed to Bognor Regis for the Channel crossing. The second element, consisting of P/Os Peers and Russell and Sgts Towell and Wright, departed Leeming between 21.45 and 22.00 and set course for Flamborough Head as their exit point. They reached the target area to find dense cloud obscuring the ground, which persuaded P/O Russell to drop his load in a single stick from 8,000 feet at 01.20, observing them to burst among docks almost two miles south-east of the primary. A number of fires were started, which continued to burn as the Whitley turned away. By this time P/O Peers had carried out two runs from a similar altitude at 00.15 and 00.18 on docks a mile south of the primary, which had been glimpsed through a gap in the eight-tenths cloud. He dropped his incendiaries on the first run and the two 500 and five 250 pounders on the second, and was able to report explosions and fires. Sgts Towell and Wright were unable to locate the aircraft factory and turned their attention upon Schiphol aerodrome away to the south-west, which they attacked more than an hour apart from a height of 7,000 feet. Similarly cloudy conditions created difficulties for the French contingent, and only S/L Ferguson and F/L Phillips located the primary target, which they bombed from 7,000 feet without observing the outcome. P/O Jones attacked the alternative target of Le Havre from 8,000 feet, while P/O Brant found Cherbourg, and unloaded his hardware from 9,000 feet. There was no report from P/O Bridson.

Four 10 Squadron Whitleys were made ready for the night of the 10/11th, when 4 Group was to launch a total of thirty aircraft from Leeming, Linton-on-Ouse, Dishforth and Topcliffe on wide-ranging operations over Germany and Holland. Despite the fact that the target for S/L Sawyer, P/O Peers and Sgts Towell and Wright was the synthetic oil refinery at Wesseling, situated on the West Bank of the Rhine south of Cologne, a target which would develop a reputation later in the war as a defensive "hotspot", it was considered to be suitable for freshman crews, who took off between 21.59 and 22.16 before setting course for the English coast at Hornsea. The weather conditions in the target area were good, and the crews were able to identify the target by the shape of the Rhine. They were forced to run the gauntlet of searchlights and accurate heavy flak as they passed over the aiming-point at between 7,000 and 10,000 feet, and S/L Sawyer's aircraft was coned during the bombing run. He forced the nose of the Whitley down and dived towards the ground, followed and still held by the searchlight beams. Finally, at 1,000 feet, and with the flak coming horizontally from the rear as they headed south, the crew gathered its wits and prepared for a second run. This time the flak was less accurate, but, probably while focussing on regaining height and positioning for a second attack, S/L Sawyer had failed to reset the bomb-release master switch, although he believed that he had done so and that the bomb load had fallen away. They experienced great difficulty then in establishing their position as they neared the English coast, and, it was only after receiving nine fixes and eleven QDMs that they eventually found base to land some three hours after the others. At debriefing it became clear that the navigator had frozen as a result of the frightening experience over the target and had failed to act on the fixes given to him by the wireless operator. While the debrief was still in progress, a message came through from flights that the bombs were still on board. The inspection would show also that the Whitley had sustained more than thirty shrapnel and small-bore bullet holes. The other three crews reported attacking the primary target and observing large explosions and fires, some of them bright green, and a sizeable red glow in the vicinity of the target, which remained visible for forty miles into the return journey. S/L Sawyer, as crew captain, accepted responsibility for the failures, and the station commander restricted the crew to training operations only for the next month.

Briefings on the 14th involved eight crews from 10 Squadron, five to attack an oil refinery at distant Stettin, situated close to the Baltic coast near the Polish frontier, and three freshmen to bomb shipping and the docks at Le Havre. They all took off between 17.25 and 17.40 with S/L Ferguson leading the Stettin-bound element and P/O Peers the freshmen, but tragedy struck the crew of Sgt Wright at 20.00. P4993 collided with a barrage balloon cable near Weybridge in Surrey, probably one of those protecting the nearby Vickers aircraft factory, and plunged to the ground killing Sgt Wright and his crew. This was some two-and-a-half hours after taking off, clearly insufficient time to reach the French coast and return, which suggests that some kind of technical issue had caused the crew to return early. P/O Peers delivered his bombs in two sticks in favourable weather conditions, and reported direct hits on basins 8, 9 and 11, followed by large fires. Sgt Towell dropped his load in a single stick from 8,000 feet, and also observed large explosions and fires visible for some time into the return journey. Meanwhile, those heading for north-eastern Germany reached their destination, which was almost certainly the I.G.Farben Hydrierwerke Politz A.G. hydrogenation plant, and all carried out attacks from between 6,000 and 10,000 feet, P/O Jones making one pass, S/L Ferguson, F/L Phillips and P/O Steyn two and F/L Tomlinson four. Large explosions, fires and smoke were observed as they turned towards the west, and all were confident that they had delivered a telling blow to Germany's vital synthetic oil industry. Diversion signals were sent out because of bad weather over the 4 Group stations, but not all picked them up, and S/L Ferguson and crew had to abandon P4952 over Northumberland at 05.20, having run out of fuel after eleven hours in the air. The Whitley came down at Otterburn on the edge of the Kielder Forest, and all crew members landed safely. Not so for F/L Tomlinson and crew, who had experienced their second major incident within six weeks some fifty minutes earlier, after similar circumstances forced them to take to their parachutes at 04.30. When the wreckage of T4143 was picked over near Thirsk on the following morning, the bodies of the observer and wireless operator were found to be still inside, and it is not known why they failed to heed the bale-out order.

F/L Tomlinson's temporary status as A Flight commander was recognized on the 16th by his elevation to acting squadron leader rank, only for the A-O-C 4 Group to cancel it on the following day. Doubtful weather conditions caused a number of operations to be cancelled over the ensuing days and the take-off time for P/O Peers and Sgt Towell was brought forward on the 19th to 17.30 to avoid another scrub. Their target was the marshalling yards at Osnabrück, which Sgt Towell and crew failed to reach after excessive vibration of the port engine forced them to turn back when one hour and forty miles out from the Yorkshire coast. The cause was traced to the loss of six inches off one of the propeller blades. P/O Peers and crew continued on over the island of Texel and reached the primary target in fine weather conditions with some ground mist to partially obscure detail. They faced a sporadic but accurate searchlight and flak response, and delivered their load from 10,000 feet shortly after 22.00, observing four orange-coloured explosions followed by three fires.

On the 21st S/L Ferguson was handed the acting rank of wing commander and put in temporary command of the squadron. He delivered the briefings to six crews later in the day, four to attack an aircraft components factory at Stuttgart in southern Germany, while F/L Tomlinson and P/O Russell took freshman crews to the Reisholz oil refinery at Düsseldorf. In the event, P/O Russell's Whitley became unserviceable, leaving F/L Tomlinson and crew to take off alone for the Ruhr at 17.26. The remaining quartet departed Leeming between 17.51 and 18.18 with F/L Phillips the senior pilot on duty, and headed for the coast at Orfordness. After about two hours P/O Brant's starboard engine began to emit smoke and flames from above the exhaust manifold, and it became necessary to turn back to ultimately land safely at Cold Kirby with the bombs still on board. P/O Steyn and crew encountered seven-tenths cloud at 4,000 feet, which hampered their attempts to locate the primary target, and they eventually bombed a flarepath and flak battery at a map reference that put them over north-western France. P/O Jones and crew were able to locate the primary target, which they bombed at 23.00 from 8,000 feet. A number of fires were started, but five-tenths cloud at 3,000 feet prevented a more detailed assessment. F/L Phillips had only recently returned to operational duties following his recovery from the severe injuries sustained in early June, and his arrival back at Leeming was awaited in vain. News would reach the squadron later that T4152 had been brought down somewhere in southern Germany with the loss of all on board.

The squadron made ready just a single Whitley on the 24th and loaded it with two 500 and five 250 pounders, some with delay fuses, and a container of incendiaries. It took off at 17.37 with the crew of P/O Peers on board, and set course for Flamborough Head en-route to the dockyards of Hamburg. Adverse weather conditions outbound and poor visibility in the target area ensured a challenging sortie, and an intense searchlight and flak response added to the general discomfort and required a degree of evasive action. The bombs were dropped in two passes from west to east and east to west from 10,000 feet, and the crew reported explosions in the target area, but nothing more detailed. On the following day four crews attended briefing for an operation against a synthetic oil refinery at Magdeburg in eastern Germany, while a similar target at Reisholz in Düsseldorf would occupy the freshman crew of P/O Russell. P/Os Brant, Jones and Steyn and W/C Ferguson and their crews took off between 22.24 and 22.46, and headed out in unfavourable weather conditions, with ten-tenths cloud at 8,000 feet obscuring both the primary target and the alternative, the oil refinery at Misburg near Hannover. P/O Jones was unable to locate either, and, on the way home, bombed the aerodrome at De Kooy on the Den Helder peninsular from 8,000 feet at 04.22, and then the nearby docks from 7,000 feet thirteen minutes later. W/C Ferguson passed this way also at the same time, and bombed the docks in two passes from 10,000 feet, while P/O Steyn brought his bombs home after an extensive but unsuccessful search for a worthwhile last-resort target. The cloud over Holland had become thin enough to see through as P/O Brant and crew headed homeward, and when an aerodrome at Arnhem presented itself, they unloaded their bomb bay in a single stick at 04.10, observing bursts on and around the flare-path. P/O Russell, meanwhile, had been forced to delay his take-off because of enemy aircraft in the area, and it was 01.07 before he finally got away.

It was all in vain, as an unserviceable rear turret ended his sortie within two hours, and his landing at Catterick was in error for Leeming.

In the late afternoon of the 27th P4959 was destroyed at its dispersal after bursting into flames. A fault in the heating system had led to a fire in the cabin, which spread eventually to the fuel tanks. Earlier in the day the crews of P/Os Russell and Peers had been briefed for a freshman operation that night against the U-Boot base at Lorient on the Brittany coast. They took off at 21.36 and 21.47 respectively, and the former successfully identified the primary target in favourable weather conditions with excellent visibility. The attack was delivered from 8,000 feet in a single pass from south to north in the face of an intense searchlight and flak response, and large, white bursts were seen in a line across the target area. Unaccountably, P/O Peers and crew failed to locate the primary target in what they described as poor visibility, but spotted Cherbourg through a gap in the clouds, and bombed the docks from 10,000 feet on a south-north heading without observing the results.

The crews of F/L Tomlinson and P/Os Brant, Jones and Steyn were briefed on the 29th for an operation that night against the synthetic oil plant at Magdeburg with the Misburg refinery at Hannover as the alternative, while the freshman crews of P/Os Peers and Russell were told that the naval port of Wilhelmshaven was to be their objective. They took off either side of 17.00, and those bound for eastern Germany all reached the target area only to be defeated by adverse weather conditions in the form of ten-tenths cloud above a layer of fog. On the way home F/L Tomlinson found a road and railway-line junction west of Amsterdam, which he bombed in two passes from 9,000 feet. The others located aerodromes as last-resort targets, P/O Jones at Rheine, situated close to the German/Dutch border, while P/Os Brant and Steyn dropped their bombs on the Frisian islands of Terschelling and Baltrum respectively. Meanwhile, the freshman crews had also encountered poor visibility over Germany's north-western coast, but had identified the target through a gap in the clouds, and each had managed to deliver an attack in a single pass, P/O Peers from 7,000 feet and P/O Russell from 10,000 feet, neither observing the results. On return, P/O Peers circled Leeming a number of times and was given permission to land, but failed to do so and flew off in the direction of Barnard Castle. A message was received later to inform flying control that P4957 had flown into a hillside near Slaggyford, some five miles south of the Kielder Forest. Remarkably, despite considerable damage to the Whitley, the crew had been able to walk away unscathed. During the course of the month the squadron operated on nine nights and dispatched forty-two sorties for the loss of five Whitleys, including the one on the ground, two complete crews and two additional crew members.

November 1940

Five crews flew over to Bassingbourn on the 2nd as a forward base for operations over Italy that night, which were subsequently cancelled because of the weather. They remained at Bassingbourn overnight with the expectation of operating on the 3rd, but this, too, was cancelled, as it was again on the 4th, and it would be the 5th before the operation could be launched. The weather had also delayed S/L Sawyer's return to operations after his enforced period of extra training, and he was looking forward to finally getting back into the war on the 5th, when the weather intervened again and the two freshman sorties were scrubbed. Over at Bassingbourn, however, everything was ready for the attack on a telecommunications factory in Milan, until the instrument panel in F/L Tomlinson's Whitley began to give problems and his participation had to be cancelled. This left P/Os Brant, Jones, Russell and Steyn to take off between 18.28 and 18.46 and head for the English coast at Orfordness, before setting course for France. The weather outbound was difficult in the extreme, with ten-tenths cloud in layers up to 16,000 feet, icing conditions from 6,000 feet, snow storms and a strong westerly wind. It seems that only P/O Jones and crew reached the target to carry out an attack, which was confirmed in a message received at 23.59. A distress signal was picked up at 06.10, eleven-and-a-half hours after take-off, from which a fix located the Whitley some ten miles out from North Foreland, but P5001 was never seen again, and, despite an extensive sea search, no trace of the crew was ever found. By this time the other three participants in the operation had long-since landed, not one of them having been able to reach the target in the conditions. P/O Steyn was trying to battle his way up through a band of icing, and had reached 10,000 feet over France when the port engine cut at 20.48. He turned around and jettisoned his bomb load some forty-five miles south-east of Charleroi in Belgium. P/O Brant and crew were persuaded by icing to turn back, and they bombed the docks at Ostend in two passes at 22.50 and 23.00. P/O Russell and crew had reached a point believed to be south of Stuttgart when, at 22.10, a port-engine issue developed, and they also abandoned their sortie. The bombs were jettisoned "safe" over what they thought was Le Havre, but, after reassessment, decided that it was probably somewhere near Dunkerque. After landing at Bircham Newton at 01.43, it was discovered that the bombs were still on board, for which a faulty jettison switch was blamed.

S/L Sawyer and crew were called to briefing on the 6th with the crews of P/O Williams and Sgt Towell, and were informed that the oil refinery at Homburg, situated on the West Bank of the Rhine at Duisburg, was to be their target for that night, with the large inland docks on the other side of the Rhine at Duisburg-Ruhrort as the alternative. Later in the war, the Homberg site would be a hotly-defended and feared destination that would claim many Bomber Command lives, but, at this stage of the war, it was considered to be a suitable freshman target. They departed Leeming either side of 18.00 at the end of what had been a fine day, and made their way to the target area via Flamborough Head and the Scheldt Estuary. P/O Williams located the primary target after searching for an hour, and bombed it in a single pass from 7,500 feet at 22.05, but was prevented by cloud from observing the results. S/L Sawyer also found the primary target hidden by cloud, and wasted no time in carrying on the short distance eastwards to the massive and distinctive port complex known as Ruhrort. The bombing run was carried out at 20.35 from 10,000 feet on a due-south heading, but the results were obscured by the cloud. Sgt Towell and crew arrived at the same target almost ninety minutes later, presumably after searching in vain for the primary, and delivered their bombs in a single stick from 9,000 feet on a northerly heading at 22.00. They, at least, were able to observe bomb bursts across the docks and reported fires breaking out.

Another future "hotspot", the oil refinery at Wesseling, south of Cologne, was posted as the target for P/O Steyn and crew on the 7th, and they took off at 18.05, pin-pointing their track to the target by means of ground features, including four large factory chimney stacks clearly visible during the final approach. The attack was carried out in four sticks dropped from 10,000 feet on a variety of headings between 21.03 and 21.52, and this was something that would be unthinkable and, frankly, suicidal, within two years. The second stick produced large explosions and the incendiaries set off fires, precisely as they were designed to do. W/C Bufton had been standing in temporarily for G/C Staton as station commander, but returned to the squadron on the 8th, allowing W/C Ferguson to relinquish his acting rank and resume his role as B Flight commander.

Six crews proceeded to Honington as a forward base for that night's operation against an aircraft component factory in the Zuffenhausen district in the north of Stuttgart, and they set off from there between 17.55 and 18.19 with S/L Sawyer first away and W/C Ferguson the senior pilot on duty. They headed out over Orfordness and the Belgian coast, before reaching the target to encounter four-tenths cloud with a base at 7,000 feet and ground haze. Only P/O Brant and Sgt Towell managed to locate the primary target, which they each bombed in a single stick from 10,000 feet at 20.30 and 9,000 feet respectively at 21.55. Both saw their bombs fall across the target area and cause explosions, and P/O Brant was able to report fires breaking out. W/C Ferguson searched in vain, but found an aerodrome at Baden-Baden to the west of Stuttgart, which he attacked in two runs from 8,000 feet, causing a number of hangars to catch fire. P/O Russell dropped his bombs in a single salvo from 6,500 feet onto an aerodrome near the city of Trier, and observed explosions among hangars and workshops. P/O Williams and crew bombed wharves and warehouses in Mainz on the way home at 12,000 feet, while S/L Sawyer found an aerodrome at Ludwigsburg, just to the north of Stuttgart, and attacked it from 10,000 feet. He then found another aerodrome to the north-west, although the 4 Group ORB mentions Tübingen, which lies to the south of Stuttgart. Later on the 9th, S/L Sawyer and crew were told that they were now fully operational again.

The crews of F/O Landale and Sgt Hickling flew over to Topcliffe on the 12th, to use it as a forward launchpad for their freshman sorties to the U-Boot base at Lorient that night. Take-off was delayed for an hour, but they eventually got away at 23.12 before setting course for the English coast near Bridport in Dorset. At 01.42 news was received that F/O Landale had flown into high ground on the edge of the Brecon Beacons between Merthyr Tydfil and Ebbw Vale in southern Wales, clearly having deviated from track. T4232 was wrecked and all on board had sustained injuries, to which second pilot, Sgt Goldsmith, succumbed almost immediately. Sgt Hickling and crew continued on to reach the general target area, which they located by a fix and e.t.a. The bombs were dropped from 10,500 feet through seven-tenths cloud with a base at 8,000 feet, and no results were observed.

Seven crews were called to briefing on the 13th, five for an operation against the oil refinery at Leuna, near Merseburg in eastern Germany, and two freshmen for an attack on a naval armaments store at Hagen in the Ruhr. S/L Sawyer and P/O Williams took off first for the latter shortly before 21.15, and they were followed into the air between 21.46 and 21.58 by four of the detailed five aircraft after engine trouble grounded P/O Russell. They set course for Flamborough Head and the Dutch coast with S/L Ferguson the senior pilot on duty, but lost the services of P/O Brant and crew after engine trouble forced them to turn back from a point fifty miles out over the North Sea. The others pressed on in challenging weather conditions, which prevented any from locating the primary target despite searching extensively. Sgt Towell had climbed to 15,000 feet in an attempt to break through the cloud-tops, but gave up and descended to 5,000 feet after being attracted by a searchlight and flak concentration through the clouds in the general target area on e.t.a. He delivered his load in a single stick at 01.00 while flying towards the west. P/O Steyn was on his way home when he also came upon a searchlight and flak concentration near Nordhausen on the southern edge of the Harz mountains between Leipzig and Kassel, and bombed it from 7,000 feet at 01.25. The last message from S/L Ferguson was received at 01.55, and his return to Leeming was awaited in vain. It is assumed that T4230 disappeared into the North Sea along with its crew, who are commemorated on the Runnymede Memorial. The loss of the long-serving S/L Ferguson was a major blow to the squadron and would be keenly felt by all who had served with him and benefitted from his experience. Meanwhile, low cloud and mist over the Ruhr thwarted S/L Sawyer's attempts to locate his primary target, and he ended up attacking searchlights and flak near Gelsenkirchen from 5,000 feet at 00.55. P/O Williams reported ten-tenths cloud and severe weather conditions, and found a last-resort target, also in the form of a searchlight and flak concentration, to the north of Mönchengladbach, which he bombed in a single stick from 7,000 feet at 00.30. On the news of S/L Ferguson's loss, F/L Tomlinson was named as his temporary successor as B Flight commander.

Hamburg was posted as the destination for five crews on the 15th, with W/C Bufton and Sgt Hickling taking freshman crews to bomb the night-fighter aerodrome at Eindhoven in southern Holland. The operation, which was to be focussed on the city's Blohm & Voss shipbuilding yards, was planned as a two-phase affair with a gap of eight hours between, and the 10 Squadron element was assigned to the early shift. P/O Steyn's aircraft became unserviceable late on, and this left just P/Os Brant, Russell and Williams and Sgt Towell and their crews to depart for north-western Germany at 17.30 to be followed into the air at 17.59 and 18.47 respectively by the freshmen. The weather conditions in the Hamburg area were excellent, and this enabled all four crews to identify the shipyards and deliver their loads in either one or two passes from between 10,000 and 13,500 feet over a thirty-six-minute period from 20.30. P/O Williams reported starting eight fires, and was able to describe them as immense as he pulled away from the target, and his assessment of the effectiveness of the attack would be supported by the other participants at debriefing. Meanwhile, W/C Bufton unloaded the contents of his bomb bay over Eindhoven aerodrome in a single stick from 6,500 feet at 20.25, and Sgt Hickling followed up a little over an hour later in two runs at 8,800 feet, both reporting fires and heavy damage to the main building complex and also to the runways.

On the 17th five crews were briefed for operations that night against one of a number of synthetic oil refineries at Gelsenkirchen in the Ruhr, while Sgt Hickling and crew would go alone to bomb the U-Boot base at Lorient. They took off first, at 16.56, in what were difficult ground conditions because of the recent volume of rain, and when the Ruhr-bound element made its way to the threshold almost an hour later, Sgt Towell's P5108 became bogged down and its participation had to be scrubbed. The others were all safely airborne by 18.56, but, after completing one circuit, P/O Brant was given permission to land because of a failed a.s.i and a distinct smell of burning. The others pressed on with W/C Bufton the senior pilot on duty, and arrived in the target area to encounter the thick blanket of industrial haze that would frustrate and thwart the Command's best efforts until the advent of Oboe in the spring of 1943. P/O Russell located the secondary target, the Scholven-Buer refinery in a northern district of Gelsenkirchen, and bombed it in two sticks from 10,000 feet between 22.10 and 22.18. The others failed to find either the primary or secondary targets, which left them searching for worthwhile last-resort objectives, P/O Williams finding an aerodrome between Krefeld and Mönchengladbach for his bombs, which were delivered in a single stick from 11,000 feet at 22.40. Three large fires resulted, which soon joined up to form one huge conflagration. After searching for the primary target for more than thirty minutes, W/C Bufton spotted a target of opportunity, a railway junction one mile east of the Berger Lake on the north-eastern edge of Gelsenkirchen, which he attacked from 5,000 feet. Sgt Hickling and crew carried out three passes over Lorient from 10,000 and 9,700 feet, in a seven-minute slot to 21.27, and reported a number of fires, which did not endure for long.

F/L Tomlinson's elevation to flight commander status was recognised with promotion to squadron leader rank on the 20th. 10 Squadron was not called into action again until the 26th, when five crews proceeded to Wyton as a forward base for an operation that night over Italy, while two others were made ready for freshman sorties against the docks at Antwerp. The latter departed Leeming shortly after 17.00, but P/O Steyn was back in the circuit within thirty minutes with a failed compass. P/O Bridson and crew located the primary target after searching for ninety minutes in poor visibility until the cloud dispersed, and delivered their bombs in a single pass from 9,000 feet at 20.30. Four large fires broke out, one of them following a large explosion, and this could be seen for fifteen minutes into the flight home. The target for the main element was the Royal Arsenal in Turin, for which four Whitleys took off between 17.55 and 18.25 with S.L Tomlinson the senior pilot on duty. Sgt Hickling's sortie was scrubbed after his P4994 was involved in a minor collision with another Whitley from 51 Squadron and suffered a damaged pitot head. P/O Russell and crew had almost reached the Swiss border when it became clear that fuel consumption had been too high, and they were forced to turn back. They intended to bomb one of the Channel ports as a last-resort target, but ten-tenths cloud over the coast prevented them from identifying one, and the bombs were jettisoned over the sea. S/L Tomlinson, P/O Brant and Sgt Towell each attacked the primary target in one or two sticks from between 8,500 and 12,000 feet either side of 23.00, and returned home to report starting fires, which could be seen to develop in intensity as they embarked on the homeward journey.

P/Os Humby and Steyn were ordered to fly over to Topcliffe on the 27th in preparation for an operation to Le Havre that night. P/O Humby's departure was delayed for an hour after P4961 became bogged down while taxiing, and, after taking off, the port wheel refused to retract, and he was forced to return to Leeming and abandon the sortie. P/O Steyn had no difficulty in reaching the primary target, where six-tenths cloud with tops at 8,000 feet allowed him sufficient sight of the ground to pick out the Seine Estuary. He attacked the docks in three sticks from 11,000 feet between 22.00 and 22.09, and reported them straddling the target area and causing fires. P/O Humby and crew got their chance to open their operational account on the 29th, when Bremen's shipyards were posted as the primary target. They took off at 16.25 as the only 10 Squadron crew to operate that night, and reached the target area to find three-tenths cloud with a base at 5,000 feet. The bombs were delivered in a single stick from 10,500 feet at 19.45 on a heading from south-west to north-east. During the course of the month the squadron operated on ten nights and dispatched forty sorties for the loss of two Whitleys and one crew.

December 1940

The new month began for 10 Squadron with a call to arms on the 2nd to provide four crews to join five others from 58 squadron to attack the U-Boot base at Lorient. P/O Steyn's aircraft became unserviceable at the last minute, and, by the time the fault had been rectified, the weather had deteriorated, and he and his crew remained at home. P/Os Brant and Russell and Sgt Hickling took off between 16.37 and 16.50, and set course for the Dorset coast, encountering six-tenths cloud over the Channel with tops at 6,000 feet. By the time that P/O Brant reached the target, the cloud had built up to ten-tenths, completely obscuring the ground, and bombing took place on e.t.a. from 9,000 feet at 20.00, without any observation of the outcome being possible. On his e.t.a. at 20.22, Sgt Hickling dropped a flare through a gap in the clouds from around 11,500 feet, but haze blanked out any ground detail, and his attempts to gain a radio-fix on the target also failed because of atmospheric interference. The descent to 7,000 feet goaded an intense searchlight response, and, in the reflected glare a coastline and estuary could be made out, which the crew identified as Lorient. The bombs were dropped in a single stick from below the cloud base at 4,500 feet, but no assessment was possible. P/O Russell found himself in ten-tenths cloud during the sea crossing, and managed to establish his position by astral-fix at 20.58 at twenty-five miles north of the Brest peninsular. He decided to head eastwards to Cherbourg, where conditions were found to be equally challenging, and the decision was taken to abandon the sortie.

Six Whitleys were made ready at Leeming on the 7th, five for an operation that night against the Derendorf marshalling yards situated about a mile north of Düsseldorf city centre, while Sgt McHale and crew were briefed to attack the docks and shipping at Boulogne. The freshman crew took off first, at 17.05, and flew out over Flamborough Head before turning south to skirt the east coast and pass over Great Yarmouth en-route to the French coast. The main element got away either side of 18.00 with S/L Tomlinson the senior pilot on duty, and made their way to the Dutch coast in challenging weather conditions characterised by strong winds and ten-tenths ice-bearing cloud, particularly over Holland. The target area, however, was clear with just haze to blot out ground detail. S/L Tomlinson identified the primary target, which he attacked in a single pass from 9,500 feet, observing large fires with intermittent explosions. P/O Russell and crew were somewhat put off by the conditions, and, suspecting that they would be unlikely to locate the primary target, found a large factory north of Cologne, upon which they dropped one 500 and three 250 pounders along with a can of incendiaries from 10,000 feet at 20.45. Continuing on to the east at the same altitude, they came across the primary target as they flew past it, and turned back to unload the remaining bombs at 21.18. After battling electrical storms and icing conditions on the way home, they were able to report explosions and fires caused by their bombs at both targets. P/O Steyn carried out three runs at the primary target, all at 10,000 feet between 21.00 and 21.20, and was rewarded with the sight of two large fires burning briskly. P/O Williams and crew failed to locate the marshalling yards, but found the alternative objective, the extensive docks in a loop of the Rhine to the south-west of the city centre. Their load was delivered in two sticks from 10,000 feet at 21.30, and they, too, were able to report a number of large explosions and fires. P/O Brant and crew had been unable to climb through the cloud because of ice-accretion, and, at one point, lost height rapidly. They contented themselves with an attack on an aerodrome to the east of Ostend, carried out in three passes at 8,000 feet either side of 21.00. On return they reported a series of huge explosions and fires, which gave the impression that an ammunition dump had been hit. Meanwhile, Sgt McHale and crew had searched intensively before eventually finding Boulogne, which they bombed in a single stick through cloud at 19.20 without observing the results.

Sgt McHale and crew were offered their chance to present themselves over the Ruhr on the 10th, when they were assigned to the massive industrial docks at Duisburg-Ruhrort. They would be the only 10 Squadron crew in action on this night, and flew over to Linton-on-Ouse in the afternoon to join two crews from 58 Squadron. They took off at 18.17 and reached the target area to identify the aiming-point through a gap in the six-tenths cloud. They carried out the attack in two sticks from 10,000 feet at 21.00, and observed huge white and yellow explosions, which continued on as the Whitley withdrew to the west. While this operation was in progress, other aircraft from the group were targeting Mannheim in small numbers, in the first of a series of raids on this southern city in retaliation for recent heavy Luftwaffe attacks on British cities, including the devastating one on Coventry on the night of the 14/15th of November. Five 10 Squadron crews were briefed to attack an electricity power station in the city on the 11th, and four of them departed Leeming between 17.32 and 17.58 with S/L Sawyer the senior pilot on duty. P/O Williams and crew were left behind after a fuel-supply issue could not be rectified in time. P/O Brant and crew were back on the ground after thirty minutes with a number of technical issues, but the others all reached the target area. P/O Russell and crew encountered three to five tenths low cloud on the way out, but this cleared as the already-burning target hove into view. They pinpointed the River Rhine to the south of the city, and dropped their bombs in a single stick from 10,000 feet at 21.35, observing them to burst and add to the existing fires. P/O Steyn and crew took twenty minutes to deliver their bombs in five passes at 10,000 feet between 21.00 and 21.20, and reported some explosions in the nearby marshalling yards. S/L Sawyer also experienced no difficulty in identifying the already-burning marshalling yards, into which he deposited his load in a single stick from 11,000 feet at 21.23. The incendiaries were seen to fall into the north-east corner of the target, but seemed to peter out as the Whitley withdrew.

The main raid on Mannheim, under Operation Abigail Rachel, was launched by C-in-C Sir Richard Peirse on the night of the 16/17th, and involved a force of 134 aircraft, the largest number yet sent to a single target. The intention had been to employ two hundred aircraft, but pessimistic forecasts for the weather over the bomber stations at landing time saw the numbers reduced. 4 Group provided thirty-five Whitleys, of which six represented 10 Squadron, and they took off between 22.23 and 22.40 with S/Ls Sawyer and Tomlinson the senior pilots on duty. The plan called for eight highly-experience 3 Group Wellington crews to set off fires in the city centre as a beacon to those following behind, but, despite clear skies, bright moonlight and excellent visibility, the initial bombing was not accurate, and the raid would become scattered. P/O Brant and crew were homing in on the target at a position about fifty miles south-south-west of Cologne, when the starboard engine failed and forced them to jettison their load and turn for home. The other 10 Squadron crews could see the burning city from forty miles away, and when P/O Steyn and crew arrived they observed a semi-circle of fires into which they delivered their load in two sticks from 10,500 feet at 02.00. P/O Williams turned up fifteen minutes later to carry out his attack from 11,000 feet, dropping the bombs on the first run and the can of incendiaries on the second. P/O Russell ran in on the target by flying parallel to an autobahn, and dropped his bombs in two sticks from 10,000 feet either side of 02.30. S/L Sawyer arrived over the aiming-point at the same time, and described now a complete circle of fires, into which he delivered his bombs in a single stick from 10,000 feet at 02.25. S/L Tomlinson carried out his attack thirty minutes later from 500 feet higher, and watched his bombs fall among the fires. Post-raid reconnaissance revealed that the operation had not achieved its aims, but 240 buildings had been destroyed or damaged, and only three aircraft had failed to return.

The residents of Mannheim were, no doubt, feeling persecuted when they were warned of the approach of another raid on the following night. This was, however, on a much smaller scale involving just nine Whitleys, of which four were provided by 10 Squadron. The plan had been to send five from Leeming to attack a naval armaments factory, but P/O Russell's T4220 became bogged down while taxiing to take-off position and could not take part. The others took off between 16.15 and 16.55, and encountered unfavourable weather conditions in the form of ten-tenths cloud and poor visibility. Only P/O Russell and crew managed to locate the primary target, which they bombed in a single stick from 10,000 feet at 20.41. Sgts McHale and Hickling attacked last-resort targets at Ostend and Dunkerque respectively, while P/O Bridson and crew brought their bombs home.

Elements of 10 and 58 Squadrons joined forces on the night of the 20/21st to send thirteen Whitleys to Berlin to attack a variable pitch airscrew and component factory. 10 Squadron put up six of the Whitleys, which took off between 16.22 and 17.16 with S/L Sawyer the senior pilot on duty. P/O Bridson and crew had been delayed by having to change to the spare aircraft at the last minute, little knowing the consequences of that. Thick ground mist presented a challenge to accurate navigation, but pinpoints were made at the Dutch coast and at Bremen by the light of flares dropped by other aircraft. Intense flak was experienced also at Bremen and at Hannover, but S/L Sawyer arrived at the western edge of the Capital to locate the sheds of a marshalling yard and attack them in a single stick at 22.30 during a glide from 14,000 down to 11,000 feet. P/O Brant reported clear skies over the target, which he attacked in one pass from 11,000 feet at 22.34, while Sgt Hickling and crew took three runs to empty their bomb bay from 14,000 feet between 22.15 and 22.30. Sgt Towell and crew failed to locate the primary target, but found an unidentified objective to the north-west of the city, which they bombed in two sticks from 12,000 feet shortly after 22.00. P/O Williams and crew reached the Berlin area shortly after 23.00, but were unable to locate a suitable target in the prevailing conditions, and back-tracked to the Dutch coast, where an aerodrome was bombed in the vicinity of Rotterdam. P/O Bridson and crew flew eastwards for five hours without ever being certain of their precise location. A decision was taken to turn back to try to locate Hamburg, but when passing south-west of Bremen, a flare-path was spotted at either Cloppenburg or Löningen, and this was attacked in a single stick from 11,000 feet. While still over Germany the starboard engine began to fail, possibly as a result of being hit by flak when south-east of Hamburg during the outward flight. Losing coolant, the engine became very hot and lost power, and the port propeller then went into course pitch and lost revolutions. The Whitley was unable to maintain height, and all removeable items were thrown overboard in an attempt to avoid ditching. The Suffolk coast was crossed at 7,000 feet, whereupon the starboard engine seized with Honington in sight but unattainable, and the pilot was the last to leave the aircraft at 5,000 feet. All landed safely, which was more than could be said for P4961, which crashed nearby at 01.10.

P/O Humby and crew proceeded to Linton-on-Ouse on the afternoon of the 21st for a freshman operation over Flushing on the island of Walcheren that night, and took off at 16.23 to find clear skies and good visibility in the target area. They bombed the docks in two sticks from 10,500 feet at 20.05, and returned home safely to report starting fires at the northern end. P/O Gough and crew took off for a training flight in P4994 shortly after 19.00 on the 22nd, and clipped the roof of the farmhouse at nearby Newton Picket Farm. The Whitley crashed and was totally consumed in the subsequent fire, and second pilot P/O Flewelling, a recent addition to the squadron, lost his life, while the pilot and two others sustained injuries. The following day brought briefings for six crews, P/Os Bridson and Williams and Sgt Hickling to continue the assault on Mannheim in company with others from 58 Squadron, and three freshmen, P/O Humby, F/O Skyrme and Sgt Hoare, to target the docks at Boulogne. They were all safely airborne by 16.20, and set course for the Yorkshire coast before turning south to head across the Channel. The freshmen encountered adverse weather conditions in the target area, with a band of nine-tenths cloud between 1,500 and 7,000 feet, despite which, Sgt Hoare and crew managed to identify the docks and bomb them in a single stick, observing strikes and a fire as a reward for their efforts. F/O Skyrme and crew were searching the French coastal area for a glimpse of the ground when an engine issue developed, persuading them to jettison their load without knowing precisely where it would fall. P/O Humby and crew were unable to locate the primary target, but found Abbeville aerodrome as a suitable recipient for their bombs, which caused five fires. The fun was not yet over for the Skyrme crew, who experienced difficulty in establishing their position over England, and almost completed a grand tour of the country before landing at Leeming almost two and a half hours after the others.

Meanwhile, the Mannheim element had reached the target area, also to find ten-tenths cloud with tops at 5,000 feet and a base that no crew dared seek out. P/O Bridson and crew dropped their load through it in a single stick from 11,000 feet, presumably on e.t.a., and failed to observe any results. Sgt Hickling descended to 4,500 feet before abandoning the search, and, for some reason, headed south-west towards the Swiss border until coming across a small town, probably Ottenheim, where he picked out a factory to bomb in two sticks from 5,000 and 4,500 feet. Two large buildings were seen to collapse and the resultant fire remained visible for a few minutes. P/O Williams located nothing worthy of his bombs, and brought them all home to return to store.

There were no operations on Christmas Day and Boxing Day, but the war resumed on the 27th for six crews from 10 Squadron and others from Topcliffe, who were briefed for an attack on the U-Boot base at Lorient. Five of the Leeming element took off between 16.15 and 16.25, leaving the newly arrived F/L Holford on the ground with a wheel stuck in the mud. It took an hour to free him and get him and his crew into the air, and they were one of five from the squadron to carry out an attack at the primary target. Despite ten-tenths cloud at 8,000 feet, the poor blackout in the port helped with identification, and bombing was carried out from between 9,000 and 10,000 feet. An assessment of the outcome was made difficult by intense searchlight dazzle and accurate heavy flak. Sgt Hoare and crew cited dazzle as the reason for seeking an alternative target, which they found further east along the coast on the Cotentin peninsular. Cherbourg was sheltering under eight-tenths cloud at 6,000 to 7,000 feet, but the Hoare crew managed to straddle the docks with its bombs released from 10,000 feet, although the results could not be observed. Sgt Hayward and crew reported that the anti-aircraft fire thrown up at them from Portsmouth dockyard was better than anything the enemy had offered.

A return to Germany beckoned at briefing on the 29th, the map showing Frankfurt-am-Main as the destination for six crews, who took off either side of 17.00 before setting course via Flamborough Head and the Scheldt Estuary for south-central Germany. The senior pilot on duty was W/C Bufton, who had recently returned from a spell of sick leave, and he was supported by S/L Sawyer, who had commandeered P/O Humby's crew for the occasion. The operation was attended by ten-tenths ice-bearing cloud all the way from base to the target, through which P/O Bridson and S/L Sawyer were unable to climb, and both had their a.s.i freeze up. The former unloaded his bomb bay over Bad Honnef, just south of Bonn, observing two large flashes reflected on the cloud, while S/L Sawyer and Sgt Hoare brought their bombs home. W/C Bufton, P/O Williams and Sgt Hickling all delivered their attacks on e.t.a from just above the cloud-tops at around 12,000 feet, without ever catching a sight of the ground, and it is unlikely that their gallant efforts resulted in any meaningful damage.

Later on the 30th, S/L Kane arrived at Leeming from 10.O.T.U as B Flight commander elect. During the course of the month the squadron operated on eleven nights and dispatched forty-nine sorties for the loss of two Whitleys in crashes at home. It had been a curious year for the Command in a number of ways, although without a precedent to go on, the crews had probably not noticed. The unreality of the "Phoney War" had been shattered in May, and from then on, the Command could do little more than present a defiant face to an all-conquering enemy, and help in the battle for survival. The fact that Britain was still in the war at the end of 1940 was a surprise to many looking on from the outside, but, if the conflict were eventually to be won, the fight had to be taken to Germany itself, and Bomber Command was the only offensive arm which could do this. Sadly, and worryingly, the coming year would find it seriously wanting in this respect.

January 1941

The New Year began as would have been expected at the time, cold in the extreme, with snow on the ground and further heavy falls due to arrive in the late afternoon and evening. The first half of the month would be dominated by attacks on German ports, principally Bremen and Wilhelmshaven, but the harsh winter conditions would effectively ground 4 Group for the final two weeks. 10 Squadron briefed seven crews for an operation on New Year's night against Bremen, although only six would take part after F/L Holford's aircraft became unserviceable. Take-off was accomplished safely by 17.52, with W/C Bufton the senior pilot on duty and the last away, but the numbers were soon depleted by the early return first of F/O Skyrme, and, ten minutes later, P/O Russell, both with failure of instruments. The others pressed on over the ten-tenths cloud that persisted most of the way to the German coast, but the skies over the target area were found to be clear. More than a hundred aircraft were involved in the operation, and fierce fires were already burning in the city as the Leeming element approached, running the gauntlet of extremely intense searchlight and flak activity to reach the aiming-point. Sgt Hoare and crew were the first from the squadron to attack, delivering their bombs in a single stick from 10,000 feet at 20.55, but losing sight of the bursts among the numerous fires and already-gutted buildings. Sgt Smith and crew followed up ten minutes later from a thousand feet higher, while W/C Bufton attacked in two sticks from 12,000 feet at 21.27 and 21.38. P/O Bridson, who had S/L Kane beside him as second pilot, let his load go from 12,500 feet at 22.15, and, on return, reported a number of fires of exceptional size that remained in sight for thirty minutes into the return journey. Post-raid reconnaissance revealed hits on the Focke-Wulf aircraft factory in the southern suburb of Hemelingen, and also the destruction of fourteen apartment blocks in the city centre.

F/L Holford's promotion to squadron leader rank was confirmed on the 2nd and backdated to the 1st of December. Four crews were briefed on the 3rd to return to Bremen that night as part of a seventy-strong force, but P/O Steyn's aircraft became unserviceable at the last minute, and the crew's participation was scrubbed. P/O Bridson, with S/L Kane again flying as second pilot, P/O Williams and Sgt Hickling and their crews departed Leeming at 17.10, only for the last-mentioned to return after forty-five minutes with an a.s.i problem. The weather conditions were as they had been two nights earlier, with ten-tenths cloud most of the way to the target. P/O Bridson delivered his attack in two sticks at 21.00 and 21.02, but was unable to pinpoint the bursts because of the fires already burning. P/O Williams was at 12,000 feet for his two runs at 21.22 and 21.32, and also failed to observe where his bombs fell. He reported that the glow of the fires could be seen for at least ninety miles into the return journey.

A last-minute change of target caused confusion on the 4th, when a recall was sent to S/L Holford and F/O Steyn after they had taken off for Düsseldorf and Hamburg respectively. S/L Holford overshot the flarepath by a considerable distance on his return and became bogged down, but was freed in time to take part in the amended operation by more than fifty aircraft, against an Admiral Hipper class cruiser which had put in at Brest. A process of elimination suggests that i

Whitley Z9227 ZA-W coming in to land

the Norwegian campaign. F/O Skyrme and crew were first of the four 10 Squadron participants to get away at 18.54, but landed five minutes later with a starboard engine problem. F/O Steyn took off at 18.59, and almost came to grief immediately after the port engine failed momentarily at 100 feet before picking up again. S/L Holford and Sgt Hickling and their crews took off eventually at 19.25, and flew over ten-tenths cloud at the English coast with tops at between 3,000 and 5,000 feet. All from Leeming reached the target area to be confronted by a continuation of the cloud and a hostile searchlight and flak reception. F/O Steyn carried out two runs at 11,000 feet at 22.12 and 22.20, and bursts were observed across the docks and the gateway to the docks. Sgt Hickling's bombs were delivered on the glow of a fire through ten-tenths cloud from 13,000 feet during two runs at 22.18 and 22.32, while S/L Holford dropped his in a single stick from 10,000 feet at 22.52, and observed bursts but nothing else.

S/L Sawyer took temporary command of the squadron on the 5th while W/C Bufton covered for G/C "Bull" Staton's ten days' leave. His other nickname was King Kong, which perfectly reflected his irrepressible spirit and belligerence towards the enemy. The weather restricted operations from then until the 10th, when Leeming was declared to be unserviceable for fully-laden aircraft, and the six crews detailed for operations that night proceeded to Linton-on-Ouse in the late morning. Their target was once more the Admiral Hipper at Brest, and they took off from Linton between 17.16 and 17.26 with S/L Sawyer the senior pilot on duty and flying with a "sprog" crew. They flew to the English coast at Bridport over ten-tenths cloud, but this dispersed to leave largely clear skies with bright moonlight for the rest of the outward flight and over the target. Ground haze was the main impediment to target identification, although the docks themselves were clearly visible from the 10,000 to 12,700 feet height range selected by the 10 Squadron crews for their attacks. All except P/O Williams dropped their load of two 500lb and six 250lb semi-armour-piercing (SAP) bombs in a single stick in the face of intense but inaccurate anti-aircraft fire between 20.27 and 21.13, but none was able to observe the precise point of impact. S/L Sawyer later reported crossing the aiming-point from north to south and awaiting the call of "bombs gone", which failed to materialize. Two further runs failed to persuade the man in the nose to "press the tit", by which time the remainder of the crew had become silent with foreboding. The delay had allowed an effective smoke-screen to hide the target vessel, and S/L Sawyer told the bomb-aimer to pick a point on the coast from which to make a run and to let the bombs go when he thought they were over the target. As they flew home the crew expressed a mutual sentiment, "if you want to do that sort of thing regularly, don't ask us to come with you".

Six freshman crews were detailed for operations from Linton-on-Ouse on the 13th, and they proceeded there in the late morning. The target was the docks at Boulogne, for which they took off either side of 17.30 with S/L Holford the senior pilot on duty. They climbed out through ten-tenths, cloud which persisted for the entire outward flight from York to the target, and ruined any chance of carrying out an effective attack. P/Os Brant and Russell and Sgt Towell brought their bombs home, while Sgt Hayward, F/O Skyrme and S/L Holford jettisoned theirs "safe" into the sea. On the 15th, a new Air Ministry directive had pointed to a critical period ahead for the German oil industry, and a list of seventeen production sites was drawn up for attention, the top nine of which represented around 80% of total output. It would be February before the directive was put into effect, but it would not be exclusive, and French and German ports would continue to feature, along with other urban targets in Germany.

The destination for eighty aircraft on the night of the 16/17th was the naval port of Wilhelmshaven, for which eleven crews from 58 Squadron and eight from 10 Squadron were briefed at Linton-on-Ouse during the afternoon. This was to follow up on a successful and destructive operation twenty-four hours earlier that 10 Squadron had sat out. They took off for this one either side of 18.30 with S/L Holford the senior pilot on duty, and encountered ten-tenths cloud over the North Sea, which extended from 1,000 up to 16,000 feet and contained icing conditions with a great deal of static electricity. P/O Humby and crew returned within thirty-five minutes having lost their intercom, and were followed in ninety minutes later by Sgt Hayward and crew, who had been unable to maintain height because of ice accretion, which had caused both engines to cut out. The bomb load was jettisoned as the Whitley descended to 2,000 feet, before the engines restarted just in time to avoid a ditching. It was also struck by a powerful static discharge, which temporarily blinded the second pilot and paralyzed his right arm. Sgt Hoare and crew were prevented by the conditions from climbing above 10,000 feet, so descended, before unloading the contents of their bomb bay onto the Frisian island of Juist, observing three bursts but nothing further. Sgt Hickling and crew were the first from the squadron to reach the target, which they bombed in two sticks, the first from 13,000 feet at 20.54 and the second from a thousand feet higher at 20.58. S/L Holford arrived over the target at 13,000 feet, and observed a large fire west of the Bauhafen before delivering his bombs in a single stick at 21.25. P/O Williams and crew carried out their attack from 12,000 feet, dropping their two 500, four 250 pounders and two cans of incendiaries at 21.30. P/O Brant and crew turned up a little later and also reported large fires already burning, to which they added when letting their bombs go in a single stick from 12,000 feet at 21.59. A message was received at 21.15 from F/O Skyrme and crew confirming that they had successfully completed their sortie, but they failed to return in T4220, and no trace of the aircraft and crew was ever found.

There would be no further operations during the month because of adverse weather conditions both at home and over enemy territory. Some good news for the squadron came with the publication of the London Gazette on the 18th, which brought news of the award of the DFC to S/L Tomlinson and F/O Steyn and a DFM to Sgt Towell. F/O Steyn, a South African, was also screened from operations at the end of an outstanding tour of duty, and would be posted to 10 O.T.U on the 30th. Sadly, P/O Steyn and the other five occupants of the 10 O.T.U Anson would lose their lives on the 13th of April in a crash on Ben More Assynt in Sutherland in Scotland. The aircraft was not discovered until twelve days later, when, in view of the inaccessibility of the site, the decision was taken that the burials should take place where the accident occurred, which remains the highest war grave in Britain and is marked by a granite memorial. During the course of the month the squadron operated on six occasions and dispatched thirty-three sorties for the loss of a single Whitley and crew.

February 1941

The weather prevented operations from taking place until the 3rd, when five crews were briefed at Linton-on-Ouse for a further attempt to hit the Admiral Hipper at berth at Brest. P/O Humby's aircraft became bogged down and the sortie had to be scrubbed, leaving P/Os Brant, Bridson and Williams and Sgt Hickling to take off between 23.42 and 00.05. On reaching the target area they were confronted by six to nine-tenths cloud with tops at around 7,000 feet, and not one was able to identify the location of the vessel. Sgt Hickling bombed the docks in two sticks from 8,000 feet, and P/O Williams did likewise from 10,500 and 8,500 feet, but neither was able to observe the results of their efforts, and it was the same for P/O Brant and crew, who attacked the docks during a single pass from 10,000 feet. P/O Bridson and crew decided to head for Cherbourg, where they attacked the docks with a single stick from 8,000 feet, again, without observing the outcome.

The squadron used Linton-on-Ouse again on the following night to dispatch P/O Russell and Sgt Smith and their crews to Calais at 18.00 to bomb the docks and shipping. Ten-tenths cloud with tops at 6,000 feet proved to be an insurmountable problem, and both turned for home with enemy fighters shadowing them but not engaging. P/O Russell brought his bombs back, while Sgt Smith jettisoned his into the sea, both landing at Driffield after fog closed Linton. Leeming was to be the launching pad for six aircraft on the 6th, and each was loaded with two 500 and four 250 pounders and two cans of incendiaries, while P/Os Brant, Bridson, Humby and Williams and Sgts Hayward and McHale were being briefed to deliver them to the docks at Dunkerque. They took off between 18.24 and 18.40, and reached the target only to find a continuation of the ten-tenths cloud that had dogged operations over the past few nights. P/Os Brant and Williams and Sgt McHale attacked Dieppe as an alternative, while Sgt Hayward and P/O Humby went for Calais and P/O Bridson Boulogne, and bursts explosions and fires suggested at least some success.

The squadron was informed on the 9th that the condition of the aerodrome at Leeming meant that future operations would have to be launched from Dishforth, although all personnel would remain at Leeming, and a bus service would be provided to ferry air and ground crews the eight miles distance between the two stations. The month's "big" effort was to be launched on the 10th, and would involve a force of 222 aircraft, the largest number yet dispatched to a single target. 4 Group made ready thirty Whitleys, twenty-three belonging to 77 and 102 Squadrons at Topcliffe and seven from 10 Squadron, which flew over to Dishforth in the morning for bombing up and crew briefings. They were accompanied by three further 10 Squadron aircraft and crews which would be conducting freshman sorties against oil-storage tanks at Rotterdam. The latter took off first at 19.30, although only S/L Sawyer and Sgt Byrne and their crews actually got away after Sgt McHale's chariot broke down at the last second. Sgt Byrne had barely reached the coast before his starboard engine began to fail, and the bombs were jettisoned into the sea. S/L Sawyer continued on alone to encounter six-tenths cloud over the Dutch coast, and only located the primary target after pinpointing on the Scheldt Estuary to the south, and making three runs across the area. The bombs were dropped in a single stick from 10,000 feet at 21.05, and burning incendiaries were the only indication of where they had landed.
The main element departed Dishforth in a thirty-minute slot either side of 23.00 with W/C Bufton the senior pilot on duty, and all but one completed the outward flight to the target area.

Sgt Hayward and crew turned back with developing engine issues, and bombed De Kooy aerodrome on the Dutch coast near Den Helder in two runs from 8,000 feet at 00.53. The first stick fell on hangars, setting off two fires, and the second fell nearby causing three explosions. The remaining six crews reached the target area to find little cloud and good visibility in which to locate the industrial targets to which they had been assigned. This was a somewhat optimistic aim at this stage of the war, and the inclusion of four cans of incendiaries in the bomb load suggested an area attack on the city itself. Five of the 10 Squadron crews delivered their attacks in a single stick from between 10,000 and 12,000 feet between 01.40 and 02.02, and only W/C Bufton made two runs. Sgt Smith and crew reported twenty-six fires burning as they left the target, and P/O Williams observed huge explosions from thirty-six miles away. The others also described bomb bursts and fires in and around the centre of the target, and it was a good night for 4 Group generally, which was able to confirm that twenty-eight of the thirty participating crews had bombed the target, and there were no losses

Orders were received at Leeming on the 16th to make ready ten Whitleys for operations that night, six to target the Fischer synthetic oil refinery at Sterkrade-Holten in Oberhausen in the Ruhr, and four for freshman sorties to the docks at Boulogne. The two sections took off together between 18.26 and 18.43 with S/L Tomlinson the senior pilot on duty among those Ruhr-bound, and S/L Sawyer leading the freshmen, again with a "sprog" crew. Sgt Byrne and crew were delayed by an engine issue, and it was 19.55 before they finally got away. The weather over the French coast was good, and Sgt McHale and crew had a clear sight of the target as they delivered their load in two sticks from 9,000 feet at 21.35. A huge fire was started on the south side of Nº4 Dock and further fires between that and Nº3 Dock. Sgt Towell arrived to find a large fire between Nºs 4 and 6 Docks, and added to these during two runs at 11,000 feet. The fires witnessed by the Towell crew could well have been those caused by S/L Sawyer, who delivered his load precisely there in a single stick from 10,000 feet in the face of heavy and accurate flak, which punched a number of holes in his wings. Sgt Byrne and crew experienced W/T failure as they made their way across the North Sea, and bombed Haamstede aerodrome on the island of Schouwen at the mouth of the Scheldt as an alternative. Meanwhile, industrial haze over the Ruhr was creating the usual difficulties for orientation, and only P/Os Brant and Humby managed to locate the primary target, which they bombed in a single pass at 9,500 and 11,000 feet at 22.10 and 21.27 respectively, each observing heavy explosions and fires. Sgt Smith and crew were caught and held by searchlights and completely dazzled to the extent that they jettisoned their bombs "live" somewhere near Duisburg. S/L Tomlinson and Sgts Hayward and Hoare all failed to find the refinery, and each backtracked the short distance to Germany's largest inland docks at Duisburg-Ruhrort, where their bombs were delivered in single sticks from between 10,000 and 11,000 feet. Only Sgt Hayward and crew observed their attack causing heavy explosions and a huge fire in a long warehouse, while the others were occupied with evading the defences or were blinded by searchlight glare.

On the 22nd, P/O Williams was posted to 35 Squadron, which had been reformed on the 5th of November to introduce the new four-engine Handley Page Halifax into squadron service and was in need of experienced crews. P/Os Brant and Bridson were also posted out at this time after completing their tours, and they would impart their experience and skills to new pilots at an O.T.U. An operation to the docks at Calais was posted on the 23rd, and eight 10 Squadron crews were briefed at Dishforth by S/L Kane, who had by now been installed as the B Flight commander. S/L Tomlinson's aircraft became unserviceable late on, and his participation was scrubbed. This left seven Whitleys to take off between 19.11 and 19.47 with S/L Holford the senior pilot on duty, but the number was depleted by the early return of Sgt Hayward and crew with a failed port-engine generator. On attempting to land at Dishforth with a full bomb load at 22.10, the Whitley overshot the flarepath, and, on touch-down, the undercarriage collapsed, causing extensive damage to the port leg, wing and engine-bearing, but, happily, no crew casualties. Back at Calais, cloud and haze prevented Sgt Hoare and crew from observing the results of their two passes at 11,000 feet at 21.10 and 21.15. As S/L Holford and crew approached the target, they observed a large fire at the northern end of warehouses on the west quay of N°6 Dock, and then watched their own bombs fall across the west side of N°6 Dock after releasing them in a single stick from 10,000 feet. Sgt Byrne and crew carried out two runs at 21.38 and 21.42 under what were now clear skies, and a direct hit was claimed on a ship, which was seen to be burning furiously as they turned away. P/O Russell and crew arrived later to deliver their bombs in two sticks from 10,000 feet at 22.12 and 22.30, and they were able to report a number of fires before local fog obscured ground detail. Sgt Smith and crew attacked the secondary target, Boulogne, and reported a large fire between N°s 4 and 7 Docks after making a single pass. Sgt Hickling failed to positively locate either the primary or secondary target, despite being informed by the intense searchlight and flak activity that he was in the vicinity, and he opted to bring his bombs home.

10 Squadron sat out a large operation against Düsseldorf on the night of the 25/26th, but detailed seven Whitleys on the 26th for participation in an attack on Cologne that night. Six were to be launched from Dishforth, while a seventh would depart from Leeming in the hands of Sgt Hickling and crew. A force of 126 aircraft was made ready, including sixteen by 4 Group, and the 10 Squadron element took off between 18.01 and 18.15 with S/Ls Holford and Tomlinson the senior pilots on duty. Sgt Hickling's sortie from Leeming was scrubbed after his aircraft became unserviceable late on. Those from Dishforth crossed the English coast at Southwold and made landfall again over the island of Schouwen, before setting course for the Rhineland Capital. The weather was fair with ground haze, and all of the 10 Squadron crews reached the target area to carry out an attack, mostly selecting 10,000 feet as the optimum altitude from which to deliver their bombs in a single stick, although S/L Tomlinson and P/O Russell made two passes, and Sgt Smith preferred a height of 13,000 feet. They were over the target between 21.30 and 22.00, but the ground haze and number of fires prevented any accurate observations of the outcome. The impression of a successful operation was not borne out by local reports, which spoke of just ten high-explosive bombs and ninety incendiaries hitting the western fringe of the city. This proved to be the final operation of a month in which the squadron had operated on seven nights, dispatching forty-four sorties without loss.

March 1941

Cologne was selected to open the new month's account, for which an overall force of 131 aircraft was made ready. 4 Group detailed thirty Whitleys, eight of them provided by 10 Squadron, and they were briefed by S/L Holford at Leeming, once the bomb load had been finally decided upon after being amended three times. The participants then flew over to Dishforth in the early afternoon, and took off for Germany between 19.50 and 19.30 with W/C Bufton the senior pilot on duty, supported by S/L Tomlinson. Unusually, all reached the target area, where they encountered varying amounts of cloud and ground haze, but managed to deliver their bombs during either one or two passes from between 9,000 and 12,000 feet. The defences were very active, but the flak was inaccurate and the searchlights ineffective, and the greatest danger came from the Luftwaffe Nachtjagd, whose aerodromes were observed to be in operation. Returning crews reported explosions and fires within the city, and the effectiveness of the attack was confirmed by local reports, which described particular damage to the docks on both sides of the Rhine. A message was received from Sgt Hoare and crew to report that they had successfully completed the operation and had picked up the order to divert, and this was followed by three S.O.S signals, the last of which was fixed at 00.48 at a point some twenty-

Inside a Whitley was quite cramped as these paras demonstrate, although there is no record that 10 Sqn aircraft ever despatched them. (Operation Colossus 1941 saw Whitleys converted for dropping paras into southern Italy from Malta).

German Poster warning French civilians what to expect if found helping Allied Airmen - males to be shot, women sent to concentration camps. 10.000Fr reward for informers.

five miles off Haamstede on track for Orfordness. Sadly, no trace of T4265 and its crew was ever found.

The third raid on Cologne in the space of six nights was planned on the 3rd, for which a reduced force of seventy-one aircraft was made ready. 4 Group contributed seven Whitleys belonging to 10 Squadron and four of 78 Squadron, and the two elements joined forces at Dishforth during the afternoon for bombing up. Sgt Smith's sortie was cancelled after his aircraft developed a problem and was returned to Leeming. The remaining six took off between 19.12 and 19.30 with S/Ls Holford and Tomlinson the senior pilots on duty. Sgt Hickling and crew were forced to turn back because of engine trouble, landing at Topcliffe in error with their bombs still on board, and became bogged down. The others pressed on via Haamstede under clear skies, but found that Cologne itself lay under low eight-tenths cloud, which, together with searchlight dazzle, made pinpointing something of a challenge. S/L Holford was assisted by an illuminated aerodrome to the west of the city, and incendiaries dropped by another aircraft. He let his bombs go in a single stick from 11,000 feet at 21.30, and watched them burst on the eastern side of the Rhine. S/L Tomlinson attacked in a single run from eight hundred feet higher, but was prevented by the cloud from observing the results. By the time that Sgt Byrne and crew carried out their bombing run at 23.29, the cloud had increased to ten-tenths with tops at 8,000 feet, and they were unable to determine the fall of their single stick. P/O Russell and crew were unable to locate the primary target, and delivered their bombs from 12,000 feet onto Neuss, situated on the West Bank of the Rhine opposite Düsseldorf. Sgt McHale and crew backtracked to Mönchengladbach, which they bombed from 10,000 feet in a single stick at 23.08. Returning crews claimed many fires, but local reports denied that any bombs had fallen within the main city area, and only the western outskirts had been hit.

On the 5th, S/L Tomlinson reverted to flight lieutenant rank following the recent arrival of S/L Kane as a flight commander, and, two days later, was posted to an O.T.U at the end of a magnificent tour of duty. On the 9th, yet another new Air Ministry directive was received, which changed the emphasis of the Command's operations from oil to maritime matters. Unacceptably high shipping losses to U-Boots in the Atlantic forced the War Cabinet to order an all-out assault on this menace, and its partner in crime, the long-range reconnaissance bomber, the Focke-Wulf Kondor. They were to be hunted down at sea, in their bases, and at the point of their manufacture, and the new campaign was to begin at Hamburg on the night of the 12/13th. It was to be a night of major activity for the Command, with eighty-eight aircraft assigned to Hamburg, eighty-six to Bremen and seventy-two to Berlin. 4 Group supported the Hamburg raid with twenty-five Whitleys, eight of which were provided by 10 Squadron, and this would be the first occasion on which the new 5 Group Avro Manchesters and Halifaxes of 4 Group's 35 Squadron operated over Germany. The 10 Squadron element departed Dishforth between 20.32 and 20.59 with S/L Sawyer the senior pilot on duty, and made their way under largely clear skies to north-western Germany. Sgt Hayward and crew turned back from the enemy coast after an engine began to fail, and the bombs were jettisoned into the sea. The others carried out their attacks from between 9,500 and 12,000 feet between 00.25 and 01.35, many taking advantage of the defences' almost total focus on P/O Humby's aircraft, which allowed them to sneak in and drop their bombs unmolested. Returning crews reported many bomb bursts on quays and buildings along with fires, and the consensus was of a successful operation. This was confirmed by local reports, which described extensive damage to the Blohm & Voss shipyards, where U-Boots were under construction, and hits on four other yards.

Hamburg was posted as the target again on the 13th, for which a larger force of 139 aircraft was assembled, twenty-four of them 4 Group Whitleys. 10 Squadron was called upon to provide four aircraft and crews, and they took off from Dishforth between 20.15 and 20.35 with S/L Holford the senior pilot on duty. They all arrived in the target area under clear skies and bright moonlight, and three of them carried out their attacks from between 10,000 and 12,000 feet between 00.08 and 00.30. Sgt McHale and crew were held in searchlights for twelve minutes, with the flak gunners firing up the beams, and they were forced down to 5,500 feet, dropping their bombs from 8,500 feet as they descended. The Whitley sustained extensive damage, including a six-inch hole caused by a shell passing through the fuselage and both auxiliary fuel tanks from port to starboard and eventually exploding in the starboard wing root. Fortunately, there was no fire and no injuries to crew members. The damage on this night exceeded that of twenty-four hours earlier, with further hits on the Blohm & Voss shipyards and a total of 119 fires, thirty-one of which were classified as large.

While a force of 101 aircraft was made ready on the 14th to operate against Gelsenkirchen that night in line with the oil campaign, 10 Squadron detailed six freshman crews, all captained by sergeant pilots, to target the oil storage tanks at Rotterdam. They were briefed at Leeming by S/L Sawyer, before covering the short distance to Dishforth for bombing up. They took off between 19.15 and 19.35, but soon lost Sgt Macdonald and crew to engine trouble, and they landed back at Dishforth seventy-five minutes after leaving. The fault was traced to a piece of official paperwork dating from 1940, which had blocked the radiator! The others all reached the target to carry out their attacks in good weather conditions from 10,500 to 13,000 feet between 22.00 and 22.15, and reported direct hits on the tanks and many fires. Sgt Watson and crew made two runs, the first of which scored a direct hit on a tank in the north-east corner of the complex. They described the target area as being in flames as they turned away, but also commented on the intensity of the searchlight and flak activity. P4956's starboard engine was hit by shrapnel, and the resultant fire was dealt with by cutting the fuel feed and ignition, whereupon a second fire started beneath the inboard starboard petrol tank. Sgt Watson descended to 500 feet with the intention of ditching rather than risk the wing being blown off, however, second pilot, P/O Spiers, and rear gunner, Sgt Boles, managed to put the flames out with an extinguisher and by filling up the heating ducts with parachute bags. This also stopped smoke and fumes from reaching the cockpit through the ducts, but oil from the flaming engine sprayed onto the rear fuselage and caused other fires. Fortunately, these burned themselves out, and, once all fire had been dealt with, Sgt Watson dragged the Whitley up to 2,000 feet on the good engine, and flew on to Bircham Newton, where a perfect wheels-up landing was carried out without injury to the crew.

A force of ninety-nine aircraft was assembled on the 18th to unleash that night against the naval and shipbuilding port of Kiel. 4 Group was to contribute twenty-five Whitleys, of which seven represented 10 Squadron, and their crews were briefed at noon by S/L Sawyer before proceeding to Dishforth later for bombing up. Sgt Smith's gyroscope became unserviceable at start-up, leaving six aircraft to take-off between 20.21 and 20.53 with P/O Russell the senior pilot on duty. Ten-tenths cloud with tops at 6,000 to 7,000 feet awaited the force as it approached the German coast, and remained between the bombers and the ground all the way to the target. Sgt Sturmey and crew were unable to pinpoint the primary target, and bombed a large fire seen through the clouds, and Sgt Farmery and crew experienced similar difficulties. They arrived in the target area at 23.45, but saw nothing of the ground, and eventually jettisoned their bombs live over a position believed to be fifteen miles south-east of the Baltic port-city of Lübeck. P/O Russell did locate Kiel, after making an approach from the north over the entrance to the Kiel Canal, and turning 180 degrees to deliver his bombs at 23.57 from 12,000 feet on a due-north heading. Sgt Griffin and crew obtained a fix on the Elbe Estuary at 22.57, from where they set course for Nordstrand, fifty miles to the north, before turning to port to cross the Schleswig-Holstein peninsular and reaching Kiel at 00.20 to drop their load from 11,000 feet. Sgt Macdonald and crew chose a due-south heading over the target, and released their bombs from 12,000 feet at 00.20. Meanwhile, Sgt Watson and crew, having recovered from the traumas of four nights earlier, believed that they had pinpointed Hamburg below, and headed north from there to the target. However, a sudden gap in the cloud revealed a town, which was believed to be Neumünster, situated some fifteen miles south of the primary target, and the bombs were dropped there from 11,500 feet a fraction after midnight. After a long flight home, T4202 passed over Dishforth at 6,000 feet at 04.50 preparing to land, when the port engine seized and caught fire. The flames spread to the fuselage, prompting the order to abandon the aircraft, which all but the pilot managed to do. It is suggested that Sgt Watson may have been overcome by smoke, and his body was found in the wreckage of the Whitley at Sutton Penn Farm near Masham. The "headless" crew would now be taken over by Sgt Jesse, who was elevated to captain status. The Kiel authorities reported the attack as the most destructive to date on the port, with damage to the Deutsche Werke U-Boot yards and many town centre-type buildings.

P/O Russell was promoted to acting flight lieutenant rank on the 20th, a day on which just one crew was detailed for operations. Sgt Macdonald and crew took off from Topcliffe at 18.56 to join others from 4 Group to attack the U-Boot base at Lorient. The skies over the Brittany coast were clear, and only ground haze hampered visibility. Sgt Macdonald was at 11,000 feet when he dropped his bombs in a single stick at 22.30 onto a point south-west of the central dry dock, but was unable to observe results in the kaleidoscope of searchlights and flak. There were no further operations for the squadron for the next week until the 27th, when Düsseldorf was posted as the target for more than forty aircraft from 4 and 5 Groups. 10 Squadron was to operate from Topcliffe, and seven Whitleys made their way to take-off from Leeming, only for Sgt Sturmey's to become bogged down. Just as the remaining six were about to take off, Sgt Hayward's rear gunner was taken ill, and their sortie had to be scrubbed.

The others took off either side of 20.00 with S/Ls Holford and Sawyer the senior pilots on duty, but the latter, who had the newly-arrived F/L Skinner beside his as second pilot, was back on the ground within thirty minutes with an unserviceable rear turret. After being airborne for fifty minutes, the rear section of Sgt Griffin's aircraft began to vibrate excessively, and he opted to turn back. The original seven was now down to three, and they encountered eight-tenths cloud from the Dutch coast to the Ruhr, which hampered target identification. S/L Holford was unable to locate Düsseldorf, but came upon an unidentified aerodrome to the north, which he bombed from 12,000 feet at 21.37, estimating the high-explosives and incendiaries to have fallen just short of the flarepath. Sgt Macdonald and crew observed the glow of a large fire, which they took to be the primary target, and bombed it from 11,500 feet at 23.05. As Sgt Byrne and crew arrived over the target, the cloud miraculously dispersed, and they spent six minutes either side of 23.30 lining up an attack, which was delivered onto existing fires in a single stick from 12,000 feet. S/L Holford and crew were cruising home at 4,000 feet over Rutland at 02.15, when both engines inexplicably cut out. The crew took to their parachutes and landed safely, while Z6477 crashed eight miles east-south-east of Grantham. The debrief for Holford's crew mentioned the dropping of tea over Breda in Holland during the outward flight. The tea planters of the Dutch East Indies, a region still perhaps a year away from becoming occupied by the Japanese, had donated 4,000lbs of tea to the Dutch government in exile in London for distribution over the Netherlands, and "tea-bombings" would, apparently, become a feature of operations during 1941.

On the 29th, the German cruisers Scharnhorst and Gneisenau were reported to be off Brest, and by the following day, they had taken up residence, thus beginning an eleven-month-long saga, which would prove to be a major distraction for Bomber Command. The first major attempt to disable them was launched on the night of the 30/31st and involved 109 aircraft, although none from 10 Squadron, which had now completed its operational activity for the month. The squadron had operated on eight nights, and had dispatched forty-four sorties for the loss of three Whitleys, one complete crew and one pilot.

April 1941

The presence of the Scharnhorst and Gneisenau at Brest would occupy much of the Command's attention during the new month, and would continue to do so until the infamous "Channel Dash" episode in February 1942 finally resolved the matter. Operations against Brest and its lodgers were mounted on the nights of the 3/4th, 4/5th and 6/7th, before a major raid on Kiel involving 229 aircraft took place on the night of the 7/8th. 10 Squadron had remained at home for the first week of the month at a Leeming that was declared each day as unfit for flying. Orders were received on the 8th to prepare for a follow-up attack on Kiel to build on the success gained twenty-four hours earlier, and this time a force of 160 aircraft was made ready, of which forty-four were Whitleys, ten of them belonging to 10 Squadron.

A Flight proceeded to Dishforth and B Flight to Linton-on-Ouse for bombing up, and they took off between 20.56 and 21.43 with S/L Sawyer the senior pilot on duty and the Krupp shipyard as their primary target. Sgt Griffin and crew were soon back on the ground at Dishforth after experiencing excessive vibration in the rear of the aircraft. Sgt McHale and crew landed at Linton at about the same time with a number of issues to report, while Sgt Smith and crew were two-and-a-half hours into the outward flight when the rear gunner reported that his turret had failed, and they, too, returned to Linton after jettisoning their bombs into the sea. S/L Sawyer encountered ten-tenths cloud over the North Sea, and also had his port generator fail, but, on arrival in the target area, found the skies to be clear and the target easily identifiable by the fires already burning. A bombing run was carried out at 11,000 feet, but only a single 500 pounder fell away, and the manual release system failed to dislodge the remainder of the load, which had to be brought home. Sgt Dodd and crew were seventy minutes out when their W/T failed completely, but they decided to press on and made landfall at the Frisians at 23.40, from where they set course for the target. They were among the first from 4 Group to arrive, but fires were already burning as they delivered their bombs from 14,000 feet at 00.10. Sgt Sturmey and crew were just two minutes behind, and dropped their load from 11,000 feet at 00.12, observing them to appear to undershoot. Sgt Hickling and crew approached the aiming-point from the south and let their bombs go from 13,000 feet at 00.39. Sgt Macdonald and Sgt Salway and their crews were also drawn on by the fires, and delivered their loads from 11,000 feet at 01.00 and 9,500 feet at 01.10 respectively, without observing the results. F/O Boxwell and crew flew through a band of icing in the cloud over the North Sea, and the windscreen was left with a thick coating, which dissuaded them from pressing on to the target. The bombs were dropped onto Bremerhaven from 13,000 feet at 00.45, and the incendiaries were seen to be burning on the canal bank.

Preparations were put in hand on the 9th for an operation that night to the "Big City", for which a force of eighty aircraft was assembled. 10 Squadron detailed nine crews, three of which fell out with sickness or the unserviceability of their aircraft, and, after another crew and Whitley had been drafted in, seven presented themselves for take-off from Dishforth and Linton-on-Ouse between 20.35 and 21.02 with S/L Sawyer the senior pilot on duty. It was his third Berlin trip, and it was one from which he would learn a valuable lesson. They adopted the favoured long route to the target, which required them to fly across the North Sea to the west coast of Denmark, before crossing the Schleswig-Holstein peninsular between Kiel and Hamburg and then swing south-east to the Capital. Despite the increased flight duration, less time was spent over hostile territory, and this was the lesser of two evils. Sgt Macdonald and crew were some twenty miles in from the coast at Brunsbüttel when the starboard engine magneto failed completely. They backtracked immediately to Brunsbüttel, where they bombed the canal locks from 11,500 feet before returning safely home. Sgt McHale and crew were so concerned about the engine performance of Z8564 and its high fuel consumption, that they cut short their outward flight, and, coming upon a railway junction at Rotenburg, between Hamburg and Bremen, dropped their bombs onto it without observing the results. Sgt Griffin and crew also experienced unusually high fuel consumption, and they aimed their load at a railway junction in Braunschweig (Brunswick) from 15,000 feet at 00.48. Sgt Salway and crew were late in making landfall over the Frisian island of Blauort at 00.35, and it was 00.48 by the time they reached the mainland coast. A decision was taken to attack the Blohm & Voss shipyards in Hamburg as an alternative, and a course was set along the Elbe Estuary into the heart of the city to Steinwerder, where the yards were located on the South Bank of the river opposite Sankt Pauli and the Altstadt. The bombs were dropped from 14,500 feet, and bursts and fires were observed.

Sgt Hickling's second pilot was thirty-nine year-old W/C Victor Bennett, who was about to be appointed to be W/C Bufton's successor as 10 Squadron's commanding officer. They enjoyed an uneventful outward flight in favourable weather conditions, but were greeted over Berlin by intense searchlight and flak activity. They spent fifteen minutes over the city, held for much of the time in searchlights, despite which, they delivered their load from 15,000 feet at 01.55, without observing the results because of searchlight dazzle. S/L Sawyer, meanwhile, had attacked the primary target from 13,000 feet, setting off a fire which soon developed into a bright, white blaze that remained visible from Lübeck. Once over the sea on the way home he decided to hand over the controls to F/L Skinner, but, first, switched to the reserve fuel tanks as was standard practice, in order to use up that supply before switching back to the main tanks. He reminded F/L Skinner to be ready to switch back at the appropriate time, and then settled down for a nap, only to be awoken about an hour later by the complete absence of engine noise. Before the second pilot knew what was happening, S/L Sawyer took the necessary action and the engines picked up smoothly. With his heart thumping in his chest, S/L Sawyer resolved never to relax his guard again, no matter how peaceful and quiet the circumstances.

On the 12th, W/C Bufton departed the squadron to convert onto Halifaxes with 35 Squadron, in preparation for taking command of the reforming 76 Squadron as the second Halifax unit. After a short period of tenure, he would be promoted and installed as station commander at Pocklington, before being appointed as Deputy, and, later, Director of Bomber Operations. He would be among those calling for the formation of a Pathfinder Force, and would continue to have an influence on bomber operations for the remainder of the war. He was replaced as commanding officer at 10 Squadron by W/C V B Bennett, not to be confused with W/C D C T Bennett, whose period of command lay in the future. W/C Bennett had been commissioned as a pilot officer in 1922, and had been serving most recently as a wing commander in the

Wing Commander Victor Bruce Bennett DSO, Commanding Officer 12 April 1941 to 3 September 1941.

Directorate of Planning before arriving at Leeming, but had no operational experience behind him. That night, five 10 Squadron crews set out from Dishforth between 19.30 and 19.38 to continue the harassment of the enemy warships at Brest as part of a force of sixty-six aircraft. S/L Holford was the senior pilot on duty, and had taken over F/L Skinner as his second pilot on the imminent departure of S/L Sawyer to pastures new. They approached the French coast at 13,000 feet in very poor weather conditions over nine to ten-tenths cloud, but picked out the easterly docks through a gap, and carried out their attack in a single pass. Bursts were observed, but the cloud prevented a more detailed assessment. Sgt Salway and crew bombed at 22.50 from 11,500 feet on an estimated position based on the quantity of searchlight and flak activity. Sgts Dodd, Griffin and Hickling were defeated by the conditions, and, like almost half of the participants, flew the fifty miles south-east to Lorient, where they delivered their attacks from between 11,000 and 14,000 feet either side of 23.30.

On the 13th S/L Sawyer, F/O Bastin, and P/Os Harding and Mulligan were posted on attachment to 35 Squadron to learn the ways of the Halifax, before joining 76 Squadron. S/L Sawyer was promoted to command 78 Squadron on the 3rd of July, and, after a period in a staff job and, later, at an O.T.U, he would return to operations in the summer of 1942 as the commanding officer of 51 Squadron and see it through its conversion to the Halifax. In May 1943 he would be promoted to group captain rank and be appointed station commander at Burn, before fulfilling similar roles at Driffield and eventually Lissett in April 1944. The same five 10 Squadron crews were detailed to return to Brest on the night of the 14/15th as part of a force of ninety-four aircraft, and departed Dishforth in an eight-minute slot from 22.00 with W/C Bennett flying as second pilot to Sgt Hickling. This time five-tenths cloud with tops at 4,000 feet allowed a slightly better view of the target area, and all from 10 Squadron carried out an attack from 13,000 feet between 01.20 and 01.50. This was accomplished in the face of an intense searchlight and flak defence, the glare from which combined with the intermittent cloud to prevent an assessment of the results.

As a result of the reduction in personnel following the postings to 76 Squadron, it was decided on the 15th to amalgamate the two flights into a single A Flight under S/L Holford in the temporary absence of S/L Kane. Bremen was posted as the primary target on the 16th, for which a force of 107 aircraft was made ready. 4 Group responded with twenty-four Whitleys, seven of which were provided by 10 Squadron, and they took off from Dishforth with P/O Gough the only commissioned pilot on duty. W/C Bennett continued his operational education by flying again with Sgt Hickling, and this was good leadership, which would have been appreciated by those under his command. Heading out over Flamborough Head they found the North Sea lying beneath nine-tenths cloud with tops at 8,000 feet, and low cloud extended over the coastal region and target area. When nearing the German coast, a frozen pipe caused Sgt Dodd's starboard propeller to become stuck in coarse pitch, which prevented the Whitley from maintaining height. The bombs were dumped live on Cuxhaven from 9,000 feet at 23.39 and a safe return made. A long line of searchlights on the banks of the River Weser traced the route to the city, where an intense searchlight and flak reception awaited the intruders. Sgt Jones and crew were the first to arrive, and they carried out their attack at 23.45 from 12,000 feet, while Sgt Griffin and crew dropped their bombs from 15,000 feet just seconds before midnight, but saw nothing of their impact. Sgt Hickling approached from the south-east and delivered his bombs from 13,000 feet at 00.15 without observing the results. Hard on their heels were Sgt Farmery and crew, who attacked at 00.20 from 15,000 feet, and Sgt Gough and crew were the last from the squadron over the target, releasing their load from 14,500 feet at 00.35. Sgt Salway and crew had requested a fix at 22.40, which put them outbound off the Dutch coast, and that was the last time they were heard from. It must have been soon afterwards that Z6557 crashed into the sea, and, the fact that all of the occupants were recovered for burial at Oldenburg, suggests that they were close to making landfall at the German coast.

Seven crews were called to briefing at Leeming on the 20th, three to be told that they would be operating that night against Cologne, while the four freshmen were to attack the oil-storage depot at Rotterdam. They were also informed that the operations would be launched, for a change, from Leeming, and it was the latter element of Sgts Farmery, Gough, Jones and Jesse that departed first, either side of 20.30. They were followed into the air between 20.58 and 21.07 by P/O Humby and Sgts Griffin and Dodd, and both sections proceeded to the North Sea via Orfordness. At Rotterdam five to six-tenths drifting cloud at 6,000 feet combined with an intense searchlight and flak defence to test the mettle of the crews, three of whom bombed from 12,500 to 13,000 feet between 23.04 and 23.32. P/O Gough saw hits on the East Bank and fires developing in the docks area, but the others observed nothing of value. Sgt Jesse and crew failed to locate the primary target, and bombed an aerodrome, believed to be at Blankenburg, situated some three or four miles to the north-west. Meanwhile, the Cologne-bound element encountered ten-tenths cloud with tops at 16,000 feet stretching for the last seventy miles to the target, and plotted their positions based on the predicted flak coming up through it. P/O Humby and crew bombed Venlo aerodrome from 13,000 feet at 00.22 as a last-resort target, while Sgts Griffin and Dodd bombed on the centre of the flak and searchlight activity from around 15,000 feet a little later.

Eight crews were briefed at Leeming on the 23rd for the next assault on Brest and its lodgers, which was to be carried out by a force of sixty-seven aircraft. The Leeming element took off between 20.05 and 20.51 with S/L Kane the senior pilot on duty, but his sortie was cut short by exactor problems, while Sgt Griffin was forced to turn back after his rear gunner was taken ill. P/O Freund and crew were over mid-Channel when excessive oil temperature and low pressure in the starboard engine persuaded them to jettison the bomb load and head for land. For some reason they landed at Squires Gate, Blackpool, where they spent the night before flying back to Leeming on the following morning. This left five crews to press on to the target, which was found to be hiding beneath a thick blanket of mist and some cloud. Intense anti-aircraft fire and searchlights added to the difficulties, and only the faint outline of the docks could be identified.

Bombing was carried out from 13,000 feet between 23.08 and 23.40, and no assessment of the outcome could be made. S/L Kane and P/O Freund and their crews were given another chance to get some experience under their belts on the 25th with freshman sorties to Bremerhaven. They took off at 20.50 only to encounter poor weather over the North Sea, including cloud that all-but obscured ground references. S/L Kane carried out an attack on what he believed to be the target, but was plotted later to be Tönning in the Schleswig-Holstein region some sixty miles further north. P/O Freund searched extensively in extreme darkness for the primary target, but ended up bombing an aerodrome on the Frisian island of Teschelling just as an aircraft was taking off.

The squadron was divided into two flights again on the 27th, with S/L Holford commanding A Flight and S/L Kane B Flight. Mannheim was posted as the main target for the night of the 29/30th, for which a force of seventy-one aircraft was put together, a figure which included seven Whitleys provided by 10 Squadron. A further thirty-one aircraft were made ready for Rotterdam, and among these was a Whitley for the crew of S/L Kane. He had operated only infrequently since his arrival on the squadron and was still viewed as a freshman. The main element took off first, between 20.12 and 20.25 with P/O Humby the only commissioned pilot on duty. S/L Kane departed Leeming at 21.03, and he reached the target area to find thick ground haze, but managed to identify the river to guide him to the aiming-point. The attack was carried out from 10,800 feet at 00.07, and several small fires broke out giving off a reddish glow. Sgt Hayward and crew were proceeding south when the port engine oil began to overheat, and it was decided to drop the bombs onto Ostend docks, which was done through three-tenths cloud from 9,000 feet at 22.32. The others all reached the target area to encounter clear skies, but also thick ground haze, into which P/O Humby dropped his bombs in a single stick from 12,000 feet at 00.30. They were seen to explode west of the target, and large fires were seen in the woods to the south. The remaining crews delivered their attacks from between 13,000 and 15,000 feet between 00.20 and 01.00, before returning safely to report observing explosions and fires but no detail. During the course of the month the squadron operated on eight nights, and dispatched fifty-seven sorties for the loss of a single Whitley and crew.

May 1941

The new month began for 10 Squadron with the briefing of nine crews on the 3rd for operations that night over Cologne, for which an overall force of 101 aircraft was made ready. The Leeming crews took off either side of 21.00 with S/L Kane the senior pilot on duty, but P/O Freund and crew landed at Honington some ninety minutes later after their compass failed. The others pressed on via Orfordness to the Belgian coast, and encountered eight to ten-tenths cloud all the way. Sgt Hayward and crew were the next to turn back early after the instruments failed and the aileron control became unserviceable. An attempt was made to jettison the bombs into the sea, but only two fell away because of a fault in the release system, and they were forced to attempt a landing with the rest on board. The pilot overshot the approach, and had to swing the Whitley sharply, causing it to run onto broken ground where a runway was under construction. The starboard undercarriage leg collapsed, after which, P5109 came to rest on its starboard wing tip, happily, without damage to the crew, and sufficiently intact to eventually be returned to flying condition. Weather conditions in the target area were not conducive to accurate bombing, and S/L Kane flew the twenty miles north to Düsseldorf, where a successful attack was carried out

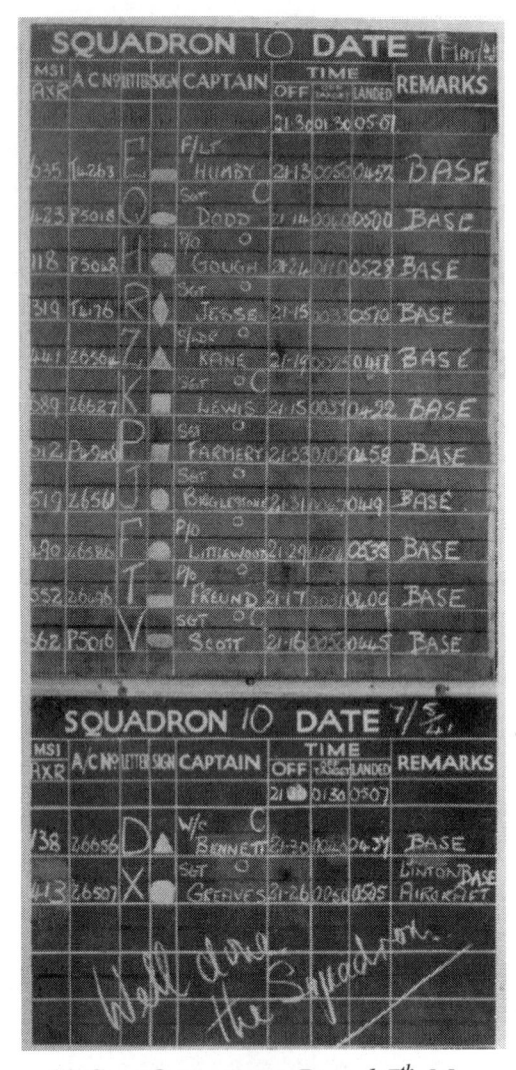

10 Sqn Operations Board 7th May 1941

from 13,000 feet at 00.41. This left six 10 Squadron crews to try their hand at the primary target in difficult conditions. Bombing was carried out from between 13,000 and 16,000 feet, with an hour elapsing between the attacks of Sgt Griffin at 00.20 and Sgt Jesse at 01.21. It was impossible to make an accurate assessment, but a local report mentioned only about ten bomb loads landing in the city, and they caused only minor damage.

Mannheim was posted as the main target for the night of the 5/6th, for which a force of 141 aircraft was made ready. 10 Squadron detailed six Whitleys for this and four others for freshman crews to take to the docks at Boulogne. The main element took off first, between 21.15 and 21.32 with S/L Kane the senior pilot on duty and W/C Bennett flying this time with Sgt Dodd and crew. Once they were safely on their way, P/O Freund and crew set off for Boulogne at 21.36, some thirty minutes before the departures of Sgts Bigglestone, Lewis and Scott. In the event, P/O Freund would return to Leeming with his bombs after four hours because of a failed port generator. Both sections met eight to ten-tenths cloud on reaching the North Sea at Orfordness and it accompanied the Mannheim force all the way to the target, while those bound for Boulogne found a slight improvement that allowed some sight of the ground. Sgts Bigglestone and Scott reached the French coast at the same time, and bombed within a minute of each other from 13,000 feet at 01.14, both reporting straddling the docks and setting off fires. Sgt Lewis and crew were unable to locate the target and jettisoned their load into the sea. S/L Kane was experiencing similar difficulties in finding Mannheim, and proceeded instead to Frankfurt, which he bombed from 15,000 feet at 01.14 and observed the incendiaries start fires. The remaining five crews all managed to locate Mannheim despite the thickness of the cloud, and they were helped by the amount of flak being thrown up at them and the glow of searchlights groping around. They carried out their attacks from 12,000 to 14,000 feet between 00.48 and 01.34, but were denied any meaningful sight of the ground and the results of their efforts.

The squadron sat out a raid on Hamburg on the night of the 6/7th, before making ready twelve Whitleys for operations against the German warships at Brest on the 7th. Eight fully operational crews and four freshmen were briefed, and they took off between 21.13 and 21.31 with W/C Bennett the senior pilot on duty and undertaking his first sortie as crew captain. S/L Kane was also on the Order of Battle, and they were part of an overall force of eighty-nine Wellingtons, Whitleys and Hampdens. Remarkably, all from 10 Squadron reached the target area, where the

The Whitley production line at Armstrong Whitworth's Baginton factory, near Coventry. After Whitley production ceased in June 1943 the factory switched to making Lancasters.

five-tenths cloud of the sea-crossing had dispersed to leave clear skies over the port and good visibility. The Leeming participants each carried out their attack in a single pass from 12,000 to 16,000 feet between 00.26 and 01.44, and returned safely to report intense searchlight and flak activity, but little in the way of an assessment. Sgt Scott's rear gunner observed two large fires break out and a heavy explosion when eighty miles into the return journey. Crews from other squadrons claimed hits on both vessels, but these were not confirmed.

The night of the 8/9th would set a new record for the Command as 321 aircraft were made ready to launch against two main targets, Hamburg and Bremen. When those assigned to minor operations were added to the numbers, a total of 364 aircraft would be operating, ninety-nine more than the previous record set in February. 3 and 5 Groups combined to send 188 aircraft to Germany's Second City, while 1 and 4 Groups assembled a force of 133 Wellingtons and Whitleys for Bremen, 4 Group contributing a record seventy-eight Whitleys and seven Mk II Wellingtons of 104 Squadron, which would be conducting its maiden operation. There was feverish activity on all bomber stations as aircraft were fuelled and bombed up, while their crews attended briefings to learn that shipyards and urban areas were to be their aiming-points. At Leeming fourteen Whitleys were loaded with two 500 pounders, two 250 pounders and four containers of incendiaries, and two extra 500 pounders were added to the bomb bays of those capable of lifting an increased load.

With the exception of P/O Gough and crew, whose aircraft became unserviceable late on, they took off between 22.06 and 22.35 with W/C Bennett the senior pilot on duty, supported by S/L Kane and the newly-promoted acting F/L Humby. When an hour out over the North Sea, P/O Freund's starboard exactor sent the propeller into fine pitch, which caused the engine to overheat. The engine cut out altogether at the moment of touching down at Leeming, causing a swing and the collapse of the starboard undercarriage leg. The aircraft sustained damage to the mainplane, but the crew was able to walk away unscathed. The others pressed on over considerable amounts of cloud with tops at 8,000 feet, but this began to disperse as the German coast hove into sight and it was down to two-tenths over the Elbe Estuary with just ground mist to contend with. W/C Bennett picked out a dummy fire south of the Altstadt (Old Town), while others would comment on the two large cones of searchlights, one to the north and the other to the south of the docks area, and fairly intense anti-aircraft fire. The primary target for the Leeming gang was the Deutscher Schiff Werke yards, upon which attacks were carried out in a single pass from 11,500 to 17,000 feet between 01.20 and 01.59. Bomb bursts and fires were observed, but it proved difficult to make an accurate assessment in the conditions. Sgt Beveridge and crew searched in vain for fifty minutes for the primary target, and, ultimately, bombed what they believed to be Cuxhaven at 01.55. A message was received from P/O Guest and crew at 01.59 to confirm successfully attacking the primary target, but nothing more was heard from them. It would be some time before news came through that P4946 had ditched off the Dutch coast and that its crew was now on extended leave in a German PoW camp. Returning crews were confident of an effective night's work, and the Bremen authorities reported widespread bombing of the town, but no hits on the shipyards. Considerable damage was also inflicted on Hamburg, where thirty-eight large fires had to be dealt with.

10 Squadron sat out the following night's attack on the I.G. Farben petro-chemicals works at Ludwigshafen, which was supported by other elements of 4 Group, but was called upon to provide eleven Whitleys on the 10th for a follow-up raid on Hamburg as part of an overall force of 119 aircraft. One Whitley became unserviceable, leaving ten to depart Leeming between 22.40 and 22.59 with W/C Bennet and S/L Kane the senior pilots on duty. F/L Humby returned at midnight with a starboard engine issue, and his landing was followed fifteen minutes later by that of Sgt Bigglestone and crew, whose wireless equipment had failed. The others continued on to be greeted over north-western Germany by clear skies and good visibility, and delivered their attacks in a single pass from 12,500 to 16,000 feet between 01.55 and 02.37. P/O Gough and crew sent a signal at 02.23 reporting that they had completed their attack, but their return was awaited in vain, and no trace of P5048 and its crew was ever found. Hamburg reported forty-seven large fires and extensive damage in the city centre.

Hamburg and Bremen were targeted again twenty-four hours later without a contribution from 10 Squadron, and further damage was inflicted upon mostly urban and commercial districts rather than the industrial docks. Seven Whitleys lined up for take-off from Leeming on the 12th, and became airborne either side of 21.30 with W/C Bennett the senior pilot on duty. They were bound for Mannheim as part of an overall force of 105 aircraft, some of which had been assigned to Ludwigshafen, the city facing Mannheim from the West Bank of the Rhine. P/O Littlewood and crew returned after an hour with W/T failure, leaving the others to push on over ten-tenths cloud with tops at 6,000 feet. Sgt Hayward and crew encountered icing conditions, which prevented the Whitley from climbing beyond 9,000 feet, and they located Dunkerque by DR (dead-reckoning), to bomb it in one stick at 23.17. Sgt Bigglestone and crew experienced an identical problem, and, after dropping two 500 pounders on a searchlight battery somewhere on the French coast at 23.24, proceeded also to Dunkerque to unload the remaining bombs from 8,000 feet at 02.12, after twice evading the attentions of an ME110 night-fighter. The cloud and thick ground haze made target identification a major challenge, and some crews were uncertain of their precise location. W/C Bennett flew over the Rhine for thirty minutes, and saw flares being dropped by other aircraft, before dropping his bombs in a single stick from 13,500 feet at 02.03 onto what he later believed was Cologne. P/O Spiers and crew couldn't positively identify Mannheim, but bombed on e.t.a from 13,000 feet at 01.30. Sgt Lewis attacked the primary target from 14,000 feet at 01.52 in the face of intense anti-aircraft fire, and Sgt Dodd believed he was over Mannheim when bombing from 13,500 feet at 01.15, but conceded later that he may have been over Cologne, some 130 miles to the north. Local reports confirmed that few bomb loads had found their way into the twin cities.

Sgts Dodd and Hayward were posted to 104 Squadron with some of their crew members on the 14th, a day on which no operations were posted by the Command. Orders were received at Leeming on the 15th to prepare seven Whitleys for the main operation to Hannover and four for freshman sorties to Dieppe on the French coast. The latter, Sgts Beveridge, Bradford, Craske and Gregory, took off between 21.45 and 22.00, to be followed into the air between 22.11 and 22.34 by the main element led by S/L Kane. Intense darkness and ground haze hampered target identification at the French coast, and only Sgt Craske and crew positively claimed to have attacked the primary target, doing so from 14,500 feet at 00.22. Sgts Bradford and Gregory bombed on e.t.a., from 14,000 and 11,500 feet respectively with almost an hour between, while Sgt Beveridge identified Calais, and bombed it from 12,000 feet at 02.15. Meanwhile, of those bound for Hannover, Sgt Lewis and crew lost their port engine almost immediately, and jettisoned their bombs safe into a field before returning to base. The others crossed the North Sea over ten-tenths cloud with tops at 8,000 feet, and made landfall at the Dutch coast somewhere near Castricum. Sgt Bigglestone and crew were unable to establish their position despite receiving a fix, and were being held in searchlights when they were engaged by a night-fighter at 01.17. Three short bursts were fired by the enemy from the starboard beam, some of which struck home, whereupon a red signal flare was sent up from the Whitley, causing the searchlights to be doused and the enemy fighter to break off the attack. The bombs had been jettisoned "live" by then in a single stick from 14,000 feet, and fell, it is believed, somewhere east of Amsterdam, probably into the waters of what is now known as the Markermeer. The others continued on, watching the cloud gradually disperse from the enemy coast to the target, where they were greeted by some wispy white stuff and ground haze. The carried out their attacks from 14,000 to 16,000 feet between 01.16 and 01.48, before returning safely to report fires but little else of use to the intelligence section. There was no report from Hannover.

Naval ports on either side of the Schleswig-Holstein peninsular were offered as the targets for elements from Dishforth, Driffield and Leeming on the 18th, with the main raid directed at Kiel on the eastern side, while three freshman crews from 10 Squadron tried their hand at Emden to the west. Seven 10 Squadron Whitleys took off for the main event between 22.13 and 22.35 with W/C Bennett the senior pilot on duty, and the freshmen followed on between 23.15 and 23.21. Clear skies over the North Sea gave way to varying amounts of cloud over northern Germany estimated at four to eight-tenths with thick ground haze, and one crew reported a heavy cloud bank to the north of Kiel. A navigational error threw P/O Spiers and crew off course, leaving them insufficient time to reach the primary target. Hamburg was within range and was found to be under clear skies but blanketed by extreme darkness. The bombs were dropped onto it in a single stick from 12,000 feet at 02.22, and the incendiaries were observed to be burning. The others carried out their attacks on the primary target from 14,000 to 15,600 feet between 02.05 and 02.14, and a number of bursts and fires were witnessed. Heading for Emden, Sgt Gregory and crew ran into a thick bank of cloud that reached up to 12,000 feet, and, by the time they reached the estimated position of the target, ten-tenths cloud lay between the Whitley and the ground. The bombs were delivered from 14,500 feet at 02.15, and a hint of burning incendiaries could be detected through the cloud. It was a similar story for Sgt Beveridge and crew, who, after failing to identify Emden, turned their attention onto a flak concentration on the Frisian island of Spiekeroog, which they bombed from 13,000 feet at 02.55. Only Sgt Craske and crew positively identified Emden, and ran through accurate flak from both flanks, but came through unscathed to deliver their load from 15,500 feet at 02.05.

On the morning of the 27th the Bismarck met her end at the hands of elements of the Royal Navy, thus avenging the loss a few days earlier of HMS Hood. At Leeming ten Whitleys were made ready for an operation against a "special" target in the centre of Cologne. They were part of an overall force of sixty-four Whitleys and Wellingtons, all but a dozen provided by 4 Group. They took off between 22.10 and 22.29 with P/O Littlewood the senior pilot on duty and all other pilots of sergeant rank. There was some disagreement about the conditions in the target area, opinions including good visibility, slight cloud, poor visibility with dense cloud and haze, and low cloud. P/O Littlewood was in clear air over Holland when he was snagged by searchlights and shot at by intense and accurate flak from the adjacent batteries. The bombs were dropped in haste from 10,000 feet at 01.35 in order to facilitate evasive action, and they fell onto an aerodrome, believed to be Gilze-Rijen, which had an illuminated flare-path. The Whitley was hit repeatedly, and was held in a low, almost horizontal searchlight cone before breaking free and running for home. Sgt Griffin and crew ran into cloud on approach to the target, and bombed the aerodrome at Woensdrecht on the Scheldt from 12,000 feet at 01.20. The others all located Cologne and carried out their attacks in a single pass from 13,000 to 17,000 feet between 02.18 and 03.00. Bursts and fires were observed, but the visibility and intensity of the defences prevented a detailed assessment from taking place. A local report suggested that only around six bomb loads landed within the city, damaging to some extent 167 buildings. This was the final operation for the squadron in a month that had seen it in action on nine nights, generating ninety-two sorties for the loss of two Whitleys and crews.

June 1941

June and July were to be significant months for the Command, as its performance began to be monitored in order to provide an assessment of its effectiveness for the War Cabinet. The project was initiated by Churchill's chief scientific advisor, Lord Cherwell, who handed the responsibility to David M Bensusan-Butt, a civil-servant assistant to Cherwell working in the War Cabinet Secretariat. The new month would be dominated by operations against Cologne, Düsseldorf and Bremen, with Kiel and Brest also receiving their share of attention. During the second half of the month Cologne and Düsseldorf would be attacked simultaneously on no fewer than eight nights by forces of varying sizes, and Bremen, including the shipbuilding yards at Vegesack, would host six raids. On the 1st, the Hipper Class cruiser Prinz Eugen arrived at Brest having evaded detection by the British following the sinking of the Bismarck. She would now join Scharnhorst and Gneisenau to form a powerful battle group that would continue to be a distraction for Bomber Command. Düsseldorf was the primary target for 150 aircraft on the night of the 2/3rd, for which 4 Group put up thirty-nine Whitleys, fourteen of them provided by 10 Squadron. They departed Leeming in a twenty-minute slot to 23.01 with S/L Kane the senior pilot on duty, and the newly-arrived F/L Webster undertaking his first sortie with the squadron. They adopted an east-south-easterly course from Flamborough Head to the Dutch coast north of Amsterdam, and continued on to Elburg, where they turned a little east of south to cross the Ruhr with the target lying directly ahead on the south-western rim of Germany's industrial heartland. The encountered ten-tenths cloud between 2,000 and 15,000 feet all the way into enemy territory, and it reduced only slightly as they neared the target area. It proved to be almost impossible to positively identify the target, and there was no chance of picking out either of the briefed aiming-points. Most established their position on the searchlight and flak activity visible through the clouds, and carried out their attacks in a single pass from 11,300 to 15,000 feet between 01.50 and 02.56. The freshman crew of Sgt Black were unable to pinpoint their position and jettisoned their bombs "safe" into the sea. When P/O Thompson and crew landed at Sealand at 05.55, they found only four gallons of fuel left in the tanks!

Small-scale operations occupied the ensuing five nights, and it was the 8th before the squadron was next called into action to make ready fourteen Whitleys for an attack that night on Dortmund. It was to be exclusively a 4 Group show involving thirty-seven aircraft, and the Leeming element got away between 22.12 and 22.31 with W/C Bennett the senior pilot on duty. P/O Littlewood and crew returned after an hour with a starboard engine issue, leaving the others to follow a route that was largely similar to the one adopted for Düsseldorf. The ten-tenths cloud encountered over the North Sea dispersed to leave clearer skies over Holland and Germany, and W/C Bennett was able to identify a dog-racing track and an autobahn as he traversed the Ruhr. The force was greeted by heavy anti-aircraft fire, and a number of returning aircraft would bear the scars of battle. Most carried out their attacks in a single pass, delivering their loads from 10,500 to 16,000 feet between 01.35 and 02.02, but industrial haze prevented them from seeing anything other than bursts and a few fires. Divert signals were sent as the force made its way home, and the majority of the 10 Squadron crews landed at Silloth on the Cumbrian coast near Carlisle.

Sixteen 10 Squadron crews were detailed for operations on the 12th, and they learned at briefing that the marshalling yard at Schwerte was to be their target in company with seventy other aircraft from 4 Group. This was just one of four yards to be raided on this night, the others, at Soest, Hamm and Osnabrück, involving a total of 234 aircraft provided by the other groups. Situated to the south-east of Dortmund, on the south-eastern edge of the Ruhr, the Schwerte yards would require the crews to adopt the now-familiar route across the Den Helder peninsular to enter Germany somewhere near Emmerich. When take-off time arrived at 22.30, the aircraft of S/L Kane and Sgt Jesse were found to be unserviceable and were withdrawn. This left fourteen Whitleys to depart Leeming in a thirty-one-minute slot with S/L Holford the senior pilot on duty for the first time in weeks, and F/L Landale now elevated to crew captain after serving the requisite number of "second dickey" sorties with F/L Humby. Sgt Gregory and crew landed half-an-hour after taking off, having been unable to retract the undercarriage, but this would be the only early return. The rest encountered ten-tenths cloud over the North Sea, and F/L Webster's windscreen iced up, but cleared sufficiently for him to pinpoint his landfall between Texel and Den Helder through a thin break in the cloud.

P/O Littlewood and crew had greater concerns to deal with when their port engine began to lose power as they approached the Dutch coast. Shortly after crossing into enemy territory, the captain decided to turn back, and the bombs were jettisoned into the sea. At that point, 00.50, the engine failed completely, and the Whitley, then at 12,000 feet, was unable to maintain height. It remained airborne until 01.35, when a ditching became inevitable and was carried out expertly, despite which the observer, P/O Stevens-Fox, was knocked out by the impact and was carried from the aircraft by the wireless operator, Sgt Wilkinson. Unfortunately, the dinghy had inflated upside down, preventing the crew from reaching the signals equipment, but they were, at least, able to clamber onto the upturned craft with great difficulty, by which time the observer had regained his senses. The Whitley sank from sight within three minutes of the ditching, leaving the crew in a perilous situation with no means to communicate. At 06.00, a Luftwaffe aircraft overflew them, and, recognising their plight, circled them while trying in vain to signal to an ASR launch. At 07.00 two Heinkel 111s came upon them, and, while one circled, the other went back and directed the launch to their position, thus saving their lives. They were picked up at 07.35 and landed at Yarmouth with nothing more than bruises and shock to show for their ordeal.

Their squadron colleagues, meanwhile, had been searching for the target through thick haze and cloud, and occasional breaks allowed some identification of ground detail like a bridge or an autobahn. On e.t.a., they were greeted by moderate flak and searchlight activity, which, more than anything else, confirmed that they were in the right place, and bombs were dropped over a wide area from 10,500 to 16,000 feet between 01.23 and 01.57. A post-raid analysis confirmed that fewer than half of the force claimed to have attacked the primary target, and it was a similar story at Soest and Hamm, while the local report from Osnabrück described a "lively" attack. On the following night 4 Group sent thirty-six Whitleys and six Wellingtons back to Schwerte, of which eleven were provided by 10 Squadron. W/C Bennett had been supposed to take part, but he ran a wheel into soft ground while taxiing to take off, and the undercarriage collapsed. This left S/L Kane the senior pilot on duty as the remainder departed Leeming between 22.42 and 22.58 and headed out south of Bridlington to encounter ten-tenths cloud and icing conditions over the North Sea. They made landfall over Vlieland, but the ground was covered by thick haze, and finding the target area would be a matter of good navigation by dead-reckoning. Some of those eventually stumbling upon the Schwerte area pinpointed on a lake to the south-west, but the whole affair was something of a lottery. Eight crews returned to report being unable to identify the railway yards and bombing the general area of the town instead from 10,500 to 15,500 feet between 01.40 and 02.02. It was impossible to assess what was happening on the ground, and a few fires and burning incendiaries was the extent of what could be observed. Sgts Bigglestone and Gregory believed that they were over Dortmund when they released their bombs, while P/O Goulding was in the Hagen area.

The night of the 15/16th brought with it the first of the simultaneous attacks on Cologne and Düsseldorf, and was supported by elements of 4 Group, although not by 10 Squadron. Poor visibility attended both operations, and the attacks were scattered and ineffective. Orders were received at Leeming on the 16th to prepare thirteen Whitleys for Cologne that night as part of an overall force of 105 aircraft. The armourers got to work loading a 1,000 pounder and three 500 pounders into six aircraft and four 500 and two 250 pounders into the others, plus four containers of incendiaries all round. Meanwhile, sixty-five Wellingtons and seven Stirlings were made ready to target Düsseldorf. The Leeming element took off on a fine summer evening between 22.38 and 22.56 with W/C Bennett the senior pilot on duty, and set course for the Scheldt Estuary and the southern approach into the target area. Sgt Gregory and crew were bang on track and had just crossed the coast into Belgium when an oil gauge suggested that an engine was about to fail. The sortie was abandoned, and the bombs jettisoned onto farmland some five miles north-east of Antwerp. The engine remained healthy all the way home, suggesting that the gauge was faulty. The others pressed on, making landfall at a variety of points between Ostend and the island of Schouwen, having made the sea crossing under clear skies. It was a night of extreme darkness, which combined with up to five-tenths cloud and dense haze to blot out ground detail in the target area, but crews were able to establish their position by glimpsing lakes, rivers, and, most prominently, the searchlights and flak in and around the target. There was no chance of picking out the briefed aiming-point, the main railway station, and crews released their bombs over the general target area from 11,000 to 14,000 feet between 01.52 and 02.27, before returning home to report fires but no significant detail. F/L Landale and crew described being attacked by a night fighter as they approached the target, which the rear gunner chased off, and four holes in the port wing supported their story. Both operations on this night failed to achieve anything of value, and the remainder of the month would follow a similar pattern.

The squadron sat out the following night's operations against Cologne and Düsseldorf, which were hampered again by thick haze and failed in their purpose. Bremen was posted as the target on the 18th, for which 10 Squadron made ready eleven Whitleys as part of an overall force of one hundred aircraft. The crews had been briefed for an unspecified "special" target, which may well have been the Tirpitz. Take-off from Leeming took place between 22.00 and 22.14 with S/L Holford the senior pilot on duty, and all made their way over thick haze to the target area, where visibility remained very poor due to low cloud and a continuation of ground haze. S/L Holford was unable to maintain height after his starboard propeller went into fully-fine pitch, and he dropped his bombs on Bremerhaven as a last-resort target. Intense flak was encountered between Wilhelmshaven and Bremerhaven, and it was particularly troublesome over Bremen itself. Attacks were carried out mostly on e.t.a., and searchlight and flak activity from 11,500 to 16,500 feet between 01.14 and 02.00, and no assessment was possible. Z6671 was last heard from at 02.50, when on its way home with the crew of Sgt Bradford, and crashed minutes later into the sea off Ameland without survivors.

Cologne and Düsseldorf were "on" again on the 21st, and 10 Squadron made ready ten Whitleys to launch against the latter in company with a further eighteen Whitleys and twenty-eight 5 Group Hampdens. They took off between 22.58 and 23.12 with W/C Bennett the senior pilot on duty, and followed the familiar route to the Belgian coast, where they were greeted by a concentrated belt of searchlights. W/C Bennett estimated that the haze in the target area extended upwards to 7,000 feet, and all he could make out was a stretch of the Rhine through that and some stratus cloud. He was forced to bomb on e.t.a., and on the position of the flak and searchlight activity, as were all of the others, from 10,000 to 15,000 feet between 01.14 and 03.08. Many fires were reported by returning crews, but local reports claimed that only two bomb loads had fallen within the city, and damage was restricted to broken windows. Three crews also report a huge explosion on the way out somewhere near Ostend at 00.50. The same two targets were posted on the 23rd, which 10 Squadron would sit out, and again on the 24th, when eleven Whitleys were made ready at Leeming to accompany twenty-one other Whitleys and twenty-two Wellingtons to Cologne, where the briefed aiming-point was the main railway station. Situated in the shadow of the city's huge and distinctive cathedral, it should have been relatively easy to locate, but would prove to be otherwise. All were safely airborne by 22.30 with S/L Kane the senior pilot on duty, planning to make landfall this time west of Ostend over Nieuwpoort and head for the target via Nivelles. However, Sgt Rickcord and crew had not even reached the English coast when an engine issue persuaded them to turn back. Thick haze and five-tenths cloud at 6,000 feet over the sea gave way to a violent thunderstorm at the Belgian coast, and Sgt Shaw and crew ran into intense flak about a dozen miles south-west of Brussels. The door to the rear turret jammed at the same time, and it was decided to find a last-resort target, which turned out to be an aerodrome south-west of Courtrai. Obstruction and landing lights aided the attack, which took place from 12,000 feet at 02.19, and was followed by bursts and a number of fires. Cologne was identified by a bend in the River Rhine and its flak and searchlight defences, but the haze obscured all other ground detail, and bombing took place on estimated positions from 10,500 to 15,000 feet between 01.55 and 02.15. Returning crews claimed to have observed bursts and fires, but none had any genuine idea as to where their bombs had fallen, and local reports again suggested an ineffective raid.

Seventy-three Wellingtons and thirty-five Whitleys were made ready for operations on the night of the 27/28th, when Bremen was the target, while a force of Hampdens also visited the city to attack the shipbuilding yards at Vegesack. 10 Squadron detailed a dozen Whitleys, which took off either side of 22.30 with W/C Bennett the senior pilot on duty. They flew out in very bad weather, which included ten-tenths cloud with tops at 17,000 feet, storms and icing conditions, and, if that were not enough, they would also face a concerted night-fighter response of unprecedented intensity. Sgt Lewis and crew did not have that additional concern to contend with, as their radio equipment failed and forced them to turn back early on. P/O Clapperton and crew were outbound through the cloud bank, when the build-up of ice Z6624's wings caused it to fall out of the sky from 14,000 at 00.35. P/O Clapperton only regained control at 4,000 feet, and, with the Whitley resisting all attempts to regain some of the lost altitude, the crew sought a last-resort target. A flashing light was spotted on the east Frisian island of Baltrum, and the bombs were dropped there at 00.49. Sgt Farmery and crew failed to locate the German coast at the intended location, and flew across the Schleswig-Holstein peninsular as far as Flensburg, which left them too short of time and fuel reserves to attack the primary target. Heading west back towards to sea, they dropped their bombs on Westerhever, near the coast, from 12,500 feet at 02.30. Sgt Jones and crew were beset with similar problems, and overshot Bremen, which they realized when they stumbled upon Hamburg, some fifty miles further on, and saw the docks laid out clearly before them. They released their bombs from 12,500 feet at 01.21, and were clearly not alone, as the Hamburg authorities recorded more than seventy bombing incidents.

Low cloud greeted the others in the briefed target area, preventing them from pinpointing the aiming-point, and most simply picked up the River Weser and made a timed run into the heart of the flak. Bombs were delivered over the target from 9,000 to 12,000 feet between 01.30 and 01.54, and returning crews reported fires without a clue as to their location. After making his attack, W/C Bennett deviated slightly from his intended course and was hit by flak near the heavily-defended Kiel Canal, which left the observer (navigator), P/O Bagnald, with a shrapnel wound to an arm. Before reaching the German coast, they were then caught in a cone of six searchlights near Tönning, which was escaped only after diving to 1,000 feet. W/C Bennett landed at Bircham Newton to allow his wounded crew member to receive medical attention, and it was whilst there that he was able to inspect the considerable damage to his Whitley. When all returning aircraft had been accounted for, four from Leeming were found to be missing, along with a further seven Whitleys from other 4 Group squadrons and three Wellingtons. P5016 crashed somewhere in north-western Germany, killing Sgt Knape and three of his crew, and only the wireless operator, Sgt Lewis, survived to become a PoW. In March 1944 he escaped, but was recaptured in July, and was reported to have been shot by the SS on the 1st of August. P5055 also came down in the Bremen/Hamburg area, with no survivors from the crew of Sgt Rickcord. Sgt Shaw was killed with his crew in T4179, almost certainly in the same region of Germany, and, finally, Z6561 was hit by flak and abandoned over Kiel Bay. Sgt Gregory and his crew landed in the sea, and were picked up by the enemy six hours later, by which time the rear gunner, P/O Watson, was no longer alive. The second pilot, Sgt Nabarro, escaped from captivity several times, and eventually arrived back in the UK via Gibraltar in November 1942. He was awarded a Distinguished Conduct Medal, and may well have been the first RAF recipient in WWII. The loss of fourteen aircraft in one night was a new record for the Command, and, it is likely, that the Luftwaffe night-fighters were largely responsible. The disproportionately high losses among the Whitley brigade, 31% of those taking part, was a concern, and, perhaps, pointed to the increasing vulnerability of the type compared with its contemporaries. However, as events were to prove, sporadic losses now belonged to the past, as the enemy defences became more organized and adept in the face of greater Bomber Command activity. A steady rate of attrition would afflict all front-line squadrons from now on, and multiple losses from a single operation would become a regular feature.

The squadron remained at home on the 28th and 29th, possibly digesting the implications of the unprecedented losses. Eight crews were called to briefing on the 30th to learn that Cologne and the Ruhr were the destinations for more than sixty aircraft that night. The 10 Squadron element was assigned to an unidentified "special" target in Duisburg, and they took off between 22.42 and 22.51 with S/L Kane the senior pilot on duty. F/L Landale and crew returned soon after take-off with a port engine issue, leaving the others to contend with ten-tenths cloud over the North Sea and enemy coast, which made pinpointing their landfall something of a challenge. Low cloud and haze over the target completely blotted out all ground features, and it was the searchlight and flak concentrations that confirmed the identity of the target area on e.t.a. F/L Webster reported observing six heavy, white explosions followed by a colossal red one, which could be seen for twenty minutes into the return flight, while others saw fires but no detail. P5018 failed to return after crashing somewhere between the Dutch border and the target, as the result of which, P/O Barrett and his observer lost their lives, while three survivors fell into enemy hands. Z6584 had just passed over Honington airfield on its way home when it was attacked by an enemy intruder, which set both engines on fire. Two members of the crew escaped by parachute before the Whitley crashed one mile north-east of Thetford in Norfolk, killing Sgt Beveridge and the rear gunner. The four-man complement of this crew reflected the new policy to dispense with the inclusion of a second pilot as standard practice. During the course of the month the squadron operated on ten nights and dispatched 118 sorties for the loss of eight Whitleys, six complete crews and two other crew members.

July 1941

Elements of the Whitley force were made ready on the 2nd to open 4 Group's July account that night at Cologne. 10 Squadron was not detailed to take part, and W/C Bennett obtained permission to allow all aircrew to spend the afternoon at the Yorkshire seaside resort of Scarborough. S/L Holford was posted from the squadron on the 3rd to take up instructional duties at 10 O.T.U., where he would be joined two days later by P/O Thompson. Suitably refreshed by the previous day's bracing sea air, eight crews attended briefing at Leeming to learn of that night's Wellington and Whitley operation to Essen, where the Krupp armaments complex and railway installations were to be the primary targets. A force of ninety aircraft was made ready, twenty-nine of them Whitleys, and those from Leeming took off either side of 23.00 with W/C Bennett the senior pilot on duty. P/O Clapperton and crew returned at 01.00 after experiencing engine trouble and the failure of the intercom connection to the rear turret, and P/O Goulding landed forty-five minutes later with an indisposed rear gunner. The others continued on to encounter ten-tenths strato-cumulus cloud over the North Sea, which obscured all ground reference and prevented them from establishing their landfall. Multiple searchlight cones co-operated with the flak batteries to provide a hot reception over the Ruhr, and thick haze over the target compounded the difficulties. W/C Bennett had run the gauntlet and picked up some damage by the time he arrived in the Essen area to drop three flares, the light from which just reflected back at him. A glide-attack was finally made on DR at 02.02 from 11,500 feet, and flashes were observed through the clouds. The remaining five crews carried out their attacks also on DR from 10,000 to 12,000 feet between 01.33 and 01.50, and could only report flashes and burning incendiaries. On the way home south of Venlo at 11,000 feet, F/L Landale and crew were engaged by a night fighter from four hundred yards astern and below. A long burst hit the Whitley's nose destroying the glass in the bomb-aimer's compartment, the frame of his seat and the lock on the front escape hatch, as well as hitting the port wing. When the enemy closed to three hundred yards it became silhouetted against searchlights, and was identified by the rear gunner as a ME110. The rear gunner returned fire with eight bursts, despite which, the enemy continued to close to fifty yards before breaking away to starboard, providing the rear gunner with the opportunity to pour more bullets into its belly and claim it as damaged.

The squadron stayed at home on the night of the 4/5th while other elements of the Whitley brigade joined Wellingtons to continue the assault on Brest and its lodgers. Leeming was busy on the 5th preparing nine aircraft for an operation that night to bomb railway communications at Münster, and they took off between 22.35 and 22.46 with F/L Webster the senior pilot on duty. For a change, the crews were greeted by good weather conditions as they crossed the North Sea, and found the cloud clearing thirty miles before making landfall over an area between the Den Helder peninsular and the Frisian island of Vlieland. The presence of a little ground haze at the target to the north of the Ruhr proved to be of no consequence, and bombing took place from 8,000 to 12,000 feet between 01.15 and 01.31. Returning crews would report a complete absence of searchlight and flak activity, and this was probably due to the presence of night fighters. Most crews had something to say on that subject, including witnessing an engagement between two aircraft at 00.58 at 11,000 feet over Holland, which resulted in one of them falling in flames. This proved to be 10 Squadron's Z6793, containing the crew of P/O Goulding, which had crossed paths with Oblt Helmut Lent of 6./NJG.1, and crashed without survivors near Coevorden on the Dutch/German frontier.

Cologne, Münster and Osnabrück were the principal targets posted for attention on the 7th, and the marshalling yards at the last-mentioned was assigned to 4 Group. Fifty-four Whitleys and eighteen Wellingtons were made ready, eight of the former at Leeming, and they took off between 22.30 and 22.40 with P/O Spiers the senior and only commissioned pilot on duty. The weather conditions were favourable as they crossed the North Sea, retracing the route of forty-eight hours earlier to make landfall between Den Helder and the Frisian island of Vlieland. The clear visibility enabled them to identify the Zweigkanal waterway, which ran south to north to a junction with the Mittelland Canal north of the town and establish their position for the bombing run. Attacks were carried out from 9,500 to 13,000 feet between 01.35 and 01.55, and returning crews reported many large fires in the marshalling yards, with long sheds seen to be well alight with fires that remained visible for up to seventy miles into the return journey. There were also hits in other parts of the yards and on the permanent way, and some bomb loads found their way into the south-western suburbs of the town, although they caused only very minor damage. Z6816 was last heard from at 04.44, when it was fixed somewhere off Flamborough Head, but it failed to appear at Leeming with the crew of Sgt Black and was lost without trace.

The important railway hub of Hamm was an important link in the communications system between the Ruhr and the rest of Germany, and its marshalling yard was posted on the 8th as the target for a 4 and 5 Group force of seventy-three Hampdens and Whitleys that night. 10 Squadron made ready ten Whitleys, and sent them skyward either side of 22.30 with S/L Kane the senior pilot on duty. P/O Spiers landed two hours later with an engine issue, having jettisoned his bombs into the sea, and P/O Littlewood followed him in some fifteen minutes later, also as a result of an engine issue. At 01.10 Sgt Craske and crew became the third early return after the rear gunner became unwell. The others pushed on intending to make landfall over southern Vlieland, but severe electrical storms over the North Sea led to some crossing the Dutch coast much further south near Amsterdam, by which time the cloud had broken up to some extent. Sgt Jones and crew reached Texel at 00.45 and considered it too late to make the primary target, so turned south to attack Schiphol aerodrome from 9,000 feet at 01.23. Those continuing on into Germany found the skies clearing to leave thick haze, but, they were able to pick out ground features by which to establish their positions. When S/L Kane and P/O Clapperton identified the Dortmund-Ems Canal to the north of Münster, they decided that they had insufficient time to reach Hamm, and decided to join in with the Wellington raid in progress at Münster. P/O Clapperton bombed from 11,000 feet at 01.40, and S/L Kane from 12,500 feet a minute later. P/O Thompson, F/L Landale and Sgt Jesse all attacked the primary target from 10,000 to 12,500 feet between 01.42 and 01.53, and returned to report bomb bursts and fires. While flying home at 8,000 feet at 03.05, and approaching the English coast a dozen miles north of Sheringham, P/O Thompson and crew spotted a light on the water, and descended to 3,000 feet to investigate. As they did so, an enemy aircraft came up from astern and opened fire, which was returned by the rear gunner after identifying it as a ME110. The enemy pressed home further attacks from the port beam and from astern on the port quarter, scoring hits to the rear turret, rear fuselage, both wings and the tail-plane. The rear gunner responded with another burst, which caused their assailant to lurch, turn on its wing and dive vertically with flames and smoke belching from its fuselage. It disappeared from sight and could only be claimed as a "probable". F/Sgt Lewis and crew failed to return in Z6627, and no trace of the aircraft or crew was ever found.

A new Air Ministry directive issued on the 9th signalled an end to the maritime diversion, which had been in force since March. It was now assessed, that the enemy's transportation system and the morale of its civilian population represented the weakest points, and that Peirse should direct his main effort in these directions. A new list of targets was drawn up, which included all of the main railway centres ringing the industrial Ruhr in order to inhibit the import of raw materials, and the export of finished products. Railways were relatively precise targets, and were to be attacked during the moon period. On moonless nights, the Rhine cities of Cologne, Düsseldorf and Duisburg would be easier to locate for "area" attacks, and, when less favourable weather conditions obtained, Peirse was to send his force to more distant objectives in northern, eastern and southern Germany.

Five fully-operational crews and three freshmen were detailed for operations to Cologne on the 10th, and actually took off between 22.32 and 23.04 before being recalled because of doubts over the weather. The weather would continue to frustrate the launching of operations, and, even when Whitleys were called into action, as at Bremen on the 14th and Hamburg on the 16th, 10 Squadron remained at home. F/L Landale was elevated to acting squadron leader rank on the 16th and P/O Thompson to acting flight lieutenant at the same time, while the London Gazette confirmed the award of the DFC to F/L Humby on the 19th. The squadron finally got back into the war on the 20th, when five fully-operational crews were briefed for an operation against railway targets in Cologne as part of an overall force of 108 aircraft, while four freshman crews would join a handful of others to attack the docks at Rotterdam. The main element took off between 22.19 and 22.30 with F/L Webster the senior pilot on duty, and G/C Wray beside him as second pilot, and they were followed away shortly before 23.00 by the freshmen crews of P/O Littlewood and Sgts O'Driscoll, Poupard and Robertson. P/O Littlewood made landfall over the Scheldt Estuary, and reached the target area soon afterwards to deliver his bombs onto the docks from 8,500 feet at 01.30. He reported a huge fire in the centre of the target area, which probably emanated from the briefed alternative target, the oil-storage facilities, and would remain visible for 140 miles into the return journey. Sgt O'Driscoll failed to pinpoint his landfall because of haze, but found the target to be under clear skies. He delivered his bomb load in a single stick in the face of a spirited searchlight and flak defence from 12,500 at 01.15, and observed flashes on docks 15, 16 and 17. The sorties of Sgts Poupard and Robertson were not recorded. Some of the Cologne element experienced difficulty in identifying the enemy coast after crossing the sea above five-tenths cloud, but it was worse in the target area, where ten-tenths cloud forced them to bomb on e.t.a., and the searchlight and flak activity. They carried out their attacks from 12,000 to 12,500 feet between 01.32 and 01.58, and observed nothing more than bursts and the glow of burning incendiaries through occasional breaks in the cloud.

On the 23rd, a reconnaissance aircraft spotted Scharnhorst at La Pallice, some two hundred miles south of where she was believed to be, at Brest. She had been moved stealthily and a large tanker substituted in her berth to disguise her absence. This raised alarm bells, that she may be about to break out into the Atlantic to begin a campaign of raiding against merchant shipping, and an operation against her was hurriedly put in hand. In fact, a major daylight assault had been planned on the warships at Brest, weather permitting, to be carried out on the 24th. Her appearance at La Pallice forced a last-minute alteration to the original plan, which had involved the use of three Fortress Is of 2 Group's 90 Squadron bombing from very high level to draw up the fighters, while a force of Hampdens performed a similar diversionary role at a less rarefied altitude under an escort of Spitfires. It was hoped that this would distract the enemy defences sufficiently to provide the unescorted seventy-nine Wellingtons of 1 and 3 Groups and 4 Group Halifaxes with a clear run on the target.

In the meantime, 4 Group mobilized thirty Whitleys to send against Scharnhorst on the evening of the 23rd, while the Halifax element would attack her in daylight on the morrow. Nine 10 Squadron crews were briefed, and they took off between 21.47 and 21.56 with F/L Webster the senior pilot on duty, accompanied by a S/L Nalder from 4 Group HQ. They set course for Bridport for the Channel crossing to St Malo, and encountered haze all the way across the sea and the Cherbourg peninsular, but found good enough visibility in the target area to establish their position. They also found intense searchlight activity, both from the mainland and from the Ile-de-Re on the western approaches to the port, and this was accompanied by moderate flak. P/O Spiers and crew were the only ones to attack in two passes, which they carried out from 10,000 feet at 02.20 and 02.25, while the others let their bombs go in a single stick from 6,000 to 11,000 feet between 02.00 and 03.10. The last-mentioned time belonged to Sgt Holder and crew, who spent so much time lining up their bombing run, that they ran short of fuel on the way home and landed at Wroughton in Wiltshire. Returning crews reported bomb bursts and fires in the docks area, but no detail, and it is unlikely that Scharnhorst was hit. The original plan for Brest went ahead on the following morning in the face of a much stronger defence than had been anticipated, at a cost of ten Wellingtons and two Hampdens for no discernible return. In the early afternoon, fifteen Halifaxes of 35 and 76 Squadrons took part in an unescorted attack on Scharnhorst, and scored five direct hits in the face of an intense flak and fighter response. Five Halifaxes failed to return and all of the others sustained battle damage. Scharnhorst was not seriously damaged, but returned to Brest where better repair facilities existed.

A mixed force of fifty-five Whitleys and Hampdens was made ready for an operation against Hannover on the 25th, six of the former provided by 10 Squadron. They departed Leeming between 22.21 and 22.30 with S/L Landale the senior pilot on duty, and ran into cloud and thunderstorms over the North Sea. The Canadian P/O Littlewood was unable to drag Z6815 above 7,000 feet, and the Whitley was caught in a cone of searchlights on the western approaches to Osnabrück. A 1,000 pounder was enough to douse the lights, and the reduction in weight allowed a further three thousand feet of altitude to be gained. The primary target could not be located, however, and the rest of the bombs were dropped from 10,000 feet at 02.27 onto an unidentified urban area in the Ruhr. The others encountered thick haze over the target, and bombed from 12,000 to 14,000 feet between 01.35 and 02.33 without being able to observe anything other than bursts, flashes and a fire. On the way home at 8,000 feet, and approaching the mid-point of the North Sea crossing, Sgt Holder and crew were engaged by a JU88 at 04.30, which made three attacks before being driven off by return fire. P/O Spiers and crew failed to return home in T4231, which had crashed some nine miles north-north west of Hasselt in Belgium with the loss of all on board. A second empty dispersal at Leeming belonged to Z6624, which had been shot down into the North Sea about ten miles south-west of Den Helder. The Whitley had crossed paths at 03.20 local time with the BF110-D-0 captained by Oblt Egmond Prinz zur Lippe-Weissenfeld of II./NJG.1 operating out of Bergen, Holland, and there were no survivors among the crew of twenty-six-year-old S/L Landale DFC. The body of the observer, Sgt George Wells, was washed ashore on the island of Texel on the 15th of August, and was buried on the following day with full military honours in Den Burg Cemetery. The remains of the second pilot, P/O George Pringle, and gunner, F/Sgt George Christie, also eventually came ashore, and now lie in Kiel Cemetery. Of five failures to return from this operation, four were Whitleys, 16% of those dispatched, which again pointed to the increasing vulnerability of this trusty old aircraft.

The loss of two such experienced crews would be keenly-felt at Leeming, but life and the war would go on, and the memory of these former colleagues would recede as new faces filled the void. The freshman crews of Sgts Baker, O'Driscoll and Poupard were dispatched either side of 22.20 to attack the docks at Dunkerque, but encountered nine-tenths cloud and such poor visibility that they were unable to gain a visual reference. They bombed on e.t.a and searchlights from 10,000 to 13,000 feet between 01.00 and 01.24, before returning safely to report flashes but nothing of significance. On the 29th F/L Webster was promoted to squadron leader rank to fill the shoes of S/L Landale as a flight commander. It was the freshmen who were called into action again on the 30th, when the crews of Sgts Baker, Craske, Lager, Poupard and Robertson and P/O Littlewood were briefed to attack the docks at Boulogne. They took off either side of midnight, but Sgt Lager turned back when over the Wash because of the failure of the intercom system. The others pressed on to encounter ten-tenths cloud over the Channel with thunderstorms and icing conditions, and similar at the French coast. Sgt Poupard descended to 3,000 feet without breaking through the cloud base, and dropped some flares to no avail, before bringing his bombs home. Sgt Baker jettisoned his bombs into the sea at 02.13, and Sgt Craske did likewise five minutes later, while P/O Littlewood and Sgt Robertson brought their bombs home, the latter turning back from the target area after the wireless operator was taken ill. During the course of the month the squadron operated on eight nights and dispatched fifty-nine sorties for the loss of five Whitleys and crews.

Sgt. George Wells and his family. Father George, Mother Ada Rose and Brother Charles of Fielding, Wellington, New Zealand.

Sgt George Wells died 25th July 1941 aged 23.

Oblt Egmond Prinz zur Lippe-Weissenfeld

*Window and memorial in Kirkmahoe, Scotland to commemorate
the life of S/L Peter Wellwood Fortune Landale, 10 Sqn. pilot of Whitley Z6624
which was shot down over the North Sea on 25 July 1941 by Oblt Egmond Prinz
zur Lippe-Weissenfeld.
All crew including observer Sgt G Wells (above) were lost.*

August 1941

4 Group opened its August account on the night of the 2/3rd, when contributing Whitleys to a raid on railway targets in Hamburg, and Halifaxes and Wellingtons to the Friedrichstrasse railway station in Berlin. 10 Squadron remained at home on this night, but made ready eight Whitleys on the following day to continue the railway theme in an assault on the main goods station at Frankfurt. The crews learned that they would be part of an all-Whitley force of thirty-nine aircraft and would be led by S/L Kane, while three freshman crews gained further experience by attacking the docks at Calais. P/O Clapperton's aircraft developed engine trouble at start-up and was scrubbed, leaving seven to take off either side of 21.30 for the main target, followed at 22.00 by the freshmen. Sgts Baker, Lager and Robertson encountered five-tenths cloud after leaving the English coast, but this dispersed to leave good visibility over Calais, where the jetties and inner harbour stood out clearly. Bombs were delivered by each in a single stick from around 9,500 feet between 00.08 and 00.40, and explosions were observed across a number of basins. Crossing the enemy coast blind further north between the Scheldt Estuary and Ostend, the Frankfurt-bound force flew above ten-tenths cloud, which persisted all the way to the target, where the tops were at just 6,000 feet. As Sgt Holder and crew crossed the Belgian frontier into Germany, the starboard engine developed an issue, and it was decided to seek a last-resort target. A road and railway junction at Gerolstein presented itself, some fifteen miles east of St Vith, and this was bombed from 12,000 feet at 00.30. The primary target could not be positively identified by S/L Kane and Sgt Poupard, and they dropped their bombs on Aachen

from 11,000 and 10,500 feet respectively at 01.59 and 02.21 on the way home. The others reached the target area without establishing an exact position, and bombed on e.t.a., DR and the considerable amount of accurate flak coming up at them through the clouds. The attacks were delivered in a single stick from 10,500 to 14,000 feet between 01.23 and 01.45, and incendiary fires and a large explosion were observed.

Bomber stations were a hive of activity on the 5th as preparations were put in hand for three operations that night to southern Germany. Ninety-eight Wellingtons and Hampdens were assigned to Mannheim, while ninety-seven aircraft, including some 4 Group Halifaxes, attended to railway targets in Karlsruhe, and forty-six Whitleys and twenty-two Wellingtons tried their hand against an unidentified "special" target at Frankfurt. 10 Squadron's contribution amounted to twelve Whitleys, which departed Leeming between 21.51 and 22.28 with S/L Webster the senior pilot on duty. Sgt Lager and crew turned back almost immediately with a failed intercom system, leaving the others to exit the English coast at Orfordness and turn towards the south-east. Nine-tenths cumulo-nimbus cloud, topping out at 7,000 feet, awaited them over the North Sea as they made their way towards landfall at Blankenberge on the Belgian coast, but this began to disperse as they passed south of Brussels, and they were greeted by clear skies over Germany. Sgt Robertson and crew believed that they were behind schedule by the time that Cologne presented itself, and they decided to take advantage of the favourable conditions to deliver their bombs there from 11,000 feet at 01.00. The others pressed on to find equally good visibility over Frankfurt, which enabled them to pick out the distinctive fingers of the docks area. They carried out their attacks in the face of an intense searchlight and flak response from 7,000 to 12,000 feet between 01.03 and 01.30, and observed many fires, one of them particularly large that remained visible, according to one crew, for a hundred miles. Just how accurate the bombing was is uncertain, but Mainz, situated some twenty miles to the south-west, also reported being hit.

The same three main targets were posted again on the 6th for much reduced forces, and just two Whitleys from 10 Squadron were detailed to return to Frankfurt, while two freshman crews would hop across the Channel to the docks at Calais. Sgts Lager and Robertson took off for the former shortly after 22.00 to join thirty-two other Whitleys and twenty-two Wellingtons to attack railway installations. Ten-tenths static and ice-bearing cloud was met over the North Sea, and this created challenging conditions for the Robertson crew when the controls froze solid and the engines began to lose power. The Whitley fell into a spin to port, and control was only recovered at 4,500 feet after the bombs had been jettisoned. The cloud accompanied the rest of the force all the way to the target, where occasional gaps allowed Sgt Lager and crew a brief glimpse of the ground. They dropped their load in a single stick from 9,500 feet at 01.46, but were unable to observe the results. A patch of clear sky over Aachen allowed them to be coned for a brief period on the way home, and a BF109 passed within a hundred yards of them without seeing them. Meanwhile, Sgt O'Driscoll and P/O Pearson had departed Leeming thirty minutes after midnight, and had had to contend with the same hostile, storm-filled cloudy conditions over the North Sea. However, according to the O'Driscoll crew, by the time that the French coast hove into view, the target lay under just three-tenths cloud with moonlight, which enabled them to identify the docks clearly, and bomb them during a second pass from 10,500 feet at 02.37. Unaccountably, the Robertson crew was unable to pinpoint the primary target because of cloud, even despite the release of three flares. After searching for some time, it became too late to seek an alternative target, and the bombs were returned to store.

Forty-two Whitleys were detailed for operations on the 8th, when briefings revealed that they would join forces with fifty Hampdens from 5 Group to attack the Deutsche Werke shipyard at Kiel, where U-Boot construction was under way. 10 Squadron made ready a dozen aircraft, which took off between 21.46 and 22.00 with F/L Webster the senior pilot on duty. Sgt Lager was forced to turn back from a position a hundred miles west of the Schleswig-Holstein coast after an engine issue required him to jettison the bombs in order to maintain height. The others pressed on over ten-tenths cloud, which had largely dispersed by the time they reached the target area. The general opinion was that good visibility was encountered over the target, which allowed the searchlights to latch on to individual aircraft. Intense and accurate flak came up at them as they sought out the aiming-point, and all attacks but one were carried out from 15,000 to 10,000 feet between 01.02 and 01.49. Sgt Clapperton was held in a searchlight cone for three minutes, which persuaded him to make a dive attack from 15,000 down to 6,000 feet, from which height he could see fires taking hold. It was an eventful night for F/L Thompson and crew, who reported being unable to determine the results of their efforts because of cloud. On the way home their Whitley was struck twice by lightning, which burned off the training aerial, rendered the TR9 unserviceable and damaged the port wingtip. Icing conditions added to the challenges, and the aircraft fell into a spin at 8,000 feet, before being recovered at 4,000 feet, at which point it was discovered that the rear gunner, Sgt Myers, had baled out. Nothing is known of his fate, and his name appears on the Runnymede Memorial. Returning crews confirmed the ferocity of the defences, and reported witnessing bomb bursts and fires, and one crew witnessed a Whitley being held in searchlights. This may have been Sgt Clapperton, but might also have been P/O Littlewood's Z6815, which failed to return home after crashing in the target area with no survivors.

Elements of the squadron were called to briefing on a number of occasions over the ensuing week, but each operation was cancelled for one reason or another, despite the fact that other types were required to take part in a number of quite major operations. Perhaps this had something to do with the increasing vulnerability of the Whitley to enemy defences, which would be confirmed on the night of the 16/17th, when railway installations in Cologne were the target for seventy-two aircraft, including twenty-nine Whitleys. 10 Squadron made ready a dozen aircraft, and launched them from Leeming between 22.02 and 22.22 with W/C Bennett the senior pilot on duty. P/O Hacking and crew experienced W/T failure, and, through faulty navigation, spent most of the five-hour-and-forty-minute flight wandering through the skies over England before landing with their load intact at Linton-on-Ouse. The others carried on over five to ten-tenths cloud with tops at 8,000 feet, and, according to the crews, this persisted in the target area to create poor visibility, which may have been made worse by haze and smoke. The 4 Group Operations Record Book (Form 540), however, described conditions over the target as "practically no cloud and good visibility with slight ground haze".

Whatever the truth, W/C Bennett reported spending thirty minutes over the target, beginning at 12,500 feet, but being forced by the cloud cover to descend to 5,000 feet, from where the bombs were released. He and his crew were subjected to intense and accurate flak for the final five minutes of the bombing run, and the unwelcome attention continued as they tried to escape, still at 5,000 feet, at which point the wireless operator sustained a wound to his hand. At 02.30, and having climbed to 7,000 feet, they flew through a searchlight belt and were attacked by an enemy fighter, which forced them down almost to treetop height. The intercom system was knocked out, which prevented communication between the cockpit and rear turret during the engagement, but the fighter was seen to stall and fall back after receiving two fifty-round bursts. Once the searchlights had been cleared, it was possible to climb to 12,000 feet to cross the Dutch coast, and a safe return was made to land at Church Fenton short of fuel. In all, six other 10 Squadron crews reported bombing the target, doing so from 11,500 to 13,000 feet between 01.03 and 01.45, while P/O Evill, who had just been elevated to crew captain status, failed to locate the primary target, and bombed Essen instead from 9,600 feet at 01.25. Seven Whitleys failed to return home, and this represented a massive and unsustainable 24% of those dispatched. Three of them belonged to 10 Squadron, beginning with Z6586, which crashed ten miles south-east of Hasselt in Belgium, killing P/O Pearson and his crew. Z6794 came down somewhere in the target area after four of the crew had baled out. The body of Sgt Lager was found in the wreckage, while that of wireless operator, Sgt Sewell RCAF, was found elsewhere after his parachute failed to deploy. The surviving three members of the crew were taken into captivity, to be joined by the entire crew of Sgt Craske, who survived the demise of Z6805. The observer, Sgt Calvert, is reported to have been involved in a mass escape from Stalag IIIE in May 1942, and was fatally shot by civil police at Dresden on the 20th.

It was on the 18th, that the previously-mentioned Butt Report was released, and its disclosures made available to send shock waves reverberating around the Cabinet Room and the Air Ministry. Having studied more than four thousand bombing photos taken on a hundred night operations during June and July, Mr Butt concluded that only a fraction of the bombs had fallen within miles of their intended targets. This swept away at a stroke any notion that the Command was having an effect on Germany's war effort, and demonstrated the claims of the crews to be over-optimistic. This was probably not a revelation to senior figures in the Command and the RAF generally, who had known all along that bombing operations were largely ineffective. Of more concern was the fact that this would provide further ammunition for those calling for the dissolution of an independent bomber force, and the redistribution of its aircraft to other causes, such as the U-Boot campaign in the Atlantic and to counter reversals in the Middle East. The report was a bitter blow to the reputation of C-in-C Sir Richard Peirse, whose period of tenure would be forever unjustly blighted by its criticisms.

Also on the 18th, the squadron was ordered to prepare for a return to Cologne that night, while providing two freshman crews for Dunkerque. Sgt Stuart and P/O Hacking took off at 20.50 and 21.00 respectively for the latter, leaving seven crews for the main operation, six of which departed Leeming between 22.10 and 22.22 after Sgt Whyte's port engine misbehaved on start-up and was withdrawn. S/L Kane was the senior pilot on duty as they made their way by the usual route, Orfordness-Blankenberge-Nivelles, to the target, and relatively clear skies promised reasonable visibility. Intense darkness and up to five tenths cloud hampered the freshmen's search for their target, but P/O Hacking located it and delivered his bombs in two sticks from 10,000 and 8,000 feet in a five-minute slot from 23.21. Flashes were observed in the western area of the docks and fires were started. Sgt Stuart and crew were unable to positively identify the primary target, and bombed the docks at Ostend from 10,000 feet at 23.05. Meanwhile, the main element reached the Rhineland Capital, where the West Station was the briefed aiming-point, but the crews were unable to identify ground detail other than the River Rhine and vague impressions of an urban sprawl. They could only bomb on the general area, which they did from 11,000 to 14,000 feet between 01.20 and 01.41 in the face of a hostile and accurate response from searchlights and flak. The newly-commissioned P/O Clapperton reported watching an aircraft being held in a cone before falling in flames, an experience that Sgt O'Driscoll and crew almost shared. They were held in searchlights immediately after bombing, and spent the next ten minutes under constant barrage, the pilot eventually sustaining an arm wound, and handing over control to P/O Godfrey. During the handover, the Whitley fell into a steep dive, which P/O Godfrey allowed to continue until pulling out at only 400 feet, still under illumination. A course was set for the Dutch coast, and gradually they escaped the clutches of the defences and were able to climb to 17,000 feet. The gyro had toppled during the evasive manoeuvres, rendering the compass useless, and their position was a matter of conjecture until the English coast was sighted and a safe landing made at Bircham Newton. Z6564 failed to return to Leeming having crashed some nine miles east-south-east of Genk in Belgium, and there were no survivors among the crew of P/O Evill. Z6672 came down on the Belgian/Dutch border ten miles east-north-east of Tongeren, killing three of the crew, while S/L Kane and one other escaped with their lives to be taken into captivity. It was another shocking night for the Whitley brigade, which lost five of the seventeen dispatched, representing 29.4%.

Two freshman crews took off for Le Havre shortly after 20.00 on the 22nd, and Sgt O'Brien and crew were outbound over the Channel when the starboard engine exactor control failed and locked the propeller in fully-fine pitch. This prevented the Whitley from climbing to operational height, and the bombs were jettisoned into the sea. P/O Liebeck RCAF and crew continued on over three-tenths cloud to reach the target and carry out an attack in a single stick from 11,500 feet at 22.25. Bursts were seen on the south side of the eastern dock N°7 before a return was made to English airspace, where, in poor visibility at 01.41, T4234 crashed into high ground on Widdale Fell, two miles from Dent in the Westmoorland region of the Lake District. The pilot and second pilot were killed, while the other three occupants survived with superficial injuries.

On the 25th, F/L Thompson was promoted to acting squadron leader rank to step into S/L Kane's shoes, and P/O Clapperton was elevated to fill the vacant position for a flight lieutenant. This marked a meteoric rise in rank for F/L Clapperton, who, just two weeks earlier had been a sergeant. It also reflected the policy of promoting from within, which would change in time to allow more senior officers in the group to be posted in to fill vacancies. Cologne was once more the destination for the Command on the night of the 26/27th, for which a force of ninety-nine aircraft had been made ready. The 4 Group element of twenty-two Whitleys included seven provided by 10 Squadron, and their brief was to aim for an unspecified marshalling yard, while others attacked the city centre, The Leeming brigade took off between 21.30 and 21.40 with F/L Clapperton the only pilot of commissioned rank. They adopted a somewhat circuitous route, which would take them from Orfordness to the Belgian coast south of Ostend, then to Valenciennes on the French side of the frontier, before swinging to port to cross the northern tip of Luxembourg and then the River Rhine to run in on Cologne from the south. Sgt Stuart and crew had just crossed the Belgian coast north of Dunkerque when a port engine issue persuaded them to turn back and return their bombs to store. The others pressed on, some to identify the town of Bad Breisig and a railway bridge over the Rhine some thirty miles south of Cologne, which provided a firm pinpoint and enabled them simply to follow the river into the heart of the city. However, the presence in the target area of eight to nine-tenths low cloud with tops at 3,000 feet, and an abundance of searchlights, produced difficult conditions in which to establish a precise position. Bombing was carried out in single sticks on approximate positions from 12,000 to 14,500 feet between 00.45 and 01.17, and no results were observed. The consensus among returning crews was of a successful operation, but local reports suggested that most of the bombing fell to the east of the city, and only minor damage occurred. While this operation was in progress, the freshman crew of Sgt O'Brien departed Leeming at 23.15 to bomb the docks at Le Havre, but were unable to find them beneath the nine-tenths cumulus cloud that stretched across the Channel to the French coast. Bombs were dropped from 7,500 feet at 02.15 onto a factory believed to belong to the Schneider munitions company, which lay at an unspecified location within fifteen miles of the primary target.

Southern Germany provided both targets for major operations planned for the 29th, and forces of 143 and ninety-four aircraft were made ready for Frankfurt and Mannheim respectively. This would be the largest operation by far against the former, and would involve sixty-two Whitleys, of which eight belonged to 10 Squadron. They took off between 19.45 and 19.57 with S/L Webster the senior pilot on duty, and made their way to the Belgian coast, and endured an uncomfortable outward flight in ten-tenths cloud with electrical storms and icing conditions. This persisted all the way to the target, which proved impossible to pinpoint, and bombs were dropped on estimated positions based on the quite considerable flak activity. Seven crews carried out their attacks in a single pass from 12,000 to 16,000 feet between 23.20 and 23.55, while F/L Clapperton dropped his load on Koblenz from 14,000 feet at 23.21. The operation was not a success, only minor damage being reported by local authorities, and it was a similar story at Mannheim.

The last night of the month brought another operation against Cologne, which 4 Group supported with a handful of Halifaxes, while forty-three Whitleys joined forces with Wellingtons to attack the Krupp works at Essen. The Leeming element of seven took off between 19.45 and 19.56 with all pilots of sergeant rank after S/L Thompson's aircraft could not be made ready in time. All reached the target to encounter ten-tenths cloud, and they delivered their bombs on estimated positions from 10,000 to 15,400 feet between 22.19 and 22.40. It was impossible to assess the outcome, but fires and bomb bursts were reported, as was the intensity of the searchlight and flak response. During the course of the month the squadron operated on ten nights, dispatching eighty-three sorties for the loss of seven Whitleys, six complete crews and three individual airmen.

September 1941

An influx of new personnel during the month, particularly of pilots, encouraged a return to a five-man crew format with a second pilot as standard, and this may have been with an eye on the expansion required to man the squadron as a Halifax unit two months hence. 4 Group sat out the opening night of the month, while other modest elements of the Command continued the almost-continuous campaign against Cologne. A number of targets were briefed at Leeming on the 2nd, until Frankfurt was finally settled upon as the primary target for 126 aircraft, including forty-four Whitleys, of which seven represented 10 Squadron. They took off either side of 20.00 with S/L Thompson the senior pilot on duty, and the freshman crews of P/Os

Godfrey and Purvis departed at the same time bound for Ostend. The former made landfall five miles to the north-east of the target, and the latter eight miles to the south-west, before converging on the port to bomb through four-tenths cloud from 10,500 and 13,000 feet respectively at 22.00 and 22.15. Bomb flashes were observed, but intense flak persuaded both crews to not loiter in the target area, and safe returns were made seventy-five minutes apart. Ten-tenths cloud accompanied the main element for most of the journey across Belgium and into Germany, and, where-ever breaks occurred, thick ground mist obscured all detail. The River Main was picked up by some crews, but none could positively identify Frankfurt. The flak was heavy but inaccurate, and probably helped to provide a rough fix for the bomb-aimers, who released their loads from 10,000 to 13,000 feet between 23.23 and 00.07, without observing anything other than flashes. S/L Thompson was unable to locate the primary target, and backtracked to bomb Koblenz from 13,000 feet at 23.27. Sgt Holder experienced similar difficulties, and attacked Mainz from 12,500 feet at 00.06.

W/C Bennett's outstanding tour as commanding officer came to an end with his posting to Dishforth as station commander on the 3rd. He had arrived in April without operational experience, and immediately set about the task of rectifying that situation to establish his credibility as the leader of already-battle-hardened men. He flew four "second dickey" operations, and added a further ten as crew captain to demonstrate good leadership from the front. Pending the arrival of his successor, S/L Webster stepped temporarily into the breach. 77 Squadron moved into Leeming from Topcliffe on the 5th, and would share the station with 10 Squadron for the next eight months. A synthetic rubber factory at Hüls, the most northerly district of Krefeld on the western edge of the Ruhr, was to be the target for a mixed force of eighty-six aircraft on the night of the 6/7th, with forty-one Whitleys the most populous type. Of these, nine were to be provided by 10 Squadron, whose crews were briefed accordingly at 16.00. It was then that they were informed that Sgt Stuart and crew, who had not been detailed to take part in the operation, had been involved in a tragic and fatal accident. While conducting an air-test in Z6932, they had become lost in poor weather and had landed at Acklington in Northumberland to get their bearings. Shortly after taking-off to return to Leeming, the Whitley had struck high-tension cables, crashed and caught fire, killing the pilot and two others and seriously injuring the rear gunner. This was the first incident in what was to be an entirely forgettable day for the squadron.

Those participating in the night's operation departed Leeming either side of 21.00 with F/L Clapperton the senior pilot on duty, but soon lost the services of Sgt Robertson and crew, who were back on the ground within minutes with a failed intercom system. The others pressed on to reach the target area, where, despite clear skies and good visibility, they experienced difficulty in identifying the aiming-point. Some of those picking up the River Lippe, the nearby canal and the lakes near Haltern situated well to the north-east, were able to navigate their way to the primary target, where five of them bombed from 10,000 to 14,500 feet between 22.50 and 23.23, P/O Purvis after gliding down from 17,000 feet. A number of large explosions and fires were observed, which remained visible for a time, but searchlights and heavy and accurate flak dissuaded any from hanging about to assess their work. P/O Godfrey and crew could not locate the primary target, and bombed a railway junction at Haltern from 11,000 feet at 22.48 as an alternative. Another bad night for the Whitley brigade was reflected in five failures to return, 12% of those dispatched, and two of the empty dispersals were at Leeming. Z6478 fell victim to the night fighter of Oblt Ludwig Becker of 4./NJG1 over Holland, and crashed at 23.00 near Oldebroek, on the eastern shore of the Ijsselmeer with no survivors from the crew of Sgt Poupard. Z6942 was also posted missing through an unknown cause, but, happily, F/Sgt Holder and all of his crew survived to be taken into captivity.

A major operation to Berlin was posted on the 7th, for which a force of 197 aircraft was made ready and the crews briefed for one of three aiming-points. 4 Group detailed thirty-one Whitleys, sixteen Wellingtons and six Halifaxes for aiming-point "C", with Sgts Robertson and Whyte representing 10 Squadron. An assault on the docks at Boulogne was also briefed out, and this would involve the 10 Squadron freshman crews of Sgts Peterson, Rochford, Schneider and Tripp. They took off together between 19.33 and 19.44, and headed into largely clear skies, which would persist all the way to the targets. The Boulogne-bound quartet all located the primary target after crossing the Channel above no more than five-tenths cloud and under bright moonlight, and carried out their attacks from 4,000 to 12,000 feet between 21.45 and 22.13. Sgt Schneider and crew had not intended to expose themselves at such a low level over a hotly-defended target, but were caught in searchlights and let their bombs go at the nadir of their hair-raising descent. All returned safely home to report hits on the docks and a fire that could be seen for around forty miles. The Schneider crew handed T4263 back to the ground crew with eight holes in the tail-plane. Meanwhile, Sgt Robertson and crew had reached the Baltic conscious of excessive fuel consumption, and decided to bomb Rostock as an alternative target. This was carried out from 11,000 feet at 22.52, upon which, searchlights sprang into action and followed the Whitley back out to sea. Despite the 4 Group ORB's assertion that there was practically no cloud over the Capital, Sgt Whyte and crew reported considerable amounts of the stuff, and bombed a marshalling yard to the east of the primary aiming-point. They reported observing the incendiaries burning as they turned away, and witnessed an aircraft being shot down in flames over Kiel on the way home at 01.30. Two-thirds of crews reported successfully bombing the target, and the effectiveness of the attack was partly borne out by local descriptions of damage to a number of war-industry factories, housing, utilities and communications, mostly in the north and east of the city. Fifteen aircraft failed to return, and, when added to three losses from other operations, this represented the highest number of bomber casualties in a single night.

On the 8th, the squadron welcomed a new commanding officer in the shape of W/C Tuck DFC, who was posted in from 19 O.T.U. He had previously served with 58 Squadron, almost certainly as a flight commander, and had been awarded his DFC at that time. He presided over his first operation that very night, although probably had little to do with the briefing and other preparations for the attack on railway workshops and a munitions factory at Kassel, an industrial city situated some seventy miles to the east of the Ruhr. A force of ninety-seven aircraft was made ready, of which just four Whitleys were to be provided by 10 Squadron. Shortly before take-off at 19.47, P/O Godfrey's sortie was scrubbed after his aircraft developed an engine issue, while Sgt O'Brien's Z6980 suffered an undercarriage collapse as it gathered speed along the runway, and was extensively damaged. The crew walked away unhurt, but this incident left just those of P/O Purvis and Sgt Baker from 10 Squadron to take part in the operation. They climbed away into ten-tenths cloud, crossed the Belgian coast south of Ostend and made their way into Germany via the standard route near Cologne, where considerable flak was encountered. Despite the presence of nine-tenths cloud in the target area, P/O Purvis identified lakes to the south-west, but could not locate the briefed aiming-point. The bombs were dropped from 10,000 feet onto a small town to the south at 00.01, and a safe return was made at 05.10. Sgt Baker and crew attacked the primary target from 12,000 feet at 23.58, observing bomb bursts but no detail.

The Baltic coast was posted as the destination for three forces of modest size on the night of the 11/12th, Rostock and Warnemünde the sites of Heinkel aircraft factories and Kiel the Deutsche Werke U-Boot yards. Eight 10 Squadron Whitleys were made ready to launch against Warnemünde as part of an all-Whitley force of thirty-two, and they departed Leeming between 20.47 and 20.58 with P/Os Godfrey and Hacking the senior pilots on duty. Sgt Peterson was back on the ground within thirty minutes with an unserviceable intercom system, leaving the others to push on over ten-tenths cloud that persisted all the way to the target area. Where-ever small gaps in the cloud appeared, the vertical visibility proved to be good, and six crews were able to identify the general target area to deliver their bombs from 10,000 to 14,000 feet between 00.28 and 01.15. Bomb bursts and fires were observed, but the conditions prevented a detailed assessment, and the crews were more concerned about eking out their fuel supplies for the long journey home. P5109 was last heard from at 04.48, reporting that it was about to ditch through a mechanical problem some eighty miles off the east coast, but, despite a search, no trace of P/O Purvis and his crew was found. Z6867 ran out of fuel and was ditched successfully off Flamborough Head by P/O Hacking at 05.55, the rear gunner sustaining a fractured left arm on impact. They managed to scramble into the dinghy, and were picked up by the destroyer, HMS

Whitley T4263 ZA-E. September 1941

Wolsey, at 07.00, shocked and bruised, but alive. They were landed at Grimsby, where they would spend two days in the naval hospital.

The freshman crews of P/Os Burdett and Miller and Sgt Wieland were the only ones from the squadron to operate on the night of the 12/13th, having been briefed for Cherbourg, while the main effort was directed at Frankfurt. They took off between 21.14 and 21.24 and encountered up to eight-tenths cloud over the Channel, which persisted over the French coast. All located the primary target and carried out their attacks from between 7,000 and 15,000 feet between 00.20 and 00.55. From such a low level, P/O Miller and crew were able to watch their bombs overshoot and fall harmlessly into the sea, while those some seven to eight thousand feet above saw nothing of the fall of their bombs. After a number of cancellations affecting the squadron over the ensuing week, during which 4 Group supported raids on Brest and Hamburg, it looked like an operation to Berlin posted on the morning of the 20th would actually go ahead. A force of seventy-four aircraft included five 10 Squadron Whitleys, which took off between 18.35 and 18.45 with P/O Miller the ranking pilot on duty. They flew out over complete cloud cover and headed east to Sylt, before crossing the Schleswig-Holstein peninsular to skirt the Baltic coast until the final turn towards Berlin. A recall signal was sent out at 22.43, which was picked up by the crews of P/O Miller and Sgts O'Brien, Robertson and Schneider, who decided to shed the weight of their bombs by releasing them on last-resort targets. P/O Miller dropped a 500 pounder on a searchlight and flak concentration on Sylt and brought the rest home, while Sgts O'Brien and Robertson relieved themselves of their entire bomb load over Rostock. Sgt Schneider emptied his bomb bay on Warnemünde, which left just Sgt Rochford and crew pressing on towards Berlin, until they, too, picked up the recall at 23.10, by which time they were closing in on the Capital from the north-west. They turned back immediately, and let their bombs go over Wismar from 14,000 feet at 00.47, setting off a flak response from the seaplane base, which scored a number of hits. Whether or not this caused a fuel leak is unclear, but Z6802 ran out of fuel and ditched off the Lincolnshire coast, from where the crew was rescued by an ASR launch from Grimsby some two hours later.

A similar situation arose on the night of the 26/27th, when 104 aircraft were dispatched on operations to Cologne, Emden, Mannheim and Genoa. Five 10 Squadron crews were on their way to Mannheim when a recall signal was sent to all operational aircraft, most of which would respond and return home. F/L Burdett landed at Waterbeach as instructed with his bombs on board, while P/O Hacking bombed an aerodrome ten miles west of Lens in north-eastern France. Sgt Schneider and crew were ten miles north of Nieuwpoort in Belgium when they picked up the signal, and they also brought their bombs back to Waterbeach, as did P/O Miller and crew. Sgt Tripp and crew bombed Dunkerque docks from 10,000 feet at 20.46, before joining their colleagues at Waterbeach.

Stettin and Hamburg were posted as the main targets for forces of 139 and ninety-three aircraft respectively on the 29th, for which 4 Group ordered what must have been a maximum effort involving fifty-six Whitleys, six Halifaxes and eleven Wellingtons to attack the former. 10 Squadron made ready eight aircraft, which took off between 18.02 and 18.36 with F/Ls Burdett and Clapperton the senior pilots on duty. Sgt Peterson and crew returned after fifty minutes with a number of technical issues, leaving the others to press on over heavy cloud, which began to disperse to some extent at the German coast. F/L Clapperton made landfall at the northern end

Whitley Z6802 ZA-P September 1941

of Sylt, but excessive fuel consumption suggested that Stettin was beyond reach, and the bombs were dropped on Warnemünde docks from 12,000 feet at 22.15. Sgt Baker and crew had made landfall at the southern end of Sylt, but had the same concerns about the state of their fuel reserves, and bombed Rostock from 12,000 feet at 22.11. Sgt Tripp and crew probably arrived at the same conclusion when much closer to Stettin, and turned back to bomb Rostock from 14,000 feet at 23.20. This left the crews of F/L Burdett, P/O Hacking, P/O Godfrey and Sgt Whyte to attack the primary target in good visibility from 9,000 to 14,000 feet between 23.11 and 23.27, and all returned safely to report observing bomb bursts and huge fires that remained visible for seventy miles into the return flight.

The last night of the month brought an operation to Hamburg, for which a force of eighty-two aircraft was made ready. 4 Group contributed ten Whitleys, eight from Leeming and two from Middleton-St-George, and the 10 Squadron trio of P/O Miller and Sgts Peterson and Schneider took off between 18.14 and 18.29. All three reached the target area and flew along the Elbe under constant flak to find the city blanketed by impenetrable cloud, which forced them to bomb on DR and e.t.a., from 13,000 to 14,000 feet between 21.16 and 21.48. No results could be determined, but the local authorities recorded fourteen fires and minor damage. During the course of the month the squadron operated on nine nights, and dispatched fifty-one sorties for the loss of seven Whitleys, four complete crews and a number of airmen.

October 1941

The adverse weather conditions characterizing the second half of September continued into the new month, and caused the recall of a modest-sized force bound for Karlsruhe on the evening of the 1st. The predominantly 4 Group raid on target "A" at Stuttgart was allowed to continue, however, 10 Squadron providing five of the twenty-seven participating Whitleys. They had departed Leeming along with the freshman crew of Sgt Joyce between 18.29 and 18.38 with S/L Webster the senior pilot on duty, and all headed for Orfordness before setting course for the Belgian and French coasts. The freshman crew was bound for the docks at Boulogne, but found that the heavy cloud from the mid-point of the Channel cloaked the French coast. Fortunately, an occasional gap allowed a brief glimpse of the ground, and the Joyce crew took advantage of one of these to drop their bombs from 9,000 feet at 21.45. No sooner had the bombs fallen away than the gap closed over, preventing a sight of the outcome. Similar conditions of between two and ten-tenths cloud had been encountered by the main element during their outward leg to southern Germany, which blighted all attempts to identify the aiming-point at Stuttgart. Bombing took place on e.t.a., from 10,000 to 14,000 feet between 22.10 and 22.55, resulting in bursts, flashes and the glow of fires. A change of wind on the way home was not noticed by P/O Godfrey's navigator, and, with the ground completely obscured by cloud, they flew across England and out over the Irish Sea. They were eventually alerted by a fix, and turned back to fly along the Bristol Channel until running out of fuel some twenty-two miles off Pembroke at 05.30. The dinghy failed to inflate and had to be cut loose, which was accomplished before Z6941 slid beneath the surface after just three minutes. They all managed to get into the dinghy, and were picked up at 09.00 by a naval trawler, which landed them at Pembroke Docks.

The group mounted a freshman operation against the docks at Dunkerque on the 3rd, for which 10 Squadron prepared and dispatched six Whitleys between 18.22 and 18.31, four of them captained by pilots of pilot officer rank and two of sergeant rank. They all reached the target under clear skies to find just a little ground haze, and identified the aiming-point without difficulty. Bombs were delivered from 9,000 to 13,000 feet between 20.40 and 22.05, and bursts were seen across Docks 2 to 8 and in a marshalling yard to the south of Docks 7 and 8. The operation provided a good opportunity for the new crews to gain some experience of the enemy's defensive response, which, on this night, amounted to intense but ineffective light flak, slight heavy flak, searchlight cones on three sides of the target area and balloons at 8,000 feet tethered to flak-ships anchored some five miles off the coast.

The Command carried out no further operations for a week, until resuming on the night of the 10/11th with the targeting of Essen and Cologne, the former supported by 4 Group without a 10 Squadron presence. Orders were received at Leeming on the 12th to prepare nine Whitleys for operations that night, six of them for the first large raid of the war on Nuremberg and three for Bremen. It was to be a busy night across the Command as a force of 152 aircraft was made ready for southern Germany, ninety-nine for north-western Germany and ninety 5 Group Hampdens and Manchesters for the synthetic rubber works at Hüls in the Ruhr. Together with a number of minor operations, this would bring the night's sortie tally to a new record of 373, an improvement of nine on the previous record set in May. The two 10 Squadron sections departed Leeming between 18.02 and 18.28, those bound for Nuremberg taking the lead and setting course for Orfordness with P/O Hacking the senior pilot on duty, while P/Os Blunden,

Kenny and the newly-commissioned P/O Joyce headed for Scarborough. Sgt Peterson and crew lost their intercom shortly after crossing the English coast, but continued on to bomb Dunkerque from 9,000 feet at 20.30 before turning back.

Generally good weather conditions accompanied the others as they continued on across Belgium, and the target area was found to be clear of cloud with only a little ground haze to contend with. P/O Hacking reported considerable cloud, however, and opted to drop his bombs on Würzburg, situated some fifty miles north-west of the target, doing so from 10,000 feet at 23.42. He reported large fires which outlined buildings and remained visible for seventy-five miles. The four remaining 10 Squadron crews reached the target, where the Siemens-Schuckert factory was their briefed aiming-point, and they carried out their attacks in good visibility from 12,000 to 17,000 feet between 22.49 and 23.18. On return they reported being unable to locate the factory because of the haze, but described bomb bursts in the city area, explosions, many fires and surprisingly little opposition. The 4 Group scribe was more expansive, reporting large fires, particularly in the northern districts, which remained visible for a hundred miles into the return flight. Bursts were observed close to the Siemens works and the Maschinen Fabrik-Augsburg-Nuremberg (M.A.N.) diesel engine factory. Seventeen large fires were counted burning at one time, and the city centre appeared to be one large fire. One unnamed crew apparently descended to 3,000 feet to clearly identify the Siemens factory, and claimed one of its buildings was ablaze with the roof girders visible. In contrast, the Nuremberg authorities reported just a few bombs in and around the city, but described many outlying communities being hit and badly damaged up to sixty-five miles away.

Meanwhile, over north-western Germany, P/O Kenny and crew had reached a point some twenty-five miles off the German coast, when a starboard engine issue prompted them to jettison their bombs and return home. Bremen was found to be concealed beneath ten-tenths cloud, leaving P/Os Blunden and Joyce with no alternative but to bomb blind on DR, which they did from 12,000 feet at around 21.40, observing the glow of fires as they turned away. On landing at Leeming, Z6828 collided with the wreckage of a 102 Squadron Whitley, sustaining extensive damage in the process, but P/O Joyce and crew walked away unscathed.
The weather caused a number of cancellations for 10 Squadron freshman crews over the ensuing days, and operations to Düsseldorf and Cologne on the night of the 13/14th and a return to Nuremberg on the 14/15th passed the squadron by. The main operation posted on the 16th was to Duisburg, and, while not detailed to take part in that, the squadron was ordered to send four freshman crews to Ostend. Sgts Lloyd, Williamson and Wisher and P/O Goldston took off between 18.05 and 18.13, and arrived in the target area towards the end of the raid, by which time the initially clear skies and good visibility had deteriorated. Nine to ten-tenths cloud enveloped the target area, leaving no chance for inexperienced crews to locate the target, and all bombs were jettisoned safe into the sea.

Bremen was posted as the main target on the 20th, and a force of 153 aircraft made ready. 4 Group was not invited to take part, and was given a "special" target of its own at Wilhelmshaven, for which a force of forty Whitleys, five Wellingtons and four Halifaxes was assembled. 10 Squadron prepared nine Whitleys, which took off between 18.24 and 19.02 with all captains of pilot officer or sergeant rank. P/O Joyce returned within thirty minutes with an engine issue, and Sgt Whyte arrived back more than two hours after that with a number of technical issues. They flew out under clear skies, until cloud began to build up as the target area approached, and it was at around three-tenths when the first crews began their bombing run. Despite reporting good visibility, P/O Godfrey and crew missed the primary target, and bombed Wesermünde as an alternative from 9,500 feet at 21.06. The others carried out their attacks from 12,000 to 13,000 feet in the face of an intense searchlight and flak response between 20.34 and 21.40, noting bomb bursts and fires, although the later arrivals were hampered by the increasing cloud. Local authorities reported scattered bombing and little damage. It is interesting to note, that in a squadron which had been characterized from the outset by the presence of senior officers in the air, there had been only one sortie by a flight commander since the arrival of W/C Tuck, and none by the commanding officer himself.

Another freshman operation was posted at Leeming on the 22nd, this one to Le Havre, for which 10 Squadron briefed four crews. One would drop out before take-off because of a sick aircraft, leaving Sgts Boothright, Lloyd and Owen to depart between 17.51 and 17.54. Cloud and haze over the Channel persisted to obscure the target area, and Sgt Boothright and crew jettisoned their bombs after being defeated by the elements. Sgt Owen and crew identified the docks, and bombed them from 9,500 feet at 20.25, observing bursts on N°7 Dock. Sgt Lloyd and crew searched for fifty-five minutes before finally pinpointing the target through a gap in the clouds and by the light of a flare dropped by another aircraft. The bombs were dropped from 12,000 feet at 21.15, and flashes were seen on Dock N°11.

Crews were briefed on the 23rd for a two-wave assault on the shipyards at Kiel that night, for which a force of 114 aircraft was made ready. 4 Group's contribution amounted to twenty-seven Whitleys, of which ten were provided by 10 Squadron. They took off as part of the first wave between 16.55 and 17.15 with F/L Burdett the senior pilot on duty, and lost the services of Sgt Rochford and crew to a port engine issue within an hour. The others pushed on across the North Sea to be greeted in the target area by ten-tenths cloud, which precluded any chance of identifying the briefed aiming-point of the Deutsche Werke shipyards. Eight crews released their bombs on estimated positions from 10,000 to 18,000 feet between 21.05 and 21.45, aided by the searchlight and flak activity, while P/O Godfrey bombed Neustadt (probably Neumünster) from 9,500 feet at 22.15 after searching extensively for the primary target.

Shortly after midday on the 24th the first Halifax II arrived at Leeming to begin the squadron's gradual conversion onto the type. On the following day W/C Tuck and a full crew climbed on board, and were flown over to Linton-on-Ouse by a ferry pilot to begin their conversion training. S/L Webster assumed temporary command of the squadron and F/L Burdett stepped into his shoes as A Flight commander. It should be noted that, despite having begun operations in the hands of 35 Squadron in March, and of 76 Squadron from June, the Halifax had been dogged by technical problems, particularly in the area of hydraulics, and had undergone periods of grounding while essential modifications were carried out. Neither squadron had been able to put double figures into the air, and the type would continue to suffer other issues, including that of being underpowered.

Such trials and tribulations still lay in the future for 10 Squadron, while it continued to put its trust in the venerable old Whitley. Sixteen of them were made ready at Leeming for an attack on Hamburg on the 26th as part of a force of 115 aircraft. The eight-strong 10 Squadron element took off between 17.10 and 18.11 with F/Ls Burdett and Clapperton the senior pilots on duty. They had been briefed to attack "special" target B, which was probably one of the shipyards earmarked as an aiming-point, along with two designated targets in the city itself. Sgt Peterson and crew abandoned their sortie over the airfield because of an engine issue, while the others flew out over the North Sea to encounter up to nine-tenths cloud all the way to the target area, with moonlight above. On arrival over Sylt, P/O Kenny became concerned about his fuel reserves and dropped his bombs onto the island from 12,000 feet at 21.30. Having found heavy cloud and haze at the enemy coast, F/L Clapperton decided to bomb Bremerhaven as an alternative target, and did so from 18,000 feet at 21.17. Once the others had located the Elbe Estuary, it could be followed all the way past the shipyards into the centre of the city, although this would require running the gauntlet of searchlights and flak from both banks. Sgt Tripp and crew found themselves victims of this very situation, and were held in searchlights for forty minutes, while violent evasive action was taken. They were forced constantly down towards the ground and were at 600 feet when the bombs were dropped at 20.40. Before they could observe the results, however, they were attacked by a BF109, which Sgt Tripp managed to evade by climbing. Sgt Blunden and crew reported being held by some forty to sixty searchlights after bombing from 12,500 feet at 21.14, and were subjected to the most intense and sustained flak barrage, during which the rear gunner, F/Sgt Clemmett, sustained a serious wound to his lower chest and abdomen. The searchlights were eventually shaken off at 5,000 feet, whereupon the gunner was brought into the fuselage to receive medical attention. They landed at Bircham Newton at 04.00, and the gunner was removed immediately to hospital The remaining three crews attacked the primary target from 10,000 to 16,000 feet between 21.10 and 21.45, but cloud, haze and searchlight glare prevented any meaningful assessment. Hamburg reported a more destructive raid than was typical for the period, with fatalities and a dozen or so fires.

Four freshman crews were called to briefing on the 28th, to learn that they would be plying their trade at Cherbourg that night. Sgts Gribben, Webb, White and Williamson took off between 17.37 and 17.54, only to encounter nine-tenths cloud at 10,000 feet over the French coast, which persuaded three of them to jettison their bombs into the sea and turn back. Sgt Williamson and crew found gaps in the cloud, through which they caught sight of the docks, and bombed them in a single stick from 13,000 feet at 20.55. Bursts were seen on Dock Nºs 4 and 5, followed by the reflection of fires. The month ended with another operation against Hamburg on the 31st, for which 10 Squadron made ready nine Whitleys as part of an overall force of 123 aircraft. The squadron also contributed three aircraft to a freshman operation to Dunkerque. The main element took off first, either side of 17.00 with P/O Godfrey the senior pilot on duty. The freshmen followed within minutes, but, as Z9221 raced towards lift-off, it swung violently in the hands of Sgt White, and crashed into a Nissen hut, causing extensive damage to the Whitley and leaving the crew shocked and bruised. The other Dunkerque-bound crews crossed the Channel over six-tenths cloud, which had increased to eight-tenths in the target area. Sgt Owen and crew made landfall at Cap Gris Nez and searched in vain for the target for twenty-seven minutes, before jettisoning the bombs into the sea and going home. Sgts Wieland and Gribben managed to locate the docks through gaps in the cloud, and carried out attacks from 12,500 and 12,000 feet respectively at 19.35 and 20.00, the former observing flashes that illuminated warehouses on the jetty between Docks 4 and 5.

The Hamburg force encountered eight-tenths cloud over the North Sea, which prevented some from identifying their point of landfall. Sgt Williamson's navigator had been taken ill during the flight out, and the pilot turned towards the target on e.t.a., without a firm indication as to his precise position. No ground detail could be seen through the cloud, and the bombs were dropped from 13,000 feet at 21.10 in the region of Aurich, some twenty miles west of Wilhelmshaven. Sgt Boothright and crew were similarly uncertain of their exact position, and dropped their bombs also from 13,000 feet at 21.09 onto what they believed to be Minden, situated about twenty-five miles east of Osnabrück. Sgt Lloyd and crew had strayed over Schleswig, twenty-five miles north-west of Kiel, and dropped the bombs there from 15,000 feet at 22.08 after gliding down. At 12,000 feet they were held in searchlights and subjected to a flak barrage, which caused some damage to the starboard mainplane. P/O Godfrey and crew searched for fifty-five minutes without ever catching a glimpse of the ground, and had almost reached the Danish frontier when the east coastline of the Schleswig-Holstein peninsular was recognised. An attack was carried out on the port of Flensburg from 10,000 feet at 23.02, which resulted in flashes and the glow of burning incendiaries. Sgt Schneider and P/O Goldston and their crews were the only ones to positively identify the actual briefed aiming-point "Altona A", which they attacked from 13,500 and 13,000 feet respectively at 21.05 and 21.35. P/Os Blunden and Kenny and Sgt Tripp reported bombing the general area of Hamburg from 12,000 to 15,000 feet between 21.08 and 22.10, without being able to assess the results. Sgt Tripp's starboard engine was damaged by flak over the target, and the port engine burst into flames just as they were about to touch down at Dishforth, but a safe landing was carried out and no casualties resulted. During the course of the month the squadron operated on ten nights, and dispatched seventy-one sorties for the loss of a single Whitley from which the crew was saved.

November 1941

The first week of the new month would pass without 10 Squadron being called upon to operate. W/C Tuck returned from his Halifax conversion course at Linton-on-Ouse on the 2nd, and the crews of S/L Thompson, P/O Godfrey and Sgts Schneider and Tripp travelled by road that morning to begin their introduction to four engines. Operations were posted and briefed over the next few days before being cancelled, largely because of the weather, and that was probably the expectation for the ten crews who attended briefing on the 7th. Undoubtedly frustrated by his inability to strike effectively at Germany, and eager to erase the stinging criticisms of the Command arising out of the Butt Report, C-in-C Pierse had planned a record-breaking night of operations. He intended to send over two hundred aircraft to Berlin, and persisted with the idea despite a late forecast of storms, thick cloud, hail and icing conditions through which the force would have to fly to reach their destination. The 5 Group A-O-C, AVM Slessor, questioned the plan, and was allowed to withdraw his contribution of seventy-five aircraft and send them instead to Cologne. A third force of fifty-three Wellingtons and two Stirlings from 1 and 3 Groups would also be operating on this night, but over southern Germany where Mannheim was the target. Together with the night's minor operations, the total of 392 sorties committed to the fray would represent a new record.

10 Squadron made ready five Whitleys for the main event with target "C" as their aiming-point, and five others to attack a "special" target at Essen, probably the Krupp works. Four of the Ruhr-bound element took off first between 19.23 and 19.55, leaving behind Sgt Wisher and

crew, who made two abortive attempts to take off. Each resulted in a violent swing, possibly because of an imbalance of power between the engines, and the commanding officer decided to scrub their sortie. The others flew out under clear skies until about twenty miles into the North Sea crossing, when they ran into eight to ten-tenths cloud, which would persist all the way to the target. Sgt Owen and crew experienced severe icing conditions that affected the performance of the engines and controls, and, with airspeed falling off, the bombs were jettisoned, and a safe return carried out. Only Sgt Williamson and crew caught a glimpse of the ground as they crossed the Dutch coast, identifying Texel and the Ijsselmeer. They, and Sgt Lloyd and crew bombed the general area of Essen from 16,000 and 15,000 feet respectively at 22.01 and 22.19, and observed flashes and fires, one large one burning with a huge white flame at its centre. Sgt Gribben and crew flew on until reaching a built-up area, which they believed was Hamm, and emptied their bomb bay upon it from 16,000 feet at 22.37.

The Berlin-bound element departed Leeming between 21.35 and 21.50 with F/L Clapperton the senior pilot on duty. They were part of an adjusted force of 169 aircraft assigned to the "Big City", and their experiences would be representative of all taking part. Cloud had continued to build up since the Essen section had passed through, and, with little prospect of gaining a visual fix, Sgt Whyte and crew attacked Sylt from 12,000 feet at 00.44. Sgt Wieland and crew crossed the Schleswig-Holstein peninsular with concerns rising over the rate of fuel consumption, and dropped their bombs in the region of Lübeck from 16,000 feet at 01.10. F/L Clapperton and crew pushed on a little further along the Baltic coast until coming upon Rostock, which they bombed from 15,000 feet at 01.30. Sgt Boothright and P/O Hacking reached the Berlin area by DR, and carried out blind attacks from 13,000 and 14,000 feet respectively at 01.58 and 02.20, and were among only seventy-three crews to report attacking the primary target. Local reports would reveal damage in Berlin to be limited to a few dozen buildings, at a cost to the Command of a new record loss in a single operation of twenty-one aircraft. 5 Group fared better in terms of losses, coming through unscathed, but unfortunately, so did Cologne. It was a similar story at Mannheim, where no bombs were reported by the city authorities, and seven Wellingtons failed to return. The minor operations cost a further nine aircraft, to bring the overall losses to thirty-seven, more than twice the previous highest number in a single night. It was a disaster, and Peirse was summoned to an uncomfortable meeting with Churchill at Chequers on the evening of the 8th to make his explanations. On the 13th the Air Ministry told Peirse to scale back operations to the minimum, while the future of the Command was debated at the highest level.

While elements of 4 Group tried their hand at Essen on the night of the 8/9th, the 10 Squadron freshman crews of Sgts Moore and Webb and P/O Murray took off shortly before 18.00 to bomb the docks at Ostend. All three located the target area under clear skies, and only some ground haze to contend with, but also considerable searchlight activity, and delivered their bombs from 2,500 and 10,000 feet between 19.57 and 20.20. Bursts were observed in the tidal harbour and west and southern quays, and a resultant fire could be seen from sixty miles away on the return flight. Following a succession of operational cancellations affecting freshman crews, one finally went ahead on the evening of the 15th involving the crews of P/O Hughes and Sgt Moore. They took off shortly after 17.00 and headed for Emden, and ran immediately into heavy cloud and icing at the English coast. Sgt Moore's port engine cut, throwing the Whitley into a spin, which was arrested by switching the air-intake into "hot". Continuing ice-accretion caused further

Halifax Mk II passing by some building cumulus..Winter 1941/42

difficulties in maintaining height, and persuaded the pilot to jettison the bombs from 3,500 feet at 18.07. P/O Hughes and crew battled the conditions to reach the target area by DR to bomb blind from 15,000 feet at 19.57.

Operations were posted daily for the next two weeks, only to be cancelled because of the weather, which also affected the Halifax training program at Leeming. A full complement of Halifaxes was on 10 Squadron charge by the 25th, allowing working up to begin in earnest under the watchful eye of W/C Tuck. The squadron was the third in the Command to receive the type after 35 and 76 Squadrons, but, despite being an improvement on the original Mk I variant, it would continue to disappoint, both in terms of performance and rate of serviceability. It was not until the last night of the month that an operation involving 10 Squadron, at last, got off the ground. The freshman crews of Sgts Barber, Moore and Tait and P/O Nelson were briefed for Emden, and took off between 16.41 and 17.00. They encountered considerable amounts of cloud over the North Sea, which began to decrease as the enemy coast drew near. Sgts Tait and Barber identified the Ems Estuary and the Dollart, the body of water immediately south of Emden, and were able to deliver their attacks on the primary target from 14,000 and 14,500 feet at 20.22 and 20.30 respectively, observing bursts, flashes and a fire. Sgt Moore and crew were unable to locate Emden, and pressed on to the east to bomb Hamburg from 8,000 feet at 20.48 without observing the results. F/O Nelson RNZAF and crew were last heard from at 19.00 while still outbound, and no trace of them or Z9166 was ever found. During the course of the month the squadron undertook just five operations on four nights, launching eighteen sorties for the loss of one Whitley and crew.

December 1941

There were no operations from Leeming until the 7th, when eight Whitleys were made ready to join 122 other aircraft for a raid on the city of Aachen, while the freshman crews of Sgts Barber and Tait targeted the docks at Dunkerque. The latter took off first, either side of 17.00, and reached the target area to encounter eight-tenths cloud with large gaps, which Sgt Tait was able to exploit. He delivered the fourteen 250 pounders and two canisters of incendiaries from 14,000 feet at 18.45, and observed them bursting on Docks 4 and 5. Sgt Barber and crew were defeated by the conditions, and decided to bring their bombs home. As they were in the final moments of their approach to Leeming, they found a 77 Squadron Whitley blocking their path, and, despite trying to regain height, hit the roof of a house and crashed near the village of Londonderry alongside the A1. The crew was able to scramble clear with only knocks and bruises before Z9162 burst into flames and was consumed in the ensuing conflagration.

There was a late take-off for the Aachen crews, and, after P/O Goldston's aircraft was side-lined with engine problems, seven Whitleys presented themselves at the threshold and departed Leeming between 00.30 and 01.17 with no pilots above pilot officer rank. They flew out over the North Sea to find seven-tenths cloud, which increased to up to ten-tenths at the enemy coast and persisted all the way across Belgium to the target, situated just across the frontier. Some crews were unable to locate the primary target, Sgt Wisher and P/O Blunden among them, and they both attacked the city of Bonn from 12,000 feet at 04.06 and 04.42 respectively. Sgt Webb searched in vain, before turning back with the intention of attacking the docks at Ostend, but failed to locate them also, and the bombs were jettisoned into the sea from 12,000 feet at 06.15. Sgt Wieland and crew bombed the town of Euskirchen, situated between Aachen and Bonn, from 16,500 feet at 03.53, but saw nothing of the outcome. P/O Murray and crew saw only snow through the few gaps in the cloud, and, thinking they were over Holland, set course for the Channel coast to employ their bombs against one of the ports. Having little clue as to their actual position, their effort was in vain, and they decided to head for home with their bombs. Sgt Boothright and P/O Joyce and their crews alone managed to locate the primary target, which they bombed from 12,500 and 13,000 feet at 04.02 and 03.56 respectively, again seeing little of the results.

When orders were received on the 11th to provide two Whitleys for Cologne that night, P/O Kenny and Sgt Rochford and their crews were called to briefing, probably not knowing that they would be the last 10 Squadron crews to go to war in a Whitley. They took off at 16.30 and 16.57 respectively as part of a force of sixty aircraft assigned to the special target "C" in the city. Eight-tenths cloud over the North Sea and ten-tenths over Rhineland Germany provided challenging conditions, which fewer than half of the participating crews would overcome sufficiently well to find the general target area. The 10 Squadron duo bombed blindly on e.t.a., Sgt Rochford from 15,500 feet at 20.08 and P/O Kenny from 12,000 feet twelve minutes later. Returning to England they ran into a violent electrical storm and strong winds which would result in the last two Whitley sorties ending unhappily. Z9188 was heading for Leeming between Pateley Bridge and Ripon at 01.43, when a powerful downdraught pushed it onto the high ground beneath, severely damaging it and injuring all members of the Kenny crew, the second pilot, Sgt Hoskin, fatally. Seven minutes later, Z9149 undershot the runway in the hands of Sgt Rochford, and crashed just outside of the airfield perimeter, fortunately without casualties.

It was on the 14th that the 10 Squadron ORB recorded that, from this day, the squadron would operate only in Halifaxes, thus bringing to an end the Whitley era, which had seen the type give unparalleled service and distinguish itself as a thoroughly reliable, dependable and tough aeroplane. Operational status was achieved in time for the squadron to participate in Operation Veracity, a daylight attack on the German cruisers, Scharnhorst and Gneisenau at Brest. Now that operations over mainland Germany had become restricted following the Berlin debacle, attention had turned once more upon these vessels, and this would be the tenth operation of varying sizes to be mounted against the port thus far during the month. The operation called for six aircraft from the three Halifax squadrons, which would join forces with eighteen Stirlings and eleven Manchesters.

The honour of being part of the first Halifax operation fell to the crews of W/C Tuck, S/L Webster, F/L Burdett, F/L Miller, F/Sgt Whyte and Sgt Schneider, who took off between 09.16 and 09.28, only for W/C Tuck's undercarriage to malfunction. The starboard leg refused to retract, and, despite strenuous efforts to rectify the problem, the sortie had to be abandoned and the four 2,000lb armour-piercing bombs were jettisoned in Filey Bay before a safe landing was carried out. S/L Webster now took command of the 10 Squadron element, which rendezvoused with the other Halifaxes over Lynton on the north coast of Devon and picked up the rest of the force over Lundy Island at 11.30, from where they proceeded to Lizard Point for the Channel

Being cold and wet was normal for ground crews at Leeming in the winter of 1941/42.

crossing. They arrived at the French coast under clear skies with excellent visibility, the 10 Squadron crews in an arrowhead formation with S/L Webster at the point, F/Sgt Whyte on the port quarter of the vic and F/L Burdett to starboard. F/L Miller and Sgt Schneider positioned themselves line astern behind S/L Webster as they ran in on the target at 15,000 feet. The Stirling element opened the attack as those following on arranged themselves into line astern to pass singly over the aiming-point, which could be clearly seen. The flak was intense and accurate, and many aircraft would sustain shrapnel damage to some extent. The 10 Squadron section delivered their bombs between 12.35 and 12.38, but could not observe the outcome because of smoke from previous bomb bursts. All returned safely to land at Boscombe Down, four of them with slight flak damage, and remained there overnight. Claims were made of direct hits on both vessels, and the 4 Group ORB stated that reconnaissance photos confirmed dense smoke pouring from them. It is believed that, in fact, Scharnhorst sustained only slight damage. On return to Leeming on the following afternoon, F/L Miller landed R9368 wheels-up at Sherburn in Elmet, east of Leeds, for which no explanation is provided.

News was received on the 29th that HM King George had approved the immediate award to S/L Webster of the DFC. That afternoon, W/C Tuck and Sgt Tripp were taking off at 15.10 from different runways for training sorties in V9981 and L9614 respectively, when they collided, writing off both aircraft. There were no serious casualties among W/C Tuck's crew, but Sgt Tripp and his wireless operator were killed and other members of the crew were injured.

Instructions were received on the 30th to prepare for Operation Veracity II, and five Halifaxes were made ready at Leeming. When take-off time arrived at 11.00, Sgt Schneider's aircraft was found to be unserviceable, leaving just four to join a dozen other Halifaxes for the attack, which would not benefit now from the presence of elements of 3 and 5 Groups after they were grounded by the weather. S/Ls Webster and Thompson were the senior pilots on duty, but the latter's port-outer engine developed a glycol leak over the English coast on the way out, and the sortie had to be abandoned. The route and tactics were the same as for the previous operation, but the prospects were not good as they flew over ten-tenths cloud all the way to the Brittany coast, where, fortunately, it dispersed to leave good visibility. S/L Thompson led the 10 Squadron trio across the aiming-point at 14,000 feet in the face of the most intense flak, and the bombs were delivered between 14.09 and 14.11. Violent evasive action prevented the results from being observed, and, having escaped the flak, the Halifaxes found Luftwaffe fighters waiting to pounce. P/O Hacking and crew were heading home to the north of Brest, when a BF109 attacked from astern and passed over the rear turret, presenting its belly to the gunner, Sgt Porritt. He poured an accurate burst into it from close range, and the entire crew watched the fighter turn onto its back, burst into flames and dive vertically into cloud. Two other BF109s came up to engage, but both were shot down by the Spitfire escort, and a third enemy fighter was driven off by the gunners. The rear gunner sustained slight wounds, but a safe return was made to St Eval in Cornwall, where an inspection revealed a burst tyre, holes in the fuselage and wing, damage to the mid-upper and rear turrets and the port-outer engine. S/L Webster's V9984 was attacked at the same time, one of its assailants closing to seventy yards before being engaged by the rear gunner, after which, it was seen to dive vertically into cloud. R9374 was badly damaged by flak, which smashed the port-outer engine, and F/Sgt Whyte was unable to maintain speed and remain with the formation. As they turned for home, north of Brest, they were attacked from astern by a BF109, which F/L Roach engaged from the rear turret. Soon afterwards the intercom became unserviceable, and cannon shells knocked out both inner engines. Now with only one good engine, F/Sgt Whyte put the nose down to gain speed, before levelling out and landing on the sea at around 14.31 some eighty miles south of Lizard Point. The flight engineer and wireless operator confirmed that F/L Roach had been killed, but could not recover his body from the turret. The Halifax remained afloat for seven minutes while the crew got into the dinghy, and they were picked up by an Air Sea Rescue launch at about 19.30.

During the course of the month the squadron undertook two night operations, dispatching twelve Whitley sorties for the loss of two aircraft, and two daylight operations involving ten Halifax sorties, losing thee aircraft. No complete crews were lost, but one pilot, one second pilot and two crew members were killed. It had been a disappointing year for the Command, which had struggled to produce an improvement on the previous year's performance, despite the introduction of a new generation of heavy bombers. The Stirling, Halifax and Manchester had each failed to meet expectations, and had undergone periods of grounding, depleting the Command's available resources. The Butt Report had exposed the frailties and failures of the strategic bombing concept, and AM Sir Richard Peirse had been unable to fulfil the often-unrealistic demands of his masters as set out in their directives. The crews had done their best in difficult circumstances, and had sustained heavy casualties in the process, but, even with the dark cloud of the possible dissolution of a dedicated bomber force overhead, salvation was close at hand. The "shining sword", the Lancaster, was already being prepared for battle by 44 Squadron, and would be ready to go to war in March, by which time a new hand would be on the tiller at Bomber Command HQ.

January 1942

The New Year began with the continuing pre-occupation with the German cruisers at Brest, and, following the fifteen raids of varying sizes sent against them during December, there would be no fewer than eleven further operations during January. W/C Tuck reported sick on the 3rd, and his health would become an issue for the remainder of his career. In his absence, S/L Webster assumed command of the squadron. The first operation of the year for 10 Squadron involved a return to Brest by four Halifaxes, which took off between 03.54 and 04.00 on the 6th with S/L Thompson the senior pilot on duty. They were part of an overall force of 154 aircraft, eighty-seven of them assigned to the warships and the remainder to the general area of the docks. The eight crews of 10 and 35 Squadrons and seventeen of 51 Squadron had been briefed to attack the dockyard power station, but nine-tenths cloud over the target ruined any chance of that. The 10 Squadron quartet delivered their bombs blind from 11,500 and 16,500 feet between 06.08 and 07.02, and very little of the outcome was observed through the few gaps. Continuing the maritime theme, 4 Group prepared twenty-seven Whitleys, Wellingtons and Halifaxes to send to St Nazaire on the 7th, while the main effort was directed at Brest. The Leeming element of four was reduced to three when F/L Miller's mount became unserviceable, leaving P/Os Godfrey, Hacking and Sgt Schneider to take off either side of 17.00. They found the target under clear skies, and picked out the Loire Estuary and dock breakwaters with ease. They carried out their attacks from 9,000 to 15,000 feet between 19.28 and 20.07, but were prevented by ground haze from observing the outcome.

W/C Tuck returned to the helm on the 13th after his sick leave, before preparations were put in hand on the 15th for the second of two raids on Hamburg on consecutive nights. Three 10 Squadron crews were briefed to take part in an overall force of ninety-six aircraft, but, for the second operation running, F/L Miller was forced to sit it out at home after technical problems grounded him and his crew. S/L Thompson and Sgt Schneider and their crews took off at 18.10 and 18.12 respectively, and encountered ten-tenths strato-cumulus cloud as they made their way across the North Sea. On reaching 4º East, the cloud began to disperse, and the Elbe Estuary was identified with ease. Searchlight and flak activity was intense and accurate as they followed the river inland over small amounts of cloud, and snow on the ground helped to highlight features through the haze. The primary target was attacked by S/L Thompson from 14,000 feet at 20.55, and, it is believed, that Sgt Schneider RCAF and crew also bombed as briefed. Sadly, the details of the sortie could not be ascertained after L9622 crashed at 23.30 one mile north of Northallerton in Yorkshire and burst into flames. Six of the crew died at the scene, and the pilot sustained such severe head injuries, that he was unable to provide a report. It was a crew of mixed nationalities, which included two other members of the RCAF and one of the RNZAF.

F/L Miller finally managed to get a Halifax off the ground and take part in an operation on the 17th, when Bremen was the target for eighty-three aircraft. He and S/L Thompson and their crews departed Leeming either side of 17.15, and headed into ten-tenths cloud that blotted out the ground and prevented all but eight crews from reaching the primary target. The 10 Squadron pair bombed on e.t.a., within three minutes of each other from 14,000 and 16,000 feet shortly

*A row of Halifax bombers under assembly at the Handley Page factory at **Cricklewood**, 1942*

before 20,00, and saw nothing of the results. F/L Miller and crew were briefed to return to Bremen on the 21st as the lone representatives of 10 Squadron in a force of fifty-four aircraft. The took off at 17.59, and once more ran into ten-tenths cloud until reaching 4°E, where it began to disperse to leave relatively clear skies over the target. Searchlights were operating in cones, some of them containing up to fifty beams, and the flak was intense and accurate as the bombs were dropped from 16,000 feet at 20.39. Searchlight glare prevented an assessment of the results, but, as only half of the force claimed to have reached the primary target, it is unlikely that significant damage was achieved.

W/C Tuck put himself on the Order of Battle on the 26th, when Hannover was posted as the target for seventy-one aircraft. He was accompanied by the crews of S/L Webster and F/L Miller in the take-off between 17.12 and 17.37, and, this time, the ten-tenths cloud persisted until 5°E before clearing to leave clear skies over the target area. S/L Webster and crew had made landfall at Cuxhaven, and were heading south-south-east towards the target area when the navigator broke his compass, thus compromising the accuracy of the navigation. They turned 180 degrees and flew up the Schleswig-Holstein peninsular as far as Friedrichstadt, where they unloaded their bomb bay onto a road and railway junction from 12,000 feet at 21.25. F/L Miller and crew arrived over Hannover at 19.56, and dropped their bombs in a single stick from 16,000 feet, before watching them burst across the city. W/C Tuck turned up almost thirty minutes later having crossed paths with a BF109 at 19.40 while at 16,000 feet. The fighter approached from below and made one attack from the port quarter, which W/C Tuck countered by turning towards it, and all contact was lost. The bombing was carried out from 14,000 feet at 20.23, but no results were observed.

Orders were received at Leeming and Middleton-St-George on the 28th to send six Halifaxes each to a forward base at Lossiemouth with a view to attacking the battleship Tirpitz at her mooring in Aasenfjord, situated some fifty miles west of Trondheim in Norway. The 10 Squadron crews were those of W/C Tuck, S/L Webster, F/L Miller, P/Os Godfrey and Hacking and Sgt Peterson, and they flew north during the afternoon to wait for the order to go. S/L Webster broke a bone in his hand in a fall, and returned to Leeming to be replaced by S/L Thompson, the latter travelling to Scotland by rail. In the event, he and the crew of Sgt Peterson would not take part, leaving the others to set off between 02.10 and 02.34 on the 30th for what would prove to be a wasted effort. They flew into ten-tenths cloud with icing conditions, and, possibly a head wind, as all crews experienced excessive fuel consumption and decided to turn back. W/C Tuck penetrated furthest into the frozen north, reaching Bremanger Island, some two hundred miles short of the target, before abandoning the sortie, and he was last to land back at Lossiemouth at 08.10, more than two hours after F/L Miller and P/O Hacking and forty minutes after P/O Godfrey. The five 76 Squadron crews reported similar experiences, but both detachments remained in Scotland awaiting a further opportunity, which, as it happened, did not materialize. During the course of the month the squadron carried out seven operations, launching nineteen sorties for the loss of one Halifax and six crew members.

February 1942

Air Chief Marshal Sir Arthur 'Bomber' Harris
AOC-in-C RAF Bomber Command from February 1942 until the end of the war.

There was no operational activity for the squadron during the first week of the new month, and the detachment finally returned from Lossiemouth on the 7th. A number of small-scale operations had been directed at Brest and its lodgers during the period, and one took place on the evening of the 11th involving eighteen Wellingtons, whose crews would have been unaware that they would be the last engaged in this seemingly endless saga. Vice-Admiral Otto Cilliax, the Brest Group commander, whose flag was on Scharnhorst, put Operation Cerberus into action shortly after the bombers had headed for home, Scharnhorst, Gneisenau and Prinz Eugen slipping anchor at 21.14, before heading into the English Channel under an escort of destroyers and E-Boats. It was an audacious bid for freedom, covered by bad weather, widespread jamming and meticulously planned support by the Kriegsmarine and the Luftwaffe, all of which had been practiced extensively during January. The planning, and a little good fortune, allowed the fleet to make undetected progress until spotted off Le Touquet by two Spitfires piloted by G/C Victor Beamish, the commanding officer of Kenley, and W/C Finlay Boyd, both of whom maintained radio silence, and did not report their find until landing at 10.42 on the morning of the 12th. 5 Group was standing by at four hours readiness when Operation Fuller, which had been planned well in advance for precisely this eventuality, ground slowly into action.

The first of a record number of 242 daylight sorties were dispatched at 13.30, and were followed by others throughout the day, but the squally conditions and low cloud prevented all but a few crews from catching sight of their quarry, and those attacks that did take place failed to find the mark. Seven 10 Squadron Halifaxes took off between 16.04 and 16.14 with W/C Tuck the senior pilot on duty, and had the intention of attacking from high level under the protection of a fighter escort. This idea was abandoned, however, as it became clear that no sighting would be possible unless aircraft came down beneath the very low cloud base. They patrolled off the Den Helder peninsular of the Dutch coast, where the squally conditions and cloud base at 2,000 feet made it almost impossible to catch a glimpse of the enemy, and harder still to carry out an attack. S/L Thompson and crew were alone in catching a momentary glimpse of a large ship through a gap in the clouds, and bombs were dropped from 9,000 feet at 18.12, whereupon the gap closed, and nothing could be observed of the results. The remaining 10 Squadron participants either jettisoned their bombs into the sea or brought them home, and, despite some claims by other units of straddling ships with their bombs, it seems that no hits were scored before the fleet made good its escape into open sea. It is known that Scharnhorst and Gneisenau struck mines laid by 5 Group Hampdens over the preceding nights, and, although their progress was slowed to some extent, all made it safely into home ports by the following morning. The whole episode was a major embarrassment to the government and the nation, but, worse still, cost the Command a further fifteen aircraft and crews on top of all of those sacrificed to this endeavour over the last eleven months. On a positive note, this annoying and distracting itch had been scratched for the last time, and the Command could now concentrate its forces against the strategic targets for which it was best suited.

Thirty-nine aircraft were detailed on the 13th to attack Cologne that night, and six crews from 10 Squadron were included and briefed to attack a "special" target. As they taxied towards a very late take-off, F/L Hacking's aircraft became bogged down and could not be freed. In trying to manoeuvre around it, P/O Godfrey also became stuck, and both sorties were scrubbed. The remaining four took off between 01.15 and 01.41 with F/Sgt Whyte probably the most senior pilot on duty, and all reached the target area to find nine to ten-tenths cloud. A number of topographical features provided a reference, and the presence of many searchlights also helped to guide the aircraft to the general area of the aiming-point, where bombs were released from 16,000 to 17,000 feet between 03.50 and 04.25.

Two days later a new Air Ministry directive decreed that the morale of the enemy population, particularly its workers, would be the new priority, thus opening the way for the blatant area bombing of German urban areas. This had, of course, been a fact of life for a very long time, despite the denials of the government, but it could now be prosecuted openly, without the former pretence that only military and industrial installations were being targeted. Waiting in the wings, and, in fact, already steaming from America's eastern seaboard in the armed merchantman, SS

Alcantara, was a new leader, who would not only pursue this policy with a will, but would also fight Bomber Command's corner against all-comers.

In the meantime, 10 Squadron detailed six Halifaxes to join forces with twenty Whitleys for a 4 Group assault on the docks at St-Nazaire on the 15th. They departed Leeming between 17.30 and 18.00 with F/L Hacking the senior pilot on duty, but soon lost the services of Sgt Gribben and crew, who took off with the pilot's escape hatch open, and could not close it while in flight. The others reached the target area, where they were hindered by thick haze, but managed to pick out the docks and deliver their attacks in the face of moderate searchlight and flak activity from 2,500 and 14,000 feet between 20.33 and 20.52. *(S/L Thompson's attack height of 2,500 feet may have been a typographical error for 12,500 feet, but he did complain about the haze and may have carried out a daring low-level pass.)* F/Sgt Lloyd and crew found it difficult to establish their bearings on return to England, and, on e.t.a at base, failed to raise flying control. A number of QDMs were received, which sent the Halifax roaming around the northlands, all the time eating into its already-diminished fuel reserves. The "Help me, I'm lost" Darky signal was sent out five or six times without response, and, when high ground was spotted by the rear gunner, F/Sgt Lloyd climbed to 5,000 feet to allow the crew to bale out. This was done successfully, leaving L9619 to crash at Angram, Yorkshire, some twenty-eight miles east-north-east of Leeming, at 01.43.

The airfield construction workers showed their humour when laying Slab No.186 on the northerly runway at Melbourne in early 1942. It is still visible today. Hitler's face is drawn in the concrete of the 6 but the 8's image is unclear as to its identity.

148

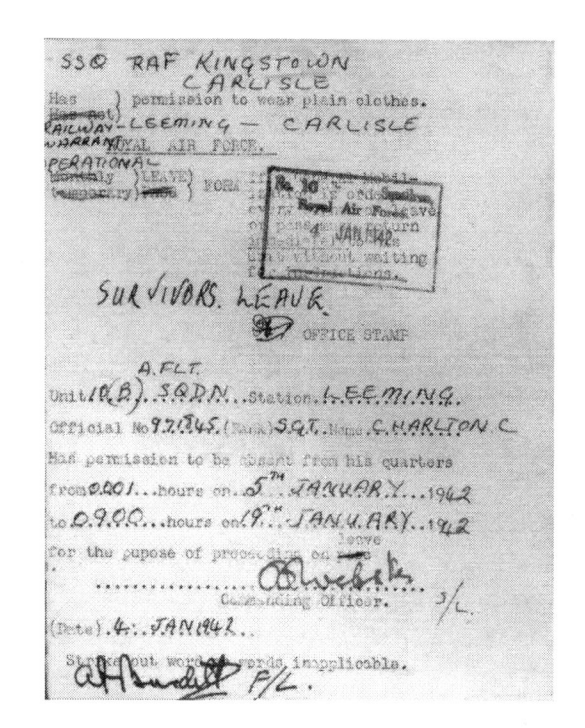

Sgt Chris Charlton

Sgt Chris Charlton was W/Op on F/Sgt Whyte's crew when their Halifax R9374, was seriously damaged by flak and an Me109, while attacking the Scharnhorst & Gneisenau battleships in Brest on 30 December 1941. Ditching some 80 miles south of the Lizard, they were picked up by an Air-sea Rescue launch after 5 hours in a dinghy. The tail-gunner Flt Lt Roach, killed before the ditching, could not be retrieved. Sgt Charlton was given 2 weeks survivor's leave.

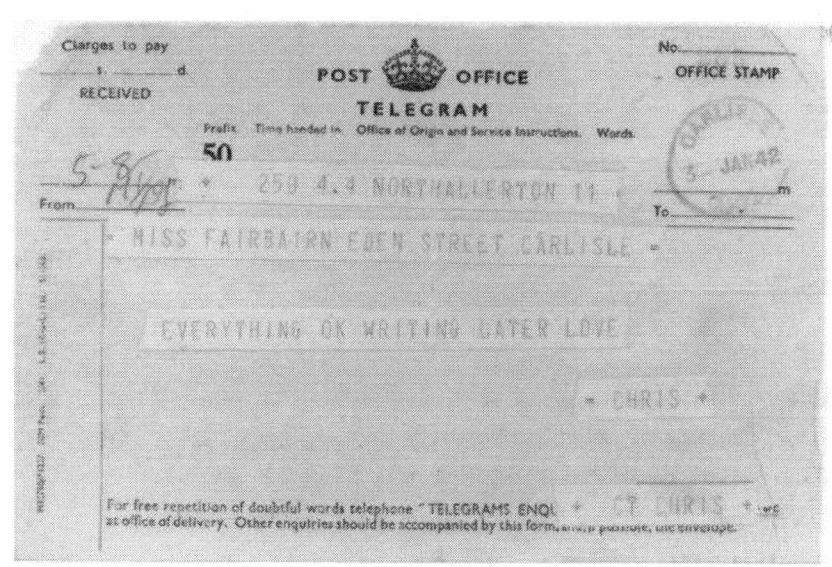

Telegrams were usually dreaded, yet occasionally brought good news: this time for Sgt Chris Charlton's girlfriend Mary Fairbairn, whom he later married in Carlisle in the spring of 1943.

4 Group sent orders out to Leeming and Middleton-St-George on the 21st to prepare aircraft for an operation that night against two aerodromes on the southern tip of Norway. After a number of sorties had been cancelled, three Halifaxes from each squadron took off in the early hours of the 22nd, W/C Tuck, S/L Thompson and F/Sgt Whyte and their crews departing Leeming between 03.53 and 04.30 bound for Mandal. They found considerable cloud over the North Sea, but this dispersed as the Norwegian coast drew near, and S/L Thompson was able to identify Mandal by its illuminated flare-path, before bombing it from 18,000 feet at 06.30. W/C Tuck and F/Sgt Whyte arrived a little later, by which time cloud had rolled in to obscure the target. Both decided to head the twenty miles west to the 76 Squadron target at Lista, which they attacked from around 10,000 feet between 07.00 and 07.09, observing their bombs to fall across the airfield and create dense clouds of smoke.

ACM Sir Arthur Harris took up his appointment as Commander-in-Chief on the 22nd, and set about the task of putting Bomber Command in order. He arrived with firm ideas already in place about how to destroy urban areas, recognising the need to overwhelm the defences by pushing the maximum number of aircraft through the target in the shortest possible time. He also recognized that built-up areas are destroyed more efficiently by fire rather than blast, and it would not be long before bomb loads reflected this. For the remainder of the month he continued with the small-scale operations against Germany's naval ports, particularly Kiel and Wilhelmshaven. and it was during an operation against a floating dock at Kiel on the night of the 26/27th, that the war threw up one of its ironies. A force of forty-nine aircraft was made ready on the 26th to target Kiel's floating dock, where, it was believed, Gneisenau was berthed, and the Deutsche Werke shipyard. The crews of six 10 Squadron Halifaxes had been briefed to attack the shipyard, and the Gneisenau if it could be located, and they took off between 18.23 and 18.42 with F/L Miller the senior pilot on duty. The heavy cloud over the North Sea gave way to clear skies in the target area, but searchlight dazzle prevented the crews from locating the warship, and all turned their attention towards the shipyard, upon which bombing was carried out from 12,000 to 18,000 feet between 21.36 and 21.55. Flashes were observed from bursting bombs, but no detail could be determined in the kaleidoscope of searchlights and exploding flak shells. V9986 failed to return to Leeming, and was lost without trace with the crew of Sgt Wieland. News eventually filtered through that a high-explosive bomb had scored a direct hit on the bow of Gneisenau, now supposedly in safe haven after enduring almost a year of bombardment at Brest, and her sea-going career was ended for good. Her main armament was removed for use as a coastal defence, and the hulk was towed to Gdynia, but never worked on.

During the course of the month the squadron operated on five occasions, dispatching twenty-six sorties for the loss of a single Halifax from which the crew parachuted safely.

March 1942

At the beginning of March, the Halifax squadrons were screened from operations to allow installation of the new navigation device "Gee" or TR1335. As a result, only a few Halifaxes were available for an operation, which would be a template for future operations and a sign of things to come. Bomber Command's evolution to war-winning capability was to be long, arduous and gradual, but the first signs of a new hand on the tiller came early on in Harris's reign with this meticulously-planned attack on the Renault lorry factory, which was located in a loop of the Seine in the district of Billancourt to the south-west of the centre of Paris. The plant was capable of producing 18,000 lorries per year, which was a massive boon to the German war effort, and the attempt to destroy it came in response to an Air Ministry request. The operation would be conducted in three waves, led by experienced crews, and would involve extensive use of flares to provide illumination. Crews were also briefed to attack from as low a level as practicable, both for the sake of accuracy and to try to avoid civilian casualties. In time, such operations would be led by Gee-equipped aircraft, but the 3 Group squadrons already employing the device were forbidden from taking part. A force of 235 aircraft was assembled on the 3rd, a new record for a single target, and 10 Squadron contributed seven Halifaxes to the 4 Group effort of forty-nine Halifaxes, Whitleys and Wellingtons.

The 10 Squadron crews were divided among the waves, and departed Leeming between 18.28 and 19.17 with W/C Tuck the senior pilot on duty and the last away. They all reached the target to find a thin layer of cloud, but good visibility below, from where the bombing would take place. S/L Thompson was the first of the 10 Squadron element to arrive, and, in the absence of any defensive response, released his bombs in two sticks from 1,000 feet at 20.15 and 20.20, observing them to score direct hits, throw debris into the air and cause buildings to collapse. P/O Godfrey let his bombs go in a single pass from 2,900 feet at 20.20, after which the rear gunner sprayed the factory with his .303s. F/Sgt Whyte's bombs were delivered from 2,500 feet at 20.37, and were observed by the crew to burst among the buildings, and it was then a further thirty minutes before W/C Tuck turned up to deliver his attack from 3,600 feet after a shallow dive. F/L Miller and F/Sgt Peterson were in the final wave, and bombed at 22.05 from 3,000 and 6,000 feet respectively, by which time the factory buildings were on fire and a strong smell of burning could be detected. Despite being the first to leave Leeming, Sgt Gribben and crew were the last from the squadron to reach the target area after being delayed by navigational problems, and were outside of the 22.15 deadline for bombing set at briefing. On the way home they bombed the flarepath at Beauvais aerodrome from 4,000 feet, and observed clouds of dust and smoke rising into the air. The operation was a major success for the loss of a single aircraft, and destroyed 40% of the buildings, halting production for a month with the loss of 2,300 vehicles. The success was marred only by the collateral deaths of 367 French civilians in adjacent residential districts, a tragedy that would be repeated in future attacks on urban targets in occupied countries. It was somewhat paradoxical that Harris, as a champion of area bombing, should achieve his first major success via a precision target.

As an industrial centre of enormous significance and home to the giant Krupp concern, Essen was to feature heavily in Harris's future plans. He mounted the first of three raids on the night of the 8/9th, when 3 Group's Gee-equipped aircraft went in first to find the aiming-point and start fires to attract those following behind. A force of 211 aircraft failed to negotiate the Ruhr's ever-present blanket of industrial haze, and the attack was scattered and ineffective. There were similarly disappointing outcomes on the following two nights, and it would soon become clear that Gee was a useful aid to navigation, but could not be relied upon as a blind-bombing device. Meanwhile on the 9th, 10 Squadron dispatched seven Halifaxes to a forward base at Lossiemouth, with a view to operating against the Tirpitz when conditions allowed. F/Sgt Whyte's R9371 crashed on landing because of defective brakes, and was damaged beyond economical repair in the process, while also slightly injuring the pilot and one other. S/L Thompson flew up a replacement Halifax and he and his crew would replace the Whyte crew on the Order of Battle. As matters turned out, no operation was mounted, and the detachment returned to Leeming on the 13th, the morning after a relatively successful raid on the Deutsche Werke and Germania Werft U-Boot construction yards at Kiel. The first successful Gee-led raid fell on Cologne that night, and caused extensive industrial and housing damage.

S/L Guthrie was posted to the squadron from 58 Squadron on the 14th at the start of a lull in operations generally. He would replace S/L Thompson as B Flight commander, he having been posted to the squadron's Conversion Flight on the same day. The King and Queen paid a visit to Leeming on the 25th, and, that night, Harris tried again unsuccessfully to hit Essen. A similar result twenty-four hours later left him frustrated but still determined, and another series of raids would be launched in the following month. The squadron dispatched eleven Halifaxes to Lossiemouth on the 27th to prepare again for an operation against the Tirpitz, and Sgt Gribben and crew joined them on the 28th. 35 and 76 Squadrons also sent detachments to operate out of Kinloss and Tain. In other respects, the Halifax squadrons continued to sit out the period on the ground, and missed out on the attack on the ancient and historic Hansastadt (free-trade) city of Lübeck on the north German coast on the night of the 28/29th. Harris believed, that, if he could provide his crews with the means to locate a target, they would hit it, and coastlines offered the most distinctive features for the purpose of identification. Hence, Lübeck, which not only lay on the Baltic coast to the east of Kiel, but also represented the perfect target for destruction by fire because of the narrow streets and half-timbered buildings in its old centre. Conducted along the same lines as the attack on the Renault factory at the start of the month, it succeeded in destroying almost fifteen hundred houses and seriously damaging almost two thousand more, in a 190-acre area of devastation that represented some 30% of the city's built-up area. It was the first major success for area bombing, and another sign of what was in store for the residents of Germany's towns and cities. There was an outcry following this unexpected attack on Lübeck, which was a vital port for the Red Cross, and an agreement was struck that ensured its future protection from bombing.

The Halifax was not suited to retrospective modifications, which meant, that each time a major alteration was required, a whole new batch of aircraft would arrive on station. Those on squadron charge with L and R serials were sent to Conversion Flights and to other squadrons, mainly 102 Squadron, to make way for new ones with W prefixes. The call to operate against the Tirpitz came on the 30th, and the 10 Squadron element of ten Halifaxes took off between 18.40 and 18.51 with W/C Tuck the senior pilot on duty. They encountered considerable cloud all the way to the Norwegian coast, and, after crossing the islands of Smøla, Hitra and Frøya, it became impenetrable and totally obscured the fjords and valleys on the approaches to Aasenfjord. Most crews jettisoned their load of four 1,000lb mines, but F/L Miller brought his back to Lossiemouth. S/L Webster DFC and crew failed to return in W1043 after crashing into the sea in the target area. S/L Webster's body was eventually found some fifty miles west of Trondheim, and he was the only member of the crew to be recovered for burial. W1044 also crashed in Aasenfjord quite close to where Tirpitz was moored, and there were no survivors from the crew of P/O Blunden RNZAF. The remains of three crew members were recovered, and lie in Stavne Cemetery in Trondheim, which is also the final resting place of S/L Webster. During the course of the month the squadron operated just twice, and dispatched seventeen sorties for the loss of two Halifaxes and crews.

April 1942

The squadron would spend the first two weeks of the new month watching from the side-lines as a new record force of 263 aircraft was sent against Cologne on the night of the 5/6th. Results were disappointing, and another failure at Essen on the night of the 6/7th increased the level of frustration at Bomber Command HQ, and preceded the preparation of yet another new record force, this time of 272 aircraft, whose crews were briefed to attack Hamburg on the night of the 8/9th. This time, twelve Halifaxes from 35 and 76 Squadrons participated, but their presence made no difference to the outcome, and few bomb-loads fell into the city. It was a similar story at Essen on the nights of the 10/11th and 12/13th, when eight and thirteen Halifaxes respectively

Tirpitz memorial Faettenfjord, Norway. The memorial erected to commemorate the air crews in the RAF Bomber Command who were killed during air attacks against Tirpitz in Fættenfjord in March and April 1942. Out of 534 men who took part in the attacks against Tirpitz 64 aircrew (12%) lost their lives. Some of them are buried at Stavne Cemetery in Trondheim. On top of the memorial stone one of the mines that was used in the attacks can be seen as well as some of the anchor chain used for Tirpitz.

of 35 and 76 Squadrons were also involved. The failures at Essen brought to an end a series of eight heavy raids against the city since the night of the 8/9th of March, during which 1,555 sorties had resulted in fewer than two-thirds of the crews claiming to have bombed in the target area, and just twenty-two bombing photos being plotted to within five miles of Essen. In exchange for this, sixty-four aircraft had been lost, industrial damage had been slight, and housing damage modest in the extreme.

When Dortmund was posted as the target on the 14th, eight 10 Squadron crews were called to briefing. They learned that they would be part of an overall force of 208 aircraft and would be the only Halifax unit operating against the primary target, while 102 Squadron would launch its first sorties with the type in a freshman operation to Le Havre. The Leeming element took off between 21.50 and 22.25 with no pilots above pilot officer rank on duty, and three of them experienced excessive fuel consumption that would prevent them from pushing through to Dortmund at the eastern end of the Ruhr. P/O Goldston had to operate his engines at high revolutions as the high-speed blower on the port-outer failed to engage, and he bombed what was believed to be Aachen from 14,000 feet at 01.12, observing a large white explosion in the prevailing good visibility that was enhanced by a flare. Sgt Rochford and crew claimed to have attacked Vogelsang aerodrome from 18,000 feet at 01.30, but there does not appear to be a location of that name within a reasonable distance of the route. P/O Hughes and crew bombed the general area of the Ruhr from 18,000 feet at 02.20, and observed bomb flashes through the haze. On the way home they experienced problems with the oxygen system, and the navigator's sextant stopped working. Having reached England the fuel situation became critical, and, at 04.45, the engines cut at 7,000 feet over Surrey. The captain ordered the crew to bale out, which they did safely, while he attempted a forced-landing. Sadly, without power, the naturally unstable R9492 spiralled in near Hindhead, killing P/O Hughes RCAF. The other squadron participants found the target area, where the inland docks were the briefed aiming-point, and carried out their attacks from 16,000 to 18,000 feet between 01.55 and 02.25. Bomb bursts were observed, as were fires over a wide area, but ground haze impeded attempts to make a detailed assessment. On return, W/O Driscoll and crew ditched W1045 at 05.30 three miles off Beer Head on the south coast of Devon, also after running out of fuel, but they were picked up safely by a rescue launch after spending some time in their dinghy, and were apparently none the worse for the experience. The operation was a failure, which sprayed bombs across a forty-mile stretch of the Ruhr, and caused very little damage in Dortmund.

On the 15th, W/C Don Bennett was posted across the tarmac from his command at 77 Squadron to replace W/C Tuck, who would return to the operational scene as the commanding officer of 51 Squadron in a month's time. Bennett, an Australian with a brilliant mind, famed for his utter lack of humour but unparalleled experience as a civil and military aviator and Master Navigator, had been disappointed at being given a Whitley squadron as his first command, but threw himself into the task of inspiring excellence and loyalty. He was a man who led from the front and thought nothing of taking a sprog crew into battle to give them confidence. Before the month was out, he would demonstrate his resourcefulness and resilience, and, before the summer was over, earn for himself an unlikely promotion that would see him secure a place in Bomber Command history. On the 16th, S/L Seymour-Price was posted in, also from 77 Squadron, to succeed the missing S/L Webster as a flight commander.

P/O L G Whyte and crew April 1942. One of the crews detached to Lossiemouth for attacks on the battleship Tirpitz.

Dortmund was raided ineffectively again on the night of the 15/16th in the absence of Halifaxes, and a modest success gained at Hamburg two nights later was followed by another disappointing attempt on Cologne by an all-Gee-equipped force on the night of the 22/23rd. During the course of the 23rd, W/C Bennett led a detachment of eleven Halifaxes to Lossiemouth in preparation for another tilt at the Tirpitz in company with elements of 35 and 76 Squadrons, which again put in at Kinloss and Tain. That night, Harris launched the first of a four-raid series on consecutive nights against the Baltic port of Rostock and the nearby Heinkel aircraft factory in an effort to repeat the success at Lübeck a month earlier. This first raid failed to impress, after most of the bombing missed the town, and the Heinkel factory escaped entirely. The factory remained untouched also after the following night's attack, but the town centre was heavily bombed, and, while that operation was in progress, the freshman crews of Sgt Wyatt and P/O Baker took off at 21.36 to attack the docks at Dunkerque and drop nickels in the general area. The weather was fine and the visibility excellent on arrival at the French coast, and the docks stood out clearly as the bombs fell away from 14,000 feet shortly before 23.30.

The assault on Rostock continued on the night of the 25/26th, when further damage was inflicted on the town, and the soon-to-be-famous W/C Guy Gibson led a small force of Hampdens to score, at last, some hits on the Heinkel works. 10 Squadron was ordered to contribute two Halifaxes to the 106-strong force being prepared on the 26th for the final raid of the series, which would be split equally between the town and the factory. P/O Clothier and Sgt Moore and their crews departed Leeming at 22.45 and 22.55 respectively, and flew across the North Sea under clear skies and bright moonlight. P/O Clothier's R9497 developed a number of technical issues, which persuaded him to jettison the bombs "live" from 8,000 feet at 00.33 and return home. Sgt Moore and crew had oil leaks and oxygen supply issues to contend with, and bombed Hörnum on the island of Sylt from 10,000 feet at 02.08 as a last resort target. On return, they reported being held in searchlights for five minutes and being chased by a JU88, which they had evaded. Also, on this night, Sgt Allen and crew carried out a freshman sortie over Dunkerque, taking off at 21.29 and returning at 01.41 to report being coned by a dozen searchlights and heavily engaged by flak, which knocked out the port-inner engine and punched a large hole in the tail-plane. The need to take violent evasive action rendered bombing an impossibility, and the load was jettisoned about three miles off the coast from 7,500 feet at 23.55. Once the dust had settled over Rostock, the mini-campaign was assessed to have been enormously effective, having destroyed an estimated 60% of the main town area and caused some damage to the Heinkel works.

Orders were received on the 27th to mount the Tirpitz operation that night from the forward bases in Scotland, and thirty-nine Halifaxes lined up for take-off along with a dozen Lancasters from 44 and 97 Squadrons. The nine 10 Squadron participants took off between 20.32 and 21.15, each carrying four of the 1,000lb spherical mines that did not quite fit into the bomb bay and prevented the doors from fully closing. Tirpitz was known to be moored some fifty feet from the steep bank at the water's edge, and the hope was, that the football-shaped mines would roll down and come to rest beneath her before detonating. All reached the target area to find excellent conditions for bombing, but also an intense flak defence from both banks of the fjord and an effective smoke-screen in operation. The attacks were pressed home from very low level, F/Sgt Rochford and crew delivering their mines from 250 feet at 01.19, and the others from 350 to 1,500 feet between 01.06 and 01.47. There would be no report from W/C Bennett and F/L Miller, who were among four Halifax and one Lancaster crews failing to return. It is believed that F/L Miller RAAF was trying to land W1037 on the frozen Lake Mevatnet after being damaged by flak, but crashed onto farmland at Elverumgaard. Two of the crew lost their lives, and, the fact that they have no known graves, suggests that they may have evacuated the Halifax by parachute and fallen into a body of water. F/L Miller and four others survived to be taken into captivity, and the loss of this experienced crew would be a blow to the squadron. W1041 was also undone by flak, which had set the starboard wing on fire and wounded the rear gunner during the descent from 2,000 feet at the start of the bombing run. The intended bomb-release height of 200 feet was attained, and the vessel's superstructure loomed large in the windscreen, before disappearing suddenly as it was enveloped by the smoke-screen, even before the bomb-aimer could let the mines go. W/C Bennett intended to go round again, and turned back towards Tirpitz only to realize that the flames were increasing and the starboard undercarriage and flap were hanging down. The mines were jettisoned, and Bennett pointed the Halifax east towards Sweden, observing a range of hills ahead with tops at 3,000 feet. It was beyond the wounded Halifax's capability to negotiate such a climb, and the order was given to bale out. According to his account in the book Pathfinder, W/C Bennett was the last to leave, flinging himself through the escape hatch as the starboard wing folded, and pulling the D-ring immediately. The parachute had barely inflated as he hit the snow near Stjørdal, on the edge of Stjørdalfjord. He met up hours later with the wireless operator, Sgt Forbes, and, together, through the courageous assistance of a number of Norwegians, they made it across the frontier into Sweden. *(Bill Chorley's Bomber Command Losses 1942 records W/C Bennett force-landing)*. One other member of the crew also evaded capture, while the remaining four soon found themselves in enemy hands.

The operation was repeated on the following night by a reduced force of twenty-three Halifaxes, of which seven represented 10 Squadron, and eleven 5 Group Lancasters. The 10 Squadron element took off between 20.32 and 20.59 with P/O Godfrey the senior pilot on duty, and were greeted once more by excellent visibility and the same hostile reception from the defences. The Tirpitz was clearly visible despite the use of the smoke-screen, which slid across the vessel as the Halifaxes raced in at low level using the cliffs as a reference. F/Sgt Rochford and crew went in at 200 feet at 01.05, skimming the smoke-screen while under intense fire, and a shell burst in the wireless operator's compartment below the flight deck, seriously wounding the occupant and the second pilot. This crew had pressed on despite losing the use of the rear turret on the way out, and returned safely to Lossiemouth, from where the wounded crew members were removed to hospital. The other crews attacked from 300 to 1,000 feet between 00.29 and 01.05, and only two managed to avoid flak damage. W/O Peterson lost an engine and had an eighteen-inch-square hole punched in his tail-plane, but made it back to a landing at 04.16 at Sumburgh

Newly appointed OC 10 Sqn, W/C D.C.T. (Don) Bennett was shot down over Norway on 27 April 1942 in a raid on the battleship Tirpitz, on his first Squadron mission. He escaped through Sweden re-joining the Squadron a month later only to leave again on 1 July to form the Pathfinder Squadron.

on Shetland, where they were joined at 05.40 by P/O Whyte and crew, who had flown back at 110 mph after the flaps were damaged and fell into the "down" position. W/O Lloyd's aircraft was holed extensively in the fuselage, and the rear gunner was wounded by shrapnel, and P/O Murray and crew came home on three engines. It had proved very difficult in the circumstances to observe the results, but P/O Godfrey and crew, who had attacked from 1,000 feet, had a better view, and reported two of his mines undershooting, one bursting very near the ship and two striking the bank. Three explosions were observed in the water, but no hits were confirmed.

Having endured a torrid time over Dunkerque on the night of the 26/27th, Sgt Allen and crew were invited to return there on the 29th, and took off at 21.22 on a night of clear skies, bright moonlight and excellent visibility. In contrast to their previous experience, they encountered only negligible opposition as they delivered their bombs from 14,000 feet at 23.35, before returning safely home to report observing bursts on the docks. The detachment returned from Lossiemouth on the 30th, when, while landing in a cross-wind, F/L Hacking's W1054 left the runway and suffered an undercarriage collapse, writing it off, fortunately without doing the same to the crew. During the course of the month the squadron operated on six nights, and dispatched thirty sorties for the loss of four Halifaxes, one complete crew, one pilot and a number of airmen.

May 1942

The 3rd of May was the centenary of the Great Fire of Hamburg, of which the Bomber Command planners may well not have been aware when they posted it as the primary target for that night. A force of eighty-one aircraft was made ready, which included twenty Halifaxes, nine of them provided by 10 Squadron, which took off between 22.43 and 23.24 with F/Ls Godfrey and Hacking the senior pilots on duty. F/L Hacking was forced to cut short his sortie at the enemy coast, after a fault in the hydraulics system prevented the bomb doors from closing fully. At a reduced speed, he reached Glückstadt on the East Bank of the River Elbe, still some twenty-five miles short of the target, and dropped his bombs there from 15,000 feet at 02.00. Engine problems persuaded W/O O'Driscoll and crew to jettison their bombs over the sea at 01.37. Seven minutes later they were attacked by an enemy night fighter, which was driven off after a brief engagement, possibly having sustained some damage. At 02.15 a JU88 tried its hand, but was skilfully evaded, and was last seen falling in flames following a burst from the rear turret. The others found ten-tenths cloud over Hamburg, and bombed on estimated positions from 14,000 to 18,000 feet between 01.27 and 02.02. They returned home with no idea that they had been part of an unusually destructive raid, which had started 113 fires, half of them classed as large.

News having filtered through from Sweden that W/C Bennett would soon be on his way home, the highly-experienced W/C James "Willie" Tait was posted in from an O.T.U on the 4th to command the squadron during his absence. It was actually a return to 10 Squadron for Tait, who had originally joined straight from Cranwell in August 1936 and remained until some time in the summer of 1939. While commanding officer of 51 Squadron, Tait had led Operation Colossus in February 1941, to drop paratroopers into southern Italy on what could be termed the forerunner of SAS operations. He then reverted to squadron leader rank to join 35 Squadron, where his vast experience was put to good use in the Command's first Halifax unit. Already

Commanding Officer 10 Sqn W/C J B Tait DSO DF, 4th May 1942 to 4th June 1942 (Temp)

wearing the ribbons of the DSO and DFC, he would be the ideal temporary custodian of 10 Squadron.

The highly industrialized city of Stuttgart had not yet been attacked in numbers, and would be the primary target for the next three nights. A force of 121 aircraft made ready on the 4th did not call upon the services of the Leeming squadrons, and those that did take part would find that Stuttgart offered quite a challenge. Situated in a series of valleys, it was often covered by cloud, but difficult to pick out even on clear nights. The 4 Group element was briefed to aim for the Robert Bosch works in the north-western suburb of Feuerbach, while the others focussed on the city generally, but ten-tenths cloud led to bombs being scattered over a wide area, and the use of a decoy fire-site at Lauffen, fifteen miles to the north, which was cleverly-defended by around thirty-five searchlights, lured away many of the bomb loads.

W/C Tait was able to pass on the good news concerning W/C Bennett's evasion on the 5th, the day on which seven crews were called to briefing, six to learn that they would be operating against Stuttgart that night, while the freshman crew of S/L Guthrie was to target the Loire docks and shipping at Nantes in north-western France. A reduced force of seventy-seven aircraft was made ready for the main event, for which 76 Squadron provided the other five Halifaxes. The 10 Squadron element took off between 21.48 and 21.58 with F/L Hacking the senior pilot on duty, and they were followed into the air by S/L Guthrie and crew at 22.07. Both targets lay under clear skies, but were enveloped in a thick blanket of haze, which prevented identification of ground features. S/L Guthrie bombed from 14,000 feet at 01.15, and observed bursts on the southern strip of Beaulieu Island in the middle of the river. Meanwhile, W/O O'Driscoll and crew had become concerned about excessive fuel consumption, and they attacked an aerodrome from 14,000 feet at 01.08 in the Black Forest region to the east of Strasbourg. F/L Hacking and crew also had fuel issues after having to use high boost and revs to persuade W7666 to climb, and they bombed Saarbrücken from 14,000 feet at 00.45. The others carried out their attacks at the primary target from 8,000 to 14,000 feet between 01.26 and 01.40, before returning with little to report other than a few fires. P/O Joyce and crew landed at Docking and described being attacked by a night fighter on the way home at 03.45, after the guns in the rear turret had become unserviceable. Damage was sustained to the fuselage and port wing root, but there were no crew casualties. According to local reports, no bombs fell in Stuttgart on this night, and the Lauffen decoy site again proved to be very effective.

The third operation against Stuttgart employed a force of ninety-seven aircraft, of which just two of the seven Halifaxes represented 10 Squadron. W/O Peterson and P/O Baker took off at 21.49 and 21.53 respectively, but the former was forced to turn back within an hour with both inner engines leaking glycol. The latter flew out under clear skies, but concerns over fuel consumption led to the decision to bomb Saarbrücken, which was carried out from 13,000 feet at 00.55, after which a large built-up area was seen to be in flames. Six minutes later the Halifax was attacked by an enemy fighter, which was shot down by the mid-upper gunner, and seen to hit the ground and burn out. The operation was another huge disappointment, that failed to land a single bomb within the city.

Orders were received at Leeming on the 8th to prepare five Halifaxes for a major operation that night against the town of Warnemünde, situated on the Baltic coast at the mouth of the Unterwarnow river north of Rostock. It was home to aircraft factories belonging to Heinkel and Arado, and, following the recent success at Rostock, offered the prospect of a relatively straightforward target. The 4 Group plan was to be carried out in three phases, beginning with a high-level attack by four Halifaxes and two Wellingtons, followed by a second high-level attack employing thirteen Halifaxes and one Wellington, at the same time as two Halifaxes and a Wellington targeted searchlights from low level. The third phase involved six Wellingtons running in at low level. A force of 193 aircraft was assembled and air-tests carried out before the bombing-up process began. F/L Hacking landed W7673 at 12.15, but ran off the runway and wrote off it off, happily, without crew casualties. However, this was the third such incident involving F/L Hacking and the second within two weeks. F/L Hacking had been operating frequently over an extended period, and it was thought that he might be suffering from fatigue. S/L Guthrie was the senior pilot on duty as the Leeming element took off between 21.48 and 22.00, and flew out under clear skies. W/O O'Driscoll and crew were attacked by an enemy night-fighter while outbound, and sustained damage before driving it off with return fire. The bombs were dropped on Sylt from 14,000 feet at 01.30, and, five minutes later, a JU88 fired a six-second burst from astern, setting the starboard-inner engine on fire, severing fuel lines and puncturing the starboard tyre and a glycol radiator. The assailant was eventually driven off with some damage of its own, the Halifax's engine fire went out, and a safe return was made to Leeming. An engine issue caused W/O Lloyd and crew to arrive too late to fulfil their brief, so they bombed the town instead from 15,000 feet at 01.05, observing the burst of their 4,000 pounder. P/O Goldston also arrived three minutes later, and they, too went for the town area from 14,000 feet at 01.09. Yet another late arrival was that of P/O Kenny and crew, who bombed

Rostock from 13,000 feet at 01.11, and they also witnessed the burst of their 4,000 pounder. S/L Guthrie had been assigned to the low-level role to be conducted at 2,000 feet, and he and his crew were killed when W7674 crashed in the target area. This was one of nineteen aircraft to fail to return, a massive 10% of those dispatched, many of them falling victim to the intense searchlight and flak defence, while others disappeared into the Baltic, probably after encountering night-fighters. 44 Squadron lost four Lancasters, including the one captained by the newly-appointed commanding officer. The outcome of the raid could not be assessed, and no local report was forthcoming.

F/L Ennis was posted in from 158 Squadron on the 14th, and was immediately elevated to squadron leader rank to replace the missing S/L Guthrie as B Flight commander. The Prime Minister paid a visit to Leeming on the 15th, and he inspected 10 Squadron's air and ground crews. A ten-day lull in operations ended on the 19th, when orders were received at Leeming to prepare for an operation that night against Mannheim, for which a force of 197 aircraft was assembled. Nine Halifaxes were made ready for the main event, and two others for the freshman crews of Sgt Wyatt and S/L Seymour-Price to take to St-Nazaire. The main element took off between 22.00 and 22.21 with F/L Godfrey the senior pilot on duty, and they were followed into the air at 23.00 by the freshmen. W/O O'Driscoll and crew turned back with a failed intercom and jettisoned their bombs into the sea, while W/O Peterson and crew were well on their way to the target when the navigator fainted, and the bombs were dropped on Trier from 16,000 feet at 00.48. The others found Mannheim under clear skies, but in extreme darkness and so cloaked by ground haze, that most carried out their attacks on DR and TR1335 (Gee), doing so from 7,500 to 18,000 feet between 01.11 and 01.30. It was impossible to make an assessment, but local reports estimated roughly ten bomb loads hitting the city, causing only modest damage. Eleven aircraft failed to return, and among them was the squadrons W1057, which disappeared without trace with the crew of P/O Baker. Meanwhile, S/L Seymour-Price had lost his port-inner engine when still a hundred miles short of St-Nazaire, and he jettisoned his bombs into the sea. Sgt Wyatt found the target under clear skies and carried out an attack from 13,000 feet at 02.28, observing bursts on the docks.

There now followed another lull in major operations as Harris prepared for his master stroke. At the time of his appointment as C-in-C, the figure of four thousand bombers had been bandied about as the number required to wrap up the war. Whilst there was not the slightest chance of procuring them, Harris, with a dark cloud still hanging over the existence of an independent bomber force, needed to ensure that those earmarked for him were not spirited away to what he considered to be less-deserving causes. The Command had not yet achieved sufficient success to silence the detractors, and the Admiralty was still calling for bomber aircraft to be diverted to the U-Boot campaign, while reverses in the Middle East also needed to be redressed. Harris was in need of a major victory, and, perhaps, a dose of symbolism to make his point, and out of this was born the Thousand Plan, Operation Millennium, the launching of a thousand aircraft in one night against a major German city, for which Hamburg had been pencilled in. Harris did not have a thousand front-line aircraft, and required the support of other Commands to make up the numbers. This was forthcoming from Coastal and Flying Training Commands, and, in the case of the former, a letter to Harris on the 22nd promised 250 aircraft. However, following an intervention from the Admiralty, the offer was withdrawn, and most of the Flying Training Command aircraft were found to be not up to the task, leaving the Millennium force well short

Prime Minister Winston Churchill visited 10 Sqn at Leeming on 15th May 1942. Escorted here by the Station Commander G/C Strang Graham and OC 10 Sqn, W/C J.B. (Willie) Tait. Graham had been a previous OC 10 Sqn from April 1937 – April 1938, when the Squadron was equipped with the Heyford bi-plane bomber.

of the magic figure. Undaunted, Harris, or more probably his able deputy, AM Sir Robert Saundby, scraped together every airframe capable of controlled flight, or something resembling it, and pulled in the screened crews from their instructional duties. He also pressed into service aircraft and crews from within the Command's own training establishment, 91 Group. Come the night, not only would the thousand mark be achieved, it would be comfortably surpassed.

10 Squadron briefed the freshman crews of Sgts Allen and Clarke on the 22nd, and sent them off to St-Nazaire shortly before 23.00, only for ten-tenths cloud to thwart them both and send them home having jettisoned most of their bombs into the sea. Over the succeeding days, the arrival on bomber stations from Yorkshire to East Anglia of a motley collection of aircraft from a variety of training units gave rise to much speculation, but as usual, only the NAAFI staff and the local civilians knew what was really afoot. The most pressing remaining question was the weather, and, as the days ticked by inexorably towards the end of May, this was showing no signs of complying. Harris was aware of the genuine danger, that the giant force might draw attention to itself, and thereby compromise security, and the point was fast approaching when the operation would have to take place or be abandoned for the time being. Harris released some of the pressure by sanctioning operations on the night of the 29/30th, for which the Gnome &

10 Sqn Groundcrew, Melbourne

Rhone aero-engine and Goodrich tyre factories at Gennevilliers in Paris were the main targets. 10 Squadron made ready five Halifaxes, which took off between 23.59 and 00.16 with S/L Ennis the senior pilot on duty, and all reached the target area. W/O Lloyd and crew described the visibility as good with bright moonlight, and bombed the target from 5,000 feet at 02.50, observing bursts in the centre of the factory. A piece of shrapnel entered the navigator's compartment through the window, and winded him, and three port fuel tanks were holed, but they returned safely to report a successful attack. The other crews reported patches of low cloud drifting across the target, but P/Os Goldston and Murray were able to deliver their bombs shortly after 03.00 from 5,500 to 6,000 feet, observing bursts on the target and a fire that could be seen for thirty miles into the return journey. The cloud prevented F/Sgt Rochford from identifying the target, and a malfunctioning port-outer engine confirmed the need to jettison the bombs. S/L Ennis was also unable to locate the target, and found an aerodrome some twenty miles to the north-west of Paris to attack from 4,000 feet at 03.20.

It was in an atmosphere of frustration and hopeful expectation, that "morning prayers" began at Harris's High Wycombe HQ on the 30th, with all eyes turned upon the chief meteorological adviser, Magnus Spence. After careful deliberation, he was able to give a qualified assurance of clear skies over the Rhineland, while north-western Germany and Hamburg would be concealed under buckets of cloud. Thus, did the fickle fates decree that Cologne would bear the dubious honour of hosting the first one thousand bomber raid in history. At briefings crews were told that the enormous force was to be pushed across the aiming-point in just ninety minutes. This was unprecedented and gave rise to the question of collisions as hundreds of aircraft funnelled towards the aiming-point. The answer, according to the experts, was to observe timings and flight levels, and they calculated also that just two aircraft would collide over the target. It is said, that a wag in every briefing room asked, "do they know which two?"

Late that evening, the first of an eventual 1,047 aircraft took off to deliver the now familiar three-wave-format attack on the Rhineland Capital, the crews having been briefed for one of three aiming-points in the north, south and centre. The older training hacks struggled somewhat reluctantly into the air, lifted more by the enthusiasm of their crews than by the power of their engines, and some of these, unable to climb to a respectable height, would fall easy prey to the defences, or would simply drop from the sky through mechanical breakdown. A total of 154 aircraft took off from 4 Group stations, 131 of them Halifaxes, of which twenty belonged to 10 Squadron and one to its Conversion Flight. They took off between 23.15 and 23.50 with W/C Tait the senior pilot on duty, supported by S/Ls Seymour-Price, Ennis and Thompson. S/L Thompson was forced to turn back after glycol leaks developed in both starboard engines, and the bombs were jettisoned into the North Sea. P/O Drake lost power on two engines, and dropped his bombs live onto a built-up area about a mile inside Germany's border with Holland, while P/O Joyce and crew were about ten miles west of Liege when an electrical fault in the bomb-release system caused the premature dropping of the entire bomb load. F/L Godfrey experienced an engine issue and icing, and dumped his bombs just off the Yorkshire coast near Scarborough, and F/Sgt Rochford did likewise off the Dutch coast after losing the use of the port-outer engine. As S/L Ennis and his scratch crew were approaching Cologne, they were picked up by searchlights and held for twenty-five minutes, which brought accurate anti-aircraft fire upon them. The rear gunner, Sgt Groves, was hit by shrapnel and sustained serious wounds to his head and body as a result, despite which, he and the mid-upper gunner fired down the beams as S/L Ennis took the Halifax down to 50 feet. The bombs were jettisoned at 02.25 at a point estimated to be a mile north of the aiming-point, and, with a dead port-outer engine, and the very real prospect of having to bale out over enemy territory, Ennis ordered the charts to be destroyed. They continued on to the Dutch coast at 400 feet, at which point it became necessary for Sgt Gibbons, the second pilot/navigator, to try to recall what had been on the charts to enable them to reach Manston, where a safe landing was carried out at 04.45, and the casualty removed immediately to hospital.

Despite the numbers being depleted by early returns and outbound losses, 868 aircraft delivered their bombs under largely clear skies and the moonlight predicted by Magnus Spence. The 10 Squadron crews carried out their attacks from 13,000 to 15,000 feet between 01.51 and 02.34 to contribute to what was by far the most effective operation of the war to date. Post-raid reconnaissance and local reports revealed that more than 3,300 buildings had been totally destroyed, and a further twelve thousand damaged to some extent, two thousand of them seriously. Thirty-six large industrial firms suffered a complete loss of production for a period, 45,000 people were bombed out of their homes and the number of fatalities was put at 470. It was not an entirely one-sided affair, however, and, in conditions which favoured attackers and defenders alike, a new record number of forty-one aircraft failed to return. This represented 3.9% of those dispatched, which, when set against the scale of success, was acceptable and sustainable. This figure included 10 Squadron's W1042, which was shot down by a night fighter, and crashed at 02.00 some nine miles south-east of Eindhoven in southern Holland. Sgt Moore died with both gunners, while the four survivors fell into enemy hands. A sad aspect of this operation was a disproportionately high loss rate among aircraft from the training units, and this trend would continue through the year until someone in authority took stock and changed policy. During the course of the month the squadron operated on eight nights, dispatching sixty-three sorties, including one by the Conversion Flight, and lost four Halifaxes and three complete crews.

June 1942

While the Thousand Force remained assembled, Harris was eager to exploit its potential again, and, what better target existed than Essen, that had so frustrated his best efforts thus far? With the warm glow of the success of Cologne still fresh, he issued instructions to prepare another mammoth force for Essen on the 1st, although losses and unserviceability left him with just 956 aircraft. 4 Group managed 136 aircraft from its front-line and training units, including eighteen belonging to 10 Squadron and its Conversion Flight. They departed Leeming in three sections of six, the first between 22.50 and 22.59, the second between 23.45 and 00.01 and the third between 00.05 and 00.33, with respectively S/L Seymour-Price, S/L Thompson and W/C Tait the senior pilots on duty, and the station commander, G/C Graham, joining the crew of W/O Peterson as second pilot. W/O O'Driscoll and crew were already experiencing an engine issue when they were attacked by a ME110 from astern at 00.30. They were able to shake it off, and jettisoned the bombs some twenty miles off the Scheldt Estuary at 00.44 before returning home. P/O Drake and crew were the last to take-off, and, once it became clear that they would not reach the primary target in the stipulated time, they bombed a flak ship off the Dutch coast, without observing the results. The others reached the target area to find ten-tenths low cloud between 3,000 and 8,000 feet, which, combined with the industrial haze, prevented any sight of ground features. Sgt Clarke and crew could not positively identify Essen, and, at 02.19, attacked a built-up area about five miles to the north-east from 12,000 feet, which would have been somewhere near the south-western fringes of Gelsenkirchen. The remaining crews from Leeming bombed on Gee-fixes and the flashes from flak and searchlight activity, doing so from 12,000 to 16,500 feet between 01.03 and 02.27, and, on return, reported the glow of many fires. W1098 crashed near Oeding in Germany, very close to the Dutch frontier, killing P/O Joyce RCAF, who was from Buenos Aires, and five members of his crew, and only the navigator survived to fall into enemy hands.

L9623 was ditched, or, more likely, crashed off the Dutch coast, and, according to Bill Chorley's Bomber Command Losses for 1942, a message was received in England on the 6th to the effect that the rear gunner had lost his life, but the remainder of the crew of P/O Senior were "safe". Bill Chorley then records the crew with a different gunner failing to return in Halifax BB201 from a raid on Emden on the night of the 20/21st, and disappearing without trace to be commemorated on the Runnymede Memorial. The problem is, that the 10 Squadron 540 makes no mention of this crew being on the squadron after the 1st, and it absolutely was not on the Order of Battle for the Emden raid, from which the 10 Squadron participants all returned. The 4 Group 540 also does not list a 10 Squadron Halifax among the casualties on this night, and, anyway, there is no record of Halifax BB201 being on squadron charge at that time. The message on the 6th must have come from a Dutch source, and the likelihood is, that it was to confirm the loss of the aircraft and all on board, and the recovery of the body of the rear gunner alone. Somehow, the message was misinterpreted, and, somehow also, records became confused, leading to the CWGC listing the crew on the Runnymede Memorial for the 21st. This is conjecture and does not explain the different rear gunner. A total of thirty-one aircraft failed to return from Essen, and a dozen of these represented training units. Among them was a Whitley from 10 O.T.U., carrying the crew of the former 10 Squadron flight commander, S/L Tomlinson DFC, who was killed with the other occupants. The operation was an abject failure,

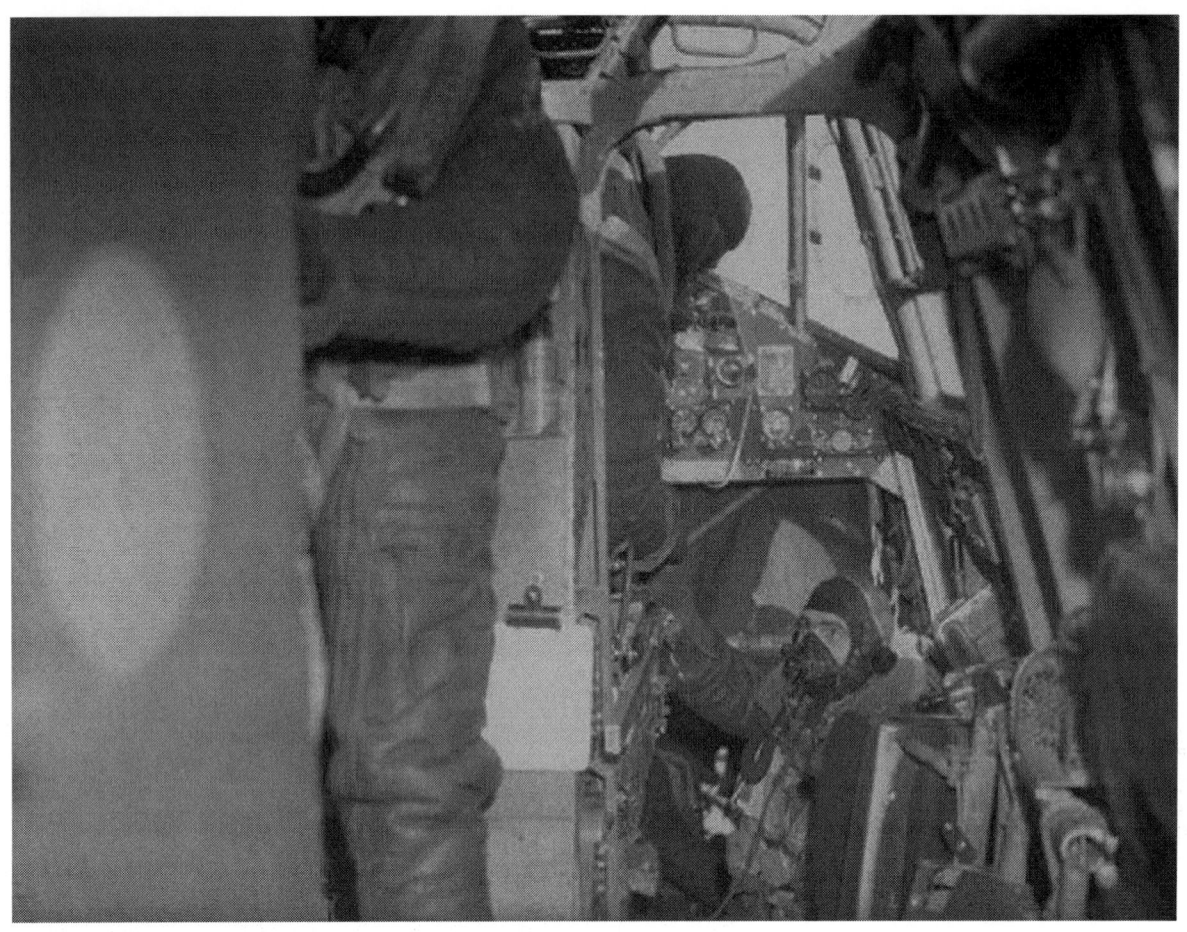

Inside a Halifax

that sprayed bombs right across the Ruhr, particularly in Oberhausen and Duisburg further to the west, while Essen reported the destruction of just eleven houses with a further 184 damaged.

197 aircraft were made ready on the 2nd for the first of a number of follow-up raids against Essen. 4 Group's conversion to four engines had gathered pace, and, with the debut of 405 (Vancouver) Squadron RCAF a few nights earlier at Cologne, there were now six Halifax squadrons to call upon, 35, 76, 10, 102, 78 and 405, and all but 76 Squadron contributed to the thirty-eight of the type detailed for this night's operation. Nine 10 Squadron aircraft took off between 23.20 and 23.41 with P/Os Drake and Kenny the senior pilots on duty, but the latter's navigator became incapacitated through ear trouble, and the sortie had to be abandoned. The bombs were jettisoned into the North Sea from 14,000 feet some forty miles out from the East Anglian coast at 02.28. The others found the entire Ruhr concealed beneath industrial haze that blotted out all but major geographical features, and bombing was carried out on e.t.a., or TR-fix from around 15,000 feet either side of 01.45. No assessment was possible, and local reports confirmed that the city had again escaped serious damage.

By the time that preparations were put in hand on the 3rd to send 170 aircraft against it that night, Bremen had been spared the attentions of a large force since the previous October. 10 Squadron briefed five crews as part of the 4 Group contribution of thirty-six Halifaxes, but F/L Hacking was taken ill at Leeming before take-off, leaving four to depart between 22.53 and 23.00 with

Pre-flight planning

S/Ls Ennis and Seymour-Price the senior pilots on duty. Shortly after crossing the Dutch coast, the latter's port-outer engine developed a glycol leak, and the bombs were dropped on some flickering lights to the east of the Ijsselmeer. The others found the target area to be covered by haze, but the employment of flares enabled the River Weser and the docks to be identified and bombed from 14,000 feet between 01.25 and 01.30. Returning crews were not confident that their efforts had been effective, but local reports confirmed the most destructive raid to date on this target, cataloguing damage to the harbour, shipyards, industrial premises and housing.

This was the final operation presided over by W/C Tait, who relinquished command on the return to duty of W/C Don Bennett on the 4th, following his speedy return from Sweden. W/C Tait was posted to RAF Station Leeming for operations room duties while his future was decided, and, in early July, he would take command of 78 Squadron, where he would remain for four months. He would leave 4 Group for 5 Group in March 1944 to fulfil the role of Base Operations Officer at Waddington, home to two RAAF squadrons, before joining the 5 Group Master Bomber fraternity at Coningsby. The most famous and well-documented period of his career came with his posting to Woodhall Spa to command 617 Squadron as successor to W/C Leonard Cheshire in July. Cheshire was a hard act to follow, but Tait endeared himself to his crews by leading them into battle at almost every opportunity, whether in a Mosquito, a Mustang or a Lancaster, and mostly by daylight during the campaigns against V-Weapon sites and U-Boot pens with the Wallis-designed six-ton Tallboy earthquake bombs. He would lead all three of the operations against the Tirpitz, his Tallboy during the first one in September actually ending the vessel's sea-going career, although this was not known at the time. He would leave 617 Squadron at the end of December after an outstanding career, during which he had undertaken 101 operations and earned a record DSO and three Bars and a DFC and Bar.

Essen was "on" again on the 5th, for which a force of 180 aircraft was made ready. Thirteen 10 Squadron Halifaxes presented themselves for take-off between 22.41 and 23.08 with S/Ls Ennis and Seymour-Price the senior pilots on duty. The former turned back almost immediately after the T1154 radio equipment began to smoke, and, giving the impression that it might burst into flames at any minute, the bombs were jettison onto farmland to the west of Louth in Lincolnshire. P/O Drake's bomb-aimer became indisposed and fainted when outbound over the North Sea, and the bombs were jettisoned some fifty miles off Sheringham. These were added to at undisclosed map references by the loads from the aircraft of P/O Murray and Sgt Clarke, both of whom cited engine issues as the cause of their early returns. The others from Leeming pushed on to the Ruhr to be greeted by the ever-present blanket of industrial haze and intense searchlight and flak activity, and delivered their bombs from 11,000 to 17,000 feet between 01.00 and 01.20, observing bursts but little detail to pass on to the intelligence section at debriefing. W/O Peterson and crew were being held in searchlights as they let their load go from 11,000 feet at 01.16, at which point all four engines cut out, and only restarted at 7,500 feet. At 02.40, while approaching Charleroi in Belgium, a ME110 passed one hundred feet overhead from starboard to port, before turning to attack from astern, scoring hits on the port wing and petrol tanks. The rear gunner returned fire with a two-second burst, which hit the enemy in the fuselage and wings, and caused the starboard engine to burst into flames. The enemy aircraft was last seen spiralling down out of control. The operation was another failure at a cost of twelve aircraft, among which was the squadron's W7696 containing the crew of the long-serving F/Sgt Rochford. The pilot and two others died in the crash some eight miles south-west of Cologne, and the four survivors, including both Canadian gunners, were taken into captivity. The raid scattered bombs over a wide area, with Oberhausen and Bottrop probably receiving the most.

The squadron sat out a heavy raid on the port of Emden on the night of the 6/7th, which destroyed approximately three hundred houses and seriously damaged two hundred others. It was back on the Order of Battle on the 8th, however, when Essen was the primary target yet again, this time for a force of 170 aircraft. Nine Halifaxes were made ready at Leeming, and they took off between 23.02 and 23.22 with S/Ls Ennis and Seymour-Price the senior pilots on duty. S/L Ennis's engines misbehaved during the start-up procedure, delaying his departure and that also of Sgt Allen and crew, to the extent that it soon became clear that neither would be able to reach the target within the stipulated time. Sgt Allen jettisoned his bombs at the mid-point of the North Sea at 00.55, while S/L Ennis had reached the Dutch/German frontier some thirty miles short of the target with overheating engines when he decided to dump his at 01.03. By this time Sgt Wiseman and crew had rid themselves of their load three miles off the Dutch coast after their aileron control failed. The others delivered their attacks over the Ruhr from 14,000 to 17,000 feet between 01.09 and 01.15, before returning home with the usual story of industrial haze and guesswork.

Polish pilot Adam Rymarz flying his Halifax

The following week saw very little operational activity across the Command other than gardening (mining), and it was the 16th before the next operation was posted at Leeming. This was the day on which S/L Ennis DFC was posted to 158 Squadron to be replaced at the end of the month by S/L Griffiths from 102 Squadron. One can imagine the reaction at briefing when Essen presented itself again, this time for a modest force of 106 aircraft. 10 Squadron made ready eleven Halifaxes, which took off between 22.40 and 23.17 with F/L Hacking the senior pilot on duty. They had been instructed at briefing to find alternative targets if visibility over the Ruhr was restricted, and the presence of nine-tenths cloud and thick haze would lead to only a handful of crews attacking the primary target. On a night of poor serviceability for the squadron, W/O Lloyd and crew had a starboard engine fail early on, and jettisoned their load over Wainfleet Sands at 23.48, while Sgt Gibbons and crew lost their port-outer engine and dumped their load south of Bruges at 00.50. P/O Murray and crew had also reached enemy territory before losing the use of their port-outer engine, and they jettisoned their bombs safe at 00.56 over north-eastern Belgium. The other 10 Squadron crews attacked Bonn as an alternative target, doing so from 16,000 to 17,000 feet between 01.09 and 01.55. Sgt Bell and crew were lucky to survive an encounter with an enemy night fighter, which inflicted damage to the rear turret, tail-plane, tail wheel, fuselage and DR compass. This operation brought to an end a series

Engine change

of five raids on Essen in a little over two weeks, during which 1,607 sorties had resulted in no industrial damage, minimal housing damage and the loss of eighty-four aircraft.

A mini-campaign of three medium-scale attacks in four nights was directed at Emden, to follow up on the successful operation earlier in the month. The force of 194 aircraft made ready on the 19th included thirty-seven Halifaxes, of which seven represented 10 Squadron. They took off between 23.15 and 23.30 with three pilots of pilot officer rank leading the way. Sgt Bell and crew continued the exciting start to their operational career with the failure to climb away in W1158 after the flaps and undercarriage refused to retract. The Halifax was crash-landed at Otterington, to the east of Leeming, and was burned out in the ensuing fire. Sgt Bell and crew walked away shaken but barely stirred by their experience. W/O O'Driscoll and crew encountered ten-tenths cloud over the primary target, and headed inland on a southerly heading in search of an alternative. Part of the flare-force had illuminated Osnabrück, situated some eighty miles from the coast, and the O'Driscoll crew joined twenty-eight other crews in bombing here from 15,000 feet at 01.39. The others all located Emden by DR and TR-fix, and carried out their attacks blind from 16,000 feet between 01.25 and 01.59. The following night brought a return to Emden by a force of 185 aircraft, 10 Squadron providing six of the thirty-eight Halifaxes. The Leeming element took off between 23.23 and 23.33 with F/L Goldston the senior pilot on duty, but it wasn't long before P/O Murray was forced to abandon his sortie with rear turret and intercom issues. The others reached the target area to be greeted by a thin layer

Close formation

of ten-tenths cloud between 4,000 and 7,000 feet, and established their positions by DR and TR-fix. Bombing was carried out from 15,500 feet between 01.31 and 01.36, and some of it found the town to cause damage to around one hundred houses. 10 Squadron sat out the final raid of the series on the night of the 22/23rd, when an initial 227 aircraft destroyed around fifty houses and much of the bombing was lured away by decoy fire-sites.

Bremen was posted as the host for the third and final 1,000-bomber raid on the 25th, for which 10 Squadron and the Conversion Flight made ready fifteen Halifaxes. They were to be part of an overall Bomber Command force of 960 aircraft, 131 provided by 4 Group, to which were added five aircraft from Army Co-Operation Command and 102 aircraft from Coastal Command, which had been ordered by Churchill himself to take part, although, its contribution was to be deemed a separate operation. However, this would represent a larger combined force than that sent to Cologne at the end of May. In preparation for the above, Sgt Wiseman took W1155 for an air-test, during which the Halifax crashed on the edge of the airfield at 14.45 and caught fire, killing the pilot and four others on board. The Leeming element took off between 22.47 and 23.50 with F/L Goldston the senior pilot on duty, but soon lost the services of F/Sgt Allen and crew, after the pilot's escape hatch blew off. Sgt Wyatt and crew suffered the failure of a number of instruments, and they jettisoned their bombs at 00.25, while F/Sgt Clarke and crew were forced to abandon their sortie after the a.s.i., failed, and bombed an unidentified town on a TR-fix from 15,000 feet at 01.00. P/O Kenny and Sgt Gibbons were defeated by the ten-

Preparing the night's load.

tenths cloud over Bremen, and back-tracked north-west to Wilhelmshaven, which they also could not see, but bombed anyway from 15,000 feet at 01.32 and 14,000 feet at 02.18 respectively. Sgt Saunders selected the town of Oldenburg by DR and TR-fix as an alternative, situated some twenty miles to the west of Bremen, and bombed it blind from 13,000 feet at 02.09. The remaining 10 Squadron participants carried out their attacks from 13,000 to 15,000 feet between 01.25 and 02.17, and returned home with little to report. The raid fell well short of what was achieved at Cologne, but surpassed by far the debacle at Essen. Even so, the destruction of 572 houses with more than six thousand damaged was a modest return for the massive effort expended and the cost of a record forty-eight aircraft, of which thirty-one came from the training units and three from Conversion units/flights.

Reversals in the Middle-East campaign had resulted in a request for heavy bombers to be sent out, and 10 and 76 Squadrons were ordered to prepare a detachment each of sixteen aircraft. As far as both squadrons were concerned this was a to be a sixteen-day sojourn for specific operations, and the first from Leeming, W1174 and W7756, departed for the staging post at Gibraltar on the 29th in the hands of S/L Seymour-Price and W/O Peterson and their crews. During the course of the month the squadron operated on nine occasions, dispatching eighty-nine sorties for the loss of four Halifaxes and three crews.

July 1942

Bremen received three follow-up raids in five nights, each with a degree of success, culminating in one by 325 aircraft on the night of the 2/3rd, an operation supported by two 10 Squadron Halifaxes. Sgt Lawer and P/O Fegan and their crews took off at 23.05 and 23.17 respectively, and that was the last that was heard from the former, whose W1056 crashed off the Dutch coast without survivors at 01.40. The latter found the target area under three-tenths cloud and haze, and bombed blindly on e.t.a., from 12,500 feet at 02.09. The raid was modestly successful, and damaged a thousand houses to some extent, while sinking one ship in the harbour and damaging others. On the 4th, W/C Bennett was told to hand over command of the squadron to the B flight commander, S/L Griffiths, and then to report as supernumerary to 4 Group HQ pending a permanent posting. S/L Carter was posted to the squadron on the 5th from 13 O.T.U, and this was the day also when seven Halifaxes left for Gibraltar, each carrying three ground personnel and spares. They were followed by the final seven on the 6th, which left the home echelon effectively bereft of aircraft and air and ground crews with which to carry on. Also on their way overseas were the squadron engineering officer, F/L Jones, and F/L Finch of Station HQ as intelligence and operations officer. In total, forty-eight NCOs and airmen of the various maintenance sections were involved in the move, but, the activities of this detachment, which would no longer fall under Bomber Command control, are outside of the scope of this profile. It is interesting to note, however, that F/L Hacking, already the survivor of three hairy incidents, was involved in yet another one on the 8th. Having taken off from Gibraltar bound for Aqir, he was forced to turn back, and crash-landed W1178, writing it off, happily, though, again without crew casualties. On arrival at Aqir, 10 and 227 Squadrons were combined to form 10/227 Squadron, while 76 Squadron was amalgamated with 454 Squadron to form 76/454 Squadron. The problem was, that both squadrons had been misled, having been posted permanently, and would soon finding themselves on standard night operations under 206 Group with no prospect of a return to Bomber Command. Ultimately, the Middle-East contingent would be absorbed into 462 Squadron, while the home echelon would continue to operate at reduced capacity while it underwent a rebuilding process.

There would be no operations for the squadron for the next two weeks, during which period fresh crews arrived from 19 O.T.U., and P/O Hillier and crew were welcomed back into the fold on the 14th, after returning from overseas as surplus to requirements following the writing off of another Halifax at Gibraltar. Leeming had been declared to be partially unserviceable at this time, and S/L Griffiths, P/O Fegan and P/O Hillier were detached to Topcliffe to participate in an operation that night against the Vulkan U-Boot construction yards in the Vegesack district of Bremen, while S/L Carter was put in command of the remainder of the squadron at Leeming. P/Os Hillier and Fegan and their crews departed Topcliffe shortly after 23.45 as part of a ninety-nine-strong all-four-engine force, and the former returned alone at 04.26 to make their report. They had encountered ten-tenths cloud at 6,000 feet, which obscured the ground, and delivered their seven 1,000 pounders on a TR-fix from 16,000 feet at 02.04. W1106 failed to return home with the crew of P/O Fegan, and was lost without trace. The operation was a complete failure, that failed to land a single bomb in Vegesack, and demonstrated again the limitations of Gee as a blind-bombing device.

A new campaign against Duisburg had begun on the night of the 13/14th, when a force of 194 aircraft encountered cloud and electrical storms. The raid failed to inflict more than minor housing damage, but, as he had done at Essen, Harris would persist with further attempts over the ensuing three weeks. 291 aircraft were made ready on the 21st for the second raid of the Duisburg series, for which two 10 Squadron Halifaxes were detailed and flown over to Topcliffe in the hands of S/L Griffiths and P/O Hillier and their crews. They took off at 23.36 and 23.48, and both arrived in the target area to find eight-tenths cloud and industrial haze, which made it difficult to identify pinpoints. They bombed on a TR-fix and by the light of flares from around 15,000 feet, but were unable to observe any results. Post-raid reconnaissance and local reports

W/C R K Wildey DFC, Commanding Officer from 26th July 1942 to 15th October 1942, when he was killed on a Cologne raid.

suggested a moderate amount of housing damage and some war-industry factories being hit, but some of the Gee-force had dropped their flares to the west of the Rhine, causing a proportion of the bombing to fall into open country. P/O Hillier and crew were the sole 10 Squadron representatives in a force of 215 aircraft sent back to Duisburg on the 23rd. They departed Topcliffe at 00.35, and ran into ten-tenths cloud from 3°E all the way to the target, where a number of breaks allowed sight of the Rhine. Bombing was still carried out on a TR-fix, however, and, although their own bomb bursts could not be identified, others were, and fires could be seen burning. The fourth raid of the series, conducted by an initial force of 313 aircraft, took place two nights later, when P/O Hillier and crew again operated on behalf of the squadron alone, taking off from Topcliffe at 00.01 and bombing the target from 16,000 feet two hours later in the face of an intense and accurate searchlight and flak defence. They observed plenty of bomb bursts and a large fire, and local reports confirmed housing damage, but on a smaller scale than during the two previous attacks.

W/C Wildey was posted in on attachment from 4 Group HQ on the 26th prior to officially taking command of the squadron and setting about the task of bringing "Shiney Ten" back up to full strength. That night, S/L Griffiths and P/Os Hillier and Black operated out of Topcliffe against Hamburg as part of a force of 403 aircraft. They took off between 23.06 and 23.15, and flew through cloud and icing conditions to reach the target, which lay under clear skies and a full moon affording excellent visibility. S/L Griffiths and P/O Black bombed from 13,000 feet and P/O Hillier from 16,000 feet between 01.32 and 01.46, and they observed many scattered fires in and around the docks area and smoke drifting across the city. The searchlight and flak defence was up to its usual intensity, and night fighters were seen to be prowling in the vicinity, S/L Griffiths twice taking evasive action as his Halifax was stalked. Local reports confirmed a highly successful operation, which caused widespread damage, particularly in residential and commercial districts, where more than eight hundred houses were destroyed and eight hundred fires had to be dealt with. It was an expensive night for the Command, however, which posted missing twenty-nine aircraft and crews, 7.2% of the force, and the loss of eight out of seventy-three Halifaxes represented an alarming 10.9%.

S/L Griffiths was posted to 102 Squadron on the 28th, while F/L Debenham came in the opposite direction on the same day. A return to Hamburg that night should have involved 4 Group, but adverse weather conditions over home bases prevented the participation of its aircraft. The weather outbound caused major problems, and the scattered remains of the original force of 256 aircraft that arrived in the target area produced little damage. The first large raid of the war on Saarbrücken was posted on the 29th, and a force of 291 aircraft made ready. P/Os Hillier and Black and Sgt Hampton were the 10 Squadron representatives and took off from Topcliffe either side of 23.15. When the occupant of Sgt Hampton's rear turret tested his guns over the sea, they were found to be unserviceable, and this forced the abandonment of the sortie and the jettisoning of the bomb load at 00.50 at a point twenty-five miles off North Foreland. The remaining pair pressed on to reach the target after flying over eight-tenths cloud with tops at 13,000 feet all the way from the Dutch coast. P/O Black attacked from 16,000 feet at 01.38, and observed bursts in the marshalling yards, while P/O Hillier bombed from 13,000 feet at 01.45, but saw nothing other than existing fires. In view of what had been expected to be a weak defence, the crews had been encouraged at briefing to bomb from as low a level as possible, and three-quarters of the force had complied from below 10,000 feet, causing much damage in central and north-western districts and the destruction of almost four hundred buildings.

F/Sgt Saunders and crew were sent over to Topcliffe on the 31st to participate in a major operation against the Ruhr city of Düsseldorf, for which a force of 630 aircraft was assembled from the front-line squadrons and the training units. This would be the first time that more than a hundred Lancasters had operated together. The Saunders crew took off at 23.50, and headed out into low cloud with a base at 1,200 feet, the pilot trying but failing to drag the Halifax above 9,000 feet because of defective blowers. The bombs were jettisoned as they approached the Dutch coast, and they landed safely at 04.07 to bring the squadron's operations for the month to and end. The attack on Düsseldorf, which spilled across the Rhine into Neuss, caused widespread damage across the two cities, set off almost a thousand individual fires and destroyed 453 buildings, while damaging thousands more to some extent. It was another night of heavy casualties for the Command, however, which registered the loss of twenty-nine aircraft. During the course of the month the squadron dispatched fifteen sorties on eight operations for the loss of one Halifax and crew.

August 1942

W/C Wildey officially took command of the squadron on the 1st, but there would be no operational activity until the 6th, when P/O Black and Sgt Hampton were sent over to Topcliffe to participate in the final raid of the series on Duisburg. They took off at 00.33 and 00.44 respectively as part of an overall force of 216 aircraft, and, for a change, encountered good weather conditions and excellent visibility over the target apart from the usual industrial haze. Sgt Hampton bombed from 15,000 feet at 03.02, and the burst of the two 4,000 pounders was observed to the east of the Rhine. P/O Black's bombs were also seen to detonate in the city, and large fires were observed from north to south of the built-up area. Despite the claims by returning crews, local reports put the level of destruction at just eighteen buildings, and this concluded another highly disappointing campaign against a major Ruhr city and massive contributor to war materials production. The five raids in three weeks, which had involved 1,229 sorties, had resulted in the destruction of 212 houses at a cost of forty-three aircraft.

P/O Hillier was posted to 405 (Vancouver) Squadron on the 8th, as new crews were posted in to help rebuild the squadron and return it to its former status. P/O Black and Sgt Hampton and their crews were sent back to Topcliffe on the 11th to participate that night in an operation to Mainz in southern Germany, while the freshman crews of F/L Debenham and Sgts Somerscales and Cobb would go to Le Havre in the company of five other Halifaxes to bomb the docks. Those bound for southern Germany took off at 22.15, and, soon afterwards, just as they were crossing the English coast, P/O Black and crew lost their a.s.i. The Halifax went into a stall and lost three thousand feet before being recovered, despite which, the outward flight was continued as far as the French coast, where they became coned in searchlights and heavily engaged by flak. Unable to take effective evasive action, they turned back and jettisoned the bombs live into the sea some ten miles south-west of Boulogne. Sgt Hampton and crew reached the target area having flown out in favourable weather conditions, and were greeted by five-tenths cloud with tops at 11,000 feet. A built-up area was seen below, and the seven 1,000 pounders were delivered from 14,000 feet at 01.01. They contributed to the substantial damage inflicted during the first major raid on this ancient and culturally-rich city, and returned safely on another night of heavy casualties amounting to twenty failures to return and others lost in crashes at home. 78 Squadron suffered the loss of four Halifaxes on this night, and 405 Squadron one, which represented a loss rate of 20% among the Halifax brigade. *(The Bomber Command War Diaries by Martin Middlebrook and Chris Everitt mention just six failures to return.)* Meanwhile, the freshman crews had taken off either side of 01.00, and all reached the target area to find good visibility and ground features easy to identify. Bombing took place from 12,000 to 17,000 feet between 03.07 and 03.34, but little was seen of the results because of searchlight glare. 35 Squadron posted missing one of its Halifaxes, to complete a bad night for the type and the group.

419 Squadron arrived at Leeming on the 12th on posting from 3 Group, but would remain for just one week before moving on to Topcliffe, from where it would continue operations on Wellingtons until becoming a founder member of the Canadian 6 Group on New Year's Day. A follow-up raid on Mainz that night did not involve 4 Group, but inflicted further damage on the city. In fact, 4 Group had been ordered to suspend operations between the 13th and the 22nd while it concentrated on intensive training. Losses from operations and training incidents among the Halifax brigade had set off alarm bells at group and Bomber Command HQs, and the most pressing problem was found to be rudder overbalance, which caused the rudders to lock to the left or right and send the aircraft into an unrecoverable spin at high level, and side-slip or flip over onto its back at low level, usually with fatal consequences for the occupants. The defect would eventually be rectified by fitting redesigned oblong fins, while other external fittings, like exhaust shrouds, which ruined the aerodynamic characteristics of the aircraft, would be removed or altered. A second problem was identified in the training of new crew captains, and this would also be addressed.

A new era for Bomber Command began on the 15th, with the formation of the Pathfinder Force, although it was two days later before the four founder heavy squadrons arrived on their stations in Huntingdonshire and Cambridgeshire. 35 Squadron moved into Graveley with its Halifaxes to represent 4 Group, and it would be the responsibility of 10 Squadron and the other front-line units to provide a steady supply of their most promising crews. The other founder members

Interior of a Handley-Page Halifax B Mk II Series I looking toward the flight engineer's in-flight position, prior to take-off. The flight engineer is sitting on the "dicky" seat on the right of the pilot, which was the flight engineer's usual position on take-off so he could assist the pilot with the throttles, which were between them. Below the flight engineer can be seen the navigator at his position with the front gunner alongside him.

were 83 Squadron, which took up residence at Wyton, the Pathfinder HQ, as the 5 Group representative operating Lancasters, while 156 Squadron retained its Wellingtons for the time-being at Warboys, and would draw fresh crews from 1 Group, and 3 Group would be represented by the Stirling-equipped 7 Squadron at Oakington. In addition to the above, 109 Squadron was posted in to Wyton, where it would spend the next six months developing the Oboe blind-bombing device and marrying it to the Mosquito under the command of W/C Hal Bufton, the brother of 10 Squadron's former commanding officer. The new force would occupy 3 Group stations, falling nominally under 3 Group administrative control and receiving its orders through that group, which was commanded by AVM Baldwin, whose tenure, which had lasted since just before the outbreak of war, was shortly to come to an end.

A "Pathfinder" force was the brainchild of the former 10 Squadron commanding officer, G/C Sid Bufton, now Director of Bomber Operations at the Air Ministry, who had used his best crews at 10 Squadron to find targets by the light of flares and attract other crews by firing off a coloured Verey light. It could be said, that the concept of target finding and marking was born at 10 Squadron. Once at the Air Ministry, Bufton promoted his ideas with vigour, and gained support among the other staff officers, culminating with the idea being put to Harris soon after his enthronement as Bomber Command C-in-C. Harris rejected the principle of establishing an elite target-finding and marking force, a view shared by the other group commanders with the exception of 4 Group's AVM Roddy Carr. However, once overruled by higher authority, Harris gave it his unstinting support, and his choice of the former 10 Squadron commanding officer, and still somewhat junior, G/C Don Bennet, as its commander was both controversial and inspired, and ruffled more than a few feathers among more senior officers. Bennett, as mentioned earlier, was among the most experienced aviators in the RAF, and a Master Navigator of unparalleled experience, with many thousands of hours to his credit. He also had the already-documented recent and relevant experience as a bomber pilot through his commands of 77 and 10 Squadrons, and had demonstrated his strong character when evading capture and returning from Norway after being shot down. Despite his reserve, and his impatience with those whose brains operated less effectively than his, he would inspire in his men great affection and loyalty, along with an enormous pride in wearing the Pathfinder badge. He would forge the new force into a highly effective weapon, although this was not immediately apparent when it operated for the first time on the night of the 18/19th, and failed to find the port of Flensburg. Situated on the eastern coast of the Schleswig-Holstein peninsular close to the Danish frontier, it should have been easily identified, but most of the bombing fell on Danish soil in what was an ignominious debut.

On the 17th, 10 Squadron had been informed that it would be moving home, and was to take up residence at Melbourne, a satellite of Pocklington in southern Yorkshire. The move was to be completed as soon as possible, and took place over the 18th and 19th, and the following eight days were spent by the air and ground crews familiarizing themselves with the lay of the land and the local watering holes. Leeming was eventually to be taken over by the Canadian 6 Group, along with the other stations in north Yorkshire, and 10 Squadron's departure would allow 408 Squadron to move in in September on temporary posting to 4 Group from 5 Group to begin conversion onto the Halifax. The second Pathfinder-led operation was directed at Frankfurt on the night of the 24/25th, and this, again, failed to produce the hoped-for results. It should be remembered that the Pathfinders, at this stage, were on hand to locate and illuminate the target with flares, and not to mark it with the target indicators that would be introduced in time as the fledgling force developed new tactics. The third outing brought an improvement at Kassel on the night of the 27/28th, when good illumination allowed the main force crews to inflict some useful if not excessive damage.

The squadron was finally recalled to action on the 28th after its long period of inactivity, and the crews of S/L Carter and Sgts Cobb and Wilmott flew over to Pocklington, the home of 102 Squadron, for bombing up. This arrangement would continue until late October while the runways at Melbourne were brought up to standard. The 10 Squadron trio took off between 20.00 and 20.07 and headed for Saarbrücken as part of an overall force of 113 aircraft, while 159 others made their way to Nuremberg. The Saarbrücken force crossed the Channel under clear skies, before picking up four to six-tenths cloud between 14,000 and 17,000 feet at the Belgian coast, which then persisted all the way to the target. While flying at 15,000 feet at 22.17 south-west of Charleroi, Sgt Cobb and crew were attacked head-on by two single-engine fighters, which fired short bursts before breaking away to starboard. Forty minutes later, south-

Melbourne airfield in 2019. Many airfields in Yorkshire and Lincolnshire were situated close to others. It was not unheard of for aircraft to land at the wrong airfield, particularly in poor visibility weather conditions (Google Maps).

east of Luxembourg, a FW190 approached four times from the starboard quarter, but evasive action threw it off before any shots were fired. Visibility was poor over the target, largely because of ground haze, but the River Saar stood out clearly as a reference. S/L Carter had the frustration of an electrical fault in the bomb-release system, and had to bring his load home, and the other two crews managed to release some of their bombs, but also suffered a partial hang-up and had to return some incendiaries to store. During the course of the month the squadron operated on just three occasions, and dispatched ten sorties without loss.

September 1942

The first half of September would bring an unprecedented run of effective attacks on targets in Germany, and 10 Squadron would return to a schedule of regular operations, even though in small numbers. The new month got off to an unpromising start, however, when Saarbrücken was selected to host its second visit from the Command in four nights. A force of 231 aircraft included the three 10 Squadron crews of W/C Wildey, F/L Debenham and Sgt Somerscales, who took off from Pocklington either side of 23.30, each carrying an all-incendiary bomb load. The ten-tenths cloud over the North Sea began to disperse at the Belgian coast, but, shortly afterwards, F/L Debenham turned back with a glycol leak in the starboard-outer engine, and jettisoned the contents of the bomb bay into the sea twenty miles off Dunkerque at 01.20. W/C Wildey identified the primary target, and bombed it from 14,000 feet in a single pass at 02.05, and Sgt Somerscales followed up nine minutes later from the same height, both crews reporting their incendiaries falling into the old town to add to the fires already burning. It was only later, that the "black" posted by the Pathfinders came to light, after the attack was plotted to have fallen onto the small, non-industrial town of Saarlouis, situated thirteen miles to the north-west on a bend in the river similar to that at the intended target. The bombing was accurate, and the town suffered extensive damage, much to the despair of its residents.

The accent remained on southern Germany on the following night, when Karlsruhe was posted as the primary target. A force of two hundred aircraft was made ready, of which just Sgt Cobb and F/Sgt Saunders and their crews would represent 10 Squadron. They departed Pocklington at 21.14 and 21.41 respectively, the former loaded with six SBCs of 4lb and six of 30lb incendiaries and the latter with four 1,000 pounders. Sgt Cobb and crew arrived early, ahead of the Pathfinders, but picked out the distinctive fingers of the Rhine docks and dropped their bombs from 14,000 feet at 01.43. F/Sgt Saunders and crew reached the target twenty minutes later and delivered their high explosives from 12,000 feet, aiming at the fires already burning. Post-raid reconnaissance revealed two hundred fires burning simultaneously, and extensive damage to housing and industrial buildings at a cost of eight aircraft.

F/L Debenham and Sgts Cobb and Somerscales were called for duty again on the 4th, learning at briefing that Bremen was to be their destination that night. The Pathfinders were developing their techniques, and this night would see the implementation of what would become standard practice for future operations. They would be divided into three distinct phases, the first, "illuminators", whose job was drop white flares to light up the general area for the second phase, the "visual markers" to drop coloured flares if they could identify the aiming-point. The third phase consisted of "backers-up", who were to drop incendiaries onto the coloured flares. A force of 251 aircraft was assembled, the 10 Squadron trio taking off either side of midnight each loaded with five 1,000 pounders. They flew out in good weather conditions, which persisted all the way into north-western Germany, where there was also a hint of moonlight. The target was located by the river, the shape of the docks and nearby woods, and, of course, the Pathfinder marking, and the bombing by the 10 Squadron crews took place from between 15,000 and 16,500 feet either side of 02.00. Sgt Cobb and crew reported the glow of fires still visible from ninety miles away. They also described being stalked by a JU88, which came up on the port quarter while they were homebound at 8,000 feet at 02.59, and positioned itself about eighty feet below the tail out of sight of the rear gunner. Sgt Cobb took evasive action without being able to break contact, before making another sharp, climbing turn to starboard, which gave the rear gunner the chance to fire a long burst. Shells were seen to enter the assailant's fuselage and its starboard engine burst into flames, before it fell away in a spin at 03.05 without once firing its guns. Reconnaissance photos revealed the destruction of 450 dwelling units and twenty-one industrial buildings of varying sizes. A further 1,361 houses were seriously damaged as were many industrial premises, and the Atlas shipyard was hit.

Harris couldn't resist another swipe at Duisburg, and a force of 207 aircraft was made ready on the 6th. 10 Squadron contributed the crew of P/O Morgan, who would be undertaking their maiden operation with the squadron. They took off in W7767 at 01.15, and were never seen again after crashing without survivors somewhere in Germany. The weather conditions in the target area were described as good, and the Pathfinder effort reported as helpful, but the reflection of their flares on the haze combined with the smoke to obliterate ground detail. The impression of returning crews was that, despite the many fires, the attack had failed to achieve concentration, and some bomb loads had fallen west of the Rhine. They were largely correct, but this was reported locally as the most effective raid on the city to date, which caused the destruction of 114 buildings and serious damage to three hundred more. The run of successes would be brought to a temporary halt at Frankfurt, for which a force of 249 aircraft was put together on the 8th. 10 Squadron contributed the crews of Sgts Cobb and Somerscales, who departed Pocklington at 20.38 and reached the general target area to find good visibility, marred only by haze. The Pathfinders were unable to establish their position, but Sgt Somerscales and crew identified the River Main, and bombed what they believed was the primary target from 16,000 feet at 23.33. Sgt Cobb and crew bombed a built-up area believed to be Mainz from 12,000 feet three minutes later, and both returned safely to report on the intensity of the searchlights and flak and the number of fires observed. Local reports suggested few bombs falling in Frankfurt, while Rüsselsheim, situated some fifteen miles to the south-west near Mainz and home to the Opel tank factory, bore the brunt of the attack.

The training units were called upon again on the 10th to bolster a force being made ready for Düsseldorf that night. A total of 479 aircraft included six 10 Squadron Halifaxes, which took off between 20.03 and 20.22 with F/L Debenham the senior pilot on duty. The Pathfinders were carrying "Pink Pansy" target indicators for the first time in converted 4,000lb bomb casings, and these were put to good use on a night of moderate visibility, enabling the crews to identify the Rhine but not ground detail through the haze. The 10 Squadron crews delivered their mixed loads of 4lb and 30lb incendiaries and 1,000 pounders from 11,000 to 17,000 feet in the face of intense searchlight and flak activity between 22.31 and 22.44, and reported many clusters of fires developing. It was clear at debriefing that the crews were fairly confident about the

The 10/227 Sqn detachment later moved from Palestine to Fayid in Egypt. Tobruk, Libya, and Iraklion, Crete were two of their frequent targets.

outcome of the raid, and comments were made concerning the effectiveness of the Pathfinder marking. Local reports confirmed this as a most destructive attack, which had caused a total loss of production at more than fifty industrial firms in Düsseldorf and Neuss. 911 houses had been destroyed and fifteen hundred others seriously damaged, and almost twenty thousand people were left without homes. It was by no means a one-sided affair, however, and the loss of thirty-three aircraft, or 7.1% of the force, was a bitter pill to swallow, particularly for the training units, to which seventeen of the missing belonged.

Despite the losses, the training units were again on hand to bolster the numbers assembled for a return to Bremen on the 13th, while 10 Squadron made ready a contribution of five Halifaxes to the overall force of 446 aircraft. They took off between 00.02 and 00.26 with P/Os Margetts and Munro the senior pilots on duty, but lost Sgt Campbell and crew to a glycol leak soon after take-off. The others pressed on to reach the target area in good weather conditions but also haze that blotted out ground detail. The general built-up area was easy to pick out by the intensity of the defences and the fires already burning, and the 10 Squadron quartet bombed from 7,000 to 15,000 feet between 02.25 and 02.55 before returning safely to home airspace. On landing at Great Massingham, BB192 ran off the end of the runway, crashed through the boundary fence and came to a halt on its belly in a severely-damaged state, but P/O Munro RAAF and crew walked away without injury. This was a highly effective raid, which, by far surpassed the results achieved in the "Thousand" raid in June. Local authorities reported the destruction of 848 houses and damage to the Focke-Wulf factory and the Lloyd dynamo works, each of which suffered a complete or partial loss of production.

A force of 202 aircraft was made ready for Wilhelmshaven on the 14th, when the trusty old Hampden would make its swansong as a front-line bomber. 10 Squadron briefed four crews, and they took off shortly after 20.00 with F/L Debenham the senior pilot on duty. They flew out over considerable amounts of cloud, which dispersed a little in the target area to seven-tenths at 5,000 feet. The target was located by the shape of the coastline, and confirmed by Gee-fix, and bombing took place from 14,000 to 17,000 feet in a five-minute slot to 22.08. It was difficult to assess the outcome, but local reports confirmed this as the most destructive raid yet on this significant naval port. The squadron had now rebuilt sufficiently to allow it to revert to a two-flight status, which prompted the promotion of F/L Debenham to acting squadron leader rank to take over B Flight, and for P/O Black and F/O Harrison to be elevated to fill the vacancies for a flight lieutenant in each flight.

Probably buoyed up by the successful series of operations, Harris sanction one against Essen, for which 369 aircraft were made ready on the 16th, the numbers once more bolstered by a contribution from the training units. 10 Squadron put up four Halifaxes, which departed Pocklington between 20.40 and 20.49 with S/L Carter the senior pilot on duty. Sgt Campbell and crew returned early with a leak in the oil cooler and falling oil pressure, and they were followed later by S/L Carter and crew. Their sortie had been cut short by excessive fuel consumption and an inability to climb, and the bombs had been jettisoned "safe" into the sea. On landing at Pocklington the brakes failed, and the Halifax ran off the end of the runway to end up with its nose on the Hull to York road, despite which, the crew walked away apparently unharmed. The remaining two attacked the primary target on e.t.a through cloud from 13,500 and 15,000 feet at 22.32 and 22.37, before returning safely with little to offer the intelligence section at debriefing. Local reports confirmed a scattered raid, but the housing and industrial damage was undoubtedly the most severe at this target to date, and the Krupp complex was hit by fifteen high-explosive bombs and a crashing bomber. It was a massively expensive night for the Command, however, costing thirty-nine aircraft, of which nineteen represented the training units.

If any period during the war could be identified as the turning point on the long road to operational effectiveness, then, perhaps, these two weeks in September 1942 was it. The evolution of equipment and new tactics was coming together at a time when the Pathfinders were getting to grips with the complexities of their demanding role, and, although failures would continue to outnumber successes for some time to come, the signs were there, and it augured ill for the people of Germany.

Saarbrücken was posted as the target for a force of 118 aircraft on the 19th, to which 4 Group contributed forty-one Halifaxes. 10 Squadron made ready five aircraft, which took off either side of 19.30 with S/L Carter the senior pilot on duty, but lost the services of Sgt Hampton and crew within fifteen minutes to a coolant leak in the port-outer engine. The others pressed on to reach the target in good visibility hampered only by ground haze, which caused problems for the Pathfinder element. S/L Carter identified the target without difficulty, and bombed it from 13,000 feet at 22.54, observing his bombs to burst in the built-up area, and, feeling unthreatened by the defences, remained over the target for ten minutes to assess the outcome. The other squadron participants carried out their attacks from 12,000 to 15,000 feet between 22.40 and 22.53, and returned with little to report. Sgt Willmott and crew were very fortunate to survive a collision with a tree on the top of the Pennines near Thrusscross Reservoir as they descended to establish their position. The starboard aileron was torn and one of the engines damaged, rendering the Halifax almost uncontrollable. The pilot climbed to allow the crew to bale out, and he was last to leave R9383, which crashed at 02.45 near West End village eight miles north-west of Harrogate in west Yorkshire, where it was consumed by fire. The navigator, Sgt McDougall, landed among rocks and failed to survive, while the rest of the crew escaped injury.

Among three small-scale operations without Pathfinder assistance mounted on the 23rd was an all-4 Group attack on the U-Boot construction yards at Flensburg, which involved twenty-eight Halifaxes. Just one crew was requested from 10 Squadron, and that of Sgt Margetts took off at 00.17 carrying six 1,000 pounders and two SBCs of 4lb incendiaries. The force encountered severe electrical storms outbound, and five-tenths cloud over the target, but the Margetts crew reported being able to see the primary target clearly, bombing it from 2,300 feet at 03.00 and observing bursts. They were among sixteen crews to claim to have reached the target on a night of heavy casualties for the group, which saw five Halifaxes fail to return, 17.8% of those dispatched. The operation was mounted again on the 26th, for which the 10 Squadron crews of S/L Debenham and Sgts Hampton and Somerscales were briefed and took off either side of 20.30. They were recalled at 23.00 after the weather conditions at home deteriorated, by which time they were over Denmark. All picked up the signal and turned back, and, shortly after jettisoning the bombs into the sea, the Somerscales crew observed a ME110 five hundred yards on the starboard quarter down. It fired two bursts, which the rear gunner returned at 150 yards, scoring hits on the starboard engine, which burst into flames, and the enemy was seen to fall and crash into the sea. During the course of the month the squadron operated on twelve occasions including the recall, and dispatched thirty-nine sorties for the loss of two Halifaxes and one complete crew.

10/227 Sqn aircrew at a pre-flight briefing in September 1942

Servicing at Aqir, Palestine in September 1942 where the Squadron detachment was renamed 10/227 Sqn to change, on its completion to No 462 Sqn.

Bombing-up for Tobruk. Pith helmets were issued to those who worked in the sun.

October 1942

There would be a disastrous start to the new month for 10 Squadron, beginning on the night of the 1/2nd, when twenty-seven Halifaxes of 4 Group resumed their quest to destroy the U-Boot construction yards at Flensburg. 10 Squadron dispatched five aircraft either side of 18,00 with P/O Jones the senior pilot on duty, and only Sgt Allan and crew returned to report their experiences after completing a round-trip of seven and three-quarter hours. The weather in the target area had been poor, with three-tenths cloud and rain showers, and when they came upon a built-up area and stretch of water, they believed it to be the Flensburg Fjord, which they bombed from 400 feet in the face of intense light flak. Bursts were observed, and a red glow remained visible for sixty miles into the return journey. W7667 fell in the target area, but not before F/Sgt Hayes and four of his crew had taken to their parachutes, and two survived similarly from F/Sgt Moller's crew in W7852. There were no survivors, however, from the crash of BB207 captained by F/O Jones, or from Sgt Campbell's DT520, which went into the sea off the south-western coast of Denmark's Langeland Island. All of the bodies from the last-mentioned were eventually recovered for burial in two cemeteries. A further eight Halifaxes failed to return home, representing a loss rate of 44%, and the light flak, which had been increased since the previous attack, was probably responsible for most of them.

The Ruhr city of Krefeld was the objective for the following night, for which a force of 188 aircraft was made ready. P/O Baxter RAAF and crew, which included four members of the RCAF, were sent over to Pocklington in W1116 as the sole representatives of 10 Squadron, and took off at 18.41 not to be heard from again. News eventually filtered through from the Red Cross that they were safe and on extended leave as guests of the Reich, but the circumstances of their survival are not known. The operation was ineffective after the Pathfinder marking was late and hampered by thick haze, the modest amount of damage being limited to a number of streets in a northern district. Aachen, Germany's most westerly city, was posted as the target on the 5th, and a force of 257 aircraft was made ready. 10 Squadron detailed four Halifaxes, loading each of them with three 1,000 pounders, six SBCs of 4lb incendiaries and six of 30lb, before dispatching them from Pocklington between 18.31 and 18.42, with W/C Wildey undertaking a rare sortie, probably as a morale-boosting measure after the recent losses. The weather was poor over England, and caused problems particularly in the Pathfinder and 3 Group region. Sgt Wilmott and crew were back home in a little over an hour because of an unserviceable gyro, while Sgt Hampton and crew inadvertently released the upper escape hatch and also reported an intercom problem. The weather remained challenging all the way to the target, where little Pathfinding took place. W/C Wildey located the target under a layer of eight-tenths cloud between 8,000 and 14,000 feet, and came down to the cloud base to bomb at 21.46, but could not make out ground detail even from that height. Curiously, P/O Munro bombed at the same time from 12,000 feet and described the visibility as good apart from a thin layer of cloud at 5,000 feet. It seems likely that they were some distance apart at the time. Although some damage did occur at the primary target, much of the effort was scattered far and wide, including onto the Dutch town of Lutterade, which would have minor consequences for the Oboe development programme in December.

The contribution made by the Squadron's ground crews can never be overestimated

The crews of Sgts Allan and Wilmott attended briefing on the 6th, before departing from Pocklington at 19.01 and 19.05 respectively as part of a force of 237 aircraft bound for Osnabrück. Both reached the target area via the Dummer See, a lake to the north-east that had been marked by the Pathfinders with flares to provide the reference for a timed run. They encountered four-tenths cloud over the town with tops at 10,000 feet, but there were sufficient gaps to allow sight of a built-up area below. Sgt Allan bombed from 13,000 feet at 21.26, and Sgt Wilmott two minutes later from 8,500 feet, neither observing the results, but noting many fires spread across the town. The operation appeared to be successful, and this was confirmed by local reports that listed 149 houses and six industrial buildings destroyed and more than five hundred other houses seriously damaged in central and southern districts.

Mining or "gardening" operations had been an integral and highly effective part of Bomber Command's remit since April 1940, when 5 Group had begun mining the waters between the German ports and Norway. The sea-lanes in which the enemy operated between the Spanish frontier in the south, Scandinavia in the north and the Polish border in the east were given horticultural code names, and were constantly resupplied with chains of "vegetables" or mines that acted like a net. It became common practice for inexperienced crews to begin their operational careers with mining sorties, and this was the case when 10 Squadron carried out its first gardening operation of the war on the night of the 10/11th. A total of forty-seven aircraft were involved off the Biscay coast and the Mussels and Nectarines regions off the Frisian islands, and four freshman crews and P/O Munro took off for the latter between 20.27 and 21.16, each carrying four 2,000lb parachute mines. They headed for Terschelling to establish a pinpoint for a timed run to the drop zone, where the mines would be delivered in a stick from low level. Three of the 10 Squadron crews were assigned to area C off the eastern end of the island (Nectarines I), and two to area A off the western end (Mussels), and all successfully completed their brief from 500 to 700 feet between 22.09 and 22.50 having faced no opposition.

It had been quite some time since the squadron had last been able to offer double figures for an operation, and it must have been something of a challenge on the 13th, when the ground crews were presented with eleven Halifaxes to make ready for Kiel that night. They took off between 18.30 and 18.42 with S/L Debenham the senior pilot on duty, and headed out over the North Sea via Flamborough Head. During the testing of his guns, Sgt Juneau's rear gunner found his turret to be unserviceable, and they were forced to turn back at 19.15. The others continued on to reach the target area, where visibility was good, despite the presence of a little low cloud and haze, and the defences were primed and ready to unleash a heavy and accurate flak barrage. As soon as the attack began, a decoy fire site was activated, and this would be very effective in attracting half of the bomb loads from the 280-strong force. The 10 Squadron crews bombed from 10,000 to 16,000 feet between 21.16 and 21.40, and all but one returned home to report fires, mostly to the west of the target, and good work by the Pathfinders. Local reports confirmed substantial damage within the town and its surrounds, particularly in south-eastern suburbs, for a modest loss to the Command of eight aircraft. Among these was 10 Squadron's W7870, which disappeared without trace with the predominantly Canadian crew of P/O Lindsay RCAF, who were on just their second operation since joining the squadron.

Cologne was posted as the target on the 15th, for which a force of 289 aircraft was assembled, eight of them representing 10 Squadron. They took off between 18.33 and 18.48 with W/C Wildey the senior pilot on duty and each Halifax containing an eight-man crew through the inclusion of a second pilot. They headed out over Southwold on course for Goeree island on the Dutch side of the Scheldt Estuary, and encountered stronger-than-forecast winds, which would create difficulties for the Pathfinders as they attempted to establish their position. The result was that there was insufficient marking at the target to attract the main force crews, although the 10 Squadron participants did comment on the Pathfinder flares illuminating the Rhine to provide a good reference point. However, the presence of a large decoy fire site was a more powerful lure, and most crews were persuaded by that to waste their effort in open country. The 10 Squadron crews reported bombing a built-up area from 13,000 to 17,500 feet between 20.48 and 20.55, but saw little of the results because of haze and defensive activity. Local reports mentioned 224 houses sustaining slight damage from the single 4,000 pounder and three other high-explosive bombs and 210 incendiaries that landed within the city, and this was out of a total of seventy-one 4,000 pounders, 231 other HE bombs and more than 68,000 incendiaries. This disappointment was compounded by the loss to the Command of eighteen aircraft, which included 10 Squadron's W1058, which was on its way home when it crashed in a western suburb of Bonn. W/C Wildey DFC and both gunners lost their lives, and the five survivors were taken into captivity.

W/C Carter was promoted from within as the new commanding officer, and would take up his post on return from leave on the 23rd. In the meantime, S/L Debenham would fill the breach, and the crews of S/Ls Catt and Barrett were posted in from 1658 Conversion Unit on the 21st. Operation Torch, the Allied landings in North Africa, which would ultimately lead to Montgomery's victory over Rommel at El Alamein, now began to make demands on the Command, and frequent trips would be mounted to Italian targets during the remainder of the year. The first operation was directed at Genoa on the night of the 22/23rd by Lancasters of 5 Group, and this was followed up twenty-four hours later by elements of 3 and 4 Groups with Pathfinder support. A force of 122 Halifaxes, Stirlings and Wellingtons was made ready for the long trip across the Alps, and nine crews were briefed at Melbourne, which could now, at last, launch operations from its own runways. Take-off took place between 18.06 and 18.21 with S/L Debenham the senior pilot on duty, and the newly-arrived S/L Barrett flying as second pilot with F/L Black. P/O Margetts swung violently off the runway during his attempt to become airborne, and his sortie was subsequently cancelled. The others set course for Dungeness on the Kent coast and Berck-sur-Mer on the other side of the Channel, and enjoyed good weather conditions until the target drew near, when ten-tenths cloud with tops at 4,000 feet obscured all ground detail. Only F/Sgt Hampton and crew admitted to being unable to locate the primary target, and attacked Savona, situated some twenty miles along the coast to the west. They identified it by the river and the form of the built-up area, and bombed it from 16,000 feet at 22.31, observing not only their own bomb bursts, but many others as well, along with numerous fires. On return, the other crews were adamant that they had attacked Genoa, doing so from 15,000 to 16,000 feet between 21.19 and 21.25, but, it seems likely that they, too, had been over Savona, from where no report was forthcoming.

Milan hosted two raids on the 24th, the first in daylight by 5 Group, while, back home seventy-one aircraft were being made ready by 1, 3 and 4 Groups and the Pathfinders for a night attack. 4 Group's contribution was five Halifaxes, of which one belonged to 10 Squadron, and, as three 102 Squadron crews were taking part, P/O Margetts and crew flew over to Pocklington for

10 Sqn Halifax ground crew

bombing up. They were airborne at 18.41, and made landfall at the enemy coast over Le Treport, before setting course in adverse weather conditions for the Alps. The storms outbound dispersed the force, and some found themselves straying into Swiss airspace, where they received a warning from the border flak batteries. P/O Margetts encountered ten-tenths cloud over what he believed to be the target area, and bombed blind on e.t.a from above cloud at 9,000 feet at 22.38. This was one of thirty-nine crews to claim to have bombed the primary target, where a local report suggested little additional damage. This was the final operation during a month in which the squadron had welcomed fifteen new crews from the 10 Squadron Conversion Flight and 1658 Conversion Unit, while operating on nine nights and dispatching forty-four sorties for the loss of seven Halifaxes and crews.

November 1942

There were no operations for the squadron during the first six nights of the new month, and this largely reflected a generally quiet period for the Command. S/L Catt and crew concluded their brief stay at 10 Squadron with a posting to 428 Squadron RCAF during w.e.f the 7th. The Italian campaign resumed at Genoa on the night of the 6/7th at the hands of an all-Lancaster force from 5 Group and the Pathfinders, and this was followed up twenty-four hours later by a larger force of 175 aircraft, which included a 4 Group contribution of forty-five Halifaxes, nine of them representing 10 Squadron. The Melbourne element took off between 17.11 and 17.19 with S/L Barrett the senior pilot on duty for the first time, but lost the services of F/Sgt Hampton and crew at 18.04 when over Cambridge after their port-outer engine failed. The bombs were jettisoned off Skegness at 18.48, and a landing made at base at 19.50, which proved to be excessively heavy, collapsed the undercarriage and culminated in W7867 being reduced to a burned-out wreck with the crew watching from a safe distance. P/O Margetts and crew were defeated by what they described as severe weather and acute icing over France, and turned back after jettisoning their bombs at 20.11. The others pushed on to the target, where they found the visibility to be good enough to identify ground features. Bombing was carried out from 13,000 to 16,500 feet between 21.35 and 22.01, and all returned safely to home airspace, where P/O Munro decided to evict his crew because of a critical fuel situation, and remained alone with DG222 to land at the 3 Group station of Downham Market. At debriefing the crews were enthusiastic about the quality of their work, and reported many fires, one large enough to remain visible from seventy miles into the return journey. Photographic reconnaissance confirmed that substantial further damage had been inflicted on the city and port.

The crews of P/O Sale and Sgts Hale and Virgo were briefed for mining sorties off the Frisians on the 8th, and took off either side of 18.00 to be greeted by scattered cloud and haze in the target area. This did not inhibit their ability to locate their pinpoints on the islands of Borkum and Juist from which to make their timed runs to the drop zone, and P/O Sale and Sgt Virgo delivered their mines from 700 feet shortly before 20.30. Sgt Hale and crew did not return in DT557, which disappeared into the sea in the target area, and only the remains of the pilot and navigator were eventually recovered for burial in north-western Germany. For the third day in a row orders were received on the 9th to prepare for operations, and this time Hamburg was the target. A force of 213 aircraft was assembled, which included nine Halifaxes belonging to 10 Squadron, but Sgt Somerscales was hit by an engine problem at start-up and his sortie had to be scrubbed. The remaining eight took to the air between 17.45 and 17.56 with W/C Carter the senior pilot on duty supported by S/L Barrett. Sgt Vinish suffered a hydraulics failure at 18.40 when seventy miles out from Flamborough Head, and turned back, and S/L Barrett abandoned his sortie at 18.42 after the oxygen system and automatic pilot failed. A night of poor serviceability was complete when W/C Carter lost one of his port engines thirteen minutes later and also turned back after jettisoning his bombs. When targeting Hamburg it was often necessary to fly through banks of towering, ice-bearing cloud, which, on this night, was a challenge compounded by an unforeseen strong wind. On reaching the target the crews were confronted by ten-tenths rain-bearing cloud and a fairly spirited heavy and light flak defence, and carried out their attacks on what they believed was the primary target from 15,000 to 17,500 feet between 20.35 and 20.53. According to local reports, many bombs fell into the Elbe or in open country, and only three of twenty-six fires were classed as large.

After a few nights of mining and minor operations, elements of 5 Group and the Pathfinders resumed the campaign against Italian cities at Genoa on the night of the 13/14th. The same target was posted on the 15th for attention from a mixed force of seventy-eight Halifaxes, Lancasters and Stirlings, for which 10 Squadron made ready eight aircraft. S/L Barrett dropped out with an engine issue at start-up, leaving the remaining seven to take off between 17.26 and 17.56 with S/L Debenham the senior pilot on duty and temporary commanding officer in the absence on leave of W/C Carter. Sgt Allan and crew were two hours out when the port-outer engine sprang an oil leak, and they were forced to turn back. The others continued on across France over heavy cloud, that dispersed east of the Alps to leave clear skies and good visibility over Genoa. Ground features could be easily identified, and the docks stood out clearly as the bombing took place from 15,000 to 16,000 feet between 22.06 and 22.13. Bursts were observed along with many fires, and the crews turned away confident that they had fulfilled their brief. On the way home at 14,000 feet and approaching the Scheldt Estuary over southern Holland, the Wilmott crew was attacked by a JU88, which came up from astern and closed to 100 yards before opening fire. The rear gunner responded with a hundred rounds, which prompted the fighter to break off and disappear. A minute later, at 00.20, a FW190 tried its luck, but its fire passed harmlessly beneath the Halifax, and it was quickly lost through evasive action.

Attention shifted to Turin on the 18th, for which a force of seventy-seven aircraft was made ready, including five Halifaxes belonging to 10 Squadron. All of the Melbourne crews was carrying a second pilot as they took off between 17.50 and 17.54 with S/L Barrett the senior pilot on duty. For a change there were no early returns, and all reached the target to find good visibility in which the crews could identify ground features like a river, bridges and a large church. P/O Munro lost his starboard-outer engine when thirty minutes short of the target, but was clear of the Alps by then and continued on to deliver his three 1,000 pounders and six SBCs of 30lb incendiaries from 15,000 feet at 22.13, observing them to fall into the western half of the city. He was the last of the squadron participants to arrive, by which time smoke had drifted across the city and fires could be seen in the built-up area. The others had carried out their attacks between 21.50 and 22.05 from 14,000 to 16,300 feet, and all returned safely to report good work by the Pathfinders, negligible opposition and burning buildings in many parts of the city including some at the Fiat works.

10 Sqn Halifaxes Melbourne

Preparations were put in hand on the 20th to return to Turin, this time with the largest force yet sent to Italy of 232 aircraft. At Melbourne the ground crews busied themselves making ready ten Halifaxes, while the armourers loaded them with a 1,000 pounder each and nine SBCs of 4lb incendiaries. They took off between 17.31 and 17.40 with S/L Barrett once more the senior pilot on duty, but he and Sgt Juneau lost their port-outer engines within minutes of each other some ninety minutes after take-off, and both jettisoned their bombs into the Channel before returning home. The others pushed on in favourable weather conditions over ten-tenths cloud as far as the Alps, where it dispersed to leave good visibility for the run-in to the target, except for some ground haze. They carried out their attacks in the light from Pathfinder flares from 14,500 to 17,500 feet between 21.52 and 22.13, and observed many fires in the city centre before smoke obscured the scene. All returned safely to give their accounts of a satisfying night's work, the effectiveness of which was confirmed by local reports and post-raid analysis.

There was a return to Germany for a force of 222 aircraft on the 22nd, of which forty-five Halifaxes and Wellingtons were provided by 4 Group, the latter belonging to two of the group's Canadian squadrons. The Melbourne element of seven was reduced to six shortly before take-off, which was accomplished safely between 17.21 and 17.34 with F/L Harrison the senior pilot on duty. Sgt Somerscales and crew were about ninety minutes out when the rear turret became unserviceable, and the bombs were jettisoned at 19.55 as they made their way home. The remaining five continued on across France to Châtillon-sur-Seine, where they turned sharply to port on course for the target. A thin layer of nine-tenths cloud and ground haze obscured the target area, and the Pathfinders failed to find the city centre, although a number of 10 Squadron crews would comment later on the accuracy and usefulness of the marker flares. Bombing took place by the Melbourne crews from 14,000 to 17,000 feet between 21.50 and 22.00, and bursts were claimed on the aiming-point along with fires near the marshalling yards. Within minutes of leaving the target P/O Brookbanks and crew were attacked from astern by a JU88, which scored hits in the fuselage, tail-plane and wings, before return fire drove it off. Seven minutes later the Halifax was set-upon in quick succession by three FW190s, which were evaded through diving from 15,000 down to 3,000 feet, and no further damage was sustained. Sgt Juneau and crew decided to come home at low level across France, and paid the price when stumbling into intense and accurate light flak, which knocked out an aileron and wounded the flight engineer in the hip and thigh. Despite bleeding profusely, he insisted on remaining at his post and assisted the pilot in bringing the difficult-to-control Halifax back to a landing at Bovingdon in Buckinghamshire. Among the ten aircraft to fail to return from the operation was 10 Squadron's DT572, which crashed in flames at Thiers-sur-Theve, some twenty-five miles north-east of the centre of Paris, after P/O Collett and his crew had parachuted into the arms of the enemy. The Canadian mid-upper gunner had been fatally wounded, however, and succumbed to his injuries within minutes. The raid was generally disappointing, hitting mostly south and south-western suburbs and outlying communities, but the main railway station was hit and sustained substantial damage.

Sgt Easton and crew were briefed on the 25th for gardening duties that night in the Nectarines region off the Frisians. They took off at 17.03 and encountered ten-tenths low cloud over the North Sea, which prevented them from locating their pinpoint and persuaded them to bring their vegetables home. The Italian campaign was to continue at Turin on the 28th, and a force of 228 aircraft was made ready on 1, 3, 4 and 5 Group stations. 10 Squadron detailed six Halifaxes, which were loaded with five 1,000 pounders each, and sent skyward between 18.09 and 18.18 with F/Ls Black and Harrison the senior pilots on duty. P/O Wann and crew turned back at 19.27 after their oxygen system failed, while F/L Black and crew had reached central France on their way to the turning point at Annecy, when the port-inner engine developed an oil leak and the Halifax was unable to maintain height. The bombs were jettisoned at 21.19 and a safe return completed with a landing at Wing in Buckinghamshire at 00.25. The remaining four crews had encountered ten-tenths cloud during the early part of the outward flight, but this had dispersed well before the target was reached, and visibility was spoiled only by ground haze as they bombed from 14,000 to 16,000 feet in a four-minute slot from 22.21 in the light of Pathfinder flares. There was a moderate flak defence in operation, but it lacked accuracy, and it was clear that the attack had been successful, with many fires visible and the Fiat works seen to be well-alight. On the way home over France, F/L Harrison and crew were attacked from astern by a BF109, and a cannon shell passed through the Perspex of the rear turret. Probably motivated by this, Sgt Culverwell responded with two short and one long burst, causing the enemy to burst into flames and dive away to be claimed as a "kill".

On the last day of the month, F/Sgt Wilmott and crew took off at 14.28 for a formation exercise in W7871, with S/L Barrett on board. Shortly afterwards the Halifax was seen to dive in from 300 feet and crash at Laytham Grange Farm, one mile south-west of the airfield, and burst into flames, killing all on board. This tragic accident bore all of the hallmarks of rudder overbalance. It will be recalled that F/Sgt Willmott and crew had used up a proportion of their good fortune when surviving a collision with a tree on return from an operation in September. During the course of the month the squadron carried out nine operations and dispatched fifty-five sorties for the loss of three Halifaxes and two crews.

December 1942

S/L Frank DFC and crew were posted in from 1652 Conversion Unit on the 2nd, and he would replace the late S/L Barrett as a flight commander. A force of 112 aircraft was made ready for an operation that night against Frankfurt, with Halifaxes representing almost half of the numbers. 10 Squadron loaded four of them with two 1,000 pounders and eight SBCs of 4lb incendiaries, and launched them from Melbourne between 01.26 and 01.30 with P/O Julian Sale the senior pilot on duty. All reached the target area, but encountered such dense haze that it was impossible to identify anything on the ground. The Pathfinders failed to establish the location of the city, and crews were left to attack what they discerned to be built-up areas. Bombs were delivered from 15,000 and 16,000 feet between 04.22 and 04.46 in the face of a quite intense searchlight and flak response, but no assessment was possible. Six aircraft failed to return, and all three missing Halifaxes were from 102 Squadron over at Pocklington. The operation was found to be a complete failure, which had deposited most of the bombs in open country to the south-west of the city.

The focus remained on southern Germany on the 6th, when Mannheim was posted as the target for a force of 272 aircraft. 10 Squadron detailed ten Halifaxes, which took off between 16.58 and 17.08 with F/L Harrison the senior pilot on duty. Sgt Juneau and F/Sgt Saunders dropped out early on after the former was unable to climb and the latter had both outer engines overheat. The weather deteriorated over Germany, and the target was found to be covered by ten-tenths cloud with occasional small gaps. Sgt Allan and crew eventually abandoned the search and jettisoned their bombs before turning back, while the others bombed blind on e.t.a, Pathfinder flares and the flashes from flak, doing so from 9,000 to 17,000 feet between 20.13 and 20.23. Only F/L Harrison and crew gained a positive reference through a gap in the clouds, which revealed a section of the River Rhine ten miles south of the city. Local reports confirmed this operation to have been a wasted effort, which landed around five hundred incendiaries and some leaflets in the city without causing meaningful damage.

The crews of Sgts Virgo and Juneau took off at 17.06 and 17.22 respectively on the 8th, and set course for the Frisians to deliver two 1,500lb mines each. The weather was good, and the sorties were fulfilled according to brief either side of 19.00 from 700 feet. Sgt Virgo was engaged from a thousand yards astern by an unidentified aircraft, but no hits were scored and there was no further contact. The main operation on this night was the first of three raids on Turin in the space of four nights, which would conclude the Italian campaign. This was a highly destructive assault by a 5 Group main force with Pathfinder support, and produced the highest casualty figures yet at an Italian target. The fires were still burning twenty-four hours later, when the next attack took place, for which 222 aircraft had set off earlier in the evening, the six 10 Squadron participants departing Melbourne between 16.40 and 16.45 with F/Ls Harrison and Munro the senior pilots on duty. Sgt Vinish and F/L Munro both dropped out with engine issues and jettisoned their loads into the sea, leaving the others to continue on to find the target in good weather conditions, but partially concealed by haze and drifting smoke. The Pathfinder marking was less efficient than on the previous night, but the crews were able to identify the built-up area and deliver their bombs from 10,000 to 16,000 feet between 21.35 and 21.39. Returning crews reported as many as thirty fires burning in the city centre, and, although it was difficult to make an accurate assessment, this was clearly an effective raid.

The final Turin operation was mounted on the night of the 11/12th, and involved eighty-two aircraft from 1, 4 and 5 Groups and the Pathfinders. 10 Squadron detailed nine Halifaxes, but one dropped out with technical issues before departure. The others took off between 16.51 and 16.57 with F/L Munro the senior pilot on duty, and flew into adverse weather conditions over the Channel in the form of a front with severe icing, which persisted all the way to the Alps and persuaded more than half of the force to abandon their sorties. Sgt Somerscales and crew were still enveloped in cloud at 20,000 feet, by which time fuel consumption had become excessive and they decided to turn back. Sgt Vinish and crew had an issue develop in both outer engines, while Sgt Virgo lost his port-inner engine, and both jettisoned their bombs before reaching the turning point at Annecy. DG222 crashed at Villiers-le-Duc, some one hundred miles south-east of Paris at 20.15 while outbound, and there were no survivors from the crew of Sgt Juneau RCAF. P/O Brookbanks ventured further towards Annecy, before he was defeated by ice-accretion, and that left just three Melbourne crews to fight their way through the conditions to reach the target area. There was some improvement east of the Alps, but it was still almost impossible to establish a position, and the bombing took place from 15,000 and 17,500 feet between 21.38 and 22.03. Some bursts were observed, but local reports confirmed that hardly any ordnance had fallen into the city.

The 14th brought another gardening operation by sixty-eight aircraft around Texel in the south and the east Frisians and Heligoland further north. 10 Squadron briefed seven crews for a drop zone off Teschelling, and dispatched them between 16.30 and 16.40 with S/L Frank the senior pilot on duty for the first time. Unfortunately, his rear turret became unserviceable, and he was forced to abandon his sortie. The others pressed on in favourable weather conditions to identify their pinpoints, before delivering their two mines each into the briefed locations from 600 and 700 feet between 18.03 and 18.19. The squadron operated for the final time during the year against Duisburg on the night of the 20/21st, when contributing eight Halifaxes to the overall force of 232 aircraft. The Melbourne element took off between 17.53 and 18.02 with F/Ls Black and Munro the senior pilots on duty, and flew out in excellent weather conditions and clear visibility. Sgt Vinish became indisposed during the outward flight, and it became necessary to turn back and jettison the bomb load over the sea. The others reached the target area, where a strong wind had blown away the haze, and left ground features standing out clearly. The bombing took place in the face of heavy and accurate flak from 13,000 to 18,000 feet between 19.52 and 19.58, and returning crews would claim a successful operation.

While the above operation was in progress, something of great significance for future operations was taking place unnoticed by all but those in the know. Six Mosquitos of 109 Squadron set off from Wyton for a power station at Lutterade in Holland, to deliver their first Oboe-aimed bombs. Since becoming a founder member of the Pathfinders in August, 109 Squadron had been fully engaged in marrying the device to the Mosquito, and conducting exhaustive trials under its commanding officer, W/C Hal Bufton. This night's operation was a calibration test to check the margin of error, for which the surrounding terrain needed to be free from damage. In the event, reconnaissance photographs showed many craters from misdirected bombs intended for nearby Aachen in October, and the three successful releases could not be identified. Further tests would be carried out in the New Year, however, and the device would be ready, if not yet fully efficient, in time for the spring offensive.

During the course of the month there was a DFC for F/L Munro, and the squadron carried out six operations, dispatching thirty-seven sorties for the loss of one Halifax and crew. It had been another tough year for the crews of 4 Group, and the Halifax was still not delivering to its full potential. An even tougher year lay ahead, with a number of challenging campaigns to test the mettle of the Command and its crews, but, at least, the effect of their efforts against the enemy would be clear for all to see.

January 1943

New Year's Day brought the formation of the Canadian 6 Group, and the departure of the 4 Group stations in north Yorkshire and Middleton-St-George in County Durham. With them went 408 Squadron with its Halifaxes and the Canadian Wellington squadrons, although 425 Squadron lingered for a couple of days and conducted mining sorties under the banner of 4 Group on the night of the 2/3rd before making the move. The organisational change left 4 Group with the recently-formed 196 Squadron, 466 Squadron RAAF and the Canadian 429 Squadron as its only Wellington units. The last-mentioned would be posted to 6 Group in April to eventually convert to Halifax Mks II and V, and the first-mentioned to 3 Group in July, while 466 Squadron would remain with 4 Group and retain the type until becoming the first in the Command to receive the much-improved Hercules-powered Mk III Halifax late in the year. There would be a gentle start to the month for the 4 Group squadrons, while further south, on the Lincolnshire stations of 1 and 5 Groups, the Oboe trials programme was in full swing. It had begun on the night of the 31st of December, when Düsseldorf was the target, after which, a total of seven operations involving 109 Squadron Oboe Mosquitos and small numbers of Lancasters were directed at Essen and one at Duisburg over the next two weeks. While this was ongoing, the Pathfinder Force was granted group status as 8 Group on the 8th, and duly took ownership of the 3 Group stations upon which it had lodged since its formation in August. For the purpose of this book the terms Pathfinders and 8 Group will be interchangeable.

Other than the gardening operation mentioned above, there was no operational activity for 4 Group until orders were received on the 9th to prepare for an extensive mining effort that night. Sixty-four Halifaxes were made ready, of which eleven would represent 10 Squadron in an overall force of 121 aircraft assigned to drop zones around the Frisians (Nectarines), the German Bight (Rosemary) and the Kattegat (Silverthorn) in Danish waters. Eight 10 Squadron crews were briefed for the Kattegat and three for the Frisians, and the former took off between 16.00 and 16.08 with S/L Frank the senior pilot on duty, while the less-experienced crews of Sgts Brunton, Fish and Illingworth followed on either side of 16.30. Both elements would benefit from favourable weather conditions, but the freshmen would face the most opposition from light flak and night fighters. With fewer miles to cover, they reached their Nectarines garden first, and Sgt Illingworth and crew were closing in on their drop zone at 18.20 when they were attacked from astern by a JU88. It closed to one hundred yards range and inflicted damage to the fuselage, control surfaces and W/T equipment before being driven off by the Halifax's gunners. Eight minutes later they delivered their vegetables into the briefed location from 900 feet, before returning safely to land at Pocklington. Sgt Brunton's aircraft was hit by light flak from the western end of the island of Juist at 18.28, and sustained damage to control surfaces and ammunition trays. The two mines were delivered into the briefed location from 800 feet at

Melbourne, East Yorks could be a cold place to be when servicing a Halifax outside in the open. Here Mk II Halifax BB194 (ZA-E) in January 1943 is being serviced. Standing at the bench on the left is engine fitter LAC George Tait.

18.44, and a safe return made. Nothing was heard from the crew of Sgt Fish until news eventually arrived to confirm that BB252 had crashed on the island of Schiermonnikoog at 18.15 with immediate fatal consequences for six members of the crew. The mid-upper gunner was critically injured, and would lose his fight for life at Leeuwarden hospital on the 15th. Meanwhile, the other element had made landfall on the Danish coast at Ringkøbing, and crossed Jutland to gain access to the waters of the Kattegat. They dropped their mines as briefed from 500 to 700 feet between 19.03 and 20.27, and returned safely to report uneventful sorties.

On the 14th, a new Air Ministry directive opened the way for the area bombing of those French ports which were home to U-Boot bases and support facilities. A list of four such targets was drawn up accordingly, Lorient, St-Nazaire, Brest and La Pallice, and, that night, Lorient was selected to open the campaign and host the first of its nine raids over the succeeding month. Between February 1941 and January 1942, the Germans had built three giant concrete structures K1, K2 and K3 on the southernmost point of the Keroman Peninsular. They were capable of housing and servicing thirty U-Boots and providing accommodation for their crews, and were impregnable to the bombs available to Bomber Command at the time. The purpose of this new campaign, therefore, was to render the town and port uninhabitable, and block or sever all road and rail communications to them. A force of 121 aircraft was assembled on this night, but a forecast of very poor weather conditions reduced the number of 4 Group aircraft involved, and fifty-two Halifaxes ultimately presented themselves for take-off, seven of them belonging to 10 Squadron. They departed Melbourne between 22.22 and 22.39 with S/Ls Debenham and Franks the senior pilots on duty, and headed into thick, low cloud which would persist throughout the operation. S/L Frank was little more than an hour out when his Halifax developed an engine issue which forced him to turn back and jettison his load. The others pressed on to be greeted by cloud with large breaks in the target area, and this allowed crews to pinpoint on Groix Island situated south-west of the Blavet Estuary. S/L Debenham had to feather his starboard-outer engine five minutes from the target, but carried on to release his two 1,000 pounders and twelve SBCs of incendiaries. Bombing was carried out from 10,500 to 17,000 feet between 01.20 and 01.48, and scattered fires were observed as the force turned for England, where the 10 Squadron crews landed safely at Colerne in Wiltshire. Post-raid analysis revealed that the Pathfinder marking had been accurate, but that the main force bombing had become wild, leading to only a modestly successful raid that destroyed some 120 buildings in the town.

Preparations were put in hand on the 15th for a return to Lorient that night, for which 10 Squadron made ready five Halifaxes in an overall force of 157 aircraft. The Melbourne quintet took off between 17.17 and 17.35 with F/O Brookbanks the senior pilot on duty and S/L Hope flying as second pilot with P/O Cobb. They all reached the target area to encounter good weather conditions and four-tenths cloud, through which the aiming-point was clearly visible. They carried out their attacks from 9,500 to 14,500 feet between 19.56 and 20.22, and returned safely to report a line of fires running from north-east to south-west across the town and the docks. This time the bombing was accurate, and at least eight hundred buildings were destroyed in a town now largely evacuated by the civilian population. Main force Halifaxes sat out two operations to Berlin on the nights of the 16/17th and 17/18th, and neither raid produced any useful damage, although the first one destroyed the ten thousand-seater Deutschlandhalle, the largest covered venue in Europe. The Annual performance of the circus was in full swing as the attack began, but not a single human or animal life was lost during the evacuation, before incendiaries burned it to the ground.

A large mine-laying effort involving seventy aircraft was announced on the 21st, for which 10 Squadron made ready six Halifaxes. They took off between 17.20 and 17.30 with S/L Debenham the senior pilot on duty, and he had the station commander, G/C Corbally, on board as second pilot. Their destination was the Nectarines garden off the east Frisians, which all reached to find patches of sea-fog, but, otherwise, favourable weather conditions. Five crews delivered their vegetables into the briefed locations from 600 and 700 feet between 19.09 and 19.20, while Sgt Vinish and crew searched for fifty-five minutes without being able to establish a pinpoint for their timed run and brought their mines home. P/O Somerscales reported one of his mines exploding on contact with the sea after the parachute failed to deploy. While Sgt Allan and crew were running in on their drop zone at very low level, DT566 was hit by flak and holed in the rear fuselage. Violent evasive action caused a wingtip to strike the sea, but the pilot skilfully maintained control and the mines were dropped accurately. Shortly afterwards the starboard-inner engine failed leaving them to come home on three.

Orders were received on the 23rd to prepare for the third raid of the series on Lorient that night, and 10 Squadron responded with ten Halifaxes, which took off between 16.56 and 17.09 as part of an overall force of 121 aircraft. F/Ls Harrison and Munro were the senior pilots on duty, and S/L Hope was flying as second pilot this time with P/O Somerscales and crew. F/Sgt Hampton and crew turned back early with engine issues, but the others continued on to the target, where fair weather conditions prevailed with patchy cloud but good visibility. The Melbourne Halifaxes were carrying all-high-explosive bomb loads consisting either of five 1,000 and six 500 pounders, or eight 1,000 pounders, and these were put to good use from 8,000 to 12,000 feet between 20.01 and 20.20. Many fires were reported, the glow from which could be seen from the English Channel, and the consensus was of a successful operation. The squadron sat out the fourth attack on Lorient on the night of the 26/27th, and contributed just F/L Black and crew to the next one on the 29th. This was a 1, 4 and 6 Group effort involving seventy-five Wellingtons and forty-one Halifaxes, for which the Black crew departed Melbourne at 17.15 on a night of heavy cloud and icing conditions. They located the target by means of a Gee-fix and the flak coming up through the ten-tenths cloud, and dropped the three 1,000 pounders and twelve SBCs of 4lb incendiaries from 13,000 feet at 20.20. There was no Pathfinder marking for this operation, and the bombing was scattered and ineffective. P/O Julian Sale and his crew were posted to 35 Squadron of the Pathfinders during the final week of the month, and he would rise through the ranks as one of the former 4 Group shining lights.

The main operation on the night of the 30/31st was one of significance for future operations, and heralded the first use of the ground-mapping radar system known as H2S, which was contained in a cupola beneath the rear fuselage of the aircraft. The device, which would eventually become standard equipment across the Command, was initially installed in Pathfinder Halifaxes and Stirlings of 35 and 7 Squadrons. A specialist operator would be fed the image onto a cathode-ray tube, and it would be his job to interpret what he saw to establish the aircraft's position. This was fine over coastlines and large rivers, but over a city it would be a much more challenging task. In time, H2S would become more sophisticated and an integral weapon in the Bomber Command armoury, but, on this night over Hamburg, it would not be effective. While this operation was in progress, 4 Group sent a dozen Halifaxes to lay mines off the Frisians, six of them representing 10 Squadron, which took off between 17.21 and 17.36 with P/Os Allan and Somerscales the senior pilots on duty. They found good weather conditions with little or no cloud, but thick sea haze prevented P/O Somerscales and crew from locating their pin-point, and they brought their mines home. The others found their pin-points on Borkum and Juist, and delivered their mines into the briefed locations from 600 and 700 feet between 19.11 and 19.23, before returning home to make their reports. Sgt Easton and crew landed at Acklington, where an oleo leg collapsed, causing extensive damage to BB243, but not to the crew. During the course of the month the squadron operated on seven nights and dispatched forty-six sorties for the loss of one Halifax and crew.

February 1943

The first major operation of the new month was directed at Cologne by an-all four-engine heavy force on the night of the 2/3rd. The crews would be relying on Oboe and H2S to locate the target, but the outcome was disappointing after scattered marking led to scattered bombing. 10 Squadron sat this one out, and, before its February operational account opened, W/C Carter concluded his spell in command, it is believed on the grounds of ill health, and was posted to Station HQ at Pocklington on the 3rd. S/L Edmonds was posted in the opposite direction from his flight commander post at 102 Squadron to assume command of 10 Squadron on promotion to acting wing commander rank. An Irishman with strong tendencies towards a disciplinarian style, he quickly became known as "The Sheriff". He presided over his first operation that very night, when Hamburg was the target for a force of 263 aircraft, of which the Halifax was the most populous type. 10 Squadron made ready seven of them, and sent them skyward between 18.29 and 18.42 with S/L Frank the senior pilot on duty. The weather conditions were appalling and typical of those that often prevailed over the Dutch and German coastal regions, barring the path into the north-western corner of the country. Sgt Easton and crew turned back after ninety minutes with an unserviceable rear turret and defective port-outer engine, while F/O Wann, Sgt Hampton and F/L Munro all used up too much fuel attempting to climb through the front and icing pockets, and turned back after jettisoning their bombs. Shortly after take-off S/L Frank discovered that his bomb doors had not fully closed, and the drag effect combined with the weather conditions meant that the target would not be reached in time. Sgt Virgo and crew battled their way through the conditions to reach the target, where they bombed through ten-tenths cloud from 17,500 feet at 21.19, observing the reflected glow of incendiaries. P/O Allan and crew arrived two minutes later and five hundred feet lower to bomb on Pathfinder skymarker flares and the flak bursts that were reaching 18,000 feet. Local reports confirmed that forty-five large fires had resulted, but damage was in no way commensurate with the effort expended and the loss of sixteen aircraft.

The first major campaign against Italian cities had concluded in December, but isolated attacks would continue until the final short, sharp series of operations in August helped to knock the country out of the war altogether. Turin was posted as the target for 188 aircraft on the 4th, for which 10 Squadron made ready six Halifaxes and launched them off the end of the Melbourne runway between 17.48 and 17.53 with S/L Frank the senior pilot on duty. P/O Allan was unable to retract his undercarriage, and continued on to a point fifteen miles out from Flamborough Head to dump his bombs, before circling the airfield to burn off petrol for the landing, which was accomplished without incident. Sgt Easton and crew were over France when a glycol leak developed in the port-outer engine, and they were unable to maintain height with the reduction in power. The bombs were jettisoned over open country at 20.59 and a safe return completed at 00.39. The others reached Turin in favourable weather conditions to find clear skies and good visibility, and delivered their loads of a single 1,000 pounder and nine SBCs of 4lb incendiaries each from 13,000 to 17,000 feet between 21.44 and 21.56 aided by accurately place Pathfinder target indicators (TIs). Many fires were observed, and it was apparent that serious and widespread damage had been visited upon the city.

Gardening operations from St-Nazaire to the east Frisians occupied the night of the 6/7th, and involved just the crew of Sgt Brunton from Melbourne, who took off at 17.30 and headed for their pinpoint on Baltrum carrying four 1,000lb mines. They encountered five-tenths cloud over the North Sea, but found their drop zone without difficulty to deliver their vegetables from 700 feet at 19.17. On the way home over the mid-point of the sea crossing, a cannon shell exploded inside the fuselage at 02.20, and punched an eight-inch gash in the roof. There were no casualties, and the Halifax landed safely at Pocklington. The seventh raid of the series on Lorient was planned for the 7th, and a force of 323 aircraft made ready for the two-wave attack. 4 Group's seventy-three Halifaxes and Wellingtons were divided between the two aiming-points A and B, with the five 10 Squadron crews briefed for the latter. F/O Dawes was the senior pilot on duty as they began to take off shortly after 19.00, but his aircraft swung violently off the runway, and his sortie was scrubbed. The others, all with sergeant pilots, got away safely by 19.20, but Sgt Brunton was forced to land at Grimsby (Waltham) forty-five minutes later because of overheating inner engines and hydraulics failure. The others reached the target to find good visibility and fires already burning to illuminate ground and water features. Bombing took place from 11,000 to 12,500 feet between 21.42 and 21.55, and post-raid reconnaissance confirmed that a devastating raid had taken place.

A force of 177 aircraft was put together on the 11th to carry out a raid that night on Wilhelmshaven, for which 10 Squadron detailed the crew of Sgt Brunton. They took off at 18.14 and proceeded to the target area to find ten-tenths cloud and Pathfinder sky-marking in progress. This was the least reliable target-marking method, and relied on H2S-laid parachute flares, which would drift across the target area at the behest of the wind. The prospects were not good

This Merlin-engined Halifax MkII DT788 failed to return from a Cologne raid on 14 February 1943. Pilot Sgt J.D. Illingworth and five of his crew were taken prisoner and W/Op Sgt H.Kay was killed. There was no mid-upper gunner on this aircraft.

as Sgt Brunton released his three 1,000 pounders and twelve SBCs of 4lb and 30lb incendiaries from 14,500 feet at 20.04, but an explosion in a naval ammunition depot at Mariensiel to the south of the target lit up the clouds for almost ten minutes, laying waste to 120 acres of built-up area and leaving substantial damage in the town and the docks area. The squadron briefed four crews on the 13th for the next round of the Lorient campaign, for which an overall force of 466 aircraft was made ready. The Melbourne quartet took off between 18.37 and 18.50 with F/Os Dawes and Espy the senior pilots on duty, each Halifax carrying four 1,000 pounders and 621 mostly 4lb incendiaries. They arrived at the Brittany coast to encounter fine weather conditions with two-tenths cloud at 2,000 feet, but good visibility spoiled only by the smoke drifting across the target area. The carried out their attacks from 9,500 to 10,000 feet between 21.14 and 21.21, before returning safely to report many fires and another highly effective operation.

Preparations were put in hand on the 14th for two operations that night, one by Lancasters of 1, 5 and 8 Groups to Milan, while 243 Halifaxes, Stirlings and Wellingtons were primed to raid Cologne. 10 Squadron loaded two Halifaxes with all-incendiary loads, and dispatched them at 16.30 in the hands of P/O Cobb and Sgt Illingworth and their crews. DT788 was caught by a night fighter while outbound over Holland, and crashed at 20.20 near Venlo, right on the border with Germany. The mid-upper gunner failed to survive, but Sgt Illingworth and four of his crew fell into enemy hands, while the rear gunner managed to evade a similar fate. Meanwhile, P/O Cobb and crew reached the target area to be greeted by ten-tenths cloud and Pathfinder sky-markers, and bombed on these from 16,000 feet at 20.24 without observing any results. Post-raid analysis revealed only modest success, with most of the bombing falling into western districts. The final raid on Lorient was planned for the 16th, and would involve 377 aircraft, including five Halifaxes representing 10 Squadron. They took off either side of 18.50 with F/O Espy the senior pilot on duty, and all reached the target to find excellent weather conditions and good visibility, aided by Pathfinder flares. Bombing took place from 10,500 to 15,000 feet either side of 21.00, and many fires and explosions were observed, including a huge flash at 21.00, which appeared to rise hundreds of feet into the air from a point south of the Port Militaire. This was another devastating raid, which left the port and its surrounds a deserted ruin.

Wilhelmshaven would receive attention on three more occasions during the month, the first of which, on the 18th, W/C Edmonds selected to be his maiden operation with the squadron. Unfortunately, his debut would have to be delayed after a fuel leak was discovered at start-up, and this left seven 10 Squadron Halifaxes to take off between 18.38 and 18.44 as part of a force of 195 aircraft, with F/L Munro now the senior pilot on duty. Sgt Vinish and crew turned back early with an unserviceable rear turret, but the others continued on to reach the target and find excellent weather conditions, and the aiming-point well-marked by Pathfinder TIs. Bombing took place from 13,000 (P/O Cobb) and 17,000 to 17,300 feet by the others between 20.34 and 20.50 and appeared to be accurate. F/L Munro and crew experienced a torrid time on the way home, when, first, a FW190 appeared astern at two hundred yards ten minutes after they had left the target. The rear gunner opened fire only for the guns to jam, and the pilot had to take violent evasive action to successfully shake off the enemy. One of the jammed guns was cleared in time for the arrival 150 yards astern of a ME110, which opened fire as the Halifax dived to port. The rear gunner managed to get in one long burst of fire at seventy-five yards range, and watched the bullets enter the enemy's wing and fuselage, causing it to explode and fall in flames.

Post-raid reconnaissance revealed a different story from that told by the crews, and demonstrated that most of the bombing had fallen into open country to the west of the town.

Twenty-four hours later a larger force of 338 aircraft set off to return to the naval port and town, the seven 10 Squadron participants departing Melbourne between 18.12 and 18.20 with W/C Edmonds and S/L Debenham the senior pilots on duty. All reached the target area where seven to ten-tenths cloud allowed major ground features like the coastline and river to be identified, and the Pathfinder ground markers could also be seen. The 10 Squadron crews carried out their attacks from 15,000 to 17,000 feet between 20.04 and 20.09, and claimed to see bursts in the target area and the glow of many fires. Unfortunately, post-raid reconnaissance revealed the marking to have been inaccurate, and, this time, the bombs had missed to town on its northern side. 4 Group sat out the next attempt at this target, which was mounted on the night of the 24/25th by 115 aircraft of 6 and 8 Groups, and again failed to find the mark.

A force of 337 aircraft was put together on the 25th to target the southern city of Nuremberg, 4 Group providing ninety Halifaxes, of which thirteen belonged to 10 Squadron and represented its best effort yet since converting. They took off between 19.17 and 19.40 with S/L Frank the senior pilot on duty, and all were over Eastern France when P/O Cobb's port-inner engine failed, forcing him to turn back at 21.40 and jettison his bombs some twenty miles south of Sedan. On reaching the city credited with being the birthplace of Nazism, the crews found the visibility to be limited by ground haze, and this was compounded by the late arrival of the Pathfinders, whose markers fell mostly to the north of the intended city-centre aiming-point. The 10 Squadron crews bombed between 23.19 and 23.33, doing so mostly from 15,000 feet, with three other bombing heights recorded at 16,500, 17,000 and 18,000. The impression gained was of a successful raid, which left many fires burning and a glow that could be seen for sixty miles into the return journey. Post-raid reconnaissance revealed that most of the bombing had fallen onto the northern fringes or the city and outlying communities up to seven miles away.

The largest operation of the month was reserved until almost the end, and involved a force of 427 aircraft, which would have the Rhineland capital Cologne as their target on the 26th. 4 Group contributed 105 Halifaxes and Wellingtons, a dozen of the former representing 10 Squadron, and they departed Melbourne between 18.54 and 19.07 with F/Ls Munro and Wood the senior pilots on duty. F/O Wann turned back early and jettisoned his bombs at 20.17 because of a malfunctioning a.s.i, and P/O Hellis followed him home after his rear guns developed a problem. The remainder pressed on in good weather conditions to reach the target, where ground haze was encountered, and Pathfinder TIs had to provide the main reference for the bomb-aimers high above. The 10 Squadron crews delivered their single 1,000 pounder each and incendiaries from 10,000 to 17,500 feet between 21.15 and 21.25, and returned home to report huge fires raging across the target that could be seen from sixty miles into the return journey. Post-raid reconnaissance and local reports confirmed that the operation had been partially successful, and had caused considerable damage to housing, small industrial units, public buildings and utilities. However, this amounted to only around a quarter of the bomb loads, the rest having missed the city altogether to the south-west.

Having dealt effectively with Lorient under the January directive, the Command now turned its attention upon St Nazaire, situated some sixty miles further south. Between February 1941 and January 1942, fourteen bunkers had been built in a three-hundred-yard long concrete structure, the first eight pens serving as dry docks, while the remaining six were standard floating berths. The first of three major attacks on the port over the succeeding four weeks was to be launched on the 28th, for which a force of 437 aircraft was assembled, a dozen of the one hundred Halifaxes belonging to 10 Squadron. They took off between 18.24 and 18.38 with S/L Frank the senior pilot on duty, and, for a change, none returned early with a technical issue. Good weather conditions prevailed throughout the operation, but a smoke screen was in operation, which combined with the usual haze to make ground features less distinct. However, the Pathfinders were on time and produced accurate marking, even managing to land some green TIs on the U-Boot pens. The 10 Squadron crews aimed for the markers from 12,000 to 16,000 feet between 21.22 and 21.33, and described the target as a mass of flames from the docks to the town. The flak was moderately heavy, and P/O Cobb's DT787 was hit in the bomb bay, and a number of incendiaries were on fire as they fell away. Post-raid reconnaissance and local reports confirmed the success of the operation, which destroyed an estimated 60% of the built-up area. During the course of the month the squadron undertook thirteen operations and dispatched eighty-one sorties for the loss of one Halifax and crew.

March 1943

The new month was about to bring the first major campaign of the year against mainland Germany, and the first campaign of the war for which the Command was genuinely adequately-equipped and prepared. Another innovation was the introduction across the Command of the Base system, which grouped together three stations, with one acting as HQ and the others as satellites. Melbourne became part of 42 Base, commanded from Pocklington. First, however, there were two other operations for the crews to negotiate, beginning with the "Big City", Berlin, on the 1st, for which a force of 302 aircraft was made ready. 4 Group offered fifty-two Halifaxes, including ten at Melbourne, which were each loaded with two 1,000 pounders, seven SBCs of 4lb incendiaries and three of 30lbs. They took off between 18.46 and 18.55 with S/L Frank the senior pilot on duty, and headed for the coast between Hornsea and Bridlington to start their six hundred-mile outward flight to eastern Germany. Remarkably, all made it to the target area, where good weather conditions prevailed, and the Pathfinders dispensed red and green marker flares after establishing their position by H2S. This operation would highlight the flaws in the early version of the device when seeking an aiming-point over a massive urban sprawl like Berlin. It would take experience and great skill on the part of the H2S navigators to interpret the jumble of indistinct images on their screens, and, on this night, the marking fell predominantly over the south-western districts, well short of the city centre. The 10 Squadron crews carried out their attacks from 17,000 to 19,500 feet between 22.05 and 22.16, in the face of fairly intense searchlight and flak activity, and returned home safely to report many fires spread across the city and all the appearances of a successful night's work. Despite the misdirection of the bombing, post-raid reconnaissance confirmed that Berlin had suffered its heaviest raid to date, with damage scattered over an area of a hundred square miles. 875 buildings, mostly houses, had been destroyed, and twenty factories and railway repair workshops had been seriously damaged at a cost to the Command of seventeen aircraft. It is interesting to analyse the percentage loss rate of each type on this night, as it would be an accurate indicator of their future fortunes. The statistics revealed the loss rate of Lancasters to be 4.5%, and those of the Halifaxes and Stirlings to be 7%.

Sixty aircraft were sent mining on the night of the 2/3rd, to ply their trade from the Frisians in the north to the Gironde Estuary in the south. 10 Squadron briefed the freshman crew of Sgt Cozens, who took off at 19.00 and set course for the pin-point at the eastern end of Terschelling. They encountered eight-tenths cloud and poor visibility in the target area, but managed to find their drop zone and deliver two 1,500lb mines from 4,000 feet at 20.24. A force of 417 aircraft was made ready for Hamburg on the 3rd, of which eighty-seven Halifaxes and Wellingtons were provided by 4 Group. 10 Squadron loaded eleven Halifaxes with two 1,000 pounders each, and filled up the available space in the bomb bays with seven SBCs of 4lb incendiaries and four of 30lbs. They took off between 18.47 and 19.00 with F/L Munro the senior pilot on duty, and headed out above ten-tenths cloud, but, otherwise, excellent weather conditions, which would hold firm for the entire operation and provide clear skies over the target. Taking off at 18.47 was Sgt Cozens and crew, who were on their way to the Terschelling area of the Frisians to continue their gentle introduction to operations by delivering two mines. F/O Brookbanks turned back from the main element with a port-outer engine issue, leaving the others to press on to the target area, where, despite the quality of the visibility and the wide River Elbe to provide good H2S returns, the Pathfinders dropped red and green TIs well to the west of the planned aiming-point and onto the town of Wedel situated thirteen miles downstream of Hamburg city centre. Other markers fell onto the Altona docks some three miles west of the centre, and both concentrations of markers attracted bombs. The 10 Squadron crews bombed from 15,000 to 18,000 feet between 21.20 and 21.26, before returning safely to report many fires and an apparently successful raid. A hundred fires had to be dealt with by the Hamburg fire brigade before they could go to the aid of Wedel, where substantial damage was inflicted on the docks and to industrial units. Meanwhile, the Cozens crew had encountered poor weather conditions and ten-tenths cloud, but managed to find the drop zone and delivered their two mines from 5,500 feet at 20.36.

After a night's rest, Harris embarked on the campaign that was to change the face of bombing and demonstrate the Command's burgeoning potential. For the next five months, Germany's industrial heartland and arsenal, situated in the fifty-mile-long urbanized part of the Ruhr Valley, would undergo a pounding unprecedented in history. No longer would the region's blanket of industrial haze conceal its towns and cities, as the electronics revolution came of age in the form of Oboe, a device now close to full operational reliability. The systematic dismantling of the region would begin at Essen, thus far Harris's nemesis, for which a force of 442 aircraft was made ready on the 5th. At Melbourne, 10 Squadron prepared a record fourteen Halifaxes to contribute to the one hundred Halifaxes and Wellingtons detailed by 4 Group, among which were the first Wellington sorties by 431 (Iroquois) Squadron RCAF. Once the marking had been carried out by Oboe Mosquitos, backed up by the Pathfinder heavy visual markers, the main force would attack in three waves beginning with Halifaxes, then the Wellington and Stirling elements, and, finally, the Lancasters.

The 10 Squadron participants took off between 18.26 and 19.07 with S/L Frank the senior pilot on duty, and made their way to Hornsea for the North Sea crossing and the northern route into the Ruhr. Among an unusually high number of fifty-six early returns, 13% of those dispatched, were two from Melbourne. P/O Hellis was unable to retract his undercarriage, and dumped his bombs in the mouth of the Humber, while F/O Dawes had reached the Dutch coast south of Den

Helder when his starboard-inner engine failed. The fallout reduced the numbers reaching the target to 362, and they found the visibility to be hampered by haze, which, in former times, would have turned the attack into a lottery. This time the bomb-aimers had accurately placed red and green TIs to aim at, and those in the 10 Squadron aircraft did precisely that from 17,000 to 18,500 feet between 20.59 and 21.12 in the face of an intense searchlight and flak defence. Many large explosions and fires were observed and reported by returning crews, and, while it was clear that a highly successful operation had taken place, perhaps the scale was not appreciated until the post-raid reconnaissance photos arrived in the hands of the interpreters. They revealed that more than three thousand houses had been destroyed, and a further 2,100 seriously damaged in an area of devastation of 160 acres between the city centre and the Krupp works, which, itself, sustained damage to fifty-three buildings. The cost to the Command of fourteen aircraft could be considered modest at a Ruhr target, particularly when compared against the scale of the success, but losses would escalate as the campaign developed over the ensuing months into a bloody and viscous war of attrition.

It would be a week before the next Ruhr operation took place, and, in the meantime, Sgt Hewlett and crew carried out a mining sortie off Schiermonnikoog on the 7th. They delivered their vegetables at 20.24 into the briefed location from 5,000 feet, and returned safely after enjoying good weather conditions and an absence of opposition. Harris switched his forces to southern Germany for the next three operations, beginning with Nuremberg, for which a force of 335 aircraft was made ready on the 8th. 10 Squadron dispatched fourteen Halifaxes between 19.17 and 19.46 with S/L Frank the senior pilot on duty, and all reached the target area to be greeted by clear skies but extreme darkness and ground haze. The target lay beyond the range of Oboe, and the marking, which had to be carried out visually and by H2S, lacked accuracy and became spread for ten miles along the line of approach. The subsequent bombing reflected this, although it may not have been apparent to the crews, most of whom failed to register the fall of their own bombs, but observed up to a hundred fires that suggested a successful attack. The 10 Squadron crews released their loads from 15,000 to 18,000 feet between 23.25 and 23.45, and all returned safely to make their reports. A post-raid analysis revealed that half of the bombing had fallen outside of the city, while the rest destroyed six hundred houses and damaged fourteen hundred others along with some important war-industry factories.

Munich was posted as the target on the 9th, and a force of 264 Lancasters, Halifaxes and Stirlings was duly made ready. 4 Group detailed fifty-three Halifaxes, of which nine belonged to 10 Squadron, and they departed Melbourne between 20.00 and 20.07, with S/L Frank once more the senior pilot on duty. F/Sgt Hampton had to turn back after his navigator was taken ill, but the others all continued on to reach the target, where strong winds pushed the marking into the western half of the city. The 10 Squadron crews reported good visibility, which enabled them to pick out some ground detail, and they delivered their attacks from 15,000 to 18,000 feet between 00.12 and 00.27. Returning crews described concentrated bombing and many fires taking hold, which suggested a successful operation. This was partly confirmed by post-raid reconnaissance, which revealed that 291 buildings had been destroyed and more than six hundred others seriously damaged. Among industrial concerns hit was the B.M.W aero-engine works, which suffered a loss of production extending to six weeks. A tragic accident during a ferry flight on the 10th cost the lives of Sgt Peck and crew, when W1039 crashed and caught fire at 17.09 near Seaton Ross, south-east of York.

The failure to return of just eight aircraft from each of the last-two operations was modest, and the trend would continue with the next one, which was to be directed at Stuttgart on the 11th. A force of 314 aircraft was assembled, to which 10 Squadron contributed ten Halifaxes, and they took off between 19.40 and 19.48 with F/L Wood the senior pilot on duty. All reached the target area, where good visibility prevailed, and ground features could be identified through the haze. The 10 Squadron element bombed from 15,000 to 17,000 feet between 23.12 and 23.25, and all returned safely to report many fires concentrated in the built-up area, and all of the appearances of a successful raid. An analysis of the operation revealed that the main force had arrived a little late, when, perhaps, some of the Pathfinder TIs had burned out, and the dummy TIs provided by the enemy were able to lure away much of the effort. The south-western suburbs of Vaihingen and Kaltental suffered the destruction of 118 buildings, mostly houses, but most of the bombing fell outside of the city boundaries into open country. Eleven aircraft failed to return, six of them Halifaxes, and, while 10 Squadron's excellent loss-free start to the month continued, it was about to end.

A week after the first operation of the Ruhr campaign, 457 crews attended briefings to learn that they would be going back to Essen to continue the excellent work begun there. 4 Group assembled a force sixty-three Halifaxes and Wellingtons, with 10 Squadron providing a dozen of the former, and they took off between 19.24 and 19.31 led by F/Ls Munro and Wood. The

P/O Tom Thackray was a flight engineer on 10 Sqn from March to August 1943. Meeting wife Dorothy whilst undergoing a course at St Athan, they were married on 19 June 1943 and celebrated their platinum anniversary in 2013. Tom edited the 10 Sqn Association Newsletter for 30 years until 2014.

route would take them from Hornsea to Egmond on the Dutch coast and then Haltern on the northern rim of the Ruhr, where they would turn sharply to starboard to approach the target from the north-west. The aiming-point for the Pathfinders was the Krupp works to the west of the city centre, and this was where the Oboe markers fell to be backed up by the heavy Pathfinders with their red and green TIs. The main force crews reported poor visibility because of industrial haze, but this no longer mattered as long as the Oboe marking was accurate, which it was. The 10 Squadron crews bombed from 15,000 to 18,000 feet between 21.20 and 21.31, and observed many explosions and fires along with smoke. While over the target, a number of flak shells exploded beneath DT789, peppering the tail-plane, bomb doors and starboard-outer engine with shrapnel, and inflicting serious wounds to the lower part of the rear gunner's body. F/Sgt Vinish brought the Halifax home to land two-and-a-quarter hours later to allow F/Sgt Barsalou to be removed immediately to hospital for treatment. At debriefing F/O Dawes and crew reported spending twenty minutes over the target trying to evade two cones of searchlights, and Sgt Geddes and crew estimated that two hundred acres of the city were ablaze, the glow from which could been seen from the Dutch coast homebound. The losses from this operation climbed dramatically to twenty-three aircraft, and there were two empty dispersals at Melbourne as the Grim Reaper returned to 10 Squadron. DT778 crashed in the target area with no survivors from the crew of Sgt Dickinson, while HR692 was shot down by a night fighter to crash eight miles north-west of Venlo at 21.15, presumably while homebound, with fatal consequences for Sgt Baker and his crew. Post-raid reconnaissance confirmed that the bombing had centred on the Krupp complex, and that 30% more damage had been inflicted upon it than in the earlier raid. Almost five hundred houses were destroyed, but some bombs also fell into other nearby towns, the boundaries of which overlapped in what was a densely urbanized region.

4 Group carried out no operations at all between the 15th and the 21st as the Command drew breath and focussed on small-scale mining operations. It was a strange fact, that despite the inherent dangers of bomber operations, crews became bored and listless if a period of inactivity stretched beyond a few days, and, there was, no doubt, a sense of release when orders came through on the 22nd to prepare for an operation against St-Nazaire that night. A force of 357 aircraft included ten Halifaxes representing 10 Squadron, which took off between 18.34 and 18.45 with W/C Edmonds and S/L Frank the senior pilots on duty. They flew out over Start Point on Devon's south coast in fine weather conditions, which would persist throughout the operation, and, despite the presence of ground haze and a smoke screen, they were able to identify the target both visually and by means of the Pathfinder TIs. Bombing took place from 14,000 to 15,000 feet between 21.49 and 22.00, and fires were seen to take hold.

A return to the Ruhr was signalled on the 26th, when, this time, Duisburg was to be the target for a force of 455 aircraft, including thirteen Halifaxes belonging to 10 Squadron. They were each loaded with two 1,000 pounders, six SBCs containing ninety 4lb incendiaries and seven SBCs filled with eight of 30lbs. They departed Melbourne between 19.27 and 19.43 with S/L Frank the senior pilot on duty, and headed via Hornsea to the Den Helder peninsular at Egmond for the northern approach to the cauldron of the Ruhr. They were guided by route-marker flares to the target area, where they found ten-tenths cloud, and scattered skymarking in progress, and bombed on e.t.a or on the red and green parachute flares from 18,000 to 19,500 feet between 21.50 and 22.17. The glow of fires was evident beneath the cloud, but no meaningful assessment was possible. What the crews didn't know was that five of the nine Oboe Mosquitos had been forced to turn back with equipment failure and another had been lost, and this severely restricted the number of markers for the Pathfinder heavy brigade to back up. The result was a disappointing, highly scattered raid that landed few bombs on the intended target and destroyed only fifteen houses.

A force of 396 Lancasters, Halifaxes and Stirlings was made ready on the 27th for the second attack of the month on Berlin. 4 Group detailed seventy-seven Halifaxes, of which a dozen were provided by 10 Squadron, and they took off between 19.54 and 20.05 with S/L Frank the senior pilot on duty. The route took them into enemy territory between the islands of Texel and Vlieland, and then on a course a little north of Hannover to a point to the south-west of the Capital for the run-in to the intended city-centre aiming-point. The Pathfinders were reliant upon H2S, and established two areas of marking, both well short, and the main force had little choice but to aim for them. There was five-tenths cloud as the Melbourne crews carried out their attacks from 15,000 to 19,000 feet between 22.55 and 23.10, before returning to report moderate flak, extensive searchlight activity and many fires within the city. The truth was, that the nearest bombs to the city centre were plotted five miles away, and the creep-back resulted in most falling between seven and seventeen miles along the line of approach. Very little damage occurred, but, at least, the losses were modest at nine aircraft. Oboe was brought into play again on the following night, when the next attack took place on St-Nazaire. A force of 323 aircraft included the 10 Squadron freshman crew of Sgt Williams, who took off at 19.20 and reached the target under clear skies to bomb from 14,500 feet on red and green TIs at 22.24. Many fires were burning, and the Williams crew reported the glow still visible from 170 miles away.

The month's final operation was posted on the 29th, when the red tape on the briefing-room wall maps ended again at Berlin. A force of 329 aircraft was made ready, of which ten were Halifaxes at Melbourne, where the armourers loaded each with the usual mix of high-explosives and incendiaries. Take-off was completed without incident between 21.35 and 21.45 with S/L Frank the senior pilot on duty, and this was the eighth time he had operated during the month. The route on this night took the bomber stream further north to cross Denmark's Jutland peninsular, but bad weather in the form of heavy ice-bearing cloud and static electricity extending from the North Sea to the Baltic forced four crews to turn for home. F/Sgt Vinish, Sgt Cozens, S/L Frank and F/O Wann and their crews landed back at Melbourne between 23.37 and 01.59, all with empty bomb bays after jettisoning their loads. The others pressed on through the front and reached the "Big City" to find good visibility that enabled them to identify the Müggelsee to the south-east of the city as a reference point from which to run in on the aiming-point. The Pathfinders were again short with their marking, and the main force arrived late, which meant that some of the markers had burned themselves out. The 10 Squadron crews bombed from 17,500 to 19,000 feet between 00.59 and 01.08 in the face of a heavy searchlight and flak defence, and set off home in the belief that the fires they had left behind, the glow from which was still visible from 150 miles away, indicated that an effective attack had been delivered. In fact, most of the bombing had been wasted in open country to the south-east of the city, and an accurate figure for damage was not forthcoming. During the course of the month the squadron operated on fourteen nights and dispatched 129 sorties for the loss of three Halifaxes and crews.

April 1943

Pre-flight briefing

April would prove to be the least rewarding month of the Ruhr offensive, largely because of the number of operations conducted outside of the region and beyond the range of Oboe. It began for 4 Group with participation in the final raids of the campaign against Lorient and St-Nazaire on the 2nd. 10 Squadron detailed the freshman crews of Sgts Beveridge and Glover and F/Sgt Hancock, and sent them off between 20.14 and 20 35 to join forty-four others at the former. They found the weather to be clear with good visibility, and picked out the coastline as they closed in on the target, where TIs were being delivered onto the aiming-point by the Pathfinder element. Bombing was carried out from 12,000 to 15,000 feet between 23.15 and 00.02, and some fires were observed. The following night brought the third operation of the Ruhr offensive against Essen, for which a force of 225 Lancasters, 113 Halifaxes and ten Mosquitos was made ready. This would be the first time that more than two hundred Lancasters had operated against a single target. 4 Group contributed ninety-one of the Halifaxes, thirteen of them belonging to 10 Squadron, and they were loaded with two 1,000 pounders and thirteen SBCs each. They took off between 19.34 and 19.49 with F/Ls Munro and Wood the senior pilots on duty, and the squadron's recent excellent rate of serviceability allowed all from Melbourne to reach the target area and find clear skies with good visibility, rather than the partial cloud predicted at briefing. The Pathfinder plan had anticipated the need for both sky and ground marking, a belt and braces approach that would become common practice in time, for which the crews would be prepared at briefing. However, there is a hint that some may have been confused to see both parachute flares and TIs on this night, although it did not adversely affect the conduct of the raid. The 10 Squadron crews carried out their attacks from 15,000 to 20,000 feet between 21.53 and 22.08 in the face of an intense searchlight and flak defence, and F/Sgt Denton's DT732 sustained some minor damage. The impression was of scattered fires over a wide area, which Sgt Geddes and crew reported were still visible for seventy miles. In fact, it had been another highly effective operation, which had destroyed 635 buildings in central and western districts, but at a cost of twenty-one aircraft, 6% of the force. The twelve missing Halifaxes represented a 10.6% casualty rate compared with a more sustainable 4% for the Lancasters.

P/O Tom Thackray, a founding member of the 10 Sqn Association.

The largest non-1,000 force to date, of 577 aircraft, was made ready on the 4th for an operation that night against Kiel. 10 Squadron detailed fourteen Halifaxes, which took off between 20.52 and 21.21 with F/Ls Munro and Wood the senior pilots on duty, and headed for the English coast at Bridlington. Sgt Williams and crew had been the last to depart Melbourne, and, after flying for almost two hours, it was clear that the target could not be reached within the time allotted for the raid, and they turned back. The bombs were jettisoned at 23.18, and, a minute later, the Halifax was attacked by a JU88, which knocked out the intercom and left the bomb doors hanging down. The rear gunner returned fire, and observed hits on the belly of the assailant, which dived away into cloud and was not seen again. At 23.59 the starboard-outer engine cut, and all fuel cocks were found to be unserviceable. The pilot decided to make for Thornaby, but the remaining engines failed at 500 feet during the approach, forcing him to crash-land at 02.31 in a nearby field. The crew walked away uninjured, but DT785 sustained serious damage, which would see it declared to be beyond economical repair. Meanwhile, the other 10 Squadron participants had arrived in the target area to find ten-tenths cloud and poor visibility, which necessitated the use of sky-marking, the least reliable method, made even more unreliable on this night by strong winds driving the parachute flares across the target area. Bombing was carried out from 18,000 to 20,000 feet between 23.19 and 23.47, and the glow of fires could be seen beneath the cloud layer. The return to Melbourne of HR699 and the crew of F/O Wann RCAF was awaited in vain, and no clue to their fate would ever be found. A number of crews commented on a strong night fighter presence off the Dutch coast, and this would seem

Leo Groak (centre) warms his hands with the rest of the ground crew who serviced F/O G. Hewlett & crew's Halifax HR691. Life-long friendships frequently resulted between the air and ground crews. In Leo's case with Tom Thackray, the flight engineer on Hewlett's crew.

to be the likely cause of the loss. The operation was an abject failure that caused minimal damage to the target at a cost of twelve aircraft.

S/L Ruffel and crew were posted in from 1652 Conversion Unit on the 5th. The Ruhr offensive continued at Duisburg on the 8th, for which a force of 392 aircraft was made ready. The 10 Squadron element of eight Halifaxes was again led by F/Ls Munro and Wood, and took off between 21.37 and 21.47, before setting course for the Dutch coast at Egmond for the northern approach to the target, followed by a southerly withdrawal via the French coast. P/O Hellis and crew were eighty minutes into the outward flight when the a.s.i froze, leaving them with little option but to turn back, the first from the squadron to do so for technical reasons for a month. The others found the target concealed beneath ten-tenths cloud, and the Pathfinder skymarking failed to provide a strong enough reference for the main force. The 10 Squadron crews bombed from 17,000 to 20,500 feet between 23.26 to 23.37 in the face of a spirited flak defence, which caused damage to a number of their aircraft. Duisburg escaped with the destruction of forty buildings, and would continue to enjoy a relatively charmed life for another five weeks, while the Command lost nineteen aircraft to compound the disappointment of the ineffective raid. 5 Group returned on the following night to find similar weather conditions, and managed to destroy fifty houses in return for a 7.7% loss.

Harris looked beyond the Ruhr for the next operation, which would be directed at Frankfurt on the 10th. A force of 502 aircraft was assembled, remarkably, with 144 Wellingtons the most populous type, some of them provided by 4 Group in an overall contribution of 114 aircraft. 10 Squadron made ready eleven Halifaxes, and sent them off between 23.32 and 23.46 with F/L Wood the senior pilot on duty. They flew out over Dungeness before setting course for Oppenheim, in order to make an approach to the target from the south-west, and all reached southern Germany to find the entire target area concealed beneath ten-tenths cloud. The Melbourne crews attacked on e.t.a on estimated positions from 16,500 and 18,000 feet between 02.46 and 03.05, and observed the glow of fires, which may have been decoys, as, according to local reports, almost no bombs fell within the city boundaries. The price of the failure was twenty-one aircraft and crews, although none from Melbourne. S/L Baird and crew were posted in from 1658 Conversion Unit on the 12th, shortly before a C Flight was formed.

The focus remained on southern Germany for the next operation, which would be against Stuttgart on the 14th. A force of 462 aircraft included a dozen Halifaxes belonging to 10 Squadron, which took off between 21.26 and 21.42 with F/Ls Munro and Wood the senior pilots on duty. They adopted a similar route to that for Frankfurt, but, for a change, not all of the Melbourne element would reach the target area. F/O Brookbanks and crew lost the use of their intercom and DR compass within ninety minutes, and were followed home by Sgt Brunton and crew, the pilot having been taken ill. The others reached the target to find clear skies and good visibility, which enabled them to pick out ground detail. The Pathfinders marked what they thought was the centre of the city, but the main force crews failed to press on to the aiming-point and a creep-back developed along the line of approach from the north-east. The 10 Squadron crews carried out their attacks from 15,000 to 16,000 feet between 01.04 and 01.14, aiming mostly at a group of green TIs, and many fires were reported, including one very large one described as being in the city centre. In fact, most of the damage occurred in the industrial north-eastern suburb of Bad Canstatt and neighbouring districts, where 393 buildings were destroyed. One tragic incident to the east of the city centre involved a direct hit on an air-raid bunker containing French and Russian PoWs, almost four hundred of whom lost their lives. Sgt Beveridge and crew returned to report the frustration of being unable to open their bomb doors over the target, and eventually jettisoned their load over Belgium on the way home. DT746 failed to return home with the crew of F/Sgt Hancock, and it was learned later that it had crashed to the east of Reims killing all but the flight engineer, who was taken into captivity.

Preparations were put in hand on the 16th for a major night of operations, which would see 327 Lancasters and Halifaxes head for the Skoda armaments works at Pilsen in Czechoslovakia, while a predominantly Wellington and Stirling force of 271 aircraft carried out a diversionary raid on Mannheim. The plan of attack for the former called for the Pathfinders to drop route markers at the final turning point, seven miles from the target, which the crews were to then locate visually in the anticipated bright moonlight, and bomb from as low a level as practicable. It was a complicated plan that invited confusion, and the outcome would question the quality of some of the briefings. 10 Squadron made ready eleven Halifaxes, loading each with four 1,000 pounders and a single 500 pounder, before dispatching them from Melbourne between 20.44 and 21.15 with S/L Frank the senior pilot on duty. They had ahead of them a round-trip of some 1,500 miles, which all of the crews would negotiate, although not without incident for some. F/Sgt Virgo and crew were outbound near Reims at 23.23 when attacked from astern by a ME110, which closed to within one hundred yards through a hail of fire from the Halifax's rear turret. Hits were observed on the enemy's port wing between the engine and the fuselage, until it broke off to leave the night fighter falling away into cloud.

All of the 10 Squadron participants arrived in the target area to find the forecast favourable weather conditions, with a layer of eight-tenths cloud at around 9,000 feet, below which, visibility was good and ground features could be made out clearly. As mentioned above, the bombing was supposed to be carried out visually from below the cloud base after making a timed run from the turning-point, which had been marked by TIs. The 10 Squadron crews bombed from 4,000 to 11,000 feet visually and on TIs, between 01.36 and 01.55, proving that they failed to comply with the instructions at briefing, and bombed the turning point, which happened to be over an asylum. They were not alone. A failure in the bomb-release system over the target prevented S/L Frank from dropping his load, and it was eventually jettisoned "live" at 02.05 some fifty miles north-east of Nuremberg. On return, F/O Dawes struck a tree while trying to land at Harwell, and ended up crash-landing HR691 without crew casualties but with extensive damage to the Halifax. F/L Wood had lost his port-outer engine to flak over the target, and then the port-inner to a similar cause at the French coast. The Channel was crossed on two engines, before a crash-landing was carried out at 05.20 near Lewes in Sussex, from where the shocked and injured crew members were ferried to hospital for treatment. After an inspection, DT791 would be declared to be beyond economical repair. Post-raid reconnaissance revealed the truth, that, despite the claims of returning crews, the factory had escaped damage, and the huge disappointment was compounded by the loss of thirty-six heavy bombers, divided equally between the two types. When added to the eighteen missing aircraft from the reasonably effective raid on Mannheim, this brought the night's total to a new record of fifty-four, making it the most expensive single night to date for the Command.

Orders were received on the 20th to prepare for another long-range operation that night, this one against the port of Stettin, situated 640 miles away as the crow flies, at the eastern end of Germany's Baltic coast. 4 Group contributed one hundred Halifaxes to the force of 339 aircraft, thirteen of them belonging to 10 Squadron. The route would take the bomber stream across the North Sea to a point north of Esbjerg on the Danish coast, before traversing Jutland to then head south-east towards the target. The distance, which was similar to that for Pilsen, dictated a reduced bomb load of a single 1,000 pounder and eleven SBCs of incendiaries each, and these were lifted into the air at Melbourne between 21.18 and 21.31 with S/L Baird the senior pilot on duty for the first time. There were targets that seemed to enjoy something of a charmed life, that frequently escaped the worst ravages of a Bomber Command attack, but Stettin was not among them, perhaps because of its location near an easily-identifiable coastline. On this night, clear skies and good visibility paved the way for the Pathfinders to deliver a perfect marking performance, which was exploited by the main force crews to devastating effect. There were no early returns among the Melbourne element, and they arrived to find the city laid out before them with the river, built-up area and the docks clearly defined, and the aiming-point marked by green TIs. S/L Baird and crew suffered the frustration of a complete hang-up, and would jettison their load into the Baltic south of Sweden on the way home. The others carried out their attacks from 11,000 to 15,500 feet between 01.01 and 01.10, and, on return, reported fires raging across the city. Twenty-one aircraft failed to return home, and among them was the squadron's JB930, which had been brought down by flak at the Danish coast outbound, and crashed near Esbjerg after Sgt Glover and his crew had parachuted into enemy hands. It was thirty-six hours before a reconnaissance aircraft captured photographs of the still-burning city, and these revealed an area of one hundred acres of devastation across the centre. Local reports confirmed that thirteen industrial premises and 380 houses had been destroyed.

A force of 561 aircraft was made ready to return to the Ruhr on the 26th for the next assault on Duisburg. 10 Squadron contributed nine Halifaxes to the 4 Group effort of 123 Halifaxes and Wellingtons, and they departed Melbourne between 00.22 and 00.57 with W/C Edmonds the senior pilot on duty. There were no early returns among the 10 Squadron element, and they approached the target in conditions of good visibility from the north-east guided by yellow route markers, from which they made a timed run. Red and green TIs awaited them at the target, and these were claimed by the Pathfinders to be on the city-centre aiming-point. Bombing was carried out from 16,000 to 19,000 feet between 02.22 and 02.48, and many fires were reported spread over a wide area. Seventeen aircraft failed to return, but there were no absentees from debriefing at Melbourne, where the consensus was of a successful night's work. This was partly confirmed by post-raid reconnaissance, but it was clear that the bombing had centred on the north-eastern districts, some spilling into other urban areas, possibly because of the tendency to bomb the first fires reached, rather than push on to the aiming-point. Even so, more than three hundred buildings had been destroyed, and this represented a victory at this elusive target.

S/L Ruffel was posted to RAF Base Pocklington on the 27th having not carried out any operational sorties during his month with the squadron, and F/L Wood was sent there also, both pending permanent postings. The first of two record mining efforts was announced on that day, for which the squadron made ready six Halifaxes for an overall force of 160 aircraft bound for the Biscay coast and the Frisians. The Melbourne element took off between 01.28 and 01.35 with S/L Baird the senior pilot on duty, and headed for the Nectarines region off the Frisians. They encountered ten-tenths cloud, heavy rain and poor visibility, which required a Gee-fix to establish positions, before the six Mk V and IV mines could be delivered into the briefed locations from 700 to 2,000 feet between 02.27 and 03.02. 458 mines were dropped on this night for the loss of a single Lancaster, but there would be a rude awakening for those imagining that mining operations were "a piece of cake", when a new mining record of 207 aircraft was set on the following night. The target areas for this night were off north-western Germany and Denmark's Baltic coasts from Læ Island in the Kattegat to the Great and Little Belts further south. 10 Squadron made ready nine Halifaxes, which took off between 20.15 and 20.30 with F/O Dawes the senior pilot on duty, and headed out in fair to good visibility to the Silverthorne garden of the Kattegat off north-eastern Denmark. Pinpoints were obtained on Skaw and on Læsø Island, and timed runs carried out to the drop zones, where the vegetables were delivered from 3,000 to 5,500 feet between 23.44 and 00.06. All returned safely from what were uneventful sorties, but twenty-two aircraft had been lost, mostly to light flak, while operating further south between Denmark's main islands. This was a record loss for a mining operation, but the 593 mines delivered into important sea lanes was also a record.

The month ended with yet another attack on Essen, for which a heavy force of 190 Lancasters and 105 Halifaxes was assembled on the 30th. 10 Squadron made ready twelve Halifaxes, which took off between 00.10 and 00.25 with S/L Baird the senior pilot on duty, and made their way via the usual northern route into the Ruhr over Egmond on the Dutch coast. An oxygen system failure forced S/L Baird to turn back after ninety minutes, at about the same time as F/O Dawes feathered his starboard-inner engine and also abandoned his sortie. The others pressed on to encounter ten-tenths cloud over the target and Pathfinder sky-marking in progress, and bombed in the face of heavy flak from 17,000 to 20,000 feet between 02.43 and 02.52. Sgt Williams and crew were attacked by a JU88 as they ran in on the target, and the bombs fell short of the aiming-point. The rear gunner returned fire, and the night fighter broke off its attack and was lost to sight. Returning crews were unable to offer an assessment, and could only report the glow of fires beneath the clouds. In fact, it had been a scattered attack, which caused fresh damage at Essen amounting to 189 buildings destroyed and further hits on the Krupp works, but ten other Ruhr towns also reported bombs falling. Six Lancasters and six Halifaxes failed to return, the telling feature being a 3.1% loss rate for the former compared with 5.1% for the latter. During the course of the month the squadron operated on twelve nights, and dispatched 121 sorties for the loss of five Halifaxes and three crews.

May 1943

May would bring a return to winning ways with some outstanding successes, and the Ruhr campaign, which, thus far, had focussed exclusively on Essen and Duisburg at the western end, would widen to include other giant centres of war production, beginning with Dortmund on the 4th. This was the day that brought S/L Hartnell-Beavis and crew to the squadron from 76 Squadron, and S/L Debenham was posted temporarily from RAF Base Pocklington as non-effective-sick. A new record non-1,000 force of 596 aircraft was made ready for Dortmund, a figure that included thirteen Halifaxes at Melbourne, which were each loaded with two 1,000 pounders, seven SBCs of 4lb incendiaries and six of 30lbs. They took off between 22.28 and 22.56 with S/L Baird the senior pilot on duty, and crossed the North Sea to make landfall over Texel, before adopting a south-easterly course to cross the Ijsselmeer on a direct heading to the target at the eastern end of the Ruhr. The weather conditions were favourable and the visibility fair as they closed in on the objective to bomb on red and green TIs from 17,000 to 19,000 feet between 01.05 and 01.34. W/O Price and crew were late, and, feeling that they would not reach the primary target in time, dropped their bombs south of Bochum, when just minutes away from Dortmund. The navigator in the crew of F/Sgt Geddes RAAF reported feeling ill as they left the target, which generally meant oxygen starvation, and the pilot reduced height for the journey home. On reaching England they were diverted to Leeming because of poor weather conditions at Melbourne, but flew into high ground at 04.43 at Hood Range, Sutton Bank near Thirsk. The pilot, flight engineer and rear gunner survived with injuries, leaving five bodies in the wreckage of JD105. On return to give their stories at debriefing, P/O Wade and crew reported observing a red flame shoot a thousand feet into the air, while others described many fires and intense searchlight and flak activity, as well as the glow of fires visible for 150 miles into the return journey. Post-raid reconnaissance revealed that some of the bombing had fallen short and a decoy fire site had attracted other loads, but half of the force had bombed within three miles of the aiming-point, and had inflicted extensive damage in central and northern districts. Local reports put the damage at 1,218 buildings destroyed and 2,100 others seriously damaged, including some important war-industry factories. The success was gained at the high price of thirty-one missing bombers, which represented a new record for the campaign, and, sadly, one that would be exceeded many times over the ensuing months.

S/L Frank DSO, DFC and his crew were posted to 51 Squadron on the 6th on promotion to succeed the former 10 Squadron stalwart, W/C Sawyer, on his elevation to group captain rank. Minor operations occupied the following week, while 10 Squadron remained at home and concentrated on a training programme, particularly for the many new crews whose arrival had swelled the ranks and facilitated the expansion to three flights. When the next operation was posted on the 12th, it was Duisburg yet again, for which a force of 572 aircraft was put together. Thirteen crews were briefed at Melbourne, and their aircraft loaded with the usual mix of high-explosives and incendiaries, although, two would be cancelled at the last minute because of mechanical problems. This left eleven to take off between 23.29 and 23.49 with S/Ls Baird and Hartnell-Beavis the senior pilots on duty, all carrying a second pilot and bound by the usual route for the western Ruhr. It was not to be a good night for the senior pilots, both flight commanders running into severe icing, which caused them to shed five hundred feet per minute, and this problem was compounded for S/L Hartnell-Beavis by the loss of his escape hatch during take-off, reducing his speed by 10 mph. Both jettisoned their loads and turned for home, where they found Sgt Williams and crew, who had experienced similar problems with icing. At 02.00, when twenty miles east-north-east of Arnhem, JB974 was engaged by a ME110, which scored hits on the Halifax, causing damage to the tail unit and bomb doors and holed Nºs 2, 3 and 4 fuel tanks. The rear gunner returned fire and observed hits on the nose and belly of the enemy, which reared up and fell away to be claimed as a probable. Sgt Beveridge had ordered the bombs to be jettisoned, and he and his crew were homebound and coming up on The Hague at 02.30, when they were attacked again, this time by a BF109, which was evaded by skilful crew co-operation.

Meanwhile, in favourable weather conditions and good visibility, the Pathfinders performed magnificently to present the city to the approaching main force crews, and, despite intense searchlight and flak activity, they pressed home their attacks on the aiming-point. The remaining 10 Squadron crews carried out their runs from 17,000 to 19,000 feet between 02.03 and 02.23, and dropped their bombs onto red and green TIs, observing large numbers of fires as they turned away. Post-raid reconnaissance confirmed that the attack had fallen on the city centre and the Ruhrort area, the largest inland docks in Germany, and that 1,596 buildings had been reduced to rubble, almost nineteen thousand tons of shipping had been sunk and a further sixty ships, amounting to forty-one thousand tons, had sustained damage. The success came again at a high price, a new record for the campaign of thirty-four aircraft, but it would not be deemed necessary to return to Duisburg again during the campaign.

Bochum became the fourth Ruhr city to be targeted and would face a force of 442 aircraft on the 13th, while 5 Group sent its Lancasters to join a Pathfinder element in what would be a vain attempt to redress the recent failure at Pilsen. Situated in the heart of the industrial region between Essen and Dortmund, Bochum's status had been built on coal mining, and its contribution to the war effort included a steel plant producing guns. 10 Squadron made ready thirteen Halifaxes, which took off between 23.42 and 00.01 with S/Ls Baird and Hartnell-Beavis the senior pilots on duty, and headed for the Scheldt Estuary to enter the target area via the southerly route to the north of Cologne. It was here that Sgt Beveridge and crew ran into a nest of searchlights while flying at 18,000 feet, and a nearby flak burst triggered rudder-overbalance,

The site near Sutton Bank's White Horse, Yorkshire where Halifax JD105 crashed on 5 May 1943. Having attacked Dortmund the aircraft was diverting to Leeming due to poor weather at Melbourne. F/Sgt R.H. Geddes the pilot, his flight engineer and the tail gunner all escaped with minor injuries. Sgt E Hill, Sgt T Cox, Sgt H Taylor, Sgt H Way and Sgt K Hart were killed.

which threw the Halifax onto its back and into a dive. The pilot regained control at 7,000 feet, by which time the mid-upper gunner had made the unilateral decision to take to his parachute.* Still held in searchlights, the bombs were jettisoned live somewhere between Cologne and Düsseldorf, possibly on Leverkusen, and the decision taken to make for home by the shortest possible route. By 03.10 they had reached South Beveland at the mouth of the Scheldt and were flying at 12,000 feet, when a JU88 with a searchlight in its nose appeared five hundred feet above and six hundred yards astern. A second JU88 then attacked from the starboard quarter, and a running battle ensued, during which the Halifax and one of the enemy fighters sustained damage, the latter being observed to emit smoke from one engine. The enemy aircraft were eventually shaken off, and the Halifax returned to base minus one crew member and displaying the scars of battle, but with no injuries to the occupants. W/O Fennell and crew were also held in searchlights for seven minutes, while being bombarded by flak, which scored some hits. During the evasive action they had lost height, and, down to 11,000 feet, they abandoned all thought of attacking the primary target. They decided to pick their way out of the Ruhr by adopting the planned return route to the north of the region and out over the Dutch coast via the Ijsselmeer, and dropped their bombs in the Dortmund area as they passed overhead at 02.08. The remaining Melbourne crews found the target in good visibility, and bombed the red and green Pathfinder TIs from 17,000 to 20,000 feet between 02.05 and 02.34. Returning crews reported a considerable number of fires and a column of smoke rising through 10,000 feet as they turned away. Twenty-four aircraft failed to return, and among them was 10 Squadron's DT732, which had been shot down by a night fighter into the Ijsselmeer on the way home, taking with it the crew of F/Sgt Mills RAAF. Thirteen of the missing aircraft were Halifaxes, which represented a 9.6% loss-rate. Post-raid reconnaissance revealed that decoy fires had drawn off some of the bomb loads intended for Bochum, but, even so, almost four hundred buildings had been reduced to ruins, and seven hundred others severely damaged.

There now followed a nine-day lull in main force activity, while the expansion programme continued apace, and sprog crews were provided with intensive training. It was during this period, on the night of the 16/17th, that 617 Squadron made headlines around the world after its epic attack on the Ruhr Dams. The "Sheriff" went on leave on the 18th, leaving the C Flight commander, S/L Debenham, in temporary command of the squadron, while F/L Badcoe stepped up to oversee the flight. It was not until the 23rd that the next operation was posted, and it would demonstrate the extent of the expansion that had taken place during the preceding month. Just three weeks earlier the Command had set a new record for a single target, when sending 596 aircraft to Dortmund. *(The "One Thousand" forces sent to Cologne, Essen and Bremen in 1942 employed aircraft from other Commands, and do not, therefore, count as exclusively Bomber Command operations for the purpose of records.)* The force assembled on the airfields of eastern England being prepared for a return to Dortmund totalled 826 aircraft, an increase of 230 aircraft, and a feat achieved by adding a C Flight to most of the established squadrons. In many cases these would be hived off eventually to form new squadrons.

10 Squadron achieved its own record by making ready twenty-one Halifaxes and launching them from Melbourne between 22.30 and 22.55 with S/L Baird the senior pilot on duty. His sortie lasted until he turned back with a failed intercom at 23.59 when twenty-five miles off the Norfolk coast, and this left F/L Wood as the senior pilot representing the squadron. The others all reached the target area to find clear weather conditions and plentiful red and green TIs marking out the aiming-point in the centre of the city. They bombed from 16,400 to 20,000 feet between 01.02 and 01.37, and observed many fires and explosions, including a vivid, orange-coloured one, before drifting smoke began to obscure the ground. Sgt Watson and crew were on their way home near the Dutch coast at 16,000 feet when they were attacked by three JU88s and a BF109 at 01.55. The ensuing battle lasted for forty-five minutes, and ended only as the English coast hove into sight, during which period the starboard-outer engine was knocked out, and further damage was sustained to the fuselage, tailplane, rudders, starboard mainplane, port tyre and the hydraulics system. The rear gunner was constantly in action, and scored hits on an

engine of one JU88, from which pieces were seen to break away as it fell towards the ground to be claimed as probably destroyed.

The records on this night continued with the failure to return of thirty-eight aircraft, the heaviest loss of the Ruhr campaign thus far, and eighteen of them were Halifaxes, which represented a 9% loss-rate compared with 2.3% for the Lancasters. There were three empty dispersals to contemplate at Melbourne on the following morning, those that should have been occupied by W1217, DT789 and HR696. The first-mentioned was shot down by the night fighter of Ofw Heinz Vinke of IV./NJG1, and crashed into the Ijsselmeer with no survivors from the crew of Sgt Hine. DT789 was last heard from by W/T at 02.27, when some seventy miles off the Lincolnshire coast and indicating that it was under attack by a night fighter. The Halifax failed to survive, and just one member of the crew of Sgt Rees eventually washed ashore for burial in Germany. The last-mentioned went down in the general target area, again with no survivors from the eight-man crew of F/Sgt Denton. Post-raid reconnaissance revealed the raid to have been a massive success, which destroyed almost two thousand buildings predominantly in central, northern and eastern districts, while causing damage to some important war industry factories.

10 Sqn "The Gunnery Section" – Smithy, Titch and Aussie.

The Ruhr offensive shifted to Düsseldorf on the 25th, for which a force of 759 aircraft was made ready, seventeen of them Halifaxes at Melbourne. They took off between 23.27 and 23.48 with S/L Debenham the senior pilot on duty, supported by F/Ls Badcoe and Wood. S/L Debenham turned back after a little more than an hour when the oxygen and intercom systems failed, but the others all continued on to reach the target area situated at the western end of the Ruhr Valley between Duisburg to the north and Cologne to the south. The route out took the bomber stream across Belgium and into Germany at a point south of Aachen, before it swung to the north-east to run in on the target. The Pathfinders were greeted by wo layers of cloud on top of industrial haze, as a result of which they were unable to establish their position with sufficient accuracy to provide the main force crews with a firm reference. Most of the 10 Squadron crews made a timed run from yellow route markers, and bombed on red and green TIs from 13,000 to 18,500 feet between 01.42 and 02.00. There may also have been decoy fire sites and markers, and the result was a scattered raid, part of which hit the primary target, but succeeded only in destroying between fifty and a hundred buildings at a cost to the Command of twenty-seven aircraft.

ZA denoted 10 Squadron's aircraft as shown here on Mk II Halifax BB324

Halifax DT776 ZA T/R. May 1943. Centre Officer may be F/L N A Cobb RCAF who left 10 Sqn to join 35 Sqn only to be killed in June 1943.

F/L Munro was posted to 10 O.T.U. on the 26th, the day on which S/L Baird and crew were posted out of 4 Group to join 3 Group's 115 Squadron, which had recently converted to Lancaster Mk IIs after spending the entire war thus far on Wellingtons. S/L Sutton and crew were posted in from 102 Squadron to replace them on the 27th. Almost four weeks after the last attack on Essen, a force of 518 aircraft was assembled on the 27th, to return there that night. The 10 Squadron element of eighteen Halifaxes departed Melbourne between 22.23 and 23.32 with S/Ls Debenham and Hartnell-Beavis the senior pilots on duty, and set course for Egmond on the Den Helder peninsular for the northern approach to the Ruhr. Sgt Belcher could not persuade DT776 to climb above 14,000 feet, and turned for home, jettisoning his bombs into the sea on the way. The others pushed on to find a thin layer of seven to nine-tenths cloud between 4,000 and 6,000 feet as they closed on the target, and made timed runs from the last turning point before bombing on red and green skymarkers from 17,000 to 19,000 feet between 00.56 and 01.24. Fires were seen through gaps in the cloud, and a large explosion was noted in the eastern side of the city at 01.03. By the end of the raid it seemed that the target was well-ablaze, the glow from which could be seen from eighty miles into the return journey. Twenty-three aircraft failed to return, eleven of them Halifaxes, a 7.2% casualty rate compared with 2.2% for the Lancasters. 10 Squadron's JB958 was shot down by the night fighter of Lt Werner Rapp of III./NJG1, and crashed at 01.47 three miles west-south-west of Emmen in north-eastern Holland. F/O Rawlinson died with four of his crew, and just two survived to fall into enemy hands. JB960 came down somewhere in or near the Ruhr to an unknown cause, and took W/O Price and his crew to their deaths, the bomb-aimer, F/O Curtis, at the tender age of eighteen. The operation was moderately successful, and destroyed 488 buildings in central and southern districts, while ten other Ruhr towns reported bombs falling.

10 Squadron had now lost five crews in just two operations, and only two of thirty-six crewmen had survived. This figure was about to become two out of forty-three with the next operation, which was to be directed at the Barmen half of the twin towns known as Wuppertal, situated on the southern fringe of the Ruhr looking out picturesque wooded countryside and lakes to the south. A force of 719 aircraft was put together on the 29th, of which seventeen Halifaxes belonged to 10 Squadron, and they took off between 22.31 and 23.09 with S/Ls Hartnell-Beavis and Sutton the senior pilots on duty. A spate of engine-related issues saw Sgts Brunton and Pinkerton and S/L Sutton turn back, leaving the others to press on across Belgium via the southerly approach to the Ruhr. They were forced to run the gauntlet of intense and accurate flak between Cologne and Düsseldorf, before arriving in the target area to find clear skies but thick haze, which obscured much of the ground detail. This would prove to be one of those rare occasions when the plan of attack worked perfectly, with accurate, concentrated marking preceding an excellent performance by the main-force crews. The 10 Squadron element bombed on Gee-fixes confirmed by red and green TIs from 16,000 to 19,000 feet between 00.49 and 01.28, and saw fires developing and an enormous explosion in the south-eastern corner of the target area at 01.28. There were ten Halifaxes among the thirty-three missing aircraft, and 10 Squadron was represented by DT787, which crashed near Dortmund soon after leaving the target, killing F/Sgt Clarke RNZAF and his crew. When the operation was assessed, it was found that around one thousand acres, or an estimated 80% of the town's built-up area, had been reduced to ruins, largely by fire, which may have reached "firestorm" proportions, although this phenomenon was not yet known. Six of the largest factories were destroyed, along with 211 other industrial premises and almost four thousand houses. A further 71 industrial buildings and

1,800 of a residential nature were seriously damaged, and the death toll, at an estimated 3,400 people, was five times the previous highest at a German target. During the course of the month the squadron operated on seven nights, and dispatched 110 sorties for the loss of eight Halifaxes, and seven complete crews.

June 1943

There would be no major operations during the first ten nights of the new month, and the only operational activity in 4 Group involved elements from the Wellington squadrons carrying out gardening sorties on the 1st, 2nd and 3rd. W/C Edmonds returned from leave on the 2nd, releasing S/L Debenham to resume command of C Flight, and Sgt Beveridge and crew were posted to 35 Squadron for Pathfinder duties. A programme of training kept the crews busy during the operational lull, and all of the squadrons were fully rested and replenished by the time that Düsseldorf was posted as the destination for a force of 783 aircraft on the 11th. It would be a milestone for the Halifax brigade, which, for the first time, could send more than two hundred aircraft to a single target. 10 Squadron made ready twenty Halifaxes, loading each with the usual mix of high-explosives and incendiaries, but W/C Edmonds's mount became unserviceable late on and was withdrawn. The remaining nineteen departed Melbourne between 22.50 and 23.35 with S/Ls Debenham and Sutton now the senior pilots on duty, and set course for the Belgian coast for the southerly approach to the target. F/Sgt Geddes, who had just returned to operations following his recovery from the injuries sustained in the crash on return from Dortmund at the start of May, and Sgt Dunlop and crews ran into severe icing at 15,000 feet at the mid-point of the North Sea crossing at 00.35 and 01.09 respectively, and were unable to maintain altitude. They jettisoned their bombs and turned for home, leaving the remaining seventeen to press on to the target, where visibility was reduced to an extent by a thin layer of cloud and ground haze. This mattered little as long as the Oboe marking provided a strong reference for the backers-up, and this part of the operation proceeded according to plan until one Oboe Mosquito accidentally released some TIs fourteen miles to the north-east. The 10 Squadron crews bombed on release-point marker flares and TIs on the ground from 16,000 and 20,000 feet between 01.16 and 02.07, and observed many individual fires, which were beginning to join together and emit large volumes of smoke as they withdrew to the north. Despite the errant markers, which, inevitably, drew off a small proportion of the bombing, post-raid reconnaissance revealed the operation to have been an outstanding success. An estimated 130 acres had been destroyed in central districts, a figure confirmed by local authorities, which reported a fire area measuring 8 x 5 kilometres covering the old and new town. There were more than 8,800 separate fire incidents, and production was halted at forty-two war industry factories. The defenders fought back to claim thirty-eight aircraft, equalling the record for the campaign thus far, but this number did not include any from 10 Squadron.

There would be a return to Bochum on the following night, for which a force of 503 aircraft was assembled. An all-Lancaster and Halifax main force included a 10 Squadron contribution of seventeen, and they took off between 23.05 and 23.32 with W/C Edmonds the senior pilot on duty supported by S/L Sutton. F/O Pennicott climbed out with the others over the airfield, but five minutes after setting course for Texel, the I.F.F failed, and he turned back, to be followed home later by F/Sgt Morley and crew with engine issues. The others reached the target area to find a thin layer of five to nine-tenths cloud at 10,000 feet, which had no effect on the Pathfinder marking performance. The 10 Squadron crews carried out their attacks on release-point flares and TIs on the ground, doing so from 18,500 and 21,000 feet between 01.29 and 01.42. Many explosions and fires were observed, and the target appeared to be a mass of flames as the crews retreated on a reciprocal course for home. W7907 was approaching the Dutch frontier when it was intercepted by Lt Hans-Heinz Augenstein of III./NJG1, who shot it down to crash at 01.56 near Gildehaus, killing the crew of Sgt Inness. The operation was highly successful, and destroyed 130 acres of built-up area, reducing to rubble 449 buildings and seriously damaging more than nine hundred others. Twenty-four aircraft failed to return, and the Halifax loss rate of 6% compared with 4.3% for the Lancaster.

The Lancasters of 1, 5 and 8 Groups maintained pressure on the Ruhr with an attack on Oberhausen on the night of the 14/15th, and then raided Cologne two nights later, both to good effect. 10 Squadron remained inactive until the 19th, when 3, 4, 6 and 8 Groups joined forces to assemble a force of 290 aircraft for an attack on the Schneider armaments works at Le Creusot in east-central France. This target was owned by the family responsible for the famous bi-annual Schneider Trophy float-plane time-trials of the 1920s and 1930s, which was competed for by Britain, France, Italy and the USA, and was won outright after three consecutive victories by Britain. The company was known as the Krupp of France, and had been attacked in daylight by 5 Group Lancasters in the previous October, but not, as it turned out, effectively. 4 Group contributed 112 Halifaxes, of which the sixteen provided by 10 Squadron were loaded with three 1,000 pounders and six 500 pounders each, before taking off between 21.58 and 22.25 with W/C Edmonds the senior pilot on duty. S/L Debenham was forced to turn back with an oil leak in the port-outer engine, and was some fifteen miles off the French coast at Dieppe at 00.15 when a BF109 was spotted at three hundred yards range on the starboard quarter. As S/L Debenham began a corkscrew to starboard, the rear gunner got in a four-second burst, which was seen to score hits on the enemy's fuselage and engine. The enemy pilot attempted to follow the Halifax's turn, but was unable to bring his guns to bear, and passed underneath before performing a climbing turn to port, which put him at the mercy of the mid-upper gunner, who fired a three-second burst, which was also seen to strike home. The persistent and resolute German pilot then closed to two hundred yards, and, while the rear gunner attempted to clear a blockage in his guns, the mid-upper fired a long burst, which forced the enemy to break off to the rear and below. Having cleared the stoppage, the rear gunner fired a five or six-second burst, and watched the assailant fall towards the sea trailing smoke. The impact was witnessed by both gunners and the second pilot, and the wreckage was seen to burn for three minutes. The Halifax landed safely, and the crew reported that the enemy aircraft had not opened fire once during the engagement.

Meanwhile, the rest of the force pressed on across France to the target, which the Pathfinders were to illuminate rather than mark, with the intention that the main force crews would identify their specific aiming-points and make two bombing runs at between 5,000 and 10,000 feet. This was asking a lot of predominantly inexperienced crews, who were used to bombing on TIs from around 18,000 feet and abdicating the responsibility for accuracy to the Pathfinders. The skies were clear as the 10 Squadron crews picked out the built-up area, factory buildings and water features, and bombed from 6,000 to 10,000 feet either side of 02.00. Many bomb bursts were observed along with a column of smoke, which began to rise and drift across the area to spoil the visibility. Only two aircraft failed to return home, both Halifaxes, and one of these was 10 Squadron's JD109, which crashed in France without survivors from the crew of Sgt Watson. Post-raid reconnaissance revealed that most of the bombing had fallen within three miles of the factory, but only about 20% of the bomb loads had hit it, some of the others falling onto residential property in the town.

A hectic round of four major operations against Ruhr targets in the space of five nights was to begin at Krefeld on the 21st. Situated on the West Bank of the Rhine south-west of Duisburg and north-west of Düsseldorf, it was the most westerly Ruhr town to be targeted, and would face a force of 705 aircraft, which were routed in over the Scheldt Estuary. 10 Squadron loaded nineteen Halifaxes with a mix of high-explosives and incendiaries, and dispatched them from Melbourne between 23.39 and 00.05 with S/Ls Debenham, Hartnell-Beavis and Sutton the senior pilots on duty. Sgt Pinkerton and crew turned back after an hour, and they were followed home by Sgt Morley and crew, both after their aircraft had developed engine issues. The others pressed on to find clear skies but the usual ground haze, which the Pathfinders would negate with a near-perfect display of target marking for the main-force crews to exploit. The 10 Squadron element carried out their attacks on red and green TIs from 16,000 to 20,000 feet between 02.03 and 02.14, and watched a concentrated area of fire develop, which would remain visible for a hundred miles into the return journey. The searchlight and flak defences were described by most as moderate, and it was the night fighters that were responsible for the majority of the forty-four missing bombers, a new record for the campaign. Seventeen Halifaxes were lost, six of them from 35 Squadron of the Pathfinders, and this represented an 8.1% loss rate for the type, which was marginally more than the 7.7% registered by the Stirlings, but appreciably in excess of the 3.4% for the Lancaster brigade. In return for this huge loss, Krefeld had suffered the destruction of 5,517 houses in an area of devastation in the centre representing 47% of the built-up area, leaving 72,000 people homeless and a death toll of 1,056.

On the following night it was the turn of Mülheim-an-der-Ruhr to face its first onslaught of the offensive, for which 557 aircraft were made ready. Situated just to the south of Duisburg, Essen and Oberhausen, the town had, no doubt, been hit many times by stray bombs, but it was a different matter to be targeted specifically by a large force at the top of its game and proficient in its tactics. 10 Squadron prepared nineteen Halifaxes, and launched them from Melbourne between 23.10 and 23.29 with S/Ls Hartnell-Beavis and Sutton the senior pilots on duty. F/Sgt Morley and crew were ninety minutes out when the engine gremlins struck again for the third time in four operations, and they turned back, as did Sgt Topp and crew at the same time with an intercom issue. The others pressed on via Noordwijk on the Dutch coast to a turning point north of the Ruhr, and reached the target to find a thin layer of three-tenths stratus cloud at 10,000 feet, through which it could be seen that the Pathfinders had produced another example of near-perfect marking. The 10 Squadron crews bombed on red and green TIs from 17,500 to 20,700 feet between 01.25 and 01.52, and observed the development of many fires, while witnessing a large red explosion at 01.34. The defenders fought back again to claim thirty-five bombers, including 10 Squadron's BB324, which was lost in the sea and took with it the crew of Sgt Pinkerton. Post-raid reconnaissance revealed an accurate and concentrated attack, which destroyed eleven hundred buildings, mostly in central and northern districts, and damaged to some extent twelve thousand more. Much damage was also inflicted upon the eastern districts of Oberhausen.

10 Sqn Halifax

Above left: Paddy Kirk. Right: Sgt L Jewsbury (M/UG in W/C D.Edmonds' crew).

After a night's rest, a force of 630 aircraft was made ready on the 24th to unleash against the Elberfeld half of Wuppertal, which was still reeling from the devastating attack on Barmen a month earlier. 10 Squadron fuelled and bombed up fifteen Halifaxes, and launched them from Melbourne between 22.52 and 23.16 with F/Ls Black and Brookbanks the senior pilots on duty. Sgt Belcher and crew were the first of three to turn back early with a number of issues possibly due to icing conditions, and F/Sgt Geddes and crew followed them home after the P4 compass, Gee and intercom systems all failed. Finally, F/L Black was forced to abandon his sortie because of the oxygen system becoming unserviceable, and this left a dozen 10 Squadron crews to press on to the target area. The weather conditions continue to favour the bombers, and relatively clear skies and accurate Pathfinder marking laid out the town to the eyes of the bomb-aimers. The Melbourne crews released their loads from 16,000 to 20,000 feet on red and green TIs between 01.14 and 01.30, and witnessed many large explosions and fires, and a pall of smoke rising through 10,000 feet as they withdrew and headed for the Dutch coast near Egmond. The glow of fires was still visible from Amsterdam, a distance of 130 miles, and it was clear to returning crews that another highly destructive raid had taken place. The cost of the success was thirty-four aircraft, and, this time, it was the Stirling brigade that sustained the highest loss rate of 10.2%, compared with the Halifax's 5.8%.

Twenty-four hours later it was the turn of Gelsenkirchen to host its first major assault by Bomber Command since 1941, when it was raided several times as part of the oil offensive. 473 aircraft answered the call to arms, eighteen of them Halifaxes provided by 10 Squadron. They took off between 23.13 and 23.41 with S/Ls Debenham, Hartnell-Beavis and Sutton the senior pilots on duty, and a G/C Thomson flying as second pilot with the first-mentioned. There is a gap in G/C Thomson's career history between August 1941 and September 1944, but, it is believed, that he spent part of that period as station commander at Melbourne, and was known to take part in operations when an opportunity arose. The route out was the standard one for a target located on the northern side of the Ruhr, with landfall over the Den Helder peninsular, passing to the north of Amsterdam, before heading south-east across the Münsterland to the final turning point towards the south. F/Sgt Baxter and crew abandoned their sortie after deviating from course, possibly through a faulty Gee-box, and being unable to make up the time to be on target within the specified window. The others arrived over the target to find ten-tenths cloud and red release-point flares and red and green stars to identify the aiming-point, and bombed from 17,500 to 20,000 feet between 01.21 and 01.50. What the main force crews did not know was that five of the twelve Oboe Mosquitos had suffered equipment failure, and that the marking was scattered, with the result that, in an echo of the past, bombs were sprayed liberally around the Ruhr, and very few of them hit Gelsenkirchen. Düsseldorf, situated some twenty-four miles to the south-west, reported twenty-four buildings destroyed, and more than three thousand damaged, mostly superficially, and a loss of production at a number of war-industry factories. The disappointment was compounded by the loss of thirty aircraft, most of which were shot down by night fighters over Holland and the sea.

A series of three operations against Cologne would span the turn of the month, beginning on the 28th, when a force of 608 aircraft was made ready. Eighteen Halifaxes were provided by 10 Squadron, and they took off between 23.00 and 23.37 with F/Ls Black and Brookbanks the senior pilots on duty. After climbing out they set course for the Belgian coast, and Sgt Walker and crew were well on their way to the target when an overheating engine prevented them from climbing above 18,000 feet, which, at this stage of the war, was not high-enough for a flak hotspot like Cologne. They turned back and jettisoned their bombs over north-eastern France, leaving the others to arrive in the target area over ten-tenths cloud between 4,000 and 10,000 feet, to find limited skymarking, the least reliable method, in progress. Again, the crews were unaware that the Oboe Mosquitos were having another bad night with equipment failure, and this had led to the marking beginning seven minutes late and being sparse and intermittent. The Melbourne crews bombed from 17,800 to 20,000 feet between 01.46 and 02.15 in the face of an intense flak defence, and all they could report at debriefing was the glow of fires reflected in the cloud. Twenty-five aircraft failed to return, ten of them Halifaxes, and two of these were 10 Squadron's HR697 and DT783. The former was shot down on the way to the target after crossing paths with a night fighter, and crashed at 01.25 near Maastricht in southern Holland, killing Sgt Geddes RAAF and all on board but the mid-upper gunner, who was taken into captivity. The latter was dispatched at 02.33 by Major Günther Radusch of I./NJG1 while homebound over Holland, and crashed twenty miles east of Tilburg without survivors from the crew of P/O Peate, who had only recently been posted to the squadron from 1652 Conversion Unit. Despite the unfavourable operational circumstances, this proved to be the Rheinland Capital's worst night of the entire war, and, with the arrival of daylight, the local authorities began assessing the damage. They came up with a list of forty-three industrial and 6,368 other buildings destroyed, and 15,000 more damaged to some extent. The death toll, at 4,300 people, was the highest of the war to date, and 230,000 people had been left without homes.

S/L Debenham received a "Mentioned in Despatches" commendation during a month in which the squadron operated on eight nights and dispatched 141 sorties for the loss of five Halifaxes and crews.

July 1943

Cologne would open the Command's July account on the 3rd, and 653 aircraft were duly made ready. 10 Squadron loaded nineteen Halifaxes with the standard city-busting mix of 1,000 pounders and incendiaries, and sent them off in a thirty-minute slot either side of 23.00 with S/Ls Hartnell-Beavis and Sutton the senior pilots on duty. F/O Pennicott and crew must have been near the Belgian coast when the port-inner engine failed at 00.43. They thought about continuing on, but 14,000 feet was the best that they could manage on three engines, and that would put them below even the Stirlings. Common sense took over, and they turned for home, jettisoning the bombs into the sea. Sgt Heppell and crew turned back shortly afterwards after the rear gunner reported a fault with his turret, which he eventually fixed, but too late to save the bomb load and the sortie. F/O Cox and crew were east of Aachen outbound when they were attacked by a JU88, which knocked out the port-outer engine and caused damage to the wing. Return fire from the rear turret was seen to strike home, and the enemy fighter was last seen diving steeply until it was lost to sight. The bombs had been jettisoned at 01.24 during the engagement, and the Halifax returned home safely.

The others continued on to find the target under almost clear skies with haze, and Pathfinder route markers pointing the way. Ground features could be identified easily to confirm the accuracy of the TIs that had fallen onto the planned aiming-point in the highly-industrialized eastern half of the city, and the 10 Squadron crews aimed for these from 16,500 to 19,500 feet

Single-engine trials for the Halifax were carried out by 1658 HCU based at Riccall, near Melbourne in July 1943. Here S/L P. Dobson determines the height loss for emergency flight on one engine.

between 01.34 and 01.52. Many large explosions were witnessed and fires on both sides of the Rhine, but predominantly to the east, and a column of smoke was rising through 10,000 feet as the bombers retreated. Thirty aircraft failed to return, and among them was the squadron's DT784, which was shot down while outbound by Lt Johannes Hager of 6./NJG1, and crashed at 01.35 near Liege in Belgium. F/Sgt Morley RAAF and his mid-upper gunner lost their lives, while the other five members of the crew were taken into captivity. This was the night on which JG300 operated for the first time, employing the Wilde Sau (Wild Boar) tactics. The brainchild of former bomber pilot, Major Hans-Joachim (Hajo) Herrmann, the unit had been formed in June with borrowed standard BF109 and FW190 single-engine day fighters to operate directly over a target, seeking out bombers silhouetted against the fires and TIs. On this night, the unit would claim twelve victories, but would have to share them with the flak batteries, which claimed them also. Unaccustomed to being pursued by fighters over a target, it would take time for the bomber crews to work out what was happening, and, until they did, friendly-fire would often be blamed for damage incurred by unseen causes. Post-raid reconnaissance and local reports confirmed another stunningly accurate and concentrated attack, in which twenty industrial premises and 2,200 houses had been destroyed, and 72,000 people bombed out of their homes. It would be left to the Lancaster brigade to complete the series of operations against Cologne on the night of the 8/9th, after which, a total of eleven thousand buildings had been destroyed, 5,500 people had been killed, and a further 350,000 rendered homeless.

Gelsenkirchen was posted as the target on the 9th, for which a force of 408 Lancasters and Halifaxes formed the heavy brigade, and they would be accompanied by ten Oboe Mosquitos. 10 Squadron made ready twenty Halifaxes, which took off between 22.45 and 23.30 with S/L Hartnell-Beavis the senior pilot on duty, and set course for the gap between Texel and Vlieland.

Sgt Belcher and F/Sgt Long turned back within eighty minutes because of engine issues, leaving the others to continue on via the northerly route to find the target concealed by ten-tenths cloud. Equipment failure among the Oboe Mosquitos led to sparse initial marking, for which the heavy markers were unable to compensate, and the main force crews had to bomb on skymarkers and the intensity of the flak coming up at them. The Melbourne crews delivered their attacks from 17,000 to 20,500 feet between 01.17 and 01.30, and could only report the glow of fires beneath the cloud. Local reports would reveal that only the southern fringe of Gelsenkirchen had sustained damage, while Bochum and Wattenscheid received many more bombs, to the extent that they were believed to have been the intended target. A more modest twelve aircraft failed to return, and seven of these were Halifaxes, but all from 10 Squadron made it home.

A main force of Halifaxes, Wellingtons and Stirlings was assembled on the 13th for an operation that night to Aachen, an important railway hub between Germany and the Occupied Countries. Only eighteen Lancasters were to participate, and they were part of the Pathfinding element. 10 Squadron made ready nineteen Halifaxes, which departed Melbourne between 23.40 and 00.01 with S/Ls Debenham and Sutton the senior pilots on duty. There were no early returns, and a strong wind brought them to the target slightly ahead of schedule to find five to nine-tenths thin, drifting cloud, which lay predominantly over the eastern half of the city at 8,000 feet. Sgt Goodall and crew lost their port-inner engine a few minutes before arriving, but pressed on to deliver their 1,000 pounders and incendiaries. Bombing was carried out mostly on red and green TIs, but also on yellow flares, from 17,000 to 20,000 feet between 01.48 and 02.07, and the crews were left with an impression of burgeoning fires and a concentrated attack. P/O Douglas and crew were attacked by a JU88 on the way home at 02.23, but it was driven off by return fire from both turrets, which was seen to strike home. At 02.37 another JU88 made a number of passes without scoring hits, and it, too, was driven off by return fire. Of the twenty missing aircraft fifteen were Halifaxes, which represented a 7% loss rate, although, one could point out that the loss of two out of eighteen Lancasters was worse at 11%. Local reports confirmed the success of the operation, which reduced 2,927 buildings to rubble, comprising 16,800 dwelling units, and caused damage to many others of an industrial, administrative and public nature.

A 165-strong all-Halifax force from 4 and 8 Groups was made ready on the 15th to send against the Peugeot motor works in the Montbeliard suburb of Sochaux, situated near France's border with Switzerland. 10 Squadron contributed twenty Halifaxes to the main force element of 134 aircraft, and they took off between 21.30 and 21.52 with S/Ls Hartnell-Beavis and Sutton the senior pilots on duty. Sgt Thackray and crew lost their starboard-inner engine while outbound over France, and turned back to jettison their bombs "safe" a few miles inland from the Normandy coast. The others reached southern France, where, according to the 4 Group ORB, a Pathfinder aircraft crashed and caused some TIs to ignite near the town of Besancon, some thirty-five miles south-west of the target. A number of bombing photos were apparently plotted at this location, but the only Pathfinder aircraft to be lost was from 405 Squadron, which crashed on the way home further north. The majority of crews ignored this distraction, however, and pushed on to the intended target, where the visibility was excellent. This enabled the factory to be identified visually and by the red and green TIs, and bombing took place from 6,000 to 9,000 feet either side of 02.00. Returning crews reported many bombs falling in the target area, and there was confidence that the factory had been hit, but this was not borne out by reconnaissance photos. They showed the main marking effort to have fallen seven hundred yards to the east and onto the town, where 123 civilians were killed, and the factory sustained only minor damage. Five of the force failed to return home, and there were two empty dispersals at Melbourne in the morning, which should have been occupied by JB961 and JD211. The former crashed at Recey-sur-Ourse, thirty-two miles north-north-west of Dijon, and a little to the east of the 405 Squadron Halifax crash, and there were no survivors from the crew of Sgt Mellor. The latter disappeared without trace with the crew of F/Sgt Pyke.*

Earlier on the 15th, 431 Squadron had left 4 Group to join the other Canadian units in 6 Group, while F/L Badcoe was posted with his crew to 77 Squadron on the 17th to take up flight commander duties. 196 Squadron departed for 3 Group on the 19th and F/O Trobe, a future 10 Squadron flight commander, came in with his crew from 1658 Conversion Unit on the 21st. This left 4 Group now with 466 Squadron as the sole operator of Wellingtons until the arrival of Mk III Halifaxes, with which it would be the first in the Command to re-equip. Although two further operations would be mounted to the region at the end of the month, the Ruhr campaign had now effectively run its course. Harris could look back over the past five months with genuine satisfaction at the performance of his squadrons, and, as a champion of technology, take particular pleasure from the success of Oboe. It was true that losses had been grievously high,

but the factories and the Empire Training Schools been able to keep pace with the rate of attrition, and feed the expansion programme.

With confidence high in the Command's ability to deliver a knock-out blow on any urban target almost at will, Harris sought an opportunity to erase a major city from the map in a short, sharp campaign. Germany's Second City, Hamburg, had been spared by the weather from hosting the

Refurbished Watch Office Melbourne

first "One Thousand" raid at the end of May 1942, but its political status and value to the war effort in terms of U-Boot construction and other war production identified it as the ideal candidate now for destruction, to, thereby, cause the maximum impact to the enemy's morale. Hamburg perfectly suited Harris's criteria also in other respects, with its location close to a coastline to make it easy to find, its relatively short distance from the bomber stations, which would enable a force to approach and retreat during the few hours of darkness afforded by mid-summer, and its easy access from the North Sea without the need for a major incursion into enemy territory. Finally, lying beyond the range of Oboe, which had proved so decisive at the Ruhr, Hamburg had the wide River Elbe to provide a solid H2S signature for the navigators high above.

The campaign under the appropriately-named Operation Gomorrah would begin on the night of the 24/25th, for which a force of 791 aircraft was assembled. The crews would be aided by the first operational use of "Window", tinfoil-backed strips of paper of precise length, which, when released in bundles into the airstream at a predetermined point, would drift down slowly in vast clouds to swamp the enemy night-fighter, searchlight and gun-laying radar with false returns and render it blind. 10 Squadron made ready twenty-one Halifaxes and sent them skyward between 22.25 and 23.07 with W/C Edmonds the senior pilot on duty supported by S/Ls Hartnell-Beavis and Sutton. Sgt Stinson and crew lost their port-inner engine soon after take-off, and had to turn back, but this was the only early return from Melbourne, and the others carried on to the point over the North Sea where the designated crew member, in most cases the wireless operator, began to dispense the Window through the flare chute. The effectiveness of the device was immediately apparent by the few combats taking place around the German coast. A few aircraft were shot down over the sea, but they were off course and outside of the protection of the bomber stream, and may even have been early-returners struggling to get home with technical problems. On reaching the target, it was apparent to the crews that there was a lack of the usual close co-ordination between the searchlight and flak batteries, and the anti-aircraft defence was random, spasmodic and ineffective. This offered the Pathfinders the opportunity to mark the target by visual reference and H2S, virtually unmolested, and, although the TIs were a little misplaced and scattered, they landed in sufficient numbers close to the city centre to provide the main force with ample opportunity to deliver a massive blow. The 10 Squadron crews, with the exception of that of F/O Jenkins, who suffered a total hang-up, bombed from 16,500 to 20,000 feet between 01.07 and 01.42, and reported numerous explosions and fires, with a column of smoke rising through 18,000 feet as they withdrew towards the south before swinging westwards to the North Sea. For whatever reason, a pronounced creep-back developed, as a result of which, a swathe of destruction was cut from the city centre, along the line of approach, out across the north-western districts and into open country, where a proportion of the bombing was wasted. Despite this, extensive damage resulted in the afflicted areas, and fifteen hundred people were killed in return for the very modest loss of twelve aircraft.

W/C Sutton, DSO DFC AFC DL with his crew. He was Commanding Officer of 10 Sqn at RAF Melbourne May 1943 – April 1944. L – R: Sgt K Wright (F/E), F/Sgt W Appleby (W/Op), F/O J Benison (Nav), S/L J.Sutton (Pilot), P/O C Crafer (BA), Sgt J. Bruce (M/UG), Sgt R. Fitzgerald (RG)

On the following night, Harris switched his force to Essen, to take advantage of the body-blow dealt to the enemy's defensive system by Window. A force of 705 aircraft included twenty Halifaxes representing 10 Squadron, which took off between 22.10 and 22.50 with S/L Hartnell-Beavis the senior pilot on duty. Sgt Walker and crew had been dealing with fluctuating revolutions in their starboard-inner engine, and, being unable to climb above 13,000 feet as they flew over the Dutch mainland, they jettisoned the bombs "live" at 00.09 and turned for home. F/Sgt Clarke and crew found themselves behind time and unable to reach the target in their allotted slot, and also turned back to jettison their load into the sea. The others pressed on to find four-tenths thin cloud over the target with good visibility, and bombed on red and green TIs from 17,500 to 21,000 feet between 00.37 and 01.07. Concentrated fires were observed around the aiming-point in the heavily-industrialized eastern half of the city, along with two large, red explosions at 00.36 and 00.39, and a column of smoke was rising through 20,000 feet as they withdrew to the west. JD207 had the misfortune to cross paths with the night-fighter ace, Major Werner Streib of I./NJG1, on the way home, and was shot down to crash at 01.20 some five miles east-north-east of Tilburg in southern Holland. S/L Hartnell-Beavis survived to fall into enemy hands, while his wireless operator retained his freedom through the courage and resourcefulness of Dutch civilians, but the remaining five crew members lost their lives. This was one of twenty-six failures to return, and the respective percentage loss rates continued to provide interesting reading and confirmation of the prevailing food chain in a mixed force. The Lancasters came out on top with a loss rate of 1.7%, followed by the Halifax at 4.5%, the Wellington at 5.9% and the Stirling at 6.7%. The operation was another outstanding success, which destroyed 2,852 houses and fifty-one industrial buildings, and caused huge damage to the Krupp complex.

After a night's rest, a force of 787 aircraft was made ready for round two of Operation Gomorrah, for which 10 Squadron bombed-up and fuelled twenty Halifaxes. They took off between 22.20 and 22.50 with F/Ls Black, Brookbanks and Wood the senior pilots on duty. It is interesting to note the reliance on NCO pilots at this stage of the war following the recent influx of new crews to feed the expansion. On this night eleven crew captains were sergeants, four were flight sergeants and only five were of commissioned rank. None of them would have any concept of the events that were to follow their arrival at Hamburg, where a previously unknown and terrible phenomenon would present itself and introduce a new word "Firestorm" into the English language. Sgt Stinson and crew turned back with an engine issue when outbound over the North Sea, leaving the others to continue on to Hansastadt Hamburg, where a number of factors would conspire on this night to seal the fate of this great city and its hapless inhabitants in an orgy of destruction quite unprecedented in air warfare. An uncharacteristically hot and dry spell of weather had left the city a tinderbox, and the spark to ignite it came with the Pathfinders' H2S-laid red and green TIs, which fell with almost total concentration some two miles to the east of the intended city-centre aiming-point, and into the densely populated working-class residential districts of Hamm, Hammerbrook and Borgfeld. To compound this, the main force, which had been drawn on to the target by yellow release-point flares, bombed with rare precision and almost no creep-back, and deposited much of their 2,300 tons of bombs into this relatively compact area. The 10 Squadron crews made their attacks from 17,000 and 20,000 feet between 01.03 and 01.32, and observed many explosions and a sea of flames developing below. Those bombing towards the later stages of the raid observed a pall of smoke rising through 20,000 feet, and the glow of fires was reported to remain visible for 190 miles into the return journey.

On the ground, individual fires began to join together to form one giant conflagration, which sucked in oxygen from surrounding areas at hurricane speeds to feed its voracious appetite. Trees were uprooted and flung bodily into the inferno, along with debris and people, and temperatures at the seat of the flames exceeded one thousand degrees Celcius. The defences were overwhelmed, and the fire service unable to pass through the rubble-strewn streets to gain access to the worst-affected areas. Even had they done so, they could not have entered the firestorm area, and, only after all of the combustible material had been consumed, did the flames subside. By this time, there was no-one alive to rescue, and an estimated forty thousand people died on this one night alone. A mass exodus from the city, which would ultimately exceed one million people, began on the following morning, and this undoubtedly saved many from the ravages of the next raid, which would come two nights later. Seventeen aircraft failed to return, reflecting the enemy's developing response to the advantage gained by the Command through Window. No gain was ever permanent, and the balance of power would continue to shift from one side to the other for the next year. For a change, it was the Lancaster brigade that sustained the highest numerical casualties on this night.

Sqn Ldr F.J. Hartnell-Beavis and his crew. Shot down during a raid on Essen on 26 July 1943, he became a POW in Stalag Luft III while W/Op. Sgt R.A. Smith evaded capture. The rest of the crew was killed.

Twenty-one crews were called to briefing at Melbourne on the 29th, to learn that they would be part of a 777-strong force returning to Hamburg that night for round three of Operation Gomorrah. They took off between 22.20 and 22.45 with S/L Sutton the senior pilot on duty, but soon lost the services of Sgts Dibben and Dixon with technical issues. The others pushed on across the North Sea to find good weather conditions and clear skies, and approach the target from the north to hit areas not yet afflicted. The Pathfinders again failed to deliver their yellow and green TIs onto the planned aiming-point, and marked an a section of the city just to the south of the firestorm area. The Melbourne crews bombed from 17,000 to 20,000 feet between 00.48 and 01.20, and were among 707 crews to deliver a total of 2,300 tons of high-explosives and incendiaries into the tortured city, initially into the already-devastated areas from the previous raid, before the creep-back took it across other residential districts of Wandsbek, Barmbek, Uhlenhorst and Winterhude. Twenty-eight aircraft failed to return, indicating that the enemy had almost fully recovered from the Window setback, but not a single 10 Squadron crew had been lost to Hamburg thus far.

An attack on the town of Remscheid on the night of the 30/31st brought down the final curtain on the Ruhr campaign and left the town 83% destroyed. 10 Squadron was not involved in the relatively small-scale operation, that employed a force of only 273 aircraft, that managed to reduce 3,115 houses to ruins, shut down industry for three months and kill 1,120 people. During the course of the month the squadron carried out eight operations, during which 160 sorties had resulted in the loss of four Halifaxes and crews.

August 1943

Briefings for the final act of Operation Gomorrah took place on the 2nd, and a force of 740 aircraft was made ready. 10 Squadron managed to offer a record twenty-two Halifaxes, and they took off between 23.15 and 23.55 with S/Ls Debenham and Sutton the senior pilots on duty. The weather conditions were good initially, but a towering bank of ice-bearing cloud built over the North Sea, which could not be circumnavigated, and, upon entering it, aircraft were thrown around by violent electrical storms. It was a hugely terrifying experience beyond anything that most crews had ever experienced, with huge flashes of lightning, thunder, electrical discharges and instruments going haywire. Many crews simply abandoned their sorties and jettisoned their bombs over Germany or into the sea, but, to their great credit, this was not the attitude of the 10 Squadron participants. They were among the proportion of the force that battled through the conditions to reach the target area, which was concealed beneath seven to ten-tenths cloud, and, in the almost complete absence of target marking, crews could only bomb blind on e.t.a. Sixteen members of the Melbourne brigade bombed from 14,000 to 18,000 feet between 02.06 and 02.37, a few on the basis of green marker flares, but Sgt Lucas and crew shed ten thousand feet between the coast and the target through the effects of the conditions, and delivered their load from 8,000 feet. Sgts Dunlop and Goodall failed to positively locate the primary target, and dropped their bombs "live" between it and the coast. F/O Douglas delivered his load on the town of Fintel to the south-west of Hamburg, and Sgt Dibben also went for a last-resort target. F/O Jenkins and crew were at 17,000 feet thirty miles west-north-west of Cuxhaven when Monica picked up the approach of an enemy aircraft at 01.53, which was identified by the rear gunner as a JU88. An engagement followed during which the Halifax sustained severe damage to the tail-plane, including the loss of both elevators, cannon and bullet holes in the wings, fuselage and port bomb door, and a burst port tyre. The JU88 was last seen spiralling down on fire to disappear into cloud. Despite the difficulty in maintaining control, F/O Jenkins brought DT792 home to Melbourne, where a controlled crash-landing was accomplished at 04.15 without crew casualties. Thereafter, the pilot would rejoice in the nickname "Bring 'em back alive, Jenkins", and would be awarded an immediate DFC, while rear gunner, Sgt Hurst RCAF, would receive a DFM for shooting down their assailant. Shortly after leaving the target, S/L Debenham's BB427 was hit by flak, which knocked out the port-outer engine and damaged the tail unit. The port-inner engine then also cut out, leaving the Halifax floundering and unable to maintain height. The rear gunner was ordered to dump ammunition to save weight, and three thousand perfectly serviceable rounds were ejected before the German coast was reached at just 4,000 feet. An attempt to restart the port-inner was successful, and they eventually landed at base at 05.45. Little further damage was inflicted on Hamburg, but the damage had already been done. The squadron's record during Operation Gomorrah was impressive, with seventy-seven of eighty-four sorties reaching and bombing the target, and it was the only squadron in 4 Group not to post missing a crew. (The Battle of Hamburg, Martin Middlebrook).

Italy was now teetering on the brink of capitulation, and Bomber Command was invited to help nudge it over the edge with a short offensive against its major cities. It began with elements of

1, 5 and 8 Groups raiding Genoa, Milan and Turin on the night of the 7/8th, and, with preparations already in hand for, perhaps, the most important operation of the war to date to be launched in ten days' time, the Turin raid was used to test the merits of employing a raid controller, or Master of Ceremonies, in the Manner of W/C Gibson during Operation Chastise. The man selected for the job was Group Captain John Searby, currently serving as commanding officer of 83 Squadron of the Pathfinders, and, although the experiment was not entirely successful, experience was gained which would prove useful for Operation Hydra. The rest of the heavy brigade remained inactive until the 9th, when a force of 457 Lancasters and Halifaxes was made ready for an operation that night against Mannheim. 10 Squadron prepared sixteen Halifaxes, which took off between 22.45 and 23.05 with F/Os Douglas and Trobe the senior pilots on duty. After climbing out they headed for the rendezvous point over Reading, before exiting England via Beachy Head on course for the French coast at Boulogne. A navigational error drew Sgt Glover and crew off track towards Le Havre, and, once this was discovered, they abandoned their sortie. The others pressed on across Belgium on a direct track to the target, but, at 01.35, when fifty-eight miles short, Sgt Whitmarsh's port-outer engine overheated and had to be feathered. The decision was taken to carry on, and the target was reached and bombed at 14,000 feet at 01.54, for which the pilot would be granted the immediate award of the DFM.

The crews were greeted by a five-tenths layer of broken cloud at 4,000 feet and eight-tenths at 10,000 feet, but visibility was fair, and the yellow skymarkers and green TIs were sufficient to provide a reference for the bomb-aimers. The Melbourne participants carried out their attacks from 17,000 to 19,500 feet between 01.40 and 01.55, and returned home to report a number of very large fires but a generally scattered raid. In fact, according to local reports, 1,316 buildings had been destroyed, forty-two industrial concerns had lost production, and more than 1,500 fires of varying sizes had had to be dealt with. Six Halifaxes and three Lancasters failed to return, but there were no empty dispersals at Melbourne.

The following night brought a return to southern Germany, this time to Nuremberg, for which a force of 653 aircraft was made ready. The presence of Stirlings, the type usually at the bottom of the food chain, might provide respite for the Halifax crews, who, in a Lancaster/Halifax force, invariably came off second best. 10 Squadron loaded nineteen Halifaxes with sufficient fuel and reserves for the 1,300-mile round-trip with an outbound load of one 1,000 pounder and ten SBCs of 4lb and 30lb incendiaries, and dispatched them between 21.25 and 21.55 with S/L Debenham the senior pilot on duty. There were no early returns to Melbourne as the climbing-out, forming-up and setting-course process took the force out over Beachy Head to follow a route similar to that of the previous night. The conditions in the target area also reflected those of twenty-four hours earlier with eight to ten-tenths cloud at 12,000 feet, despite which, the Pathfinders chose to ground-mark. There were no release-point flares to draw the main force on, but the green TIs were visible to most, and the Melbourne crews delivered their bombs from 15,500 to 17,000 feet between 01.07 and 01.32. At debriefing crews reported a good concentration of fires, the glow from which remained visible for 150 miles into the return journey. Sgt Dibben and crew were absent from the post-raid ritual, and JD198's dispersal pan stood empty on the following morning. It would be some time before news came through that they had ditched in the Channel on the way home, and had drifted for twenty-four hours towards the enemy-occupied coast, before falling into enemy hands. It was their fifth sortie, still one short of the half-dozen reckoned to be the most dangerous for a sprog crew. The operation was

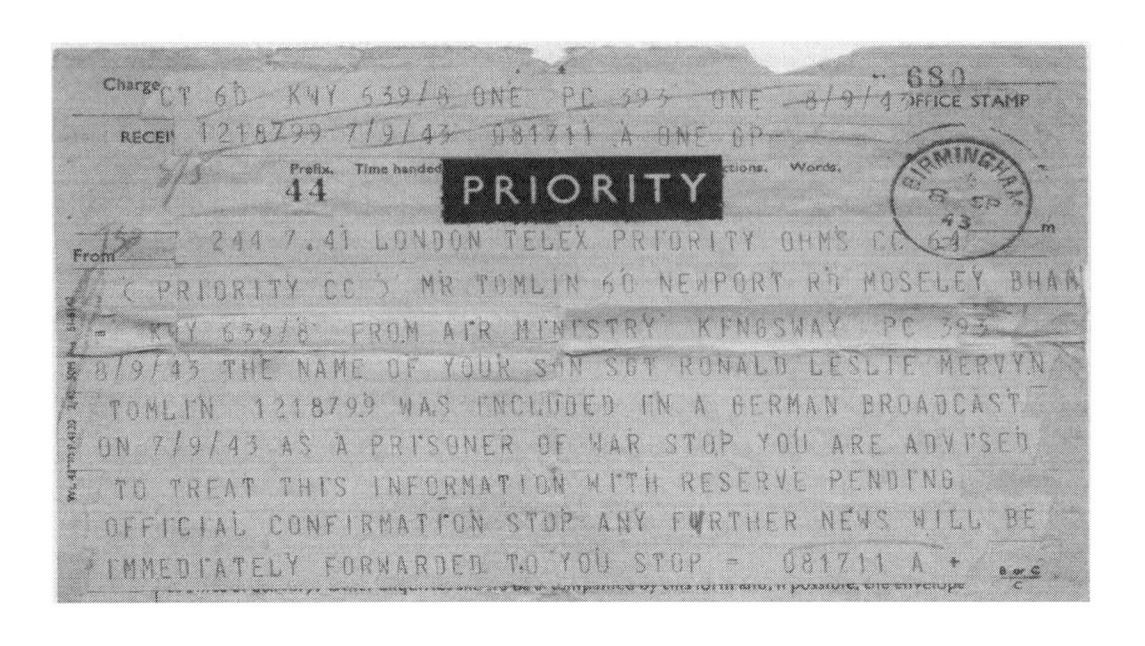

Telegram and letter sent to the father of Sgt RLM Tomlin, bomb aimer in Halifax JD198 which ditched in the English Channel after a Nuremburg raid on the 11th August 1943. All the crew became POWs.

moderately successful, and caused substantial damage in central and southern districts for the modest loss of sixteen aircraft, seven Halifaxes, six Lancasters and three Stirlings, which, in percentage terms, was respectively 3.2, 1.9 and 2.5.

The mini-Italian campaigned continued on the 12th, when Milan and Turin were the targets, the former for a force of 504 aircraft, while 152 aircraft from 3 and 8 Groups attended to the latter. 10 Squadron made ready seventeen Halifaxes, which took off between 20.45 and 21.10 with W/C Edmonds the senior pilot on duty before he headed off on leave on the 15th. The route took the bomber stream via Selsey Bill to Cabourg on the Normandy coast, and then south-east in a straight leg across central France to the northern tip of Lake Bourget, to cross the Alps and skirt southern Switzerland before the final run-in on the target. This represented a round-trip of some sixteen hundred miles, and all of the 10 Squadron crews completed the outward leg to arrive at the target under clear skies with just ground mist to spoil the view. They bombed visually or on yellow flares and green TIs from 15,500 to 18,500 feet between 01.11 and 01.30, and observed large fires in the city centre which could be seen for a hundred miles into the return flight. Local reports, though short on detail, confirmed that four important war-industry factories had sustained serious damage during August, and most of it probably occurred on this night. This was 4 Group's only contribution to the Italian campaign, which would be concluded on the night of the 16/17th. S/L Debenham, whose time on the squadron was about to conclude, stood in for W/C Edmonds as commanding officer, and F/L Black was given acting squadron leader rank.

Since the very beginning of the war, intelligence had suggested that Germany was researching into and developing rocket technology, and, although scant regard was given to the reports, photographic reconnaissance had confirmed the existence of an establishment at Peenemünde at the northern tip of the island of Usedom on the Baltic coast. Churchill's chief scientific adviser, Professor Lindemann, or Lord Cherwell as he became, steadfastly refused to give credence to the existence and feasibility of rocket weapons, and held stubbornly to his viewpoint even when presented with a photograph of a V-2 taken by a PRU Mosquito in June 1943. It required the combined urgings of Duncan Sandys and the brilliant scientist, Dr R V Jones, to persuade Churchill to act. Through Ultra intercepts, Dr Jones had been able to monitor V-1 trials over the Baltic, and gain vital information concerning the weapon's range, which would ultimately be used to feed disinformation to the enemy through "turned" spies. Operation Hydra was planned for the first available opportunity, which occurred on the night of the 17/18th. Earlier in the day, the USAAF 8th Air Force had carried out its first deep-penetration raid into Germany to attack Schweinfurt and Regensburg, and, to the shock of its leaders, had learned the harsh lesson that daylight raids in 1943 were not viable. The folks at home were not told that sixty B17s had failed to return. It was vital that the Peenemünde installation be destroyed, ideally, at the first attempt, and, consequently, a maximum effort was called for. In the event, not all of the Stirlings of 3 Group were available after being diverted on their return from Italy the night before, and a somewhat depleted force of 596 aircraft and crews answered the call.

The operation had been meticulously planned to account for the three vital components of Peenemünde, the housing estate, where the scientific and technical staff lived, the factory buildings and the experimental site. Each was assigned to a specific wave of aircraft, which would attack from medium level, with the Pathfinders bearing the huge responsibility of shifting

the point of aim accordingly. After last minute alterations, 3 and 4 Groups were given the first mentioned, 1 Group the second, and 5 and 6 Groups the third. The whole operation was to be overseen by a Master of Ceremonies (referred to hereafter as Master Bomber), and the officer selected for this hazardous and demanding role was G/C Searby of 83 Squadron, who had stepped into Gibson's shoes at 106 Squadron after Gibson was posted out to form 617 Squadron. Searby's role was to direct the marking and bombing by VHF, and to encourage the crews to press on to the aiming-point, a task requiring him to remain in the target area throughout the attack, a role, as already mentioned, that he had practiced during the not-entirely successful operation on Turin on the night of the 7/8th. In an attempt to protect the
bombers from the attentions of enemy night-fighters for as long as possible, eight Mosquitos of 139 Squadron were to carry out a spoof raid on Berlin, led by the highly experienced, and former 49 Squadron commander, G/C Len Slee.

10 Squadron made ready eighteen Halifaxes, which departed Melbourne between 20.45 and 21.15. Remarkably, on a night when many squadron commanders and flight commanders had put themselves on the order of battle, only three of the squadron's aircraft were captained by officers, the most senior being F/L Cox in JB314. F/Sgt Kilsby and crew deviated from track because of a faulty Gee-box, and abandoned their sortie, and P/O Belcher was taken ill and turned back from a point about a hundred miles west of the Danish coast. Sgt Holdsworth's DT786 was hit by flak from the German coast, and lost both starboard engines, which forced him to drop his bombs on an island to the north of Rostock from 10,000 feet at 00.06. Despite the damage, they would make it home safely to land at 04.25. The others reached the target area under clear skies with moonlight to provide excellent visibility, and ran in on their aiming-point to bomb on green TIs from 6,000 to 11,000 feet, but mostly from around 8,000 feet, between 00.16 and 00.34 in accordance with the instructions from the Master Bomber. Sadly, the initial markers fell more than a mile south of the intended aiming-point, and highlighted the Trassenheide forced workers camp, which contained hundreds of men from the Occupied Countries, some of whom had been responsible for getting the intelligence about the site to London. Trapped inside their wooden barrack buildings, many of them were killed and injured, but, once rectified, the attack proceeded more or less according to plan, and a number of important members of the scientific team were killed. The 1 Group second-wave crews encountered strong crosswinds over the narrow section of the island where the construction sheds were located, but this phase of the operation largely achieved its aims, and they were on their way home before the night-fighters arrived from Berlin, having been attracted by the glow of fires well to the north. Once on the scene they proceeded to take a heavy toll of bombers, both in the skies above Peenemünde and on the route home along the Baltic coast. Losses among the first two waves were low compared with those suffered later on, when predominantly 5 and 6 Group aircraft were attacking. Forty aircraft failed to return, of which just three were from 4 Group, while twenty-nine came from the final wave, 5 Group suffering a 14.5% loss rate and 6 Group 19.7%, and many of these fell to a new weapon in the armoury of the Luftwaffe's Nachtjagd. Upward-firing cannons, christened Schräge Musik (jazz music), had been installed in the ME110s, which allowed the fighters to sit unobserved below a bomber and, from as close as fifty yards, fire at a point between the engines to ignite the fuel tanks. By employing non-tracer rounds, their victims were taken completely by surprise and would not know from where the attack had come. 10 Squadron welcomed all but one of its aircraft home, the missing JD200 having disappeared without trace, presumably into the sea, taking with it the eight-man crew of

F/Sgt Long. The operation was sufficiently successful to set back development of the V-2 by at least a number of months, and force the Germans to abandon Peenemünde in favour of caves in the Harz Mountains south of Hannover, where production would continue employing slave labour in harsh conditions. The testing was moved to Poland, out of range of Harris's bomber force.

A rare training accident cost the squadron F/L Smith and four of his crew, who were killed when JD119 shed a propeller during a cross-country exercise on the evening of the 20th, and crashed at 23.15 near Market Harborough in Leicestershire. The navigator and bomb-aimer were the only survivors. S/L Debenham was posted to 20 O.T.U., on the 21st, and, with W/C Edmonds still on leave, S/L Black took temporary command of the squadron. However, an entry in the ORB for September suggests that S/L Debenham came back to 10 Squadron until the posting was completed finally on the 10th of September. S/L Black presided over his first operation on the 22nd, when the Ruhr city of Leverkusen was posted as the target for a heavy force of 449 Lancasters and Halifaxes with 8 Group Oboe-Mosquito support. The aiming-point was to be a factory belonging to the infamous I.G. Farben chemicals company, which was engaged in the development and production of synthetic oil, and employed slave labour at all of its factories, including 30,000 from the Auschwitz concentration camp, where it built a plant. One of the company's subsidiaries manufactured the Zyklon B gas used during the Holocaust to murder millions of people. 10 Squadron made ready seventeen Halifaxes, which departed Melbourne between 20.45 and 21.05 with F/L Cox the senior pilot on duty, and headed for the Belgian coast at Knokke. It was a well-worn route to the southern Ruhr, but passed through the searchlight and flak belt near Cologne, which always provided a hot welcome. All from 10 Squadron made it safely through to reach the target, where ten-tenths cloud blanketed the area, and most crews were reduced to bombing on e.t.a in the absence of markers through Oboe-equipment failures. The glow of fires became an aid to bombing as the raid developed, although a small number of crews spotted green TIs on the ground. Bombing was carried out in the face of intense flak from 17,500 to 20,000 feet between 00.09 and 00.37, and the glow of fires and the flash of explosions was the only confirmation of something happening under the cloud, until a column of smoke was observed to be rising through 12,000 feet. Local reports would reveal that up to a dozen neighbouring towns were hit, Düsseldorf suffering the destruction of 132 buildings.

Harris had long held the view that, as the seat and the symbol of Nazi power, Berlin was more than just the capital city, and that its destruction would do more to hasten a German collapse that any other target. On the 23rd he issued the order for the first of an eventual nineteen raids on the "Big City" that, with an autumn break, would drag on until the following spring, and test the resolve of the crews to the absolute limit. It would also seal the fate of the Stirlings and the Mk II and V Halifaxes. There are varying opinions concerning the true start date of what became known as the Berlin offensive or the Battle of Berlin, some commentators believing these first three operations in August and September to be the start, while others point to the sixteen raids from mid-November. However, there was little doubt in Bomber Command circles that this was it, a fact demonstrated by the comments in numerous squadron ORBs, which speak of the "long-awaiting Berlin campaign" and similar sentiments. A force of 727 aircraft was assembled, of which 158 Halifaxes represented 4 Group, seventeen of them belonging to 10 Squadron, the smallest contribution in the group, and they took off between 20.10 and 20.46 with just two officer pilots on duty, F/O Harden the more senior. There would be a Master Bomber on hand for this operation, and the officer chosen was W/C Johnny Fauquier, the commanding officer of 405 (Vancouver) Squadron of the Pathfinders, and former 4 Group favourite. The route had been planned to take the bomber stream to a rendezvous point over the North Sea, before crossing the Dutch coast near Haarlem and setting course to pass between Bremen and Hannover to bypass the southern rim of Berlin. The intention was then to turn back to approach the city from the south-east and, after bombing, pass out over the Baltic coast and make for the Schleswig-Holstein peninsular. W/O Fotheringham and crew turned back at 22.16 from a point some fifty miles off the Dutch coast because of icing and an unserviceable Gee-box, and, shortly afterwards, Sgt Walker and crew also abandoned their sortie, citing the icing conditions and being behind schedule as the causes.

Those reaching the target area found clear skies, but the Pathfinders were unable to identify the aiming-point in the centre of the city, a result of the inherent difficulties of interpreting the H2S images, and marked the southern outskirts instead. Many main force crews then cut the corner to approach the city from the south-west rather than south-east, and this would result in the wastage of many bomb loads in open country and on outlying communities. The 10 Squadron crews bombed visually and on red and green TIs from 17,000 to 19,000 feet between 23.50 and 00.19, and reported intense searchlight activity with moderate flak. Sgt Dunlop and crew had their port-outer engine set on fire and the port-inner and wing holed, while Sgts Thackray and Lucas were engaged by an enemy night-fighter, the former over the target and the latter during the approach. Sgt Lucas's assailant was seen to burst into flames and fall away to be claimed as destroyed. Large explosions and many fires were observed, the glow from which was visible for at least 140 miles, and a pall of smoke was beginning to rise to meet the bombers as they turned towards the north-east. Curiously, there was no mention at debriefing of instructions being received from the Master Bomber. A new record of fifty-six aircraft failed to return, twenty-three Halifaxes, seventeen Lancasters and sixteen Stirlings, representing a loss rate

MkII Halifax. Note both starboard engines have been shut down.

respectively of 9.1, 5.1 and 12.9, which perfectly reflected the food chain when all three types operated together. Berlin experienced a scattered raid, but, because of the numbers attacking, extensive damage was caused, a little in or near the centre, but mostly in south-western residential districts and industrialized areas a little further east. 2,611 buildings were reported to have been destroyed or seriously damaged, and the death toll of 854 people was surprisingly high, caused largely, perhaps, by a failure to heed the alarms and go to the assigned shelters. 10 Squadron operated without loss, while 158 Squadron sustained the group's highest casualties, posting missing five crews.

S/L Dean was posted in from the training station at Holme-on-Spalding-Moor on the 27th, the day on which orders were received to prepare for an operation that night against Nuremberg. A force of 674 aircraft ultimately lined up for take-off in mid-evening, fifteen of them at Melbourne, and they took to the air between 20.42 and 21.06 with F/L Cox the senior pilot on duty. F/O Harden and W/O Kennedy each lost a port engine, the former turning back when twenty miles short of the French coast, and the latter a little later when thirty-five miles inland. The others pressed on across France until crossing into Germany south of Luxembourg on course for the target, where clear skies and intense darkness prevailed. F/O Trobe and crew were attacked by a JU88 when fifteen miles south-west of Mannheim at 00.20, but return fire from both turrets scored hits and drove it off. The Pathfinders had been briefed to check their H2S equipment by dropping a 1,000 pounder on Heilbronn, and some crews complied, while others, it seems, experienced technical difficulties. The initial marking was accurate, but a creep-back developed, which the backers-up and the Master Bomber could not correct, and this resulted in many bomb loads falling into open country, while others hit south-eastern and eastern districts. The 10 Squadron crews aimed at green TIs from 17,000 to 19,000 feet between 00.36 and 01.08, and gained an impression of a fairly concentrated and accurate attack, which produced many fires. On the way home at 01.20, when passing by Frankfurt, F/Sgt Clarke and crew became coned by searchlights and bombarded by flak, which inflicted extensive damage and knocked out the electrical system. They dived from 17,000 down to 4,000 feet to escape the clutches of the beams, and, afterwards, discovered that the bomb-aimer had taken the unilateral decision to abandon ship. Despite the damage, they made it home safely to land at 03.34. Thirty-three aircraft failed to return, eleven of each type, which again confirmed the vulnerability of the Stirlings and Halifaxes when operating alongside Lancasters. The loss rate on this night was 3.1% for the Lancaster, 5% for the Halifax and 10.6% for the Stirlings. 10 Squadron posted missing the crew of Sgt Baker in JD368, which was shot down by a night-fighter on the way home, and crashed at 03.30 seven miles south-east of Mons in Belgium. The pilot and five of his crew ultimately evaded capture, while the mid-upper gunner fell into enemy hands and the rear gunner was killed.

The twin towns of Mönchengladbach and Rheydt were posted as the targets for a two-phase operation on the 30th, and it would be the first major attack for both of them. Situated some ten miles west of the centre of Düsseldorf in the south-western Ruhr, they would face an initial force of 660 aircraft in what, for the crews, was a short-penetration trip across the Dutch frontier, which would be a welcome change from the recent long slogs to eastern and southern Germany. The plan called for the first wave to hit Mönchengladbach, before a two-minute pause in the bombing allowed the Pathfinders to head south to mark Rheydt. 10 Squadron made ready thirteen Halifaxes, whose crews had been briefed to bomb in the first wave, and they took off between 23.51 and 00.22 with F/O Harden the senior pilot on duty. There were no early returns, and all reached the target to find good visibility, but seven to ten-tenths cloud at 8,000 feet. A near perfect display of target-marking by Oboe delivered red and green flares to draw on the main force to bomb with scarcely any creep-back, the 10 Squadron element doing so from 16,000 to 19,000 feet between 02.07 and 02.37. On return they would report many fires, the glow from which could be seen from the Dutch coast homebound. Photo-reconnaissance confirmed a highly accurate and concentrated attack, which destroyed more than 2,300 buildings in the two towns, 171 of them of an industrial nature and 869 residential properties. Twenty-five aircraft failed to return, and Halifaxes again sustained the highest numerical casualties.

The month ended with preparations for the second of the Berlin operations on the night of the 31st, for which 622 aircraft were made ready, more than half of them Lancasters. W/C Edmonds returned from leave on this day, and relieved S/L Black of his onerous responsibilities for overseeing the squadron. 10 Squadron bombed and fuelled up sixteen Halifaxes, but three were cancelled late on because of technical problems, leaving the remaining thirteen to take off between 20.14 and 20.37 with F/L Cox the senior pilot on duty. Sgt Dixon turned back with an engine issue shortly after leaving the English coast, P/O Walker was unable to coax more than 11,500 feet out of JD273 and gave up at the mid-point of the North Sea crossing, while P/O Goodall was within twenty-five miles of Texel when the engine "gremlins" curtailed his sortie. The route on this night took the bomber stream on an east-south-easterly heading across Texel to a position between Hannover and Leipzig, before turning to pass to the south-east of Berlin and approach the city-centre aiming-point on a north-westerly track. The return leg would involve a south-westerly course to a position south of Cologne for an exit over the French coast, but despite the attempts to outwit the enemy night-fighter controller, he was able to predict to some extent where to concentrate his fighters. This would be the first occasion on which the Command registered the German use of "fighter flares" to mark out the path of the bombers to and from the target. The Pathfinders encountered five to six-tenths cloud in the target area, and this combined with H2S equipment failure and a spirited night-fighter response to cause the markers to be dropped well to the south of the planned aiming-point. The main force crews became involved in an extensive creep-back, which would stretch some thirty miles into open country and outlying communities. The 10 Squadron crews reported up to five-tenths thin cloud, and bombed on green TIs from 17,000 to 19,000 feet between 23.41 and 00.07, observing many fires over a wide area. It was noted by some that two groups of green TIs were ten miles apart, and both attracted attention from the main force. The outcome was a major disappointment, brought about by woefully short marking and a pronounced creep-back, and resulted in the destruction of just eighty-five houses, a figure in no way commensurate with the effort expended and the loss of forty-seven heavy bombers.

The percentage loss rates made alarming reading at Bomber Command HQ, the Lancasters with an acceptable and sustainable 3%, the Halifaxes with 11.3% and the Stirlings with 16%. During the course of the month the squadron carried out ten operations, and dispatched 167 sorties for the loss of four Halifaxes, three complete crews and five individuals from the training crash.

September 1943

It was left to the Lancaster squadrons to conclude this opening salvo of the Berlin campaign on the night of the 3/4th, which they did with modest success at a cost of twenty-two aircraft. 4 Group sent half-a-dozen Halifaxes mining in northern waters on the following night, but it was the 5th before its stations were stirred into concerted action to prepare 120 Halifaxes to contribute to the overall force of 605 aircraft being assembled for that night's operation against the twin cities of Mannheim and Ludwigshafen, which face each other from the East and West Banks of the Rhine respectively. The plan was to exploit the creep-back phenomenon that attended most large operations by approaching the target from the west, and marking the eastern half of Mannheim, with the expectation that the bombing would spread back along the line of approach across western Mannheim and into Ludwigshafen. 10 Squadron loaded each of sixteen Halifaxes with a single 1,000 pounder and ten SBCs, five containing ninety 4lb incendiaries and five containing eight of 30lbs. They took off between 19.17 and 19.35 with S/Ls Black, Dean and Sutton the senior pilots on duty, and set course for Beachy Head and the Channel crossing. P/O Baxter turned back with engine issues when thirty-five miles out from the English coast, leaving the others to continue on in good weather conditions to find clear skies over the target. The marking plan worked perfectly, and the 10 Squadron crews bombed on red, yellow and

The Comet Escape Line's 'Monique' (in blue) with another Resistance worker, Irma Caldow taken in Gosselies Cemetery, on a visit to the grave of 10 Sqn Sgt G.R.M. Warren RCAF Air Gunner, killed over Belgium on 28 August 1943. These very brave ladies were both still alive in 2015 and aged 95 and 100 years. Right: Sgt George R M Warren RCAF Aged 19

green TIs from 16,000 to 19,000 feet between 23.10 and 23.39, those arriving towards the later stages of the raid being drawn on by the burgeoning fires fifty miles ahead. A number of large, red explosions were observed, one at 23.27 followed by a purplish-red mushroom of fire, and the glow from the burning cities was visible for 120 miles into the return journey. Searchlights were numerous, but the flak negligible, and it was the abundance of night-fighters that posed the greatest risk, three crews reporting at debriefing that they had been involved in inconclusive engagements. Thirty-four aircraft failed to return, thirteen each of Lancasters and Halifaxes and eight Stirlings, and the percentage loss rates continued to tell the same story. JD322 did not return to Melbourne, with the crew of P/O D'eath after crashing in the target area with the loss of all on board.* Local reports confirmed that both Mannheim and Ludwigshafen had suffered catastrophic destruction, with almost two thousand fires in the latter alone, 986 of them classed as large. Mannheim's reporting system broke down completely, and little detail emerged of this raid, although it would recover in time for the next assault in less than three weeks' time.

Munich was posted as the target on the 6th, for which the squadron made ready fifteen Halifaxes to contribute to the overall force of 257 Lancasters and 147 Halifaxes in the absence of the Stirling brigade. They departed Melbourne between 19.03 and 19.24 with S/L Sutton the senior pilot on duty, carrying the same bomb load and adopting the same route as for the previous night. P/O Goodall and crew were at the mid-point of the Channel crossing when an engine issue forced them to turn back, and they were followed home by F/Sgt Mayers and crew who had experienced a fuel-feed problem. Conditions in the target area on this night were not ideal, with cloud varying between five and nine-tenths, although some ground features, like the river, could be identified and the red, yellow and green TIs seen. The 10 Squadron crews bombed from 16,000 to 19,500 feet between 23.35 and 23.50, and a large number of fires were observed to be grouped around the markers. The searchlights were ineffective because of the cloud, but large numbers of night-fighters were again evident, and, during the final approach to the target, F/Sgt Lindsey and crew were alerted by a searchlight in the nose of an ME210, which was creeping up on them from fifteen hundred yards astern. Sight of the enemy was lost when the light was extinguished, but it came on again at 250 yards range astern and below, temporarily blinding both gunners, who opened fire. The assailant performed a diving turn to starboard under constant fire from the Halifax's rear turret, and its starboard engine and wing suddenly burst into flames. All on board the Halifax, except for the navigator and wireless operator, watched it fall in flames until it exploded and disintegrated. Sixteen aircraft failed to return, thirteen of them Halifaxes, a percentage loss rate of 8.8, compared with 1.2 for the Lancasters. Two empty dispersals at Melbourne told their own stories, that JD364 and JD166 were missing with the crews of Sgt Davies and F/O Douglas respectively. No trace of the former would ever be found, but news filtered through eventually that the latter had fallen to a night-fighter at Kaufbeuren west-south-west of the target, killing the pilot and rear gunner and delivering the rest of the crew into enemy hands.

A week-and-a half would elapse before the squadron was next called into action, and this was for a predominantly Halifax and Stirling operation by elements of 3, 4 and 6 Groups with 8 Group support against the Dunlop rubber factory at Montluçon in central France. The squadron made ready sixteen Halifaxes on the 15th, as part of an overall force of 369 aircraft, and dispatched them between 20.00 and 20.30 with S/Ls Dean and Sutton the senior pilots on duty. Sgt Culverhouse and crew turned back with leaky hydraulics, leaving the others to press on to the target, where eight to nine-tenths cloud at 4,000 feet failed to prevent a view of the factory and the red, green and yellow TIs marking it out. A Master Bomber, in the form of W/C Deane of 35 Squadron, was on hand to direct the attack, and the 10 Squadron crews bombed in bright moonlight from 4,500 to 9,500 feet between 23.31 and 23.58. It wasn't long before black smoke was seen to rise through 10,000 feet from the developing fires, and it was clear to all that the factory complex had been severely damaged. Opposition was negligible, and just two Halifaxes and a Stirling failed to return, among them 10 Squadron's HR920, which contained the crew of the appropriately-named Sgt Dunlop. This Halifax crashed near l'Aigle in the Normandy region of north-western France, killing the pilot and three others and delivering two into enemy hands, while the wireless operator managed to evade a similar fate.

On the following day, the same groups were alerted to an operation that night against the important and extensive railway yards at Modane, situated on the main line between France and Italy in the foothills of the Alps in south-eastern France. 10 Squadron made ready eleven Halifaxes to contribute to the 340-strong force, and they took off between 19.35 and 20.00 with S/L Sutton the senior pilot on duty. F/Sgt Lindsey and crew turned back shortly after taking-off with intercom and rear turret issues, while P/O Glover had crossed the Normandy coast when the W/T gave up the ghost and curtailed his sortie. A number of crews ran into icing conditions as they approached the target area, and this forced F/L Jenkins to jettison his bombs and turn for home. P/O Heppell and crew were some seventy miles from the target and flying at 17,000 feet at 23.40, when ice-accretion caused the Halifax to fall suddenly into a spin with the controls locked. With great difficulty the pilot rescued the situation and levelled out, only for the same thing to happen again almost immediately, upon which he ordered the bombs to be jettisoned and warned the crew to prepare to abandon aircraft. Again, he regained control with the Halifax now at 10,500 feet, when it was discovered that the navigator and wireless operator had taken to their parachutes.* The bomb-aimer assumed navigational duties, and the Halifax eventually landed at Tangmere with the Gee and most of its instrument unserviceable. Meanwhile, the

10 Sqn F/S Moggridge (B/A), Sgt E Jones (MU/G), Sgt E Jenkins (W/Op), Sgt C H Glover (Pilot) Sgt J Hamnett (RG), Sgt D Gerrard (FE), P/O J Whitton (Nav.)

P/O Jack Heppell and his crew. On the 16th September 1943, attempting to cross the Alps to bomb Montlucon, the aircraft suffered severe icing and started to spin. The crew were ordered to bale out. At the second order, F/Sgt B Booth (Nav) and Sgt C Varley (W/Op) jumped before the order was retracted. They both returned to England within three months. P/O Heppell and all his then crew were killed on the 22nd October 1943 when his Halifax JD315 crashed on a Kassel bombing raid.

others pushed on to find moderate to good visibility, with haze in the deep valley, and some were able to pick out ground features. They bombed on green TIs from 14,000 to 15,000 feet between 00.15 and 00.39, and the impression was gained that the attack was concentrated around the yards and adjacent railway station, but, it seems that the marking was misplaced, and the operation failed in its purpose.

Another week of inactivity preceded the first of a series of four operations over a four-week period against Hannover beginning on the 22nd, for which a force of 711 aircraft was assembled. Situated in northern Germany midway between the Dutch frontier and Berlin, the city was home to much industry, with oil, rubber and tank production of particular significance to the raid planners of Bomber Command, and was also the location of seven concentration camps. According to Martin Middlebrook and Chris Everitt in Bomber Command War Diaries, the first three operations produced concentrated bombing, but mostly outside of the target, while only the third one succeeded in causing extensive damage, which, if the figures are to be believed, seem to be massively out of proportion. The author contends that the reports of the crews after the first two operations suggest strongly that the damage to Hannover was accumulative over the first three raids and did not result from just one, as will be explained in the following narrative. The telling feature is, perhaps, that no reports came out of Hannover to corroborate the testimony of the crews on the first two raids, although post-raid reconnaissance by the RAF after the second one did show that some of the bombing had fallen into open country, and the Pathfinders admitted to at least one poor performance.

10 Squadron prepared sixteen Halifaxes, which took off between 18.50 and 19.22 with S/Ls Black and Dean the senior pilots on duty. P/O Cockrem and W/O Kennedy both returned within ninety minutes because of instrument and Gee failure respectively, but the remaining Melbourne crews all reached the target area, where good visibility prevailed, but stronger-than-forecast winds would play their part. F/Sgt Lindsey could not coax JD146 to climb above 12,000 feet, which gave him and his crew a premium view of the target, and possibly helped them to avoid the intense searchlights and heavy flak, which was bursting way above them at 18,000 feet. They bombed on red and green TIs at 21.27, and observed their bombs to fall about three hundred yards to the north of the aiming-point. F/L Jenkins and crew had been attacked while on approach to the target by a ME110, which shot away the H2S cupola, holed both sides of the fuselage and destroyed the hydraulics system. An attempt was made to bomb the target, but the hardware remained resolutely in the bomb bay and refused to be dislodged. They turned for home, reporting their predicament on arrival, and were told to fly the wounded HR924 to the coast east of Hull, and point it out sea before baling out, which they accomplished safely at 01.40. Meanwhile, 430 miles away, their squadron colleagues were bombing Hannover on red, green and yellow TIs from 13,500 to 20,000 feet between 21.32 and 21.49, and some observed a line of fires developing from west to east, with smoke rising through 14,000 feet. F/Sgt Plant and crew reported fires running from the aiming-point in a north-north-westerly direction across the city, and other crews from across the Command claimed that the glow of fires was still visible from the Dutch coast, a distance of two hundred miles. On leaving the target the Plant crew was attacked by a BF109, which they promptly shot down. Twenty-six aircraft failed to return, twelve of them Halifaxes, which, again sustained the highest numerical losses, and, this time, at 5.3%, even exceeded the Stirling's loss rate.

Now let us examine the claim that the main weight of bombs fell two to five miles south-south-east from the city centre, and that the operation largely failed. Firstly, two to five miles in any city means that the bombing fell within the boundaries, and, therefore, within the built-up area. Secondly, the majority of crews, if not all, reported a highly successful raid with fires right across the city, smoke rising to 14,000 feet as they left the scene and the glow visible from the Dutch coast. It is true that crews were very frequently mistaken in their belief that an attack had been successful, but the evidence on this occasion would seem to confirm their testimony. Decoy fire-sites do not produce a glow visible from a distance of two hundred miles, or sufficient volumes of smoke to climb to 14,000 feet during the short duration of a raid, and be dense enough to be visible at night.

The WAAFs of RAF Melbourne

Mannheim was selected on the 23rd to host its second major raid of the month, and would face a force numbered at take-off of 628 aircraft. 10 Squadron contributed eleven Halifaxes, which took off between 18.45 and 19.05 with no pilots on duty above pilot officer rank. P/Os Baxter and Cockrem and F/Sgt Clarke returned early respectively because of a defective engine, unserviceable turrets and an inability to climb beyond 13,000 feet. The others reached the target area to find good visibility and the Pathfinders marking the northern districts, which had not been hit so severely during the previous operation. The marking was accurate and concentrated, allowing the Melbourne crews to attack on red, green and yellow TIs from 12,500 to 18,300 feet between 22.01 and 22.18. F/Sgt Wardman and crew were nine minutes into the return journey when they were attacked by what they believed was a JU88 at extreme range. Severe damage was inflicted on the starboard mainplane and the tail unit, but further contact was evaded, and the Halifax completed a safe return. Sadly, it seems that this crew had used up its ration of good fortune. Later bombing spilled over into the northern fringe of Ludwigshafen and out into the nearby towns of Oppau and Frankenthal, where much damage resulted. 927 houses and twenty industrial premises were destroyed in Mannheim, and the I.G Farben factory suffered severely in Ludwigshafen. Thirty-two aircraft failed to return, and, this time, the Lancasters were hardest-hit with eighteen missing, compared with seven each for the Halifaxes and Stirlings, which gave a loss-rate of 5.7%, 3.6% and 6% respectively.

The WAAFs of RAF Melbourne – date unknown. One Halifax flight engineer used to find a pair of 'blackouts' (RAF issue ladies' bloomers) resting on the aircraft throttles before each flight. After a safe return they were always there again the next night.

Hannover was posted as the target again on the 27th, and a force of 678 aircraft made ready. 10 Squadron answered the call with eighteen Halifaxes, which took off between 19.15 and 19.45 with F/Ls Cox and Pont the senior pilots on duty. Poor weather conditions were encountered over the North Sea, and it was at this stage that P/O Kennedy's a.s.i failed, forcing him to turn back, and he was followed home by P/O Lucas and crew, who had reached a position some twenty-five miles off the Norfolk coast before an engine failed. The others carried on in the wake of the Pathfinders, who were unaware that they were operating in accordance with incorrectly-forecast winds, which would push the marking some five miles from the city centre towards the north of the city. The weather improved markedly over Germany to present the crews with clear skies over the target, and the 10 Squadron crews bombed on red, yellow and green TIs from 16,000 to 19,000 feet between 22.04 and 22.21, observing many fires with smoke rising to 15,000 feet. Sgt Whitmarsh and crew landed on three engines and reported the glow of fires visible from the Dutch coast, and confidence in the success of the operation was unanimous across the Command, giving lie to the claim that little damage resulted. Post-raid photos did reveal many bomb craters in open country, but the fire and smoke evidence did not support decoy fire-sites, and no local report was forthcoming. The loss of thirty-eight aircraft was probably something of a shock, but, at least, common sense returned to the statistics to re-establish the status-quo after the topsy-turvy outcome of the Mannheim raid. Seventeen Halifaxes, ten Lancasters, ten Stirlings and one Wellington failed to return, giving loss-rates for the four-engine types of 9% for the Stirling, 7.3% for the Halifax and 3.2% for the Lancaster. Three of the missing Halifaxes belonged to 10 Squadron, HR922 falling in the target area, with just one survivor from the crew of F/Sgt Wardman, while HX159 was the victim of a night-fighter also close to the target, and P/O Cockrem RAAF died with four of his crew, leaving the three survivors to be taken into captivity. Sgt Rostron and his entire crew were killed in JD272, which, based on their final resting place in Reichswald, probably means that they came down close to the Ruhr, and were moved there after being interred initially close to their crash site.

The month ended with an operation to Bochum on the 29th, for which 10 Squadron made ready eight Halifaxes in an overall heavy force of 343 aircraft. They took off between 18.00 and 18.25 with the inordinately large number of four pilots of flight lieutenant rank, Cox, Jenkins, Pont and Wilkinson as the senior pilots on duty. F/L Wilkinson returned early because of a faulty aileron control, which prevented him from turning to port. The bombs were jettisoned off Bridlington before a landing was carried out safely at Lissett. P/O Heppell and crew found themselves running late and unable to comply with the briefed concentration times, and also turned back. The others reached the target area to find good visibility, which enabled them to identify their position visually, but two route markers ignited at 20,000 feet to confirm that their approach was on track, and green TIs marked out the aiming-point. The bombing was carried out from 17,000 to 19,500 feet between 20.58 and 21.07 in the face of a strong searchlight and moderate flak defence, and the target was described by some as a mass of flames, with smoke rising rapidly to meet the bombers. At debriefing, F/Ls Pont and Cox reported being attacked outbound by single engine fighters, the latter claiming his assailant as destroyed. Bochum sustained extensive damage, local reports stating 527 houses destroyed and 742 seriously damaged. During the course of the month W/C Edmonds was awarded a DFC, and there were DFMs for three gunners, two wireless operators and one bomb-aimer. The squadron operated on eight occasions, dispatching 111 sorties for the loss of seven Halifaxes and crews.

Sgt R.B. Carpenter (last in line and later commissioned with award of DFM). He was usually in F/Sgt Virgo's crew. Halifax MkII of 10 Sqn.

October 1943

There was a hectic start to October for the Lancaster squadrons, elements of which were called on to operate six times during the first eight nights. The Halifaxes enjoyed a more leisurely

Sgt R.B Carpenter in bomb aimer's position

introduction to the month's operational schedule, 4 Group contributing twenty of the type to extensive mining operations on the 2/3rd while elements of 1, 5 and 8 Groups were raiding Munich. Five 10 Squadron crews were assigned to the waters of Kiel Bay, probably in the Radishes, Quinces and Pumpkins gardens, and took off between 18.00 and 18.06 with F/L Jenkins the senior pilot on duty. The pin-point for him and his crew was to be Vejsnæs on the southern tip of Ærø Island, from where they would make a timed run to the drop zone, but they were unable to locate it because of sea mist and unserviceable H2S equipment. Shortly after turning for home, and while crossing southern Denmark, having discovered that their guns were inoperable, they were approached by a Dornier 217, which then tailed them for thirty minutes without opening fire. P/O Dixon and crew found an alternative location in the Great Belt, and delivered their mines from 5,800 feet at 21.29. Almost an hour later as they approached the west coast of Denmark, they were attacked by a JU88 and a BF109, and sustained cannon-shell holes in the rudder, but claimed the former as probably destroyed. The others dropped their vegetables through five to ten-tenths cloud into the assigned locations from 5,200 to 6,500 feet between 20.53 and 21.19, before returning safely.

Kassel, an industrial city located some eighty miles to the east of the Ruhr, would receive two visits from the Command during the month, the first on the 3rd, for which a force of 547 aircraft was made ready, consisting of 223 Halifaxes, 204 Lancasters and 113 Stirlings. 10 Squadron supported the operation with sixteen Halifaxes, which took off between 18.00 and 18.20 with S/L Dean the senior pilot on duty. Unfortunately, a 25% rate of early returns removed the crews of F/Ls Jenkins and Wilkinson and Sgts Green and Wilson from the proceedings, leaving a dozen to continue on to find clear skies over the target area, but thick ground haze. The Pathfinder H2S "blind" markers overshot the planned aiming-point, and, because of the haze, the backers-up, whose job was to confirm their accuracy by visual means, were unable to correct the error. As a result, the main weight of the attack fell onto the western suburbs, where the Henschel and Fieseler aircraft factories were hit, but a stray bomb load also detonated an ammunition dump at Ihringshausen, situated close to the north-eastern suburb of Wolfsanger, which was left devastated by the blast. Twenty-four aircraft failed to return, fourteen Halifaxes, six Stirlings and four Lancasters, which gave a loss-rate of 6.3%, 3.2% and 2.9% respectively.

Frankfurt was posted as the target twenty-four hours later, and a force of 406 aircraft made ready. A small number of American 8th Air Force B17s had been flirting with night raids alongside their RAF colleagues since the first Hannover raid, and this night would bring their final involvement. 10 Squadron briefed ten crews and launched them from Melbourne between 17.20 and 17.45 with S/L Dean the senior pilot on duty. They had to follow a somewhat circuitous route, which departed England over the Sussex coast and tracked across Belgium as if heading for southern Germany, before swinging to the north-east and passing to the west of Frankfurt for the final run-in of around eighty miles. This added significantly to the mileage, but avoided the flak hotspots from the Dutch coast and north of the Ruhr. An engine issue developed in Sgt Thackray's aircraft over Reading at 19.15, which persuaded him to feather it and turn for home. However, the engine was restarted five minutes later, and the sortie resumed. Sgt Evans and crew had progressed only as far as south of London when the navigator was taken ill with oxygen starvation, after puncturing his hose while sharpening a pencil, and this caused the sortie to be abandoned. The others pushed on to reach the target area after a four-hour outward flight, although an hour of that was generally accounted for in climbing-out and gaining height before setting course. Frankfurt was found to be clear of cloud, and the Pathfinders produced a masterful marking performance to leave the city at the mercy of the main force. The 10 Squadron crews bombed on red and green TIs from 16,000 to 19,500 feet between 21.34 and 21.46, and witnessed a highly-concentrated attack taking place that left the eastern half of the city and the docks area a sea of flames. S/L Dean's JD967 was hit by flak over the target, damaging the port mainplane and the fuselage, and a 4lb incendiary somehow found its way into the fuselage without igniting, before being promptly thrown out through the flare-chute. A large red explosion was observed at 21.37, which threw flames up to 3,000 feet, and smoke was rising through 8,000 feet as the bombers turned away, some crews returning to report the glow from the burning city to be visible for 120 miles into the homeward leg. The success was gained at the modest cost of ten aircraft, half of which were Halifaxes.

Crew of Halifax II JB974 ZA-T. Pilot F/L H Wilkinson and all his crew died on 22/23 October 1943 on a raid to Kassel. Crew: Pilot - F/L Herbert Henry Vincent Wilkinson; Flight Engineer - Sgt Harold Kearsley[1]; Navigator - F/O Robert Lionel Harman Ball; Bomb Aimer - F/O Frank Hewitt; Wireless Operator - Sgt Kenneth Lomas; Air Gunner - Sgt Richard Thomas Burman ; Air Gunner - Sgt Ronald Lascelles Jenkins

A new weapon in the Command's armoury was introduced for the first time in numbers on the night of the 7/8th, when aircraft from 1 Group's 101 Squadron participated in an all-Lancaster operation to Stuttgart equipped with "Jostle", a night-fighter-communications-jamming device. It required a specialist operator in addition to the standard crew of seven, who, though not necessarily a German speaker, could recognise the language, and, on hearing it, jam the signals on up to three frequencies by broadcasting engine noise over them. At 101 Squadron the device was referred to as ABC or Airborne Cigar, and, once proved to be effective, ABC Lancasters would be spread through the bomber stream for all major operations, whether or not 1 Group was otherwise involved. The Lancaster would also carry a full bomb load reduced by 1,000lbs to compensate for the weight of the equipment and its operator. Five crews from 10 Squadron, each, unusually, with an officer pilot, would spend this evening gardening in the Hawthorn III region, on the approaches to Esbjerg off Denmark's south-western coast. They took off either side of 20.30 with F/Ls

Sgt Ronald Jenkins

Pennicott and Trobe the senior pilots on duty, and reached the target area to find three to eight-tenths cloud. F/L Trobe was unable to locate his pin-point in the poor weather conditions with unserviceable navigational aids, and brought his mines home. The others delivered theirs into the briefed locations by H2S from 2,000 to 6,000 feet between 23.00 and 23.19, and returned safely to report uneventful sorties.

W/C Edmonds concluded his tour as commanding officer on the 8th, and was succeeded by W/C Sutton on his promotion from within. The third raid of the series on Hannover was posted that day, and a force of 504 aircraft duly assembled. 10 Squadron made ready sixteen Halifaxes, but that number would be reduced by one after F/L Wilkinson's flight engineer was struck on the head by a propeller, and had to be removed to sickbay, where his injury was found to be not serious. The remaining fifteen departed Melbourne between 22.35 and 23.00 with F/Ls Jenkins and Trobe the senior pilots on duty. P/O Walker returned early with engine issues, and P/O Heppell after his mount refused to climb above 14,000 feet. The others set course for Hornsea and then the northern tip of Texel, before reaching the target area to find clear skies and red and green TIs marking out the city-centre aiming-point. The Melbourne crews bombed from 16,000 to 19,000 feet between 01.32 and 01.38, and, having arrived in the early stages of the attack, saw fires just beginning to take hold. It was clear as they retreated westwards that the fires were developing into a serious conflagration, but, curiously, despite the claim by some commentators that this was the one successful raid of the series, there was no mention of the glow being visible from a considerable distance, as had been the case with the first two operations. This time a local report did emerge, which described heavy damage in all districts except for those in the west, with 3,932 buildings destroyed, and thirty thousand others damaged to some extent, with a death toll of 1,200 people. These statistics seem somewhat excessive for a single operation by fewer than five hundred aircraft, particularly in the absence of the kind of crew reports common to the first two raids, and this adds weight to the author's contention, that the damage was accumulative over the three operations. HX163 sustained flak damage to the undercarriage and flaps, and was declared a write-off after crash-landing in the hands of P/O Cameron and crew, who walked away unscathed.

The final raid of the series against Hannover was conducted by an all-Lancaster heavy force on the night of the 18/19th, when thick cloud prevented the Pathfinders from marking accurately, and most of the bombs fell into open country to the north and north-west. Eighteen Lancasters failed to return, and this brought the final casualty figure to 110 aircraft from 2,253 sorties. Two nights later another all-Lancaster force tried to hit Leipzig, but appalling weather conditions rendered the attempt futile, and the attack was scattered and ineffective. The final major operation of the month was the second one against Kassel, for which preparations were put in hand on the 22nd. A force of 569 ultimately stood ready to take off in the early evening, the 10 Squadron element of nineteen becoming airborne between 17.15 and 17.47 with S/L Dean the senior pilot on duty. It was not to be a happy night for "Shiney Ten", with five crews returning early to land between 20.50 and 22.15, three because of severe icing and two with technical issues. The others pushed on to the target, where the H2S "blind" markers overshot the city-centre aiming-point, leaving the success of the operation reliant upon the visual marker crews backing up, and they did not disappoint. The red and green TIs were concentrated right on the aiming-point, and the main force followed up with accurate and concentrated bombing with scarcely any creep-back. The 10 Squadron crews carried out their attacks from 14,700 to 20,000 feet between 23.53 and 21.02, and observed the fires just beginning to take hold as they turned away. It was after the sound of their engines had receded that the fires joined together to engulf the city in what, in some areas, was a firestorm, though not one as fierce as that experienced in Hamburg. It was not a one-sided contest, however, and the defences brought down forty-three bombers, twenty-five of them Halifaxes, and three of these represented 10 Squadron. HX174 exploded near the target, throwing clear the bomb-aimer, before crashing six miles north of the target killing P/O Plant RAAF and the rest of his crew. This was very close to the crash site of JD135, in which P/O Heppall and his seven-man crew perished. JB974 came down in a northern suburb of Hagen in the eastern Ruhr on the way home, and was clearly well south of the intended course to the North Sea via northern Holland. F/L Wilkinson and his crew paid the ultimate price for their navigational error. In Kassel the shell-shocked inhabitants were emerging from their shelters to find their city devastated and unrecognizable. After 3,600 fires had been dealt with, it would be established eventually that 53,000 apartments had been destroyed or damaged, leaving up to 120,000 people without homes, and in excess of six thousand others killed. 155 industrial buildings had also been destroyed or severely damaged, along with numerous schools, hospitals, churches and public buildings.

S/L Maw and crew were posted in from 1663 Conversion Unit on the 25th, while S/L Black was posted to 1652 Conversion Unit on the 27th at the end of his tour of operations. He took with him a DFC, and other past and present pilots, S/Ls Dean and Hartnell-Beavis and F/Ls Brookbanks, Cox and Wood were similarly rewarded for their service. During the course of the month the squadron operated on six nights, and dispatched seventy sorties for the loss of four Halifaxes and three crews.

November 1943

The new month would bring a resumption of the Berlin offensive, but, first, in a memo to Churchill on the 3rd, Harris stated that, with the assistance of the American 8th Air Force, he could "wreck Berlin from end to end", and win the war without the need for the kind of bloody and protracted land campaigns that he had witnessed personally during the Great War. The Americans, however, were committed to victory on land, where the cameras could capture the glory, and there was never a chance of enlisting their support.

Düsseldorf was selected to open the month's operational account that very night, and, no doubt, while the Prime Minister was digesting Harris's epistle, a force of 589 aircraft was being prepared for action. 10 Squadron made ready eighteen Halifaxes, loading eight of them with a 2,000 pounder each and ten SBCs of 4lb incendiaries and three of 30lbs, eight others with two 1,000 pounders plus incendiaries, and two with a slight variation on the above. They took off between 16.35 and 17.10 with W/C Sutton the senior pilot on duty, but soon lost the services of P/O Culverhouse and crew to an unserviceable Gee-box and F/O Hall and crew to an inability to persuade JD202 to climb above 15,000 feet. P/O Dixon and crew were outbound over Belgium and some fifteen miles short of the German frontier when they were attacked by a JU88 at 19.38, which set the port-outer engine on fire and holed two fuel tanks. The bombs were jettisoned, the fighter was evaded, and a safe return was made on three engines. F/L Trobe and crew had crossed into Germany when they, too, were set upon by four enemy fighters at 19.42. The bombs were jettisoned and the crew fought for their lives as HR921 sustained damage to the W/T equipment, hydraulics, fuel tanks, bomb doors and port-inner engine, which stopped.

F/L 'Timber' Wood and crew, Bill Knott 2nd from right and Frank Morton 2nd from left

The engagement lasted for four minutes, during which the flight engineer and wireless operator were wounded and the mid-upper gunner, also slightly injured, claimed one of the attackers as probably destroyed. Somehow the fighters were shaken off, and a normal landing was carried out on three engines, but, such was the state of the Halifax, that it was declared to be beyond economical repair. The crew would be well-rewarded for their efforts, receiving between them a CGM, a DFC and two DFMs.

Meanwhile, over the south-western Ruhr, the other Melbourne crews had encountered small patches of low cloud and smoke beginning to drift across the target. However, visibility was generally good, and the Pathfinders employed both sky and ground markers to good effect to identify the aiming-point in the city centre. Bombing took place on red and green TIs and skymarkers from 15,000 to 19,500 feet between 19.48 and 20.11, and fires were observed to be developing on both sides of the Rhine with black smoke rising through 6,000 feet as the bombers turned away. At debriefing, Sgt Evans and crew reported witnessing a large, red explosion at 19.50 as they were on their bombing-run and three minutes from release, then described losing an engine at the Dutch coast on the way home, but landing safely on three. HX179 limped over the Norfolk coast shortly after 21.00, clearly having returned early and carrying some kind of damage. At 21.16 the Halifax crashed at Park Farm, one mile north of the American base at Shipdham, and was consumed by fire. The only survivor from the crew of P/O Cameron was the rear gunner, who was dragged clear by a member of the Home Guard, but, sadly, succumbed to his injuries on the 5th. His rescuer, Mr Ernest Bowman would be awarded a BEM for his brave actions. It will be recalled that this crew had walked away from a landing-crash on return from Hannover a month earlier. Eighteen aircraft failed to return, and, unusually, eleven were Lancasters and seven Halifaxes. JN947 was among the latter, having crashed in the target area, killing F/L Harden, his flight engineer and both gunners, and delivering the three survivors into enemy hands.

Following a period of operational inactivity, during which the squadron focussed on training, nine crews were called to briefing on the 11th to learn of their destinations for that night. Four crews were to join a force of 124 Halifaxes and ten Lancasters of 4, 6 and 8 Groups to attack the marshalling yards at Cannes in southern France, on the main coastal line to Italy. While this operation was in progress, elements of 617 Squadron led by W/C Leonard Cheshire would be attempting but failing to destroy the Antheor Viaduct further west along the coast. The other five crews at briefing were bound for the Nectarines garden off the Frisians, and they waited at the threshold while the Cannes element took off between 18.00 and 18.06 with F/L Jenkins the senior pilot on duty. The gardeners followed them into the air a minute later, and reached their allotted target area long before their Riviera-bound colleagues. P/O Ayres turned back from a position close to Terschelling after something fell on the bomb-release switch and smashed it. The others found seven-tenths cloud with a base at 4,000 feet, and used their navigational aids to establish their positions. P/O Dixon was unable to gain a firm fix, and brought his vegetables home, leaving F/Sgts Holdsworth, Kilsby and Lindsey to deliver their mines into the briefed locations from 2,500 to 5,500 feet between 20.01 and 20.16.

It took four-and-a-half hours for the main element to climb out, rendezvous and reach the target area eight hundred miles away in southern France. They found clear skies and excellent visibility, which enabled them to make a visual identification of the coastline before concentrating on the red and green TIs placed from 5,000 feet by the Pathfinder element. There was negligible opposition as they bombed from 13,000 to 14,000 feet between 22.31 and 22.46, after which, a number of fires were observed, although it was difficult to make an accurate assessment of the outcome. P/O Culverhouse and crew thought the bombing to be scattered and to the east of the aiming-point, and this was confirmed by local reports, which suggested that the railway installations remained untouched, while adjacent residential districts had sustained damage and fatalities.

It would be a further week before operations were on again, and then there would be a flurry of five operations in eight nights to conclude the month's offensive activity. The long and rocky road to Berlin was re-joined on the 18th, for which a heavy force of 440 Lancasters was made ready. A diversion was planned to divide the enemy's night-fighter force, and Mannheim and Ludwigshafen were selected as the destination to put three hundred miles between the two elements. 394 aircraft, made up of 248 Halifaxes, 114 Stirlings and thirty-three Lancasters, were drawn from 3, 4, 6 and 8 Groups for the latter, and 10 Squadron contributed eighteen of the Halifaxes, which departed Melbourne between 16.25 and 17.05 with F/Ls Jenkins, Pont and Trobe the senior pilots on duty. P/O Ayres and crew returned early after their oxygen-supply system failed, leaving the others to continue on across France to reach the target under clear skies and with good visibility. Stronger-than-forecast winds had driven the bomber stream to the target a little ahead of time, which upset the planned schedule to a degree, and may have led to what became a scattered attack. Some crews made a visual identification of the aiming-point after following yellow route markers, and confirmed their positions by H2S, while others relied on the red and green TIs and bombed from 14,000 to 20,000 feet between 20.27 and 20.51. Local reports confirmed that the northern and north-eastern districts of Mannheim had borne the brunt of the attack, and it here that most of the destruction occurred, before some of the bombing also spilled into Ludwigshafen. Four industrial premises, including the Daimler-Benz car factory, and 325 other buildings were destroyed at a cost to the Command of twenty-three aircraft. Among the twelve missing Halifaxes was 10 Squadron's HX190, which crashed at Rapscourt in the Marne region of France, killing P/O Lindsey RAAF and all but his rear gunner, who was taken into captivity. Neither operation was an outstanding success, but the diversion was successful in keeping night-fighters away from the Capital, from which a modest nine Lancasters failed to return.

The Lancasters stayed at home on the 19th, while 3, 4, 6 and 8 Groups combined to put 170 Halifaxes, eighty-six Stirlings and 10 Mosquitos into the air for Leverkusen. 10 Squadron contributed eleven Halifaxes, which took off between 16.15 and 16.35 with F/Ls Jenkins, Pont and Trobe the senior pilots on duty. P/O Dixon and crew returned early because of the failure of the port-inner engine, and they were followed home by F/Sgt Wilson and crew, who had suffered wireless-receiver and Gee-box issues. P/O Baxter and crew were at 20,000 feet over Holland when engine problems persuaded them to abandon their sortie, and their bombs were dropped through cloud onto an alternative target at 19.06, which, according to their map references, was a wood in north-eastern Belgium. When the others reached the target area, they were greeted by ten-tenths cloud and an absence of marking, which was caused by equipment failure among the Oboe Mosquitos. A few green TIs were spotted some five to ten miles to the north-west of the target during the approach, but the crews were left to establish their positions on the basis of their own H2S, which, over a region as densely built-up as the Ruhr, was a challenge. Bombing took place from 16,000 to 20,000 feet between 19.20 and 19.28, but no results could be observed. Only five aircraft were missing from the operation, but 10 Squadron lost two to crashes in England on return. F/Sgt Holdsworth tried to land HX181 at Tangmere, but crashed into a hangar at 21.35, killing all on board.* Almost ninety minutes later, a flak-damaged JD473 crashed at Ford after over-shooting the landing, and this resulted in injuries to P/O Lucas and three of his crew. The operation was a complete failure, which sprayed bombs over twenty-seven towns in the Ruhr, mostly to the north of Leverkusen.

Harris called for a maximum effort on Berlin on the 22nd, and 764 aircraft were made available, of which sixteen of the 234 Halifaxes were contributed by 10 Squadron. They took off between 16.45 and 17.20 with S/L Dean the senior pilot on duty, and briefed to adopt an outward route similar to that employed by the Lancaster force four nights earlier. This took them from Texel to a point north-west of Hannover, where a slight dogleg to port would put them on a due-easterly heading directly to the target. Unlike the previous raid, however, rather than the circuitous return south of Cologne and out over the French coast, they would come home via a reciprocal route. This was based on a forecast of low cloud and fog over Germany, which would inhibit the night-fighter effort, while broken, medium-level cloud over Berlin would facilitate ground marking. An additional bonus was the availability to the Pathfinders of five new H2S Mk III sets, while a new record of thirty-four aircraft per minute passing over the aiming-point would be achieved by abandoning the long-standing practice of allocating aircraft types to specific waves. On this night aircraft of all types would be spread through the bomber stream, which was bad news for the Stirlings, which, by the very nature of their design, would be below the Lancaster and Halifax elements, and in danger of being hit by friendly bombs.

F/Sgt Wilson's sortie was effectively over before it began after his escape hatch blew open during take-off, and could not be closed against the power of the slipstream. Sgt Hullah and crew arrived back shortly afterwards because of a faulty Gee-box. On arrival by the remainder at the target, it became clear that the forecast had been inaccurate, and that the city was hidden under a blanket of ten-tenths cloud with tops at around 12,000 feet. This meant that ground marking would be largely ineffective, and that the least reliable method, skymarking, would have to be employed. As F/O Clarke and crew closed on the target, the navigator collapsed through oxygen starvation, despite which, the captain decided to carry on. No markers were visible by the time they ran into intense predicted flak and a mass of searchlights, and they spent the next ten minutes trying to shake off the unwelcome attention. Failing to do so, the bombs were dropped at 20.04 onto what they believed was the south-eastern outskirts of the city. The other 10 Squadron crews aimed at red and green TIs and release-point flares, confirming their positions by H2S, and bombed from 17,000 to 20,000 feet between 20.08 and 20.25. The glow of fires was observed beneath the clouds, and a very large explosion lit up the sky at 20.10. The impression was of a successful operation, but an assessment through the clouds was impossible. Twenty-six aircraft failed to return, and two of the ten missing Halifaxes were from Melbourne. JD146 was lost without trace with the crew of F/L Pont, and JD367 came down at Achmer, close to the Mittelland Canal, two miles west-south-west of Bramsche with no survivors from the crew of F/O Hall. Post-raid reconnaissance and local reports confirmed that this attack on Berlin had been the most effective of the war to date, and had caused a swathe of destruction from the city centre through the western residential districts of Tiergarten and Charlottenburg as far as the suburb town of Spandau. A number of firestorm areas were reported, and the catalogue of destruction included three thousand houses and twenty-three industrial premises. Many thousands more sustained varying degrees of damage, costing 175,000 people their homes and an estimated two thousand their lives, and, by daylight on the 23rd, the smoke had risen to almost 19,000 feet.

The Command posted missing twenty-six aircraft, with a loss-rate among the types 2.3% for the Lancaster, 4.2% for the Halifax and 10.0% for the Stirling, which proved to be the final straw for Harris as far as the last-mentioned was concerned. The Stirling, which was restricted by its short wing design to a low service ceiling, and by the configuration of its bomb bay to small calibre bombs, lacked development potential, and was immediately withdrawn from future operations over Germany. It would still have an important role to play on secondary duties, however, bombing over occupied territory, mining, and, in 1944, it would replace the Halifax to become the aircraft of choice for the two SOE squadrons, 138 and 161, at Tempsford. Many of those released from Bomber Command service would find their way to 38 Group, where they would give valuable service as transports and glider-tugs for airborne landings.

Lancasters carried out another highly accurate and destructive attack on the "Big City" on the following night, guided by the glow of fires still burning beneath the clouds. 4 Group remained at home, until being invited on the 25th to join forces with elements of 6 and 8 Groups for an attack in Frankfurt. A force of 262 aircraft included seventeen Halifaxes from 10 Squadron, which departed Melbourne between 23.20 and 23.59 with S/L Dean the senior pilot on duty.

P/O Scott turned back from mid-Channel with a dead port-outer engine, but the others all made it to the target, where complete cloud cover obscured the ground, and crews were drawn on by red route markers and red, green and yellow sky-markers, which coincided with e.t.a. Bombing was carried out from 16,000 to 20,000 feet between 02.38 and 03.00, and a bright glow was evident beneath the clouds along with a number of brilliant flashes. Local reports described a modest amount of housing damage, and 3,500 people were bombed out of their homes in return for the loss of eleven Halifaxes and a single Lancaster.

It again fell to the Lancaster squadrons to continue the assault on Berlin on the 26/27th, while 157 Halifaxes and twenty-one Lancasters carried out a diversionary raid on Stuttgart. 10 Squadron made ready a dozen Halifaxes, which took off between 16.42 and 16.59 with S/L Dean the senior pilot on duty, but lost the services of Sgt Borthwick and crew almost immediately on the discovery that the petrol cap and filter had been left off Nº 5 port tank. The two forces followed the same route over France until diverging shortly before Frankfurt was reached, and this did confuse the night-fighter controller for a time. The Stuttgart element reached the target, assisted by excellent route-marking by the Pathfinders, but the six to nine-tenths thin cloud swallowed up the red and green parachute flares, making it difficult for the bomb-aimers to draw a bead on them. Positions were confirmed by the 10 Squadron crews by H2S and the bombs dropped from 16,000 to 20,000 feet between 20.22 and 20.49. The glow of fires beneath the cloud, which remained visible for some time into the return journey, suggested a degree of success, but this was not borne out by local reports, which described a widely scattered raid and no significant damage. The diversion did draw off some of the night-fighter force, but twenty-eight Lancasters failed to return from Berlin, demonstrating the vulnerability of the type when operating without Halifaxes and Stirlings. S/L Dean was posted to 1652 Conversion Unit at the end of the month, and W/C Sutton and F/L Trobe were among recipients of the DFC. During the course of the month the squadron carried out eight operations on seven nights, and dispatched 101 sorties for the loss of seven Halifaxes and six crews.

December 1943

December began for 4 Group with the hugely significant introduction to operations of the Hercules-powered Mk III Halifax in the hands of 466 Squadron RAAF, which was the first unit in the Command to receive the type. Once fully-equipped, the group would be transformed, and have an aircraft equal or even superior in performance to the Lancaster, although it would never come close in terms of bomb-carrying capacity. Its introduction to war work came with a dozen gardening sorties in northern waters on the night of the 1/2nd, in company with Stirlings, while the rest of the bomber force remained at home. The following night brought round five of the renewed Berlin campaign, for which an all-Lancaster main force was dispatched in the late afternoon. Incorrectly-forecast winds spread the bomber stream out, resulting in a widely scattered raid across mostly southern districts, which caused some useful industrial damage, but not the destruction commensurate with the size of the force and the effort expended. The disappointment was compounded by the loss of forty bombers, thirty-seven of them Lancasters, two Halifaxes from 8 Group's 35 Squadron and a Mosquito.

Having been spared by the weather from experiencing a major visitation from the Command in October, Leipzig found itself on the 3rd at the end of the red tape on briefing-room wall-maps from County Durham to Cambridgeshire. A force of 527 aircraft included sixteen Halifaxes provided by 10 Squadron, which took off between 23.15 and 23.50 with F/L Pennicott the senior pilot on duty. F/Sgt Green and crew turned back with an engine issue when just short of the Dutch coast, and F/Sgt Burcher and crew abandoned their sortie at around the same time after being unable to climb to a respectable height. The bomber stream was routed towards Berlin as a feint, passing north of Hannover and Braunschweig, before turning towards the south-east, while Mosquitos continued on to carry out a diversion at the Capital. Night-fighters had already infiltrated the stream at the Dutch coast, and HX191 was attacked by one shortly after crossing into Germany. The second pilot was killed in the engagement, and the order to bale out was issued seconds before the Halifax exploded and crashed near Cloppenburg at around 02.25. P/O Walker and five of his crew lost their lives when into the final third of their tour, and only the navigator and wireless operator survived to fall into enemy hands. The feint had the desired effect, and few night-fighters were encountered in the target area, where ten-tenths cloud prevailed, and the Pathfinders marked by H2S with green skymarkers. The 10 Squadron crews bombed on these from 17,000 to 20,000 feet either side of 04.00, having confirmed their positions by means of their own H2S. A strong glow beneath the clouds and black smoke emerging through the tops suggested that an accurate and concentrated attack had taken place, and the smoke remained visible for a hundred miles into the return journey south-east towards the French frontier. Had many aircraft not then strayed into the Frankfurt defence zone, the losses may have been fewer, but twenty-four aircraft failed to return, fifteen of them Halifaxes. Local reports confirmed this as a highly successful operation, the most destructive visited upon the eastern city during the war, although, it would have its revenge in time.

A long period of inactivity now ensued for the Halifax squadrons, which was exploited at Melbourne to carry out intensive training. In the meantime, an all-Lancaster heavy force attacked Berlin again on the night of the 16/17, which will forever be remembered for the carnage that occurred as exhausted crews with dwindling fuel reserves sought out a place to land in low cloud. The 1, 6 and 8 Group regions were the worst-affected, and twenty-nine Lancasters crashed, many of them abandoned by their crews, and around 150 airmen lost their lives when so close to home and safety. It was the 20th before the Melbourne crews were next called to briefing, when they learned that Frankfurt was to be the target for 647 Lancasters and Halifaxes, while elements of 1 and 8 Groups carried out a diversion at Mannheim, some forty miles to the south. 10 Squadron supported the operation with nineteen Halifaxes, which took off between 16.25 and 16.55 with W/C Sutton and S/L Maw the senior pilots on duty. W/C Ayling had also been due to take part, but his aircraft became unserviceable shortly before take-off. He had been seconded to the RNZAF in 1940, and came to 10 Squadron on attachment to gain up-to-date operational experience prior to being appointed to the command of 51 Squadron at the start of February 1944.

After climbing out, the crews set course for Southwold and the North Sea-crossing to the Scheldt Estuary, before passing north of Antwerp and flying the length of Belgium to the German frontier north of Luxembourg. The German night-fighter controller had picked up transmissions from the bomber stream as soon as it left the English coast, and was able track it all the way to the target and vector his fighters into position. Many combats took place during the outward flight, and the diversion failed to draw fighters away from the main action. While experiencing navigational problems, Sgt Evans and crew were lured away by TIs from the diversion at

Mannheim, and dropped their bombs there from 18,000 feet at 19.34. The problems continued at the primary target, where the forecast clear skies failed to materialize and the crews were greeted by four to nine-tenths cloud, which allowed some of them to pick out ground features, while others fixed their positions by H2S. The Pathfinders had prepared a ground-marking plan in expectation of good vertical visibility, and dropped red, green and yellow TIs, while the Germans lit a decoy fire-site five miles to the south-east of the city. The 10 Squadron crews bombed from 16,000 to 19,500 feet between 19.32 and 19.48, and contributed to a moderately successful raid, which was achieved largely as the result of the creep-back from the decoy site falling across the suburbs of Offenbach and Sachsenhausen, situated on the southern bank of the River Main. 466 houses were destroyed and more than nineteen hundred seriously damaged, despite which, the operation fell well short of its aims, and the loss of forty-one aircraft was a heavy price to pay. The Halifaxes suffered heavily, losing twenty-seven of their number, a loss-rate of 10.5%, compared with the Lancaster's 3.6%. It was another bad night for 10 Squadron, which had three empty dispersals to contemplate at Melbourne on the following morning. HX164 contained the eight-man crew of F/L Whitmarsh, who, it will be recalled, had been awarded a DFM as a sergeant pilot back in August, and had risen swiftly through the ranks since. The navigator was the sole survivor from the aircraft, and he was taken into captivity to be joined by the flight engineer, navigator and bomb-aimer from Sgt Borthwick's crew in HX186, and the flight engineer, navigator, wireless operator and mid-upper gunner from the crew of Sgt Morris in JD474.

10 Sqn enjoying Christmas   L – R: Archer, Sheddon, Lucas, Young, Proud, McLeod, Charles Sheppard (NZ), Taffy, Pye, Harrison, MacPhie, Kelly, Hegon. (Photo: Charles Sheppard NZ)

An all-Lancaster main force continued the assault on Berlin on the night of the 23/24th, and failed to produce the hoped-for outcome after the Pathfinder "blind" markers experienced problems with their H2S equipment. The Christmas period passed in peace and traditional style before the "Big City" was posted as the target again on the 29th, for what, for the Lancaster operators, would be the first of three raids on it in five nights spanning the turn of the year. A force of 712 aircraft included 252 Halifaxes, of which twenty represented 10 Squadron, and they took off either side of 17.00 with S/L Maw the senior pilot on duty. It was at this juncture that the intolerable strain on the crews of successive long-range flights in difficult weather conditions would begin to become manifest in some squadrons through the rate of early returns. The bomber stream was routed out over the Dutch Frisian islands pointing directly for Leipzig, and, having reached a point just to the north of that city, was to turn to the north towards Berlin, while Mosquitos carried out spoof raids on Leipzig and Magdeburg. JD314 had the misfortune to cross paths with the night-fighter of ace Oblt Heinz-Wolfgang Schnaufer over Holland, and crashed at 18.50 near Meppel, without survivors from the crew of F/Sgt Green. The others reached the target area to find ten-tenths cloud and red and green Pathfinder release-point flares hanging over the city, upon which they aimed their bombs from 16,000 to 20,000 feet between 20.10 and 20.49 after confirming their positions by H2S. Two minutes before releasing their load, the Burcher crew's LW322 was hit by flak, which set the starboard-outer engine on fire. They were also hit by two falling incendiaries, which cut some internal cables and damaged the starboard flaps, despite which, they delivered their bombs and returned home safely. At debriefing crews reported observing a considerable red glow beneath the clouds, which remained visible for a hundred miles, and gave the impression of a concentrated and successful assault. This was not entirely borne out by local reports, which revealed that the main weight of the raid had fallen onto southern and south-eastern districts, and also into outlying communities to the east. 388 buildings were destroyed, although none of significance, and ten thousand people were bombed out of their homes. Eleven Lancasters and nine Halifaxes failed to return, a loss-rate of 2.4% for the former and 3.5% for the latter.

During the course of the month the squadron operated on just three nights, and dispatched fifty-five sorties for the loss of five Halifaxes and crews. It had been a tough year for the crews, but a highly successful one for the Command, which had laid waste to much of the Ruhr, helped to knock Italy out of the war, stemmed the progress of V-Weapons and delivered a message to all corners of the Reich that nowhere was beyond Harris's reach. A long and challenging first quarter of the coming year would test the courage and resolve of the crews to the absolute limit, but they would not be found wanting. For the crews in Yorkshire, there was the promise of going to war in the new and much-improved Mk III Halifaxes, which were now filtering through to the squadrons of 4 and 6 Groups.

January 1944

One can assume with some degree of certainty, that the beleaguered residents of Berlin and the hard-pressed crews of Bomber Command shared a common hope for the coming year, that Germany's Capital city would cease to be the focus of Harris's attention. Proud to be Berliners first and Germans second, the residents were a hardy breed, and, just like their counterparts in London during the blitz of 1940, they bore their trials with fortitude and humour. During this, their "winter of discontent," they paraded banners in the streets, which proclaimed, "You may break our walls, but not our hearts", and the melodic song, Nach jedem Dezember kommt immer ein Mai, After every December comes always a May, was played endlessly over the air waves, hinting at a change of fortunes with the onset of spring. Both camps would have to endure for some time yet, however, and before New Year's Day was over, a force of 421 Lancasters would be winging its way towards the Capital, most of them to arrive overhead in the very early hours of the 2nd. The operation was a failure, which was repeated twenty-four hours later at a combined cost to the Command of fifty-five Lancasters.

While the main force Halifax brigade remained on the ground, an all-Lancaster force inflicted heavy damage on Stettin on the night of the 5/6th, before, finally, 4 Group put preparations in hand for its first operational activity of the new year on the 6th. Twenty-four Halifaxes were made ready to join other elements for gardening duties off the Frisians and the Biscay ports,

Sgt Jesse Smith and his bride Eluned Hughes at their wedding in Kent just months before his death.

and it was to the former that the 4 Group crews headed in the early hours of the 7th. 10 Squadron launched seven aircraft from Melbourne in a five-minute slot to 04.25 led by F/L Pennicott, and all reached their allotted gardens to encounter five to ten-tenths cloud. They fixed their positions by H2S on either Norderney or Schiermonnikoog, and made timed runs to the drop zones, where five crews delivered their vegetables from 6,000 feet and one from 7,000 feet between 06.12 and 06.34. F/Sgt Taylor brought his mines home after they hung-up and refused to be dislodged, while F/Sgt Simmons and crew experienced a similar problem, but managed to release them manually on a second run.

Minor operations held sway thereafter until the 14th, when 496 Lancasters and two Halifaxes were dispatched to carry out the first major raid of the war on Braunschweig (Brunswick), situated some thirty-five miles east-south-east of Hannover in northern Germany. While this operation was in progress, 10 Squadron contributed four Halifaxes to another mining effort off the Frisians, for which they took off between 16.46 and 16.57 with S/L Maw the senior pilot on duty. The arrived in the target area to find haze but no cloud, and delivered their mines as briefed from 6,000 and 7,000 feet between 18.42 and 19.19, before returning from uneventful sorties. The Braunschweig raid was not successful and cost thirty-eight Lancasters, mostly to night-fighters, which had been fed into the bomber stream early on through the Sahme Sau (Tame Boar) running commentary system. This had revolutionized the efficiency of the Luftwaffe's Nachtjagd since replacing the old arrangement of night-fighter boxes in a direct response to the introduction of Window.

It had been a disastrous start to the year for the Pathfinders, whose losses had been particularly heavy, 156 Squadron alone having posted missing fourteen crews in total from the two Berlin operations and Braunschweig. These were experienced men who could not easily be replaced, and sideways postings became necessary to ensure a leavening of senior crews in each squadron until the numbers could be rebuilt. Orders were received across the Command on the 20th to prepare for the next round of the Berlin offensive, for which a force of 769 aircraft was assembled. 10 Squadron made ready seventeen Halifaxes, which took off between 16.01 and 16.47 with the newly-promoted S/L Trobe the senior pilot on duty. Having climbed out, they headed for the west coast of the Schleswig-Holstein peninsular at a point opposite Kiel, before turning to the south-east on a more-or-less direct course for Berlin. F/O Le Cudenec and crew deviated from track off the German coast through a navigational error, and could not correct it in time to continue, and F/Sgt Beveridge and crew attacked a flak battery between Hamburg and Bremen as an alternative target after their gyro unit and artificial horizon failed. The others pressed on and soon found themselves being hounded by night-fighters, which had begun to infiltrate the bomber stream east of Hamburg, and would remain in contact until a point between Leipzig and Hannover on the way home. Diversionary raids by Mosquitos on Kiel and Hannover would be completely ignored by the night-fighter controller. Berlin was found to be concealed beneath ten-tenths cloud, and the main force delivered its attack on red and green skymarkers, the 10 Squadron crews doing so from 14,000 to 20,000 feet between 19.37 and 19.54, after confirming their positions by H2S. On return the crews commented on the lack of flak activity over Berlin, and reported the glow of large fires under the cloud and smoke rising through the tops. Thirty-five aircraft failed to return, twenty-two of them Halifaxes, which

Sgt D.F. Ling with his crew of JD891 whose graves are in the British Military Cemetery, Berlin. Sgt Smith is left rear. January 1944

represented an 8.3% casualty rate compared with 2.6% for the Lancasters. 102 Squadron at Pocklington posted missing five aircraft and lost two more to crashes at home. F/Sgt Arthur and crew were absent from debriefing at Melbourne, after JD470 crashed in the general target area, and only the navigator and bomb-aimer survived to fall into enemy hands. There were no survivors from the crew of P/O Cruthers in JN899, which came down at Grüneberg, some twenty miles north of the city when about to start the bombing-run. It took a little time for an assessment of the operation to be made because of continuing cloud over north-eastern Germany, by which time four further raids had been carried. It seems that the eastern districts may have received the heaviest weight of bombs, although no details emerged from local sources to confirm or deny.

On the 21st, Magdeburg was posted to receive its first major raid of the war, and a force of 648 aircraft was duly made ready. Situated some fifty miles from Braunschweig and slightly to the south of east, it was on an increasingly familiar route as far as the enemy night-fighter controllers were concerned, and within easy striking distance of the night-fighter assembly beacons. 10 Squadron loaded eighteen Halifaxes with the standard city-busting mix of high-explosives and incendiaries, and dispatched them from Melbourne between 19.34 and 20.06 with W/C Sutton the senior pilot on duty. They flew out over the North Sea to a point some one hundred miles off the west coast of the Schleswig-Holstein peninsular, before turning to the south-east to pass between Hamburg and Hannover. Enemy radar was able to detect H2S transmissions during night-flying tests and equipment checks, and the night-fighter controller was, thereby, always aware of an imminent heavy raid. On this night, the night-fighters were able to infiltrate the bomber stream even before the German coast was crossed, and the recently-introduced "Tame Boar" night-fighter system provided a running commentary on the bomber stream's progress, enabling the fighters to latch onto the bombers and remain in contact. The final turning-point was twenty-five miles north-east of the target, but F/L Culverhouse and crew became confused by what they took to be dummy fires and TIs over to port. They assumed that this was Magdeburg, but it was actually Berlin, where a small 5 Group Lancaster force was trying to create a diversion. They did not discover the error until the primary target failed to appear on e.t.a., by which time it was too late to backtrack, and they ended up bombing an alternative target, which was probably Halberstadt, from 20,000 feet at 23.12.

The grave of Sgt J.C. Smith tail gunner killed with all his crew over Berlin on 29 January 1944 in Halifax JN891. The poppy cross was placed there by present-day 10 Sqn members on a visit to the graves in 2014. Never forgotten

The conditions over Magdeburg varied according to the time of arrival, the early birds encountering seven to nine-tenths thin cloud at around 6,000 feet, while those turning up towards the end of the raid found the northern half of the city completely clear with cloud over the southern half. Stronger-than-forecast winds drove some aircraft to the target ahead of the Pathfinders, and some of these bombed on their own H2S without waiting for TIs to go down. This and dummy fires were cited by the Pathfinders as the reason for their failure to produce concentrated marking, but, as far as the 10 Squadron crews were concerned, they were able to bomb from 16,000 to 20,000 feet on red and green TIs, confirmed either by H2S-fix or visual reference, between 22.57 and 23.48 and in the face of fairly modest opposition. Returning crews reported observing explosions and fires or their glow, and smoke beginning to rise as they turned away. A record fifty-seven aircraft failed to return, thirty-five of them Halifaxes, and this provided another alarming statistic of a 15.6% loss-rate compared with 5.2% for the Lancasters. Full conversion to the Mk III could not happen soon enough. HX165 crashed near Uslar to the west of the Harz mountains on the way home, and the experienced F/L Dixon DFC perished with all but two of his crew, who fell into enemy hands.

On the night of the 27/28th an all-Lancaster heavy force began what would turn out to be the final concerted effort to destroy Berlin. This was the first of three raids on the Capital in the space of an unprecedented four nights, and was moderately successful at a cost of thirty-three Lancasters, It was to be back to the "Big City" on the following night for a force of 677 aircraft, of which 241 were Halifaxes, twenty-one of them representing 10 Squadron. This was to be an appalling night for "Shiney Ten", although that lay in the future as they departed Melbourne between 23.45 and 00.25 with S/L Maw the senior pilot on duty. They were routed out over southern Denmark before turning south-east on a direct course for the target, with an almost reciprocal return and various diversionary measures to distract the night-fighter controller. Between 02.13 and 04.35, the crews of Sgts Hewitt, Sutton and Regan, F/Sgt Aston, P/O Ayres and F/L Pennicott all returned early to Melbourne, five because of technical issues and one because of severe icing. Those reaching the target area encountered ten-tenths cloud, and a mixture of sky and ground-marking to aim at. The 10 Squadron crews delivered their bombs on red and green release-point flares from 17,000 to 20,000 feet between 03.18 and 03.32, and P/O Hullah and crew reported a huge explosion at 03.16 as they were on final approach to bomb, describing it as lighting up the sky over a radius of fifty miles. Their two 2,000 pounders and some incendiaries hung-up, probably as a result of freezing, and they were dropped from 17,000 feet onto an aerodrome on the way home at 04.12. The impression was of a concentrated and effective attack, and this was partly borne-out by local reports of heavy damage in western and southern districts, where 180,000 people were bombed out of their homes, but seventy-seven outlying communities were also afflicted. The defences again exacted a heavy toll among the bombers, and forty-six failed to return, twenty-six of them Halifaxes, four belonging to 10 Squadron. HR952 crashed ten miles south-east of the centre of Berlin, killing F/O Large and five of his crew, and JD273 came down at Abenra on Denmark's south-eastern coast with no survivors from the crew of Sgt O'Connor. Four crewmen managed to parachute to safety from JN891 after it was shot down by a night-fighter over Germany on the way to the target, but Sgt Ling and both gunners were found in the wreckage. F/L Kilsby RAAF and crew were some fourteen miles west-north-west of the target on final approach to bomb when JP133 was shot down by a night-fighter to crash at 03.17. Five men had time to abandon the stricken Halifax, but the pilot and wireless operator failed to survive. All of those surviving the loss of their aircraft soon found themselves in enemy hands.

The squadron was not involved in the Berlin operation mounted on the night of the 30/31st, when Mk III Halifaxes were among the 534-strong heavy force. They inflicted heavy damage predominantly on central and south-western districts, but on other areas of the city too, while hitting many outlying communities and killing more than a thousand people at a cost to the Command of thirty-two Lancasters and a single Halifax. During the course of the month the squadron operated on five nights, dispatching sixty-seven sorties for the loss of seven Halifaxes and crews.

February 1944

Bad weather during the first two weeks of February allowed the crews to draw breath and the squadrons to replenish. Harris had intended to maintain the pressure on Berlin, and would have launched a further attack, had he not been thwarted by the conditions. As a result, the time was filled with training and mining operations, and fourteen crews were called to briefing at Melbourne on the 2nd to learn of their part in that night's proceedings. 4 Group would be sending twenty-eight Halifaxes to the Forget-me-not region, the Kiel Canal, and the 10 Squadron crews took off either side of 02.00 with S/L Trobe the senior pilot on duty. All but one crew reached the target area in the western Baltic, where cloud ranged from two to ten-tenths with tops at between 6,000 and 9,000 feet, and positions were established by H2S-fix. The mines were delivered into the briefed locations from 12,000 to 15,000 feet between 04.26 and 04.33, F/Sgt Aston and crew requiring two runs before theirs dropped away. F/Sgt Clarke and crew had reached southern Denmark when their H2S equipment let them down, and they returned their vegetables to store. On the way home, P/O Ayres was forced to shut down the starboard-outer engine because of falling oil pressure, and then the port-inner engine overheated and also had to be cut. The starboard-outer was restarted, but burst into flames, which were extinguished by the Graviner system, and the same thing happened when the port-inner was restarted, only, this time, the flames went out after the engine was shut down again. By this time they were close to the Yorkshire coast and down to 2,000 feet, and a safe landing was carried out on two engines on the emergency landing strip at Carnaby.

Two nights later 10 Squadron was the only 4 Group unit to operate, when sending ten Halifaxes to the Beeches and Cinnamon gardens off St-Nazaire and La Rochelle respectively. They departed Melbourne between 17.57 and 18.24 with F/Ls Kennedy and Pennicott the senior pilots on duty, and all made it safely to their respective drop zones. Those in the Beeches garden encountered up to ten-tenths cloud below 7,000 feet, and established their positions by H2S, before delivering their mines from 11,000 and 12,000 feet between 20.34 and 21.00. The skies over the Cinnamon garden contained varying amounts of cloud between two and ten-tenths, but the visibility was good, and these crews also employed H2S to confirm their positions before

F/Sgt Jack Walker and crew prior to them being shot down by an Me110 on 20 February 1944. All parachuted to safety and became POWs. Jack re-joined 10 Sqn flying VC 10s in 1969.

dropping their two vegetables each from 11,000 to 12,000 feet between 20.51 and 21.27. Sgt Cartwright and crew had been three minutes from release when a ME110 attacked, but return fire and evasive action shook it off, and they made a fresh pinpoint before fulfilling their sortie as briefed. G/C Thomson went on leave on the 12th, leaving W/C Sutton as temporary "Station Master", and the recently-arrived S/L Guy Maxwell Brisbane DFC occupying the squadron commander's chair. The details of S/L Maxwell's posting were not made manifest in the 10 Squadron ORB, but it is known that he was a navigator.

When the Pathfinder and main force squadrons next took to the air, it would be for a record-breaking effort to Berlin on the 15th, and would also be the penultimate operation of the campaign, and, indeed, of the war by Bomber Command's heavy brigade, against Germany's Capital City. The force of 891 aircraft represented the largest non-1,000 force to date, and, therefore, the greatest-ever to be sent against the Capital, and it would be the first time that more than five hundred Lancasters and three hundred Halifaxes had operated together. They would carry in their bomb bays the greatest-ever tonnage of bombs, and among them were eighteen Halifaxes belonging to 10 Squadron, which took off between 17.12 and 17.40 with S/L Maw the senior pilot on duty, each with two 500lb cluster bombs and ten SBCs of 4lb and 30lb incendiaries on board. The route out took the bomber stream to the western coast of Denmark, before crossing Jutland and entering Germany via the Baltic coast between Rostock and Stralsund, with a direct heading, thereafter, for the target. The return route required the bombers to pass south of Hannover and Bremen, and cross Holland to the North Sea via Castricum. Extensive diversionary measures included a mining operation in Kiel Bay ahead of the arrival of the bombers, a raid on Frankfurt-an-Oder to the east of Berlin by a small force of 8 Group Lancasters, and Oboe Mosquitos attacking five night-fighter airfields in Holland. F/L Kennedy lost his port-inner engine soon after take-off to end his participation, while F/Sgt Walker and crew were at the mid-point of the North Sea crossing when the overload tank failed to release fuel and forced them to turn back. P/O Ayres abandoned his sortie after low boost in the port-inner engine prevented him from climbing, and W/O Porter and crew turned back because of an engine issue at 19.38 with the Danish coast almost in sight. The others pressed on to find the target blanketed by ten-tenths clouds, and checked their positions by H2S before bombing on the Pathfinders' red release-point flares with green stars from 15,000 to 20,000 feet between 21.17 to 21.35. Returning crews reported the markers to be highly effective and well-concentrated, and the burgeoning glow beneath the clouds convinced them that they had taken part in a successful operation. This was borne out by local reports, which confirmed that the 2,642 tons of bombs had caused extensive damage in central and south-western districts, but had also spilled out into surrounding communities. A thousand houses and more than five hundred temporary wooden barracks were destroyed, and important war-industry factories in the Siemensstadt district were damaged at a cost to the Command of forty-three aircraft, twenty-six Lancasters, (4.6%) and seventeen Halifaxes, (5.4%). Perhaps slightly disturbing was the fact that eight of the missing Halifaxes were Mk IIIs, only one fewer than the nine Mk II/Vs. 10 Squadron's JN833 crashed somewhere in the target area, and there were no survivors from the crew of F/O Clarke.

Orders were received on the 19th to prepare for a major assault on Leipzig that night, which would employ another massive force, this time of 823 aircraft. Seventeen 10 Squadron Halifaxes presented themselves for take-off, which occurred without incident between 23.22

and 23.49 with S/L Trobe the senior pilot on duty. After climbing-out, they headed for the Dutch coast, where a proportion of the Luftwaffe Nachtjagd was waiting for them, while others had been drawn away by a mining diversion off Kiel. F/O Allen and crew turned back with an engine issue from a position on the Dutch coast south of Harlingen, leaving the others to become embroiled in a running battle all the way into eastern Germany. It was on this leg of the outward flight that LW324 was shot down north of Braunschweig by a JU88 at 03.00, when still a hundred miles short of the target. F/Sgt Walker and his crew took to their parachutes, and all fell safely into the arms of their captors.* Inaccurately forecast winds caused some aircraft to arrive at the target early, and they were forced to orbit, while they waited for the Pathfinders to arrive to mark the target. The local flak batteries accounted for around twenty of these, while four other aircraft were lost through collisions. The 10 Squadron crews arrived to find ten-tenths cloud with tops at around 9,000 feet, and confirmed their positions by H2S before bombing on green skymarkers from 17,000 to 21,000 feet between 03.59 and 04.30. It seems that there was a brief period during the attack when skymarking stopped and led to some scattering of bombs, but the marker-flares were soon replenished with the arrival of more backers-up, and a considerable glow beneath the cloud, that remained visible for some fifty minutes into the return journey, gave the impression of a successful assault. When all of those aircraft returning home had been accounted for, there was a massive shortfall of seventy-eight, a record loss by a clear twenty-one aircraft. Forty-four Lancasters and thirty-four Halifaxes had failed to return, with a percentage loss-rate of 7.8 and 13.3% respectively. HR805 was the second 10 Squadron Halifax to go missing, and only the navigator survived as a PoW from the crew of F/Sgt Davenport RCAF. This prompted Harris to take the decision to immediately withdraw the Mk II and V Halifaxes from further operations of Germany, which, at a stroke, removed a proportion of 4 Group's fire-power, including that of 10 Squadron, from the front line until they could be re-equipped with the Mk III Halifax. In the meantime, the Mk II and V operators would focus their energies for the remainder of the month on gardening duties.

An operation was called and then cancelled on the 20th, when, despite the horrendous losses of the previous night, 598 aircraft of the frontline squadrons took off to attack Stuttgart. A North Sea sweep and a diversion at Munich drew up many night-fighters two hours before the bomber stream passed across enemy territory, and a modest nine aircraft were lost in return for a scattered but destructive raid that caused much damage in central districts and in the northern quadrant. 10 and 102 Squadrons each provided five Halifaxes on the 21st for mining sorties in the Deodars region, off Bordeaux in south-western France. The Melbourne element took off between 18.08 and 18.20 led by S/L Maw, and, after climbing out, set off for the coast at Lyme Regis for what would be a three-and-a-half-hour outward flight. They found ten-tenths cloud at 8,000 to 10,000 feet obscuring the ground, and fixed their pinpoints on Pointe-de-la-Coubre by means of H2S. The mines were delivered totally unopposed from 14,000 feet between 21.40 and 21.46, and all returned safely from uneventful sorties. Ten crews actually took off for another mining operation twenty-four hours later, this time in the Silverthorn garden in the Kattegat region of the western Baltic, but they were recalled within thirty minutes by group because of anticipated adverse weather conditions.

A new tactic was introduced at this point in an effort to address the problem of unsustainable losses incurred since the turn of the year. The force was to be split into two distinct waves separated by two hours, in the hope that the night-fighters would be on the ground re-arming and refuelling as the second wave passed through. The ball-bearing production centre of Schweinfurt was selected as the Guinee-pig on the 24th, for which a force of 734 aircraft was made ready and divided into waves of 392 and 342. While this operation was in progress, extensive diversionary measure would be put in hand that involved more than three hundred aircraft. Among them was a large mining contingent, which included fifteen 10 Squadron Halifaxes and twenty-nine others from 77 and 102 Squadrons, for a re-run of the mining operation in the Silverthorn garden that had been recalled four nights earlier. The Melbourne element took off between 16.55 and 17.14 with S/L Maw the senior pilot on duty, but soon lost the services of W/O Porter and P/O Kiltie with H2S and engine issues respectively. Because this operation was to act as a diversion, it was important to create as large a presence as possible, and this was achieved by Pathfinder aircraft dropping yellow route markers over Mandø Island, south of Esbjerg, shortly after 20.00. On reaching the target area they encountered nine to ten-tenths cloud at around 8,000 feet, and delivered their mines on yellow Pathfinder flares confirmed by H2S-fix from 15,000 feet. The timings suggest that the attacks were carried out in two sections, the first either side of 20.30, and the second shortly after 21.00. P/O Wilson and crew suffered the frustration of their bomb doors jamming, preventing the mines from falling away, and they was forced to bring them home. Sgt Sims and crew observed the marker flares ignite some fifteen miles ahead, but they had gone out by the time they arrived, and they also returned their mines to store. The Schweinfurt operation was only modestly successful after much of the bombing fell short, but 50% fewer aircraft were lost from the second wave in an overall loss of thirty-three, and this suggested some merit in the tactic.

The main operation on the following night was directed at the beautiful and culturally significant southern city of Augsburg, which was home to a major Maschinenfabrik Augsburg Nuremberg (M.A.N) diesel engine factory, which had been the target for an epic low-level daylight raid by 5 Group Lancasters in April 1942. On this night 594 aircraft were divided into two waves, and dispatched towards the Belgian coast, while thirteen 10 Squadron Halifaxes joined others from 77 and 102 Squadrons to mine the waters of the Forget-me-nots garden in the Kiel Canal. They departed Melbourne between 19.50 and 20.21 with S/L Maw the senior pilot on duty, but F/O Allen and Sgt Sutton were soon on their way back with an engine and a compass issue respectively. The others continued on in fair weather conditions with up to eight-tenths cloud between 4,000 and 8,000 feet, and established their positions by H2S and or release-point flares. Some crews arrived early because of wrongly-forecast winds, and this caused F/L Culverhouse and crew to miss their opportunity. They began to orbit to kill time, but another change of wind then delayed them, and, by the time they returned to the drop zone, the release-point flares had burned out. F/Sgt Fenney and crew failed to spot any route markers, and could not obtain a firm Gee-fix, so also brought their mines home. F/O Burgess and crew saw a release-point flare at 23.06, but, after being unable to open their bomb doors, orbited until another flare ignited at 23.16. The same thing happened, and they turned for home, only for a crew member to succeed in persuading the doors to open, upon which they returned to the drop zone and fulfilled their brief at 23.36. The others delivered their mines from 15,000 and 16,000 feet between 22.57 and 23.17, and returned safely to make their reports. Meanwhile at Augsburg, all facets of the plan came together in perfect harmony, and this spelled disaster for the ancient city, the heart of which was ripped out by fire, destroying forever centuries of cultural history. The loss of twenty-one aircraft seemed to confirm the benefits of splitting the forces, and this tactic would remain an important part of Bomber Command planning for the remainder of the war. During the course of the month the squadron operated on seven nights, and dispatched ninety-two sorties for the loss of three Halifaxes and crews.

March 1944

March opened with Stuttgart posted as the target on the 1st, for which a force of 557 aircraft took off in the late evening. This was the second of three attacks on this city during the period, and was successful in causing further extensive damage in central, western and northern districts, where a number of important war-industry factories were hit. There was no work for 10 Squadron on this night, but orders were received at Melbourne on the 2nd to prepare for an operation that night. The target was to be the S.N.C.A aircraft factory at Meulan-les-Meureaux, situated fifteen miles north-west of Paris, for which a force of 117 Halifaxes and six Mosquitos was drawn from 4, 6 and 8 Groups. 10 Squadron contributed twenty of the former, which took off between 00.27 and 01.05 with W/C Sutton and S/L Trobe the senior pilots on duty. F/O Burgess and crew lost the pilot's escape hatch during take-off, despite having checked it, and that ended their interest in proceedings. The others formed up as they passed over reading en-route to Selsey Bill for the Channel crossing, but F/L Hampton turned back at this stage with an engine issue, leaving the remainder to press on over thickening cloud, which, at the target, was five to seven-tenths with tops at between 6,000 and 8,000 feet. On the way out, F/L Le Cudenec's gunners frightened off a FW190, which had closed to eight hundred yards without firing, and they arrived in one piece to carry out their attack on red TIs from 7,500 feet at 03.17. Some confirmed their position by H2S before also aiming at the TIs from 5,000 to 8,000 feet between 03.13 and 03.21, and the only crew to reach the target and miss out was that of F/Sgt Blackford. They were the first to arrive, at 03.10, before the first TIs went down, and, in the absence of a reference, turned for home, only to see a single red TI ignite behind them at 03.15, but too late for them to backtrack. Returning crews reported bomb bursts and fires in and around the factory buildings, and post-raid reconnaissance revealed that the factory had been severely damaged.

On the following day the squadron prepared nine Halifaxes to mine the waters of the Cinnamon garden off La Rochelle, and dispatched them between 19.05 and 19.28 with F/L Pennicott the senior pilot on duty. They all arrived in the target area to find clear skies and visibility at fifteen miles, and found their pinpoints by means of H2S before making timed runs to the release-point. The mines were delivered unopposed into the briefed locations from 8,000 to 15,000 feet between 22.16 and 22.28, and a safe return made from an uneventful night's work.

The first salvos of a new campaign of interdiction would be fired on the 6th by a heavy force of Halifaxes, which would include the remaining MKs II and V before their retirement from the front-line. The Transportation Plan called for the dismantling of the French and Belgian railway systems by bombing, to prevent their use by the enemy to bring forces to bear against the coming invasion. Until the Command as a whole had concluded the winter campaign, and could release the Lancaster squadrons to join in, it would be left largely to the Halifaxes and Stirlings to set the ball rolling. The first target was the marshalling yards at Trappes, situated on the south-western outskirts of Paris, for which 261 Halifaxes and six Mosquitos were made ready, and, among the former were nineteen representing 10 Squadron. They departed Melbourne between

10 Squadron – Melbourne. March 1944 Halifax ZA-N NX326 L – R: Sgt L Oaks (M/UG), Sgt D Kirkland (Nav), Sgt K Walker (B/A), S/L Mike Maw (Pilot), P/O B Bellinger (RG), P/O Des Fitzgerald (F/E), Sgt H Williams (W/Op)

18.40 and 19.08 with W/C Sutton and S/L Trobe the senior pilots on duty, and S/L Brisbane undertaking his first sortie with the squadron as second air-bomber to F/L Lucas. There were no early returns among the 10 Squadron participants, and they arrived at the target to find clear skies and good visibility, which enabled them to make a visual identification of ground features, particularly the Saint-Quentin Lake just to the north. They bombed on red TIs from 10,000 to 13,000 feet between 21.18 and 21.30, and observed bursts among the railway tracks and fires at both ends of the yards. There was virtually no opposition, and no aircraft were lost.

The first examples of the Mk III Halifax arrived on squadron charge on the 7th, and the conversion and working-up process would occupy the next two weeks. Attention turned to the marshalling yards at Le Mans in north-western France that night, for which a force of 242 Halifaxes, fifty-six Lancasters and six Mosquitos of 3, 4, 6 and 8 Groups was made ready. 10 Squadron filled thirteen with the standard Halifax-load for this kind of target of 1,000 and 500 pounders, and launched them between 19.03 and 19.21 on what would be the final operation for Merlin-powered Halifaxes in 10 Squadron hands. W/C Sutton was the senior pilot on duty, and

F/O D Evans DFC, 1944 and more recently. Doug went on to a long flying career with British Airways and Gulf Air before becoming a founder member of the 10 Sqn Association.

he and his crew were the first to leave the ground, reaching the target two hours and forty minutes later to find eight to ten-tenths cloud between 4,000 and 8,000 feet. They and seven others from the squadron bombed on the glow of red TIs from 5,500 to 12,500 feet between 21.40 and 22.01, and a large white flash was observed along with a widespread red reflection. Five crews withheld their bombs after failing to positively identify the target in the absence of TIs. They observed the large red glow beneath the clouds, and some orbited while trying to determine whether or not it was from TIs, but decided it was too imprecise over France to risk collateral damage, and jettisoned their bombs before returning home. Local reports confirmed that the raid was successful in destroying 250 wagons, cutting track and damaging locomotives and other installations, and was achieved without loss.

10 Squadron's A Flight began conversion training on the 10th, B Flight on the 13th and C Flight on the 14th, and, each day thereafter, crews were airborne on a variety of exercises to familiarize themselves with their new aircraft. While they were absent from the operational scene, other elements of the Command returned to Le Mans on the night of the 13/14th and to Stuttgart on the 15/6th, the latter costing thirty-seven aircraft in return for only modest gains. That night also brought an attack on the marshalling yards at Amiens, which received another visit twenty-four hours later. The first of two massive raids on Frankfurt took place on the night of the 18/19th, and left a swathe of destruction from west to east, right across the centre, and destroyed or seriously damaged more than six thousand buildings, including many of an industrial nature.

After two weeks on the side-lines, thirteen crews were called to briefing on the 22nd to learn of their participation in that night's operation, which was to be the second one against Frankfurt. They were to be part of a total force of 816 aircraft, and took off between 18.57 and 19.19 with S/L Maw the senior pilot on duty. After climbing out they adopted an unusual route for a target in southern Germany, crossing the enemy coast over Vlieland and Teschelling, before passing to the east of Osnabrück on a direct course due south for the target. F/L Le Cudenec and crew were just short of Terschelling when a leak in a fuel line forced them to turn back at 20.47 and leave the others to push on in favourable weather conditions. F/O Barnes and crew were a little off course to the west of Osnabrück when their port-outer engine failed some 150 miles short of the target. Part of the bomb load was jettisoned to save weight, and they carried on to complete their sortie. The bomber stream arrived at the target to find five to six-tenths thin, low cloud, and the 10 Squadron crews established their positions by H2S before focussing their attention on the release-point flares and red and green TIs marking out the aiming-point. W/O Aston and crew were hounded by one or more JU88s as they approached to bomb, and faced six attacks between 22.05 and 22.17, sustaining severe damage to most parts of the aircraft, including the hydraulics system and P4 compass. All guns jammed early on, possibly because of the icing conditions, and they eventually dropped their bombs onto an alternative target five miles or so north of Frankfurt. Fortunately, none of the crew sustained injury and the four Hercules kept turning to bring the Halifax home to a safe landing. The others bombed from 20,000 to 23,000 feet, (Oh, the joy of having Hercules power!) between 21.54 and 22.16, and observed a massive rectangular area of unbroken fire across the centre, the glow from which could be seen for at least a hundred miles into the return flight. Returning crews reported numerous searchlights lighting up the cloud, and moderate to intense flak that reached up to the bombers' flight level of 20,000 feet. Local reports confirmed the enormity of the devastation, which was particularly severe in western districts and left this half of the city without electricity, gas and water for an extended period. More than nine hundred people lost their lives and a further 120,000 were bombed out of their homes, at a cost to the Command of twenty-six Lancasters and seven Halifaxes, a loss-rate of 4.2% and 3.8% respectively.

The stage was now set for the nineteenth and final operation of the campaign against Berlin, which had begun back in August. It was more than five weeks since the main force had last visited the Capital, and 811 aircraft were made ready on the 24th for what would be the final raid of the war by RAF heavy bombers on Germany's Capital. Ten Halifaxes were made ready by 10 Squadron, and they took off between 18.50 and 19.10 with F/Ls Kennedy and Le Cudenec the senior pilots on duty. They had a long flight ahead of them, which would take them across the North Sea to the Danish coast near Ringkøbing and then to a point on the German Baltic coast near Rostock. When north-east of Berlin they were to adopt a south-westerly course for the bombing run, and, once clear of the defence zone, dogleg to the west and then north-west to pass around Hannover on its southern and western sides, before heading for Holland and an exit via the Castricum coast. The extended outward leg provided a time-on-target of around 22.30, but an unexpected difficulty would be encountered, which would render void all of the meticulous planning. The existence of what we now know as "Jetstream" winds was unknown at the time, and the one blowing from the north with unprecedented strength on this night pushed the bomber stream south of its intended track. Navigators, who were expecting to see the northern tip of Sylt on their H2S screens, were horrified to find the southern end, which meant that they were thirty miles south of track, and about to fly over Germany rather than Denmark.

Wing Commander D S Radford DSO DFC AFC
10 Sqn Commanding Officer 1April 1944 to 9 October 1944.

A "wind-finder" system had been set up to help with navigation, and this used designated crews to establish wind strength and direction and send their findings to the raid controllers, who would collate the figures, adjust them as necessary and rebroadcast them to the whole force. The problem on this night was that the wind-finders refused to believe what their instruments were telling them. Winds in excess of one hundred m.p.h had never been encountered before, and, fearing that they would be disbelieved, many modified the figures downward. The same thing happened at raid control, where the figures were modified again, so that the information rebroadcast to the bomber stream bore no resemblance to the reality of the situation.

F/L Kennedy and crew realized that they were fifty-five miles south of track by the time they reached Westerhever on the west coast of the Schleswig-Holstein peninsular, and set course for the north to regain track and avoid the defences that would be met if they turned east over Germany. It soon became clear that they had lost forty minutes and would not reach the target in the allotted window, so turned for home and jettisoned their load. The others reached the target to find four to nine-tenths low cloud, onto which yellow release-point flares were sinking, and through which, red TIs could be seen marking out the aiming-point. The 10 Squadron crews confirmed their positions by H2S before bombing from 20,000 to 21,000 feet between 22.30 and 23.05, and observed what appeared to be a scattered attack in the early stages, until fires began to become more concentrated. The defences were very active with moderate flak and intense night-fighter activity. The 10 Squadron crews all made it home safely, but they were the lucky ones, as seventy-two aircraft failed to return, two-thirds of them having fallen victim to the Ruhr flak batteries after being driven into that region's defence zone by the wind on the way home. Post-raid analysis revealed that the wind had played havoc with the marking and bombing, and had pushed the attack towards the south-western districts of the Capital, where most of the damage occurred, while 126 outlying communities also received bombs. 10 Squadron had participated in eight of the nineteen main force raids on the Capital during the offensive, and lost ten aircraft from 133 sorties, with fifty-eight men killed and twelve surviving as PoWs. (The Berlin Raids, Martin Middlebrook).

W/C Radford DFC, AFC arrived from 1652 Conversion Unit on the 26th in preparation to succeed W/C Sutton as commanding officer a few days hence. That night the squadron was asked to provide two Halifaxes to join in an attack on the marshalling yards at Aulnoye, situated on the French side of the border with Belgium on the main railway line to Mons, about a dozen miles to the north. F/Sgts Livesey and Sutton took off just before 19.15, and reached the target to find clear skies and ground haze, and bombed on red and green TIs from 8,000 feet one minute either side of 22.00. There were two aiming-points, and there appeared to be fires at both, with an explosion and yellow flame emanating from the one at the western end. Post-raid reconnaissance revealed that the marking at each aiming-point had been slightly misplaced to the north-east, and that a proportion of the bombing had fallen wide of the target. However, this was an on-going campaign of destruction and rapid repair, for which local civilians were often pressed into service, and each of the major marshalling yards would be attacked multiple times.

The winter offensive still had a week to run, and two more major operations for the crews to negotiate, the first of which was to be against Essen on the 26th. 10 Squadron made ready eighteen Halifaxes to contribute to the overall force of 705 aircraft, and they departed Melbourne between 19.54 and 20.19 with S/Ls Maw and Trobe the senior pilots on duty. They climbed out and headed for the Dutch coast to pass north of Haarlem and Amsterdam before swinging to the south-east on a direct run to the target. There were no early returns among the 10 Squadron contingent, and all reached the target area to find ten-tenths cloud with tops at around 12,000 feet. Red and green TIs could be seen burning beneath the cloud, and positions were checked by H2S before the bombing took place from 19,000 to 22,000 feet between 22.00 and 22.11. Returning crews reported many flashes on the ground and an impression of a successful operation, but, in truth, had little of value to offer at debriefing. Absent from that procedure were the crews of P/Os Simmons and Wilson in HX295 and LV859 respectively, both of which crashed on the way home via the southerly route to the south of Cologne. The former came down somewhere in Belgium, by which time both gunners had saved themselves, ultimately to evade capture, while the latter fell to a night-fighter between Cologne and Coblenz with no survivors. Post-raid reconnaissance and local reports confirmed this as another extremely accurate and concentrated raid, and it thus continued the remarkable run of successes against this once elusive city since the introduction of Oboe to main force operations twelve months earlier. More than seventeen hundred houses had been destroyed and forty-eight industrial building severely damaged at a cost to the Command of six Lancasters and three Halifaxes.

The period known as the Battle of Berlin, but which was better referred to as the winter campaign, was to be brought to an end on the night of the 30/31st, with a standard maximum-effort raid on the birthplace of Nazism, Nuremberg. The plan of operation departed from normal practice in only one important respect, and this was to prove critical. It had become standard routine over the winter to employ diversions and feints to confuse the enemy night-fighter controllers. Sometimes they were successful and sometimes not, but with the night-fighter force having clearly gained the upper hand with its "Tame Boar" running commentary system, all possible means had to be adopted to protect the bomber stream. During a conference held early on the 30th, the Lancaster Group A-O-Cs expressed a preference for a 5 Group-inspired route, which would require the aircraft to fly a long straight leg across Belgium and Germany, to a point about fifty miles north of Nuremberg, from where the final run-in would commence. The Halifax A-O-Cs were less convinced of the benefits, and AVM Bennett, the Pathfinder chief, was positively overcome by the potential dangers and predicted a disaster, but he was overruled. A force of 795 aircraft was made ready, of which fifteen Halifaxes were to be provided by 10 Squadron, and the crews attended briefings to be told of the route, wind conditions and the belief that a layer of cloud would conceal them from enemy night-fighters. Before take-off, a Meteorological Flight Mosquito crew radioed in to cast doubts upon the weather conditions, which they could see differed markedly from those that had been forecast. This also went unheeded, and, from around 21.45 for the next hour or so, the crews took off for the rendezvous area, and headed into a conspiracy of circumstances, which would inflict upon Bomber Command its heaviest defeat of the war.

At Melbourne, three sorties were scrubbed because of technical issues with the aircraft, and this left twelve to take-off between 21.56 and 22.29 with F/Ls Burgess, Kennedy and Le Cudenec the senior pilots on duty. It was not long into the flight before they and the other crews began to notice some unusual features in the conditions, which included uncommonly bright moonlight, and a crystal clarity of visibility that allowed them the rare sight of other aircraft in the stream. On most nights, crews would feel themselves to be completely alone in the sky all the way to the target, until, bang on schedule, TIs would be seen to fall and other aircraft would make themselves known by the turbulence of their slipstreams as they funnelled towards the aiming-point. P/O Hullah and F/Sgts Cartwright and Sutton returned over the ensuing three hours because of engine issues, and F/L Burgess was the last to abort after a fault developed in the hydraulics system. Once at cruising altitude, the others noted that the forecast cloud was conspicuous by its absence, and, instead, lay beneath them as a white tablecloth, against which they were silhouetted like flies. Condensation trails began to form in the cold, clear air to further advertise their presence to the enemy, and the Jetstream winds, which had so adversely affected the Berlin raid a week earlier, were also present, only this time from the south. As the final insult, the route into Germany passed close to two night-fighter beacons, which the enemy aircraft were orbiting while they awaited their instructions.

The carnage began over Charleroi in Belgium, and from there to the target, the route was signposted by the burning wreckage on the ground of eighty Bomber Command aircraft. Among these was the squadron's LV881, which crashed near Hungen in Germany, some 120 miles short of the target, killing F/Sgt Regan and three of his crew and delivering the three survivors into enemy hands.* The wind-finder system broke down again, and those crews who either failed to detect the strength of the wind, or simply refused to believe the evidence, were driven up to fifty miles north of their intended track, and, consequently, turned towards Nuremberg from a false position. This led to more than a hundred aircraft bombing at Schweinfurt in error, and together with the massive losses sustained before the target was reached, this reduced considerably the numbers arriving at the briefed destination. The eight 10 Squadron crews arrived over Nuremberg to encounter eight to nine-tenths cloud with tops at around 12,000 feet, and bombed on red and green TIs and sky-markers after confirming their positions by H2S. They were mostly at 22,000 feet and slightly above the Lancaster fraternity, and carried out their attacks between 01.13 and 01.28, observing many fires, the glow from which, according to some reports, remained visible for 120 miles into the return journey. Ninety-five aircraft failed to return home, and many others were written off in landing crashes or with battle damage to severe to repair. The shock and disappointment was compounded by the fact that the strong wind had driven the marking beyond the city to the east, and Nuremberg had, consequently, escaped serious damage.

During the course of the month the squadron operated on nine nights and dispatched 116 sorties for the loss of three Halifaxes and crews. It had been a gruelling winter campaign, and represented the Command's lowest point, when, perhaps for the only time, the morale of the crews had been in question. What now lay before the hard-pressed crews was in marked contrast to that which had been endured over the seemingly interminable winter months. In place of the long slog to Germany on dark, often dirty nights, shorter range hops to France and Belgium in improving weather conditions would become the order of the day. However, these operations would be equally demanding in their way, and would require of the crews a greater commitment to accuracy, to avoid casualties among friendly civilians. Despite this, a decree from on high insisted that such operations were worthy of counting as just one third of a sortie towards the completion of a tour, and, until this flawed policy was rescinded, an air of mutiny would pervade the crew rooms. Despite the horrendous losses of the winter campaign, the Command was in remarkably fine fettle to face its new challenge, and Harris was in the enviable position of being able to achieve what had eluded his predecessor, namely, to attack multiple targets simultaneously with enough weight to be effective. Such was the hitting-power now at his disposal, he could assign targets to individual groups, to groups in tandem, or to the Command as a whole, as dictated by operational requirements.

April 1944

10 Squadron began the spring offensive under a new commanding officer, as W/C Radford succeeded W/C Sutton DFC, DSO on his posting to Bomber Command HQ on the 1st. That night 4 Group contributed a dozen Halifaxes to mining operations in the Limpet and Trefoil gardens between Den Helder and the southern tip of Texel. The three 10 Squadron crews of P/Os Hullah and Keltie and F/Sgt Cartwright took off either side of 19.50, and each reached the target area to find clear skies and excellent visibility. They were able to identify their pinpoints visually, and the drop zone by means of H2S-fix, before delivering their vegetables unopposed from 8,000 feet at around 21.30.

As already documented, the pre-invasion campaign against the French and Belgian railway networks had begun in March at the hands, largely, of the Halifax and Stirling squadrons withdrawn from the main battle. Now the rest of the Command was available to join in, and the first briefings were held on the 9th, when crews learned that they would be involved in one of two operations planned for that night. The Lille-Delivrance goods station and marshalling yards would face a force of 239 aircraft drawn from 3, 4, 6 and 8 Groups, while the marshalling yards at Villeneuve-St-Georges, in a southern suburb of Paris, was to be targeted by 225 aircraft from all groups. 10 Squadron made ready sixteen Halifaxes for the former, and they departed Melbourne between 21.42 and 22.03 with W/C Radford and S/L Maw the senior pilots on duty. They all reached the target area to encounter up to seven-tenths patchy cloud at 8,000 feet, but good visibility and favourable bombing conditions, and confirmed their positions by H2S before bombing on red or red and green TIs from 15,000 feet between 00.38 and 00.45. Two vivid blue explosions were witnessed soon after the bombing started, and many others lit up the area as the attack developed, with black smoke rising through the clouds as the crews turned away. The operation was highly successful, and destroyed more than two-thirds of almost three thousand items of rolling stock, while also ripping up track and damaging buildings. Unfortunately, many stray bombs fell into adjacent residential districts, where five thousand houses were destroyed or damaged and 456 people lost their lives. The question of collateral damage was always uppermost in the minds of the raid planners at targets in the Occupied Countries, but it was an impossible dream to think that large numbers of aircraft could concentrate their thousands of bombs in a defined area, and further tragedies would occur. The other operation was also successful, but collateral damage resulted in ninety-three fatalities.

On the following night, four similar targets were posted, those at Tours, Tergnier, Laon and Aulnoye in France and Ghent in Belgium, and they were handed respectively to 5 Group, 4 Group, 3, 6 and 8 Groups, 1 Group and 6 Group. 5 Group had its own Mosquito target-marking force, and 8 Group Mosquitos were on hand at the other locations to provide the marking. 10 Squadron made ready twenty Halifaxes to support the 157-strong force for Tergnier, a town situated in north-eastern France, and they took off between 21.00 and 21.35 with S/Ls Maw and Trobe the senior pilots on duty. F/L Culverhouse's sortie was over immediately after take-off because of the failure of the flaps and undercarriage to retract, but this was the only early return to Melbourne. The others continued on to reach the target, where they found two to three-tenths low cloud and haze, which blotted out ground detail. H2S and red and green TIs took care of any doubts about the location of the aiming-point, and bombing took place from 10,000 to 11,000 feet between 00.02 and 00.10. Bombs were seen to burst across the TIs, and post-raid reconnaissance would confirm severe damage to the yards. The success was gained at a cost of ten Halifaxes, including LV858, in which F/L Barnes DFC and his rear gunner lost their lives. Three of the survivors fell into enemy hands, and three managed to evade a similar fate, almost certainly due to the selfless dedication of the resistance organisations that were supported in their work by Bomber Command's secret 138 and 161 Squadrons.

4 Group did not take part in a heavy and destructive area attack on Aachen on the following night, but 10 Squadron loaded eleven Halifaxes with two 1,500lb parachute mines each and dispatched them between 20.25 and 20.51 with F/Ls Allen, Burgess, Hampton and Le Cudenec the senior pilots on duty. Their destination was the Silverthorn garden in the Kattegat region of the western Baltic. F/L Hampton and crew made it as far as the west coast of Jutland before H2S-equipment failure ended their sortie, and they returned the mines to store. The others reached the target area to find five-tenths cloud and mist that reduced visibility to around seven hundred yards, but fixed their positions by H2S, using the southern tip of the Ebeltoft peninsular as one of their pinpoints for a timed run to the drop site. Mines were delivered from 12,000 feet between 23.06 and 23.28 in the face of very little opposition, and only F/L Le Cudenec returned with minor battle damage courtesy of heavy flak.

From the 14th, the Command became officially subject to the requirements of the Supreme Headquarters of the Allied Expeditionary Force (SHAEF) in preparation for the invasion, and would remain thus shackled under the command of Dwight D Eisenhower until the Allied armies were sweeping towards the German frontier in late summer. However, while Harris remained at the helm, old style city-busting would never be totally abandoned in favour of other considerations, and, whenever an opportunity presented itself, he would strike. 4 Group had been inactive for a week before targets were posted on the 18th, which revealed that the night was to be devoted largely to marshalling yards and mining operations, both of which would be supported by the group. A return to Tergnier was briefed out to thirteen 10 Squadron crews and 125 others from 4 Group, which would be joined by 24 Lancasters from 3 Group and eight Oboe Mosquitos, while six other 10 Squadron crews were to take care of mining duties in the Forget-me-not and Daffodil gardens in Kiel Bay and the Kiel Canal. The gardeners departed Melbourne first, between 20.50 and 20.59 with S/L Trobe the senior pilot on duty, and they were followed into the air between 21.08 and 21.25 by the main element led by W/C Radford. They would arrive in their respective target areas within minutes of each other, but 450 miles apart, and each element would find favourable weather conditions in the form of clear skies over France and two to five-tenths patchy cloud with good visibility over the Baltic. Three salvoes of red and green TIs marked out the aiming-point at Tergnier, after which, bombing took place from 13,000 feet between 23.32 and 23.39, and resulted in many bomb bursts and large, orange explosions that confirmed the accuracy of the attack. Post-raid reconnaissance would reveal that fifty railway lines had been blocked, but also that housing had been hit south-west of the yards with unknown casualties. Meanwhile, the horticultural brigade had delivered their vegetables into the briefed locations from 14,000 feet on green flares between 23.41 and 23.47. The flares were fortuitous as far as F/L Burgess was concerned, having lost the use of his H2S shortly after take-off. P/O Scott and crew had been engaged by a JU88 over the west coast of Jutland, and sustained damage to the starboard wing and N°3 fuel tank, but the gunners returned fire to damage and beat off their assailant, and they continued on to fulfil their brief.

On the 20th, Harris found the opportunity to take another swipe at Cologne with an all-Lancaster heavy force, while 5 Group undertook its first full-scale operation as an independent unit, employing its Mosquito-based low-level marking system. Both operations were highly successful, and while they were in progress, 4 Group provided a Halifax main force for an attack on the marshalling yards at Ottignies, situated ten miles south-east of Brussels in central Belgium. Twenty-one 10 Squadron aircraft had departed Melbourne between 21.07 and 21.33 with S/Ls Maw and Trobe the senior pilots on duty. There had been no early returns, and the two-wave force arrived in the target area to find relatively clear skies with ground haze, and release-point flares igniting bang on schedule. The red TIs were more than a minute later, however, and this caused the two waves to close up and create a degree of congestion on the run-in. An early TI fell a little wide of the mark, but the presence of a Master Bomber for the first time since Berlin in August, rescued the situation before many bomb loads were lured away. The 10 Squadron crews carried out their attacks on red and green TIs in accordance with the Master Bomber's instructions, doing so from 11,000 to 13,000 feet between 23.19 and 23.26. A large number of bomb bursts were observed across the target, and dense smoke was seen to be rising as the bombers left the scene. Post-raid reconnaissance confirmed the effectiveness of the operation, particularly in the area of the southern aiming-point.

Düsseldorf was posted as the target on the 22nd, as Harris continued to pursue his own city-busting agenda, for which a force of 596 aircraft was made ready. 10 Squadron bombed and fuelled up twenty Halifaxes, and they took off between 22.24 and 22.53 with W/C Radford and S/Ls Maw and Trobe the senior pilots on duty. Again, there were no early returns among the Melbourne crews, who all reached the target area, W/C Radford and crew doing so after being engaged by a BF109. The enemy appeared on the port quarter with the target ten minutes away, and fired at a range of one thousand yards before being shaken off by evasive action. The skies were clear, and the Rhine was easily identified visually despite the glare from cones of thirty or more searchlights. A cluster of four red TIs and a number of greens went down onto the aiming-point, and these were bombed by the 10 Squadron crews from 16,000 to 20,500 feet between 01.14 and 01.26. A mass of fires was observed, particularly in northern districts, and a belt of flames about a mile wide covered the marshalling yards, while black smoke could be seen rising through 8,000 feet as they turned away. The operation was a massive success, which destroyed or seriously damaged two thousand houses and fifty-six large industrial premises, and local reports would reveal that more than a thousand people had lost their lives. The defenders fought back with a stark reminder that the Ruhr remained a highly dangerous region to visit, and brought down twenty-nine aircraft, sixteen of them Halifaxes. Flight commander, S/L Trobe DFC RAAF and crew failed to return in LV867, which was partially abandoned over Holland, before being force-landed near Griendtsveen in the south-east of the country. The captain and four others evaded capture, while both gunners were taken into captivity. Also lost on this operation was S/L Somerscales, who, it will be recalled, had begun his operational career as a sergeant pilot with 10 Squadron back in August of 1942, before being posted to 76 Squadron, where he rose through the ranks during his second tour to be appointed flight commander.

114 aircraft were made ready on the 23rd for mining operations in five areas of the Baltic. 4 Group provided thirty-three Halifaxes for the Sweet Pea garden off Rostock, of which thirteen represented 10 Squadron, six of them tasked with dropping flares for the benefit of aircraft not equipped with H2S. They departed Melbourne either side of 21.00 with F/L Lucas the senior

pilot on duty, and, after flying out over ten-tenths cloud with tops at 10,000 feet, the skies began to clear over some parts of the garden to five-tenths. Mines and flares were released on an H2S-fix just off the coast some fifteen miles north-east of Rostock and in other adjacent drop zones, mostly from 13,000 and 14,000 feet either side of midnight, and all returned safely to report successful and uneventful sorties.

The busy month of operations continued on the 24th, with briefings for a heavy raid on Karlsruhe in southern Germany. A force of 637 aircraft included eighteen 10 Squadron Halifaxes, which took off between 21.52 and 22.17 with six pilots of flight lieutenant rank leading the way. There were no early returns, and the flight out was relatively uneventful until 23.40, when they ran into an electrical storm between Liege and Strasbourg that lasted for an hour and affected some H2S sets. Sixty to seventy searchlights were operating as they passed close to Mannheim, and it was here that W/O Murtha and crew delivered their bombs in error from 20,500 feet at 00.39, having been misled by the compass, which provided a false reading after taking a battering during the storm. Those reaching Karlsruhe were greeted by moderate flak coming up through the nine to ten-tenths thin cloud that reached up to 18,000 feet, and P/O Pearson and crew overshot the aiming-point until spotting the glow of red TIs four miles to starboard. The pilot decided to orbit to get his bearings, but banked too steeply and threw the artificial horizon out of kilter, while losing height quickly to 16,000 feet. On levelling out they noticed scattered fires over a wide area, and bombed the largest of these at 00.45. F/Sgt Blackford and crew orbited for fourteen minutes on e.t.a., checking their position by H2S in the absence of any release-point flares or TIs, and eventually bombed the largest concentration of fires from 21,000 feet at 00.57. The others mostly found red and green TIs and red and yellow release-point flares, and delivered their bombs from 17,500 to 21,000 between 00.42 and 00.57. F/L Hampton and crew had become victims of the icing conditions while in the storm clouds, and lost height at one thousand feet per minute until reaching the target at 12,000, where they bombed the fires at 00.45. F/Sgt Lavalley and crew were attacked three times by a night-fighter on the way home, but sustained no damage or crew casualties. Local reports confirmed that the strong winds had pushed the attack onto the northern districts of the city and beyond, and nine hundred houses were destroyed or seriously damaged. This was achieved at a cost to the Command of nineteen aircraft.

After a night's rest, nineteen crews were called to briefing on the 26th to learn that Essen would be their target for that night as part of an overall force of 493 aircraft, while 5 Group tried out its low-level marking system at Schweinfurt and other elements of 4, 6 and 8 Groups attended to the marshalling yards at Villeneuve-St-Georges. Two 10 Squadron crews dropped out with technical issues late on leaving seventeen to take-off between 22.57 and 23.23, with pilots of flight lieutenant rank leading the way, and S/L Brisbane undertaking only his second operation with the squadron and flying with F/L Lucas and crew. He was recorded as second pilot on this occasion, having been recorded as second air-bomber on his first sortie, but was, as already mentioned, a navigator by trade. All reached the target area, where conditions were favourable with just patchy cloud and condensation trails to slightly inhibit the view, and most crews found ground detail on which to orient themselves, particularly the River Lippe and parallel canal running east to west on the northern fringe of the Ruhr. Having confirmed their positions by H2S-fix, all but two bombed on red and green TIs from 20,000 feet, and the odd ones out from 18,000 and 21,000 feet, all between 01.32 and 01.41. A large yellow explosion was observed at

01.28, an orange one at 01.34 and these were followed by a third one at 01.36. All crews commented on the abundance of searchlights operating in cones of about thirty, they also described thick smoke rising from a line of fires across the aiming-point and beginning to obscure the target. It was clear that a very destructive raid had taken place, at a cost to the Command of a modest seven aircraft. The single missing Halifax was HX326 of 10 Squadron, captained by F/L Allen, which was brought down from 21,000 feet by a combination of flak and a night-fighter on the way home over Belgium. The pilot and four others lost their lives, and one of the two survivors evaded capture.

On the following night elements of 4, 6 and 8 Groups combined to send a force of 223 aircraft, predominantly Halifaxes, for another shot at the marshalling yards at Aulnoye. Eighteen crews lined up for take-off at Melbourne, and fifteen made it safely into the air between 01.04 and 01.36, before P/O Burcher swung off the runway in LV863, which eventually came to a halt with its back broken. The crew emerged unscathed from the bowels of the wreck, but its close proximity to the runway persuaded W/C Radford to cancel the final two sorties waiting to take-off. F/L Kennedy suffered a hydraulics failure during take-off, which prevented him from raising his flaps and undercarriage and forced him to jettison his load before returning to land safely. The remaining fourteen 10 Squadron crews reached the target to find clear skies and good bombing conditions, which they exploited when delivering their high-explosive loads of 1,000 and 500 pounders onto red and green TIs from 13,000 to 14,000 feet between 03.01 and 03.09, all under the watchful gaze and instructions of a Master Bomber. The attack was concentrated around the markers, and post-raid reconnaissance confirmed that severe damage had been inflicted on the yards.

On the last night of the month, someone gave P/O Burcher and crew another Halifax so that they and the crews of P/Os Pearson and Lassey could join fifteen others from the group to mine the waters of the Nectarines garden off the Frisians, and those of Deodars (Bordeaux) and Cinnamon (La Rochelle). The 10 Squadron trio took off between 21.37 and 21.48 and headed for La Rochelle on the Biscay coast, which they reached to find clear conditions with sea haze. They fixed their positions by H2S on the Ile-de-Re and Pointe-du-Grouin, and delivered their mines unopposed into the briefed locations from 11,000 and 12,000 feet between 00.42 and 00.49. This concluded a busy month, during which the squadron had operated on eleven nights, and dispatched 176 sorties for the loss of three Halifaxes and crews.

May 1944

With the invasion now just five weeks away, the new month would be devoted to attacks on railway targets and coastal defences. In the case of the latter, the focus would be on the Pas-de-Calais region of France, to try to reinforce the enemy's belief that the landings would take place there. 4 Group detailed 110 Halifaxes on the 1st as the main force for an assault on the railway yards at Mechelen (Malines), situated on the main line between the port of Antwerp and Brussels in Belgium. 10 Squadron made ready ten aircraft for this operation and six to join others on gardening duties in the Hyacinth (St-Malo), Upas Tree (Morlaix), Greengages (Cherbourg), Scallops (Le Havre) and Cinnamon (La Rochelle) regions of north-western France. The latter element departed first between 21.20 and 21.29 with S/L Maw the senior pilot on duty, and bound for La Rochelle. The bombing element followed them into the air between 21.57 and 22.09 led by five pilots of flight lieutenant rank, including F/L Hart, who had just been posted in from 41 Base. Having a shorter distance to travel, they arrived in their target area first, where they encountered three to ten-tenths thin cloud and thick haze, which not only prevented a visual identification of ground features, but also inhibited sight of the red and green TIs and red spotfires marking out the aiming-point. The 10 Squadron crews bombed from 12,000 to 13,000 feet between 23.40 and 23.53, but the markers were not concentrated, and the Master Bomber did not provide strong direction. The result was that some of the bombing hit the locomotive sheds, but much of it fell into adjacent residential districts of the old-town, where more than thirteen hundred houses were destroyed or seriously damaged, and 171 people lost their lives. P/O Lassey and crew failed to return in HX347, which exploded and crashed between the target and Brussels, killing the pilot and six others. The wireless operator was the sole survivor, and he was aided by the Belgian resistance in retaining his freedom. Meanwhile, the gardeners had found clear skies, bright moonlight and good visibility, and delivered their mines unopposed by H2S and visual reference from 11,000 to 12,000 feet between 00.37 and 01.05.

A few nights away from operations preceded a briefing at Melbourne on the 6th for an operation that night against railway installations in the Gassicourt district of Mantes-la-Jolie, a town situated some twenty-five miles to the north-west of the centre of Paris. Fourteen Halifaxes were made ready as part of the 4 Group element of seventy-seven aircraft, which were to join forces with sixty-four Lancasters and eight Mosquitos of 8 Group. They took off between 23.59 and 00.20 with the newly-promoted S/L Kennedy the senior pilot on duty, and all reached the target area, where clear skies and bright moonlight afforded a visual identification of the target. The Pathfinders dropped white illuminator flares and red and green TIs, and the bombing took place from 10,000 to 10,500 feet between 02.16 and 02.22 in accordance with the Master Bomber's instructions. Post-raid reconnaissance revealed damage to stores depots and locomotive sheds, but also identified areas of collateral damage in the old-town, where 128 houses and other buildings were destroyed, and many others damaged to some extent, while fifty-four civilians were killed.

While elements of 4 Group made preparations to attend to other matters on the 8th, eight 10 Squadron Halifaxes were loaded with four or six 1,500lb mines each to deliver to the Scallops, Greengage and Sultanas II (Brest) gardens between St Malo and Le Havre. They departed Melbourne between 21.40 and 21.55 with all but one crew captained by an officer. They reached the target areas under clear skies to find good visibility, which enabled them to identify their pin-points and check them by H2S before delivering their mines into the briefed locations from 8,000 to 12,000 feet between 23.39 and 00.30. The target for the squadron on the following night would be a coastal battery at Berneval, north-east of Dieppe, for which thirteen Halifaxes were made ready. This was one of seven similar targets, the others situated further north in the Pas-de-Calais region. Take-off from Melbourne was accomplished without incident between 21.56 and 22.13, with S/L Brisbane flying as second air-bomber in the crew of F/L Culverhouse. The recent run of high serviceability continued on this night, and all reached the target area to find clear skies and slight ground haze. The Pathfinders were a little late in opening the raid, and some TIs fell short and into the sea before the marking was rescued to some extent and bombing took place on green TIs from 9,000 feet between 23.54 and 00.08. Bomb bursts were

A photograph from 22 May 1944. The end of Ops tour of F/L Doug Evans and his crew. His dedicated ground crew squat in front of Halifax MkIII LV908 F-Freddie. Below: Sgt Martin Gilbert, Halifax rear gunner on Sgt J. Saynor's crew, May 1944. It was a cold and lonely place of work.

seen to be scattered over a wide area, and returning crews expressed doubt that the operation had been effective. In truth, it didn't matter, as long as it confirmed to the enemy that this area of coastline was being softened-up for the forthcoming invasion, and, in that regard, it was effective.

For the third day in a row the squadron was ordered on the 10th to prepare their Halifaxes for operations, this time twelve for marshalling yards at Lens in the Pas-de-Calais, and four others for mining duties in the Scallops and Greengages gardens. They took off together between 21.30 and 21.50 with S/L Kennedy leading the bombers and F/L Hampton the mining brigade, and all reached their respective target areas to encounter clears skies and good visibility. Ground features could be identified visually, but the gardeners checked their positions by H2S before delivering their two 1,850lb mines each into the briefed locations from 8,000 feet between 23.44 and 23.51. Further north the bombers were benefitting from illuminator flares and red spot-fires, which they attacked from 8,500 to 9,500 feet between 23.24 and 23.31, observing many bomb bursts across the target and a major explosion that created a huge pall of smoke. On their way out of the target area, HX232 collided with another Halifax that came up suddenly from below. F/L Keltie took immediate evasive action, but was unable to avoid contact, and severe damage resulted to the fuselage and port wingtip. There were no crew casualties, and the pilot regained control to bring the aircraft home to a safe landing at 01.40, after which they were able to report a successful sortie.

Z for Zebra Halifax Mk III after 37 ops., 29th May 1944, 10 Squadron, Melbourne. F/Sgt Bert Field (W.Op); F/Sgt Allen Bruce DFC (Pilot); Sgt Ron Day (RG) Sgt Jack Anderton(MUG) F/O Jack Lee DFC (BA) F/Sgt Tom Bigley DFC (Nav) Sgt Archie Tolmie (FE) Albert (Armourer) Name Unknown (Fitter's Mate) Tom (Rigger) Jock (Fitter)

Marshalling yards featured prominently at briefings on the 11th, as plans were put in hand to attack those at Boulogne in France and Louvain (Leuven) and Hasselt in Belgium, while 5 Group attended to a military camp at Bourg-Leopold, also in Belgium. 10 Squadron was to support a 4 Group effort against a gun battery at Trouville, situated about ten miles in from the French coast at Fecamp. Eight Halifaxes were made ready at Melbourne, four of which were loaded with three 1,000 and fourteen 500 pounders, and the others with six 1,000 and ten 500 pounders, and they took off between 22.45 and 22.59 with F/Ls Burgess, Culverhouse and Le Cudenec the senior pilots on duty and S/L Brisbane flying as second navigator with the second-mentioned. Wrongly forecast winds delayed the arrival of some of the 10 Squadron element, and four of them found that the TIs had burned-out by the time they turned up. All aimed at small fires from 11,000 feet between 00.51 and 01.00, but F/O Henderson and crew experienced a total hang-up, and abandoned their sortie. Unaccountably, the other four crews, who were over the target at the same time, saw red TIs and bombed them from 11,000 feet, observing many bursts across the aiming-point.

The two Belgian marshalling yards were scheduled for another visit from the Command on the 12th, for which 10 Squadron detailed eleven Halifaxes, loading each with three 1,000 and fourteen 500 pounders. They took off between 22.13 and 22.47 led by W/C Radford and bound for the Hasselt yards in the north-east of the country, which they all reached to find thick haze obscuring ground features. An H2S-fix helped them to establish their positions, and red and green TIs took care of the marking of the aiming-point, which was bombed from 8,000 to 8,500 feet between 00.28 and 00.33. A good concentration of bombing was reported, along with a large, yellow explosion north of the marked area at 00.34. While leaving the target, F/O Murray's LK812 was hit in the port-inner engine by a missile, believed to be a friendly bomb, and the damage allowed the propeller to work its way forward along its shaft until it fouled the port-outer propeller, slicing eight inches off each blade. It then wrapped itself round its cowling, despite which F/O Murray retained control and brought his aircraft and crew home to a safe landing. Post-raid reconnaissance would reveal that only a few bombs had hit railway lines, and most had fallen into open country.

F/L Lucas was posted to 20 O.T.U., on the 13th at the end of his tour, while his former colleagues enjoyed a few days off the Order of Battle after a hectic first half of the month. When they returned to the fray on the 19th, it would be for the first of six nights of operations over the ensuing nine days. A busy day ahead for ground staff was confirmed by the detailing of a record twenty-four Halifaxes, which were to be divided equally between that night's attack by the group on Boulogne marshalling yards, and a mining effort to take place between the Brest peninsular and Ouessant Island (Sultanas), and off Brest (Jellyfish), Lorient (Artichokes) and St-Nazaire (Beeches). The Boulogne operation was a 4 and 8 Group affair, and was one of five raids on railway targets, while smaller forces attended to gun batteries in the Pas-de-Calais. The gardeners departed Melbourne first, between 21.57 and 22.23, with S/L Maw the senior pilot on duty and only two NCO captains among them. They were well on their way by the time that the bombers took off between 23.22 and 23.40, led by a number of pilots of flight lieutenant rank. There were no early returns from either element, and the gardeners arrived in their target areas off the Biscay coast to find four to ten-tenths low cloud with tops up to 8,000 feet. Positions were fixed by H2S, and mines delivered into the briefed locations from 11,000 to 12,500 feet between 00.40 and 01.07, the latter time coinciding with the opening of the attack some 350 miles to the east. Clear skies greeted the bombing brigade as they arrived over north-eastern France, and this enabled the crews to identify ground features visually and the aiming-point courtesy of red and yellow TIs. The attacks were delivered mostly from 12,000 feet, between 01.06 and 01.09, and at least one large explosion was witnessed, which illuminated a wide area. A local report confirmed extensive damage to the main railway station, and thirty-three civilians killed.

Duisburg and Dortmund received their first major raids for a year on the nights of the 21/22nd and 22/23rd respectively, both at the hands of all-Lancaster heavy forces. Each was highly destructive, but at a cost to the Command of twenty-nine and eighteen Lancasters respectively. Elements of 4 Group went alone to bomb railway installations at Orleans during the latter, while 10 Squadron contributed twelve Halifaxes to a further mining effort in four gardens off the Biscay coast, having been briefed for those at Lorient (Artichokes) and St-Nazaire (Beeches). They took off between 22.05 and 22.35 with S/Ls Kennedy and Maw the senior pilots on duty, but F/L Evans lost his starboard-inner engine immediately after take-off, and returned his mines to store. The others reached their respective target areas to find up to nine-tenths patchy cloud with tops at 6,000 feet with haze below, and established their positions by H2S-fix before delivering their vegetables into the assigned locations from 10,000 feet between 00.56 and 01.13.

On the following night, nine Halifaxes departed Melbourne between 22.49 and 23.03 for gardening duties off the Elbe Estuary and south-western corner of the Schleswig-Holstein peninsular (Rosemary). F/Ls Evans, Le Cudenec and Taylor were the senior pilots on duty as they headed for the North Sea via Hornsea, and all reached the target area to encounter five to seven-tenths scattered cloud with tops at between 6,000 and 8,000 feet. W/O Blackford and crew lost the use of their H2S while outbound, and brought their mines home. The others established their positions by H2S, and delivered their mines into the briefed locations from 15,000 feet between 00.46 and 00.53, before returning safely from uneventful sorties.

The important railway hub of Aachen, Germany's most westerly city, was earmarked for attention on the 24th, for which 10 Squadron made ready nine Halifaxes as part of an overall force of 442 aircraft. While this operation was in progress, five other 10 Squadron crews would be involved in an attack on a coastal battery at Colline-Beaumont, one of four similar targets in the Pas-de-Calais, while six others were to continue the relentless mining campaign, this time south of Lorient (Artichokes). The gardeners took off first, between 22.16 and 22.24 with W/C Radford the senior pilot on duty, and they were followed into the air by those bound for north-eastern France between 22.28 and 22.38, and the Aachen-element between 22.54 and 23.04 led by S/Ls Kennedy and Maw. There was not a single early return, and the crews at Colline-Beaumont were on their way home by 00.23 after bombing the target on green TIs, confirmed by H2S, from 10,500 feet in the space of barely two-minutes. Meanwhile, the main element had reached Aachen, where the two marshalling yards at Aachen-West and Rothe Erde in the east were the aiming-points. The 10 Squadron crews were assigned to the latter, where they encountered poor visibility, caused, initially, by thin, low cloud, and, later, by smoke. Red and green TIs were visible on the ground, which were bombed from 16,000 to 17,000 feet between 00.52 and 00.59, and bomb bursts were observed followed by a pall of smoke rising upwards as the force withdrew. The losses from this operation harked back to earlier days, with eighteen

Halifaxes and seven Lancasters failing to return. The loss rates were respectively 11.1% and 2.6%, and among the former was the squadron's LV906, which had already notched up thirty-two sorties by the time it took off on this night in the hands of W/O Blackford and crew. Shot down by flak to crash near Sittard in southern Holland, the entire crew survived to fall into enemy hands, although the rear gunner, F/O Singh RAAF, sustained injuries severe enough to keep him in hospital for most of his period of captivity. The mining brigade enjoyed clear skies and good visibility over the coast of north-western France, and delivered their vegetables into the briefed locations from 10,000 feet between 01.10 and 01.14.

The squadron learned on the 26th that eight crews would be required for that night's return to the Jellyfish (Brest) and Beeches (St-Nazaire) gardens, and they took off between 22.09 and 22.18 with F/L Taylor the senior pilot on duty. All reached the target areas to be met by clear skies and just a little haze to spoil the view, and positions were established by H2S before the vegetables were planted in the assigned locations from 10,000 feet between 01.11 and 01.25. The final operations of the month from Melbourne were posted on the 27th, and the main one was to be against a previously-attacked military camp at Bourg Leopold in northern Belgium. The force of 331 aircraft contained 267 Halifaxes, of which nine would represent 10 Squadron, but it was three gardening NCO-captained crews who took off first, at 22.40, bound for the Artichokes region off Lorient. The main element departed Melbourne between 00.01 and 00.26 with F/O Henderson the senior pilot on duty, and, while they were still thirty minutes or more from their target, the mining trio arrived at theirs to find up to three-tenths cloud and a little sea haze. They attracted some moderate and accurate flak from the Lorient area, and F/Sgt Lavalley and crew were held in a searchlight cone for ten minutes. Despite that, all crews established their positions by H2S-fix before delivering their wares into the assigned locations from 12,000 feet between 00.33 and 00.41. Meanwhile, the skies were clear over Belgium, and a Master Bomber was on hand to direct the marking and bombing. Red, green and yellow TIs marked out the aiming-point, and the main-force obliged with an accurate attack, delivered by the 10 Squadron crews from 10,500 to 14,000 feet between 02.05 and 02.18. One Oboe TI had landed right on the aiming-point, and post-raid reconnaissance revealed that the camp had sustained extensive damage. While 10 Squadron remained at home for the last few nights of the month, other elements of the Command continued to attack pre-invasion targets such as radar stations, coastal batteries and railways. During the course of the month the squadron operated on thirteen nights, and dispatched 171 sorties for the loss of two Halifaxes and crews.

June 1944

As the invasion approached, the rate of operations increased, with radar stations and airfields being added to the list of targets. 4 Group's target for the night of the 1/2nd was the main German RDF station, located at Ferme-d'Urville on the Cherbourg peninsular to the west of the planned landing grounds. 10 Squadron made ready twenty-three Halifaxes to contribute to the force of 101, which would have eight Oboe Mosquitos on hand to carry out the marking. The Melbourne element took off between 22.51 and 23.25 with F/Ls Burgess, Culverhouse and Kiltie the senior pilots on duty, the H2S-equipped aircraft carrying nine 1,000 and four 500 pounders each, and the non-H2S-equipped an additional 500 pounder. F/Sgt Horne and crew turned back after the starboard-outer engine caught fire and had to be shut down, while F/O Murray and crew were unable to squeeze sufficient airspeed out of MZ576 to keep up, and they turned back also when it became clear that they would not reach the target in time. P/O Hullah and crew also lost their starboard-outer engine at 00.35 before crossing the English coast outbound, but decided to press on and complete the sortie. They and the others reached the target to find it largely obscured by six to ten-tenths cloud with tops at 7,000 feet, and a combination of red and green Pathfinder release-point flares, H2S and Gee to establish their positions over the aiming-point. P/O Hullah and crew released their bombs from 8,500 feet, and the rest of the squadron from 13,000 to 14,000 feet between 01.10 and 01.15, although F/Sgt Bond experienced the frustration of a total hang-up, and jettisoned his on the way home. It was impossible to assess the outcome, and post-raid reconnaissance revealed that it had not been a successful raid. 5 Group would have a go two nights later and would flatten it.

Seventeen crews were called to briefings at Melbourne on the 2nd, twelve to learn the "gen" for their attack that night on the marshalling yards at Trappes in the west of Paris, and five for mining duties in the Iris garden off the West-Scheldt and the Hook of Holland. The main element took off between 22.28 and 22.43 with F/Os Henderson and Murray the senior pilots on duty, and, after climbing out, rendezvoused with the rest of the 124-strong heavy force, which included 1 Group Lancasters, probably of the ABC variety belonging to 101 Squadron. The gardeners took to the air between 23.17 and 23.34 led by F/L Burgess, and, according to plan, the two elements reached their respective target areas simultaneously but separated by some 240 miles. Paris lay under cloudless skies and the conditions for the attack were ideal, allowing the main force crews to identify the aiming-point visually. The red and Yellow TIs were mostly well-placed, and the instructions of the Master Bomber clear as the 10 Squadron crews bombed from 10,500 to 12,500 feet between 00.51 and 00.55. W/O Kite witnessed a large explosion, and, like the others, reported little opposition from the ground in the target area, but evidence of night-fighters on the way home. The loss of fifteen Halifaxes and a Lancaster, 12% of the force, gave lie to the suggestion from on high that French targets warranted only one-third of a sortie status, and this lesson would he hammered home time and again as the summer progressed. 10 Squadron lost two aircraft, both of which fell to night-fighters, and, while the routes in and out were similar, almost certainly, they occurred on the way home. LV882 crashed onto farmland near Epernon to the south-west of the target, killing Sgt Kumar and all but the wireless operator, who ultimately evaded capture. MZ630 had both port engines and the mainplane set on fire, and was partially abandoned by the crew, before crashing some forty miles to the west of Paris. F/O Murray and his wireless operator lost their lives, four men were captured, while the mid-upper gunner managed to retain his freedom.* Post-raid reconnaissance revealed that the main weight of the attack had fallen into the eastern half of the yards. Meanwhile, the gardeners had encountered three-tenths low cloud, but good visibility, and had identified their pin-points visually and by H2S before dropping their vegetables into the briefed locations from 12,000 feet between 00.51 and 00.54.

On the following night, while 5 Group attended to the RDF station at Ferme-d'Urville, other elements of the Command continued the programme of deception by bombing coastal defences in the Pas-de-Calais region, while 10 Squadron contributed ten Halifaxes to the mining of coastal waters off Brest (Jellyfish) and the West-Scheldt (Iris). The six bound for north-western France departed Melbourne between 22.31 and 22.40 with S/Ls Kennedy and Maw the senior pilots on duty, five of them carrying two 1,500lb mines and one of them four. They were

10 Sqn Ops Record Book F541 for a raid two days after D-Day when 11 out of the planned 12 aircraft successfully bombed the railway yards at Juvisy just west of the River Seine, south of the modern Paris Orly Airport.

followed an hour later by a quartet led by F/L Keltie, who headed towards the south-east, two with four 1,500lb mines on board and two with four of 1,850lbs. The skies over the Best area were clear with good visibility, and the mines were laid in the allotted locations by H2S-fix from 15,000 feet between 01.22 and 01.33. Five to eight-tenths broken cloud lay over the Scheldt Estuary, but conditions were favourable, and the stores were delivered on H2S-fixes as briefed from 12,000 feet between 00.59 and 01.08.

10 Squadron remained at home on the night of the 4/5th, while other elements of the group and the Command attacked three coastal batteries in the Pas-de-Calais, and another at Maisy, situated between the Normandy beaches code-named Omaha and Utah, which were soon to be the scene of American landings. The weather over the Channel had been giving cause for concern, delaying the invasion with cloud-filled skies, gusty winds and choppy seas, and, when the decision was finally taken to launch Operation Overlord in the early hours of the 6th, there was a distinct sense of uncertainty at HQ. Briefings took place on all bomber stations during the course of the 5th, but there was no direct reference to the invasion itself. Instead, crews were warned to adhere strictly to specified flight-levels, and were prohibited from jettisoning bombs over the sea. 1,012 aircraft were to be involved in the bombing of ten coastal batteries covering the landing areas, and twenty-three of the 220 Halifaxes of 4 Group were provided by 10 Squadron. They took off between 02.07 and 02.45 with S/L Kennedy the senior pilot on duty, and headed for their target at Mont-Fleury, located right in the centre of the landing grounds. On the way they rendezvoused with elements from 51, 76, 78 and 578 Squadrons, which were all assigned to the same target. They all arrived to find ten-tenths thin cloud, the "Y" aircraft, those equipped with H2S, using their equipment to confirm their positions, while the others employed Gee. With the exception of F/Sgt Horne and crew, who saw no TIs, the 10 Squadron element bombed on red and green TIs seen dimly through the cloud from 9,000 to 12,000 feet between 04.36 and 04.48. Some crews reported seeing bomb bursts among the TIs, but it was difficult to make an accurate assessment.

Another thousand aircraft were made ready to take part in operations on D-Day night, when road and railway communications were to be bombarded in and around nine towns leading to the beachhead to prevent enemy reinforcements from reaching it. 4 Group committed 213 Halifaxes to attacks on Chateaudun and St Lo, 108 of them from 10, 76, 77, 78, 102 and 346 (Free French) Squadrons assigned to the latter, situated to the south of the American landing areas. The twenty-two-strong 10 Squadron element departed Melbourne between 22.05 and 22.38 with S/Ls Kennedy and Maw the senior pilots on duty, and each bomb bay loaded with up to eighteen 500 pounders for use against enemy troop concentrations. They all reached the target area to find complete cloud cover at around 5,000 feet, but, in the almost complete absence of opposition, the Master Bomber called them down below the cloud base, where the TIs were clearly visible. The 10 Squadron crews bombed from 2,000 to 3,000 feet on red, yellow and white TIs between 00.51 and 00.57, and only W/O Kite and crew missed out after their Gee-box was jammed, causing them to overshoot the aiming-point. When no TIs were visible on e.t.a., the sortie was abandoned and a proportion of the bomb load jettisoned. Returning crews reported a large column of smoke rising through 2,000 feet as they turned away, and a concentrated pattern of bombing was confirmed by post-raid reconnaissance.

The hectic pace of operations continued on the 7th with preparations for an attack that night on the marshalling yards at Juvisy, situated in a southern suburb of Paris, while others were assigned to gardening duties. At Melbourne a dozen Halifaxes were loaded with 500 pounders for the main target and seven with mines for delivery to the sea lanes off Brest (Jellyfish) and St Nazaire (Beeches). They took off together between 22.56 and 23.28, with F/L Le Cudenec leading the horticultural brigade and W/C Radford and S/L Maw the bombers, but the latter element soon lost the services of Sgt Davies and crew due to starboard-inner engine failure as they flew over the 5 Group stations of Woodhall Spa and Coningsby. The remainder pressed on to their respective targets, those bound for Paris arriving first to encounter fair weather conditions with good visibility, and a Master Bomber on hand to direct the bombing. Red and green TIs were clearly visible from the bombing height of 3,500 to 6,000 feet, and the 10 Squadron crews carried out their attacks in accordance with the Master Bomber's instructions between 01.07 and 01.18. On the way home, P/O Henderson and crew spotted a FW190 approaching to attack from the port-quarter, but, before it had time to open fire, it was engaged by both of the Halifax's turrets, and was seen to spiral down in flames to explode on the ground. Sgt Peacock and crew returned to claim a BF109 destroyed. Meanwhile, the gardeners had employed H2S to establish their pinpoints, and had delivered their vegetables into the briefed locations from 12,000 feet between 01.52 and 01.57, with only F/Sgt Hedley and crew missing out after experiencing a fault in the electrical release system. Post-raid photographs of Juvisy revealed a few stray bombs to the north-west, but the majority being concentrated around the aiming-point.

F/O Leitch RAAF took off on a night cross-country exercise in mid-evening on the 8th as part of his initial training on the Mk III Halifax, and, on return at 00.59, held off too long after misjudging his height, and landed heavily. The impact thrust the starboard undercarriage up through the wing, resulting in LW371 being damaged beyond repair. F/O Leitch and his crew emerged unscathed to fight another day, but, sadly, it would be a very brief reprieve. 10 Squadron remained at home on this night, while other elements of 4 Group and the Command attended to railway targets at five locations in France in an attempt to cut off Normandy from the south. Four airfields to the south of the battle area were targeted on the 9th with the same purpose in mind, and 10 Squadron made ready thirteen Halifaxes to send to Laval, situated between Rennes to the west and Le-Mans to the east, while a further ten were loaded with mines destined for the waters off Lorient (Artichokes) and St-Nazaire (Beeches). They departed Melbourne first, between 22.43 and 22.56, with F/Ls Burgess and Hampton the senior pilots on duty, and were divided equally between the two gardens, where five to eight-tenths cloud was met between 5,000 and 6,000 feet. Visibility was moderate to good, and there was no opposition at St-Nazaire, but fifteen searchlights and accurate heavy flak made life a little uncomfortable at Lorient. H2S bearings were taken and positions established before the mines were delivered into the briefed locations from 10,000 to 11,000 feet at around 01.35.

The bombing element took off between 00.20 and 00.42 led by F/L Le Cudenec, and it was when over the Thames Estuary that P/O Burcher lost his starboard-inner engine, but decided to continue on to the target, anyway. Sgt Bond and F/Sgt Bowmer reached the target, and heard the Master Bomber, but failed to see TIs through the ten-tenths cloud that was down to around 3,000 feet, so brought their bombs home. F/L Le Cudenec came down below the cloud base to bomb on yellow TIs from 2,800 feet at 03.06, exposing his aircraft to quite intense light flak and the risk of being hit by friendly bombs, which were falling from other 10 Squadron aircraft from 3,400 to 8,000 feet from 03.03 onwards. They were aiming at red TIs, which had been extinguished by the time that P/O Burcher arrived, having been delayed by the loss of an engine, and he confirmed his position by Gee before letting his load go onto the glow of fires from 7,500 feet at 03.22. On return, F/L Le Cudenec reported observing three large areas of fire, while W/O Kite and crew described an encounter with a FW190, which was hit by return fire and was seen to turn over and dive steeply into cloud. All of the airfield attacks were successful, and the only losses were two Halifaxes, both from the Laval raid and both belonging to 10 Squadron. MZ532 crashed about two miles west of the target, while MZ684 came down about five miles to the south-east after being hit by flak, and there were no survivors from the crews of P/O Henderson RAAF and F/O Willem Van Stockum respectively. The latter was a Dutch academic with an established reputation in the field of General Relativity.

Above left: Sgt Vijendra Kumar, shown here with his mother Chandra, was the captain of Mk3 Halifax LV882, which crashed at Hermeray, France on 3 June 1944. All but Sgt Alec Hunter, the W/Op who escaped, were killed. Above right: Kumar's Tail Gunner, Sgt Gerald O'Leary.

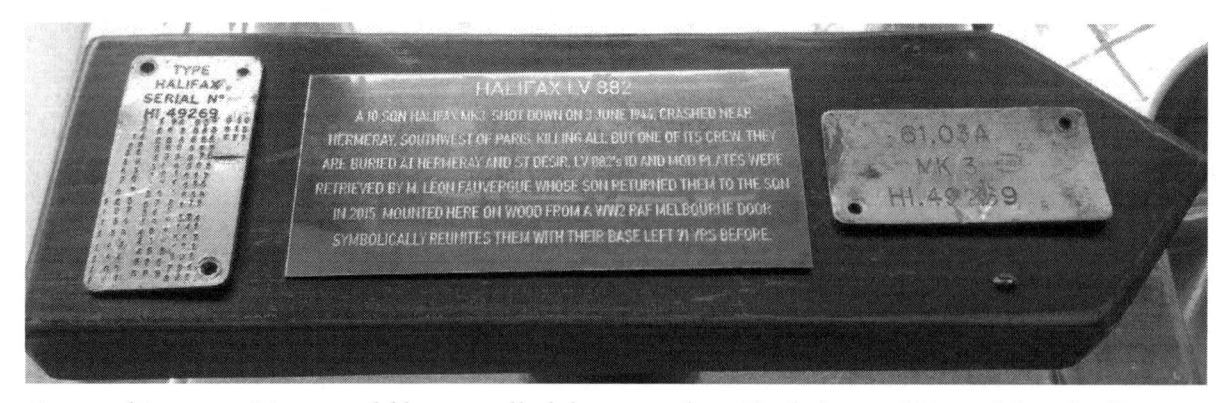

Bernard Leroy, a 14-year-old boy recalled the event described above. A French local villager, Léon Fauvergue, recovered the aircraft's ID & modification plates from the wreckage. In 2015 his son Pierre returned them to 10 Sqn and they are now mounted on part of a wooden door from wartime RAF Melbourne with a plaque describing the event.

S/L Maw was posted out to Leconfield on the 12th on promotion to acting wing commander rank to take command of 640 Squadron, and he was succeeded temporarily as B Flight commander by F/L Hampton. Melbourne resounded to the clamour of activity during the day as twenty-four Halifaxes were made ready for battle that night, nineteen of them to join 652 other aircraft drawn from 4, 5, 6 and 8 Groups to target communications, mostly railways, at six locations in France. 4 Group was assigned to two marshalling yards at Amiens in north-eastern France, at St-Roche, close to the city centre, and Longueau in a south-eastern suburb, and it was for the latter that the 10 Squadron element took off between 21.59 and 22.26 with F/Ls Burgess and Hampton the senior pilots on duty. They were to join forces with eighty-one other Halifaxes from 51, 76, 78 and 346 Squadrons as they set course towards the south to exit England via the Kent coast. Meanwhile, five gardening crews, all with pilots of pilot officer rank, had taken off either side of 22.00 to plant vegetables in the Jellyfish garden (Brest), but P/O Burcher was forced to turn back after his H2S equipment failed. He reported being engaged by coastal flak from north of Torquay both out and inbound, despite signalling the letter of the day. There were no early returns from the main element, which was greeted at the target by four-tenths cloud at 13,000 feet. A Master Bomber was on hand to oversee the bombing, and he kept a firm hand on proceedings, directing the crews to aim for red, yellow or white TIs according to requirements shifting from one moment to the next. The Melbourne crews delivered their loads of 500 pounders mostly from 12,000 feet, but with exceptions at 10,500 and 15,000 feet, between 00.11 and 00.21, and observed what appeared to be a concentrated attack, with much smoke rising to meet them. Five minutes after bombing, F/Sgt Bowmer and crew were attacked five times from astern by a single-engine fighter, which was seen to crash and explode after being hit by return fire from both turrets. At 00.48 a JU88 attacked from the port quarter, and this, too, was seen to have both engines on fire before crashing and exploding. While this was happening, P/O Rosen and crew had attracted the attention of two single-engine fighters, one of which, with a white light in its nose, closed to attack at 00.42. Return fire from both turrets set the assailant's engine on fire, and it was seen to explode on impact with the ground. The second fighter had by then broken away and was observed to shoot down a Halifax. While these events were in progress, the quartet of 10 Squadron gardeners had found five to ten-tenths cloud between 5,000 and 8,000 feet and had established their positions off Brest by H2S. They delivered their mines into the briefed locations from 15,000 feet, between 01.20 and

01.30, and returned safely to report little opposition other than ineffective flak from the port. It was a night of heavy losses, which cost seventeen Halifaxes and six Lancasters from the operations over France, all from 4 and 6 Groups. Also, on this night, a new oil campaign had begun, and seventeen Lancasters had failed to return from a highly successful attack by elements of 1, 3 and 8 Groups on the Nordstern synthetic oil plant (Gelsenberg Aktien Gesellschaft) at Gelsenkirchen.

There were now three major campaigns running concurrently, oil, communications and tactical support, and to these was about to be added a fourth, against the mounting threat from V-1 flying bombs. F/L Neill and crew were posted to the squadron from 41 Base on the 14th, and the first daylight raids for a year took place late that evening in a highly-successful two-phase attack on German light naval craft at Le Havre,

F/L H.A. 'Homer' Lawson DFC, Navigator on The 'Ol Ram, survived the war.

which were posing a threat to the beachhead. While this was in progress, a force of 337 Halifaxes and Lancasters of 4, 5 and 8 Groups joined forces to hit enemy vehicle and troop positions around Caen in support of the Allied break-out, and 330 others of 4, 6 and 8 Groups prepared to prosecute the communications campaign at Cambrai, St-Pol and Douai. Twenty 10 Squadron Halifaxes were assigned to the last-mentioned, situated in the north-eastern corner of France close to the Belgian frontier, where a locomotive depot was the specific target. They departed Melbourne between 23.39 and 00.04 with F/Ls Burgess and Hart the senior pilots on duty, only for F/L Burgess to lose his starboard-outer engine over Suffolk and have to turn back. The others pressed on to find the target under largely clear skies with good visibility, and bombed on red and green TIs from 12,000 feet between 01.58 and 02.06 in accordance with the instructions of the Master Bomber, F/L Hewitt of 582 Squadron. Six minutes after bombing, Sgt Bond and crew were descending to clear a patch of thin cloud, when they collided with a FW190, which robbed them of five feet of their port wing. The enemy aircraft was seen to spiral down in flames until impacting the ground, while the Halifax made a safe return to land on the emergency strip at Woodbridge on the Suffolk coast at 03.00. Sadly, Master Bomber F/L Hewitt and crew were all killed on the way home after being shot down by a night-fighter over Belgium. Seven of the eight men on board were holders of the DFC or DFM.

Boulogne suffered severe damage on the 15th, when elements of 4 Group joined in a daylight evening attack on fast, light enemy naval craft, in a carbon copy of the previous night's destruction at Le Havre. 10 Squadron made ready eighteen Halifaxes as part of a 4 Group force of ninety-nine aircraft to be dispatched that night to an ammunition dump at Fouillard, located a mile or so to the north-east of Rennes in Brittany. They departed Melbourne between 21.09

and 21.31 with F/Ls Burgess, Hart and Le Cudenec the senior pilots on duty, and all reached the target to find slight cloud and a Master Bomber on hand to direct proceedings. The all-500 pounder loads were delivered onto red and green TIs from 7,000 and 8,000 feet between 00.03 and 00.12 in accordance with instructions, and huge explosions were witnessed at 00.05 and 00.07. The shockwave from the latter was felt in some aircraft, and these explosions were followed by a series of smaller detonations and a developing glow at 00.10, which gave rise to flames and much smoke. The fires remained visible for around eighty miles into the return flight, during which P/O Hewitt and crew claimed a JU88 as a "probable".

A busy night of operations on the 16th heralded the second new campaign of the month, against flying-bomb sites, while the second raid of the new oil campaign would target the Sterkrade-Holten refinery at Oberhausen in the Ruhr. The large concrete flying-bomb storage and launching structures in the Pas-de-Calais were referred to in Bomber Command circles as "constructional works" and it was one at Domleger, situated some dozen miles inland from the Baie-de-la-Somme, east-north-east of Abbeville, that was the target for 4 Group, while elements of 1, 5, 6 and 8 Groups plied their trade at three other sites. The eleven 10 Squadron participants took off between 00.14 and 00.34 with F/Ls Burgess and Hampton the senior pilots on duty, but, at around 00.50, LV825 span in and exploded on impact at Pastures Farm, Rawcliffe, near Goole in Yorkshire. P/O Leitch RAAF and five of his crew were killed, the lone survivor, the rear gunner, having narrowly escaped by parachute. The others pushed on to the target, where ten-tenths cloud was encountered with tops at between 6,000 and 8,000 feet, which caused problems. The 10 Squadron crews attacked from 14,000 to 15,000 feet on the glow of red Oboe TIs on the ground or on others cascading towards the clouds, and one or two bombed on the glow of fires after confirming their positions by H2S and Gee. There was no opposition, and all returned safely to have the success of their efforts eventually confirmed by post-raid reconnaissance. The raid on the oil refinery had not gone well, had inflicted no significant damage on the plant and had cost thirty-one aircraft, twenty-two of them Halifaxes, 13.6% of those dispatched. 77 Squadron lost seven of twenty-three Halifaxes, and 102 Squadron five out of twenty-three.

Flying bomb-related sites would dominate proceedings for the remainder of the month, but all of the concurrent campaigns would require attention, forcing the Pathfinders to spread themselves thinly in order to provide a presence at each target. While 10 Squadron remained at home, 4 Group sent ninety Halifaxes to a flying bomb store at St-Martin-l'Hortier on the night of the 17/18th. Bombing took place through cloud, and it would be deemed necessary to return to this target in due course. Thirteen 10 Squadron Halifaxes departed Melbourne late on the 19th to return to Domleger, but were recalled within ninety minutes, resulting in a large number of perfectly serviceable 500 pounders ending up on the bed of the North Sea. Following a number of days on stand-by, orders were received at Melbourne on the 22nd to prepare twenty Halifaxes for an operation that night against the marshalling yards at Laon in north-eastern France. They were part of a 4 Group force of one hundred aircraft, and took off between 22.44 and 23.10 with F/L Fenny the senior pilot on duty. There were no early returns, and all reached the target area to encounter good weather and clear skies, that enabled the crews to make a visual identification of the aiming-point, before bombing on mostly red TIs from 10,000 to 14,000 feet between 01.00 and 01.06. A Master Bomber was on hand, and, although not all heard his broadcasts, he rescued the operation by diverting attention away from a stray cluster of markers to the north.

D-Day Log Book – 'Homer' Lawson (Nav) and crew, attacking targets in Normandy.

No mean achievement – Completion of First Operational Tour

The crew of LV825, who apart from their tail gunner, all lost their lives in a crash at Rawcliffe near Goole on 17 June 1944. R:(L-R) Sgt R. Crawford (FE), Sgt C. Lewington (W/Op) Sgt C. Dummer (M/UG)F/Sgt M.J. Coleman (R/G). F:(L-R) Sgt R.F. Pearce (Nav) P/O N.C.C. Leitch RAAF (Pilot), F/Sgt W.J.McCarroll (B/A)

Post-raid reconnaissance would reveal that two TIs in the yards had attracted most of the bombs, and that extensive damage had resulted. F/Sgt Bowmer and crew had just turned for home when they were attacked by a ME210 from the starboard quarter. The pilot threw the Halifax into a corkscrew, while the two gunners returned fire and observed their assailant burst into flames, dive and explode on the ground. Not to be outdone, P/O Cembrowski's mid-upper gunner shot down a FW190, which had opened fire from four hundred yards shortly after the bombing run, and this was also seen to fall in flames before impacting the ground.

Briefings took place on various 1, 4, 6 and 8 Group stations on the 24th for operations that afternoon against three flying-bomb sites in the Pas-de-Calais. For 10 Squadron, at least, this would be the first genuine daylight operation for two years, and signalled a new phase of bombing operations to bring the formerly nocturnal force out of the shadows. The 10 Squadron scribe initially referred to flying bombs on the Form 540 as "doodle-bugs", but these references were crossed out, and hand-written amendments of "flying bomb" substituted, probably on the instructions of the commanding officer after signing it off at the end of the month. Twenty-two Halifaxes were loaded with 500 pounders at Melbourne, and took off for Noyelle-en-Chausee between 15.30 and 15.57 with W/C Radford the senior pilot on duty. First to leave the ground was F/L Hampton, whose sortie ended immediately on the failure of his undercarriage and flaps to retract. The others all reached the target area to find excellent visibility, and bombed on red

All that remained of LV825 when an engine fire after take-off resulted in the aircraft crashing on Cuckoo Park Farm, Rawcliffe, on 16 June 1944. Note the rear gun turret on the left; the tail gunner, F/Sgt Coleman was the only survivor.

TIs in accordance with the Master Bomber's instructions from 17,000 to 18,000 feet between 17.20 and 17.22. The 4 Group ORB recorded ninety-eight aircraft releasing their loads onto the TIs in just three minutes, almost all of them falling within half-a-mile of the aiming-point, and a large proportion within a quarter-of-a-mile. At debriefing, F/O Rosen reported that two of his bombs had hit another Halifax, which exploded and took out another nearby Halifax, and a total of three parachutes were observed. In Bomber Command Losses for 1944, Bill Chorley cites a mid-air collision between aircraft of 77 and 102 Squadrons, which may, in fact, have related to this incident.

There was an early start for elements of 1, 4, 6 and 8 Groups on the following day, as 323 aircraft were made ready to attack three further flying-bomb sites. Twenty-one Halifaxes departed Melbourne between 07.30 and 07.51 bound for Montorgueil, with F/Ls Burgess, Hampton, Hart and Neill the senior pilots on duty. There were no early returns, and the good conditions prevailing in the target area allowed the crews to identify the aiming-point visually and aim for the red and yellow TIs from 17,000 to 18,000 feet either side of 09.30. The entire attack was over in three minutes to leave the target enveloped in rising smoke, and post-raid reconnaissance confirmed the bombing to have been concentrated around the aiming-point.

Another busy day across the Command on the 27th saw 721 aircraft made ready for operations against six flying-bomb sites that night, including the one at Mont Candon, situated close to the Normandy coast south-west of Dieppe, which was to be the target for fifteen Halifaxes of 10 Squadron. The squadron scribe actually described the target as a pilotless-plane base on this occasion. The 10 Squadron element would be part of a 4 Group effort amounting to 103

Halifaxes, while a further eight Halifaxes were prepared at Melbourne for mining duties in the Jellyfish garden off Brest. The bombers took off first, between 22.23 and 22.41, with F/Ls Hart and Neill the senior pilots on duty, and all reached the target area to be greeted by four-tenths cloud with good visibility. Bombing took place almost completely unopposed on red TIs from 16,000 to 18,000 feet between 00.17 and 00.22, and was seen to be concentrated. Post-raid photographs revealed that the TIs had fallen slightly to the east of the aiming-point, and that the target had not received the full weight of bombs. Meanwhile, the gardening element had taken off between 22.54 and 23.07 led by F/Ls Burcher, Hewitt and Murtha and their crews. The last-mentioned were some thirty-five miles off Cherbourg when the port-inner engine caught fire, causing the Halifax to lose height, and it looked like a ditching might be the only option, until the fire was successfully extinguished, and a safe return completed. The others found good weather conditions but ten-tenths cloud, and established their positions by H2S before delivering their vegetables into the briefed locations from 12,000 to 15,000 feet between 02.06 and 02.15.

There would be a sting in the tail for 4 Group at the end of a hectic month of operations, the penultimate one of which was to be against marshalling yards at Blainville-sur-l'Eau, situated south-east of Nancy in eastern France. Ninety-seven Halifaxes were made ready, of which nineteen were loaded with fifteen 500 pounders each at Melbourne, and they took off between 22.02 and 22.29 with F/Ls Burcher, Hewitt and Neill the senior pilots on duty. They made their way to the target via a route that passed to the west of Reims, and it was here that enemy night-fighters infiltrated the bomber stream. F/L Hewitt and crew (not to be confused with the recently lost crew of the same name) were attacked three times between 00.43 and 01.14, first by a

'The 'Ol Ram'. Apart from the bombs denoting the raids carried out by this aircraft three swastikas denote the fact that this aircraft's gunners shot down three enemy aircraft.

FW190 and later by an unidentified twin-engine aircraft, neither of which scored hits. Finally, a ME210 was spotted at seven hundred yards range, and received five four-second bursts from the mid-upper turret, which resulted in the assailant falling away with its starboard wing in flames, before exploding on the ground. It is highly likely, based on the locations of the wreckage, that two 10 Squadron aircraft were lost at this stage of the outward flight. LV870 crashed near Perles, killing the rear gunner, and delivering P/O Taylor and two of his crew into enemy hands, while three others retained their freedom.* LW717 came down near Crepy-en-Valois some twenty-five miles further to the west, and there were no survivors from the crew of P/O Livesey. The remainder, including the Hewitt crew, arrived in the target area to find ideal conditions, and a Master Bomber on hand to direct proceedings. The first red TIs appeared to be slightly misplaced, and not all crews were able to hear the Master Bomber's attempts to rectify the situation. As a consequence, the initial bombing was a little scattered, but matters improved thereafter, and a good concentration of bombing was achieved with a slight drift to the western side of the yards. The 10 Squadron crews attacked from 9,500 to 11,000 feet between 01.30 and 01.36, and many bomb bursts were observed along with copious amounts of smoke. Eleven Halifaxes failed to return, almost certainly victims of night-fighters, and for the second time in less than two weeks, 102 Squadron lost five aircraft.

F/L Culverhouse was posted to 10 O.T.U at the end of the month on completion of an outstanding tour of operational duty. During the course of the month the squadron operated on seventeen occasions, and dispatched 328 sorties, including those recalled, for the loss of eight Halifaxes and crews.

July 1944

The squadron was in action immediately at the start of the new month, when contributing seventeen Halifaxes to a 4 Group force of 101 aircraft assigned to attack the flying-bomb site at St-Martin-l'Hortier, situated some fifteen miles south-east of Dieppe, by daylight on the 1st. They departed Melbourne between 15.05 and 15.37 with F/Ls Burcher, Hewitt and Murtha the senior pilots on duty, and all reached the target to find nine-tenths cloud with tops at 8,000 feet. Most crew had to establish their position by H2S or Gee, although some claimed to have seen TIs burning dimly through the cloud. The conditions made it difficult to achieve concentration, and the Master Bomber's instructions did not reach the 10 Squadron crews, who bombed from 13,000 to 14,000 feet between 17.15 and 17.21. Returning crews reported about ten heavy flak guns protecting the target, and one of these accounted for MZ584, which was observed by other 10 Squadron crews to be hit and to descend in a controlled glide. There were reports that parachutes were seen, but F/O Rosen and five of his crew, who had arrived from 41 Base at the end of May, lost their lives when the Halifax crashed just beyond the target, and only the rear gunner got out in time, ultimately to retain his liberty. A number of bombing photos were plotted near the aiming-point, while others showed an area three to four miles to the south-south-east, and it was clear that the raid had been scattered and the target would have to be revisited.

The Squadron made ready twenty Halifaxes on the 4th as part of a 4 Group force of 103 aircraft detailed to return to St-Martin-l'Hortier, and they took off between 12.01 and 12.32 with five pilots of flight lieutenant rank taking the lead. There were no early returns, and all reached the target, by which time the seven-tenths cloud that had all-but obscured the Channel had broken to leave a large gap. Clusters of red and yellow TIs, and, according to some, white ones, were clearly visible, and a Master Bomber was on hand to direct proceedings, although, not all crews could hear or understand his instructions. Those that could complied, while the others aimed at the TIs, the 10 Squadron crews bombing almost as one from 15,000 to 16,000 feet between 14.15 and 14.16. As the crews turned away, they could see a large volume of smoke rising from where the TIs had been, and the impression was of a fairly concentrated attack. It was learned later, that the Master Bomber's aircraft had been hit by flak, though not fatally, and this was the cause of the loss of his signal.

S/L Turner was posted in on the 5th as the new A Flight commander, and presided over his charges' first operation that night, which was a return to St-Martin-l'Hortier. 10 Squadron made ready nineteen Halifaxes as part of a 4 Group force of 102 aircraft, and it was actually the 6th before the Melbourne crews took off, between 01.41 and 02.04, with five pilots of flight lieutenant rank leading the way. They all reached the target area to find fine weather conditions with clear skies and good visibility, and bombed on red TIs from 15,000 to 16,500 feet between 03.50 and 03.56, observing in the process that most of the bursts were occurring around the markers. Post-raid reconnaissance confirmed the accuracy of the attack, and it would not be necessary to return. Most of the 10 Squadron crews who had taken part in this operation were roused from their beds in the early afternoon in order to be ready for an early-evening take-off for a flying-bomb site at Croixdalle, located south-east of Dieppe. Twenty Halifaxes were waiting for them as they vacated the crew room and made their way to the transports that would take them out to the dispersals. They were airborne between 18.51 and 19.18 with F/Ls Hewitt, Janes, Murtha and Hart the senior pilots on duty and C Flight commander, S/L Brisbane, flying as second air-bomber with the last-mentioned. As they made their way towards the Sussex coast, they joined up with eighty-three others from the group, and all arrived at the target at the same time as a large gap opened in the clouds. This would remain for the duration of the raid, which enabled the crews to identify the aiming-point, a wedge-shaped gap in the woods. The initial red TIs overshot by a hundred yards, but this was soon corrected, and some crews aimed for the point where an access road entered the woods. Crews checked their positions by H2S and Gee, particularly if they had failed to pick up the Master Bomber's instructions, and bombing took place from 11,000 to 17,000 feet between 21.13 and 21.18 in the face of intense and accurate flak. Six crews handed slightly flak-damaged Halifaxes back to the ground crews before attending debriefing, where the consensus was of an effective attack.

The squadron remained on stand-by over the ensuing five days, and was not involved in the first major tactical support operation for the ground forces, which took place in daylight on the evening of the 7th. 467 aircraft from 1, 4, 6 and 8 Groups were sent to bomb a series of fortified villages north of Caen to clear the path for the Canadian 1st and British 2nd Armies. The decision to bomb open ground between the villages and Caen, rather than the villages themselves, proved to be an error and was, ultimately, counter-productive. S/L Leggate was posted in from 41 Base on the 11th to assume command of B Flight, but, in the event, would barely have time to settle in before being posted out again. The squadron made ready a record twenty-six Halifaxes on the 12th, six for mining duties and the remainder for a flying-bomb storage site at Thiverny, north of Paris. The latter would benefit from daylight, and the Melbourne element took off between 18.07 and 18.31 as part of an overall 4, 6 and 8 Group force of 222 aircraft. S/L Turner was the senior pilot on duty as they made their way south to pass west of London and exit the English coast near Brighton, but P/O Freeman and crew had to turn back from north of Sheffield after their starboard-outer engine failed. The others pressed on to reach the target, which was largely obscured by nine-tenths cloud, forcing the crews to establish their positions by H2S and Gee, while listening out for the instructions of the Master Bomber. Some caught sight of red TIs as the ground became visible at intervals, and the 10 Squadron crews bombed from 14,500 to 16,000 feet between 20.22 and 20.25 in the face of moderately heavy flak in barrage form. Returning crews reported a scattered attack, and there was little confidence in its effectiveness, but, at least, the enemy fighters had stayed away and no aircraft were lost. They were heading for their post-operational meal and thinking of bed by the time the gardeners took off between 00.05 and 00.12 with F/Ls Hewitt and Murtha the senior pilots on duty. They set course for the Rosemary garden off the west coast of the Schleswig-Holstein peninsular, where they encountered good visibility above the eight-tenths cloud. Positions were established by H2S and the vegetables delivered from 15,000 feet between 01.52 and 01.58, and all returned home safely to report evidence of flak and searchlights, but nothing troublesome.

Two days on stand-by preceded the next operation, which was posted on the 15th and was to be against a flying-bomb supply site in a wood at Nucourt, situated some twenty-five miles north-west of Paris. This would be the target's second attack of the day, and would follow a daylight effort by a small 8 Group force, the results of which could not be assessed because of complete cloud cover. The Melbourne element of sixteen Halifaxes took off between 23.24 and 23.45 with S/L Turner the senior pilot on duty, but soon lost the services of two of the most experienced crews when F/L Burgess turned back with an intercom issue while still over England, and F/L Murtha followed later from over the Channel because of a failed port-inner engine. The others reached the target to find nine-tenths cloud with a base at 8,000 feet and tops between 10,000 and 12,000 feet, but red TIs could be seen through gaps, and bombing took place in accordance with the Master Bomber's instructions from 8,000 to 12,000 feet between 01.42 and 01.46. Returning crews reported many bomb bursts around the markers, and bombing photos and post-raid reconnaissance confirmed an effective operation.

F/L Burcher was posted to 27 O.T.U on the 17th at the conclusion of his tour, while, later in the day, twenty-two Halifaxes were made ready for an operation that evening against the flying-bomb launching site at Mont-Candon. They took off between 18.55 and 19.26 led by pilots of flight lieutenant rank, and with the station commander, G/C Thomson, flying as second pilot with F/L Hampton. This was one of three similar targets to receive attention from a total of 132 aircraft, and there were no early returns among the Melbourne element, which were the only 4 Group representatives at this particular target. The weather in the target area was fine and clear, and bombing took place in accordance with the instructions of the Master Bomber on red TIs from 14,000 to 15,000 feet in a three-minute slot either side of 21.00. Returning crews reported concentrated bombing and no opposition, and no aircraft were lost from any of the raids.

W/C D S Radford (centre) and the crew of the MkIII Halifax LW 167 (ZA-O) - 'Farouk' at RAF Melbourne between April and October 1944. The following is a possible list of names.: On Radford's right the Navigator wearing the 'O' observer brevet was probably F/L Hensby. On his right is F/Sgt Cartwright the Wireless Operator and on his right at the end, could possibly be a F/O Taylor the Tail Gunner. He was Canadian and the RCAF had slightly darker uniforms than the RAF 'blue' material.

Stations across the Command were alerted on the 17th to a large-scale tactical operation, which would take place at dawn on the 18th in support of the British 2nd Army's Operation Goodwood. 942 aircraft were made ready to attack five fortified villages to the east of Caen, 4 Group providing 105 Halifaxes for aiming-point H-1, and 103 for H-2, and it was for the latter that 10 Squadron was called upon to provide just six aircraft. They departed Melbourne between 04.11 and 04.17 with S/L Turner the senior pilot on duty, and they flew out in ideal weather conditions, which held firm in the target area. The Master Bomber's instructions were not heard clearly by all crews, but ground features could be identified, and yellow TIs seen marking out the aiming-point. Bombing was carried out in the face of some heavy flak from 6,000 to 8,000 feet between 06.04 and 06.12, and was well-concentrated around the markers. Volumes of smoke began to drift upwards and across the target area as the force turned away, and crews were confident that they had contributed to an effective attack. American aircraft were also involved, but the RAF dropped 5,000 of the 6,800 tons of bombs, and two German divisions in particular suffered a torrid time.

F/L D Stewart RCAF and his crew

Another crew which flew 'Farouk' was that of Halifax LW187 ZA-O. L-R: Sgt G Smith (M/UG), Sgt P Galloway (RG), P/O. M Kutyn RCAF (Nav), F/L D Stewart RCAF (Pilot), F/O. G Kingsbury (BA), P/O H Lorimer (W/Op), Sgt E Cummings (FE)

FIDO Installation at RAF Melbourne 21 July 1944. View of tank and bunds

FIDO Installation at RAF Melbourne 21 July 1944. Rear view of engine pump unit.

The day's activities were not yet over for seventy-one 4 Group crews, who were briefed for an operation against marshalling yards at Vaires in company with a small number of others from 6 and 8 Groups. Nineteen Halifaxes were made ready at Melbourne, and they took off between 15.23 and 15.46 with G/C Thomson flying this time with F/L Hart. The weather was excellent all the way to the target, situated some ten miles to the west of Paris, and crews were able to identify ground features before bombing on red and yellow TIs from 12,000 to 14,500 feet between 17.53 and 18.01. Many bombs were seen to explode on the aiming-point, and smoke was rising through 5,000 feet as the force withdrew. All returning crews reported accurate flak, much of it coming from a wood north-east of the target, and seven 10 Squadron Halifaxes were handed back to their ground crews with holes in them.

S/L Leggate was posted out to 78 Squadron on the 20th, and was succeeded immediately by F/L Hart on his promotion to acting squadron leader rank. Meanwhile, twenty-four Halifaxes were made ready at Melbourne for a foray into the Ruhr to attack a synthetic oil plant at Bottrop, situated on the northern edge of the industrial region. This was to follow on the heels of two very successful attacks two nights earlier on the refineries at Wesseling and Scholven-Buer, and would be conducted on this night simultaneously with one at Homberg in the north-west of Duisburg. 4 Group provided the entire main force element of 149 Halifaxes, and also supported a small-scale operation against a flying-bomb site at Ardouval. The 10 Squadron aircraft took off between 22.52 and 23.34 with S/L Turner the senior pilot on duty, but lost the services of P/O Roberts and crew, who turned back with a dead port-outer engine when equidistant from the Norfolk coast and the Dutch mainland. F/L Hewitt and crew were just short of the Dutch coast on course for Haarlem when their port-outer engine also failed, and a fuel leak developed in the port-inner. The others pressed on, and a number of crews reported a Halifax falling in flames and exploding on the ground at 01.16. On reaching the target area some crews found up to ten-tenths cloud with tops at 3,000 to 5,000 feet, while others reported nothing other than thick haze, but there was agreement concerning the intensity of the flak, which, exploding at between 17,000 and 21,000 feet, caused damage to four Melbourne aircraft. The glow of red and green TIs could be seen through the cloud or haze, and the 10 Squadron crews checked their positions by H2S and Gee before aiming for them from 16,500 to 20,000 feet between 01.33 and 01.38. It appeared to some crews that the markers were scattered to the north of the aiming-point, and a large explosion was observed to the south at 01.36, which emitted a sheet of red flame followed by two pillars of black smoke. F/Sgt Yates and crew lost both starboard engines, but managed to reach the emergency landing strip at Woodbridge, where they landed safely. Seven Halifaxes and a Pathfinder Lancaster failed to return, and, in addition to the one mentioned above, two other Halifaxes were seen to fall in flames on the way home at 01.40 and 01.53. The former may have been 10 Squadron's MZ312, which crashed at about that time in southern Holland after being hit by flak, which killed the rear gunner. F/O Bond and the remainder of the crew parachuted to safety, but were unable to evade capture and would spend the rest of the war as guests of the Reich. LV912 came down near Schöppingen at 01.30 when on final approach to the target, and only the mid-upper gunner survived from the eight-man crew of F/O Hadley. On the credit side, the synthetic oil plant was badly damaged, as was that at Homberg, although twenty Lancasters were lost from that raid, seven of them belonging to 75(NZ) Squadron. These two operations further reduced the production capacity of this vital industry, and the effects were beginning to be felt, particularly with regard to the availability of aviation fuel.

Having not indulged in city-busting for two months, Harris issued orders for a major attack on the naval port and town of Kiel, for which a force of 629 aircraft was assembled on the 23rd. 10 Squadron answered the call by providing twenty Halifaxes, which took off between 22.41 and 23.12 with an entire posse of flight lieutenant pilots leading the way. Extensive Radio Countermeasures (RCM) provided by 100 Group allowed the force to appear suddenly and with complete surprise from behind a "Mandrel" jamming screen, and it was only at the last minute that the enemy night-fighter controllers realised that this was more than just a mining operation. All of the 10 Squadron crews reached the target area to encounter ten-tenths thin cloud with tops at 3,000 to 4,000 feet, and confirmed their positions by H2S and Gee before bombing on red and green TIs from 17,250 to 20,000 feet between 01.20 and 01.37. Flak was mostly in barrage form and exploding at 15,000 to 22,000 feet, but was not overly troublesome, and crews were able to assess that the bombing was concentrated and effective, despite being unable to hear the Master Bomber's instructions. A large yellow explosion was observed at 01.34, and the glow of fires remained visible as the force withdrew to the North Sea. Local reports confirmed that all parts of the town had been hit, with particularly severe damage in the port area and in the shipyards, and the town remained in a state of semi-paralysis for the next eight days.

The first of a three-raid series of operations against Stuttgart was posted on the 24th, for which 10 Squadron made ready twenty-one Halifaxes as part of an overall force of 614 aircraft. They departed Melbourne between 21.32 and 21.57 with S/L Hart the senior pilot on duty, but lost the services of F/O Bowmer and crew to a defective rear turret as they passed close to

Back to Melbourne, one of the few airfields to have FIDO which enable landings in foggy conditions. The acronym FIDO stayed in common use after its original 'Fog Investigation Dispersal Operation' trials.

Above left: F/Sgt R M Dixon FIDO Operator. Above right: F/Sgt R M Dixon and Colleagues

Cherbourg, and P/O Roberts and crew to an engine issue over north-central France. The others arrived in the target area over ten-tenths cloud with tops at 5,000 feet, and bombed on e.t.a, H2S and green skymarkers with yellow stars from 18,000 to 20,000 feet in accordance with the Master Bomber's instructions. The Melbourne crews were over the target between 01.43 and 01.54, and reported a glow of fires covering an area of perhaps five square miles, which remained visible for eighty miles into the return journey. No local report came out of Stuttgart for this night, but it was clearly a successful and destructive raid, although gained at a cost of seventeen Lancasters and four Halifaxes.

The second raid on Stuttgart was scheduled to take place on the night of the 25/26th, but would not involve 10 Squadron, which had other fish to fry. This was a night on which 4 Group split its strength between two flying-bomb sites and the synthetic oil refinery at Wanne-Eickel in the Ruhr. A flying-bomb site at Ferfay, situated some thirty miles to the south-east of Calais, was earmarked for attention by thirty Halifaxes, after an attack on the previous night had been abandoned part-way through by the Master Bomber. 10 Squadron put up nineteen of the aircraft and 78 Squadron the remainder, and they departed Melbourne between 22.14 and 22.42 with F/Ls Henderson, Janes and Neill the senior pilots on duty. They all arrived in the target area, where the weather was good, the red and green TIs were clearly visible, and the Master Bomber's broadcasts could be heard. Bombing took place on his instructions from 9,500 and 13,500 feet between 00.13 and 00.17, and appeared to be well-concentrated around the markers. F/L Henderson missed out after his bomb-release system failed at the critical moment. Bombing photos revealed four distinct clusters of TIs, north, south, east and south-west of the target, but smoke and haze prevented a positive assessment of the damage to the aiming-point.

A flying-bomb storage site in the Foret-de-Nieppe was posted as the target for a number of individual attacks by 4 Group aircraft in daylight on the 28th. There were to be two attacks on aiming-point G and two on aiming-point H, with 10 Squadron providing sixteen Halifaxes for the second one on the former. They took off between 16.23 and 16.40 with S/L Hart the senior pilot on duty, but lost W/O Kite almost immediately because of R/T failure. The weather was perfect over the Channel, and the crews were able to pick out the target in north-eastern France from twenty miles away even before crossing the coast. They identified the aiming-point visually, before bombing almost as one from 16,000 to 18,000 feet within a minute from 18.38. Many bomb bursts were observed to be concentrated around the aiming-point before the site became obscured by a thick mushroom of smoke rising out of the woods. That night, two further attacks were carried out by 4 Group, the second one by sixty Halifaxes, of which eight belonged to 10 Squadron. They took off between 02.19 and 02.27 with F/Ls Body and Fawdon the senior pilots on duty, and all reached the target to find good bombing conditions and red TIs marking out the aiming-point. The attack took place from 10,000 to 11,000 feet either side of 04.00, and was observed to be concentrated on the markers.

The final raid of the three on Stuttgart was carried out on this night to complete the destruction of the city's central districts. However, bright moonlight assisted the German night-fighters to infiltrate the bomber stream outbound over France, and thirty-nine Lancasters failed to return. A simultaneous raid on Hamburg, the first for a year, was only moderately successful, and cost a further eighteen Halifaxes and four Lancasters. During the course of the month, the squadron operated on fifteen days/nights, and dispatched 273 sorties for the loss of three Halifaxes and crews.

August 1944

Flying-bomb sites would continue to provide the main employment at the start of August, and 777 aircraft were detailed to attack numerous targets on the 1st. 4 Group was assigned to the sites at Prouville, Noyelle-en-Chausee and Chapelle-Notre-Dame and prepared forces accordingly. Twenty-four 10 Squadron crews were briefed for the first-mentioned, and departed Melbourne between 15.54 and 16.34 with F/Ls Body, Henderson, Janes and Neill the senior pilots on duty. F/L Neill lost his starboard-outer engine on the way out and turned back, leaving the others to press on to what they found to be a cloud-covered target situated some ten miles to the east of Abbeville. At 18.14, an order was received from the Master Bomber to abandon the operation because of the conditions, and dozens of perfectly serviceable 500 pounders found their way onto the seabed, along with thousands more from most of the other operations. W/C James was on attachment to the squadron at this time, undergoing conversion training before being appointed to command 578 Squadron at Burn.

10 Squadron remained on the ground on the 2nd, while the campaign continued at the hands of others, but orders on the 3rd had the ground crews toiling to prepare twenty-five Halifaxes to throw against the flying-bomb storage facility at Bois-de-Cassan to the north of Paris. They were part of a 4 Group force of 178 aircraft, and took off between 11.35 and 12.08 with pilots of flight lieutenant rank leading the way. There were no early returns among the Melbourne element, and they arrived at the target to find four-tenths cloud and good visibility, which enabled them to make a visual identification of the aiming-point. They bombed in accordance with the Master Bomber's instructions from 14,000 to 16,000 feet between 14.03 and 14.08, and observed many bomb bursts concentrated around the TIs and smoke passing through 1,000 feet as they turned away. Just seven of the squadron's crews were required for operations on the 4th, and they would be mining the waters of the Jellyfish garden off Brest. They took off between 22.10 and 22.17 with F/L Janes the senior pilot on duty, but lost F/O Cembrowski and crew to

F/Sgt Allen Bruce and crew. L-R: Sgt Jack Anderton (MUG) F/Sgt Bert Field (W.Op) F/O Jack Lee DFC (BA) F/Sgt Allen Bruce DFC, (Pilot), F/Sgt Tom Bigley DFC (Nav,) Sgt Ron Day (RG), Sgt Archie Tolmie (FE).

a failed H2S set. The others reached the target area some eleven miles off Cap-de-la-Chevre, and delivered their mines in good visibility from 15,000 feet between 00.47 and 01.01.

Preparations were put in hand of the 5th to assemble 742 aircraft of 4, 5, 6 and 8 Groups to be divided between the flying-bomb storage sites in the Foret-de-Nieppe and at St-Leu-d'Esserent, the latter in chalk caves north of Paris, formerly used to grow mushrooms. Twenty 10 Squadron crews took off between 11.13 and 11.42 with S/L Hart the senior 10 Squadron pilot on duty, and W/C James undertaking his first sortie as a Halifax pilot. F/Sgt Beeby and crew lost their port-outer engine shortly after take-off, and added their bombload to the increasing volume of ironware resting on the seabed. The others pushed on in good conditions to reach the target area under clear skies, and bombed on yellow TIs from 14,000 to 16,500 feet between 13.03 and 13.09, all under the watchful eye of the Master Bomber. Returning crews reported the bombing to be concentrated around the aiming-point, and smoke rising as they turned away. Following a day away from operations on the 6th, the squadron was alerted to a major activity on the 7th involving 1,019 aircraft, which would be providing tactical support for the British 2nd Army at five enemy strongpoints south of Caen. 10 Squadron made ready twenty Halifaxes, which departed Melbourne for May-sur-Orne between 20.49 and 21.13 with W/Cs Radford and James the senior pilots on duty, supported by S/L Turner. The bombing at all five aiming-points was carefully controlled by a Master Bomber, and, not satisfied with the conditions, the one at May-sur-Orne called for the operation to be abandoned at 23.05. Only 660 aircraft were allowed to bomb at the various aiming-points, and they left the ground and surrounding roads well-cratered.

Fifteen 10 Squadron Halifaxes lined up for take-off at Melbourne in the early evening of the 8th, their crews having been briefed for a flying-bomb launching site at St Philibert-Ferme, one of four such targets to be assigned to small 4 Group forces. Fourteen actually got away safely between 18.08 and 18.29 with W/C James and S/L Hart the senior pilots on duty, but HX343's elevators jammed as it tried to leave the ground in the hands of F/Sgt Thorne and crew, causing it to career off the runway and crash into trees. The Halifax was declared a write-off, but, happily, the crew emerged from the wreckage shaken but not stirred. The others continued on towards the target via the French coast at Dunkerque, and, between there and St Omer, intense flak caused damage to a number of aircraft. The skies over north-eastern France were clear, and bombing took place on red TIs from 10,000 feet in a four-minute slot either side of 20.00. It appeared to be a very concentrated attack, which caused large volumes of smoke to rise as the crews headed for home. On the following morning, 4 Group detailed 147 Halifaxes to represent the main force for a daylight attack on a fuel storage dump in the Foret-de-Mormal, situated on the Franco-Belgian border south of Mons. 10 Squadron made ready twenty-one Halifaxes, which took off between 11.08 and 11.32 with W/C James and S/L Turner the senior pilots on duty. F/Sgt Rose and crew were thwarted by the failure of their port-outer engine, leaving the others to reach the target unopposed and with good visibility to aid their cause. Yellow TIs marked out the aiming-point, and the Master bomber maintained a grip on the bombing, warning crews against bombing a stray marker to the south. The attack was carried out by the 10 Squadron crews from 8,500 to 10,000 feet between 13.05 and 13.10, and appeared to be well-concentrated around the aiming-point. A column of smoke, rising up through 8,000 feet, obscured the target from those arriving at the tail-end of the raid, and they were ordered to aim for the base of the column. Returning crews reported a number of red explosion occurring between 13.05 and 13.10, and bombing photos revealed bursts along the entire length of the dump.

4 Group detailed 104 Halifaxes on the 10th to send against the marshalling yards and a railway junction at Dijon in eastern France that night. 10 Squadron made ready twenty-one aircraft, which took off between 20.39 and 21.09 with S/L Turner the senior pilot on duty. He and his crew were led off track by a navigational error as they headed across France, and, at zero hour, found themselves to be some twenty-five miles to the west of the target, and unable to reach it in time to participate. The others had, by then, arrived at their destination to find clear skies and good visibility, and awaited the instructions of the Master Bomber. The first red TI fell slightly to the west of the planned aiming-point, and was followed by two pairs of TIs to the east. The Master Bomber ordered the bombing to be focussed on the nearer of the pairs, and the Melbourne crews complied from 9,000 to 11,000 feet between 00.20 and 00.28. Bombing photos revealed that the early stage of the attack had been well-placed, but a slight creep-back had led to a degree of undershooting, which spread across the southern reception sidings. Returning crews reported large explosions and much smoke, and, taken as a whole, the operation was deemed to be a success.

The relentless programme of operations continued on the 11th, when 4 Group was ordered to attack four flying-bomb sites with ten Halifaxes each, supported by five Pathfinder Mosquitos to carry out the marking. 10 Squadron was assigned to the Foret-de-Nieppe site, and dispatched its element from Melbourne between 17.17 and 17.30 with F/Ls Neill and Stewart the senior pilots on duty. They all reached the target to find clear conditions and good visibility, and were able to identify it visually, aided by the volume of bomb craters from previous attacks. Bombing was carried out on TIs from 13,000 to 14,500 feet between 19.29 and 19.32, and, although the markers had been a little to the north of the planned aiming-point, sufficient bombs hit the target for the raid to be considered successful. S/L Kennedy was posted to the Group Tactical School on this day, and would take with him a hard-earned DFC.

Such were the demands upon the Pathfinders to provide cover for each operation across the four campaigns currently in progress, that it was decided to launch an experimental raid on the 12th, to gauge the ability of crews to find and attack a target on H2S alone without 8 Group support. The target selected was Braunschweig (Brunswick), a culturally significant city with a long history, situated in northern Germany to the east of Hannover. It had been attacked by the Command in January and by 5 Group in April, but, on neither occasion, with outstanding success. A force of 379 Lancasters and Halifaxes was made ready, of which 4 Group provided eighty-nine of the latter, including eleven belonging to 10 Squadron. They departed Melbourne between 21.23 and 21.36 with W/C Radford the senior pilot on duty, and all but one reached the target area to find thin, scattered cloud and good visibility. The absentee was MZ773, which contained the crew of F/O Saynor, who were on their thirty-eighth and probably final operation of their tour. They had just crossed the German coast over the Ems Estuary, and were at 18,000 feet, when they fell victim to a "friendly fire" incident involving another Halifax. The port-outer engine and N°4 fuel tank caught fire, and the Halifax was abandoned to crash at 00.10 a mile-and-a-half north of Papenburg, while the crew landed safely in the arms of their captors. Meanwhile, some 150 miles to the east, their squadron colleagues were establishing their positions by H2S before delivering their bombs from 16,000 to 18,000 feet between 00.10 and 00.22. They observed what appeared to be a concentrated attack that caused explosions and fires, but was, in fact, scattered with no point of concentration, and some bombs fell onto outlying communities up to twenty miles to the south. The local flak defence were moderate in intensity, but night-fighters were much in evidence, and it would be an expensive night for the Command. Seventeen Lancasters and ten Halifaxes failed to return, which compounded the disappointment that main force crews were not able to perform to the highest standard without a Pathfinder presence.

A day off on the 13th allowed the crews to draw breath before being roused from their beds on the 14th to prepare for a tactical support operation. The targets were enemy ground forces facing the 3rd Canadian Division in the Normandy battle area, for which twenty-three Halifaxes were fuelled and bombed up at Melbourne. They were to join forces with eighty-three others from the Group, as part of an overall force of 805 aircraft assigned to seven aiming-points. Each was to be marked initially by Oboe, and backed up visually by the Pathfinder heavy brigade, and, because of the close proximity of friendly troops, a Master Bomber and deputy would be on hand to direct the attacks. The 10 Squadron crews were divided between Tractable 21A and Tractable 22, eighteen for the former and five for the latter, and the first element took off between 11.41 and 12.06 with S/L Hart the senior pilot on duty and W/C James guesting with the squadron for the final time before moving on to 578 Squadron. There were no early returns, and all crossed the French coast north of Caen in perfect conditions, listening out for the instructions from the Master Bomber. They carried out their part in the proceedings from 6,000 to 7,500 feet between 14.02 and 14.06, aiming for the centre of a cluster of red TIs or on the smoke in accordance with instructions. The second element took off between 12.42 and 12.45, and also bombed on yellow TIs from 6,500 to 7,000 feet at 14.39. It was during this stage of the operation that bombs began to fall among Canadian troops, who identified their positions with yellow flares, which may have been confused with the yellow TIs. The Canadians claim that the bombing came first, while Bomber Command asserted that the flares preceded the bombing. Whatever the truth, thirteen Canadian soldiers lost their lives, fifty-three sustained injury, and many guns and vehicles were hit.

In preparation for his new night offensive against Germany, Harris launched a thousand aircraft by daylight on the 15th against nine night-fighter airfields in Holland and Belgium. 4 Group was assigned to Eindhoven in Holland and Tirlemont/Gassoncourt in Belgium, and twenty 10 Squadron crews were briefed for the latter along with eighty-nine others. They took off between 09.41 and 10.06 with S/L Turner the senior pilot on duty, and all reached the target area to find excellent conditions. Depending on the state of the target on their arrival, crews bombed on red TIs, smoke and or visual identification, but all in accordance with the Master Bomber's instructions, and entirely unopposed. The bombing appeared to be concentrated across the airfield and on hangars and buildings, and post-raid reconnaissance confirmed the effectiveness of the operation.

The return to Germany began on the night of the 16/17th, when Lancasters went to Stettin, and destroyed fifteen hundred houses and twenty-nine industrial premises, while sinking or damaging 20,000 tons of shipping and killing 1,150 people. A simultaneous raid on Kiel by a mixed force achieved only moderate success, while 10 Squadron remained at home. On the 17th, 4 Group gathered a force of seventy-nine Halifaxes to attack shipping at Brest, for which 10 Squadron detailed twenty-three aircraft. They took off between 13.09 and 13.39 with S/Ls Hart and Turner the senior pilots on duty, and all reached the target to find seven to ten-tenths cloud partially obscuring the view. Fifteen crews managed to identify ground features as in the coastline, breakwaters and docks, and released their bombs from 13,000 to 14,000 feet between 16.00 and 16.12, while the remaining eight tried their best before giving up and going home. Some returning crews reported observing bomb bursts, but the majority were unable to offer an assessment, and two sustained slight flak damage.

It was still somewhat risky to fly over the Ruhr by daylight, and so an attack on the synthetic oil refinery at Sterkrade, a northern suburb of Oberhausen, was planned for the night of the 18/19th, while a simultaneous raid was visited upon Bremen and other operations were directed elsewhere to involve more than a thousand sorties in all. 10 Squadron made ready eighteen aircraft for the 210-strong all-Halifax main force, for which 8 Group Mosquitos and Lancasters would mark. Preceding them into the air between 21.13 and 21.20, and led by F/Ls Janes and Stewart, were four gardeners, whose destination was the Gironde Estuary that led to the port of Bordeaux. The main element departed Melbourne between 22.14 and 22.37 with F/Ls Body, Henderson, Neill and Pearson the senior pilots on duty, and lost the services of F/O Blackwell and crew, whose DR compass and air-positioning indicator (API) failed. The others reached the target to find thin four-tenths cloud but excellent visibility, and bombed on red TIs from 15,000 to 20,000 feet between 00.56 and 01.01. F/O Horne and crew had to make a second run after his bomb doors failed to open first time around, and they reported a good concentration of bombing, as did other returning crews. A large red explosion was witnessed at 00.56, and others, including one with yellow/orange flash, were observed at 01.02 and shortly thereafter. A post-raid analysis concluded that this was a highly effective operation that had caused extensive damage to the plant and would have cost production. Meanwhile, the gardeners had planted their vegetables into the briefed locations off Pointe-de-la-Coubre by H2S-fix from 8,000 feet at around 01.20, and returned safely to report no opposition and uneventful sorties all round.

After a week away from operations for most squadrons, crews were probably beginning to get fidgety at the lack of action by the 25th, when, during the course of the evening and night, 1,460 sorties would be launched. The main operation of the night was against the Opel motor works at Rüsselsheim near Frankfurt, while 5 Group tried its hand at nearby Darmstadt and 334 aircraft were sent against eight coastal batteries in the Brest area. First, though, 4 Group sent 125 Halifaxes to three flying-bomb sites in the Pas-de-Calais at Chapelle-Notre-Dame, Wemars Cappel and Watten, ninety-two of them assigned to the last-mentioned, of which seven were provided by 10 Squadron. They departed Melbourne between 18.32 and 18.41 with no senior pilots on duty, and all arrived at the target to find good visibility, red TIs marking out the aiming-point, and a Master Bomber on hand to direct proceedings. The bombing was carried out on red TIs from 12,000 to 14,000 feet between 20.31 and 20.34, and all but two aircraft returned safely. One of the missing was 10 Squadron's MZ844, which crashed beyond the target after bombing, killing F/O Walton and four of his crew, while the two survivors managed to retain their freedom. As the above crews were closing in on the target, seventeen other 10 Squadron crews were taking off between 19.54 and 20.15 bound for one of eight coastal batteries in the Brest region. The squadron ORB refers to Ronsceval as the target, but the group ORB cites Pont-Scorff, which is situated a little to the north of Lorient. F/L Pearson lost his port-inner engine immediately after take-off, leaving the rest of the Melbourne element to reach the target area, where they found a band of ten-tenths cloud at 4,000 to 5,000 feet, which completely obscured the ground. The illuminator flares were disappearing into the cloud tops as they approached, and the Master Bomber called some crews down to below the cloud base, from where the yellow TIs could be seen. F/O Horne dropped through the cloud to 2,500 feet, and bombed from there at 23.25, while F/L Henderson descended to 4,000 feet and made three runs across the aiming-point before bombing at 23.36. These were the only two 10 Squadron crews to carry out an attack before the Master Bomber abandoned the operation and sent the crews home with their bombs.

Eleven 10 Squadron Halifaxes were made ready on the 26th to participated in mining operations in the Forget-me-not garden in Kiel Bay, where they would hope to sneak in under cover of a major raid on the port by more than 350 aircraft, while 5 Group ventured further east at extreme range to bomb the port of Königsberg (now Kaliningrad in Lithuania). They departed Melbourne between 21.33 and 21.46 with F/Ls Fawdon, Henderson, Pearson and Stewart the senior pilots on duty, and all reached the garden area to find good enough conditions to identify pinpoints visually, before confirming them by H2S and delivering the mines into the briefed locations from 15,000 feet between 00.30 and 00.43.

On the 27th, 4 Group was handed the unenviable task of sending a force of 216 Halifaxes in broad daylight to bomb the Rhein-Preussen synthetic oil refinery at Homberg in the Ruhr, with 8 Group Oboe Mosquitos and Lancasters to take care of the marking. This would be the first major daylight operation over Germany by the Command since August 1941, and the two-wave attack would benefit from an umbrella of nine squadrons of Spitfires outbound and seven on the return journey. Just seven 10 Squadron crews were briefed, and they took off as part of the first wave between 11.58 and 12.12 with F/L Body the senior pilot on duty. The nose of F/Sgt Rebick's aircraft began to fill with smoke, forcing him to turn back, but the others continued on to the target, where a large gap in the clouds provided a clear sight of the ground in good visibility, and the Master Bomber's broadcasts were strong and clear. Bombing was carried out on his instructions on green TIs from 17,000 to 19,000 feet between 14.01 and 14.06, and appeared to be well-concentrated around the aiming-point. A heavy explosion and sheet of red flame was witnessed at 14.01, and a large column of blue smoke was rising through 10,000 feet as the force turned away. Cloud and smoke created more challenging conditions for the second wave, and rendered an accurate assessment impossible, although some bombing photos showed that Duisburg and its environs had been hit.

With the Pas-de-Calais about to fall into Allied hands, the final operations against flying bomb launching and storage sites were carried out by small forces at twelve locations by daylight on the 28th in the absence of 4 Group. The squadron operated for the final time in the month on the night of the 29/30th, when dispatching a dozen Halifaxes on gardening sorties to the Sweet Pea region of the Cadet Channel in the western Baltic. They took off between 22.38 and 22.53 with F/Ls Fawdon and Janes the senior pilots on duty, and all reached the target area to encounter eight to ten-tenths cloud at around 7,000 feet. Positions were fixed by H2S and the mines delivered into the briefed locations from 15,000 feet either side of 02.00. During the course of a busy month, S/L Brisbane was awarded a DSO, and the squadron operated on eighteen days/nights, dispatching 316 sorties for the loss of three Halifaxes and two crews.

September 1944

The principal theme in September was the campaign to return to Allied control the three French ports still in enemy hands, Le Havre, Boulogne and Calais, and this would occupy a large part of the month. Although the flying-bomb threat had been nullified, that of the V-2 had not, and twenty-two 10 Squadron crews themselves at briefing before dawn on the 1st to learn of their part in the forthcoming operation against a rocket storage site at Lumbres, situated fifteen miles south-east of Calais. They were to join forces with twenty-four others from 78 Squadron, while fifty Halifaxes drawn from six 4 Group squadrons attended to a similar target at La Pourchinte, each element supported by 8 Group Mosquitos and Lancasters. The Melbourne crews took off between 06.05 and 06.41 with W/C Radford the senior pilot on duty, but lost the services of W/O Horne RAAF and crew, whose port-inner engine failed at 07.58 shortly after crossing the English coast at Beachy Head. They turned east towards Dungeness on the Kent coast, only for the port-outer engine to fail at 08.30, at which point they jettisoned part of their bomb load into the sea and set course for Manston. They were three miles short of landing when it became necessary to put the Halifax down in a field to the west of the airfield, whereupon the port-outer engine erupted in flames. The crew scrambled clear unscathed, and extinguished the blaze, but could not save MZ847 from being declared a write-off. This was the second hairy incident for the Thorne crew, who had survived a take-off crash three weeks earlier. The others, meanwhile, had reached the target to find excellent conditions, and were able to identify the northern aiming-point both visually and with the aid of markers, and most were able to hear the instructions from the Master Bomber. They bombed unopposed from 13,000 to 14,000 feet between 08.20 and 08.28, and observed what appeared to be a concentrated and effective attack.

As they withdrew, the 78 Squadron element arrived at the southern aiming-point, and carried out their part in the operation with equal effectiveness. On return, F/O Lavalley reported being unable to release his load after the failure of the master switch, and some bombs were jettisoned over the sea during the return flight. A post-raid analysis revealed that the marking for the northern aiming-point had drifted towards the south, while that for the southern aiming-point had drifted to the north, and while the operation was entirely successful, it was likely that the southern aiming-point had received the greater weight of bombs.

A force of 675 aircraft was assembled on the 3rd to attack six airfields in southern Holland, for which 10 Squadron made ready nineteen Halifaxes as part of a 4 Group contribution of 105 aircraft assigned to Soesterberg, situated some twenty-five miles south-east of Amsterdam. A second 4 Group force, also of 105 Halifaxes, would attack the aerodrome at Venlo, perched on the frontier with Germany west of the Ruhr. The Melbourne element took off between 15.46 and 16.14 with W/C Radford the senior pilot on duty,

Sgt Betty Allan, an MT driver at Melbourne in 1944

supported by S/L Hart, and all reached the target to encounter five-tenths rain-bearing cloud with tops at 6,000 feet and moderate visibility. Despite the conditions, most crews were able to identify the aiming-point visually through the gaps, and bombed on red TIs in the centre of the airfield in accordance with instructions from the Master Bomber. The attack took place in the face of moderate flak from 14,500 to 18,000 feet between 17.30 and 17.42, and was concentrated around the markers. A large explosion was witnessed at 17.37, and returning crews also reported the runways to be cratered.

The first of six operations to be mounted against enemy strong-points around Le Havre was launched on the 5th, while 10 Squadron remained at home and focussed on training for the ensuing four days. Further operations to unseat the Germans from Le Havre and its surrounds took place on the 6th, 8th and 9th, although poor weather conditions severely restricted the numbers actually bombing on the 8th, and the raid of the 9th was abandoned entirely. Eight aiming-points were earmarked for attention at various times during the 11th, and these operations would involve 992 aircraft. 10, 76 and 78 Squadrons each made ready seventeen Halifaxes for the early shift to attack a coastal battery outside the port, and the Melbourne element took off between 06.06 and 06.31 with S/L Turner the senior pilot on duty. There were no early returns, and all reached the target to find a layer of three to five-tenths cloud between 6,000 and 12,000 feet, but, otherwise, good visibility. The Master Bomber instructed the crews to ignore the green TIs and to bomb the most northerly of the reds, and, apart from a few bombs seen to fall into the sea, the majority were concentrated around the markers. Sixteen 10 Squadron crews attacked from 6,000 to 10,000 feet between 07.59 and 08.11, but P/O Bridgett and crew suffered a total hang-up and brought part of his load home after jettisoning the rest.

The day's activities were not yet over for six 10 Squadron crews and ninety-seven others from the group, who were assigned to attack an aiming-point coded Alvis I, while similar numbers from the group attended to Alvis II. The Melbourne crews were airborne between 15.02 and 15.12 with F/L Stewart the senior pilot on duty, and all reached the target to find up to five-tenths patchy cloud at 4,000 to 5,000 feet, but, otherwise excellent bombing conditions. The Master Bomber instructed the crews to bomb the red TIs and ignore the greens, which the 10 Squadron crews complied with from 9,000 to 10,000 feet between 16.43 and 16.53, and observed their hardware to fall around the markers. A few hours after the final assault on the 11th, which also included a 4 Group contribution, the German garrison surrendered to British forces. 10 Squadron was not involved, but was active, never the less, on gardening duties in the Silverthorn region of the Kattegat off north-eastern Jutland. The ten Halifaxes took off between 19.48 and 19.59 with F/Ls Janes and Stewart the senior pilots on duty, but F/O Cembrowski and crew abandoned their part in the operation at Flamborough Head because of technical issues, and F/Sgt Beeby and crew were forced to turn back at 22.05 after the starboard-inner engine failed with Esbjerg in sight. The others pressed on across Jutland to find excellent conditions in the target area, and all mines were deposited by H2S-fix into the briefed locations from 15,000 feet between 22.41 and 23.00. That night, 5 Group went to Darmstadt in southern Germany, and devastated the relatively intact city of 120,000 residents. An estimated 12,300 people lost their lives and seventy thousand were rendered homeless in a demonstration of the power invested in the hands of just one single group.

A busy day for 4 Group on the 12th began with participation in a daylight attack on the Scholven-Buer synthetic oil plant to the north of Gelsenkirchen in the Ruhr, while other elements from 6 and 8 Groups went for similar targets at Dortmund and Wanne-Eickel. Twelve 10 Squadron crews took off between 11.04 and 11.23 with S/L Turner the senior pilot on duty, and joined up with the rest of the 134-strong 4 Group force as they made their way to the southern coast of Holland. S/L Turner and crew abandoned their sortie when the starboard-inner engine failed with the Dutch coast on the horizon, while P/O Moss and crew made it to the Scheldt Estuary before turning back with a feathered port-inner engine. The others pressed on to reach the target under clear skies with ground haze, and a smoke-screen added to the challenge of identifying ground features. The red TIs fell within the boundaries of the target, one cluster to the north-west of the aiming-point and two others to the south and south-east, and these were bombed by the 10 Squadron crews from 17,000 to 19,000 feet between 13.32 and 13.38 in accordance with the Master Bomber's instructions. Flak was intense, causing various degrees of damage to sixty aircraft, but the overriding impression was of thick, black smoke rising skyward as the bombers turned away, and this prevented an assessment of the results.

The above aircraft had landed by the time that ten Halifaxes lined up for take-off from Melbourne to join forces with 109 others from the group for a city-busting attack on Münster, the first on this target for fifteen months. They took to the air between 16.01 and 16.23 with F/L Fawdon the senior pilot on duty, and all reached the flatlands to the north of the Ruhr to find cloudless skies and ground haze. The bombing was carried out onto red TIs from 17,000 to

19,600 feet between 18.39 and 18.45 in accordance with the Master Bomber's instructions, and started in the marshalling yards before spreading throughout the town, and setting off many fires. The flak was intense, and many aircraft sustained damage, among them MZ309, which was hit four minutes after bombing as it left the target in the hands of P/O Winter and crew. The starboard-inner engine had to be feathered, and the journey to the Dutch coast began with two Halifaxes from other squadrons flying alongside as escorts. One sped off as they reached the North Sea, but the other remained in contact until the Suffolk coast was reached, and a safe landing was carried out at the emergency strip at Woodbridge, where, after an inspection, the Halifax was declared to be beyond economical repair. F/O Bowmer and crew had their starboard wing and N°5 tank holed over the target, and, when smoke began to trail behind the starboard-outer engine, two Lancasters appeared to dispense Window in large quantities, and six Spitfires escorted the wounded Halifax out of the target area. F/O Cembrowski also returned on three engines and F/O Harrison and crew handed MZ793 back to the ground crew with holes in the fuselage. That night, 1, 3 and 8 Groups pounded the western half of Frankfurt, while 5 Group went to Stuttgart and flattened the northern and western districts close to the centre, creating a mini-firestorm in the process.

4 Group sent out orders on the 13th to prepare for a daylight operation against the Nordstern Synthetic oil plant (Gelsenberg A. G.) at Gelsenkirchen, and one hundred Halifaxes were made ready, seventeen of them provided by 10 Squadron. They departed Melbourne between 15.56 and 16.25 with S/L Turner the senior pilot on duty, and all reached the target area to be greeted by small amounts of low cloud with haze, large amounts of heavy flak and an effective smoke-screen. The red TIs fell about eight hundred yards to the south-east of the aiming-point, and the Master Bomber called upon the crews to undershoot, those from 10 Squadron delivering their attacks from 19,000 to 21,000 feet between 18.31 and 18.34. F/O Brown made two runs across the target without spotting any TIs, but picked out a canal and the racecourse before dropping his load on the marshalling yards. He and his crew were not alone in failing to locate the primary target, as bombing photographs and post-raid analysis revealed that the attack had been very scattered, and that only around thirty aircraft had aimed for the markers, while most of the others had area-bombed within the boundaries of Gelsenkirchen and neighbouring Wattenscheid. About seven crews had strayed over Recklinghausen and set off fires within the town, but, despite reports of large explosions by returning crews, the operation against the oil plant was not an outstanding success and cost two Halifaxes and crews.*

A day off on the 14th preceded a return to night operations for sixteen 10 Squadron crews on the 15th, as they were detailed to be part of a force of 490 aircraft from 1, 4, 6 and 8 Groups bound for Kiel. The Melbourne element took off between 22.08 and 22.33 with S/L Turner the senior pilot on duty, and flew out in poor weather conditions which improved in the target area to just three-tenths cloud cover. Most crews were able to pick out some ground detail, aided by illuminator flares, but bombing took place on yellow, red and green TIs from 16,500 to 22,000 feet between 01.15 and 01.22. Returning crews were confident of a successful night's work, and the glow from the burning town could be seen from 120 miles into the return journey. Bombing photos were plotted at between two and four miles to the north-east of the planned aiming-point, and two explosions were witnessed at 01.20 and 01.23 which emitted large amounts of smoke. A post-raid analysis based on the bombing photos revealed extensive damage to the old town and port area, and this was confirmed by local reports, which also commented on the number of bombs falling outside of the built-up area.

With Le Havre now back in Allied hands, attention turned upon Boulogne, and a force of 762 aircraft was put together on the 17th to use against enemy strong-points in and around the port. 4 Group was assigned to aiming-points 1B and 5, and detailed seventy-two Halifaxes for the former and 105 for the latter, including eighteen provided by 10 Squadron. They took off between 09.26 and 09.52 with F/Ls Body, Henderson and Janes the senior pilots on duty, and all reached the target area to find two to three-tenths cloud with tops at 7,000 feet and good visibility. A Master Bomber was on hand to direct the attack, but, many crews failed to hear him or found his broadcasts too indistinct to be understood, and this left them to their own devices. Those bombing towards the end of the attack seemed to have better reception and followed his instructions, the Melbourne element bombing on red or green TIs from 9,000 to 10,000 feet between 11.08 and 11.14. Post-raid analysis revealed that the markers had fallen in three distinct clusters, five hundred and a thousand yards west of the aiming-point and fifteen hundred yards north-west, and these had attracted the main weight of bombs. Never the less, three thousand tons of bombs were sufficient to persuade the enemy of the futility of resistance, and the port fell into Allied hands soon afterwards.

The first of series of attacks on enemy positions around Calais was mounted on the 20th, when more than six hundred aircraft produced good results in favourable conditions. 10 Squadron remained at home and had been away from the operational scene for six days when orders were received on the 23rd to prepare twenty-two aircraft for that night's operation to Neuss in the Ruhr. They were to join 527 other aircraft from 1, 3, 4 and 8 Groups, and took off between 18.55 and 19.33 with F/Ls *, Fawdon and Kerr the senior pilots on duty. P/O Winter turned back after his bomb-aimer became ill, but the others continued on to find ten-tenths cloud completely obscuring the target, and through which the TIs were barely visible. It appears that the Pathfinders had not prepared a skymarking plan, and there was no Master Bomber to direct the attack, leaving the crews to bomb on estimated positions and the glow of fires. The 10 Squadron crews delivered their loads from 15,000 to 19,500 feet between 21.31 and 21.36 without being able to assess the outcome, but there were many reports of bomb bursts and large explosions lighting up the clouds. Bombing photos were plotted as being over the docks and industrial districts, and this was confirmed by a short local report, which mentioned 617 houses and fourteen public buildings being destroyed or seriously damaged. Five Lancasters and two Halifaxes failed to return, of which MZ574, and the crew of P/O Kite RCAF represented 10 Squadron. News eventually came through that the pilot and mid-upper gunner had died in the crash in Belgium on the way to the target, but that five others were safe, albeit in enemy hands.

A force of fewer than two hundred aircraft carried out the second raid on Calais and its surrounds, but very low cloud persuaded the Master Bomber to call a halt to proceedings after two-thirds had bombed. 10 Squadron received orders on the 24th to make ready twenty Halifaxes for the following day to join a force of 872 aircraft detailed to continue the assault on the port and its occupants. 4 Group was assigned to two aiming-points, and the Melbourne crews took off between 06.32 and 07.03 bound for 2B with S/L Turner the senior pilot on duty. On arrival in the target area the cloud base was found to be below 2,000 feet, and the Master Bomber abandoned the operation at 08.24. It was a similar story at some of the other aiming-points, and

10 Sqn Halifax III MZ315 ZA G. F/L G Neill and crew, September 1944. P/O A Perry (B/A), Sgt E Hart (RG), F/L G Neill (Pilot), P/O R Mason, Sgt R Jones, (M/UG) F/Sgt C Thorne (W/Op), Sgt I Underwood (FE)

only a third of those dispatched were allowed to bomb. It was on this day that 4 Group Halifaxes were pressed into service to carry motor transport petrol to airfields in Belgium. Seventy sorties were flown on this day by aircraft from 77, 102, 346 and 347 Squadrons, each loaded with 165 jerricans, which represented 750 gallons per aircraft, and these flights would continue for eight days, by which time 435 sorties would have been completed to deliver 325,000 gallons.

10 Squadron's effort on the 26th, and that of eighty-five others from the group, was to be directed against a heavy gun position of Cap Gris Nez, which had been firing at Bomber Command aircraft during the previous attacks. The Melbourne element of eighteen Halifaxes got away between 08.02 and 08.43 with S/L Hart the senior pilot on duty, and all arrived in the target area to find excellent conditions, no opposition and a Master Bomber to direct proceedings. Red TIs marked out the aiming-point, and these were bombed accurately from 8,500 to 10,000 feet between 10.05 and 10.11 in accordance with instructions. Many bomb bursts were observed as was a large explosion at 10.06, and smoke was rising through 6,000 feet as the force turned away. It was similar fare on the following day, when sixteen Halifaxes departed Melbourne between 08.50 and 09.28 with F/Ls Fawdon, Henderson, Neill and Stewart the senior pilots on duty. They were part of an overall force of 341 aircraft from 1, 3, 4 and 8 Groups, and were assigned to a coastal battery at aiming-point 14 in company with twenty-six other Halifaxes belonging to 76 and 578 Squadrons. The target area was concealed by ten-tenths cloud with a base at between 4,000 and 6,000 feet, but the Master Bomber called the force down beneath the

murk from where the red TIs were clearly visible. Bombing took place from 4,000 to 5,000 feet between 10.44 and 10.46 in accordance with instructions, and returning crews confirmed that most of the bombing had fallen within the marked area. Two large explosions were witnessed at 10.43 and 10.45, and a number of crews reported a bridge disintegrating before their eyes.

The final operations towards the recapture of Calais took place on the 28th, when four aiming-points were targeted around the port and six at Cap Gris Nez, shortly after which, Canadian forces marched in to take the garrison's surrender. During the course of the month, W/C Radford was awarded a DSO to add to his DFC and AFC, and the squadron carried out operations on twelve days/nights, dispatching 223 sorties for the loss of two Halifaxes and one crew.

October 1944

Having now discharged his primary obligation to SHAEF, Harris would turn his attention fully towards industrial Germany, with a particular emphasis on oil production. A gentle start to the new month saw 10 Squadron inactive until the 4th, when nine crews were briefed for mining operations in the Silverthorn garden of the Kattegat, where they would be joined by ten others from 78 Squadron. The Melbourne element took off between 17.03 and 17.48 with F/Ls Fawdon and Stewart the senior pilots on duty, and all reached the target area without incident to find seven to ten-tenths cloud with tops at between 10,000 and 14,000 feet and good horizontal visibility. Positions were established by H2S, before the mines were delivered into the briefed locations from 15,000 feet between 20.38 and 20.54, and safe returns made to report spirited but ineffective flak activity from the Danish coast.

4 Group ordered a maximum effort on the 6th after receiving orders to conduct operations over the Ruhr against the synthetic oil refineries at Scholven-Buer on the edge of Gelsenkirchen, and Sterkrade-Holten in Oberhausen. 128 Halifaxes, including fourteen from 10 Squadron, were assigned to the former, and 126 to the latter, while forty-six 8 Group Lancasters and twenty Mosquitos were divided between them to take care of the marking. The Melbourne element took off between 14.10 and 14.50 with F/Ls Fawdon and Stewart the senior pilots on duty, and soon lost P/O Yates and crew to an engine issue. The others reached the target area to be greeted by the anticipated intense and accurate heavy flak, but, at least, the visibility was good enough for some crews to establish their positions visually. There was a choice of red, green and yellow TIs for the crews to aim at, and those from 10 Squadron bombed mostly on the reds from 17,000 to 18,500 feet between 17.00 and 17.03 in accordance with the Master Bombers instructions. As thick smoke began to obscure the target, he was unable to correct a drift towards the south-west, and a proportion of the bombing probably fell a little wide of the mark. Four Halifaxes and two Lancasters were lost, three of the former belonging to 78 Squadron, two of which were involved in a collision over Holland, and eleven 10 Squadron aircraft would arrive home with flak damage. They were still over the North Sea homebound when five Halifaxes departed Melbourne between 17.54 and 18.06 and set course for the Rosemary garden in the Heligoland Bight, between the island of Heligoland itself and the Elbe Estuary. F/Ls Body and Henderson were the senior pilots on duty as all five reached the garden in good weather conditions to find varying amounts of thin cloud from nil to five-tenths at 2,000 to 3,000 feet. They established their positions by H2S before planting their vegetables as briefed from 12,000 feet between 20.13 and 20.19.

The new Ruhr offensive opened that night at Dortmund, for which a force of 529 aircraft was made ready, 293 of them provided by the Canadian 6 Group. The operation was an outstanding success, and a foretaste of what was in store, not just for the Ruhr, but towns and cities in wider Germany also, many of which had not been targeted before. While this operation was in progress, 5 Group devastated Bremen, where almost five thousand buildings were destroyed or seriously damaged, and much of the city's industry, including its shipyards and aircraft factories, suffered major disruption to production. 10 Squadron's work for the day was over by this time, but the morrow would bring further activity, and much pain to the towns of Kleve (Cleves) and Emmerich, which were just four miles apart to the south and north

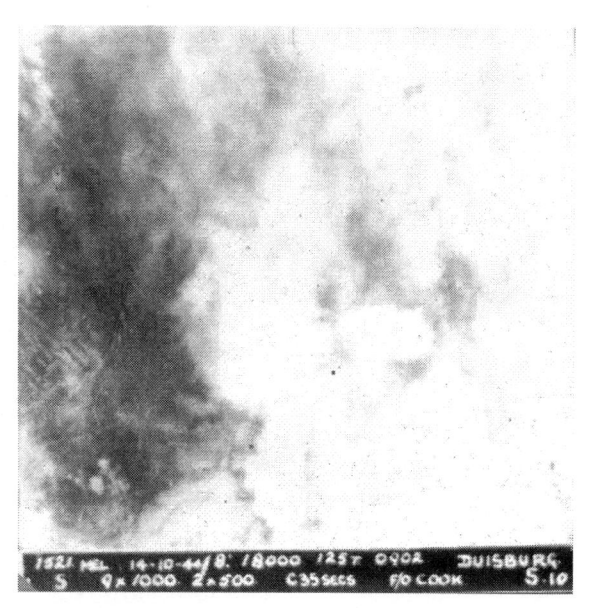

10 Sqn Target photo 14th October 1944 Duisburg Pilot F/O Cook

respectively of the River Rhine close to the Dutch frontier. They were to be dismantled by bombing to disrupt enemy communications in the area of the recently failed Operation Market Garden. 10 Squadron made ready eighteen Halifaxes to contribute to 4 Group's effort of 249 aircraft, which would join elements of 3 and 8 Groups to form an overall force of 351 aircraft. The 10 Squadron element departed Melbourne between 11.35 and 12.02 with F/Ls Evans, Kerr and Stewart the senior pilots on duty, and there were no early returns as they made their way in good conditions to make landfall at the Dutch coast near The Hague. F/O Moss and crew lost their starboard-inner engine at 13.10, but jettisoned some bombs to lighten the load and continued on to the target, where cloud was encountered with a base at around 13,000 feet. The Master Bomber called the crews down to make their attacks from beneath it, where the visibility was excellent apart from a little haze, and ground features could be identified. Red and green TIs marked out the aiming-point, and these were bombed from 9,500 to 13,500 feet between 14.02 and 14.07 in accordance with the Master Bomber's instructions. The bombing fell initially a little to the north, before spreading back to leave the entire town enveloped in smoke, and it was clear that massive damage had been inflicted. It was a similar story on the other side of the Rhine, where more than 2,400 buildings were destroyed.

W/C Radford was posted to Bomber Command HQ during w.e.f the 9th, and was succeeded by W/C Shannon, who came in from 41 Base, and began his conversion to the Mk III Halifax under the guidance of F/L Fawdon on the 8th. Bochum was posted as the target on the 9th, for which a force of 435 aircraft was assembled, 375 of them Halifaxes representing 4 and 6 Groups. They would be accompanied by ABC Lancasters of 101 Squadron to provide a RCM screen and 8 Group Lancasters and Mosquitos to take care of the marking. Twenty 10 Squadron Halifaxes departed Melbourne between 17.11 and 17.41 with S/Ls Hart and Turner the senior pilots on duty, and made their way via the southern approach to the Ruhr over the French coast at Calais. F/O Brown and crew were well on their way when the port-outer engine failed and persuaded them to turn back. The others pressed on to reach the target, where five to ten-tenths thin cloud prevailed at 12,000 feet, and red and yellow skymarkers were deployed by the Pathfinder element in large numbers but not in concentration. This led to a scattering of bombs, the 10 Squadron crews releasing their loads from 15,000 to 20,000 feet between 20.32 and 20.43, and observing many explosion and the glow of fires reflected in the cloud. The impression was of an effective attack, and this was the thought of returning crews at debriefing. Local reports admitted to damage in southern districts and the destruction of or serious to 140 houses, but this was not commensurate with the effort expended.

Operation Hurricane was devised by the leaders of the RAF and the USAAF 8th Air Force as a series of massive operations against major industrial centres to demonstrate to the enemy the overwhelming power of the Allied bomber forces ranged against it. The first target for Bomber Command was to be Duisburg, for which a force of 1,013 aircraft was made ready for an early launch on the 14th, to arrive on target shortly after breakfast time. 4 Group contributed 256 Halifaxes, of which twenty-three represented 10 Squadron, and they departed Melbourne between 06.30 and 07.06 with S/L Turner the senior pilot on duty. F/L Sifton and crew returned early after losing both starboard engines, leaving the others to press on to the French coast near Dunkerque, and bypass Lille before turning sharply to port to cross Belgium between Antwerp and Brussels for the run to the target. They arrived to find three to ten-tenths thin cloud at 10,000 feet, but, otherwise, favourable weather conditions, and most were able to establish their position visually before bombing on red TIs from 17,000 to 19,000 feet between 09.01 and 09.10 in accordance with instructions from the Master Bomber. The cloud prevented some crews from observing the fall of their bombs, while others specified the marshalling yards, the Rhine docks and the built-up area generally as the points of impact. P/O Bishop and crew lost their starboard-outer engine on the bombing-run, but carried on and would arrive home safely, while W/O Davies and crew survived being hit by flak shortly after bombing, and sustained damage to the electrical system and the port-outer engine. The flight engineer picked up a leg wound, but they, also, would return safely to land at Manston on three engines. P/O Bridgett and crew landed at Carnaby with a damaged wing and hydraulics issues. Returning crews described a concentrated attack, and the target area appearing to be on fire from end to end, with thick smoke beginning to obscure the ground as they withdrew.

A total of 4,500 tons of bombs had been dropped on the already-ruined city, but its ordeal was not yet over, as plans were already in hand to turn-round the force and send it back that night. 4 Group managed to offer 228 Halifaxes to the force of 1,005 aircraft being made ready during the course of the day, and 10 Squadron had seventeen Halifaxes fuelled and bombed up in time for take-off between 00.33 and 00.59, with S/L Turner the senior pilot on duty. F/O Yates and crew suffered a hydraulics issue while climbing-out, and they were forced to abandon their sortie, leaving the others to follow a similar course to that adopted for the earlier raid. The skies were almost clear of cloud as the bombers approached, and, despite haze and lingering smoke, it was possible to visually identify a distinctive bend in the Rhine and the large Ruhrort docks area. The bombing by the Melbourne element took place on a selection of red, green and yellow TIs from 17,000 to 19,000 feet between 03.24 and 03.32, and W/O Banks and crew were lucky to survive being hit by bombs from above which damaged both wings. Although the squadron ORB makes no mention of the event, LV908 apparently crash-landed at base with flak damage, but F/O Atkins and his crew emerged unscathed from the wreckage. Returning crews reported a concentrated attack, with many explosions and fires, the latter remaining visible for a hundred miles into the return flight. It was a remarkable feat to prepare and dispatch 2,018 bombers in eighteen hours, and it hammered home the message of "overwhelming" superiority. Another remarkable fact was the absence from both operations of 5 Group, which took advantage of the commotion over the Ruhr on this night to finally land a devastating blow on Braunschweig (Brunswick).

S/L J H Calder arrived from 51 Squadron on the 15th to assume command of C Flight, presumably to succeed the rarely-mentioned S/L Brisbane, but the ORB offers no clue as to the date of his departure or his destination. There was no immediate respite from operations as preparations were put in hand on the 15th to attack Wilhelmshaven that night. Crews would have done their best to catch up on sleep as the work of the day went on around them, and six of those who had landed at dawn were up, briefed and fed in time to join five others for an early evening take-off between 17.33 and 17.46, led for the third time in thirty-six hours by S/L Turner. They were part of an overall force of 506 aircraft drawn from all but 5 Group on what would turn out to be the last of fourteen major raids on this naval port during the war. F/O Lightfoot and crew returned early because of a hydraulics issue, but the others all made it to the target, which they found to be concealed beneath ten-tenths cloud. F/L Neill and crew reported being unable to climb above the cloud, so descended through it until finding themselves in clear air at 14,000 feet over red and green TIs, which they bombed immediately at 19.54. Bombing was carried out by the other 10 Squadron crews between 19.48 and 19.54 from 13,300 to 19,000 feet on the markers, and flashes and explosions were observed reflected in the cloud. P/O Bishop and crew were hit by flak on approach to the target and again on withdrawal, causing damage to the starboard mainplane and undercarriage. On lowering the undercarriage of LV908 on return, the starboard wheel fell off, and a wheels-up landing was carried out, from which the crew emerged without a scratch. LV878 failed to return with the crew of F/Sgt Owen, and no trace of the Halifax and crew was ever found.

While this operation was in progress, six 10 Squadron crews were gardening off north-eastern Jutland (Silverthorn) and between Læsø Island and the mainland (Yew Tree). They had departed Melbourne between 18.35 and 18.42 led by S/L Hart, and arrived in the target area under clear skies with a little haze. Positions were confirmed by H2S-fix, and the mines delivered into the briefed locations from 15,000 feet between 21.21 and 21.43. On return, F/L Body and crew reported a Halifax being shot down over eastern Jutland, and the failure to return of S/L Hart and crew in MZ826 confirmed it to have been them. News eventually came through that the Canadian navigator had been the only survivor, and he had evaded capture. S/L Allan was posted in from 1658 Conversion Unit on the 20th to fill the vacancy for a flight commander created by the loss of S/L Hart.

10 Squadron remained at home for the next week, during a period of largely small-scale operations by the Command generally. The exceptions were attacks on Stuttgart and Nuremberg by all-Lancaster heavy forces on the night of the 19/20th, and a recalled operation against Hannover by Halifaxes of 4 and 6 Groups two nights later. The Hurricane force had lain dormant since Duisburg, but was roused from its sleep on the 23rd, when Essen was posted as the target for a record 1,055 aircraft that evening, for which 10 Squadron made ready nineteen Halifaxes. Once again, this massive force would be achieved without the involvement of 5 Group. During the day, W/C Shannon completed his conversion training, and would soon put himself on the

Order of Battle. The Melbourne crews took off between 16.14 and 16.54 with F/Ls Harrison, Neill and Stewart the senior pilots on duty, and were part of a 4 Group contribution of 263 aircraft, of which a disturbing thirty-four returned early. F/O Davies and crew were among these, after losing the use of the starboard-inner engine. Essen was covered by ten-tenths cloud at around 10,000 feet, and bombing was carried out on red and green skymarkers from 18,000 to 21,000 feet between 19.30 and 19.52. The bomb loads consisted of ninety-percent high-explosives, as it was assumed that most of the combustible buildings had been consumed in earlier raids. It was impossible to observe the fall of the bombs, but an intense glow on the cloud told its own story that there was, indeed, something left to burn in the tortured city, and local reports confirmed the destruction of 607 buildings along with a death toll of 667 people.

Harris had not yet done with his old enemy, and ordered another attack, this time by daylight on the 25th. 771 aircraft were made ready, including twenty-two at Melbourne, and they took off between 12.30 and 13.00 with W/C Shannon the senior pilot on duty for the first time. F/L Harrison was back on the ground at 14.30 after losing the use of his starboard-inner engine, and he was followed home ten minutes later by F/L Neill, who had been unable to raise his undercarriage. A further ten minutes saw the return of F/O Bleakley and crew, whose port-outer engine had failed while climbing-out. The others pressed on across Belgium to enter Germany near Aachen, and it was as the German frontier drew near that F/O Gibbs and crew lost their port-inner engine and their port-outer lost power. They began to lose height and speed, and were down to 16,000 feet when part of the bomb load was jettisoned over Stommeln, a town to the north-west of Cologne at 15.26. This did not arrest the loss of height, and a further four 500

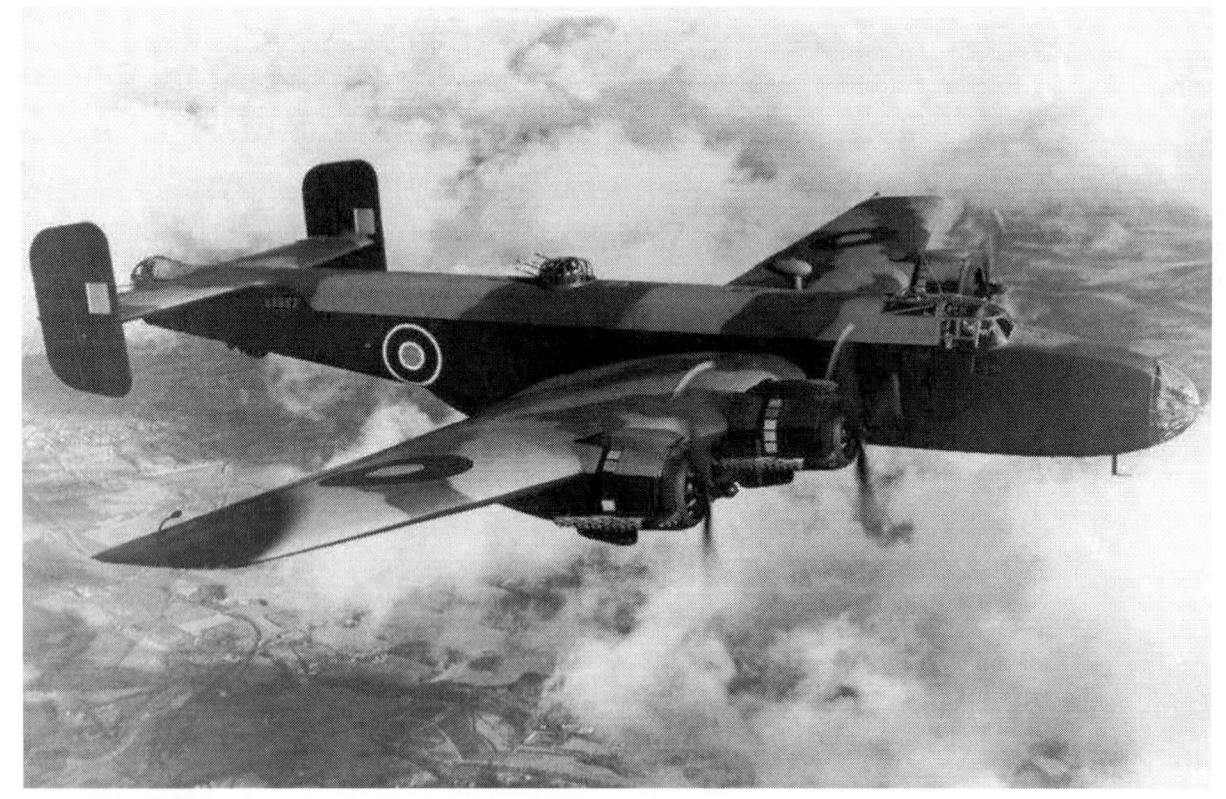

The Halifax MkIII had more rectangular tail fins than those of the Mk II and Bristol Hercules engines replaced the older Merlins.

pounders were let go over Haan, a small community east of Düsseldorf. By the time that Essen hove into view they had clawed back 500 feet, and let the remaining bombs go onto red skymarkers over ten-tenths cloud from 16,500 feet at 15.37. Their squadron colleagues encountered the same seven to ten-tenths cloud at 8,000 feet, and some were able to establish their position by identifying ground detail through the gaps, while others employed an H2S-fix before aiming at the red skymarkers from 17,500 to 21,000 feet between 15.33 and 15.37. Many bomb bursts and volumes of smoke were evident through the clouds, and it was clear to all that another devastating blow had been visited up the city, which had, by now, lost its status as a major centre of war production. Local reports confirmed the destruction of 1,163 buildings, almost twice the number resulting from the larger attack thirty-six hours earlier, and the death toll was also greater at 820 people.

The month would end with a three-raid mini-campaign against the Rhineland Capital, Cologne, which would be conducted during a three-day period from the 28th. The last time that the Command had targeted Cologne in such a way was in June/July 1943 over the course of ten days, and this had resulted in the destruction of 11,000 buildings, 5,500 fatalities and 350,000 people rendered homeless. The operation was to be conducted in two phases, with one aiming-point in the district of Müllheim, to the north-east of the city centre, and the other in Zollstock to the south-west. The Melbourne element of twenty-one Halifaxes took off between 13.03 and 13.29 with S/L Allan leading for the first time, and, after climbing-out, they headed for Orfordness on course for Dunkerque. They were part of a force of 733 aircraft and a 4 Group effort of ninety-one Halifaxes, a dozen of which turned back early. MZ576 lost its port-outer engine over the Channel and could not maintain height, leaving F/O Bleakley and crew with no choice other than to jettison the bombs "safe" into the sea. Despite this, the Halifax continued to sink and was at 10,000 feet when the port-inner engine also cut out. A distress signal was sent and the Halifax pointed towards the English coast, but the imbalance of having two dead engines on one side created control problems, causing the aircraft to fly in circles as it descended further towards the sea. A controlled ditching was achieved, and the dinghy deployed after some initial difficulties with the automatic pump, and the crew spent four hours and fifteen minutes afloat before being picked up by HMS Middleton to be put ashore near Portsmouth. W/O Davies and crew were an hour out when they lost the use of their starboard-inner engine, and they were also forced to turn back for an eventual landing at Ridgewell. W/O Grayshan and crew were the last to abandon their sortie, at 14.37, and this was also due to the failure of an engine. F/O Murphy and crew noticed their port-inner engine beginning to overheat at 14.40, so climbed to 20,000 feet before shutting it down, and then continued on to the target, where the 4 Group element had been assigned to aiming-point G. They were down to 14,000 feet on arrival at Cologne, and found five-tenths thin cloud, through which they bombed the centre of the smoke at 15.35 as ordered by the Master Bomber. S/L Allan and crew had lost an engine at about the same time, and reached the target to bomb from 15,000 feet at 15.54. Their squadron colleagues bombed on red TIs and by visual identification of the Rhine from 18,000 to 21,000 feet between 15.30 and 15.50, and reported the attack to be well-concentrated around the markers. Both aiming-points were devastated, local reports confirming the destruction of 2,239 blocks of flats and fifteen industrial premises, along with many other buildings of a public nature, and severe damage to power stations, railway and river docks installations.

Cologne was posted as the target again on the 30th, for which 10 Squadron again made ready twenty-one Halifaxes in a 4 Group contribution of 235 to an overall force of 905 aircraft. The Melbourne element took off between 17.37 and 18.05 with W/C Shannon and S/L Allan the senior pilots on duty. On a night of very poor serviceability, six of the 10 Squadron crews returned early, four with engine issues and two with Gee failure. The most serious incident involved the crew of F/O Scott, whose starboard-outer engine cut, caught fire and shed its propeller and reduction gear. Nine of the others reached the target to find ten-tenths thin cloud and red, white and green Oboe skymarkers to guide them to the aiming-point, where they confirmed their positions by Gee and H2S-fix before bombing from 17,000 to 20,000 feet between 21.08 and 21.16. F/L Janes and crew failed to release their load after the navigator forgot to activate the master bombing switch. Returning crews reported many bomb flashes and the glow of fires, but were unable to make an assessment because of the cloud. A post-raid analysis suggested a scattered attack, but local reports confirmed heavy damage in south-western suburbs, where housing, communications and utilities were the principal casualties. Earlier in the day, F/L Janes had been elevated to acting squadron leader rank to assume control of C Flight.

A 1, 3, 4 and 8 Group force of 493 aircraft was made ready on the 31st to complete the series of raids on Cologne, 4 Group providing 143 Halifaxes, including fourteen belonging to 10 Squadron. They departed Melbourne between 18.04 and 18.32 with S/L Allan the senior pilot on duty, and only F/O Findlay returned early after his hydraulics system failed. The others found the target to be covered by ten-tenths thick cloud with tops at 6,000 to 10,000 feet, and established their positions by Gee and H2S-fix before bombing on Oboe-laid red, white and green skymarkers from 17,000 to 19,000 feet. Returning crews reported concentrated bombing and a large red glow beneath the clouds as they turned for home. Local reports confirmed that the southern districts had received the main weight of bombs, but the reporting system was breaking down and precise details were not forthcoming. It is likely, that the city had largely been evacuated by this stage, and all future operations would be directed at its numerous and extensive marshalling yards. During the course of the month the squadron operated on eleven days/nights and dispatched 209 sorties for the loss of four Halifaxes and two crews.

November 1944

The squadron's relatively light losses or recent times would continue for the remainder of the year, and this was indicative of the overwhelming numerical superiority of the Allied air forces, the advent of American long-range escort fighters, and the success of the oil campaign in drastically reducing the output of vital aviation fuel from the refineries. 4 Group was not involved in the operations against oil targets at Homberg and Oberhausen on the 1st, but detailed 220 Halifaxes for an attack on Düsseldorf on the 2nd, of which sixteen would represent 10 Squadron. They took off between 16.24 and 16.48 with S/L Allan the senior pilot on duty and W/C Shannon flying as second pilot to W/O Banks, but lost F/O Dark and crew shortly after take-off with a dead engine and F/L Kerr over Reading with a variety of issues including navigational equipment and engine failure. The remainder reached the target to encounter excellent conditions, and bombed on red TIs from 17,000 to 19,500 feet between 19.23 and

19.34. Returning crews reported the bombing to have been concentrated around the markers, and commented on the number of explosions and fires and the volume of smoke.

4 Group detailed 210 Halifaxes on the 4th for a raid that evening on Bochum in the Ruhr, and they would be part of an overall force of 749 aircraft drawn from 1, 4, 6 and 8 Groups. 10 Squadron briefed nineteen crews, and they took off between 17.21 and 17.52 with F/L Kerr the senior pilot on duty. He was probably still over England when his navigational equipment let him down again, and he was compelled to turn back, leaving the others to continue on via The Hague to the target. An eventful sortie for F/O Sifton and crew began at this point, when they were hit by light flak squirted up from the Dutch Capital, but it did not inhibit their progress to the target, while P/O Gibbs and crew had to jettison part of their load to maintain height after their port-inner engine overheated. Very thin cloud of up to three-tenths was encountered at 5,000 feet over Bochum, through which the red and green TIs were clearly seen to be concentrated around the aiming-point, and attracted the majority of the bombs. The 10 Squadron crews delivered their loads from 15,700 to 19,000 feet between 19.35 and 19.43, with the flak bursting below them at around 14,000 feet. Even so, P/O Tudberry and crew sustained damage to both wings, a fin, rudder and the rear fuselage generally. As they left the target area eight minutes after bombing, the Sifton crew found themselves being stalked by an unidentified twin-engine aircraft astern, which the mid-upper gunner engaged, and saw strikes on one engine. The rear-gunner then also fired, upon which the enemy aircraft turned away before breaking up in the air. They were engaged by a second enemy aircraft immediately afterwards, but that was driven off with neither combatant sustaining damage. F/O Daffey and crew were an hour into the homeward run when two hydraulics pipes broke, causing the flaps, bomb doors and tail-wheel to flop down and create drag that reduced their speed by sixty m.p.h, but they made it safely to a landing at Woodbridge. Returning crews reported many explosions and fires, and their confidence in the success of the operation was confirmed by post-raid reconnaissance and local reports, which confirmed that the city centre and industrial districts had borne the brunt of the attack, with four thousand buildings destroyed or seriously damaged, and almost a thousand people killed. However, the defences demonstrated that they were not yet spent, and brought down twenty-eight aircraft, twenty-three of them Halifaxes. It was a bad night for 4 Group, which posted missing seventeen crews, five of them from the Free French 346 Squadron at Elvington. 10 Squadron was represented among the missing by LW716, which failed to return with the crew of F/Sgt Harris RNZAF, and only the mid-upper gunner survived to fall into enemy hands.

10 Sqn Target Photo Essen 28/29 November 1944.

Bochum's neighbour, Gelsenkirchen, was posted as the target on the 6th, for which a force of 738 aircraft was put together and the crews briefed to aim for the Nordstern Synthetic oil plant. 10 Squadron made ready sixteen Halifaxes in a 4 Group contribution to the raid of 208 aircraft, and they took off between 11.47 and 12.12 with S/Ls Janes and Turner the senior pilots on duty. There were no early returns, and the Melbourne crews approached the target to find six to eight-tenths cloud with tops at around 9,000 feet. In the early stages it was possible to see green TIs through the gaps, but these began to close and thick smoke spread across the area to obscure any sight of the ground. The Master Bomber initially ordered the crews to bomb the TIs, and then the smoke obscuring the TIs, and, eventually, to focus on the built-up area generally. The 10 Squadron crews established their positions by Gee and H2S on e.t.a., and bombed from 19,000 to 20,000 feet in the face of accurate heavy flak, which inflicted damage on a number of aircraft. Many explosions were witnessed, and the consensus was of a concentrated attack, although it was impossible to make an accurate assessment. Local reports confirmed that a "catastrophe" had befallen the town, and that more than five hundred people had lost their lives.

The pace of operations slackened somewhat thereafter, and, although a number of major operations were undertaken by individual groups, largely against oil-related targets, 4 Group mounted a single mining operation during the ensuing ten days. As the American 1st and 9th Armies prepared to advance eastwards between Aachen and the Rhine, the three towns of Düren, Heinsberg and Jülich, located in an arc from north to east of Aachen, stood in their way, and a request was made for Bomber Command to erase them from the map. A massive force of 1,188 aircraft was prepared across the Command on the 16th and the crews assigned to one of the three targets. 4 and 6 Groups were to join forces as the main force at Jülich, and they would benefit from marking by elements of 8 Group. 4 Group contributed 254 Halifaxes to the overall force of 413 aircraft, twenty-one of them provided by 10 Squadron, and they departed Melbourne between 12.33 and 12.59 with W/C Shannon the senior pilot on duty. F/O Atkins turned back early with an engine issue, leaving the others to press on over cloud across Belgium, turning sharply to the north-east when twenty miles south of Liege for the approach past Aachen to the unsuspecting target. Four to five-tenths low cloud lay over the town, but this did not inhibit a visual identification or conceal the red TIs around the aiming-point, which the 10 Squadron crews bombed from 12,000 to 14,500 feet between 15.30 and 15.37. The bombing was well-concentrated, and the town was soon enveloped in smoke, into which the later arrivals delivered their bombs. All three operations achieved their purpose, and while reports came out of Düren and Heinsberg, there was nothing from Jülich. Düren had not been evacuated and suffered 3,127 fatalities, while Heinsberg had been all-but emptied of civilians, but almost half of the 110 who remained lost their lives.

4 Group detailed 210 Halifaxes on the 18th for an operation against the heavily-garrisoned city of Münster, situated some twenty-five miles from the north-eastern edge of the Ruhr, and they would join forces with elements of 6 and 8 Groups to produce an overall force of 479 aircraft. 10 Squadron dispatched fifteen Halifaxes between 12.25 and 12.43 with S/L Allan the senior pilot on duty, but lost F/O Smith and crew to an engine issue as they climbed to operational altitude. The others continued on to find the target concealed beneath a blanket of heavy cloud, and bombed on somewhat scattered red and green skymarkers from 15,000 to 19,500 feet between 15.05 and 15.16. There was no chance of observing the results, but the impression was of a scattered raid, and little information came out of the city to confirm or deny this.

Twenty-two crews were briefed at Melbourne on the 21st for a return to nocturnal activities that night. The target for the all-4 Group main force of 232 Halifaxes was the synthetic oil refinery at Sterkrade-Holten in the north of Gelsenkirchen, for which the Melbourne crews took off between 17.17 and 17.42 with W/C Shannon the senior pilot on duty. F/O Scott and crew returned early after the mid-upper gunner became indisposed, probably through oxygen starvation, and they were followed home by F/L Bridgett and crew with engine issues. The others reached the target to encounter five to ten-tenths thin cloud with tops at around 5,000 feet, through which red and green TIs could be seen marking out the aiming-point. Bombing was carried out from 19,000 to 21,000 feet between 20.59 and 21.08, and appeared to be concentrated, this seemingly confirmed by a number of large explosions that produced black, oily smoke. The flak was bursting well below the bombers at around 14,000 to 15,000 feet, and was not troublesome, and the two failures to return resulted from a mid-air collision between aircraft of 51 and 346 Squadron over Belgium. Post-raid reconnaissance revealed the disappointing fact that the refinery had not been hit.

Halifax RG442 ZA E Crew. L-R David 'Jock' Small (Nav), Johnny Horsham (Flt.Eng.), Fred Thompson (W.Op) Dick Morris (Pilot), Tony Greerson (RG), Bill Doyle (BA), Roy MacGoldrick (M/UG)

Another period of operational inactivity restricted most of 4 Group to training until the 28th, when the first of two further operations to the Ruhr would see out the month. Essen was posted as the target for that night, for which a force of 316 aircraft was made ready, consisting of a main force of 270 Halifaxes from 4 Group, a handful of ABC Lancasters from 1 Group's 101 Squadron and 8 Group Lancasters and Mosquitos to take care of the marking. Twenty-three Halifaxes were prepared at Melbourne, and they took to the skies between 02.22 and 02.51 with W/C Shannon and S/Ls Allen and Janes the senior pilots on duty. There were no early returns, but P/O Tudberry RAAF and crew lost their port-outer engine while outbound, and sank gradually until arriving at the target at 12,500 feet to find ten-tenths cloud below them with tops at 2,500 feet. The Pathfinders had prepared a ground and skymarking plan, and main force crews confirmed their positions by H2S and Gee-fix based on red and yellow marker flares. Apart from the Tudberry crew, the 10 Squadron element bombed from 19,000 to 21,000 feet between 05.32 and 05.42, and observed many bomb bursts and a large red glow beneath the clouds. As P/O Rebick and crew were leaving the target area in LW545 six minutes after bombing, they were attacked three times by a ME110, which was eventually struck by return fire from the rear turret, before breaking away with its starboard engine on fire. Meanwhile, the Tudberry crew was still struggling to maintain height in MZ789, and it was decided at 06.26 to make for Manston as Melbourne was out of the question. At 07.05 the port-outer engine threatened to burst into flames, and the extinguisher was activated to prevent that from happening. With the Channel crossing looming, P/O Tudberry opted for a forced-landing in Allied territory, and put the Halifax down in a field at Guines, about five miles south of Calais, at 07.15. They would return to the squadron on the 1st of December. Bomber Command claimed a successful raid, which was confirmed by local reports of 405 houses destroyed and 673 seriously damaged.

S/L Bond, a bomb-aimer, was posted to the squadron from the Pathfinder station of Little Snoring on the 30th, probably arriving at Melbourne in the midst of preparations for that evening's heavy raid on Duisburg, for which 576 aircraft were made ready by 1, 4, 6 and 8 Groups. 10 Squadron fuelled and bombed up twenty-two Halifaxes to contribute to the 4 Group effort of 234, and they took off between 16.23 and 16.47 with W/C Shannon the senior pilot on duty. Again, there were no early returns, and the 10 Squadron element reached the target to find similar conditions to those of two nights earlier, ten-tenths cloud with tops at around 5,000 feet. The usual positional checks were carried out by Gee and H2S-fix before the bombing took place from 18,000 to 20,000 feet onto red TIs visible through the cloud and red and yellow skymarkers drifting over it. The Melbourne crews were over the target between 20.00 and 20.07, and could only report bomb bursts and the glow of fires and the likelihood of a scattered attack. In reality, it had been more destructive than the Command suspected, local reports confirming the destruction of 528 houses with serious damage to more than eight hundred others. During the course of the month the squadron operated on eight days/nights, and dispatched 154 sorties for the loss of two Halifaxes and one crew.

December 1944

It was becoming increasingly difficult to find worthwhile targets to attack in a country so laid waste by continuous bombing, and a number of quite small and seemingly insignificant towns and cities would find themselves in the firing line over the ensuing months. The city of Hagen became the first target for 10 Squadron in the new month, for which twenty-two Halifaxes were made ready to contribute to an overall force of 504 aircraft drawn largely from 4 and 6 Groups, with 1 and 8 Group support for RCM cover and target marking. Perched on the south-eastern edge of the Ruhr to the south of Dortmund, it had not been attacked by the RAF since the 1st of October 1943, when it had been severely damaged. One of the many factories hit at that time was the main supplier of accumulator batteries for U-Boots, and this had led to a serious slowing of production of the vessels. The Melbourne crews took off between 17.35 and 18.02 with W/C Shannon and S/Ls Allan and Turner the senior pilots on duty, and flew out in very unfavourable weather conditions, which included sleet and hail storms and icing over the French coast. At the target they were met by ten-tenths thick cloud, which prevented sight of the markers, and it seems that no skymarking took place. The crews established their positions by Gee and H2S-fix on e.t.a., before bombing from 15,000 to 21,000 feet between 20.59 and 21.12, and observing many large explosions along with the glow of fires. F/Ls Harrow and Kerr returned on three engines, and, like the other crews, had nothing to offer the intelligence section at debriefing, and the assumption at high level was that the raid had been scattered. In fact, it had been hugely destructive, and had destroyed or seriously damaged 1,658 houses, ninety-two industrial buildings and many others of a public nature. The U-Boot accumulator factory was completely wrecked and many of the other factories lost up to three months production.

The squadron remained at home on the following two nights, while, on the 5th, 5 Group went alone to Heilbronn in southern Germany, which had the misfortune to sit astride a north-south railway line. More than 80% of the built-up area was destroyed, almost certainly as the result of a firestorm, and around 7,000 people lost their lives. The town of Soest, situated a few miles to the north of the now famous Möhne Dam, was one of a number of important railway hubs linking the Ruhr with greater Germany, and its marshalling yards were posted as the target for 497 aircraft from 1, 4, 6 and 8 Groups on the 5th. 10 Squadron made ready twenty-one Halifaxes, and launched them skyward between 17.51 and 18.26 with W/C Shannon and S/Ls Janes and Turner the senior pilots on duty. They all reached the target area, where good conditions prevailed, some crews describing clear skies and other up to five-tenths thin cloud with tops at around 10,000 feet. Red and green TIs could be seen clearly marking out the aiming-point, and bombing was carried out from 19,000 to 21,000 feet between 21.20 and 21.35. F/L Stephens and crew were the odd ones out, having been unable to see any TIs on arrival at 21.32, and then completing a slow orbit to eventually drop their bombs twenty minutes later than planned at 21.57. Returning crews reported a concentrated attack, punctuated by large explosions, and the resultant fires could be seen for a considerable distance into the return flight. Local reports confirmed that the main weight of the attack had fallen in the northern half of the town, where the railway yards were situated, and that a thousand houses had been destroyed along with fifty-three other buildings.

Group Captain U Y Shannon, 10 Sqn Commanding Officer 9 October 1944 to 29 January 1945.

The night of the 6/7th was to be a busy one for the Command, as almost twelve hundred aircraft were made ready for three major operations to be mounted against an oil refinery at Leuna in eastern Germany, railway yards and the town centre of Giessen in central Germany and railway yards at Osnabrück, north of the Ruhr. 4 Group was assigned to the last-mentioned in concert with elements from 1, 6 and 8 Groups to produce an overall force of 453 aircraft, of which sixteen Halifaxes were provided by 10 Squadron. The departed Melbourne between 16.00 and 16.35 with S/Ls Allan and Turner the senior pilots on duty, and fifteen are known to have reached the target, which had not been attacked in numbers for more than two years. They found it covered by ten-tenths cloud with tops at around 6,000 feet, and icing prevented them from descending to a lower altitude to obtain a better view. Few could pick out the red and green TIs, and, in the absence of instructions from the Master Bomber, who could do nothing in the circumstances, they bombed on H2S and Gee-fix on e.t.a., doing so from 19,000 to 21,000 feet between 19.41 and 19.50. A large, reddish explosion was witnessed at 19.45, and there appeared to be three distinct areas of fire developing as the bombers withdrew. F/O Dark and crew were on their way home at 20.06 when they were approached from the port beam by a ME110, which closed to two hundred yards before opening fire. Return fire from both turrets resulted in the enemy aircraft falling away with both engines on fire, and a number of crew members observed it to impact the ground. Seven Halifaxes and a Lancaster failed to return, and 10 Squadron posted missing the crew of F/O Welsh, who were lost without trace in LK827. The raid was only partially successful, and caused only slight damage to the railway installations, but four factories sustained damage and 203 houses were destroyed.

There followed a lull in major operations thereafter, until Essen was posted as the target for 540 aircraft on the 12th. 4 Group put up 163 Halifaxes, of which ten were provided by 10 Squadron, and they departed Melbourne between 16.24 and 16.47 with S/L Turner the senior pilot on duty. They all arrived over the Ruhr to find ten-tenths cloud at 14,000 feet, and accurately-placed red, yellow and green skymarkers drifting down on parachutes, which, after confirmation of positions by Gee and H2S-fix, were bombed from 19,000 to 21,000 feet between 19.38 and 19.50. It was impossible to assess the results, but returning crews reported many fires and a large glow beneath the clouds, and it was established later that this last night raid of the war on Essen had been highly destructive, and had hit vital war-industry factories, including the Krupp complex.

The French Ardennes village of Taillette now has a plaque on its War Memorial commemorating the British and Canadian Halifaxes which collided over the village on 18th December 1944.

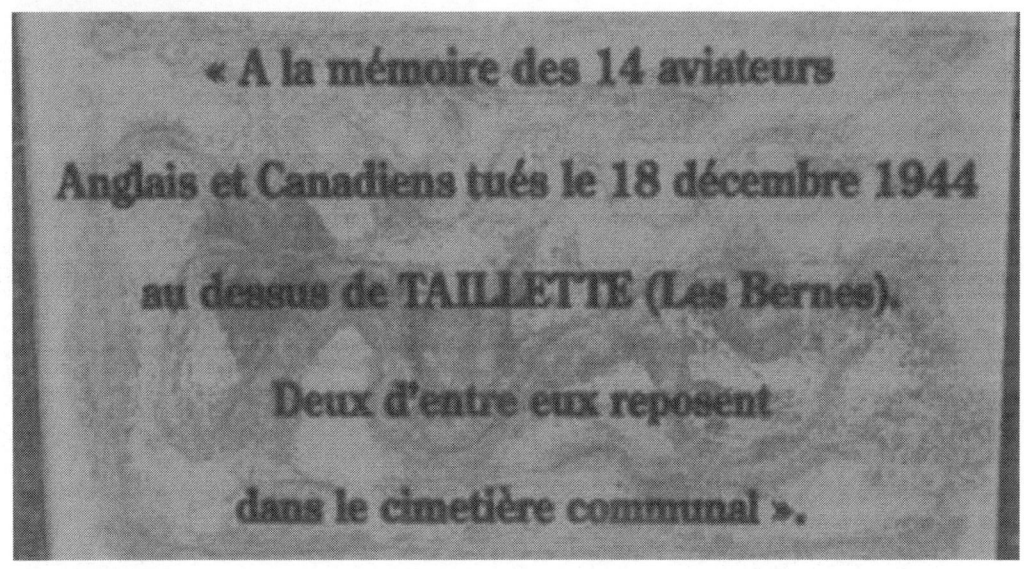

« A la mémoire des 14 aviateurs

Anglais et Canadiens tués le 18 décembre 1944

au dessus de TAILLETTE (Les Bernes).

Deux d'entre eux reposent

dans le cimetière communal ».

David Mole was 7 days old when his father was killed in Halifax LV818 ZA-W/K/F on Duisburg bombing raid on18 December 1944. After many years of research and administrative effort he succeeded in having this plaque erected in the village where his father is buried in the local cemetery.

Gardening operations occupied a number of 4 Group squadrons on the ensuing two nights, and involved four 10 Squadron Halifaxes and five from 78 Squadron on the 14th. Their destinations were the garden areas of the Kattegat (Silverthorn), the Læsø Channel (Yew Tree) and the Lim Fjord between Alborg and Hals (Krauts), and it was for the first-mentioned that the 10 Squadron quartet set course after taking off between 15.35 and 15.50 with F/Ls Davies and Murphy the senior pilots on duty. They found the area concealed beneath ten-tenths cloud with tops at 7,000 feet, and established their positions by H2S before delivering their mines into the briefed locations from 15,000 feet. On the following night, F/Os Dark, Moss, Tudberry and Whitbread and their crews took off between 15.11 and 15.28 bound for the same area, this time to plant their vegetables in the Læsø Channel (Yew Tree) off the eastern coast of Jutland. They encountered ten-tenths cloud with tops at around 8,000 feet with clear skies above, and the mines were dropped into the briefed locations by H2S from 15,000 feet between 18.32 and 18.40. The Tudberry crew were no strangers to challenging situations, and, on their way home at 17.00, they ran into severe icing conditions, which temporarily knocked out the intercom. By the time they were on final approach, they had lost both aerials and the starboard-outer engine, and were diverted to Carnaby, where a safe landing was carried out. It was on the 16th that the Germans began their unanticipated advance through the Ardennes in an attempt to recapture Brussels and Antwerp and split the Allied armies in two. This would become known as the Battle of the Bulge, and made swift progress after taking the Americans by surprise.

Above left : F/O Douglas Mole (W/Op on F/L Body's crew). His son David was a former chairman of 10 Sqn Association. Above right: The graves of F/O J H Waldron and F/O D J Mole in Taillette, northern France.

There was a late take-off for twenty-one 10 Squadron crews bound for Duisburg on the night of the 17/18th, and it was actually between 02.56 and 03.20 that they departed Melbourne with W/C Shannon and S/Ls Allan and Turner the senior pilots on duty. S/L Turner and crew had just passed Rouen when their Gee-box failed, and the ten-tenths cloud precluded any chance of navigating by ground features, leaving them with no option but to turn back. F/L Body and crew had almost reached the Franco-Belgian frontier when LV818 crashed west-north-west of Rocroi, following a collision with a 432 Squadron Halifax captained by F/O Krakowsky RCAF, who was the only survivor from both aircraft. The 10 Squadron crew was highly experienced, and, on this night, included a second pilot, F/L Tatam.* The others pressed on to reach the target, where they and the rest of the 520-strong force were divided between two aiming-points, neither of which was visible through the cloud. Bombing was carried out by the Melbourne crews on the basis of Gee and H2S-fix from 16,000 to 20,000 feet between 06.18 and 06.32, and, as a glow developed around both aiming-points, the later arrivals aimed for these. It was impossible to assess the outcome, but it was established eventually that 346 houses had been destroyed along with other unspecified buildings. While this operation was in progress, a 1 Group main force destroyed almost 82% of the city of Ulm in southern Germany in a twenty-five-minute orgy of destruction. The city contained two major lorry manufacturing plants and railway installations, which made it a legitimate target, but it had not been attacked before, and, fortunately, following the horrors of the recent attack on Heilbronn, the city authorities had urged the civilian population to evacuate the city. Many thousands had heeded the call, but more than six hundred others perished under the bombs.

The dismantling of Germany's railway infrastructure continued with attacks on installations at Trier, Bonn and Cologne on the 19th and the 21st, and then it became 4 Group's turn to join in on the 22nd. The target was the marshalling yards at Bingen-am-Rhein, a town to the west of Mainz with a direct link to the Ardennes battle area. This was to be a 4 Group show involving 104 Halifaxes, after forty-five other sorties were cancelled because of poor weather conditions at home. The 10 Squadron element of twenty aircraft departed Melbourne between 14.50 and 15.15 with S/Ls Allan and Turner the senior pilots on duty. After climbing out, F/L Stephens and crew set course twenty minutes late through confusion over timings, and, on reaching France, realized that they could not reach the target in the allotted time. The bombs were dropped "live" onto a rural area some thirty miles inside Germany before they turned back. The crews of F/L Davies and F/Os Atkins and Cook returned early with engine issues, and F/O Yates with hydraulics failure. After touching down on the FIDO runway at 16.25, NA627 ran off the end through lack of brake pressure and the undercarriage collapsed. The Halifax was declared a write-off, while the crew emerged without injury for what would be only a temporary reprieve. The others found the target area in better conditions than of late, and some crews were able to identify the aiming-point through the four-tenths thin, shifting cloud with tops at around 6,000 feet. The Pathfinder element provided red and green parachute flares and TIs, and bombing took place on these or visually from 17,000 to 19,000 feet between 18.39 and 18.47. Returning crews reported concentrated bombing and a number of red explosions that left a glow in the clouds, and smoke was rising steadily as the bombers turned for home. A post-raid analysis confirmed that all of the bombs had fallen into the yards or the Rhine, and that no buildings in the town had suffered more than blast damage, while a local report confirmed no fatalities. This highly successful operation cut off all rail traffic to the battle front and helped to slow the German advance, which was already beginning to run out of steam.

Christmas Eve brought daylight attacks on the aerodromes at Lohausen (Düsseldorf) and Mülheim (Essen) for which 338 aircraft from 4, 6 and 8 Groups were made ready. 4 Group's contribution of 151 Halifaxes was assigned to the latter, and the 10 Squadron element of fifteen took off between 11.23 and 12.00 with S/L Allan the senior pilot on duty. F/O Taylor became ill and brought his crew home early, leaving the others to continue on under clear skies to visually identify the intersection of the runways. The Master Bomber gave clear instructions, and ordered a two-second overshoot of the eastern edge of the smoke, which was already beginning to drift and obscure the ground. The Melbourne crews bombed from 20,000 feet between 14.35 and 14.44 in the face of intense and accurate heavy flak, and seven of them sustained slight damage. Two large explosions were observed at 14.38, followed by clouds of yellow smoke, which soon covered the airfield to prevent a further assessment, but all crews headed homeward confident in the quality of their work. They were diverted to a variety of stations on return because of fog at base, and, by the time they returned to Melbourne, bombing photos were available to confirm the success of the operation.

The final wartime Christmas period was interrupted on Boxing Day for some crews across the Command by the need to deal with the now encircled remnant of German infantry in the Ardennes. For the first time since October, elements of all of the groups came together in a force of 294 aircraft to attack enemy troop positions at St Vith in south-eastern Belgium. F/Os Yates, Sifton, and Winter took off at 11.50, 12.46 and 13.11 respectively, and reached the target to find clear skies and smoke already rising from the earlier bombing. The Sifton and Winter crews bombed from 14,000 feet at 15.33 by visual identification and green TIs, and watched their high-explosives fall into the marked area, before returning safely to Dyce in Scotland because of fog over the Yorkshire stations. Messages were received from NR246 at 16.33 and 16.36, but it did not return with the crew of F/O Yates, and it was seen to crash into the sea off the Kent coast at Margate at 16.40. It is believed that three bodies were recovered for burial. Five 10 Squadron crews were called to briefing on the 27th to learn of their part in an attack on railway yards at Opladen to the north of Leverkusen in the Ruhr. A force of 328 aircraft was made ready for what would be an early start on the 28th, and 122 of the Halifaxes were provided by 4 Group. The Melbourne element took off between 03.16 and 03.34 with F/L Kerr the senior pilot on duty, and all reached the target to find ten-tenths thin cloud with tops at around 10,000 feet. Red and green TIs were clearly visible and well-concentrated, and bombing was carried out from 18,000 to 20,000 feet between 06.30 and 06.40. Cloud and smoke obscured the results, but a large explosion, followed by a yellow glare, was witnessed at 06.38, and the impression was of a successful raid.

Two marshalling yards at Koblenz were providing the main railway access to the Ardennes region, and the Mosel yards to the south of the city centre and the Lützel yards to the north were to be attacked respectively by forces of 192 aircraft from 4 and 8 Groups and eighty-five of 3 Group. 10 Squadron detailed twenty Halifaxes, which took off between 11.12 and 11.55 with S/L Janes the senior pilot on duty. They reached the target to find around seven-tenths stratus cloud at 3,000 feet and low mist, which hampered identification, and the Master Bomber was not heard clearly by all because of jamming by the enemy. Never the less, most crews could pick out the River Rhine and the Mosel branching off it, and confirmed their positions by Gee and H2S and the smoke trails of the red TIs. The bombing took place from 18,500 to 19,500 feet between 15.02 and 15.05, and appeared to be concentrated on the eastern end of the yards, from where smoke was rising through 5,000 feet as the bombers turned away. It was only then that F/O Smith and crew realized that their load of eight 500 and eight 250 pounders had hung-up, and these were eventually jettisoned over the sea. Although the flak had not been particularly fierce, five Halifaxes returned to Melbourne bearing the scars of battle. A local report commented that these attacks completed the damage inflicted by the Americans on the previous day, and left the railway system blocked, with the Lützel railway bridge out of action for the remainder of the war.

The final operation of the year for 10 Squadron was another in the series against the German railway system, and, this time, involved an attack on the Kalk-Nord marshalling yards on the East Bank of the Rhine in the centre of Cologne. 470 aircraft from 4, 6 and 8 Groups were made ready, seventeen of the 356 Halifaxes representing 10 Squadron, and they departed Melbourne between 17.18 and 17.41 led by five pilots of flight lieutenant rank. They all arrived at the target to find ten-tenths cloud with tops at between 7,000 and 12,000 feet, and established their positions by Gee and H2s before bombing on red and green skymarkers from 16,000 to 20,000 feet between 21.00 and 21.09. F/L Blackwell lost his starboard-outer engine fifteen minutes before bombing, and was responsible for the lower bombing height recorded above, which was two thousand feet below his nearest squadron colleagues. F/O Taylor and crew reported that the bombing appeared to be concentrated in two areas two miles apart, and the glow of fires was reflected in the clouds. A series of five large, red explosions was observed at 21.06, and the overwhelming impression of returning crews was of a successful outcome. This was confirmed by a local report, which mentioned at least two ammunition trains blowing up, two passenger stations sustaining severe damage along with nearby autobahns, and the destruction of 116 houses and three industrial premises in adjacent areas.

During the course of the month the squadron operated on thirteen days/nights, and dispatched 178 sorties for the loss of four Halifaxes and three crews. 1944 had been a much better year for the squadron, principally because of the vastly improved performance and flying characteristics of the Hercules-powered Halifax. There had also been a break from the punishing round of operations to Germany during the pre and post-invasion periods, and even plenty of daylight operations to provide some variety. The New Year approached with the scent of victory in the air, but no-one knew how long it would take to subdue the stubborn resistance of a determined enemy. Any thoughts that the defences were spent were misplaced, and many more crews would have to be posted missing before the end finally came.

January 1945

The New Year got off to a resounding start with the launching of the Luftwaffe's ill-conceived and, ultimately, ill-fated Operation Bodenplatte at first light on New Year's Morning. The intention of catching Allied aircraft on the ground at the liberated airfields of France, Belgium and Holland was only partially effective, and cost the enemy day fighter force (Tagjagd) 250 of its frontline aircraft, and many of its pilots, who were killed, wounded or captured. Any losses sustained by the Allies could be made good within hours, but not so for the Lufwaffe, which would never recover. The three main operations on New Year's Night involved 5 Group at the Mittelland Canal, 3 Group at the Vohwinkel railway yards and 105 Halifaxes of 4 Group attacking the Hoesch benzol (coking) plant at Dortmund with a Pathfinder Lancaster and Mosquito element to provide the marking. 10 Squadron supported the operation with eighteen Halifaxes, which took off between 16.11 and 16.35 led by pilots of flight lieutenant rank. F/O Winter lost his starboard-outer engine soon after take-off when at 2,000 feet, and proceeded out to sea to jettison the bombs before landing. On final approach to Melbourne he realised he was too high, and, in attempting to abort the landing for a go-around, LV785 struck a tree and crashed into a field at Laytham Grange Farm to the south of the airfield. The wreckage burst into flames, and the severely injured navigator had to be dragged clear by members of his crew and the farmer. Sadly, the wireless operator and rear gunner lost their lives, while two other members of the crew sustained superficial injuries and all suffered from shock. This was not the only early return, F/O Hurrell and crew having noticed their port-outer engine smoking as they set course for the target. Despite this, they carried on until a hundred miles out over the North Sea, when the engine caught fire, a situation dealt with by activation of the graviner switch.

The others pressed on towards the Ruhr via the Dutch Frisians, and found clear skies with excellent visibility and snow on the ground, which enabled the crews to identify features before bombing visually and on red and green TIs from 18,000 feet between 19.14 and 19.24. A large explosion was observed at 19.19 which gushed smoke, and this was believed to be a gas-holder or fuel tank, and a large fire could be seen in the docks area. Smoke was billowing upwards as the bombers turned for home, and the glow of fires could be seen from as far away as Antwerp. F/O Dade and crew experienced the frustration of a total hang-up, which was not at first appreciated. The bomb-aimer pressed the tit, the camera operated and the photo-flash went off, and it was only after the bomb doors had closed that the truth was revealed. A number of attempts to dislodge them on the way home failed, until, finally, they fell away over the sea. Despite the apparently successful operation, the benzol plant escaped damage. Operation Bodenplatte had resulted in a bunch of very twitchy and trigger-happy American anti-aircraft gunners in Belgium who shot first and asked questions later, and two 3 Group Lancasters were hit, and one of them brought down with fatal consequences for the crew.

Two I G Farben chemical factories, one in Ludwigshafen and the other close by in Oppau, were posted as the Group's target for the following night, in company with elements of 6 and 8 Groups. A Halifax main force of 351 aircraft was made ready, of which eighteen were provided by 10 Squadron, and they departed Melbourne between 14.47 and 15.17 with S/Ls Janes and Turner the senior pilots on duty. F/L Stephen and crew had been airborne for two-and-a-quarter hours when they were forced to turn back with a dead starboard-inner engine, leaving the others to push on to the target, where they encountered between three and ten-tenths thin, low cloud, through which they were able to distinguish ground features. Red and green TIs marked out the aiming-point, and bombing took place with great concentration from 18,000 to 20,000 feet between 18.43 and 18.55. A series of explosions culminated with one of abnormal ferocity and brilliance, which lit up the entire area, and, as the bombers withdrew, both factories were seen to be ablaze. The success of the operation was confirmed by local reports that five hundred high-explosive bombs had fallen within the confines of the two factories, along with many thousands of incendiaries. This had put an end to all production of synthetic oil, and adjacent industrial buildings, residential property and railway installations had also been destroyed. While this operation was in

10 Sqn Target Photo, Dortmund 1/2 January 1945 Pilot F/O Cook.

progress, five hundred Lancasters of 1, 3, 6 and 8 Groups pounded Nuremberg, destroying two thousand preserved medieval houses and many thousands of residential units in housing blocks, and also causing extensive damage to industrial areas.

Hannover was posted as the target on the 5th, for which a force of 664 Halifaxes, Lancasters and Mosquitos was made ready. 10 Squadron fuelled and bombed up twenty-one aircraft, which took off between 16.29 and 17.00 with W/C Shannon and S/L Turner the senior pilots on duty. F/L Scott and F/O Sifton each carried an extra crew member as a ventral (mid-under) gunner, which had first been tried in Halifaxes in February 1944, at a time when H2S sets were in great demand for retro-fitting and for new aircraft. As the manufacturers could not meet the demand, the H2S cupola was used to house the remotely-operated gun, which was intended to be a response to the enemy's upward-firing cannons. F/L Harrow and crew had been airborne for a little over an hour when a fractured pipe allowed exhaust fumes to enter the fuselage, forcing them to turn back and jettison the bombs. The others continued on to enter enemy territory over northern Holland for an approach to the target from the north-west, and encountered ten-tenths cloud with tops at 6,000 to 10,000 feet. The Pathfinders dropped red skymarkers with green stars and green TIs, and the Master Bomber and Deputy were both heard to instruct the crews to bomb on the centre of the red skymarkers. The 10 Squadron crews complied from 18,000 to 19,500 feet between 19.20 and 19.31, and assessed the attack to be well-centred on the aiming-point, from where two large, orange explosions erupted at 19.26 and 19.28. F/O Hurrell and crew flew all the way to the target, only for the bombs to hang-up. It turned out to be a costly operation, from which twenty-three Halifaxes and eight Lancasters failed to return, among them 10 Squadron's NA114. This was shot down by a night-fighter on the way home, and crashed at Lemgo, some thirty miles south-west of Hannover, killing the eight-man crew of F/O Sifton. Local reports confirmed an effective, if scattered attack, which destroyed 493 buildings, most of them residential apartment blocks.

Crew of Halifax ZA-N NA618. F/Sgt D. Elsome (W/Op), Sgt F. Paxton (Nav), Sgt R. Tuck (R/G), F/O A. Marshall (Pilot), Sgt H. Griffiths (F/E) Sgt J. Thornley (M/UG) F/Sgt D. Lawrence (B/A). Marshall, Griffiths and Thornley were killed when their aircraft was shot down by a night fighter near Hannover in January 1945.

The busy first week of January continued with an operation against an important railway junction in the town of Hanau, situated on the Rhine some five miles east of Frankfurt. A force of 482 aircraft from 1, 4, 6 and 8 Groups contained seventeen 10 Squadron Halifaxes and reflected the importance of the target. The Melbourne element became airborne between 15.06 and 16.32 with S/L Turner the senior pilot on duty, but soon lost the services of F/O Cardwell and crew because of an intercom issue. Shortly after taking off, F/O Smith and crew discovered that the pump to the starboard overload tank was unserviceable and incapable of drawing fuel. Rather than turn back, it was decided to remain a little below the briefed height and micro-manage the engine performance, by which means they were able to complete their sortie. They pressed on with the others, and, it is believed, that 10 Squadron's LV909 and MZ456 of 415 (Swordfish) Squadron collided while outbound, probably at the final turning point north-west of the target, the former crashing at Oberscheld and the latter at Eibach, a mile to the north-west, with fatal consequences for both crews. F/L Harrow was a most experienced pilot with more than thirty operations to his credit, and must have been close to completing his tour. The target was found to be covered by ten-tenths cloud with tops at 9,000 to 10,000 feet, and the early arrivals observed red and green TIs falling into the cloud before becoming lost to sight. Thereafter, crews relied on red and green skymarkers, which those from Melbourne bombed from 18,000 to 20,000 feet between 19.02 and 19.13, observing the development of a gradual glow beneath the clouds. It was not possible to assess the outcome, but a local report confirmed damage in the area of the railway junction, and also in other parts of the town resulting in the destruction of 40% of the built-up area.

Five crews each from 10, 77, 78 and 102 Squadrons were called to briefing on the 12th to learn of their mining operation that night in the Forget-me-not garden of Kiel Harbour. The Melbourne quintet took off between 17.34 and 17.49 with F/Ls Blackwell and Neill the senior pilots on duty, and all reached the target area to find seven to ten-tenths cloud with tops at between 4,000 and 7,000 feet. Positions were confirmed by H2S and the mines delivered into the allotted locations unopposed from 15,000 feet a few minutes either side of 21.00, and all returned safely from uneventful sorties. Twenty-four Halifaxes were made ready at Melbourne on the 14th for three separate operations during the day and night, the main one against the marshalling yards at Saarbrücken, for which fourteen crews were detailed as part of a 4 Group force of 107 aircraft. This would be the third attack in twenty-four hours on this important target. *(The Bomber Command War Diaries does not mention this operation, but cites one by 3 Group Lancasters.)* They took off between 11.01 and 11.28 with F/Ls Bridgett, Grant, Scott and Stephen the senior pilots on duty, and all reached the target area under clear skies to identify the yards visually, the tracks standing out starkly against the snow-covered ground. Red and green TIs marked out the aiming-point, and the bombing was carried out from 18,000 feet in a three-minute slot from 15.00 in accordance with instructions from the Master Bomber. The target soon became covered by smoke, through which a number of explosions were observed, and all returned home safely. The Luftwaffe had put in an appearance, and seven of its fighters were claimed by the escorts as destroyed, with another as a probable.

The above crews had been debriefed and fed by the time that F/L Blackwell and F/Os Dark and Smith departed Melbourne shortly before 19.30 as part of a 4 Group main force of 115 Halifaxes bound for oil-storage facilities at Dülmen, situated some fifteen miles north of the eastern end of the Ruhr. They were followed immediately into the air by seven aircraft led by W/C Shannon, who had been briefed to mine the waters of the Silverthorn garden in the Kattegat. The weather to the north of the Ruhr was clear and the visibility good as the Pathfinders marked the aiming-point with great accuracy, and the 10 Squadron trio bombed on red and green TIs from 19,000 feet between 23.17 and 23.19, observing a large blue flash at 23.20 and a considerable explosion at 23.24. However, there was no evidence of the tell-tale signs of an exploding fuel store, and there was some doubt at group as to whether or not the target had been hit. Meanwhile, the gardeners had encountered four to nine-tenths cloud with tops at 6,000 to 8,000 feet, and had delivered their vegetables by H2S-fix from 15,000 feet between 22.51 and 23.07.

When Magdeburg was posted as the target on the 16th, 4 Group responded by detailing 185 Halifaxes as part of an overall force of 371 aircraft in concert with 6 and 8 Groups. This was to be a city-busting operation, while three other major attacks were taking place on oil refineries in the Ruhr, eastern Germany and western Czechoslovakia. F/O Marshall and crew were first off the ground at Melbourne at 18.31, and it took more than an hour to dispatch the twenty-one others, F/L Murphy lifting off last at 19.34. S/L Allan was the senior pilot on duty as they set course for Flamborough Head and thence to enter Germany via Jade Bay before passing to the south of Hamburg on their way to the eastern target city. F/L Bridgett's sortie was over instantly on take-off after a fractured hydraulics pipe prevented the undercarriage from being raised. F/O Thorne and crew had been airborne for under ten minutes when the starboard-inner engine

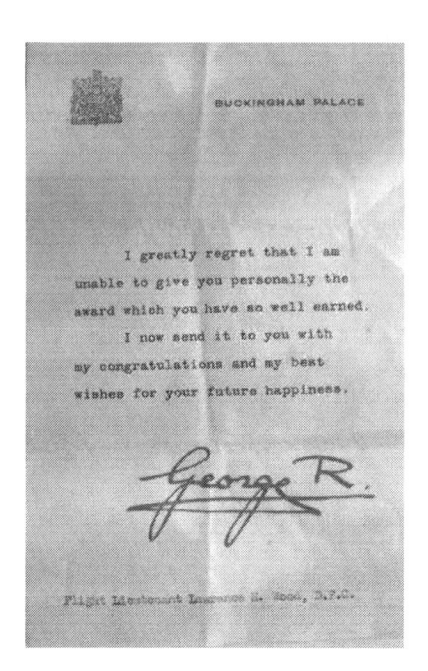

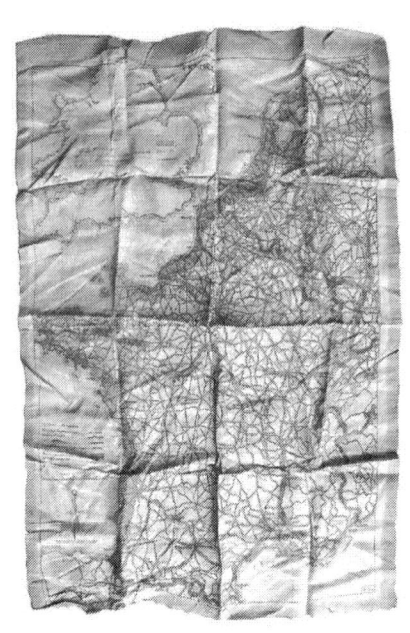

Above left: F/L Lawrence Henry Wood's DFC (Distinguished Flying Cross). Wood was a Melbourne Halifax pilot from 1944-45, who like so many, was given this award for bravery. .Centre: A letter to F/L Wood from HM King George VI. Above right: F/L Wood's silk escape map of France. These were issued to all crews.

failed, and the starboard-outer began to falter, ending their part in the proceedings. The others pressed on into the night, and reached the target after an outward flight of almost four hours. The skies were clear and the visibility excellent as the Pathfinders marked out the aiming-point with red and green TIs, and the 10 Squadron crews bombed them from 18,000 to 20,500 feet between 21.42 and 22.05 in accordance with the instructions of the Master Bomber. The early stages of the raid fell into the southern districts, but spread gradually into other parts of the city, and, by the time that the force withdrew, the built-up area appeared to be on fire from end to end, and the glow could be seen from a hundred miles into the return flight. It was not a one-sided affair, a fact made manifest by seventeen empty dispersals that should have been occupied by Halifaxes, and two of the absentees belonged to "Shiney Ten". NA237 was shot down by a night-fighter on the way home, and crashed at 22.30 some ten miles south of Hildesheim, killing F/O Marshall and two of his crew, and delivering the survivors into enemy hands. LW167 disappeared without trace and took with it the crew of F/O Whitbread. Post-raid reconnaissance confirmed the success of the operation, and Bomber Command claimed that 44% of the city's built-up area had been destroyed.

By the time that the next operation was posted at Melbourne on the 28th, the crews were probably tearing their hair out with boredom after twelve days of nothing but lectures and training. The target was the Hirth aero-engine factory at Zuffenhausen, a northern suburb of Stuttgart, and was the second part of a two-phase operation by an initial 602 aircraft with a gap of three hours between them, both supported by 4 Group. The first phase, by 226 aircraft, was to be directed at the marshalling yards in the town of Kornwestheim, situated just beyond the northern boundary of Stuttgart. The Melbourne element of ten Halifaxes took off between 19.53 and 20.08 with F/Ls Bridgett, Grant, Murphy and Stephen the senior pilots on duty, but F/L Stephen lost his port-outer engine as he was heading south-east across France, and had little option but to turn back. The others reached the target to find eight to ten-tenths thin cloud with tops at 10,000 to 12,000 feet, and bombed on red/yellow and green/red skymarkers from 19,000 to 20,000 feet between 23.35 and 23.43. Large explosions were witnessed at 23.36 and 23.38, and the glow of fires beneath the clouds confirmed a torrid time for those on the ground, although not all bombs fell where intended, and many parts of the city were hit. A decoy fire site also attracted some bomb loads as the Germans fired dummy TIs into the air. This would prove to be the last of fifty-three major raids on the important industrial city, which had now been largely destroyed.

W/C Shannon had flown eleven sorties with the squadron by the time of his promotion to group captain rank and posting to Full Sutton as station commander on the 29th. He was succeeded as 10 Squadron's commanding officer by W/C Alan Dowden, who was one of the few non-pilots to rise to squadron commander status, and had served as an observer (navigator) on Whitleys and Halifaxes with 78 Squadron before moving to 1659 Conversion Unit. On taking command of 10 Squadron he chose to fly as a bomb-aimer, and would have forty-four sorties to his credit by war's end. During the course of the month the squadron operated on eight days/nights and dispatched 135 sorties for the loss of five Halifaxes and four crews plus two airmen.

February 1945

The weather would prove to be something of a challenge over Germany during a hectic first week of the new month, which began with three major operations on the night of the 1/2nd. While 5 Group attended to Siegen, situated some forty miles to the east of Cologne, and elements of 1, 6 and 8 Groups attacked Ludwigshafen in the south, 206 Halifaxes of 4 Group joined forces with elements of 6 and 8 Groups to target communications in and through Mainz, also in the south, to hamper enemy troop movements. Twenty-three Halifaxes departed Melbourne between 15.54 and 16.31 with S/Ls Allan and Turner the senior pilots on duty. F/Os Dade and Jones returned early with starboard-outer engine failure, leaving the others to push on over cloud to reach the target after a three-hour outward flight. The early arrivals found gaps in the cloud that enabled them to see TIs on the ground, but the cloud cover soon became complete, and the main part of the bombing took place on red and green skymarkers, the position of which was confirmed by Gee and H2S. The 10 Squadron crews carried out their attacks from 18,500 to 20,000 feet between 19.29 and 19.39, and observed bomb bursts, explosions and the glow of fires. H2S photos were plotted at between one-and-a-half and two miles south-east of the aiming-point, and local reports confirmed that no significant damage was achieved.

On the following day, nineteen crews were called to briefing at Melbourne to learn that the Ruhr would be their destination that night in company with elements of 6 and 8 Groups. Specifically, they would be targeting the synthetic oil refinery in the Wanne-Eickel district of Herne, a town in the Gelsenkirchen conurbation, where they could expect to meet a hostile reception from searchlights and flak. An overall force of 323 aircraft was made ready, the main-force element consisting of 277 Halifaxes, among which the 10 Squadron contingent took off between 20.17 and 20.54 with S/Ls Janes and Turner the senior pilots on duty. F/Sgt Parsons and crew turned back after an hour with engine and intercom issues, but the others all made it to the target, where ten-tenths cloud prevailed, and positions had to be checked by Gee and H2S. A red glow beneath the cloud was too bright to be a fire, and crews, believing it to be a red TI, bombed it from 18,000 to 20,000 feet between 23.20 and 23.45 in the face of intense and accurate flak. Among the four missing Halifaxes was the squadron's RG443, which crashed in south-eastern Holland on the way home, killing F/O Gibbs and all but the bomb-aimer, who was taken into captivity. It was not possible to assess the outcome of the raid, but it was considered most likely to have missed the aiming-point.

Ruhr benzol plants were to provide the main fare on the 3rd, on a night of reduced operational activity, while six 10 Squadron Halifaxes were loaded with four mines each, and dispatched between 17.15 and 17.30 bound for the Yams garden in Jade Bay off Wilhelmshaven. F/O Findlay and crew were two hours out and over the North Sea when their H2S failed and ended their part in the proceedings. The others reached the drop zone to find eight to ten-tenths cloud with tops at 7,000 feet, and four delivered their mines as briefed from 15,000 feet at around 19.30, while F/L Wood and crew suffered a hang-up and had to bring their mines home. 4 Group supported two operations on the 4th, one against the synthetic oil plant at Gelsenkirchen, and the other, for which 10 Squadron made ready nineteen Halifaxes, against military road communications in Bonn. 202 Halifaxes from 4 and 6 Groups constituted the main-force element, and the Melbourne contingent took off between 17.38 and 18.15 with S/Ls Allan and Turner the senior pilots on duty. F/O Davies lost his hydraulics immediately after take-off, but the others all reached the target area, where the persistently cloudy conditions concealed the aiming-point. Red and green skymarkers provided the main-force crews with a reference, and those from 10 Squadron bombed them from 15,000 to 20,000 feet between 20.44 and 21.02. A bright, red glow began to develop in intensity beneath the clouds, and one crew insisted that it remained visible for 150 miles into the return flight, while others suggested a more conservative forty to one hundred miles. What caused it remains unknown, but most of the bombing missed the target to the south.

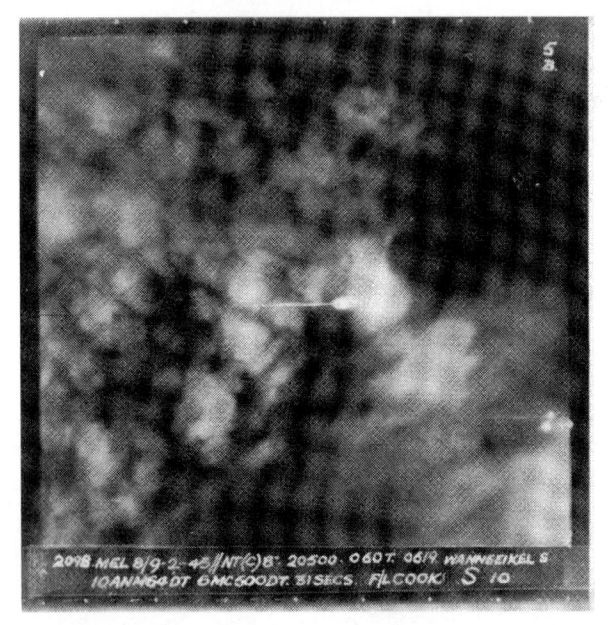

10 Sqn Target Photo 8/9 February 1945 Wanne-Eickel. Pilot F/L Cook.

The towns of Cleves and Goch are separated by around eight miles and lie east of the Reichswald and to the south of the Rhine, where the British XXX Corps was preparing to advance. 464 aircraft of 4, 6 and 8 Groups were made ready on the 7th to attack the latter, which was part of the enemy's defensive line, while a predominantly 1 Group force dealt with the former. Fourteen 10 Squadron Halifaxes formed part of the 195-strong 4 Group contribution, and they departed Melbourne between 18.57 and 19.35 with S/L Turner the senior pilot on duty. Taking off amongst them, between 18.23 and 19.31, were eight crews heading for the Forget-me-not garden of Kiel Harbour to lay mines, and they were led by four pilots of flight lieutenant rank. On arrival at Goch the crews encountered ten-

tenths thin cloud with a base at around 5,000 feet, prompting the Master Bomber to bring the main-force crews down to provide them with a view of the aiming-point. Four 10 Squadron crews, those of F/O Bowen, and F/Ls Atkins, Ballantine and Bridgett, were among 155 who bombed red and green TIs between 22.18 and 22.23 before smoke concealed the aiming-point and the Master Bomber called a halt. One violent explosion was observed, and a burgeoning red glow beneath the cloud suggested that the attack was effective. Meanwhile, the gardening brigade had encountered eight to ten-tenths cloud with tops at between 5,000 and 8,000 feet, and delivered their vegetables into the briefed locations from 15,000 feet between 21.57 and 22.14, before returning home to report uneventful sorties. A post-raid analysis of the Goch raid revealed extensive damage to the town, which had been evacuated by the civilian population, and most of the casualties would appear to have involved foreign-national forced workers.

The oil refinery at Wanne-Eickel was posted as the target across the Halifax stations of 4 and 6 Groups on the 8th, and fifteen crews from 10 Squadron attended briefing to learn of a very early start planned for the following morning. No fewer than seven pilots of flight lieutenant rank were on duty as the Melbourne element took off between 03.11 and 03.38, and all but F/L Atkins and F/L Murphy reached the target area to find conditions ranging from clear skies to ten-tenths thin cloud with tops at between 5,000 and 10,000 feet. F/L Atkins had turned back after two hours because of a dead starboard-outer engine, and F/L Murphy was outbound at 18,000 feet when the port-outer engine failed, and the Halifax was unable to maintain height. As it descended through 17,000 feet it began to collect ice, and, at 14,000 feet, it was decided to bomb the first alternative objective, which, according to a Gee-fix, was a cloud-covered Mönchengladbach. The others established their positions over the primary target by Gee and H2S-fix, before bombing on red and green TIs from 19,000 and 21,000 feet between 06.16 and 06.26. The bombing appeared to be concentrated, and a large explosion was observed along with much smoke, but it was not possible to accurately assess the damage, which was established later to be only very minor.

A series of Churchill-inspired attacks on Germany's eastern cities under Operation Thunderclap began at Dresden on the night of the 13/14th. The two-phase operation was opened by 244 Lancasters of 5 Group, with its own Mosquitos carrying out the low-level marking, and was completed three hours later by 529 Lancaster of 1, 3, 6 and 8 Groups. The result was a firestorm, which left 25,000 people dead, and also gave rise to controversy and outrageous accusations by Germans and the liberal element in this country, that Harris and his crews were war criminals, and this has continued to tarnish their reputations to this day. The Halifaxes of Bomber Command sat this one out, and Dresden is not, therefore, part of the 10 Squadron story, although twenty-three of its crews were to operate that night over eastern Germany, as part of a force of 368 aircraft from 4, 6 and 8 Groups detailed to target the Braunkohle-Benzin plant at Böhlen, some seven miles to the south of Leipzig. The Melbourne crews took off between 18.10 and 18.45 with S/Ls Allan and Turner the senior pilots on duty, and headed for the French coast at Dunkerque. P/O Steel and crew were tracking France's north-eastern frontier with Belgium when the starboard-inner engine failed, forcing them to turn back. The others completed the three-and-a-half-hour outward flight, and found the target area concealed beneath ten-tenths cloud with tops, according to a number of reports, ranging from 6,000 to 14,000 feet. Positions were established by Gee and H2S-fix before bombing took place on red and green TIs from

16,500 and 19,000 feet in accordance with the instructions of the Master Bomber, at least, by those who picked up his broadcasts. Large explosions and the glow of fires suggested an accurate attack to the retreating crews, who had to battle through severe icing conditions to reach home. A post-raid analysis concluded that the operation had failed to find the mark, and further attempts would be made to destroy it over the ensuing weeks.

Operation Thunderclap moved on to Chemnitz on the following night, and, this time, 499 Lancasters and 218 Halifaxes from all but 5 Group would operate together. Fifteen Halifaxes were made ready at Melbourne for the main event, while four others were prepared for mining duties in the Sweet Peas garden of the Kadet Channel in the western Baltic. The bombers took off between 16.56 and 17 28 with S/L Turner the senior pilot on duty, and they were followed into the air between 18.06 and 18.11 by the mining quartet led by F/L Scott. All of the bombers reached the target area to find ten-tenths thin Cirrus cloud, through which a plentiful array of red and green TIs could be seen. The Master Bomber ordered crews to bomb the centre of the greens, and those who could make out his transmissions complied from 16,500 to 20,000 feet between 21.05 and 21.21, and the many bomb bursts observed in the marked area convinced most that the raid had been concentrated and accurate. Fires appeared to be taking hold across the target area, and the glow was visible for at least an hour into the homeward flight. Post-raid reconnaissance confirmed that many parts of the city had been hit, but much of the effort had been wasted in open country. Meanwhile, three of the 10 Squadron gardeners had returned from their sorties to report encountering eight to ten-tenths cloud with tops at 7,000 feet, and

Aircrew V-Victor Halifax Mark III

No. 10 Squadron Royal Air Force — No. 4 Group — Bomber Command — Melbourne Yorkshire England

Completed 38 Operations — July 30, 1944 to Feb. 18, 1945   Photo: Feb. 20, 1945

delivering their mines into the briefed locations from 15,000 feet between 21.03 and 21.08. Absent from debriefing was the crew of P/O Grayshan, who had failed to survive an encounter with a night-fighter in MZ793 and had crashed at Asmindrup on the north-western edge of the main Danish island of Zealand. The pilot and navigator lost their lives, while the flight engineer and both gunners evaded capture, leaving the other two crew members in enemy hands.

The town of Wesel had the misfortune to sit on the East Bank of the Rhine a dozen or so miles north of Duisburg, and directly in the path of advancing Allied ground forces. By the end of the war it would claim to be the most destroyed town of its size in Germany, and its ordeal began with a raid by 3 Group on the 16th. Twenty-four hours later, 247 Halifaxes and twenty-seven Lancasters were made ready to carry out the second attack using the marshalling yards as the aiming-point, with twenty-four Mosquitos of 8 Group in attendance to carry out the Oboe marking. 10 Squadron dispatched twenty-two Halifaxes between 11.24 and 11.51 with S/L Janes the senior pilot on duty, and all reached the target area, although F/O Dade and crew only after experiencing a testing time. The port-outer engine cowling broke away at 12.00, allowing the slipstream to enter the wing and attempt to inflate it, a situation which became more serious as the journey continued. The skin of the wing was bursting by the time the Master Bomber gave the order to abandon the operation in the face of ten-tenths cloud layered up to 25,000 feet. Eight aircraft had bombed before the order was given, and F/O Dade ordered his load to be jettisoned live on the first available target of opportunity, which was ascertained by Gee-fix, after which, a safe return was made to Eye in Suffolk. F/Ls Bridgett and Dark also found alternative targets at Gladbeck and Homberg respectively, before returning to diversion airfields because of fog at Melbourne. Wesel was attacked again on the 18th and the 19th by 3 Group using its G-H blind-bombing system, and would then be left in peace for a number of weeks before its destruction was completed in March.

The busy month of operations continued for 10 Squadron on the 20th, when sixteen crews were called to briefing to learn of their part in a raid that night on the Rhenania-Ossag oil refinery at Reisholz, a south-eastern suburb of Düsseldorf. A 4 Group main-force of 156 Halifaxes would be supported by Lancasters and Mosquitos of 8 Group, and the Melbourne element took off between 21.42 and 22.05 with S/L Turner the senior pilot on duty. They were confronted by ten-tenths cloud over the target, through which the glow of red TIs could be seen, and positions were checked by navigational aids before bombing took place from 17,000 feet between 01.27 and 01.32. It was impossible to assess the outcome, but some bombing photos were plotted at between five hundred and two thousand yards from the aiming-point. It was established later that the operation had been successful and had halted all production at the site.

Two major operations were planned for the 21st, one against Duisburg by a main-force of Lancasters, while Halifaxes carried out the first and only area raid of the war on the southern city of Worms, for which 8 Group would provide the marking. 10 Squadron made ready sixteen Halifaxes and launched them between 16.41 and 17.15 with S/L Janes the senior pilot on duty, and, it is believed, that all reached the target area to find the luxury for a change of clear skies and good visibility. The roads leading into the city were clearly identified, which was of interest to the crews, who had been told at briefing that the purpose of the operation was to cut road and rail communications. The Pathfinders delivered red and green TIs onto and around the planned aiming-point, and the bombing by the 10 Squadron crews took place from 17,000 to 19,000 feet between 20.35 and 20.44. A large explosion was witnessed at 20.34 to the south-east of the aiming-point, and the pattern of burning streets was discernible and still developing as the force turned away. The flak defence had been moderate, but it was the night-fighters that posed the greatest risk, and F/O Daffey's gunners opened fire on a FW190 seen to be attacking another Halifax. Ten of the type and a Lancaster would fail to return home, and among them were two from 10 Squadron. NR189 contained the crew of F/Sgt Parsons, who all survived, all but the wireless operator in enemy hands, and they were joined by five members of F/L Hurrell's crew, who had escaped from RG426 before it crashed, killing the pilot and rear gunner. Post-raid reconnaissance confirmed that Worms had sustained massive damage, amounting to the destruction of an estimated 39% of its built-up area.

297 Halifaxes and twenty-seven Lancasters constituted the heavy element of a 4, 6 and 8 Group force to be sent to bomb Essen by daylight on the 23rd, for which 10 Squadron made ready seventeen aircraft. They departed Melbourne between 12.09 and 12.45 with S/L Turner the senior pilot on duty, and all reached the target area to encounter ten-tenths cloud in layers between 12,000 and 18,000 feet. The Pathfinders dropped green smoke-puff skymarkers, which the 10 Squadron crews bombed from 15,500 to 17,500 feet between 15.13 and 15.17 after confirming their positions by Gee and H2S. F/O Jones and crew failed to spot any markers on e.t.a., or, indeed, any other aircraft, and brought their bombs home. The results could not be assessed, but local reports revealed this to have been a highly accurate attack, which delivered three hundred high-explosive bombs and eleven thousand incendiaries onto the Krupp complex, causing massive damage. That night a force of 360 aircraft from 1, 6 and 8 Groups delivered 1,825 tons of bombs from 8,000 feet onto the city of Pforzheim in twenty-two minutes, and created a firestorm that left 17,000 fatalities in its wake.

A series of attacks on a synthetic oil plant located in the Bergkamen district of Kamen, a town on the north-eastern edge of the Ruhr, began on the 24th at the hands of a force of 340 aircraft drawn from 4, 6 and 8 Groups. 10 Squadron made ready nineteen Halifaxes to contribute to the 4 Group effort of 180 aircraft, and they departed Melbourne between 13.04 and 13.31 with S/Ls Allan and Janes the senior pilots on duty. P/O Ryan was climbing out when a hydraulics failure ended his crew's part in the proceedings, leaving the others to press on and cross the battle front with cloud at five-tenths. This thickened to ten-tenths with tops at 6,000 to 8,000 feet by the time the target was reached, and, as no markers were visible, the Master Bomber ordered the crews to bomb on the information provided by their navigational aids. The 10 Squadron crews complied almost as one from 17,000 feet at 16.45, and, apart from smoke rising through the clouds, had nothing to offer the intelligence bods at debriefing. A local report made no mention of the refinery, stressing instead the damage to the centre of the town.

The same Groups were called upon on the 27th to provide 458 aircraft to carry out a daylight attack on the city of Mainz, for which 10 Squadron made ready nineteen Halifaxes. They took off between 13.02 and 13.30 with S/L Turner the senior pilot on duty and W/C Dowden undertaking his first sortie with the squadron as bomb-aimer in the crew of F/L Atkins. There were no early returns, and all reached the target after an outward flight of more than three hours. They were greeted by ten-tenths cloud as anticipated, and were instructed by the Master Bomber to aim for the centre of the plentiful and concentrated green smoke-puff skymarkers. This they did from 18,000 feet between 16.38 and 16.46, and were rewarded with the sight of smoke spiralling up through the cloud tops at 9,000 feet as they turned away. It emerged later that this attack, during which 1,545 tons of bombs had been dropped, had devastated the city and resulted in the destruction of 5,670 buildings, wiping out the historic Altstadt and killing more than even hundred people. During the course of the month the squadron operated on fourteen days/nights and dispatched 255 sorties for the loss of four Halifaxes and crews.

March 1945

March opened for the Command with the final heavy raid of the war on Mannheim by daylight on the 1st, which spilled also into Ludwigshafen on the other side of the Rhine. The reporting system in the former had broken down, and no report emerged, while the Ludwigshafen authorities confirmed another punishing blow. With Cologne now almost on the front line, it, too, was earmarked for its final attack of the war on the morning of the 2nd, for a which a two-phase operation was planned. 10 Squadron's twenty-two Halifaxes were to be part of the larger first wave of 703 aircraft, and took off between 06.52 and 07.38 with S/Ls Allan and Turner the senior pilots on duty. F/O Jones returned early with an unserviceable air-positioning-indicator unit (a.p.i), leaving the others to press on towards Beachy Head for the Channel crossing. All reached the target to find near perfect bombing conditions with a little cloud with tops at around 6,000 feet, and a Master Bomber on hand to tell them where to bomb, although the city's landmarks, the cathedral and nearby main railway station, stood out in the sunshine, almost inviting the bombs to fall. The 10 Squadron crews carried out their attacks on red and blue smoke-puff markers mostly from 18,000 feet between 10.07 and 10.12, and many, for a change, were able to see the fall of their bombs. It wasn't long before a mushroom of black smoke began to conceal the ground, and later crews were instructed to bomb the up-wind edge of that. The main concentration of bombing was on the western side of the Rhine, and the western end of the Hohenzollern railway bridge appeared to have been demolished. The second wave by 3 Group was ruined by the failure of a G-H station in England, and had to be halted after only fifteen aircraft had bombed. It mattered little, as the once proud city fell to American forces four days later.

4 Group detailed 201 Halifaxes for a return to the Bergkamen oil refinery on the 3rd, of which twenty-two would be provided by 10 Squadron. According to the squadron ORB, the purpose of the operation was to disrupt enemy troop movements in the town, but this is unlikely and is probably an error on the part of the scribe. The Melbourne element took off between 18.15 and 18.42 with S/L Janes the senior pilot on duty and W/C Dowden flying as bomb-aimer with F/L Stephen. F/Sgt Beaumont and crew lost their starboard-outer engine as they headed south towards Reading, and had to abandon their sortie. The remainder carried on over the Channel to the French coast, before turning towards the north-east from south of Cambrai to by-pass Brussels en-route to the Ruhr. They arrived to find up to ten-tenths thin cloud at 8,000 feet, through which the glow of red and green TIs could be clearly identified. The markers appeared to have fallen in two distinct areas some three miles apart, which the 4 Group ORB recorded as causing a lack of concentration of bombing, although this was not apparent to the 10 Squadron crews, who confirmed the accuracy of the markers by H2S and Gee before bombing from 20,000 feet between 22.00 and 22.10. They reported large explosions lighting up the cloud, but could not accurately assess what was happening on the ground. As they approached the English coast homebound, they received warnings of Luftwaffe activity over the bomber stations, which

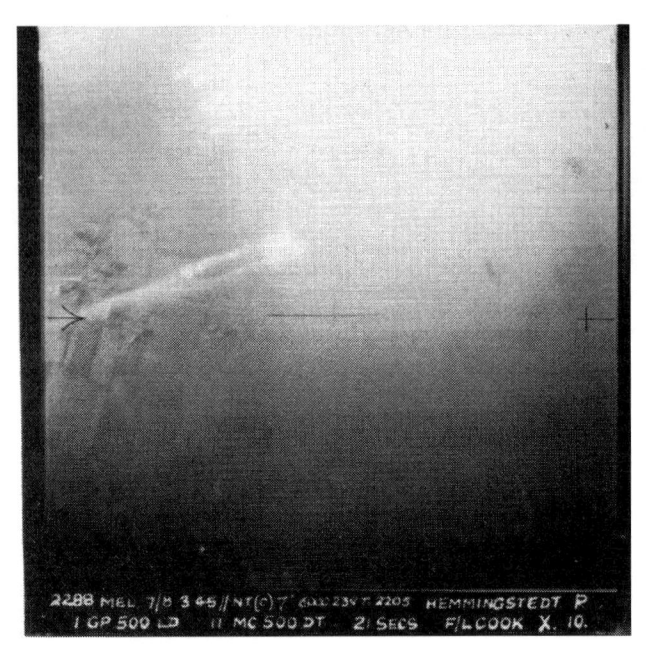

10 Sqn Target photo Hemmingstedt 7/8 March 1945 F/L Cook.

would ultimately be identified as Operation Gisella, a concerted intruder effort by two hundred aircraft. It turned into a highly effective undertaking, which caught the returning bombers at the most vulnerable stage of their flight, the approach to landing. Twenty bombers were shot down, eight of them 4 Group Halifaxes, and among them was 10 Squadron's HX332, which had on board the eight-man crew of F/L Laffoley. Flying below 3,000 feet, the Halifax was hit by canon fire from a JU88, and crashed at 01.45 on Spellow Hill, Staveley, a few miles south-east of Ripon, killing F/L Laffoley RCAF, who was on his thirty-third operation, and four others, while the three survivors sustained serious injury. Post-raid reconnaissance confirmed the success of the operation, and all oil production ceased for the duration of the war.

On the following night, 10 Squadron prepared six Halifaxes to support a small 4 Group mining operation in the Rosemary garden, off the western coast of the Schleswig-Holstein peninsular. This was linked to the port of Kiel on the east coast by a canal, through which U-Boots could pass from the Elbe Estuary to the Baltic, and the purpose of the operation was to disrupt such movement. They took off between 17.49 and 18.00 with S/L Turner the senior pilot on duty and headed eastwards to join up with a similar number from 51 Squadron. They found eight-tenths broken cloud in the target area, with good visibility above, and established their positions by H2S before delivering their mines into the briefed locations from 15,000 feet between 20.00 and 20.04.

Having escaped serious damage in mid-February, Chemnitz remained of interest and was earmarked to face a major operation on the 5th, for which a force of 760 aircraft was prepared. 4 Group detailed 196 Halifaxes, of which twenty-two were made ready at Melbourne, and they took off between 16.54 and 17.29 with S/Ls Allan and Turner the senior pilots on duty. The route suggests that NR131 crashed outbound at Mühlhausen, some one hundred miles short of the target, killing F/L Stephen and his crew, whose bodies were recovered from the wreckage by PoWs from the nearby Stalag IXC camp. This was another highly experienced crew like that of F/L Laffoley, and their presence would be sorely missed at Melbourne. P/O Currie's starboard-outer engine seized as he and his crew approached the Frankfurt area, and, unable to maintain height, they dropped their bombs live to the north-west of the city, not far from the Dulag Luft interrogation centre at Oberursel, where many bomber Command captives spent an uncomfortable few weeks before moving on to other camps. The others pressed on and reported being targeted by predicted flak in the Leipzig area, which had probably been stirred-up by a simultaneous attack by 5 Group on the Böhlen oil refinery. As they approached the target area, they were greeted by ten-tenths cloud with tops up to 13,000 feet, and listened out for the Master

Bomber's instructions as they lined up for the bombing-run. They observed cascading red and green skymarkers, and were told at 21.50 to bomb them with a twelve-second overshoot. When the skymarkers went out at 21.55, they were ordered to bomb the glow in the clouds, before further skymarkers appeared and the original order was repeated. The 10 Squadron crews carried out their attacks from 15,000 to 17,500 feet between 21.41 and 21.59, but were unable to assess the outcome, reporting only a bright glow beneath the clouds that seemed to cover an area a mile wide. They turned south towards the Czechoslovakian frontier for the homeward flight across southern Germany, where some were pestered by enemy night-fighters, one of which was probably responsible for the failure to return of MZ948. Before it crashed, however, F/L Moss and two of his eight-man crew managed to take to their parachutes and drifted down into the arms of their captors. It was established eventually that the operation had been a major success, which had destroyed by fire much of the central and southern area of the city. It also resulted in damage to some important war-industry factories, and the destruction of the Siegmar tank-engine works.

The main operation on the 7th was to be against the virgin target of Dessau, a city in eastern Germany between Berlin to the north-east and Leipzig to the south. While this was in progress, elements of 4, 6 and 8 Groups were to target an oil refinery at Hemmingstedt on the western side of the Schleswig-Holstein peninsular, while 5 Group went for a similar target at Harburg on the south side of the River Elbe opposite Hamburg. 4 Group detailed 156 Halifaxes for the Deutsche Erdöl refinery, of which nineteen were made ready by 10 Squadron, and they departed Melbourne between 18.27 and 18.45 with S/L Janes the senior pilot on duty. There were no early returns, and clear skies provided ideal bombing conditions as they approached the target at medium level to give themselves the best chance of achieving accuracy. The target was identified in the light of illuminator flares, and the aiming-point was marked out by red, green and yellow flares, which the 10 Squadron element bombed from 6,000 to 10,500 feet between 21.59 and 22.08. The attack seemed to be concentrated on the green TIs, and the crews returned home confident of a successful outcome. Unaccountably, the attack had missed the target by two to three miles, but, at least, the other two operations did achieve their aims.

The pace of operations refused to slacken, and, what, perhaps, should have been a wind-down towards the German capitulation, became one of the most intense operational periods in 10 Squadron's war. With five operations already behind it during the first week of the month, the second week began with orders on the 8th for the squadron to provide twenty Halifaxes for an attack on the Blohm & Voss U-Boot yards in Hamburg, where the new Type XXI vessels were under construction. They were to be part of a 312-strong force drawn from 4, 6 and 8 Groups, while 5 Group conducted the last major raid of the war on the already-devastated city of Kassel. The Melbourne crews took off between 18.20 and 18.38 with F/L Tudberry probably the senior pilot on duty. They all reached the target to find up to nine-tenths thin, drifting low cloud with tops at 6,000 to 8,000 feet, which would eventually conceal the green TIs and force the Pathfinders to dispense red and green skymarkers. A Master Bomber was on hand to direct the bombing, and he ordered the crews to aim for the middle of three skymarkers, which the 10 Squadron element complied with from 18,000 to 20,000 feet between 21.28 and 21.37. Two very large explosions were witnessed at 21.33 and 21.36, and another a minute later that lit up the area for five or six seconds. Returning crews were optimistic that the operation had been successful, but no post-raid reconnaissance took place and local reports were sparse.

A new record was set on the 11th when the largest force ever assigned to a single target was assembled to attack Essen in preparation for the arrival of American ground forces. 1,079 aircraft were drawn from all groups, 199 of the Halifaxes provided by 4 Group with 10 Squadron responsible for twenty-two of those. They departed Melbourne between 11.30 and 12.03 with S/Ls Allan and Janes the senior pilots on duty, but F/L Bastard lost his port-outer engine while climbing out over base, and aborted his sortie. The others arrived over the Ruhr to encounter ten-tenths cloud with tops up to 7,000 feet, and bombed on Oboe-laid blue smoke-puff markers in accordance with the Master Bomber's instructions from 18,000 to 20,000 feet between 15.06 and 15.12. There was no opposition either from flak or fighters as the city succumbed for the final time to a Bomber Command assault, and evidence of the destruction going on at ground level came with a mushroom of dark-brown smoke seeping through the cloud-tops. MZ433 was diverted to Carnaby because of a hydraulics issue, and took off again about ninety minutes later after a hasty repair had fixed the problem sufficiently for a return to Melbourne. W/O Poley landed rather heavily at 19.45, causing the Halifax to balloon back into the air, before coming to earth again in a manner that was too much for the undercarriage, which collapsed. The crew scrambled clear without injury as a fire broke out, and the Halifax was declared to be beyond economical repair. Little information came out of Essen following this operation, but a figure of 897 fatalities gave an indication of the destruction caused by 4,661 tons of bombs.

The record of the 11th lasted just a little over twenty-four hours, before being surpassed by the preparation of a force of 1,108 aircraft to be sent against Dortmund, which would stand to the end of the war as the largest single force ever dispatched by the Command. 4 Group again detailed 199 Halifaxes, of which nineteen would represent 10 Squadron, and they took off between 13.00 and 13.26 with S/L Janes the senior pilot on duty. All reached the target to find conditions similar to those of the day before, with ten-tenths cloud topping out at between 5,000 and 7,000 feet. The Master Bomber instructed crews to bomb on green and blue smoke-puff markers, and those from 10 Squadron confirmed their positions by Gee and H2S before complying from 18,000 to 20,000 feet between 16.37 and 16.43, observing black smoke to rise through the clouds as they turned away. A new record of 4,851 tons of bombs hit mostly central and southern districts and left the city in a state of paralysis.

Despite having been almost totally destroyed in May 1943, the Barmen half of Wuppertal was posted as the target for 354 mostly Halifaxes belonging to 4, 6 and 8 Groups on the 13th. 10 Squadron contributed twenty-two aircraft, which departed Melbourne between 12.34 and 13.00 led by no fewer than eleven captains of flight lieutenant rank. There were no early returns, and all reached the target on the southern fringe of the Ruhr to find seven to ten-tenths cloud in two layers with tops at between 4,000 and 12,000 feet. Positions were established by means of navigational aids before bombing took place on red and blue smoke-puff skymarkers in accordance with instructions from the Master Bomber. The 10 Squadron crews attacked from 18,000 to 20,000 feet between 16.01 and 16.06, and some crews reported a large red fire through gaps in the cloud, while others commented on the flash of high-explosive bomb bursts and dark-brown smoke merging with the cloud tops as they turned away. Post-raid reconnaissance revealed another devastating assault, which had hit the eastern half of the town and its surrounds, and left 562 fatalities in its wake. The series of three daylight raids in three days on the Ruhr had involved 2,541 sorties, which delivered 10,650 tons of bombs at a cost to the Command of just five aircraft.

General Patch's 7th US Army was pushing eastwards in a wide swathe between Strasbourg in the south and Koblenz in the north, and Bomber Command was tasked with bombing the towns of Zweibrücken and Homberg to help clear the path. *(There are a number of Hombergs in Germany, and this one should not be confused with the location of the same name near Duisburg containing the synthetic oil refinery).* 4 Group put up 127 Halifaxes as the main force assigned to the latter, and the 10 Squadron element of fifteen took off between 17.11 and 17.36, again led by pilots of flight lieutenant rank. All reached the target area to the east of Saarbrücken to find clear skies but considerable haze, and established their positions initially by means of H2S and Gee. The aiming-point was marked out by illuminator flares and red and green TIs, and bombing took place in accordance with the Master Bomber's instructions from 12,000 feet between 20.30 and 20.36. The attack seemed to be concentrated in the built-up area, and large explosions were observed at 20.37 and 20.41, before smoke obscured the ground to prevent further assessment.

Benzol plants at Bottrop and Castrop-Rauxel in the Ruhr would occupy elements of 4, 6 and 8 Groups on the 15th, 4 Group detailing eighty Halifaxes for the former, seven of them provided by 10 Squadron. They departed Melbourne between 13.13 and 13.23 with F/L Tudberry the senior pilot on duty, and headed for the Mathias Stinnes plant, where clear skies prevailed, but haze presented challenging condition for identifying what the squadron ORB described as the smallest Bomber Command target. Positions were confirmed by H2S and Gee-fix, before bombing took place on red and green TIs under the watchful eye of the Master Bomber. The Melbourne crews attacked from 19,000 feet between 16.17 and 16.20, and observed a huge explosion at 16.19 which gave off dense volumes of black smoke. Flak was moderate and accurate, and claimed one 77 Squadron aircraft, from which all but one crew member escaped with their lives. That night, 4, 6 and 8 Groups put together a force of 267 Lancasters, Halifaxes and Mosquitos for an area raid on the town of Hagen, situated on the south-eastern corner of the Ruhr some eight miles south of Dortmund. 10 Squadron was called upon to provide nine Halifaxes, the crews of which were informed at briefing of the need to disrupt railway communications to prevent the movement of troops to meet Montgomery's advance. They departed Melbourne between 17.03 and 17.16 led again by pilots of flight lieutenant rank, and all reached the target to find clear skies and industrial haze. Positions were confirmed by navigational aids and the aiming-point identified by illuminator flares, before bombing took place on red and green TIs from 19,000 to 20,000 feet between 20.30 and 20.40. Fires were observed to gain hold, and the glow of the burning town could be seen from a hundred miles into the return flight. Such was the level of destruction in central and eastern districts, which had been ravaged by more than fourteen hundred fires, that local reports estimated eight hundred aircraft to have been involved.

10 and 78 Squadrons made ready six Halifaxes each on the 16th to send to the Baltic that night to mine the waters of the Rosemary 3 and 5 gardens. The 10 Squadron element was assigned to the former, off Denmark's Sejerø Island to the north of the main Zealand Island, and took off between 17.47 and 17.53 with F/L Tudberry the senior pilot on duty. All reached the drop zone, where they encountered up to ten-tenths cloud with tops between 2,000 and 8,000 feet, and

established their positions by means of H2S-fix. The mines were delivered into the briefed locations, between seven and ten miles from the island, from 12,000 feet between 21.18 and 21.24, and all returned safely to report successful and uneventful sorties.

S/L Janes was posted to 44 Base on the 17th at the end of his tour, and S/L Black arrived at the same time from 1669 Conversion Unit. The rest of the squadron, meanwhile, enjoyed an entire twenty-four-hour break from operations, which ended with a call to briefing for nineteen crews on the 18th. They learned that they were to be part of a heavy bomber force of 304 aircraft, 259 of them Halifaxes, provided by 4 and 6 Groups, with twenty 8 Group Mosquitos to carry out the Oboe marking. The target was to be Witten, a town towards the eastern end of the Ruhr, south-west of Dortmund, for which the Melbourne element took off between 00.24 and 01.01 on the 19th with S/L Allan the senior pilot on duty. There were no early returns among the 10 Squadron element, who used navigational aids to confirm their arrival at the target, where clear skies and good visibility prevailed. The Pathfinder element had prepared for both ground and skymarking, and the aiming-point, the marshalling yards, was clearly identified by red and green TIs and red and green parachute flares, which the 10 Squadron crews bombed from 15,000 to 16,500 feet between 04.13 and 04.20. Returning crews reported explosions and fires taking hold as they withdrew to leave the town enveloped in smoke, and the glow was still visible thirty minutes into the homeward flight. Post-raid photographs revealed that 129 acres of the town had been destroyed, which represented 62% of its built-up area, and that the Ruhrstahl steel works and Mannesmann tube factory had been severely damaged.

Orders were received on the 19th for a further operation to the Ruhr on the morning of the 20th, this time to Recklinghausen, a town in the north-east of the region close to Gelsenkirchen. The railway yards were given as the aiming-point for the force of 141 aircraft, mostly Halifaxes, drawn again from 4 and 6 Groups with 8 Group Mosquitos to provide the Oboe marking. 10 Squadron dispatched fourteen aircraft between 10.09 and 10.24 led by pilots of flight lieutenant rank, but with S/L Black flying as second pilot in the crew of F/O Halstead. They ran into headwinds, which delayed their arrival at the target, where they encountered large patches of cloud with tops in places as high as 9,000 feet. The wind and cloud combined to disperse the red and blue smoke-puff skymarkers, and obscure them to an extent, while allowing occasional glimpses of the ground, where the built-up area and river docks could be identified. Bombing took place in accordance with the Master Bomber's instructions from 18,000 to 19,000 feet between 13.06 and 13.16, but it was clear that there was no point of concentration, and many crews in the force generally, including that of F/O Giles, attacked alternative targets.

10 Squadron was excluded from an operation against railway yards in the small Münsterland town of Rheine on the 21st, but was called upon on the 22nd to contribute eighteen Halifaxes to a 4 Group main-force of 106 aircraft bound for Dülmen, a very small town situated some ten miles to the north of the Ruhr at its eastern end. They departed Melbourne between 11.26 and 11.53, led by numerous pilots of flight lieutenant rank, and all arrived in the target area to find clear skies and ground haze. Positions were established by means of Gee and H2S, and bombing took place on green TIs in accordance with the Master Bomber's instructions. Smoke soon obscured the ground, however, and crews were then ordered to bomb the upwind edge of that, the 10 Squadron crews complying almost as one from 12,500 to 13,500 feet in a one-minute

slot from 14.22. Returning crews reported concentrated bombing and large volumes of smoke, and it is likely that few buildings remained standing after the raid.

The final phase of the ground war began on the 24th with the crossing of the Rhine near Wesel and the landing of airborne troops. Bomber Command focussed on the enemy's oil industry and communications on this day, sending forces of moderate size to the Ruhr locations of Gladbeck, Dortmund, Bottrop and Sterkrade. It was for the last-mentioned that 4 Group made ready 155 Halifaxes, of which twenty-two were provided by 10 Squadron, and they departed Melbourne between 09.11 and 09.37 bound for the railway yards led by numerous pilots of flight lieutenant rank. Some thirty minutes later, W/O Rogers RCAF and crew began their take-off for a training sortie in RG438, but lost their starboard-outer engine and veered off the runway to crash through the FIDO installation piping. The Halifax was declared to be beyond economical repair, but the crew emerged unscathed to continue their training. Their colleagues, meanwhile, reached the Ruhr under clear skies and identified the target visually, before bombing on red TIs as instructed by the Master Bomber from 18,000 feet between 13.15 and 13.19. The bombing was observed to be highly concentrated around the aiming-point, causing a large explosion among the engine sheds at 13.14 and the destruction of a nearby factory soon afterwards. A pall of black smoke hung over the area as the bombers withdrew, and all returned home safely to report a successful operation which had faced only token flak opposition. This was the day on which S/L Turner was officially posted to 84 O.T.U at the end of an outstanding tour as a flight commander.

4 Group detailed 131 Halifaxes on the 25th to act as the main-force for an attack on the marshalling yards at Osnabrück in the Münsterland region of Germany north of the Ruhr. 10 Squadron made ready twenty aircraft, and dispatched them between 06.50 and 07.16 with captains of flight lieutenant rank leading the way. F/L Best returned early with a failed port-inner engine, leaving the others to press on to the target, where clear skies allowed a visual identification of the aiming-point. A Master Bomber was on hand to direct the bombing onto red TIs, the 10 Squadron crews carrying out their attacks almost as one from 16,000 feet within two minutes of each other either side of 10.05. A number of Melbourne Halifaxes sustained damage from accurate heavy flak over the target, but all made it back to report another successful and destructive operation, which turned out to be the last of the month.

Thereafter, the Command mounted minor and small-scale operations, the exception being an attack by more than 450 aircraft on the Blohm & Voss shipyards at Hamburg on the 31st, to hit construction of the type XXI U-Boots. The bombing was conducted through ten-tenths cloud, and was confirmed by local reports to have caused extensive damage in the city, but no mention was made of the shipyards. A spirited response by the Luftwaffe Tagjagd resulted in the loss of eleven bombers, but this would be the final double-figure casualty figure sustained by the bomber force. During the course of the month, the squadron carried out eighteen day/night operations, and dispatched three hundred sorties, the third highest monthly tally of the war, losing five Halifaxes and the better part of three complete crews in the process.

April 1945

For most heavy squadrons the new month would bring with it the end of the bombing war, but there was still time for a scare or two, and for 10 Squadron to register its final missing aircraft and crew. By the time that twenty-two crews attended briefing at Melbourne on the 4th, the squadron had been off the Order of Battle for nine days, and was fully rested and replenished. The 4 Group target for that evening was the Rhenania oil plant at Harburg, a town facing Hamburg from the South Bank of the Elbe, for which the Melbourne element took off between 19.38 and 20.25 with S/L Black the senior pilot on duty and W/C Dowden flying as bomb-aimer with F/L Bowen and crew. They were part of an overall 4, 6 and 8 Group force of 327 aircraft engaged in one of three major raids on oil refineries, the other two taking place in eastern Germany. They were carrying either sixteen 500 pounders or ten 500 and six 250 pounders, which F/O Steel was forced to jettison safe after losing his a.s.i on take-off to end his crew's interest in the proceedings. The remainder all reached the target area, where clear skies prevailed and illuminator flares helped the identification of the aiming-point, which the Pathfinders marked accurately and backed up until thick smoke obscured it from view. The Master Bomber instructed crews to bomb initially on mixed red and green TIs, then to port of the greens, and, finally, on the developing fires, and the 10 Squadron crews complied from 18,000 feet between 22.27 and 22.35. Returning crews reported a number of large, red explosions, many fires and black smoke rising through 8,000 feet as they turned away. Post-raid reconnaissance confirmed that extensive damage had been inflicted on the plant.

F/L R. Halstead and his crew. Sgt John Kilroy (M/UG), P/O Jack Munzt (Nav), F/L Bob Halsted (Pilot), P/O Bill Houghton (W/Op) Sgt Bob Evans (FE), Sgt Harry Lightfoot (B/A).

440 crews of 4, 6 and 8 Groups were notified of a return to the same area on the 8th, this time to target the Blohm & Voss U-Boot construction yards and naval installations in Hamburg, and this was to take place just a few hours after an attack by the American 8th Air Force. Twenty-one 10 Squadron Halifaxes departed Melbourne between 19.20 and 19.48 with S/L Black the senior pilot on duty, and headed for the English coast at Whitby, before setting course for the Schleswig-Holstein peninsular to approach the target from the north. They arrived to find ten-tenths, very thin cloud with tops at 2,000 to 3,000 feet, through which the red and green TIs could easily be seen. The 10 Squadron crews able to hear the Master Bomber's instructions complied with them and bombed on the edge of the markers, doing so from 19,000 to 20,000 feet between 22.31 and 22.40. All but one returned home to report what appeared to some to be a scattered attack, while others assessed it either as concentrated or failed to observe the results, and post-raid reconnaissance was unable to attribute damage specifically to either the RAF or American attacks. It is likely, that the principal objectives, the shipyards, escaped serious damage during what was the final heavy raid on Germany's Second City. Among the three Halifaxes and three Lancasters failing to return was 10 Squadron's LK753 containing the crew of P/O Currie RNZAF. Some months after the publication of my original 10 Squadron Profile in the late nineties, I received a letter from Norman Mackenzie of Wellington, New Zealand, the cousin of the pilot concerned, to whom I am indebted for kindly providing me with the following account, which I reproduce verbatim.

"However, the sad truth of the matter is, that whilst there was a severe engine vibration, and the port-inner had to be shut down, this was not the real problem. On the way to the target area, the starboard-outer engine had to be shut down, but worse, a parachute was lost when a crew member, unable to cope with the situation, baled out, but unfortunately in doing so, dislodged the navigator's parachute, which fell out of the aircraft through the open hatch. With the plane losing height on two engines, and only five parachutes among six men, a shocked and, no doubt, traumatized crew decided that, rather than leave one of their number without a parachute, they would all remain in the aircraft in the belief that a safe crash-landing could be achieved. Fate was against them, and what was thought to be the River Rhine, turned out to be a wet street in the middle of Düsseldorf. In the darkness of the night, the reflection had led my cousin, who was piloting the aircraft, and the navigator who was sitting alongside, into thinking that they were about to set down in the hoped-for softness of the Rhine River. The plane burst into flames on impact, and split in half at the bulkhead. The only survivor was the wireless operator, Sgt Sinnett, who staggered out of the aircraft with substantial burns to his legs, hands and the area of his face that had not been covered by his hands. In addition, a boot had been ripped off, and his leg was severely gashed. He spent two weeks in a German hospital before the area was captured by the Americans. He was then taken to an army hospital in Devon, where he spent the next eight weeks before being sent to Cosford to debriefing, prior to being sent home on sick leave."

The above account raises a number of questions concerning the timing of the crash and the location in Düsseldorf, which was not close to either the outward or return route. The outward flight was over the North Sea as far as the Schleswig-Holstein peninsular, then due south to the target, with a withdrawal to the south across Holland to the Scheldt Estuary. It seems most unlikely that the events recorded above occurred on the way to the target, but a navigational error in the difficult circumstances experienced by the crew on the way home, could account for them being east of the planned track, perhaps attempting to reach Allied-held territory in Belgium. In Bomber Command losses for 1945, Bill Chorley confirms that those killed were initially buried in the Nordfriedhof in Düsseldorf, before being removed to the Reichswald CWGC post-war, which means that the location of the crash is not in question. A second 10 Squadron aircraft came to grief on this night when returning from Hamburg, but F/Sgt Hicks and his crew emerged unscathed after RG424 suffered an undercarriage collapse on landing and was written-off.

Eighteen Halifaxes were made ready for operations on the 9th, eleven to target Stade aerodrome to the south of the Elbe, west of Hamburg, as a diversion for a major raid on Kiel, while seven others were loaded with four mines each to deliver into the Wallflower garden in Kiel harbour. The two elements took off together between 19.39 and 20.05 with pilots of flight lieutenant rank leading each, and those bound for Stade rendezvoused with eleven Halifaxes of 78 Squadron on the way out. They all reached the target to find eight to ten-tenths low cloud or haze, above which red and green skymarkers were deployed, and green TIs could be seen on the ground. Bombing took place mostly from 18,000 feet between 22.24 and 22.32, and appeared to be concentrated, although it was difficult to make an accurate assessment. Forty minutes after bombing, the crew of F/Sgt Beaumont lost their starboard-inner engine, which could not be feathered because of low oil pressure. A violent vibration threatened to tear HX286 apart, and, when the defective engine began to emit flames, the crew was ordered to bale out, which they did safely over territory held by the British 2nd Army near Rees in Germany. Meanwhile, the gardeners had encountered three to eight-tenths broken cloud over the western Baltic, through which they delivered their mines into the briefed locations from 12,000 feet between 22.34 and 23.06.

4 and 8 Groups were the only ones operating on the 11th, when they were briefed to combine forces for two operations again marshalling yards at Nuremberg and its neighbour Bayreuth, situated some thirty miles to the north-east. 129 Halifaxes were assigned to the former and one hundred to the latter, and it was for the latter that twenty-seven 10 Squadron aircraft departed Melbourne between 10.57 and 11.38 with S/L Black the senior pilot on duty. All reached the target area to be greeted by clear skies and good visibility, and identified the aiming-point visually and by red TIs. Bombing was carried out from 12,000 to 15,000 feet between 15.01 and 15.09 in accordance with instructions from the Master Bomber, with F/L Holes and crew responsible for the later time after losing sight of the gaggle in the cloud. The bombing was accurate and concentrated around the railway yards, which were enveloped in smoke as the force withdrew, and extensive damage was confirmed by post-raid reconnaissance. F/Sgt Hicks and crew found themselves attached to the Nuremberg gaggle by mistake, and remained with it to bomb from 16,000 feet at 15.04. F/Sgt Beer and crew experience an issue affecting both starboard engines and descended out of the formation while they sought a cure. That done, they also joined up with the Halifaxes and Lancasters bound for Nuremberg, and bombed from 14,500 feet at 15.05.

Six crews were called to briefing at Melbourne on the 13th to learn of their part in a mining operation in the Carrotts region of the western Baltic in the Aabenraa Fjord, the purpose of which was to bottle up elements of the Germany navy. They took off between 20.56 and 21.04 with S/L Black the senior pilot on duty, and reached the target area to find clear conditions and

An age-speckled photo of Charles Brignell, the wireless operator (rear left) on this crew. He went on to serve with the Squadron on Dakotas in India before becoming a surveyor after his demob.

F/O Fred "Nugget" Worker RNZAF Pilot, F/O Ken Stewart (Nav), F/O) Fred Wilkinson RNZAF (B/A), F/Sgt Fred Tiller (M/UG), F/Sgt Ian Rowlands RNZAF (W/Op). Unknown who was only with the crew for a few days, in the absence of their Canadian (F/E), and F/Sgt Bob Woollard (R/G) with their ground crew.

no opposition. Positions were established by H2S and the mines delivered into the briefed locations from 11,000 and 12,000 feet between 23.21 and 23.40.

Orders were received at Melbourne on the 18th to prepare to move 10 Squadron to Full Sutton during the following week, but, first, there was other business to attend to. A force of 969 aircraft had been assembled on that day to attack the naval base, airfield and town on the island of Heligoland. 10 Squadron made ready twenty-six Halifaxes as part of a 4 Group contribution of 218 aircraft, and they departed Melbourne between 11.07 and 11.34 led by numerous pilots of flight lieutenant rank. P/O Thomas and crew turned back early after their port-inner engine feathered itself as they crossed the coast near Flamborough Head, leaving the others to press on in good weather conditions to find the target under clear skies. F/L Bastard and crew had to feather an engine while outbound, but restarted it to gain height for the attack, and then shut it down again for the homeward journey. Bombing was carried out on red and yellow TIs from 14,000 to 17,000 feet between 13.24 and 13.49 according to their assigned wave and under the instructions of the Master Bomber. The island was soon covered by black smoke, a large column of which rose steadily from the south-eastern end, and this hid from view what photographs would reveal later to be a surface that resembled a cratered moonscape. F/L Smith and crew brought PN447 home without any sign of damage, but the Halifax was eventually struck off charge as beyond economical repair. Heligoland's ordeal was not yet over, as, on the following day, it faced an attack by 617 and 9 Squadrons, the former carrying 10-ton Grand Slams and 6-ton Tallboys and the latter Tallboys. If not already totally evacuated, the island certainly was after this operation.

There was no further activity for 4 Group for a week, during which period the final attacks were carried out on enemy railway communications, and Allied ground forces advanced further into the German homeland. The order to prepare to move to Full Sutton was rescinded on the 23rd, when the squadron was informed that it would remain at Melbourne, and revert to a two-flight status on that day. S/L Bond, the bomb-aimer in F/L Bowen's crew, was appointed A Flight commander and S/L Black B Flight commander, while S/L Allan was posted out to a new role to do with Bomber Command's emergency airfield administration.

The 25th brought the final operations for the main-force heavy squadrons, beginning in the early morning with the dispatch of 359 Lancasters of 1, 5 and 8 Groups to Hitler's Eaglesnest retreat and the nearby SS barracks at Berchtesgaden in the Bavarian mountains. Later that afternoon, a force of 482 aircraft from 4, 6 and 8 Groups set out for the Frisian island of Wangerooge to target heavy gun positions barring the approaches to German ports. 10 Squadron dispatched twenty Halifaxes between 14.40 and 14.59 led by twelve pilots of flight lieutenant rank. On the way out, two Lancasters of 431 Squadron RCAF collided off Norderney and crashed without survivors, and similar tragic incidents caused the loss of two 76 Squadron Halifaxes and one each from 408 and 426 Squadrons RCAF in the target area, with just one survivor among them. All of the 10 Squadron crews arrived at the target to find excellent conditions with, perhaps, three-tenths cloud at 3,500 feet, but not sufficient to inhibit sight of TIs clearly marking out the aiming-point. The Master Bomber instructed the force to overshoot the red TIs, before switching attention to the yellows, and, once they became obscured, he focussed the bombing on the edge of the smoke. The 10 Squadron crews carried out their attacks in the face of a spirited flak response from 8,000 to 10,000 feet between 16.59 and 17.07 and observed the bombing to be concentrated on the marked area. All returned safely, and, when W/O Flower and crew touched down at 19.16, they had the honour of bringing to an end the squadron's wartime operational service. That night, 5 Group carried out an attack on an oil refinery in southern Norway, and then, for the heavy brigade, at least, it was all over.

The war ended on the 8th of May, from which date Melbourne and 10 Squadron became part of Transport Command, the crews swapping their mighty four-engine Halifaxes for twin-engine Dakotas. The contribution by 4 Group to Bomber Command's offensive cannot be overstated. 10 Squadron was one of the mainstays of the group and the Command throughout a long and exacting war, and, apart from its short period of depletion, when the bulk of the squadron was detached overseas, it remained at the forefront of operations. It carried out the highest number of overall operations in 4 Group, and the second highest number of sorties, the third highest number of overall Halifax operations in Bomber Command and fourth highest number of Halifax sorties. Its fine record of service bears comparison with any, and stands as a permanent reminder of the sacrifice, heroism and commitment of all who served it in whatever capacity, whether in the air or on the ground. 10 Squadron remains operational at RAF Brize Norton in Oxfordshire as an air-refuelling and transport unit.

Author's Notes

1943

13/14th May: What happened to Sgt McCoy RCAF, Beveridge's gunner, who baled-out, is not known and he is commemorated at Runnymede.

15/16th July: The Besancon crash – my understanding is that this involved both F/Sgt Pyke's JD211 <u>and</u> a Do217 and that, by 2015, the AHB was asking CWGC to acknowledge this after work by relatives. If memory serves, there was a Service there by a new headstone in/around June 2015.

5/6th September: Possibly of interest, excavation of the JD322 crash site began over a year ago.

16/17th September: P/O Heppell's Nav and WOP both fell in with Resistance groups after baling-out and both got home, about a month apart, via Spain.

19th November: Plans are in hand for a memorial to Holdsworth's crew, as near as can be estimated to the position of the crash at Tangmere, hopefully at some date this summer.

1944

19/20th February: F/Sgt Jack Walker would eventually re-join 10 Squadron as a VC10 captain in 1967.

30/31st March: The Nuremberg Raid. Excavation of the site where F/Sgt Regan's aircraft (LV881) crashed was carried out in 2014/15, with a commemoration Service held there in September 2015, attended by relatives, a 10 Sqn delegation, and German dignitaries.

2/3rd June: MZ630's crew …. Navigator, F/O Stan Booker, and flight engineer Sgt Ossleton were at first with the Resistance until they were betrayed by a collaborator and handed over to the SS and NOT to the Luftwaffe. Imprisoned near Paris, they were moved out to the Concentration Camp at Buchenwald as the Allies advanced on the city. They were but two of 168 Allied airmen similarly mistreated until an eventual transfer to Luftwaffe control.

9/10th June: F/O Willem Van Stockum, captain of one of the missing aircraft, was Dutch, and an academic with an established reputation in the field of general relativity.

28th June: After being downed, P/O Ralph Taylor was another airman initially betrayed to the SS like Booker and Ossleton, again ending up in Buchenwald.

13th September: P/O Winter's landing at Woodbridge – A booklet published by Arthur Smith, his bomb-aimer, records that, as they landed, there was a Lancaster, flown by its bomb-aimer, landing in the opposite direction! The F/O Bowmer in trouble that day is another to be identified as returning to 10 Squadron in 1967 as one of the first VC10 captains.

A total of 156 aircraft from 10 Squadron were lost on WWII operations comprising 47 Whitleys and 109 Halifaxes, 839 aircrew men from 10 Squadron were killed on active flying service between September 1939 and December 1945. This figure includes the deaths of POWs and casualties from flying training accidents, but it does not include victims of non-flying accidents or deaths from natural causes.

10 Sqn War Memorial, Melbourne, Yorks

Miscellany of 10 Sqn Photographs

Any information about the people and aircraft in these photographs would be very welcome. Please contact the author at *bombercommandbooks@gmail.com*

Melbourne Football Team

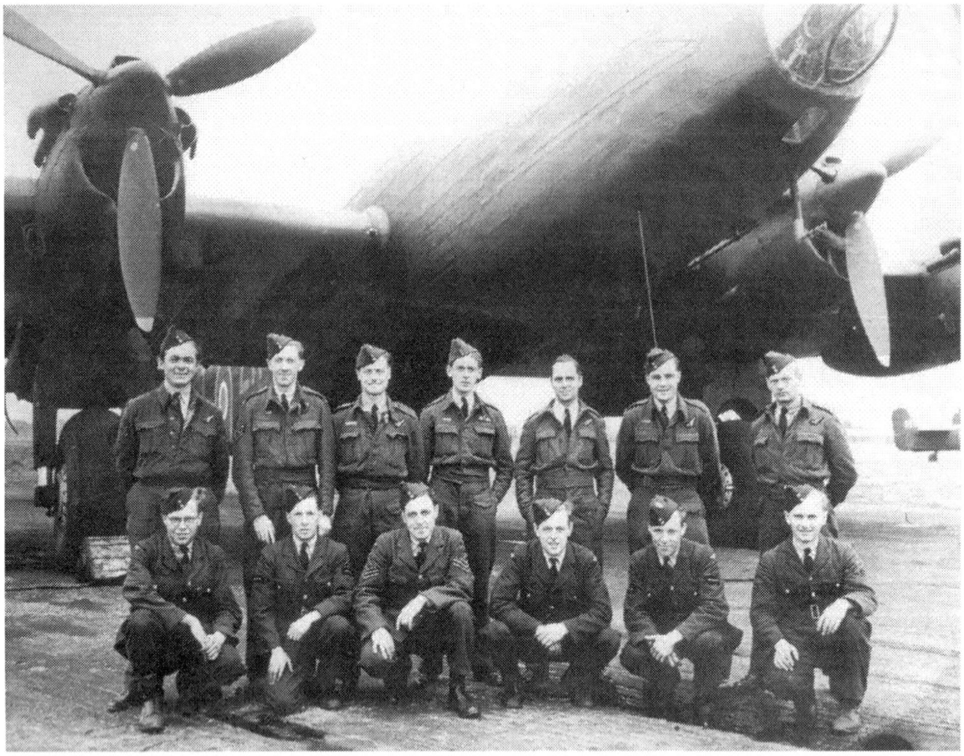

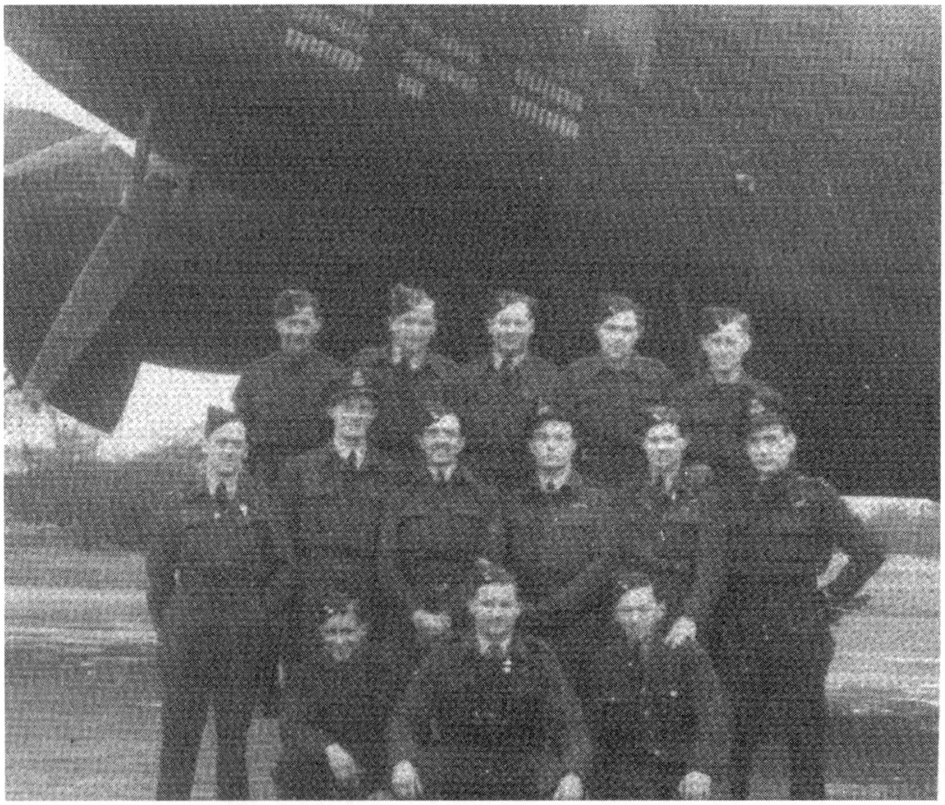

10 Sqn Crew (Photo from Sgt N Henshaw)

Fg Off Tubby Lawrence, the Sigs Leader, presenting the Adjutant with a 'Flying Adjutant' badge that used a quill pen as the wing.

M.U.G.   B/A   WT/OP   SKIPPER   N.   E.   T/G.
FREDDIE. KEN. ANDY. "PENNY" ROY. GEORGE. BILL.

Ground Crews

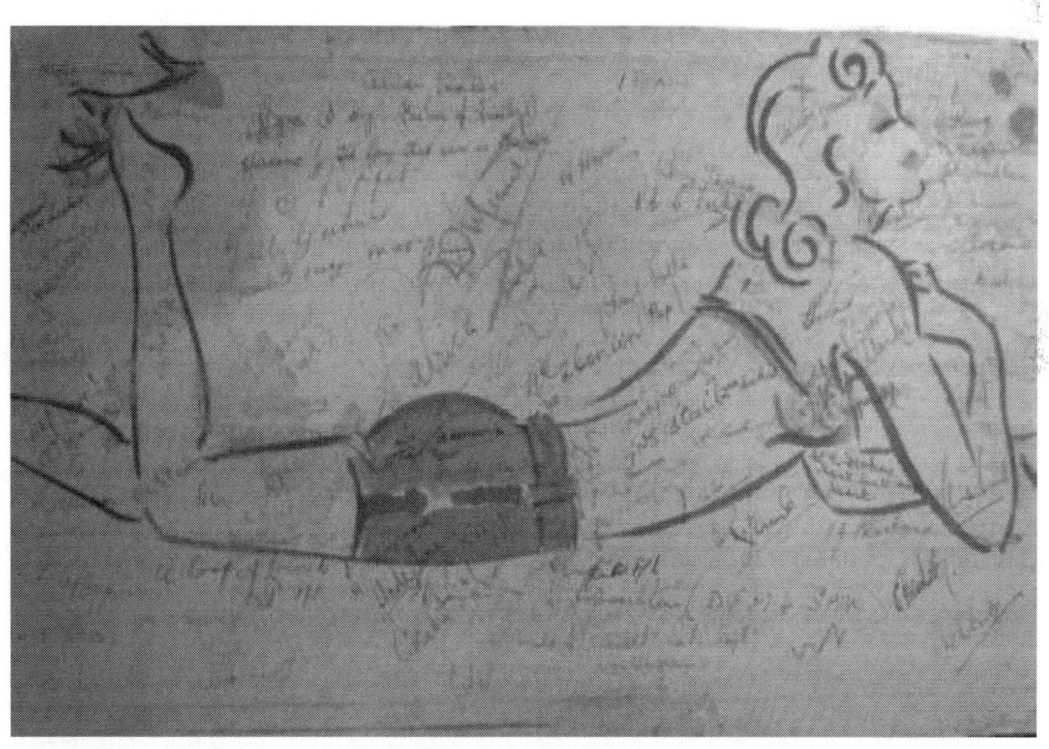

'The Painted Lady'. A panel from above a bar at RAF Melbourne signed at an end of Ops tour party in early 1945. Reframed in 2015 it now hangs in the 10 Sqn HQ.

Mid Upper Gunner

'Cook's Tours' were flown over Germany immediately after the war to show ground crews the results of their past labours, but Cologne Cathedral's towers are left still standing.

RAF Melbourne has now become Melrose Farm and the old main runway is often used by a motor sports club. In an old taxiway light mounting this plaque outside their HQ encourages present-day enthusiasts to reflect on past times.

Melbourne crew bar picture, now reframed at Brize Norton

Melbourne Band

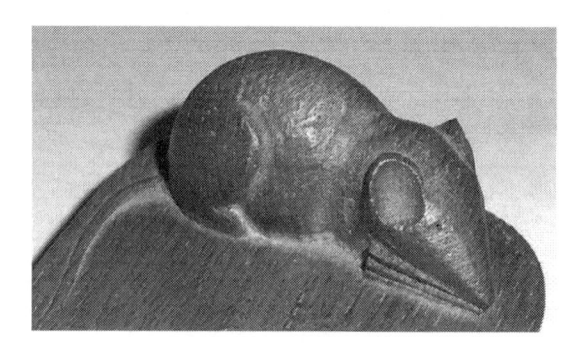

Whitley K 9018 failed to return on the night of 1/2 October 1939 when 10 Sqn carried out the first raid of WW2 on Berlin, dropping leaflets. The Whitley was last heard on R/T when abeam St Abbs Head. A wooden 'Mouseman' plaque in the Squadron commemorates the event and the loss of the crew.

The Seaton Ross Mill, close to Melbourne, was a welcome sight after a long night on Ops.

10 SQUADRON

MOTTO REM **ACU TANGERE** (To hit the mark) Code **ZA**

STATIONS

DISHFORTH	25.01.37. to 08.07.40.
LEEMING	08.07.40. to 19.08.42.
MELBOURNE	19.08.42. to 06.08.45.
POCKLINGTON (Temporary detachment)	28.08.42. to 23.10.42.

COMMANDING OFFICERS

WING COMMANDER W E STATON DSO* MC DFC	10.06.38. to 10.07.40.
SQUADRON LEADER J N H WHITWORTH	10.07.40. to 21.07.40.
WING COMMANDER S O BUFTON DFC	21.07.40. to 12.04.41.
WING COMMANDER K S FERGUSSON (Temp.)	21.10.40 to 08.11.40.
WING COMMANDER V B BENNETT DSO	12.04.41. to 03.09.41.
WING COMMANDER J A H TUCK DFC	08.09.41. to 15.04.42.
WING COMMANDER D C T BENNETT DSO	15.04.42. to 27.04.42.
WING COMMANDER J B TAIT DSO DFC (Temp)	04.05.42. to 04.06.42.
WING COMMANDER D C T BENNETT DSO	04.06.42. to 04.07.42.
SQUADRON LEADER E D GRIFFITHS (Temp)	04.07.42 to 26.07 42.
WING COMMANDER G P SEYMOUR-PRICE (Middle East Det)	04.07.42.
WING COMMANDER R K WILDEY DFC	26.07.42. to 15.10.42.
WING COMMANDER W CARTER	16.10.42. to 03.02.43.
WING COMMANDER D W EDMONDS DFC	03.02.43. to 08.10.43.
WING COMMANDER J F SUTTON DFC AFC	08.10.43. to 01.04.44.
WING COMMANDER D S RADFORD DSO DFC AFC	01.04.44. to 09.10.44.
WING COMMANDER U Y SHANNON	09.10.44. to 29.01.45.
WING COMMANDER A C DOWDEN	29.01.45. to 01.06.46.

AIRCRAFT

WHITLEY IV	05.39. to 05.40.
WHITLEY V	03.40. to 12.41.
HALIFAX II	12.41. to 03.44.
HALIFAX III	03.44. to 08.45.

OPERATIONAL RECORD

OPERATIONS	SORTIES	AIRCRAFT LOSSES	% LOSSES
609	6233	156	2.5

CATEGORY OF OPERATIONS

BOMBING	MINING	OTHER
533	61	15

WHITLEY

OPERATIONS	SORTIES	AIRCRAFT LOSSES	% LOSSES
223	1430	47	3.3

CATEGORY OF OPERATIONS

BOMBING	MINING	OTHER
208	0	15

HALIFAX

OPERATIONS	SORTIES	AIRCRAFT LOSSES	% LOSSES
386	4803	109	2.3

CATEGORY OF OPERATIONS

BOMBING	MINING
325	61

Aircraft histories

WHITLEY		**To December 1941.**

K9017 ZA-A	To 78Sqn.
K9018	FTR from leafleting sortie 1/2.10.39.
K9019	To 10 OTU.
K9020 ZA-L	To 78Sqn.
K9021	To 51Sqn.
K9022 ZA-M	Damaged beyond repair attempting to land at Dishforth training 3.3.40.
K9023 ZA-E	To 10 OTU.
K9024	To 51Sqn.
K9025	To 10 OTU.
K9026 ZA-O	To 78Sqn.
K9027	To 19 OTU.
K9028 ZA-P	To 10 OTU.
K9029 ZA-D	To 10 OTU.
K9030	To 19 OTU.
K9031 ZA-G	To 10 OTU.
K9032	Crashed near Grimsby on return from reconnaissance sortie 7.4.40.
K9033	To 10 OTU.
K9034 ZA-S	To 78Sqn.
K9035 ZA-H	To 10 OTU.
K9036 ZA-T	To 10 OTU.
K9037 ZA-J	To 10 OTU.
K9044 ZA-U	To 10 OTU.
N1354	From 77Sqn. To 10 OTU.
N1482 ZA-K	To 10 OTU.
N1483 ZA-I	Ditched in the Irish Sea on return from Berlin 1.10.40.
N1484	To 10 OTU.
N1487	To 78Sqn.
N1488	To 51Sqn.
N1489	To 102Sqn.
N1490	To 78Sqn.
N1491	To 9BGS.
N1492	To 19 OTU.
N1493	To 19 OTU.
N1494	To Hendon.
N1495	To 19 OTU.
N1496	FTR Kiel 8/9.7.40.
N1497 ZA-B	FTR Milan 15/16.8.40.
N1498	To Hendon.
P4935	FTR Berlin 6/7.9.40.
P4937	To 78Sqn.
P4946 ZA-P	FTR Bremen 8/9.5.41.
P4952 ZA-H/R	Abandoned over Northumberland on return from Stettin 15.10.40.

P4953 ZA-F/X	To 10 OTU.
P4954 ZA-T	FTR French battle area 11/12.6.40.
P4955 ZA-G	FTR Jena 16/17.8.40.
P4956 ZA-O	To 10 OTU.
P4957 ZA-E	Crashed in Northumberland on return from Wilhelmshaven 29/30.10.40.
P4958 ZA-K	To 78Sqn.
P4959 ZA-A	Destroyed by fire on the ground at Leeming 27.10.40.
P4960 ZA-S	Crashed on approach to Honington on return from Antwerp 20.6.40.
P4961 ZA-D	Abandoned over Suffolk on return from Berlin 21.12.40.
P4962 ZA-P	To 10 OTU.
P4963 ZA-B	Force-landed in Suffolk on return from Homberg 4.6.40.
P4965 ZA-H	Crashed off Kent coast on return from Turin 13/14.8.40.
P4966	Ditched off Yorkshire coast when bound for Antwerp 14.9.40.
P4967 ZA-J	Crash-landed in Yorkshire on return from Berlin 4.9.40.
P4990 ZA-T	FTR Milan 26/27.8.40.
P4993 ZA-V	Collided with balloon cable and crashed in Surrey on return from Le Havre 14.10.40.
P4994 ZA-U	Crashed on take-off from Leeming while training 22.12.40.
P5001 ZA-S	FTR Milan 5/6.11.40.
P5016 ZA-V	FTR Bremen 27/28.6.41.
P5018 ZA-Q	FTR Duisburg 30.6/1.7.41.
P5048 ZA-H	FTR Hamburg 10/11.5.41.
P5055 ZA-G	FTR Bremen 27/28.6.41.
P5094 ZA-B	Crash-landed at Leeming on return from Ostend 9.9.40.
P5109	FTR Warnemünde 11/12.9.41.
T4130	FTR Berlin 30.9/1.10.40.
T4143 ZA-J	Abandoned over Yorkshire on return from Stettin 15.10.40.
T4152 ZA-Z	FTR Stuttgart 21/22.10.40.
T4157 ZA-A	To 19 OTU.
T4176 ZA-N/R	To 58Sqn.
T4179 ZA-U	From 10 OTU. FTR Bremen 27/28.6.41.
T4202 ZA-N	Abandoned over Yorkshire on return from Kiel 19.3.41.
T4220 ZA-S	FTR Wilhelmshaven 16/17.1.41.
T4230 ZA-R	FTR Merseburg 13/14.11.40.
T4231 ZA-A	FTR Hanover 25/26.7.41.
T4232 ZA-V/W	Crashed in Wales when bound for Lorient 13.11.40.
T4234 ZA-Z	Crashed in Westmoreland on return from Le Havre 23.8.41.
T4263 ZA-E	From 51Sqn. To 19 OTU.
T4265 ZA-J	FTR Cologne 1/2.3.41.
Z6477 ZA-D	Abandoned over Lincolnshire on return from Düsseldorf 28.3.41.
Z6478 ZA-S	FTR Hüls 6/7.9.41.
Z6496 ZA-T	Badly damaged in crash. To A&AEE.
Z6557	FTR Bremen 16/17.4.41.
Z6559	From 51Sqn. To 77Sqn.
Z6561 ZA-J	From Leeming. FTR Bremen 27/28.6.41.

Z6564 ZA-Z	FTR Cologne 18/19.8.41.
Z6582	To 77Sqn.
Z6584 ZA-N	Crashed in Norfolk on return from Duisburg following attack by intruder 1.7.41.
Z6586 ZA-F	From 102Sqn. FTR Cologne 16/17.8.41.
Z6624 ZA-O	FTR Hannover 25/26.7.41.
Z6627 ZA-K	FTR Hamm 8/9.7.41.
Z6630	From 102Sqn. To 77Sqn.
Z6656 ZA-B	To 58Sqn.
Z6669 ZA-B	To 1485Flt.
Z6671	From 77Sqn. FTR Bremen 18/19.6.41.
Z6672	FTR Cologne 18/19.8.41.
Z6721	Ditched when bound for Schwerte 12/13.6.41.
Z6793	FTR Münster 5/6.7.41.
Z6794	FTR Cologne 16/17.8.41.
Z6802 ZA-P	Ditched off Withernsea on return from Berlin 21.9.41.
Z6805	FTR Cologne 16/17.8.41.
Z6814	To 58Sqn.
Z6815	FTR Kiel 8/9.8.41.
Z6816	FTR Osnabrück 7/8.7.41.
Z6817	To 78Sqn.
Z6828 ZA-Q	To 102Sqn.
Z6864	To 78Sqn.
Z6867 ZA-Z	Ditched off Yorkshire coast on return from Warnemünde 12.9.41.
Z6932	Crashed on take-off from Acklington during air-test 6.9.41.
Z6941 ZA-O	Ditched off Milford Haven on return from Stuttgart 2.10.41.
Z6942	FTR Hüls 6/7.9.41.
Z6954	To 19 OTU.
Z6976 ZA-U	From 51Sqn. To 10 OTU.
Z6979 ZA-Z	To 10 OTU.
Z6980	To 10 OTU.
Z9119 ZA-C	To 58Sqn.
Z9143	To 77Sqn.
Z9149 ZA-F	To 1481Flt.
Z9156 ZA-A	To 19 OTU.
Z9160	To 161Sqn.
Z9161 ZA-G/R	To 102Sqn.
Z9162 ZA-Y	Crashed on approach to Leeming after early return from Dunkerque 7.12.41.
Z9163 ZA-H	To 77Sqn.
Z9166 ZA-O	FTR Emden 30.11/1.12.41.
Z9188 ZA-V	Crashed in Yorkshire on return from Cologne 12.12.41.
Z9221 ZA-T	To 77Sqn.
Z9225	To 77Sqn.
Z9226 ZA-K	To 77Sqn.
Z9227 ZA-W	To 58Sqn.

HALIFAX.   **From December 1941.**

L9524	From 35Sqn. To 1659CU.
L9569	From 35Sqn. To 1658CU.
L9614	Collided with V9981 during take-off at Leeming while training 29.12.41.
L9619 ZA-E	Abandoned over Yorkshire on return from St Nazaire 15/16.2.42.
L9621 ZA-P	To 78CF.
L9622 ZA-G	Crashed in Yorkshire on return from Hamburg 15.1.42.
L9623 ZA-O	FTR Essen 1/2.6.42.
L9624 ZA-C	To 78Sqn.
R9365 ZA-U	To 76Sqn via 76CF.
R9366 ZA-Y	To 76Sqn via 76CF.
R9367	To 35Sqn via HCF.
R9368	To 78Sqn via 1652CU.
R9369 ZA-B	To 78CF.
R9370	To 35CF.
R9371 ZA-J/Z	Crashed on landing at Lossiemouth whilst in transit 9.3.42.
R9373	To 76Sqn.
R9374 ZA-K	Ditched off Cornwall on return from Brest 30.12.41.
R9376 ZA-D	To 138Sqn and back. To 10CF and back. Force-landed near Melbourne 14.11.42.
R9382	To 76CF.
R9383 ZA-A	From 102Sqn. Abandoned over Yorkshire on return from Saarbrücken 20.9.42.
R9384 ZA-W	From 76Sqn. To 1659CU.
R9387	From A&AEE. To 1658CU via 76CF.
R9392 ZA-A	From 35Sqn. To 1658CU via 10CF.
R9421 ZA-N	From 102Sqn. To 10CF. Belly-landed at Linton-on-Ouse 17.11.42.
R9428 ZA-Y	From 35Sqn. To 1661CU via 10CF.
R9430	Conversion Flt only. To 76CF.
R9491	To 102Sqn.
R9492 ZA-G	Crashed in Surrey on return from Dortmund 15.4.42.
R9493 ZA-E	To 35CF.
R9495 ZA-M	To 102Sqn.
R9497 ZA-V	To 102Sqn.
R9498	To 102Sqn.
R9528	To 102Sqn.
R9529	To 102Sqn.
V9980	From 76Sqn. To 1658CU via 10CF.
V9981	Collided with L9614 on take-off from Leeming while training 29.12.41.
V9984 ZA-F/A	To 1659CU.
V9985 ZA-V	To A&AEE.
V9986 ZA-M	FTR Kiel 26/27.2.42.
V9988	To 1658CU via 10CF.

W1003 ZA-K		To 158CF.
W1006		Conversion Flt only. To 78Sqn.
W1007		Conversion Flt only. To 78Sqn.
W1010 ZA-X		To 10CF and back. To 1658CU.
W1013		To 78Sqn.
W1037 ZA-U		FTR Aasenfjord (Tirpitz) 27/28.4.42.
W1038 ZA-O		To 158Sqn.
W1039 ZA-O		Crashed near Melbourne during ferry flight 10.3.43.
W1040 ZA-P		To 158Sqn.
W1041 ZA-B		FTR Aasenfjord (Tirpitz) 27/28.4.42.
W1042 ZA-T		FTR Cologne 30/31.5.42.
W1043 ZA-F		FTR Aasenfjord (Tirpitz) 30/31.3.42.
W1044 ZA-D		FTR Aasenfjord (Tirpitz) 30/31.3.42.
W1045 ZA-J		Ditched off South Devon on return from Dortmund 15.4.42.
W1052 ZA-K		To 102Sqn.
W1054 ZA-H		From 102Sqn. Crashed on landing at Leeming whilst in transit 30.4.42.
W1055 ZA-Z		From Dishforth. To 102Sqn.
W1056 ZA-N		From Dishforth. FTR Bremen 2/3.7.42.
W1057 ZA-X		FTR Mannheim 19/20.5.42.
W1058 ZA-L/S		From Dishforth. FTR Cologne 15/16.10.42.
W1098 ZA-W		FTR Essen 1/2.6.42.
W1106 ZA-A		To 76Sqn.
W1116 ZA-P		FTR Krefeld 2/3.10.42.
W1146		To 35Sqn and back. To 78Sqn.
W1151 ZA-H		To Middle East.
W1155 ZA-U		Crashed at Leeming during air test 25.6.42.
W1158 ZA-T		Crashed near Leeming when bound for Emden 19.6.42.
W1160		From 35Sqn. Damaged February 1943 and SOC 16.3.43.
W1170 ZA-U		To Middle East.
W1171 ZA-X		To Middle East.
W1172 ZA-Q		To Middle East.
W1174 ZA-G		To Middle East.
W1176 ZA-Z		To Middle East.
W1178 ZA-T		To Middle East.
W1181		To 102Sqn.
W1217 ZA-Z		From 158Sqn. FTR Dortmund 23/24.5.43.
W1271		From 102Sqn. To 419Sqn.
W1276		From 10CF. To 1652CU.
W7659 ZA-F		To Middle East.
W7666 ZA-J		Crashed on approach to Leeming during air test 24.5.42.
W7667 ZA-G		FTR Flensburg 1/2.10.42.
W7673		Crashed on landing at Leeming during air test 8.5.42.
W7674 ZA-U		FTR Warnemünde 8/9.5.42.
W7678 ZA-B/P		From 78Sqn. To 76Sqn.
W7679 ZA-C		To Middle East.
W7695 ZA-D		To Middle East.

W7696 ZA-H	FTR Essen 5/6.6.42.
W7697 ZA-R	To Middle East.
W7716 ZA-I	To Middle East.
W7717 ZA-G/J	To Middle East.
W7718	To 405Sqn.
W7756 ZA-L	To Middle East.
W7757 ZA-W	To Middle East.
W7758 ZA-Y	To Middle East.
W7767 ZA-O	FTR Duisburg 6/7.9.42.
W7772	From 51Sqn. To 1654CU.
W7811 ZA-C	To BDU.
W7852 ZA-K	FTR Flensburg 1/2.10.42.
W7855 ZA-E	Crashed on landing at Snaith while training 25.2.43.
W7865	From 158Sqn. To 1658CU.
W7867 ZA-F	Crashed on landing at Melbourne following early return from operation to Genoa 7.11.42.
W7869 ZA-K	To 419Sqn.
W7870 ZA-G	FTR Kiel 13/14.10.42.
W7871 ZA-B/C	Crashed near Melbourne while training 30.11.42.
W7881	To 35Sqn.
W7909 ZA-Z	From 102Sqn. FTR Bochum 12/13.6.43.
BB192 ZA-B	Crashed on landing at Great Massingham on return from Bremen 14.9.42.
BB193	To 158CF.
BB194 ZA-E	To 1658CU via 10CF.
BB201	FTR Emden 20/21.6.42.
BB207 ZA-M	From 158Sqn. FTR Flensburg 1/2.10.42.
BB220 ZA-D	To 158Sqn and back. To 1652CU.
BB240 ZA-A	To 51Sqn.
BB241	From 78Sqn. To 51Sqn.
BB243 ZA-G	From 102Sqn via 102CF. To 1661CU.
BB248 ZA-J	From 77Sqn. To 1658CU.
BB249	To 158Sqn.
BB252 ZA-X/Y	From 77Sqn. FTR from mining sortie 9.1.43.
BB300 ZA-A	From 76Sqn. To 1658CU.
BB324 ZA-D/X	From 76Sqn. FTR Mülheim 22/23.6.43.
BB427 ZA-X	From 77Sqn. To 1658CU.
DG222 ZA-Q	FTR Turin 11/12.12.42.
DG226 ZA-H	From 35Sqn via 10CF. To 158Sqn.
DG230 ZA-V	To 1652CU.
DT500 ZA-S	From 35Sqn. To 419Sqn.
DT520 ZA-J	FTR Flensburg 1/2.10.42.
DT541 ZA-V	From 76Sqn. To 1658CU.
DT546 ZA-R	To 408Sqn.
DT549 ZA-B	To 1658CU.
DT552 ZA-T	To 51Sqn.

DT557 ZA-U		FTR from mining sortie 8/9.11.42.
DT561 ZA-L		To 51Sqn.
DT566 ZA-X		To 1652CU.
DT567		From 78Sqn. To 51Sqn.
DT572 ZA-M		FTR Stuttgart 22/23.11.42.
DT667		To 1652CU.
DT720 ZA-L		From 158Sqn. To 466Sqn.
DT732 ZA-X		FTR Bochum 13/14.5.43.
DT746 ZA-S/Y		FTR Stuttgart 14/15.4.43.
DT776 ZA-T/R		To 466Sqn.
DT778 ZA-N		FTR Essen 12/13.3.43.
DT783 ZA-Q		FTR Cologne 28/29.6.43.
DT784 ZA-M		FTR Cologne 3/4.7.43.
DT785 ZA-H		Crash-landed at Thornaby on return from Kiel 5.4.43.
DT786 ZA-X/P		To 1652CU.
DT787 ZA-S		FTR Wuppertal 29/30.5.43.
DT788 ZA-E		FTR Cologne 14/15.2.43.
DT789 ZA-G/B		FTR Dortmund 23/24.5.43.
DT791 ZA-K		Crash-landed in Sussex on return from Pilsen 17.4.43.
DT792 ZA-F/D/O		Crash-landed at Melbourne on return from Hamburg 3.8.43.
HR691 ZA-K/W		To 1658CU.
HR692 ZA-R		FTR Essen 12/13.3.43.
HR695 ZA-D		To 1658CU.
HR696 ZA-G		FTR Dortmund 23/24.5.43.
HR697 ZA-F		FTR Cologne 28/29.6.43.
HR698 ZA-G/E		Crashed on take-off from Melbourne during training 1/2.8.43.
HR699 ZA-J		FTR Kiel 4/5.4.43.
HR757		To 158Sqn.
HR805 ZA-H		From 405Sqn. FTR Leipzig 19/20.2.44.
HR860 ZA-C		From 405Sqn. To 1652CU.
HR873 ZA-B		From 35Sqn. To 102Sqn.
HR879		From 35Sqn. To 1663CU.
HR920 ZA-L/C		FTR Montlucon 15/16.9.43.
HR921 ZA-D		Damaged beyond repair by night fighter during operation to Düsseldorf 3/4.11.43.
HR922 ZA-P		FTR Hanover 27/28.9.43.
HR924 ZA-N		From 102Sqn. Abandoned over Yorkshire on return from Hannover 23.9.43.
HR952 ZA-T		From 51Sqn. FTR Berlin 28/29.1.44.
HX156 ZA-N		From 102Sqn. To 1652CU.
HX159 ZA-L		FTR Hannover 27/28.9.43.
HX163 ZA-L		Damaged beyond repair during operation to Hannover 8/9.10.43.
HX164 ZA-K		FTR Frankfurt 20/21.12.43.
HX165 ZA-J		FTR Magdeburg 21/22.1.44.
HX170 ZA-O		To 1652CU.
HX171 ZA-E		To 102Sqn.

HX172 ZA-F	To 1652CU.
HX174 ZA-H	FTR Kassel 22/23.10.43.
HX179 ZA-L	Crashed near Shipdham on return from Düsseldorf 3.11.43.
HX181 ZA-K	Crashed on landing at Tangmere on return from Leverkusen 19.11.43.
HX184	To 102Sqn.
HX186 ZA-E	FTR Frankfurt 20/21.12.43.
HX190 ZA-E	FTR Mannheim 18/19.11.43.
HX191 ZA-J	FTR Leipzig 3/4.12.43.
HX232 ZA-E	From 35Sqn. To 1658CU.
HX281 ZA-R	Completed 100 operations.
HX286 ZA-R	From 35Sqn. FTR Stade 9/10.4.45.
HX295 ZA-A	From 35Sqn. FTR Essen 26/27.3.44.
HX323 ZA-M/C	From 35Sqn. To 1658CU.
HX326 ZA-N	From 35Sqn. FTR Essen 26/27.4.44.
HX327 ZA-N	From 35Sqn.
HX332 ZA-P/V	From 35Sqn. Shot down by intruder over Yorkshire on return from Kamen 3/4.3.45.
HX343	From 415Sqn. Crashed on take-off from Melbourne when bound for St Philibert Ferme 8.8.44.
HX347 ZA-Q	From 35Sqn. FTR Mechelen 1/2.5.44.
HX357 ZA-J	From 35Sqn.
JB899 ZA-M	From 405Sqn. To 1662CU.
JB910 ZA-T/J	To 1658CU.
JB930 ZA-H	FTR Stettin 20/21.4.43.
JB958 ZA-W	FTR Essen 27/28.5.43.
JB960 ZA-N	FTR Essen 27/28.5.43.
JB961 ZA-R	FTR Montbeliard 15/16.7.43.
JB974 ZA-T	FTR Kassel 22/23.10.43.
JD105 ZA-K	Crashed in Yorkshire on return from Dortmund 5.5.43.
JD106	To 1666CU.
JD109 ZA-Y	FTR Le Creusot 19/20.6.43.
JD119 ZA-C	Crashed in Leicestershire during cross-country exercise 20.8.43.
JD120 ZA-H	To 1658CU.
JD146 ZA-B/V	FTR Berlin 22/23.11.43.
JD166 ZA-G	FTR Munich 6/7.9.43.
JD198 ZA-N	FTR Nuremberg 10/11.8.43.
JD199 ZA-W	To 1659CU.
JD200 ZA-S	FTR Peenemünde 17/18.8.43.
JD202 ZA-Z	To 1658CU.
JD207 ZA-V	FTR Essen 25/26.7.43.
JD211 ZA-Y	FTR Montbeliard 15/16.7.43.
JD255 ZA-R	From 158Sqn. To 1658CU.
JD272 ZA-F	FTR Hannover 27/28.9.43.
JD273 ZA-Y	FTR Berlin 28/29.1.44.
JD314 ZA-Q/X	FTR Berlin 29/30.12.43.
JD315 ZA-R	FTR Kassel 22/23.10.43.

JD322 ZA-V		FTR Mannheim 5/6.9.43.
JD364 ZA-T		FTR Munich 6/7.9.43.
JD367 ZA-O/Q-/Z		FTR Berlin 22/23.11.43.
JD368 ZA-A		FTR Nuremberg 27/28.8.43.
JD470 ZA-S		FTR Berlin 20/21.1.44.
JD473 ZA-X		Crashed on landing at Ford on return from Leverkusen 19.11.43.
JD474 ZA-R		FTR Frankfurt 20/21.12.43.
JN883 ZA-S		From 51Sqn. FTR Berlin 15/16.2.44.
JN891 ZA-P		From 102Sqn. FTR Berlin 28/29.1.44.
JN899 ZA-T		From 51Sqn. FTR Berlin 20/21.1.44.
JN907		From 158Sqn. To 1652CU.
JN917 ZA-S		From 51Sqn. To 1658CU.
JN947 ZA-F		From 102Sqn. FTR Düsseldorf 3/4.11.43.
JN948		To 102Sqn.
JP118 ZA-D		SOC 15.11.46.
JP133 ZA-D		FTR Berlin 28/29.1.44.
LK753 ZA-T ZA-S/Q/C/V		From 51Sqn. FTR Hamburg 8/9.4.45.
LK812 ZA-T/Y		From 51Sqn. To 1658Sqn.
LK827 ZA-X/E/I		From 51Sqn. FTR Osnabrück 6/7.12.44.
LL445		From 644Sqn. To 1658CU.
LL588		To 78Sqn.
LL606 ZA-D-/B-		From 76Sqn.
LV785 ZA-A/M/Q/C		From 35Sqn. Crashed while trying to land at Melbourne on return from Dortmund 2.1.45.
LV818 ZA-W/K/F		From 35Sqn. FTR Duisburg 17/18.12.44.
LV822		From 35Sqn. To 51Sqn.
LV825 ZA-G		From 35Sqn. Crashed at Rawcliffe when bound for Domleger 17.6.44.
LV832		From 35Sqn. To 51Sqn.
LV857		From 35Sqn. To 51Sqn.
LV858 ZA-J		From 35Sqn. FTR Tergnier 10/11.4.44.
LV859 ZA-C		From 35Sqn. FTR Essen 26/27.3.44.
LV860 ZA-C		From 35Sqn. To 415Sqn.
LV862		From 35Sqn. To 51Sqn.
LV863 ZA-O		From 35Sqn. Crashed on take-off from Melbourne when bound for Aulnoye 28.4.44.
LV865		From 35Sqn. To 51Sqn.
LV866		From 35Sqn. To 429Sqn.
LV867 ZA-D		From 35Sqn. FTR Düsseldorf 22/23.4.44.
LV870 ZA-H		From 35Sqn. FTR Blainville-sur-L'Eau 28/29.6.44
LV878 ZA-V		From 35Sqn. FTR Wilhelmshaven 15/16.10.44.
LV880		From 35Sqn. To 51Sqn.
LV881 ZA-V		From 35Sqn. FTR Nuremberg 30/31.3.44.
LV882 ZA-R/D		From 35Sqn. FTR Trappes 2/3.6.44.
LV906 ZA-K/F/Q		From 35Sqn. FTR Aachen 24/25.5.44.

LV908 ZA-F/J		From 35Sqn. Belly-landed at Melbourne on return from Wilhelmshaven 15.10.44.
LV909 ZA-L/A/P		From 35Sqn. FTR Hanau 6/7.1.45.
LV912 ZA-A		From 35Sqn. FTR Bottrop 20/21.7.44.
LW167 ZA-O		FTR Magdeburg 16/17.1.45.
LW234		From 77Sqn. To 1663CU.
LW289 ZA-Y		From 51Sqn. To 1663CU.
LW314 ZA-K		From 158Sqn. To 1652CU.
LW322 ZA-P		To 102Sqn.
LW324 ZA-J		From 78Sqn. FTR Leipzig 19/20.2.44.
LW332 ZA-G		To 102Sqn.
LW336 ZA-L		To 102Sqn.
LW371 ZA-B		From 35Sqn. Crashed on landing at Melbourne on return from Laval Airfield 9.6.44.
LW445 ZA-Y		To 51Sqn.
LW545 ZA-E/N/Z ZA-D/L		From 51Sqn.
LW716 ZA-S/D/Y/Z		FTR Bochum 4/5.11.44.
LW717 ZA-W		FTR Blainville-sur-L'Eau 28/29.6.44.
LW718		To 158Sqn.
LW719		To 158Sqn.
LW720		To 158Sqn.
MZ290 ZA-L/J/O		From 102Sqn.
MZ300 ZA-I/K		From 102Sqn.
MZ309 ZA-D/B		From 76Sqn. Damaged beyond repair during an operation to Münster 13.9.44.
MZ312 ZA-E		FTR Bottrop 20/21.7.44.
MZ315 ZA-G		
MZ344		To 640Sqn.
MZ345 ZA-G		To 640Sqn.
MZ346 ZA-S/P		From 640Sqn.
MZ354 ZA-M		From 76Sqn.
MZ361		From BDU. To 78Sqn.
MZ398		To 462Sqn.
MZ403		To 462Sqn.
MZ406		To 640Sqn.
MZ409		To 640Sqn.
MZ410		To EANS.
MZ411 ZA-M/A		To Leconfield.
MZ413 ZA-B		To 96Sqn.
MZ417 ZA-E		From 78Sqn.
MZ421 ZA-Z/X		From 76Sqn.
MZ430 ZA-W		To Leconfield.
MZ433 ZA-X		Crashed on landing at Melbourne during transit from Carnaby after returning from Essen 11.3.45.
MZ464		From 433Sqn. To 96Sqn.

MZ532 ZA-Z		FTR Laval Airfield 9/10.6.44.
MZ534 ZA-Z		To 1663CU.
MZ574 ZA-V/W		FTR Neuss 23/24.9.44.
MZ576 ZA-T		Ditched off Lincolnshire coast on return from Cologne 28.10.44.
MZ584 ZA-V		FTR St Martin L'Hortier 2.7.44.
MZ630 ZA-S		FTR Trappes 2/3.6.44.
MZ684 ZA-B		FTR Laval Airfield 9/10.6.44.
MZ732		To 76Sqn.
MZ746 ZA-S		
MZ751 ZA-J		
MZ773 ZA-Y		FTR Brunswick 12/13.8.44.
MZ789 ZA-H		From 78Sqn. Belly-landed in France on return from Essen 28/29.11.44.
MZ793 ZA-X		FTR from mining sortie 14/15.2.45.
MZ810		To 78Sqn.
MZ826 ZA-M		FTR from mining sortie 15/16.10.44.
MZ844 ZA-D		FTR Watten 25.8.44.
MZ847 ZA-A		Belly-landed in Kent on return from operation to V2 rocket stores at Lumbres 1.9.44.
MZ902 ZA-R		From 76Sqn.
MZ919 ZA-L		
MZ948 ZA-E		FTR Chemnitz 5/6.3.45.
NA114 ZA-K		From 76Sqn. FTR Hanover 5/6.1.45.
NA149		To 76Sqn.
NA162 ZA-W		To EANS.
NA195 ZA-F/R		
NA198 ZA-W		From 76Sqn. To EANS.
NA228 ZA-D		
NA237 ZA-C		FTR Magdeburg 16/17.1.45.
NA275		To 78Sqn.
NA506		To 346Sqn.
NA627 ZA-Y		Crashed on landing at Melbourne on return from Bingen 22.12.44.
NP993 ZA-Q		From 78Sqn. To Leconfield.
NP994 ZA-K		
NR130		To 78Sqn.
NR131 ZA-N		FTR Chemnitz 5/6.3.45.
NR188 ZA-M		
NR189 ZA-Z		FTR Worms 21/22.2.45.
NR245 ZA-H		To 51Sqn.
NR246 ZA-Y		FTR St Vith 26.12.44.
PN447 ZA-B		SOC following operation to Heligoland 18.4.45.
RG345 ZA-Y		
RG354 ZA-O		
RG422 ZA-C		From 96Sqn.
RG423 ZA-P		From 96Sqn.
RG424 ZA-T		From 96Sqn. Undercarriage collapsed on landing at Melbourne on return from Hamburg 9.4.45.

RG425 ZA-Z　　　　　From 96Sqn.
RG426 ZA-X　　　　　From 96Sqn. FTR Worms 21/22.2.45.
RG427 ZA-N/V　　　　From 96Sqn.
RG428 ZA-F　　　　　From 96Sqn.
RG429 ZA-H　　　　　From 96Sqn.
RG431 ZA-Z　　　　　From 96Sqn.
RG434 ZA-A　　　　　From 78Sqn.
RG435 ZA-Y/G　　　　From 77Sqn.
RG438 ZA-S/N　　　　Crashed on take-off from Melbourne while training 24.3.45.
RG439 ZA-Q/K　　　　From 346Sqn.
RG440 ZA-T/M　　　　From 78Sqn.
RG442 ZA-C/E　　　　From 77Sqn.
RG443 ZA-Q　　　　　From 77Sqn. FTR Wanne-Eickel 2/3.2.45.
RG444　　　　　　　　To 76Sqn.

HEAVIEST SINGLE LOSS

27/28.06.41.　Bremen.　　4 Whitleys.
01/02.10.42.　Flensburg.　4 Halifaxes.
28/29.01.44.　Berlin.　　　4 Halifaxes.

Key to Abbreviations

A&AEE	Aeroplane and Armaments Experimental Establishment.
AA	Anti-Aircraft fire.
AACU	Anti-Aircraft Cooperation Unit.
AAS	Air Armament School.
AASF	Advance Air Striking Force.
AAU	Aircraft Assembly Unit.
ACM	Air Chief Marshal.
ACSEA	Air Command South-East Asia.
AFDU	Air Fighting Development Unit.
AFEE	Airborne Forces Experimental Unit.
AFTDU	Airborne Forces Tactical Development Unit.
AGS	Air Gunners School.
AMDP	Air Members for Development and Production.
AOC	Air Officer Commanding.
AOS	Air Observers School.
ASRTU	Air-Sea Rescue Training Unit.
ATTDU	Air Transport Tactical Development Unit.
AVM	Air Vice-Marshal.
BAT	Beam Approach Training.
BCBS	Bomber Command Bombing School.
BCDU	Bomber Command Development Unit.
BCFU	Bomber Command Film Unit.
BCIS	Bomber Command Instructors School.
BDU	Bombing Development Unit.
BSTU	Bomber Support Training Unit.
CF	Conversion Flight.
CFS	Central Flying School.
CGS	Central Gunnery School.
C-in-C	Commander in Chief.
CNS	Central Navigation School.
CO	Commanding Officer.
CRD	Controller of Research and Development.
CU	Conversion Unit.
DGRD	Director General for Research and Development.
EAAS	Empire Air Armament School.
EANS	Empire Air Navigation School.
ECDU	Electronic Countermeasures Development Unit.
ECFS	Empire Central Flying School.
ETPS	Empire Test Pilots School.
F/L	Flight Lieutenant.
Flt	Flight.
F/O	Flying Officer.
FPP	Ferry Pilots School.
F/S	Flight Sergeant.

FTR	Failed to Return.
FTU	Ferry Training Unit.
G/C	Group Captain.
Gp	Group.
HCU	Heavy Conversion Unit.
HGCU	Heavy Glider Conversion Unit.
LFS	Lancaster Finishing School.
MAC	Mediterranean Air Command.
MTU	Mosquito Training Unit.
MU	Maintenance Unit.
NTU	Navigation Training Unit.
OADU	Overseas Aircraft Delivery Unit.
OAPU	Overseas Aircraft Preparation Unit.
OTU	Operational Training Unit.
P/O	Pilot Officer.
PTS	Parachute Training School.
RAE	Royal Aircraft Establishment.
SGR	School of General Reconnaissance.
Sgt	Sergeant.
SHAEF	Supreme Headquarters Allied Expeditionary Force.
SIU	Signals Intelligence Unit.
S/L	Squadron Leader.
SOC	Struck off Charge.
SOE	Special Operations Executive.
Sqn	Squadron.
TF	Training Flight.
TFU	Telecommunications Flying Unit.
W/C	Wing Commander.
Wg	Wing.
WIDU	Wireless Intelligence Development Unit.
W/O	Warrant Officer.

Printed in Germany
by Amazon Distribution
GmbH, Leipzig